THE DYNAMICS OF ORGANIZATION THEORY

Gaining a Macro Perspective

Structure and design

D0217512

The West Series in Management

Consulting Editors:

Don Hellriegel—Texas A&M University
and
John W. Slocum, Jr.—Southern Methodist University

SECOND EDITION

THE DYNAMICS OF ORGANIZATION THEORY

GAINING A MACRO PERSPECTIVE

JOHN F. VEIGA and **JOHN N. YANOUZAS**
The University of Connecticut

WEST PUBLISHING COMPANY
St. Paul New York Los Angeles San Francisco

Cover art: "Fabric of Human Involvement" by Clark
Fitz-Gerald, owned by Mr. and Mrs. Robert U. Redpath,
Jr., South Orange, New Jersey. Photograph by
Werner Wolff, Black Star. Used with permission.

Library of Congress Cataloging in Publication Data

Main entry under title:

The Dynamics of organization theory.

 (The West series in management)
 Includes bibliographies.
 1. Organization—Addresses, essays, lectures.
2. Management—Addresses, essays, lectures. I. Veiga,
John F. II. Yanouzas, John N. III. Series.
HD31.D96 1984 658.4 83–16827
ISBN 0–314–77852–7
1st Reprint—1985

CONTENTS

2 ENVIRONMENTAL FIT 74

3 STRUCTURE and DESIGN 150

MANAGEMENT PRACTICE

EXERCISES

4 POWER, CONFLICT and POLITICS 252

READINGS

MANAGEMENT PRACTICE

EXERCISES

5 REVITALIZATION **336**

READINGS

MANAGEMENT PRACTICE

EXERCISES

PREFACE TO THE SECOND EDITION

TO: Students of Organization Theory

FROM: John F. Veiga and John N. Yanouzas

SUBJECT: *Gaining a Macro Perspective*

It is only appropriate that we begin a book on organization theory with a memo. Even though our book does not deal with memo writing *per se*, memos often become artifacts of organizational actions—actions which this book is about.

The primary objective of the book is to help you develop a way of looking at organizations which transcends merely examining organizational parts and then deducing the whole. To achieve this view, you will have to take off the sets of glasses through which you typically view behavior in organizations and put on a pair of "macro glasses." We want you to develop more than just a *top down* view of organizations. Such a view implies that the concepts would be relevant to you only if, and when, you achieve a top management position. Macro glasses are intended to correct vision not only from the top down, but also from the bottom up. It is our feeling that waiting to put on such glasses until you reach the top in an organization would be a great loss.

Gaining a macro perspective involves two components: first, actual organizational experience; and second, the development of conceptual models of organizations through which to filter and better understand that experience. The first component we hope to provide for you through the use of structured exercises and examples of management practice. While this experience can never fully duplicate your own "real world" experience, it will provide a basis for reflection, and an opportunity to try out your new glasses. The second component will develop as you study the relevant literature in organization theory. While the term *theory* is often reacted to negatively by students and practitioners alike, we have carefully selected readings which have been written for practitioners. These readings express an understanding of organizations which has evolved as theorists have begun to distill the wisdom of the management practitioner.

While these two components can be treated as mutually exclusive, it is our view that they should not be. As a

without the vision of conceptual models, you must
~~~ously reinvent the wheel. Yours would be a world
~~~l and error. In early career you would have a man-
~~~ial blind spot. Your decisions would not reflect an
~~~erstanding of the total organization and your efforts
~~~ improve the organization may be wasted. Your perspective would lack the wisdom of managerial seasoning, and
your mistakes, as well as your successes, would not contribute as much to your own learning and development as
they might have. As a senior manager, assuming you survive these trials and errors, you would be in a better
position to view the total organization, but your knowledge would be primarily based on intuition and hence be
difficult to explain and defend. Also, you may not have
as clear an understanding or awareness of the impact of
your decisions on the behavior of people below you because
you failed to be sensitive to such relationships in early
career. In contrast, heavy reliance on conceptual models
and theories alone would result in your having a stilted
and abstract view of the real world realities facing you.
Management is still an art and organization theory remains
incomplete. The artist who spends too much time studying
technique loses the potential for truly creative work.
This book is an attempt to help you integrate both of
these components.

While every organization has unique characteristics, many
of the problems each faces is universal. To some degree,
organizations experience the problems of evolution and
survival, adaptation, power, politics and conflict, as
well as revitalization. To that end, because organization
theorists have not focused on any single type of organization, we have selected articles on management practice
from many settings in both the private and public sectors.
The choice of such vastly different settings as a bank, an
electronics firm, a computer manufacturer, an advertising
agency, a drug council, a hospital, a film making firm, an
airline, a trucking firm, and a television network, was
deliberate to demonstrate the universality of the concepts
and to keep from limiting the focus of potential applications you may discover. We strongly recommend that *all*
the articles in the management practice section be read in
order for you to gain a better sense of realities of organizational life.

While the title of the book may have implied emphasis on
abstract theories, our hope is to build a bridge between
theory and action. We have designed several exercises
which provide you with a first-hand opportunity to cope
with organizational problems. To magnify such problems,
the exercises were designed to exaggerate their real world
counterparts. By requiring you to analyze situations,
make decisions, and then take actions, the exercises provide a results-oriented testing ground for the theories.
As you progress through the book, the exercises will

require you to continually utilize your accumulated knowledge and experience, thereby providing a foundation of
management experiences that can be built upon in later
career. By analyzing your successes and failures you will
begin to improve your abilities to learn from your own
experiences and develop a perspective on organizations
that would normally have taken many years of management
experience to develop.

We have attempted to provide a good balance between theory
and practice in the readings. The readings represent current thought in the field. Organization theory continues
to evolve as a field through research. Hence, while several of the readings were written within the last five
years, a few of the readings are over twenty-five years
old. The age of an article was not a factor in its selection—its contribution to understanding and knowledge was.
In some instances we have included an article because it
addressed an important issue even though we recognized you
would have some difficulty in comprehending the concepts.
We have also included readings in the management practice
section which are not espousing a theory *per se*, but were
written to stimulate thought or offer insight into the
dilemmas and paradoxes faced by real world managers and
administrators.

The book was designed to provide a variety of vehicles for
learning. We do not advocate any single approach, but
feel that some balance is desirable. Exercises are fun
and involving, discussing management practices make the
concepts and problems more universal and common and, readings provide the wisdom to be challenged and the stimulus
for new insights. The book can be used as the primary
text or as a supplemental text for an introductory course
at the junior-senior level or graduate level. We have
used the material with undergraduate management majors and
M.B.A.'s, as well as with graduate administration majors
from several fields, including public administration, educational administration, health care, etc. The material
has also been used many times in management training and
executive development programs.

The five sections of the book are organized around organizational issues with which we feel managers of the future
must learn to cope. We have not covered all of the topics
and issues currently being studied by organizational theorists. However, we carefully surveyed the field and used
our own consulting and management training experience as a
basis for our selections. Each section has some brief
introductory comments designed to acquaint you with the
central theme and to provide you with some overall
learning objectives. While there is no overall master
plan for the sequence of each section, our classroom experience tells us that this sequence does provide a basis
for the continued building upon and refinement of con-

cepts. The book culminates in Part 5 with a testing ground for all the concepts learned as you grapple with applying your macro perspective to achieve organizational revitalization.

Many people have helped in the development of this material. In developing exercises, our wives Mo and Eleni, and our children were the first to be experimented on and were kind enough not to laugh at some of our crazier ideas. Our many students, as well as the hundreds of managers in training programs, provided criticism and praise which shaped the contents. Our colleagues, who liked the material well enough to pirate it, provided indirect encouragement. We would also like to acknowledge the assistance of Lillian Marchand who typed many earlier versions of the exercises as we experimented. And lastly, we would like to express our debt to our parents who instilled in us the values necessary to stay with this project and to keep searching yet for better ways of doing things.

SECOND EDITION

THE DYNAMICS OF ORGANIZATION THEORY

Gaining a Macro Perspective

1 Evolution and Survival

■ **LEARNING OBJECTIVES**

1. To examine the process by which organizations evolve

2. To explore the implications of a turbulent environment on the evolution and survival of an organization

3. To examine the need for organizational renewal and some of the obstacles that may prevent it

■ OVERVIEW

Most organizations will readily identify survival as one of their primary goals. And yet many organizations are often unaware of a major threat to their existence until it is too late. No organization, regardless of its size, is immune from obsolescence. To understand this phenomenon, we need to begin by looking at the process by which organizations evolve and how effective they are at responding to their environment.

An organization facing a stable environment may not need to renew itself as often as one faced by continual pressures for change. The problem, however, is that very often an organization becomes conditioned by its environment so that in long periods of stability the organization and its leaders become myopic and inattentive to the environment. This lack of vigilance coupled with increased organizational rigidity often sets into motion patterns of organizational response that can inadvertently lead to decay and the eventual demise of the organization.

If we can view organizations as living systems, capable of growth as well as decay, then the process by which they adapt bears closer examination. For living systems such as human beings, the adaptation process needed to respond to changes in the environment is relatively slow and not subject to intragenerational modification. Hence, in truly hostile and changing environments, people may not be able to adapt quickly enough to insure survival. The same, however, is not necessarily true for organizations. There are few limits placed on the organization other than those imposed by people. Hypothetically, the organization could modify its structure and strategy very rapidly to meet changes in its environment. Unfortunately, many organizations are not able to adapt in time because of their limited capacity for renewal. In Part 1, we will explore some of the human constraints that limit organizational renewal—those "mind-forged manacles" that Gardner tells us more often prevent renewal than do factors external to the organization.

3

Readings

■ Putting Excellence into Management

THOMAS J. PETERS

What makes for excellence in the management of a company? Is it the use of sophisticated management techniques such as zero-based budgeting, management by objectives, matrix organization, and sector, group, or portfolio management? Is it greater use of computers to control companies that continue to grow even larger in size and more diverse in activities? Is it a battalion of specialized MBAs, well-versed in the techniques of strategic planning?

Probably not. Although most well-run companies use a fair sampling of all these tools, they do not use them as substitutes for the basics of good management. Indeed, McKinsey & Co., a management consultant concern, has studied management practices at thirty-seven companies that are often used as examples of well-run organizations and has found that they have eight common attributes. None of those attributes depends on "modern" management tools or gimmicks. In fact, none of them requires high technology, and none of them costs a cent to implement. All that is needed is time, energy, and a willingness on the part of management to think rather than to make use of management formulas.

The outstanding performers work hard to keep things simple. They rely on simple organizational structures, simple strategies, simple goals, and simple communications.

The eight attributes that characterize their managements are:

- A bias toward action.
- Simple form and lean staff.
- Continued contact with customers.
- Productivity improvement via people.
- Operational autonomy to encourage entrepreneurship.
- Stress on one key business value.
- Emphasis on doing what they know best.
- Simultaneous loose-tight controls.

Although none of these sounds startling or new, most are conspicuously absent in many companies today. Far too many managers have lost sight of the basics—service to customers, low-cost manufacturing, productivity improvement, innovation, and risk-taking. In many cases, they have been seduced by the availability of MBAs, armed with the "latest" in strategic planning techniques. MBAs who specialize in strategy are bright, but they often cannot implement their ideas, and their companies wind up losing the capacity to act. At Standard Brands, Inc., for example, Chairman F. Ross Johnson discovered this the hard way when he brought a handful of planning specialists into his consumer products company. "The guys who were bright [the strategic planners] were not the kinds of people who could implement programs," he lamented to *Business Week*. Two years later, he removed the planners.

Another consumer products company followed a similar route, hiring a large band of young MBAs for the staffs of senior vice-presidents. The new people were assigned to build computer models for designing new products. Yet none of the products could be manufactured or brought to market. Complained one line executive, "The models incorporated eighty-three variables in product planning, but we were being killed by just one—cost."

Companies are being stymied not only by their own staffs but often by their structure. McKinsey studied one company where the new-product process required 223 separate committees to approve an idea before it could be put into production. Another company was restructured recently into 200 strategic business units—only to discover that it was impossible to implement 200 strategies. And even at General Electric Co., which is usually cited for its ability to structure itself according to its management needs, an executive recently complained, "Things become bureaucratic with astonishing speed. Inevitably when we wire things up, we lose vitality." Emerson Electric Co., with a much simpler structure than GE, consistently beats its huge competitor on costs—manufacturing its products in plants with fewer than 600 employees.

McKinsey's study focused on ten well-managed companies: International Business Machines, Texas Instruments, Hewlett-Packard, 3M, Digital Equipment, Procter & Gamble, Johnson & Johnson, McDonald's, Dana, and Emerson Electric. On the surface, they have nothing in common. There is no universality of product line: Five are in high technology, one is in packaged goods, one makes medical products, one operates fast-food restaurants, and two are relatively mundane manufacturers of mechanical and electrical products. But each is a hands-on operator, not a holding company or a conglomerate. And while not every plan succeeds, in the day-to-day pursuit of their businesses these companies succeed far more often than they fail. And they succeed because of their management's almost instinctive adherence to the eight attributes.

BIAS TOWARD ACTION

In each of these companies, the key instructions are *do it, fix it, try it*. They avoid analyzing and questioning products to death, and they avoid complicated procedures for developing new ideas. Controlled experiments abound in these companies. The attitude of management is to "get some data, do it, then adjust it," rather than to wait for a perfect overall plan. The companies tend to be tinkerers rather than inventors, making small steps of progress rather than conceiving sweeping new concepts. At McDonald's Corp., for example, the objective is to do the little things regularly and well.

Ideas are solicited regularly and tested quickly. Those that work are pushed fast; those that don't are discarded just as quickly. At 3M Co., the management never kills an idea without trying it out; it just goes on the back burner.

These managements avoid long, complicated business plans for new projects. At 3M, for example, new product ideas must be proposed in less than five pages. At Procter & Gamble Co., one-page memos are the rule, but every figure in a P & G memo can be relied on unfailingly.

To ensure that they achieve results, these companies set a few well-defined goals for their managers. At Texas Instruments Inc., for one, a typical goal would be a set date for having a new plant operating or for having a designated percent of a sales force call on customers in a new market. A TI executive explained, "We've experimented a lot, but the bottom line for any senior manager is the maxim that more than two objectives is no objective."

These companies have learned to focus quickly on problems. One method is to appoint a "czar" who has responsibility for one problem across the company. At Digital Equipment Corp. and Hewlett-Packard Co., for example, there are software czars, because customer demand for programming has become the key issue for the future growth of those companies. Du Pont Co., when it discovered it was spending $800 million a year on transportation, set up a logistics czar. Other companies have productivity czars or energy czars with the power to override a manfuacturing division's autonomy.

Another tool is the task force. But these companies tend to use the task force in an unusual way. Task forces are authorized to fix things, not to generate reports and paper. At Digital Equipment, TI, HP, and 3M, task forces have a short duration, seldom more than ninety days. Says a Digital Equipment executive, "When we've got a big problem here, we grab ten senior guys and stick them in a room for a week. They come up with an answer and implement it." All members are volunteers, and they tend to be senior managers rather than junior people ordered to serve. Management espouses the busy-member theory: "We don't want people on task forces who want to become permanent task force members. We only put people on them who are so busy that their major objective is to get the problem solved and to get back to their main jobs." Every task force at TI is disbanded after its work is done, but within three months the senior operations committee formally reviews and assesses the results. TI demands that the managers who requested and ran the task force justify the time spent on it. If the task force turns out to have been useless, the manager is chided publicly, a painful penalty in TI's peer-conscious culture.

SIMPLE FORM AND LEAN STAFF

Although all ten of these companies are big—the smallest, McDonald's, has sales in excess of $1.9 billion—they are structured along "small is beautiful" lines. Emerson Electric, 3M, J & J and HP are divided into small entrepreneurial units that—although smaller than economies of scale might suggest—manage to get things done. No HP division, for example, ever employs more than 1,200 people. TI, with ninety product customer centers, keeps each notably autonomous.

Within the units themselves, activities are kept to small, manageable groups. At Dana Corp., small teams work on productivity improvement. At the high-technology companies, small autonomous teams, headed by a product "champion," shepherd ideas through the corporate bureaucracy to ensure that they quickly receive attention from the top.

Staffs are also kept small to avoid bureaucracies. Fewer than 100 people help run Dana, a $3 billion corporation. Digital Equipment and Emerson are also noted for small staffs.

CLOSENESS TO THE CUSTOMER

The well-managed companies are customer driven—not technology driven, not product driven, not strategy driven. Constant contact with the customer provides insights that direct the company. Says one executive, "Where do you start? Not by poring over abstract market research. You start by getting out there with the customer." In a study of two fast-paced industries (scientific instruments and component manufacturing), Eric Von Hippel, associate professor at Massachusetts Institute of Technology, found that 100% of the major new product ideas— and 80% of the minor new product variations—came directly from customers.

At both IBM and Digital Equipment, top management spends at least thirty days a year conferring with top customers. No manager at IBM holds a staff job for more than three years, except in the legal, finance, and personnel departments. The reason: IBM believes that staff people are out of the mainstream because they do not meet with customers regularly.

Both companies use customer-satisfaction surveys to help determine management's compensation. Another company spends

12% of its research and development budget on sending engineers and scientists out to visit customers. One R & D chief spends two months each year with customers. At Lanier Business Products Inc., another fast growing company, the twenty most senior executives make sales calls every month.

Staying close to the customer means sales and service overkill. "Assistants to" at IBM are assigned to senior executives with the sole function of processing customer complaints within twenty-four hours. At Digital Equipment, J & J, IBM, and 3M, immense effort is expended to field an extraordinarily well-trained sales force. Caterpillar Tractor Co., another company considered to have excellent management, spends much of its managerial talent on efforts to make a reality of its motto, "twenty-four-hour parts delivery anywhere in the world."

These companies view the customer as an integral element of their businesses. A bank officer who started his career as a J & J accountant recalls that he was required to make customer calls even though he was in a financial department. The reason: to insure that he understood the customer's perspective and could handle a proposal with empathy.

PRODUCTIVITY IMPROVEMENT VIA CONSENSUS

One way to get productivity increases is to install new capital equipment. But another method is often overlooked. Productivity can be improved by motivating and stimulating employees. One way to do that is to give them autonomy. At TI, shop floor teams set their own targets for production. In the years since the company has used this approach, executives say, workers have set goals that required them to stretch but that are reasonable and attainable.

The key is to motivate all the people involved in each process. At 3M, for example, a team that includes technologists, marketers, production people, and financial types is formed early in a new product venture. It is self-sufficient and stays together from the inception to the national introduction. Although 3M is aware that this approach can lead to redundancy, it feels that the team spirit and motivation make it worthwhile.

Almost all these companies use "corny" but effective methods to reward their workers. Badges, pins, and medals are all part of such recognition programs. Outstanding production teams at TI are invited to describe their successes to the board, as a form of recognition. Significantly, the emphasis is never only on monetary awards.

Autonomy to encourage entrepreneurship. A company cannot encourage entrepreneurship if it holds its managers on so tight a leash that they cannot make decisions. Well-managed companies authorize their managers to act like entrepreneurs. Dana, for one, calls this method the "store manager" concept. Plant managers are free to make purchasing decisions and to start productivity programs on their own. As a result, these managers develop unusual programs with results that far exceed those of a division or corporate staff. And the company has a grievance rate that is a fraction of the average reported by the United Auto Workers for all the plants it represents.

The successful companies rarely will force their managers to go against their own judgment. At 3M, TI, IBM, and J & J, decisions on product promotion are not based solely on market potential. An important factor in the decision is the zeal and drive of the volunteer who champions a product. Explains one executive at TI, "In every instance of a new product failure, we had forced someone into championing it involuntarily."

The divisional management is generally responsible for replenishing its new product array. In these well-managed companies, headquarters staff may not cut off funds for divisional products arbitrarily. What is more, the divisions are allowed to reinvest most of their earnings in their own operations. Although this flies in the face of the product-portfolio concept, which dictates that a corporate chief milk mature divisions to feed those with apparently greater growth potential, these companies recognize that entrepreneurs will not be developed in corporations that give the fruits of managers' labor to someone else.

Almost all these companies strive to place new products into separate startup divisions. A manager is more likely to be recognized—and promoted—for pushing a hot new product out of his division to enable it to stand on its own than he is for simply letting his own division get overgrown.

Possibly most important at these companies, entrepreneurs are both encouraged and honored at all staff levels. TI, for one, has created a special group of "listeners"—138 senior technical people called "individual contributors"—to assess new ideas. Junior staff members are particularly encouraged to bring their ideas to one of these individuals for a one-on-one evaluation. Each "contributor" has the authority to approve substantial startup funds ($20,000 to $30,000) for product experimentation. TI's successful Speak'n'Spell device was developed this way.

IBM's Fellows Program serves a similar purpose, although it is intended to permit proven senior performers to explore their ideas rather than to open communication lines for bright comers. Such scientists have at their beck and call thousands of IBM's technical people. The Fellows tend to be very skilled gadflies, people who can shake things up—almost invariably for the good of the company.

The operating principle at well-managed companies is to do one thing well. At IBM, the all-pervasive value is customer service. At Dana it is productivity improvement. At 3M and HP, it is new product development. At P & G it is product quality. At McDonald's it is customer service—quality, cleanliness, and value.

Stress on a key business value. At all these companies, the values are pursued with an almost religious zeal by the chief executive officers. Rene McPherson, now dean of Stanford University's Graduate School of Business but until recently Dana's CEO, incessantly preached cost reduction and productivity improvement—and the company doubled its productivity in seven years. Almost to the day when Thomas Watson, Jr., retired from IBM he wrote memos to the staff on the subject of calling on customers—even stressing the proper dress for the call. TI's ex-chairman Patrick Haggerty made it a point to drop in at a development laboratory on his way home each night when he was in Dallas. And in another company, where competitive position was the prime focus, one division manager wrote 700 memos to his subordinates one year, analyzing competitors.

Such single-minded focus on a value becomes a culture for the company. Nearly every IBM employee has stories about how he or she took great pains to solve a customer's problem. New product themes even dominate 3M and HP lunchroom conversations. Every operational review at HP focuses on new products, with a minimum amount of time devoted to financial results or projections—because President John Young has made it clear that he believes that proper implementation of new-product plans automatically creates the right numbers. In fact, Young makes it a point to start new employees in the new-product process and keep them there for a few years as part of a "socialization" pattern. "I don't care if they do come from the Stanford Business School," he says. "For a few years they get their hands dirty, or we are not interested." At McDonald's, the company's values are drummed into employees at Hamburger U., a training program every employee goes through.

As the employees who are steeped in the corporate culture move up the ladder, they become role models for newcomers, and the process continues. It is possibly best exemplified by contrast. American Telephone & Telegraph Co., which recently began to develop a marketing orientation, has been hamstrung in its efforts because of a lack of career telephone executives with marketing successes. When Archie J. McGill was hired from IBM to head AT&T's marketing, some long-term employees balked at his leadership because he "wasn't one of them," and so was not regarded as a model.

Another common pitfall for companies is the sending of mixed signals to line managers. One company has had real problems introducing new products despite top management's constant public stress on innovation—simply because line managers perceived the real emphasis to be on cost-cutting. They viewed top management as accountants who refused to invest or to take risks, and they consistently proposed imitative products. At another company, where the CEO insisted that his major thrust was new products, an analysis of how he spent his time over a three-month period showed that no more than 5 percent of his efforts were directed to new products. His stated emphasis therefore was not credible. Not surprisingly, his employees never picked up the espoused standard.

Too many messages, even when sincerely meant, can cause the same problem. One CEO complained that no matter how hard he tried to raise what he regarded as an unsatisfactory quality level he was unsuccessful. But when McKinsey questioned his subordinates, they said, "Of course he's for quality, but he's for everything else, too. We have a theme a month here." The outstanding companies, in contrast, have one theme and stick to it.

Sticking to what they know best. Robert W. Johnson, the former chairman of J & J, put it this way: "Never acquire any business you don't know how to run." Edward G. Harness, CEO at P & G, says, "This company has never left its base." All the successful companies have been able to define their strengths—marketing, customer contact, new product innovation, low-cost manufacturing—and then build on them. They have resisted the temptation to move

into new businesses that look attractive but require corporate skills they do not have.

Simultaneous loose-tight controls. While this may sound like a contradiction, it is not. The successful companies control a few variables tightly, but allow flexibility and looseness in others. 3M uses return on sales and number of employes as yardsticks for control. Yet it gives management lots of leeway in day-to-day operations. When McPherson became president of Dana, he threw out all the company's policy manuals and substituted a one-page philosophy statement and a control system that required divisions to report costs and revenues on a daily basis.

IBM probably has the classic story about flexible controls. After the company suffered well-publicized and costly problems with its System 360 computer several years ago—problems that cost hundreds of millions of dollars to fix—Watson ordered Frank T. Cary, then a vice-president, to incorporate a system of checks and balances in new-product testing. The system made IBM people so cautious that they stopped taking risks. When Cary became president of IBM, one of the first things he did to reverse that attitude was to loosen some of the controls. He recognized that the new system would indeed prevent such an expensive problem from ever happening again, but its rigidity would also keep IBM from ever developing another major system.

By sticking to these eight basics, the successful companies have achieved better-than-average growth. Their managements are able not only to change but also to change quickly. They keep their sights aimed externally at their customers and competitors, and not on their own financial reports.

Excellence in management takes brute perseverance—time, repetition, and simplicity. The tools include plant visits, internal memos, and focused systems. Ignoring these rules may mean that the company slowly loses its vitality, its growth flattens, and its competitiveness is lost.

■ Obstacles to Corporate Innovation

SHELBY H. McINTYRE

Robert J. Mayer, a vice-president at Booz, Allen and Hamilton management consultants, recently noted that the lack of innovation "poses a significant threat to U.S. dominance of world wide markets in the 1990s." It has also been suggested that the lag in U.S. productivity behind such world market competitors as West Germany and Japan can be traced, at least in part, to sagging American innovativeness, a phenomenon that has been called "the graying of America." These observers seem to feel that the U.S. needs more innovation if our economy is to prosper. Where is such innovation to come from? Can it be expected from the large corporations with vast resources?

First, I should make clear the distinction between "innovations" and "inventions." Whereas an invention is the creation of a new idea or new knowledge, an innovation is the commercial exploitation of such knowledge.

And where do innovations originate? Perhaps surprisingly, large industrial enterprises, with their vast resources and huge research laboratories, are frequently not the source of the innovations that one might most expect from them. Large corporations turn out their fair share of patents, but do not seem to excel in the commercial exploitation of those patents. For instance, granola was introduced by the back-to-na-

ture movement of the sixties, not by General Foods, General Mills, or Quaker Oats; instant photography was introduced by the then-fledgling Polaroid Corporation, not by giant Eastman Kodak; computer-based switchboards (PBXs) were introduced by the then-tiny Rolm Corporation, not by huge AT & T; micro-computers were introduced by the entrepreneurs at Intel and not by mammoth IBM or Fairchild; Xerography was introduced by the Haloid Corporation (later named Xerox), and not by Addressograph-Lithograph; start-up company Federal Express introduced the overnight package delivery service, via a special jet fleet, even though Emery Air Freight and United Airlines were much better equipped to make such a move; Tandem Computers, a new start-up company, recently established an extremely successful commercialization of a fail-safe computer with dual processors running in tandem, even though IBM and the other computer giants have toyed with this idea for years. This list could be greatly extended.

Such examples suggest that large industrial enterprises do not have an edge with respect to being innovative, even though they devote more resources to research and development than do all the smaller firms combined. In fact, Henry E. Riggs states, "To an amazing extent, major new products incorporating new technology have been brought to the market by new companies, rather than by those companies with large investments in fundamental research . . .. Indeed, it is difficult to name any major new industry that has been created by large companies."

Shelby H. McIntyre, *Business Horizons*, January/February 1982. Copyright © 1982, by the Foundation for the School of Business at Indiana University. Reprinted by permission. References deleted. See original work.

OBSTACLES TO INNOVATION

With such clear advantages—the vast resources and sophisticated labs, experienced marketing departments, economic media buys, well-known corporate names, existing channels of distribution, and so on—why aren't large corporations developing more of the successful and innovative new products and services? Why are large organizations continually beaten to the marketplace by smaller firms with many fewer resources? The obstacles to innovation stem from the nature of large corporations, whose principal purpose and strength is to manage and maintain an already achieved base of success. The conservatism and inertia in large organizations give rise to the following difficulties.

Very large organizations foster resistance to change. A large corporation is a formalized structure that maintains and manages the successes of the past. Procedures have been designed to achieve efficiency in "doing what we do best." Innovation disrupts the stable state of corporate society, interfering with the corporation's vigorous and continuing efforts to be efficient at what it does and, therefore, to stay as it is. In a large, established organization, innovation thus meets a wall of resistance to change.

Innovation may threaten current successes. Frequently, large corporations are reluctant to innovate in areas that would compete with their already existing products, markets, and/or technologies. Honeywell, for instance, might not be expected to develop a digital thermostat because it currently commands the dominant position in the mechanical thermostat market. In addition, huge sums have been spent to automate the production of its mechanical thermostat. The company is not likely to risk losing market share and its capital investment for the sake of innovation.

The corporate hierarchy breeds conservative subordinates. The relationship of boss and subordinate may lead to conservatism. Subordinates who take risks are exposed to the possibility of bad outcomes. Since bosses tend to spend more time worrying about problems than thinking about successes, bad outcomes are more likely to be noticed and remembered than good outcomes. The subordinate who takes risks thus may turn up as the one who seems to cause the most problems. When the subordinate and the boss are not in daily contact, it is difficult for the boss to evaluate the appropriateness of the subordinate's risk-taking. At higher organizational levels, where subordinates and bosses have even less frequent contact, negative consequences of risk-taking by subordinates may be more pronounced. To the extent that this observation of corporate life pertains, truly innovative people are not as likely to be promoted and rewarded in a large corporation as are their more conservative counterparts. As a result, large corporations tend to be staffed with more conservative people.

Product/market boundary charters sometimes preclude innovation. When development work goes on within a corporate divisional structure, division business charters sometimes cut off potentially successful innovations because they do not match the current narrow objectives of that division.

In a large organization, the separation of power constitutes a "weakest link" constraint on innovation. Innovation requires both development and marketing of the product. These functions are usually separated in large organizations because specialization is believed to enhance efficiency. As a result, coordination is more difficult, and inflexibility is likely. The separation of development and marketing leads to a "propose and dispose syndrome," where each function is free to propose something that must be disposed of, or acted upon, by the other function. Since enthusiasm and vision are critical to innovation, it is difficult for one function to sell its idea to the other. The result is conservative moves that satisfy the minimal vision of both functions.

The politics of large organizations can lead to compromises that decrease the effectiveness of attempts at innovation. The balance of organizational power can lead to other difficulties, ones exemplified by the old adage that "a camel is a horse designed by a committee." V. Stefflre observes that new product champions sometimes try to form a coalition of committed advocates for a project by delegating out selected components of the development process so that each group involved gets something that they personally want.

The largest firms tend to emphasize short-run efficiency. Large organizations use management control systems that emphasize financial measures. Short-term profits, the bottom line, and return on investment become the objectives. These are measured on a yearly basis. But the payoff from innovation is typically at least five or more years.

The rotation system of training managers at large corporations develops a short-run perspective in managers. Large enterprises train their managers by rotating them through the organization. Assignments for fast-track, bright managers are seldom made for more than two years. Thus, these individuals do not see innovations as being within their horizons on any particular assignment.

Large organizations can only get excited about something big. Frequently, large corporations view a given market opportunity as too small to be interesting. However, these small market niches sometimes mushroom into sizable markets over time when proper market development is practiced (as happened, for instance, with the markets for granola, fiber optics, and lasers). Spin-off firms are often started by individuals who leave a large firm because it does not allow them to pursue an innovative project. Sometimes these spin-offs become very successful. The Control Data Corporation is a prime example. CDC was a spin-off from the Univac division of Sperry Rand in 1957; now CDC dwarfs its parent organization.

Large firms have marketing departments that follow, rather than lead, the market. Narrow and inappropriate application of the marketing concept has sometimes led companies to be driven by market needs that are extant and to ignore latent or potential needs. If too much reliance is placed on market surveys, consumer questionnaires, and test panels for new product ideas, the tendency is to develop incremental product improvements or changes in existing products rather than to develop new products for which there may be no readily perceived or existing market.

For large organizations, growth opportunities exist through acquisition. Sometimes large organizations think in terms of achieving growth through acquisition. Such a strategy is essentially evidence of the greater difficulty of being innovative within the existing corporate structure. But the decision to emphasize a strategy of absorbing already successful innovations may discourage new developments at home.

OVERCOMING OBSTACLES

The typical entrepreneurial business, which has brought us so many innovations in the past, suffers far less from the above problems. The entrepreneur is an individual who does not answer to a given boss on short-run outcomes, who can appreciate and thus integrate both the capabilities of the firm and the need of the market, who sees beyond the short-term financial figures, and who does not rotate through the organization and thus can develop a long-run perspective. Furthermore, the entrepreneur, by definition, has a vision of what could be, rather than what is, and sees the reward of going after a small, fledgling market. Finally, the entrepreneur has no vested interest in the existing technology or market due to fear of cannibalization.

It should be remembered that many of the weaknesses of large corporations, from the point of view of innovation, are the very strengths that generate great economic efficiencies in managing already developed products, markets, and technologies. As H.I. Ansoff and R.G. Brandenburg point out, performance objectives for business are often inherently incompatible. For instance, it is not possible to maximize both current operating efficiency and strategic responsiveness.

Does all this mean that large corporations should avoid innovation? Certainly not. But it does suggest that large organizations must be cognizant of the fact that innovation will not happen easily; it must be fostered, nurtured, and actively pursued. There are a few large corporations that have been successful over the long term at being innovative, such as 3M, Texas Instruments, Hewlett-Packard, International Harvester, and Wang Laboratories. These exceptional corporations have a spirit of innovation at the top of the organization, and this spirit is communicated and reflected down the hierachy. To overcome the obstacles to innovation, these companies use the following techniques:

Goals are set for innovative achievement. At 3M, for instance, every division is expected to get 25 percent of its sales each year from products that did not exist five years earlier. As Daniel J. MacDonald, general manager of 3M's Occupational Health and Safety Products Division, comments, "Our top executives are never interested in what you've already got on the market. They want to know what's new."

Managers are encouraged to take a long-term perspective. As Dr. J. Elder, General Manager of the New Business Ventures Division of 3M, notes, "We only think of Cinderella on the night of the Ball, but we tend to forget she was around being formed for eighteen years before that. So it is with new technology and new ventures."

Successful innovation is rewarded. At International Harvester, inventors are given large cash bonuses and lavish praise. An $11,000 banquet was recently thrown for one inventor.

Failures are accepted as part of the game. Managers and researchers who spawn a loser often are given a second and third chance by companies that realize that even the most effective innovator faces a high risk of failure in the extremely complex and competitive business of innovation.

Engineers and research scientists are encouraged to meet the customer. A recent survey of high technology firms noted that business unit managers in successful, high-technology companies encourage their product development engineers to get out into the field. These managers want their designers to meet users directly in their own environment rather than having users' needs communicated to designers via the marketing department. Hank Gauthier, a division manager at Coherent Corporations, notes:

> There is a danger that the marketing identification of an opportunity will not get translated down to the lab inventors in a way that they can completely appreciate. To overcome that, you have to have the lab people get out to see the customer, to appreciate his point of view. These are things that are very difficult to communicate through a written report. These customer interactions can trigger creative thought on the part of the design engineer that may never really come to the mind of the marketer. This relationship between the design engineers and the customer also has a motivational component. The marketing department doesn't have to work as hard to sell the designer what features and characteristics the product needs to have.

Special unrestricted funds are made available to explore innovative ideas without upper-level approval. For instance, Texas Instruments has a program called IDEA that allows forty program representatives throughout the company to finance long-shot projects without any higher-level approval.

Customers are carefully screened to identify new ideas. User groups and customer conferences are continually held to identify customer reactions, problems, ideas, and innovative suggestions. Hewlett-Packard and Wang Laboratories have institutionalized these procedures.

Large corporations face substantial obstacles to innovation. If top management is not vigorous enough at encouraging and stimulating innovation, it is unlikely to occur. But the obstacles to corporate innovation *can* be overcome, and some leading corporations have created the appropriate climate. There appears to be no panacea, such as the much touted corporate-venture groups approach. It takes creative, planned, long-term determination and emphasis by top management to generate the innovative result.

■ The Analysis of Goals in Complex Organizations

CHARLES PERROW

Social scientists have produced a rich body of knowledge about many aspects of large-scale organizations, yet there are comparatively few studies of the goals of these organizations. Most studies of the internal operation of complex organizations, if they mention goals at all, have taken official statements of goals at face value. There are two major categories of goals, official and "operative." ✗Official goals are the general purposes of the organization as put forth in the charter, annual reports or public statements by key executives, and other authoritative pronouncements. For example, the goal of an employment agency may be to place job seekers in contact with firms seeking workers. The official goal of a hospital may be to promote the health of the community through curing the ill, and sometimes through preventing illness, teaching, and conducting research. Similar organizations may emphasize different publicly acceptable goals. A corporation, for example, may state that its goal is to make a profit or adequate return on investment, or provide a customer service, or produce goods.

Official goals are purposely vague and general and do not indicate two major factors that influence organizational behavior: the host of decisions that must be made among alternative ways of achieving official goals and the priority of multiple goals, and the many unofficial goals pursued by groups within the organization. The concept of "operative goals" will be used to cover these aspects. ✗Operative goals designate the ends sought through the actual

Abridgement of Charles Perrow, "The Analysis of Goals in Complex Organizations," *ASR*, Vol. 26, 1961, pp. 854–866. Reference deleted. See original source.

operating policies of the organization; they tell us what the organization actually is trying to do, regardless of what the official goals say are the aims. For example, where profit-making is the announced goal, operative goals will specify whether quality or quantity is to be emphasized, whether profits are to be short run and risky or long run and stable, and will indicate the relative priority of diverse and somewhat conflicting ends of customer service, employee morale, competitive pricing, diversification, or liquidity. Decisions on all these factors influence the nature of the organization, and distinguish it from another with an identical official goal. An employment agency must decide whom to serve, what characteristics they favor among clients, and whether a high turnover of clients or a long-run relationship is desired. In the voluntary general hospital, where the official goals are patient care, teaching, and research, the relative priority of these must be decided, as well as which group in the community is to be given priority in service, and whether these services are to emphasize, say, technical excellence or warmth and "hand-holding." Operative goals are tied more directly to group interests. While they may support, be irrelevant to, or subvert official goals, they bear no necessary connection to them.

The Task—Authority— Goal sequence

Every organization must accomplish four tasks: (1) secure inputs in the form of capital sufficient to establish itself, operate, and expand as the need arises; (2) secure acceptance in the form of basic legitimization of activity; (3) marshal the necessary skills; and (4) coordinate the activities of its members and the relations of the organization with other organizations and with clients or consumers. All four are not likely to be equally important at the same time. Each of these task areas provides a basis for control or domination by the group equipped to

meet the problems involved. The operative goals will be shaped by the dominant group, reflecting the imperatives of the particular task area that is most critical, their own background characteristics (distinctive perspectives based upon their training, career lines, and areas of competence), and the unofficial uses to which they put the organization for their own ends.

The relative emphasis upon one or another of the four tasks will vary with the nature of the work the organization does and the technology appropriate to it, and with the stage of development within the organization. An organization engaged in manufacturing in an industry where skills are routinized and the market position secure may emphasize coordination, giving control to the experienced administrator. An extractive industry, such as mining, with a low skill level in its basic tasks and a simple product, will probably emphasize the importance of capital tied up in land, specialized and expensive machinery, and transportation facilities. The chair of the board of directors of a group within the board will probably dominate such an organization. An organization engaged in research and development, or the production of goods or services that cannot be carried out in a routinized fashion, will probably be most concerned with skills. Thus engineers or other relevant professionals will dominate. It is also possible that all three groups—trustees, representatives of critical skills, and administrators—may share power equally. Of course, trustees are likely to dominate in the early history of any organization, particularly those requiring elaborate capital and facilities, or unusual legitimization. But once these requisites are secured, the nature of the tasks will determine whether trustees or others dominate.

Where major task areas do not change over time, the utility of the scheme presented here is limited to suggesting possible relations between task areas, authority structure, and operative goals. The more interesting problems involve organizations that experience changes in major task areas over time. If the technology or type of work changes, or if new requirements for capital or legitimization arise, control will shift from one group to another. Let us see how this shift takes place in a hospital.

GENERAL HOSPITALS

Hospitals can be dominated by trustees, by the medical staff (an organized group of those doctors who bring in private patients plus the few doctors who receive salaries or commissions from the hospital), by the administration, or by some form of multiple leadership. There has been a general development among hospitals from trustee domination, based on capital and legitimization, to domination by the medical staff, based upon the increasing importance of their technical skills, and, at present, a tendency towards administrative dominance based on internal and external coordination. (The administrator may or may not be a doctor.) Not all hospitals go through these stages, or go through them in this sequence.

Trustee domination. Trustees legitimate the non-profit status of the organization, assure that funds are not misused, and see that community needs are being met. Officially, they are the ultimate authority in voluntary hospitals. They do not necessarily exercise the legal powers they have, but where they do, there is no question that they are in control.

The functional basis for this control is primarily financial. They have access to those who make donations, are expected to contribute heavily themselves, and control the machinery and sanctions for fundraising drives. Financial control allows them to withhold resources from recalcitrant groups in the organization, medical or non-medical. They also, of course, control all appointments and promotions, medical and non-medical.

Where these extensive powers are exercised, operative goals are likely to reflect the role of trustees as community representatives and contributors to community health. Because of their responsibility to the sponsoring community, trustees may favor conservative financial policies, opposing large financial outlays for equipment, research, and education so necessary for high medical standards. The administrator in such a hospital—usually called a superintendent under the circumstances—will have little power, prestige, or responsibility. For example, trustees have been known to question the brand of grape juice the dietician orders, or insist that they approve the color of paint the administrator selects for a room. Physicians may disapprove of patient selection criteria, chafe under financial restrictions that limit the resources they have to work with, and resent active control over appointments and promotions in the medical staff.

Medical domination. It is sometimes hard to see why all hospitals are not controlled by the medical staff, in view of the increasing complexity and specialization of the doctors' skills, their common professional background, the power of organized medicine, and the prestige accorded the doctor in society. Furthermore, they are organized for dominance, despite their nominal status as "guests" in the house. The medical staff constitutes a "shadow" organization in hospitals, providing a ready potential for control. It is organized on bureaucratic principles with admission requirements, rewards and sanctions, and a committee structure that often duplicates the key committees of the board of directors and administrative staff. Nor are doctors in an advisory position as are "staff" groups in other organizations. Doctors perform both staff and line functions, and their presumptive right to control rests on both. Doctors also have a basic economic interest in the hospital, since it is essential to most private medical practice and career advancement.

They seek extensive facilities, low hospital charges, a high quality of coordinated services, and elaborate time and energy-conserving conveniences.

Thus there is sufficient means for control by doctors, elaborated far beyond the mere provision of essential skills, and sufficient interest in control. Where doctors fully exercise their potential power, the administrator functions as a superintendent or, as his co-professionals are wont to put it, as a housekeeper. The importance of administrative skills is likely to be minimized, the administrative viewpoint on operative goals neglected, and the quality of personnel may suffer. A former nurse often serves as superintendent in this type of hospital. Policy matters are defined as medical in nature by the doctors, and neither trustees nor administrators, by definition, are qualified to have an equal voice in policy formation.

The operative goals of such a hospital are likely to be defined in strictly medical terms, and the organization may achieve high technical standards of care, promote exemplary research, and provide sound training.

Various unofficial goals may be achieved at the expense of medical ones, or, in some cases, in conjunction with them. There are many cases of personal aggrandizement on the part of departmental chiefs and the chief of staff. The informal referral and consultation system in conjunction with promotions, bed quotas, and "privileges" to operate or treat certain types of cases, affords many occasions for the misuse of power. Interns and residents are particularly vulnerable to exploitation at the expense of teaching goals. Furthermore, as a professional, the doctor has undergone intensive socialization in his training and is called upon to exercise extraordinary judgment and skill with drastic consequences for good or ill. Thus he demands unusual deference and obedience and is invested with "charismatic" authority. He may extend this authority to the entrepreneurial aspects of his role, with the result that his "service" orientation, so taken for granted in much of the literature, sometimes means service to the doctor at the expense of personnel, other patients, or even his own patient.

Administrative dominance. Administrative dominance is based first on the need for coordinating the increasingly complex, non-routinizable functions hospitals have undertaken. There is an increasing number of personnel that the doctor can no longer direct. The mounting concern of trustees, doctors themselves, patients, and pre-payment groups with more efficient and economical operation also gives the administrator more power. A second, related basis for control stems from the fact that health services in general have become increasingly interdependent and specialized. The hospital must cooperate more with other hospitals and community agencies. It must also take on more services itself, and in doing so its contacts with other agencies and professional groups outside the hospital multiply. The administrator is equipped to handle these matters because of his specialized training, often received in a professional school of hospital administration, accumulated experience, and available time. These services impinge upon the doctor at many points, providing a further basis for administrative control over doctors, and they lead to commitments in which trustees find they have to acquiesce.

The administrator is also in a position to control matters that affect doctors' demands for status, deference, and time-saving conveniences. By maintaining close supervision over employees or promoting their own independent basis for competence, and by supporting them in conflicts with doctors, the administrator can, to some degree, overcome the high functional authority that doctors command. In addition, by carefully controlling communication between trustees and key medical staff officials, he can prevent an alliance of these two groups against him.

If administrative dominance is based primarily on the complexity of basic hospital activities, rather than on the organization's medical-social role in the community, the operative orientation may be toward financial solvency, careful budget controls, efficiency, and minimal development of services. For example, preventive medicine, research, and training may be minimized; a cautious approach may prevail towards new forms of care such as intensive therapy units or home-care programs. Such orientations could be especially true of hospitals dominated by administrators whose background and training were as bookkeepers, comptrollers, business managers, purchasing agents, and the like. This is probably the most common form of administrative dominance.

However, increasing professionalization of hospital administrators has, on the one hand, equipped them to handle narrower administrative matters easily, and, on the other hand, alerted them to the broader medical-social role of hospitals involving organizational and financial innovations in the forms of care. Even medical standards can come under administrative control. For example, the informal system among doctors of sponsorship, referral, and consultation serves to protect informal work norms, shield members from criticism, and exclude noncooperative members. The administrator is in a position to insist that medical policing be performed by a salaried doctor who stands outside the informal system.

Multiple leadership. So far we have been considering situations in which one group clearly dominates. It is possible, however, for power to be shared by two or three groups to the extent that no one is able to control all or most of the actions of the others. This we call multiple leadership: a division of labor regarding the determination of goals and the power to achieve them. This is not the same as decentralized power, where specialized units of the organization have considerable autonomy. In the latter case, units are free to operate as they choose only up to a point, when it be-

comes quite clear that there is a centralized authority. In multiple leadership there is no single ultimate power.

Multiple leadership is most likely to appear in organizations in which there are multiple goals that lack precise criteria of achievement and admit of considerable tolerance with regard to achievement.

PROFIT-MAKING ORGANIZATIONS

If profit-making is an overriding goal of an organization, many operative decisions must be made that will shape its character. Even where technology remains constant, such organizations will vary with regard to personnel practices, customer services, growth, liquidity, an emphasis upon quality or quantity, or long- or short-run gains.

When asked, "What are the aims of top management in your company?" the responses of executives of 145 business firms showed: "to make money, profits, or a living" mentioned as the first aim by 36 percent of the executives; "to provide a good product; public service" by 21 percent, and "to grow" was third with 12 percent. When the first three aims spontaneously mentioned were added together, profits led; employee welfare tied with "good products or public service" for second place.

Some writers have asserted that in large corporations it is the executive group, rather than stockholders or the board of trustees, that generally dominates. One study of the role of trustees showed that trustees exercise leadership mainly in times of crisis. The common pattern of evolution shows active leadership by owners in the early years of the firm. Leadership is then passed on to new generations of the families concerned, and gradually responsibility for decision-making passes to professional executives who frequently have been trained by the original leaders. Goals likewise shift from rapid development and a concern with profits to more conservative policies emphasizing coordination, stability, and security of employment.

But does this mean that for profit-making organizations in general there are only two alternative sources of domination, trustees (including owners) and professional administrators? Certainly within the organizations dominated by professional managers there is ample opportunity for a variety of operational goals less general than, say, stability and security of employment. It has been suggested that the "historical background" of a company and especially the training received by its leading executives may be a powerful factor in shaping management decisions. It is the "Rockefeller tradition" rather than the present Rockefeller holdings that has actively conditioned management decisions in Standard Oil. This tradition is largely responsible for present methods of management organization and internal control, use of the committee system, and the domination of boards of directors by company executives.

Domination by skill groups is possible in two ways. On the one hand, a department—for example, sales, engineering, research and development, or finance—may, because of the technology and stage of growth, effectively exercise a veto on the executive's decisions and substantially shape decisions in other departments. Second, lines of promotion may be such that top executives are drawn from one powerful department, and retain their identification with the parochial goals of that department.

Thus, goals may vary widely in profit-making organizations, and power may rest not only with trustees or professional administrators, but with skill groups or administrators influenced by their skill background. Of course, one task area may so dominate a firm that there will be no shifts in power, and operative goals will remain fairly stable within the limits of the changing values of society. But where basic tasks shift, either because of growth or changing technology, the scheme presented here at least alerts us to potential goal changes and their consequences. A typical sequence might be: trustee domination in initial stages of financing, setting direction for development and recruitment of technical or professional skills, then dominance by the skill group during product or service development and research, only to have subsequent control pass to coordination of fairly routinized activities. As the market and technology change, this cycle could be repeated. During the course of this sequence, operative goals may shift from quantity production and short-run profits as emphasized by trustees, to the engineers' preoccupation with quality at the expense of quantity or styling, with this succeeded by a priority upon styling and unessential innovations demanded by the sales force, and finally with an emphasis upon the long-run market position, conservative attitude towards innovation, and considerable investment in employee-centered policies and programs by management. While formal authority structure may not vary during this sequence, the recruitment into managerial positions and the actual power of management, trustees, or skill groups could shift with each new problem focus. Multiple leadership by all three is also possible.

How to Cope with Organizational Future Shock

HAZEL HENDERSON

Why do all organizations, including corporations, experience difficulties in adapting to changing conditions? To paraphrase Alvin Toffler, why do they suffer "organizational future shock" when faced with accelerating social and technological change—now a common problem of all industrialized societies? And how will organizations learn to cope with the new shock waves that may be in store for them if societies must readapt to the slower-growth, less capital-intensive and energy-rich conditions that many futurists now predict?

Today, individuals are learning faster than institutions, causing many to feel enmeshed and constrained by them. As sociologist Bertram Gross notes, organizations are devices for screening out reality in order to focus attention on their own specific goals. Thus they regularly intercept, distort, impound, or amplify information, structuring it for their own needs and channeling employees' efforts toward their own goals. In the extreme, this can lead to what Joseph Coates, deputy director of the U.S. Office of Technology Assessment, calls "functional lying," a step beyond the mere overzealous public relations efforts of most organizations.

In addition, to unify their participants around a common purpose, institutions develop their own folklore and pep talk as well as more structured methods such as management information systems and man-

agement-by-objectives programs. Unfortunately, during periods of rapid societal change, these objectives themselves must be changed. At a recent World Future Society Assembly, systems scientist Magorah Maruyama pointed out that not only must organizational goals be changed but also the old logic behind the industrial era based on standardization, competition, and hierarchy must be replaced by a new logic for the post-industrial era based on destandardization, heterogeneity, interaction, and a new ethics in harmony with nature.

THE ENTROPY STATE: DEATH OF A SYSTEM

These information-structuring activities of organizations are functional only in early growth phases; as organizations grow larger, their ability to distort information and screen out feedback increases and eventually becomes dysfunctional. Commenting on how this affects management's performance in pyramidally structured organizations, futurist Robert Theobald notes, "Any person with power gets no valid information at all." Thus attempts to grow and dominate more variables in the immediate environment eventually become self-defeating, causing loss of feedback and maladaption.

The basic evolutionary law that "nothing fails like success" is the mechanism that keeps human society in balance. It eventually checks overgrowth of subunits that have reached the dinosaur stage and prevents diseconomies of scale while encouraging diversity, experimentation, and continual learning and adaption of the whole system to change.

In fact, human societies and their economic subsystems operate within the basic laws of physics and conform to the evolutionary processes of growth and decay: the syntropy/entropy cycles of all natural systems. Just as the decay of last year's leaves provides humus for new growth the following spring, some institutions must decline and decay so that their components of capital, land, and human talents can be used to create new organizations.

But the idea that obsolete organizations should be allowed to die often alarms many individuals; many of them have grown so large and employ so many people that their decline can cause great social dislocations. Yet as resources, energy, and capital become more scarce and precious, less-productive organizations can wastefully divert resources and human talent, sometimes starving needed innovation and new organizations.

Often, however, many organizations can be revitalized by restructuring themselves and changing their goals. Some can only survive by devolving to a lower level of superstructure. Some must decline and pass from the scene, such as those too rigidly programmed to fill needs that are becoming saturated or those relying on resource inputs that become so scarce or expensive that profit margins in production erode to the vanishing point. These companies may even have to mount "demarketing" campaigns as they phase out unprofitable products.

Other organizations become too complex and diverse and begin to spend more effort transacting with themselves than in producing their desired output. They create so many interdependent variables and interfaces that they can no longer be modeled accurately, and any system that cannot be modeled accurately cannot be managed. Corporations, government bureaucracies, and even nations are suscepti-

ble to this syndrome—"the entropy state"—in which an organization's own weight gradually winds it down into a state of equilibrium where no further useful work or output is possible.

Some familiar examples of organizations approaching the entropy state include conglomerates that have been forced to spin off some of the divisions they acquired during the 1960s and government bureaucracies (as in New York City) that suffer from diseconomies of scale and unmanageable complexity. As energy and transportation become more realistically priced, we will see a return to regional and local patterns of production and distribution—just as in our personal lives we are substituting for market value, use value, or even psychic value as we learn how to repair our own houses, appliances, and cars, and to grow more of our own food.

LEARNING AT THE WATER COOLER

How can we help our organizations to adapt and alleviate their future shock?

First, we need to recognize the different roles of "insiders" and "outsiders" and how they can mesh creatively to promote the vital adaption process. Both can function in the role that organization theorist Warren Bennis calls the "change agent."

Most people are insiders, employed or otherwise enmeshed within organizations, both the primary ones in which they earn their livelihoods and the secondary ones such as clubs, churches, and voluntary associations. Most people also have a pretty good sense of how much these organizations lag in adapting to new conditions and absorbing new perceptions, values, and goals.

When many individuals begin to notice that these institutional lags and discrepancies exist, they coalesce into informal groups and networks within their organizations, sharing their perceptions with each other at the water cooler, in the cafeteria, or elsewhere. Such interactions are frequent in openly administered organizations, which are based on Douglas McGregor's now famous Theory Y principles of participatory, cooperative, integrative functioning (as opposed to the more hierarchical, competitive, authoritarian style of Theory X). But in more rigidly structured organizations, new insights sometimes are repressed, either by superiors or through fear of "sticking one's neck out." And if these insights are valid, they will be shared by large numbers of other employees and will find expression in discontent, faster turnover, reduced productivity, or increased apathy and alienation.

In some cases, alienation has even prompted workers to take over corporate production facilities and lock out management (at a French plant and a British shipyard, for example). Or sometimes insiders feel compelled by their own consciences to "blow the whistle," as did cost accountant Ernest Fitzgerald, who complained of cost overruns on Department of Defense contracts and was fired for his trouble. Many organization theorists endorse the concept of whistle blowing, either to a professional society (perhaps when its safety standards are being violated) or to public interest researchers and the press. Such seemingly drastic action is sometimes the only recourse if the upward flow of vital information is impeded.

At the 1975 World Future Society Assembly, panelists Donald Schon of the Massachusetts Institute of Technology, Donald Michael of the University of Michigan, and Daniel Gray of Arthur D. Little, Inc., argued that our very survival now depends on the renewal of our institutions. These experts in organizational adaption discussed the need for supporting people in their efforts to change rules and redefine problems, permitting employees to learn from failure. In this way people may overcome their fear of making decisions and learn to develop group skills and greater self-knowledge.

SKIRTING THE ISSUE

These brave sentiments, however, neatly avoid one organizational taboo—the taboo against questioning whether an organization itself has outlived its usefulness or whether its purposes or products have become irrelevant or even counter-productive. In such cases, outsiders in the form of consultants and other corporate critics are the only ones likely to raise this issue, even though their message will be screened out or rejected. But often consulting firms themselves are large and carry heavy overhead costs, and consequently they may become overanxious to please their clients. Thus they may confirm, rather than buck, prevailing corporate values.

If management cannot always hear its own well-motivated insiders or rely on outside consulting firms, how can it develop less orthodox ways of scanning society and picking up the often faint signals that may, if correctly interpreted, portend awesome change?

TECHNOLOGICAL FORECASTING AD ABSURDUM

Many of the methods used for mapping change rely on the traditional tools of technological forecasting: cost/benefit analysis, demand forecasting, and planning, programming, and budgeting systems. However, these linear, extrapolative methods are only of limited usefulness in situations where many variables in the social, political, and economic environment are interacting and changing simultaneously.

Systems and input-output analyses, technology assessments, environmental impact statements, Delphi techniques, cross-impact analyses, and relevance trees are some of the developing methods for trying to predict how these multiple, shifting variables may interact with each other over time. Most of these methods are still highly experimental and try to design nonlinear, dynamic models to map such complexities. But ironically, each order of magnitude of technological mastery and managerial virtuosity inevitably requires greater orders of magnitude of sophistication in modeling techniques and greater coordination and control. Eventually, the law of diminishing returns sets in as it becomes increasingly more difficult to define the boundaries of the system under study. Ultimately, nothing less than an "all-by-all matrix" may be required.

Economists are lagging behind in their attempts to expand predictive models and include more variables. Indeed, economists already have lost their former preeminence in planning and forecasting, both because of their glaring failures in this field and in macroeconomic management and because of the rise of new, more inclusive methods such as technology assessment. Similarly, microeconomic tools, such as cost/benefit analysis, are also in trouble. Often these methods are used to mask difficult political choices as if they were pseudo-technical questions of feasibility or efficiency rather than matters of conflicting values and social equity.

For example, cost/benefit analyses too often average out costs and benefits per capita, thus obscuring who will pay the costs and who will receive the benefits. Not surprisingly, these basic conflicts soon erupt into public opposition to projects justified by mere intellectual sleight of hand.

INTUITION—THE MISSING LINK?

The purpose of economists' calculations of the benefits of performing research is to provide information that significantly reduces uncertainty for decision-makers. Paradoxically, the more likely result of the information gathered through broader research methods such as technology assessments and environmental impact statements actually *increases* uncertainty for the poor decision-makers, only telling them more about *what is not known.*

As new quantitative methods develop, it becomes clearer to their practitioners that all suffer from what Alfred North Whitehead called "the fallacy of misplaced concreteness." Such quantitative, inductive, linear, and logical methods are based on a world view inherited from Aristotle and the French philosopher Descartes. It assumes that wholes can be understood by examining their parts.

But the development of human knowledge and, hopefully, wisdom requires both imaginative hypothesis and careful validation by logical, quantitative methods. Currently, organization theorists are showing much interest in reintegrating intuitive processes into management sciences, which have grown excessively quantitative and reductionist and consequently miss important, nonquantifiable variables, particularly in human behavior.

Society's dynamically changing values and goals, far from being peripheral, are the dominant, driving variables in all human systems. Since these values change consumer preferences and create and destroy markets for corporations, managers must learn to use some of the more informal methods of tapping imagination, intuition, and artistic expression to monitor the social scene.

Todd A. Britsch of Brigham Young University in Utah believes that most forecasting techniques, with their emphasis on quantification, have ignored the uses of art and literature as social indicators. Britsch points out that the insights of artists and writers are often predictive of perceptual shifts before they become obvious in actual societal value changes or innovations. Perhaps the best example of this is the famous novel by British writer George Orwell, *1984,* which still qualifies as one of the best futuristic scenarios of the darker possibilities of the computer age—even though it was written in 1949. But until now, only science fiction has been widely utilized by futurists. Britsch suggests that social forecasters monitor novels, plays, and poems for key words and attitudes on topics such as the work ethic, divorce, and child bearing and then compare this data to sociological material for the same period and for subsequent years.

Similarly, Britsch notes that satire is generally a social indicator, telling us that new iconoclasts are emerging to challenge the old order. Indeed, corporations perhaps should monitor "little" magazines and other obscure journals for signs of value shifts and use them to plot possible consumer preference changes. Such monitoring methods have been adopted by the Institute for Life Insurance's Trend Analysis Program, the Urban Research Institute, and other organizations.

COUNTERCULTURE CONSULTANTS

Citizen movements for social change are obviously social indicators of high visibility, whether their causes are consumer and environmental protection, peace, social justice, or economic opportunity. But too often, corporate and government executives prefer not to confront these groups directly; instead, they prefer to purchase very expensive, second-hand information from public relations firms, further contributing to the general confusion.

Social scientists are constantly constructing more easily quantifiable social indicators such as data on park acreage per citizen, educational levels, health statistics, and other objective indicators of the quality of life. However, much more work on subjective social indicators is needed—for example, polling citizens on how they perceive the changing quality of their own lives or implementing exercises in "anticipatory democracy" such as Hawaii 2000 and Alternatives for Washington, where whole communities are linked by communications media and feedback devices in order to explore regional values and goals.

Consulting unorthodox, imaginative dropouts from our highly institutionalized society provides still another innovative approach to monitoring value changes. The president of one large corporation, for instance, maintains regular communication with a long-haired, bearded poet who was a prominent counterculture "Yippie" leader in the 1960s. Since money is of little interest to this unorthodox "consultant," the company underwrites the purchase of the books on his huge reading list and gives him copying and mailing facilities to help him stay in contact with his far-flung network of equally brilliant, iconoclastic friends.

■ Transforming Organizations: The Key to Strategy Is Context

STANLEY M. DAVIS

I once asked an executive vice-president who was responsible for the future development of a very large corporation, "What is the thing you worry about most on your job?" His answer was startling. "I worry most about what my people don't know that they don't know. What they know that they don't know, they are able to work on and find the answers to. But they can't do that if they don't know that they don't know."

What does it mean not to know that you don't know? In some ways, this is the condition of "Ignorance is bliss." It is only when a problem is identified and defined that people can go to work resolving it. Before that time, there is no problem. The same events may have occurred long before the identification of the phenomenon as an issue, but they are meaningful only because meaning has been attached to them.

The way in which people perceive a problem, a question, an event determines what they will be able to know about it. The newborn, for example, is not able to distinguish itself from its environment; it must sense the environment as "not me" before it can develop any distinct sense of "me." The infant moves from not knowing that it doesn't know there is a difference to knowing that it doesn't know what is "out there" beyond itself. Initially, this is frightening and confusing. There is both terror and exhilaration in being on the existential edge. From this new place, knowing that it doesn't know, the infant then goes on to knowing. Exploration, growth, mastery, and maturation all therefore involve a three-step process, moving from: (1) not knowing that you don't know to (2) knowing that you don't know to (3) knowing.

In the world of business, knowing is the realm of daily activities, the operating company, today's job; and "knowing that you don't know" is represented in the corporate planning and research and development functions. Most people and organizations pay attention to the move from (2) to (3). Very few consider the shift from (1) to (2)—and quite naturally, for you cannot consider what you don't even know that you don't know.

The shift from (1) to (2) is generally referred to as "a major breakthrough." This shift raises more questions than it answers. That is its purpose. Before this shift, no one ever thought of asking such questions. The questions raised in the first shift are then answered in the second shift, from knowing that we don't know (2) to knowing (3). The second shift gives us the *content* that was missing. The first shift transforms the *context*.

Here are some examples of transformations of context:

■ From physics: When Einstein theorized that mass and energy are the same thing expressed differently ($E = mc^2$), he transformed the context in which we understood reality. Mass and energy are *content,* the relationship expressed by the equation is *context.*

■ From psychology: Freud's work on the unconscious transformed the *context* in which one must examine the mind. What goes on in the unconscious is part of the *content* of the mind.

TRANSFORMING CONTEXTS

Contexts are the unquestioned assumptions through which all experience is filtered. Context has no meaning—yet it provides, in Paul Tillich's phrase, the "ground of being" from which content derives. An elementary example of this might well be useful here.

A context for "two" is illustrated in section A of exhibit 1.1, where two lines of equal length are shown. Another context for "two" is shown in section B of exhibit 1.1. Again, two lines are shown, only now one looks longer than the other. Actually they are the same length—but presented in a different context, they are not perceived as equal.

Context creates a reality, and the reality it creates is the content. Most managers manage the content, and only during a major strategic shift is the context brought into question. An operating budget or a two-year plan mainly provides content within a given and unquestioned context. The func-

tion of a ten-year plan is to provide the context. An organization's leadership will have implemented a long-range strategic plan when they manage the *context,* not the content.

ASKING THE RIGHT QUESTIONS

How are contexts created? Leaders should spend as much time posing questions as they do attempting to answer them. Perhaps they should spend even more time framing them.

Context is created by the drawing of a boundary—the frame. What lies within the boundary becomes content. The reason that asking the right question is so important is that it determines the boundaries of the inquiry that is to follow. A question focuses attention, provides direction, and tells people where to look for the answer. Given that the boundary of inquiry is determined by the formulation of the question, what is inside that boundary becomes what we know that we don't know, and what we focus our attention on. What is outside the boundary of the question is, in effect, what we don't know that we don't know and therefore pay no attention to.

If the wrong question is posed, the inquiry will focus on the wrong data, and the outcome is sidetracked even before the search gets underway. If the focus is too narrow and specialized, the investigator will fail to comprehend the larger context bearing on the issue. If the focus is too broad, it becomes impossible to know what content is meaningful or how the pieces relate to one another. Asking the right question is thus the most important first step in determining the answer. Only a good question can yield a worthwhile answer.

STRATEGY AND ORGANIZATION

You have to know what you want to do before you can do it. The two elements of this

---

EXHIBIT 1.1 Contexts for Two

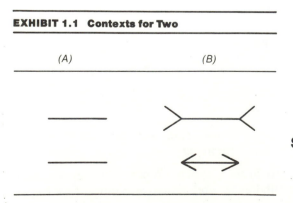

(A)　　　　　　　(B)

statement—knowing what to do and knowing how to do it—are definitions of strategy and organization, respectively. Organization, here, refers to the culture, structure, systems, and people in the corporation.

Strategy is the plan for future survival. Organization is the current arrangement for day-to-day living. In principle the relation between the two is that a team, company, army, or nation should be organized in the manner that will best implement the strategy. A good strategy with poor organization is a thoroughbred without a rider, trainer, stable, or track. In principle, strategy precedes organization. Also in principle, the two are closely related; in practice, often they are not.

The proposition is that, by definition, *organization always lags behind strategy.* You have to know what it is you want to do before you can know how to do it. According to this logic, unless there are no changes in the environment or in the strategy, all organizations are created for businesses that either no longer exist or are in the process of going out of existence!

That is a terrible state of affairs. The inherent weakness of the model is that no organization can ever be totally appropriate for carrying out its mission or purpose. The mission, objectives, and strategy of the firm will always come first; they will always be ahead of the structure and organization. The lag between formulating a strategic plan and implementing it may be thought of as the distance between a strategy and its appropriate form of organization.

Organizations can do no better than catch up to the present, and there is even a Catch-22 to catching up: When you get there, "there" isn't there any more. Strategy is always focused on the future; organization may focus on the future, but it is rooted in the present, or even in the past if management is inefficient.

The name of the game, managerially and organizationally, is to catch up as quickly as posssible. The shorter the lag between strategy and organization, the more efficient

is the firm. Reduce the lag by which organization follows strategy and, all else being equal, you will increase your success by whatever measurements you choose.

This is a very inert conception of organization. Organization does not have to be *pulled* along by the strategy. Organization can be used to *push* the strategy toward its realization. An organization's culture, structure, systems, and people can implement a strategic plan without the lag.

FROM EXTRAPOLATION TO INTERPOLATION

When strategic planning was in its infancy, it was little more than extrapolation of the past into the future. As the field became more sophisticated, practitioners engaged in various assessments of that likely future, as in the environmental scans and future scenarios. From these tools a clearer statement of strategy emerged: "This is what our company is going to look like at a point in the future." Thus interpolation replaced extrapolation in strategic planning: "If this is what our firm looks like today, and this is what we intend it to look like X years from now, then we can know *what* changes must be made to become that newly described entity."

This is one way of describing what has since become the very sophisticated area of strategic planning and the formulation of strategy. Organization planning, or the implementation of strategy, however, is still not that sophisticated. Remember the logic: Organization lags behind strategy. There is a lag in the evolution between strategic planning and organization planning just as there is a lag between strategy and organization. Organization planning, to the extent that it exists at all, is still largely extrapolative:

Our sales have grown at X percent for the past ten years, and the number of our employees has grown at 80 percent of X during that same period. Given our expected size at a future time, we will therefore have to hire ___ people during the next ___ years.

Planning the future organization should be accomplished in the same way that the strategy for the future is determined—interpolatively. Each element of organization that will be appropriate for the future should be spelled out in detail. They should say, for example:

> Given the kind of business that we intend to be, what is the appropriate structure for *that* business? How does it differ from the current structure? What steps are necessary to move it from here to there?

Is organizational lag necessary? Theoretically, there must be some; practically, there should be as little as possible. Remember, strategy is the allocation of future resources to anticipated demand. Strategy tells you what the business is going to look like; organization tells you how you are going to get it to be that way. Once the organization is "that" way, it has implemented the strategy; and when this has occurred, "that" is no longer the strategy. By definition there is no organization whose culture, structure, systems, and people are completely appropriate for its strategy. If all components of the organization were completely appropriate, the strategy would be realized; that is to say, it would be operational and no longer strategic. Successful strategy self-destructs. An objective, once accomplished, is no longer an objective. The realization of strategy is always futuristic. Because organization is the mechanism for implementing strategy, it is therefore the mechanism for realizing the future.

This is the appropriate orientation to take. Organization is too often taken to be the current framework, at best, or the inadequate and unresponsive framework, at worst. Literature on organization, organization consultants, and most personnel, for example, deals with organization from a remedial point of view: how to cure what is wrong with it, how to make it better, how to get it to somewhere that it is not. The organization is thought of as some lethargic giant that never quite does what you want it to do, and you have to pull and tug at it to get it to go where you want it to be. Those who focus on organization in each case have a sense of what it should be, and when they look at what the current organization is, their conclusion is, "This is not it."

From this viewpoint, the organization retards the implementation of strategy. The valence is always negative; it is only a question of how much. Reduce the negatives, remove the impediments, improve the organization, and you will reduce the lag between the formulation of strategy and its realization. Most restructurings, management development programs, reward systems, information processing techniques, and other elements of organization are aimed at such improvements.

Most parents have dreams for their children. Some want their children to be doctors, some musicians, and all want them to be healthy, wealthy, and wise. These are parents who raise their children by focusing on content. Following in father's footsteps, or in the footsteps father never had and therefore wants for his son, are well-known examples of this approach. Other parents, however, raise their children by focusing on context. In Helen Keller's famous phrase, their dream is, "Be all you can be." The orientation here is to "parent" the context, and let the child discover the content.

The same distinctions can be made in a corporation. To reiterate, an operating budget or a two-year plan mainly provides content within a given and unquestioned context. *The function of a ten-year or other long-range plan is to provide the context.* Managers will have implemented a long-range plan if they manage the context, not the content. When this is done, every action taken is both discovery and implementation of the content. It is management as source, not as outcome.

■ Evolution and Revolution as Organizations Grow

LARRY E. GREINER

A small research company chooses too complicated and formalized an organization structure for its young age and limited size. It flounders in rigidity and bureaucracy for several years and is finally acquired by a larger company.

Key executives of a retail store chain hold on to an organization structure long after it has served its purpose, because their power is derived from this structure. The company eventually goes into bankruptcy.

A large bank disciplines a "rebellious" manager who is blamed for current control problems, when the underlying cause is centralized procedures that are holding back expansion into new markets. Many younger managers subsequently leave the bank, competition moves in, and profits are still declining.

The problems of these companies, like those of many others, are rooted more in past decisions than in present events or outside market dynamics. Historical forces do indeed shape the future growth of organizations. Yet management, in its haste to grow, often overlooks such critical developmental questions as: Where has our organization been? Where is it now? And what do the answers to these questions mean for where we are going? Instead, its gaze is fixed outward toward the environment and the future—as if more precise market projections will provide a new organizational identity.

Companies fail to see that many clues to their future success lie within their own organizations and their evolving states of development. Moreover, the inability of management to understand its organization development problems can result in a company becoming "frozen" in its present stage of evolution or, ultimately, in failure, regardless of market opportunities.

My position in this article is that the future of an organization may be less determined by outside forces than it is by the organization's history. In stressing the force of history on an organization, I have drawn from the legacies of European psychologists (their thesis being that individual behavior is determined primarily by previous events and experiences, not by what lies ahead). Extending this analogy of individual development to the problems of organization development, I shall discuss a series of developmental phases through which growing companies tend to pass. But, first, let me provide two definitions.

1. The term *evolution* is used to describe prolonged periods of growth where no major upheaval occurs in organization practices.

2. The term *revolution* is used to describe those periods of substantial turmoil in organization life.

As a company progresses through developmental phases, each evolutionary period creates its own revolution. For instance, centralized practices eventually lead to demands for decentralization. Moreover, the nature of management's solution to each revolutionary period determines whether a company will move forward into its next stage of evolutionary growth. As I shall show later, there are at least five phases of organization development, each characterized by both an evolution and a revolution.

KEY FORCES IN DEVELOPMENT

During the past few years a small amount of research knowledge about the phases of organization development has been building. Some of this research is very quantitative, such as time-series analyses that reveal patterns of economic performance over time. The majority of studies, however, are case-oriented and use company records and interviews to reconstruct a rich picture of corporate development. Yet both types of research tend to be heavily empirical without attempting more generalized statements about the overall process of development.

A notable exception is the historical work of Alfred D. Chandler, Jr., in his book *Strategy and Structure*. This study depicts four very broad and general phases in the lives of four large U.S. companies. It proposes that outside market opportunities determine a company's strategy, which in turn determines the company's organization structure. This thesis has a valid ring for the four companies examined by Chandler, largely because they developed in a time of explosive markets and technological advances. But more recent evidence suggests that organization structure may be less malleable than Chandler assumed; in fact, structure can play a critical role in influencing corporate strategy. It is this reverse emphasis on how organization structure affects future growth that is highlighted in the model presented in this article.

From an analysis of recent studies, five key dimensions emerge as essential for building a model of organization development:

1. Age of the organization.
2. Size of the organization.
3. Stages of evolution.
4. Stages of revolution.
5. Growth rate of the industry.

I shall describe each of these elements separately, but first note their combined effect as illustrated in exhibit 1.2. Note especially how each dimension influences the other over time; when all five elements begin to interact, a more complete and dynamic picture of organizational growth emerges.

After describing these dimensions and their interconnections, I shall discuss each evolutionary revolutionary phase of development and show (a) how each stage of evolution breeds its own revolution, and (b) how management solutions to each revolution determine the next stage of evolution.

Age of the Organization

The most obvious and essential dimension for any model of development is the life span of an organization (represented as the horizontal axis in exhibit 1.2). All historical studies gather data from various points in time and then make comparisons. From these observations, it is evident that the same organization practices are not maintained throughout a long time span. This makes a most basic point: management problems and principles are rooted in time. The concept of decentralization, for example, can have meaning for describing corporate practices at one time period but loses its descriptive power at another.

The passage of time also contributes to the institutionalization of managerial attitudes. As a result, employee behavior becomes not only more predictable but also more difficult to change when attitudes are outdated.

EXHIBIT 1.2 Model of Organization Development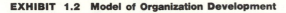

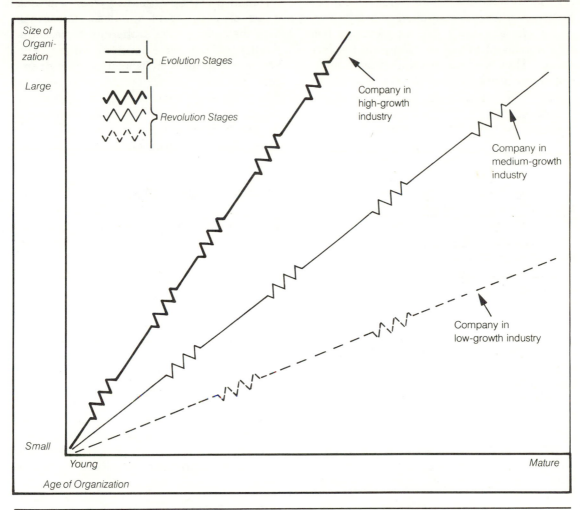

Size of the Organization

This dimension is depicted as the vertical axis in exhibit 1.2. A company's problems and solutions tend to change markedly as the number of employees and sales volume increase. Thus, time is not the only determinant of structure; in fact, organizations that do not grow in size can retain many of the same management issues and practices over lengthy periods. In addition to increased size, however, problems of coordination and communication magnify, new functions emerge, levels in the management hierarchy multiply, and jobs become more interrelated.

Stages of Evolution

As both age and size increase, another phenomenon becomes evident: the prolonged growth that I have termed the evolutionary period. Most growing organizations do not expand for two years and then retreat for one year; rather, those that survive a crisis usually enjoy four to eight years of continuous growth without a major economic setback or severe internal disruption. The term evolution seems appropriate for describing these quieter periods because only modest adjustments appear necessary for maintaining growth under the same overall pattern of management.

Stages of Revolution

Smooth evolution is not inevitable; it cannot be assumed that organization growth is linear. *Fortune's* "500" list, for example, has had significant turnover during the last fifty years. Thus we find evidence from numerous case histories that reveals periods of substantial turbulence spaced between smoother periods of evolution.

I have termed these turbulent times the periods of revolution because they typically exhibit a serious upheaval of management practices. Traditional management practices, which were appropriate for a smaller size and earlier time, are brought under scrutiny by frustrated top managers and disillusioned lower-level managers. During such periods of crisis, a number of companies fail—those unable to abandon past practices and effect major organization changes are likely either to fold or to level off in their growth rates.

The critical task for management in each revolutionary period is to find a new set of organization practices that will become the basis for managing the next period of evolutionary growth. Interestingly enough, these new practices eventually sow their own seeds of decay and lead to another period of revolution. Companies therefore experience the irony of seeing a major solution in one time period become a major problem at a later date.

Growth Rate of the Industry

The speed at which an organization experiences phases of evolution and revolution is closely related to the market environment of its industry. For example, a company in a rapidly expanding market will have to add employees rapidly; hence, the need for new organization structures to accommodate large staff increases is accelerated. While evolutionary periods tend to be relatively short in fast-growing industries, much longer evolutionary periods occur in mature or slowly growing industries.

Evolution can also be prolonged, and revolutions delayed, when profits come easily.

For instance, companies that make grievous errors in a rewarding industry can still look good on their profit and loss statements; thus they can avoid a change in management practices for a longer period. The aerospace industry in its infancy is an example. Yet revolutionary periods still occur, as one did in aerospace when profit opportunities began to dry up. Revolutions seem to be much more severe and difficult to resolve when the market environment is poor.

PHASES OF GROWTH

With the foregoing framework in mind, let us now examine in depth the five specific phases of evolution and revolution. As shown in exhibit 1.3, each evolutionary period is characterized by the dominant *management style* used to achieve growth, while each revolutionary period is characterized by the dominant *management problem* that must be solved before growth can continue. The patterns presented in exhibit 1.3 seem to be typical for companies in industries with moderate growth over a long time period; companies in faster growing industries tend to experience all five phases more rapidly, while those in slower growing industries encounter only two or three phases over many years.

It is important to note that *each phase is both an effect of the previous phase and a cause of the next phase.* For example, the evolutionary management style in Phase 3 of the exhibit is "delegation," which grows out of, and becomes the solution to, demands for greater "autonomy" in the preceding Phase 2 revolution. The style of delegation used in Phase 3, however, eventually provokes a major revolutionary crisis that is characterized by attempts to regain control over the diversity created through increased delegation.

The principal implication of each phase is that management actions are narrowly prescribed if growth is to occur. For example, a company experiencing an autonomy crisis in Phase 2 cannot return to directive man-

EXHIBIT 1.3   The Five Phases of Growth

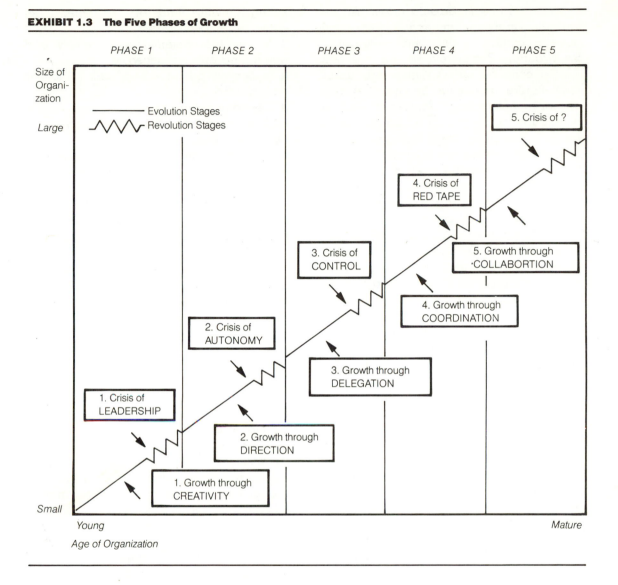

agement for a solution—it must adopt a new style of delegation in order to move ahead.

Phase 1: Creativity . . .

In the birth stage of an organization, the emphasis is on creating both a product and a market. Here are the characteristics of the period of creative evolution:

■ The company's founders are usually technically or entrepreneurially oriented, and they disdain management activities; their physical and mental energies are absorbed entirely in making and selling a new product.

■ Communication among employees is frequent and informal.

■ Long hours of work are rewarded by modest salaries and the promise of ownership benefits.

■ Control of activities comes from immediate marketplace feedback; the management acts as the customers react.

. . . *& the leadership crisis:* All the foregoing individualistic and creative activities are essential for the company to get off the ground. But therein lies the problem. As the company grows, larger production runs require knowledge about the efficiencies of manufacturing. Increased numbers of employees cannot be managed exclusively through informal communication; new employees are not motivated by an intense dedication to the product or organization. Additional capital must be secured, and new accounting procedures are needed for financial control.

Thus the founders find themselves burdened with unwanted management responsibilities. So they long for the "good old days," still trying to act as they did in the past. And conflicts between the harried leaders grow more intense.

At this point a crisis of leadership occurs, which is the onset of the first revolution. Who is to lead the company out of confusion and solve the managerial problems confronting it? Quite obviously, a strong manager is needed who has the necessary knowledge and skill to introduce new business techniques. But this is easier said than done. The founders often hate to step aside even though they are probably temperamentally unsuited to be managers. So here is the first critical developmental choice—to locate and install a strong business manager who is acceptable to the founders and who can pull the organization together.

Phase 2: Direction . . .

Those companies that survive the first phase by installing a capable business manager usually embark on a period of sustained growth under able and directive leadership. Here are the characteristics of this evolutionary period:

■ A functional organization structure is introduced to separate manufacturing from mar-

keting activities, and job assignments become more specialized.
■ Accounting systems for inventory and purchasing are introduced.
■ Incentives, budgets, and work standards are adopted.
■ Communication becomes more formal and impersonal as a hierarchy of titles and positions builds.
■ The new manager and his key supervisors take most of the responsibility for instituting direction, while lower-level supervisors are treated more as functional specialists than as autonomous decision-making managers.

. . . *& the autonomy crisis:* Although the new directive techniques channel employee energy more efficiently into growth, they eventually become inappropriate for controlling a larger, more diverse and complex organization. Lower-level employees find themselves restricted by a cumbersome and centralized hierarchy. They have come to possess more direct knowledge about markets and machinery than do the leaders at the top; consequently, they feel torn between following procedures and taking initiative on their own.

Thus the second revolution is imminent as a crisis develops from demands for greater autonomy on the part of lower-level managers. The solution adopted by most companies is to move toward greater delegation. Yet it is difficult for top managers who were previously successful at being directive to give up responsibility. Moreover, lower-level managers are not accustomed to making decisions for themselves. As a result, numerous companies flounder during this revolutionary perod, adhering to centralized methods while lower-level employees grow more disenchanted and leave the organization.

Phase 3: Delegation . . .

The next era of growth evolves from the successful application of a decentralized organization structure. It exhibits these characteristics:

■ Much greater responsibility is given to the managers of plants and market territories.
■ Profit centers and bonuses are used to stimulate motivation.
■ The top executives at headquarters restrain themselves to managing by exception, based on periodic reports from the field.
■ Management often concentrates on making new acquisitions that can be lined up beside other decentralized units.
■ Communication from the top is infrequent, usually by correspondence, telephone, or brief visits to field locations.

The delegation stage proves useful for gaining expansion through heightened motivation at lower levels. Decentralized managers with greater authority and incentive are able to penetrate larger markets, respond faster to customers, and develop new products.

. . . *& the control crisis:* A serious problem eventually evolves, however, as top executives sense that they are losing control over a highly diversified field operation. Autonomous field managers prefer to run their own shows without coordinating plans, money, technology, and human resources with the rest of the organization. Freedom breeds a parochial attitude.

Hence, the Phase 3 revolution is underway when top management seeks to regain control over the total company. Some top managements attempt a return to centralized management, which usually fails because of the vast scope of operations. Those companies that move ahead find a new solution in the use of special coordination techniques.

Phase 4: Coordination . . .

During this phase, the evolutionary period is characterized by the use of formal systems for achieving greater coordination and by top executives taking responsibility for the initiation and administration of these new systems. For example:

■ Decentralized units are merged into product groups.
■ Formal planning procedures are established and intensively reviewed.
■ Numerous staff personnel are hired and located at headquarters to initiate companywide programs of control and review for line managers.
■ Capital expenditures are carefully weighed and parceled out across the organization.
■ Each product group is treated as an investment center where return on invested capital is an important criterion used in allocating funds.
■ Certain technical functions, such as data processing, are centralized at headquarters, while daily operating decisions remain decentralized.
■ Stock options and companywide profit sharing are used to encourage identity with the firm as a whole.

All these new coordination systems prove useful for achieving growth through more efficient allocation of a company's limited resources. They prompt field managers to look beyond the needs of their local units. While these managers still have much decisionmaking responsibility, they learn to justify their actions more carefully to a "watchdog" audience at headquarters.

. . . *& the red-tape crisis:* But a lack of confidence gradually builds between line and staff, and between headquarters and the field. The proliferation of systems and programs begins to exceed its utility; a red-tape crisis is created. Line managers, for example, increasingly resent heavy staff direction from those who are not familiar with local conditions. Staff people, on the other hand, complain about uncooperative and uninformed line managers. Together both groups criticize the bureaucratic paper system that has evolved. Procedures take precedence over problem-solving, and innovation is dampened. In short, the organization has become too large and complex to be managed through formal programs and rigid systems. The Phase 4 revolution is under way.

Phase 5: Collaboration . . .

The last observable phase in previous studies emphasizes strong interpersonal collaboration in an attempt to overcome the red-tape crisis. Where Phase 4 was managed more through formal systems and procedures, Phase 5 emphasizes greater spontaneity in management action through teams and the skillful confrontation of interpersonal differences. Social control and self-discipline take over from formal control. This transition is especially difficult for those experts who created the old systems as well as for those line managers who relied on formal methods for answers.

The Phase 5 evolution, then, builds around a more flexible and behavioral approach to management. Here are its characteristics:

■ The focus is on solving problems quickly through team action.
■ Teams are combined across functions for task-group activity.
■ Headquarters staff experts are reduced in number, reassigned, and combined in interdisciplinary teams to consult with, not to direct, field units.
■ A matrix-type structure is frequently used to assemble the right teams for the appropriate problems.
■ Previous formal systems are simplified and combined into single multipurpose systems.
■ Conferences of key managers are held frequently to focus on major problem issues.
■ Educational programs are utilized to train managers in behavioral skills for achieving better teamwork and conflict resolution.
■ Real-time information systems are integrated into daily decision-making.

■ Economic rewards are geared more to team performance than to individual achievement.
■ Experiments in new practices are encourged throughout the organization.

. . . *& the ? crisis:* What will be the revolution in response to this stage of evolution? Many large U.S. companies are now in the Phase 5 evolutionary stage, so the answers are critical. While there is little clear evidence, I imagine the revolution will center around the "psychological saturation" of employees who grow emotionally and physically exhausted by the intensity of teamwork and the heavy pressure for innovative solutions.

My hunch is that the Phase 5 revolution will be solved through new structures and programs that allow employees to periodically rest, reflect, and revitalize themselves. We may even see companies with dual organization structures: a "habit" structure for getting the daily work done, and a "reflective" structure for stimulating perspective and personal enrichment. Employees could then move back and forth between the two structures as their energies are dissipated and refueled.

One European organization has implemented just such a structure. Five reflective groups have been established outside the regular structure for the purpose of continuously evaluating five task activities basic to the organization. They report directly to the managing director, although their reports are made public throughout the organization. Membership in each group includes all levels and functions, and employees are rotated through these groups on a six-month basis.

Other concrete examples now in practice include providing sabbaticals for employees, moving managers in and out of "hot spot" jobs, establishing a four-day workweek, assuring job security, building physical facilities for relaxation *during* the working day, making jobs more interchangeable, creating an extra team on the assembly line so that one team is always off for reeducation, and switching to longer vacations and more flexible working hours.

The Chinese practice of requiring executives to spend time periodically on lower-level jobs may also be worth a nonideological evaluation. For too long U.S. management has assumed that career progress should be equated with an upward path toward title, salary, and power. Could it be that some vice-presidents of marketing might just long for, and even benefit from, temporary duty in the field sales organization?

IMPLICATIONS OF HISTORY

Let me now summarize some important implications for practicing managers. First, the main features of this discussion are depicted in exhibit 1.4, which shows the specific management actions that characterize each growth phase. These actions are also the solutions that ended each preceding revolutionary period.

In one sense, I hope that many readers will react to my model by calling it obvious and natural for depicting the growth of an organization. To me this type of reaction is a useful test of the model's validity.

But at a more reflective level I imagine some of these reactions are more hindsight than foresight. Those experienced managers who have been through a developmental sequence can empathize with it now, but how did they react when in the middle of a stage of evolution or revolution? They can probably recall the limits of their own developmental understanding at that time. Perhaps they resisted desirable changes or were even swept emotionally into a revolution without being able to propose constructive solutions. So let me offer some explicit guidelines for managers of growing organizations to keep in mind.

Know where you are in the developmental sequence. Every organization and its component parts are at different stages of development. The task of top management is to be aware of these stages; otherwise, it may not recognize when the time for change has come, or it may act to impose the wrong solution.

Top leaders should be ready to work with the flow of the tide rather than against it; yet they should be cautious, since it is tempting to skip phases out of impatience. Each phase results in certain strengths and learning experiences in the organization that will be essential for success in subse-

EXHIBIT 1.4 Organization Practices During Evolution in the Five Phases of Growth

Category	Phase 1	Phase 2	Phase 3	Phase 4	Phase 5
Management Focus	Make & Sell	Efficiency of Operations	Expansion of Market	Consolidation of Organization	Problem-solving & Innovation
Organization Structure	Informal	Centralized & Functional	Decentralized & Geographical	Line-staff & Product Groups	Matrix of Teams
Top Management Style	Individualistic & Entrepreneurial	Directive	Delegative	Watchdog	Participative
Control System	Market Results	Standards & Cost Centers	Reports & Profit Centers	Plans & Investment Centers	Mutual Goal-setting
Management Reward Emphasis	Ownership	Salary & Merit Increases	Individual Bonus	Profit-sharing & Stock Options	Team Bonus

quent phases. A child prodigy, for example, may be able to read like a teenager, but he cannot behave like one until he ages through a sequence of experiences.

I also doubt that managers can or should act to avoid revolutions. Rather, these periods of tension provide the pressure, ideas, and awareness that afford a platform for change and the introduction of new practices.

Recognize the limited range of solutions. In each revolutionary stage it becomes evident that this stage can be ended only by certain specific solutions; moreover, these solutions are different from those that were applied to the problems of the preceding revolution. Too often it is tempting to choose solutions that were tried before, which makes it impossible for a new phase of growth to evolve.

Management must be prepared to dismantle current structures before the revolutionary stage becomes too turbulent. Top managers, realizing that their own managerial styles are no longer appropriate, may even have to take themselves out of leadership positions. A good Phase 2 manager facing Phase 3 might be wise to find another Phase 2 organization that better fits his talents, either outside the company or with one of its newer subsidiaries.

Finally, evolution is not an automatic affair; it is a contest for survival. To move ahead, companies must consciously introduce planned structures that not only are solutions to a current crisis but also are fitted to the *next* phase of growth. This requires considerable self-awareness on the part of top management, as well as great interpersonal skill in persuading other managers that change is needed.

Realize that solutions breed new problems. Managers often fail to realize that organizational solutions create problems for the future (i.e., a decision to delegate eventually causes a problem of control). Historical ac-

tions are very much determinants of what happens to the company at a much later date.

An awareness of this effect should help managers to evaluate company problems with greater historical understanding instead of "pinning the blame" on a current development. Better yet, managers should be in a position to *predict* future problems, and thereby to prepare solutions and coping strategies before a revolution gets out of hand.

A management that is aware of the problems ahead could well decide *not* to grow. Top managers may, for instance, prefer to retain the informal practices of a small company, knowing that this way of life is inherent in the organization's limited size, not in their congenial personalities. If they choose to grow, they may do themselves out of a job and a way of life they enjoy.

And what about the managements of very large organizations? Can they find new solutions for continued phases of evolution? Or are they reaching a stage where the government will act to break them up because they are too large?

CONCLUDING NOTE

Clearly, there is still much to learn about processes of development in organizations. The phases outlined here are only five in number and are still only approximations. Researchers are just beginning to study the specific developmental problems of structure, control, rewards, and management style in different industries and in a variety of cultures.

One should not, however, wait for conclusive evidence before educating managers to think and act from a developmental perspective. The critical dimension of time has been missing for too long from our management theories and practices. The intriguing paradox is that by learning more about history we may do a better job in the future.

Management Practice

■ W.T. Grant's Last Days—As Seen from Store 1192

RUSH LOVING JR.

At 9:30 in the morning last February 10, lawyers for the creditors' committee of W.T. Grant Co. walked into a federal courtroom in New York with a surprising proposal. For months, Grant's had been trying to reorganize under the protection of a bankruptcy court, and the once vast retail chain had shrunk from 1,100 stores to 359, and from 75,000 employees to 30,000. With no warning, the creditors' lawyers declared that the seventy-year-old business should be liquidated at once.

Two days later Federal Bankruptcy Judge John J. Galgay granted the committee's request, and the company's stores were padlocked to await a closeout sale. It was the final chapter in the largest bankruptcy proceeding in the history of retailing—the company's debt totaled more than $800 million.

Fighting for Their Livelihood

The liquidation of a multimillion-dollar enterprise is a poignant business drama even as it is played out where the public most often views it—at the level of the lawyers, the accountants, and the creditors' committees. But Grant's decline and fall takes on a different, more human perspective when it is

Reprinted from the April 1976 issue of *Fortune Magazine*, by special permission. Copyright © 1976 Time Inc.

perceived at store-level, so to speak, where men and woman were fighting for their livelihood as well as for the survival of the organization. The view from Store 1192, Grant's branch in Westerly, Rhode Island, also tells a good deal about what went wrong with the company and why it couldn't keep itself off the rocks.

The manager of Store 1192 was Albert J. Duclos (pronounced "du-close"), forty-one, a man whose hazel eyes sparkled with an enthusiasm that seemed almost unquenchable. He is methodical and, surprisingly for one so immersed in detail, articulate as well. His thoughts roll out decisively in a voice edged with the clipped, harsh accents of southeastern Massachusetts. His decisiveness helped to dispense confidence, and some small measure of comfort, among the eighty employees of Store 1192 during Grant's last uncertain hours.

A District Leader

Duclos spent nineteen years with Grant's, his entire working career, and over the past ten years he managed six Grant's stores in various New England towns. In that decade his annual income multiplied from $8,000 to $37,000, largely because of bonuses. He was so successful a manager that he led his district in sales and profits for six years.

Duclos took over the Westerly store in 1971. A seacoast town on the Connecticut border, Westerly is a marketing center for 140,000 families. Many shoppers come from across the state line, where the sales tax is a penny higher, and during the summer extra thousands from New York and central New England fill the shingled cottages that line the nearby beaches. Most of these people shop at the Franklin Plaza Shopping Center, a strip of sixteen stores just outside town. The largest of the stores was Grant's.

The year-round residents, many of whom work at the submarine yards of General Dynamics in Groton, Connecticut, shopped in Store 1192 for such staples as work clothes, cosmetics, and housewares. The vacationers, who knew the Grant's name from back home, came for fishing tackle, toothpaste, and similar traveling needs. And both groups patronized the Bradford Room, the store's restaurant. One of the most popular eating establishments in Westerly, the Bradford Room earned thirty cents on the dollar, making it the most profitable department in the store.

During his years in Westerly, Duclos played to this market well. Within two years after his arrival he had increased his store's sales by 19 percent, to more than $2.5 million, while doubling profits to $245,000. This 10 percent return on sales was about twice the average for all America's retailers. Under Duclos, 1192 became Grant's twenty-third most profitable store, and continued to make a little money even after the company had fallen into the red.

Every morning Duclos made the hour-long drive to Westerly from his home in Attleboro, Massachusetts. The commute was inconvenient, but not unusually long for that part of New England, and Duclos and his wife, Val, preferred Attleboro to Westerly as a place to bring up their two daughters. The store was open from 10:00 A.M. until 9:00 P.M., and Duclos was always there an hour or more before opening time. He rarely left before 6:30 or 7:00 P.M.

Cutting His Teeth on Kool-Aid

At the store Duclos was used to feeling like the captain of a ship—in charge of just about everything that went on. With the aid of his merchandise manager and two assistant managers, he oversaw all orders for new stock and plotted the mix of goods that Grant's offered Westerly's shoppers. He could raise or lower prices at will to beat the competition, and he had the power to concoct special promotions, even drawing up his own newspaper and radio ads. Once his bosses in New York City tried to keep him from stocking swimming pools, on the ground that pools wouldn't sell in a seaside community. Duclos went ahead anyway and ordered $5,000 worth, selling out in a week. Duclos had been in love with merchandising since the age of eleven, when he set up a Kool-Aid stand outside the neighborhood grocery in Fall River.

Duclos felt his first qualms about Grant's policies in the early 1970s. New York headquarters had ordered the stores to begin selling furniture and large appliances. To bolster those sales, the company had entered the hazardous credit-card business full steam ahead. Clerks were offered $1 bounties for each customer they signed up for a card, and Duclos was ordered to push the credit-card campaign above everything else. The pressure grew so intense that at one point his district credit manager called hourly asking how many accounts he had opened. "We hated the goddam things," says Duclos.

On New York's insistence, only cursory credit checks were conducted. When one manager insisted on making thorough inquiries, New York threatened to fire him. Meanwhile, the new card holders were using their new credit to haul away hundreds of dollars worth of washing machines and beds. Duclos and virtually every other manager warned that the cards were brewing trouble, but New York didn't listen. By last year Grant's credit-card receivables totaled $500 million, and half of that was deemed uncollectible.

Undoing Disaster

The day of reckoning finally came early last year when the company plunged into the red—$177 million for fiscal 1975. Despite the immensity of the loss, Duclos's hope still ran high; he'd heard rumors that the directors were already searching for a new president who could turn the company around. And, sure enough, one morning last April, Duclos's district manager called to say that the directors had found their man. His name was Robert H. Anderson; he was a merchandising vice-president from Sears.

Through the summer Duclos thought Anderson really might be able to do the job. The new boss sent order after order from New York undoing disastrous policies of the old regime. The best news Duclos got was a bulletin from headquarters telling him to stop issuing credit cards; Anderson had ordered the entire operation to be phased out. At a meeting of managers came more good news: Duclos was ordered to close out appliances and furniture. These higher-priced stocks turned over too slowly and did not generate enough sales per square foot of floor space. His district manager told Duclos to rearrange the store so that the first thing customers saw when they entered was women's fashions. Someone in New York had finally discovered that 80 percent of Grant's customers were women.

Despite these favorable signs, Duclos kept hearing rumors that Grant's might go bankrupt. After his district manager informed him that there would be no semiannual bonus coming up in September, Duclos canceled plans for his family's annual vacation trip. He spent the three-week holiday in July on a ladder painting the house, because now he also could not afford to hire anyone for the job.

One morning several months later, a customer walked into the Westerly store and told a clerk that she had just heard on the radio that Grant's had gone bankrupt. The report spread rapidly across the sales floor. In the office Duclos and his immediate subordinates clustered around a portable radio on a secretary's desk as the 10:30 news came on. The news about Grant's was all they had feared—the company had indeed plunged into bankruptcy.

There had been no warning from New York, no word at all. Everyone stood there in stunned silence. Finally Duclos spoke up, trying to reassure his people. "This could be the best thing for this company that could happen to us," he said. He tried to explain that bankruptcy would permit them to get out of some bad contracts. "This may be the best way to save the company."

The Nest Egg Gets Fried

But for all his reassurances, the bankruptcy hit Duclos with a jolt. In Grant's better days he had invested more than $20,000 in company stock, drawing on most of his savings and borrowing from a bank to finance his purchases. Now his holdings were virtually worthless, and he still owed the bank $5,000.

Several days after the bankruptcy five clerks came to his office and announced that each of them would raise $10,000 and buy the store if he would run it for them. Duclos was moved, but he told them the idea would not work—they would need more backing than they could get. But Duclos was impressed by their morale.

Meanwhile, his own morale was being severely shaken. Hundreds of his fellow managers, many of them respected friends, were laid off as New York headquarters closed down their stores. Val Duclos, an outgoing and equally outspoken woman in her late thirties, kept telling him to quit, that the company was doomed. But Duclos was determined to stick it out.

Into the winter word kept coming down that Anderson was changing the chain's merchandise mix, orienting it more to a narrow line of items that sold the fastest. In November, just as Grant's biggest selling season got underway, Duclos was told to begin a series of clearance sales. He fretted about the timing. November and December are the months that can determine a chain's year-end profit, and when managers are ordered to slash prices at such times, profits can only suffer. The creditors' committee was watching the turnaround from the sidelines. Duclos feared that if Anderson misjudged the committee's mood, climbing losses might impel the creditors to push for liquidation.

A Day in "Grant's Tomb"
In mid-January Duclos and his fellow managers were summoned to New York for a special briefing. It was the only time he had ever been inside "Grant's Tomb," which is what employees called the fifty-three-story headquarters building on Times Square that had been completed only five years before. They assembled in a third-floor auditorium, one wall of which sported a banner proclaiming: "Best of the Stores . . . Best of the Items!" Remembering the many old friends who were not there because their stores had been closed, Duclos resented the insensitivity of the slogan.

In a marathon of speeches and slide shows, Anderson and his key executives outlined a bold new plan for creating a "New Grant's." First off, they said, all stores would be "fashionized," a term Anderson had coined; it meant emphasizing women's fashions. And, since they were discontinuing slow-selling items, the managers would have to put their stores through "compaction," another Anderson coinage meaning to squeeze the sales area into a smaller space. They must also "colorize" their stores, i.e., paint counters and walls a

selection of bright colors, in shades and types of paint decreed by New York.

Anderson warned his managers that every store must be spotless. "If the windows are washed at nine o'clock, and it rains at ten, they'll be washed again at eleven," he snapped. "That's the way we're going to run our stores." Anderson said the New Grant's would be launched on February 1, the beginning of their new fiscal year. They would open with a "supersale," featuring drastic markdowns of such items as boots, toasters, and electric saws.

On the evening train back to Providence, Duclos pondered the day's events. He was elated by a promise that, come spring, he and the other managers would get those canceled bonuses after all. Of far more importance to company and career, he felt a sense of excitement about the New Grant's. Here at last was something definite and creative, a plan a real merchant could get enthusiastic about.

Yet, there were things that troubled Duclos. More than once during that day at Grant's Tomb, they had been told to charge all the costs of the transformation to the current fiscal year. Duclos worried that this would push the company's year-end losses higher than the creditors might stand for. On a more personal level, he and the other managers were rankled by the New York office's increasingly patronizing attitude, signalized by the excruciating detail of its edicts for paint hues and merchandise mixes. "We did something wrong, but we're not all stupid," Duclos had grumbled during a coffee break. As he and the other managers had reminded one another, it had not been they who had bankrupted Grant's, but the executives who sat in New York.

Selling the Wrong Goods
Within days, Duclos was well on his way toward creating a new store. His clerks and stockboys were painting the counters, and Duclos had "compacted" the sales floor from 60,000 square feet to 41,000. Over on one side, two dozen shoppers picked

over the clearance sale, where everything not on New York's checklist of approved merchandise had been stacked and marked down 75 percent. The checklist had not included such popular items as paper towels and barbecue grills, meaning that Duclos had to put them in the sale. Then, it turned out that New York, incredibly, had sent out an incomplete list. So Duclos had to reorder paper towels to replace those that he had sold at a loss.

The carpenters arrived to rebuild some of the walls. A floor man showed up and began replacing cracked tiles. Duclos juggled his maintenance budget and hired a cleaning contractor to strip old wax and polish the floor. "I can feel it all coming together," he said happily.

But then the district manager, Paul Carlson, a jovial but nervous little man, called with the news that Anderson had decided to make an inspection tour of the area on February 4, just after the scheduled opening of the New Grant's and the Westerly store would be his first stop. Duclos was unshaken. But Carlson was jittery; he began pushing Duclos hard to create a perfect store.

Carlson had good reason to worry, because on a previous visit to New England Anderson had been displeased with the stores he had seen and had abruptly dismissed Carlson's predecessor. "Come on now, Paul, calm down," Duclos joked. "If they fire me, they fire you first. It'll take them so long to get to me it'll be like having two weeks' notice."

The Mannequin Crisis

Word of the president's visit spread through the store, and everyone seemed to work more feverishly. While they toiled, a clerk talked about Anderson's previous trip to Rhode Island. "Mr. Duclos and the others stood at the door waiting," she recalled. "Someone was on the telephone calling that he was forty minutes away, then thirty minutes away, but he never came."

By early afternoon five regional and district merchandising and display men had arrived; they had been dispatched urgently from Massachusetts. The regional office near Boston seemed to have been swallowed up by panic, but Duclos was philosophical: presidential inspections create panic in every corporation.

Duclos showed his visitors how low he was on stock and displays. His own people had called New York and the warehouses, pushing for shipments, only to be rebuffed. One display man looked around the fashions department and turned to Duclos in surprise: "You don't have any mannequins at all?" "Just toss-ups," said Duclos—meaning simple cardboard figures. The display man hurried off to call New York and round up some mannequins. All afternoon the store's two phone lines were tied up, as the five men made call after call, using their authority—and the imminence of Anderson's visit—to get quick deliveries of displays and goods.

While Duclos wandered about the sales floor checking on the progress of the stockboys and clerks, one of the regional men informed him that the bright yellow paint on the infant's-wear counters was the wrong shade. Together they called the display manager in New York who confirmed that he had just changed the specifications. "A bulletin is in the mail to you," he said cheerily. Duclos hung up, disgusted. Now they had to paint the department all over again.

Soon the two regional men were back; one of them announced that his colleague did not like the layout of the candy counters. "It's not according to the plan from New York," he explained. The Westerly store had never received the candy-department plan.

It became obvious that what really troubled the regional men was the layout of the entire store. They thought it should have the broad aisles and affluent look of a department store. Duclos was happy to hear this, because he and his merchandise manager had proposed just that sort of layout when they had gone through their "compaction." The regional office had turned them down.

"Get God to Make it Snow!"

Duclos and his visitors tried out new counter arrangements, shifting one department and then another, but after each move a neighboring area would cry out for a change of its own. Into the evening a half dozen stockboys and the older men sweated and puffed and pushed and pulled counter after counter. Five of the stockboys were teenagers who had been off from school that day because of snow. Duclos had hired them part-time, and at nine o'clock they put on their jackets to leave.

"Al! You're letting the boys go?" called a display man.

"They have school tomorrow."

"Get God to make it snow! Hasn't He ever heard of Bob Anderson?"

Wherever possible, during the coming days, Duclos used Anderson's visit to help get his store remade. When the tape of the background music began to drag, he called the Boston company that leased the equipment and asked for a new player. The man in Boston said it would take ten days. "My president is visiting next week," replied Duclos, "and if he hears that thing dragging he'll probably order your machines pulled out of all Grant's stores." The new machine arrived in two days.

Jotting Notes at 55 mph

Duclos worked ceaselessly, arriving at 8:00 A.M., leaving at 10:00 P.M. for the hour-long drive home. Sometimes he jotted down reminders for the next day on folded pieces of notepaper while steering his Vega down Interstate 95 with his knees. After he got home he would sit for an hour or more making more notes and sipping a Seven and Seven (Seagram's 7 with 7-Up).

The thing that plagued him increasingly was the lack of merchandise. He even rented a truck and dispatched an assistant to a Grant's warehouse in Windsor Locks, Connecticut, to bring back a special load of auto accessories. Despite this effort at self-help, Duclos found himself trying to serve his customers from a stockroom and shelves that remained too bare. The warehouses seemed unable to distribute fast enough; the flow of goods to all stores was so slow that Carlson called to say that New York had ordered the supersale delayed. Now the New Grant's would open on the very day of Anderson's visit.

As the big day loomed, the truckloads of merchandise began arriving at last, and the shelves and racks were filling with goods. But then Carlson called again: Anderson was not coming. He could not leave New York—something about a meeting with the creditors.

The New Grant's blossomed forth on schedule. Shoppers poured in. Some women asked if this were a new store; others commented on the fresh colors. Sales for the day reflected the customers' positive attitude; volume was up 60 percent from a normal Wednesday.

Sales were still running high the next week. Monday two vice-presidents visited and offered nothing but praise. But soon after he arrived at the store on Tuesday morning, Duclos received a severe jolt. The manager of another New England store telephoned to say that he had just called a New York buyer about some needed goods, and the buyer had told him that the creditors were going to court to ask that Grant's be liquidated. Duclos called his wife, who had planned a shopping trip that day. "Don't spend any money," he warned.

$1 Million for the Boss

He was on the phone the rest of the day seeking information. A manager in Warren, Rhode Island, told him that the creditors had pulled the plug after discovering that the year's losses were running higher than they had been led to expect. Duclos had feared just that reaction. Another manager passed the word that the bonus was now dead.

Like the other managers, Duclos was growing increasingly bitter with each call, especially when he remembered that the same bankers who were now closing the company had guaranteed Anderson's salary for five years, to the tune altogether of $1,050,000. Through the entire day there was never any word from New York. "I figure we'll get notified when the guy is putting the lock on the door," Duclos grumbled.

Duclos kept hoping that the report of liquidation was merely another rumor. But late that afternoon a friend called to report that New York had put out a press release confirming everything. "What can I say?" Duclos said, his voice hollow. "It was a great company." He was close to tears.

But only as Duclos drove home that night did he finally realize what this all really meant: he had to find another job. "This is it, boy," he said to himself. "You'd better get moving." What kind of work should he seek? Did he want to stay in retailing and put up with the long hours? Duclos thought of the past two weeks. "I loved it," he thought. "That's the kind of thing I want to do."

That night the emotions and the shock kept thundering over him. He drank five Seven and Sevens, sitting in the family room. When he went to bed he could not sleep; he just lay there watching a Frankenstein movie on TV.

Wednesday morning Duclos performed the most heartrending task of his entire career. Although he still had heard nothing from New York, he broke the news to his clerks, calling them into a conference room that the carpenters had just finished paneling. "It's nothing official," he said. "I have nothing official, but it looks like the Grant Co. will go out of business." Several women wept.

Thursday afternoon the judge signed the order to liquidate. All stores were to be locked that night. Duclos received his instructions about 6:30. It was the first direct word he'd had from New York in all those three days.

Friday the Thirteenth

The next morning Duclos was sitting with his merchandise manager in the restaurant silently sipping coffee and staring out the window at the jammed parking lot. The other stores at Franklin Plaza were beginning their Washington's birthday sales. It was Friday the thirteenth. While they sat there one of the district display men came in.

"Sit down and have a cup of coffee," Duclos said dejectedly. "It may be your last cup of coffee at Grant's."

"We were really up after Monday," said the merchandise manager.

"Yeah, we were 400 ahead in sales," said Duclos.

"Then someone zapped us."

Duclos looked out the window again. "Look at all those cars out there," he said wistfully.

After a while they got up and went back to the sales floor. Most of the lights were out, and they wandered among the counters, thinking how beautiful it looked and how the customers at the liquidation sale would ravage it. The floor seemed to gleam brighter than ever. All the merchandise sat in neat rows. The store was immaculate. "Now the animals will come," Duclos blurted out angrily.

"They'll tear the place up," said the display man, Bob DeBroisse. "You'll never recognize it by the first night."

The tape of background music was still running, and as they passed a counter of coffee makers and toasters that were about to be marked down for the liquidation, it blared gaily into "The Best Things in Life Are Free."

They walked on, and the display man began worrying about being out of work. Duclos suddenly regained some of his old bounce and tried to cheer him up.

"You've known hard times before, Bob."

"Yeah, but I never had a big house to unload fast."

"They're not going to take your house," Duclos said, putting his hand on the man's shoulder. "The banks don't want your house."

But no sooner had the display man left than Duclos was somber again. Head down, thinking, he walked once more through the empty store with a friend who had come to commiserate with him. Through the fashions, down the back row past the draperies, back up along the housewares and the toys, past the records and the jewelry. He stopped and leaned against a checkout stand and looked into the gloom of the unlighted store. He stayed there for some time thinking, remembering. Two customers came to the door, read the "Closed" sign and walked off to Fishers Big Wheel, the discount store down the way.

A Very Tight Company

"I really think it would have worked," he spoke up at last. "But Anderson went about it the wrong way. He went too fast. You don't give away a quarter of a billion in merchandise in the last quarter of the year. If we'd come up with a better profit picture for last year I think the creditors would have gone along.

"This has always been a very tight company," Duclos went on, his voice rising, the words now tumbling out. "His idea of cleanliness has always been in my book, but . . . goddamit! . . . you don't do it in a year when you're not making money. I don't mean leaving crud on the floor, but . . . goddam! . . . you don't paint the whole goddam store in a bad year! He said: 'Get it all done; get all the expenses in this year and get it clear before 1976,'" Duclos paused. His tired, black-rimmed eyes looked over the store once more, and he said bitterly: "There wasn't any 1976."

■ A Call for Vision in Managing Technology

RICHARD N. FOSTER

Competing in a world of rapidly changing technologies can be likened to playing a video game. The target constantly moves, and new opponents zoom in from various vectors. Focusing solely on one target

Reprinted from the May 24, 1982 issue of *Business Week* by special permission, Copyright © 1982 by McGraw Hill, Inc., New York, N.Y. 10020. All rights reserved.

sometimes means losing the game to an unexpected foe that has been overlooked in the fray. To play the game well, a new set of skills is required: heightened reflexes plus the ability to anticipate challenges and to make fast, rational decisions.

A number of companies have discovered the risks in this game. Among them is AM International Inc., which lost $245 million in 1981 as it faltered in an attempt to shift from its traditional electromechanical lines to electronic ones. AM is now in Chapter 11. A decade earlier, National Cash Register Co. was forced to write off $139 million when it tried a similar game. RCA, General Electric, and Sylvania—leaders in vacuum tube technology—lost out when transistor technology revolutionized the business.

The record is uncomfortably clear. Technology leaders tend to become technology losers. A few companies manage transitions to new technological fields effectively, but many others are unable even to begin the process, and most find it impossible to complete the move successfully.

The strategic implications of technological change are not limited to high-tech industries. The development of steel minimills has drastically altered the requirements of scale in steel manufacturing. Biotechnology may radically change the nature of the chemical and paper industries. If the commercial banking business continues its move to automated teller machines and electronic funds transfer, companies such as Citicorp may find themselves overseeing research and development budgets that rival those of large manufacturing companies—and wondering about the long-term attractiveness of branch banking.

One of the reasons technology has proved so hard to manage is that most companies focus their attention on the efficiency of their technological efforts—attempting to determine, for example, how well their labs are run, how closely the labs are tied to production or marketing, or the amount of money spent on "long-shot" programs. Under conventional management, a lab might be reorganized, a research program might be canceled, or a new liaison between production and marketing might be established. These are tidy, cosmetic solutions, but they miss the critical factors in R & D effectiveness:

■ Which technology to pursue and when to pursue it.
■ How to manage the transition from one technology to another.

■ How to prepare the corporation for technological change.

These three elements determine a company's ability to manage technological transitions steadily, and they are the basis of effective technology management.

In any field, technological improvement is eventually limited by the laws of nature. The ultimate strength of a fiber is limited by the strength of its intermolecular bonds. The number of transistors that can be placed on a silicon chip is limited by the crystal structure of the silicon material. The goal of technical management is to identify the limits of any given technology early, as a first step in determining what finally can be accomplished with it.

Industry, though, is usually far from these natural limits, and it is more likely to come up against practical, physical barriers that represent the current state of the art. The difference between the technical and the state-of-the-art limits determines the technology's potential for performance improvement; the greater the distance, the more the potential. This can have dramatic strategic implications.

When a major manufacturer of a mature product looked at its business from a context of technical limits, for example, the company was surprised. Each year its lab's goal had been to improve productivity over the past year. Using that amorphous target, productivity had increased 20 percent in the previous ten years. But by defining the best that could be done, the company boosted productivity 40 percent in just two months.

Once a company becomes aware of what it can hope for by defining the limits of its technology, it can then determine how far it wants to go to approach these limits. It accomplishes this by applying research—knowledge acquisition—and development—knowledge application—to narrow the gap between the state of the art and the natural limit. In the early stages of a typical R & D program, progress is slow. Lines of inquiry are drawn and tested, and some are discarded. Recombinant genetic theory was postulated in the 1920s, for example, but work on industrial applications began only ten years ago, and another ten years may be required for any major exploitation.

During this early phase, extensive effort goes into achieving only limited performance improvement. But once the knowledge base is established, progress accelerates rapidly, reaching its greatest momentum about halfway toward its limit. At that point improvements slow. Should the limit actually be reached, improvements, of course, drop to zero. The process can be depicted as an S-curve.

If there is a better technology for doing something, there will be more than one S-curve in a given chart. These multiple S-curves are not connected, and switching to a new one requires different efforts. Transistors did not evolve from vacuum tubes; there was no subtle shift from one technology to another. They were revolutionary.

Evidence and experience show that breaks between technologies occur more frequently and are more important strategically than is commonly assumed. In packaging, for instance, the move from three- to two-piece cans was just such a discontinuity. The development of the retort pouch to replace conventional canning may be another. Still photography, based on the chemical processes Eastman Kodak Co. understands, is one technology, but Sony Corp.'s recently exhibited line of cameras based on electronic imaging is surely another.

If companies can assess the limits of their own technologies, as well as those of alternate approaches, they can begin to answer strategic questions about which areas to pursue. They can then prepare to manage a transition. Careful study may show that engineers with different skills will be needed, new approaches will have to be taken in production and marketing, new financing must be arranged.

Viewing tire cords in terms of S-curves illustrates the strategic importance of knowing what the limits of varying technologies are. The cords, which add strength, resilience, and blowout protection to tires, were made first from cotton, then rayon, then nylon, and finally polyester. Each succeeding technology outperformed its predecessor, but those who championed the earlier ones lost market leadership to the newcomers. During the late stages of nylon cord development, for example, when the polyester version was being developed, the return on R & D for the latter was some 4.5 times greater than for the former. Polyester had proved itself superior, enabling Celanese Corp. to get far more for its research dollar than could Du Pont Co. No company can support that level of cost disadvantage for long. Clearly, in technology, the economics of attack are frequently superior to those of defense.

By trying to protect its own technology instead of moving to a more promising alternative, each successive leader actually made it easier for challengers to enter the tire cord business. New competitors developed new technologies in areas where there was no entrenched competition. Suppose, instead, that in the late stages of nylon cord development, 25 percent of a company's R & D budget had gone toward polyester cords. Since the return on polyester was 4.5 times greater, the 25 percent investment would have improved the company's overall return on R & D investment by more than 100 percent.

Switching from products that are based on a mature technology to ones based on a new technology is not easy. Management must be certain that old customers are not left in vulnerable positions. Nor can resources be withdrawn too quickly from existing products that, though mature, may still be making money. But the risks inherent in making transitions are not nearly as great as those of avoiding them. On the classic S-curve, less than half the potential for improving a given product or process remains when R & D productivity reaches its peak. Once the rate of improvement starts to slow, it is a signal that perhaps the optimum time has come for beginning the move to a new technology.

This observation may seem obvious, but it goes against the straight economic view. It is just at this point that a business, based on the existing technology, is beginning to make significant profits for the company.

There is a difference, then, between economic and technological performance. If technological efforts are not shifted early enough, economic performance, once it begins to deteriorate, will collapse. This was demonstrated in the transistor industry in 1966, when silicon solid-state devices outsold germanium products for the first time. Even then, germanium sales increased 11 percent. But when they finally lagged, they plunged. By 1967 sales of germanium solid-state products were 27 percent lower than the year before, and by 1972 germanium was eking out a mere 5 percent of the market. Germanium producers did not understand their predicament until very late in the game. Although sales crested in 1966, the number of germanium vendors did not peak until the following year.

Such competitive myopia is common. Even when they recognize the superiority of a new technology, managers are loath to switch. They tend to assume that change will always occur at the same rate and pace as the changes of yesterday. In technology, such is not the case, but managers typically discover this after technological development has bumped up against the natural limit or a new and better technology.

NCR Corp.'s evolutionary progress up the electromechanical S-curve came to just such an abrupt halt when the company's most advanced products were suddenly made obsolete by radically new electronic technology. When NCR announced that it planned to switch to electronics, it evinced awareness of alternative technology. But when it continued to invest heavily in its obsolete products, it acted as if a choice could be made about when—or even whether—to switch. No company has such a choice. If it is unable to come to grips with limitations and discontinuities, it cannot manage technological change.

But if the concept of technical limits is well understood and thoughtfully acted on, the management puzzle solves itself. Through an informal process of estimating the company's proximity to its technological limits, managers can begin to assess their next moves. This is best done analytically, although it can be started as an intuitive process. There are ten key signals that suggest trouble when the company approaches the limits of an existing technology:

■ An intuitive sense among top managers that the company's R & D productivity is declining.

■ A trend toward missed R & D deadlines. This is often misinterpreted as a signal that the department is losing effectiveness, when in realty improvement is becoming more difficult to achieve.

■ A trend toward process rather than product improvement. Typically, as limits are approached, process improvements are easier to attain.

■ A perceived loss of R & D creativity.

■ Disharmony among the R & D staff.

■ Lack of improvement from replacement of R & D leaders or staff.

■ Profits that come from increasingly narrow market segments.

■ Loss of market share—particularly to a smaller competitor—in a specialized market niche.

■ Little difference in returns despite spending substantially more—or less—than competitors over a period of years. When significant variations in expenditures produce no significant differences in performance, the technology is near its limits.

■ Smaller competitors that are taking radical approaches that ''probably won't work.''

If they do work, larger competitors may suddenly become smaller ones.

Assessing each of these points is likely to spark a rigorous investigation of the company's technologies. It may prompt the company to consider alternatives, and management may discover previously unnoticed discontinuities and the potential for future transitions. One thing is certain: Assumptions grounded in evolutionary, incremental thinking will be severely tested.

Since technical limits are ultimately scientific ones, any assumptions are tenuous in the absence of scientific investigation. Yet most companies simply do not do the basic homework. Instead, they rely on trial-and-error experimentation. That served well in the past for such giants as Thomas Edison and Alexander Graham Bell, but it no longer meets the needs of huge corporations developing massive computer systems, advanced aircraft, or even tire cords.

Still, many companies remain devoted to tinkering, focusing on near-term results and understanding only enough science to satisfy their present needs. They are likely to pursue the first product or process that works, rather than push on to the best that can be developed.

One example is Oxirane Corp., a company with a short but enviable history of developing novel processes for the chemical industry. In the 1970s, Oxirane announced plans to introduce a new, cheaper method to produce ethylene glycol (used in antifreeze and polyester) and vinyl acetate (used in paints and adhesives) simultaneously. Intending to tap the market potential quickly, the company skipped the pilot-plant phase of development, counting on correcting significant corrosive problems inherent in the process while the plant was starting up.

But the problems could not be solved. The plant was never opened, and Oxirane went out of business. Preliminary research might have provided the answer, but even if it did not, at least it would have defined the magnitude of the problem. Alert managers could have redirected the development process or terminated the project.

Clearly, companies must perform that underlying research. And they can achieve better and faster results by investing in new R & D support tools, such as computer-aided research and development devices (CARD). These use techniques similar to computer-aided design and manufacturing (CAD/CAM), enabling investigators in theoretical physics, chemistry, and mathematics to answer "what if" questions with greater speed and accuracy than ever before.

While not all companies are interested in such basic research, most do want to get and keep a competitive edge. Those that are not tuned in to scientific research typically give an inordinate amount of attention to market research. Frequently, such an approach distorts technological reality because it ties investment decisions in new technology to customer needs. But customers cannot be relied on to judge what might be possible from technology. Asking laymen whether they prefer metal to ceramic engines is likely to "prove" that metal engines are the wave of the future. In fact, that may be false. Similarly, few customers could have conceptualized a need for something called "Pac-Man" five years ago, before video games existed.

Managers want competitive edges, but many resist technological change. They may not understand a new technology's potential. Or, because they are familiar with an existing technology and are ignorant of its limits, they may believe it can be improved indefinitely. There may be a strong aversion to risk—and technological risk is often perceived as chanciest of all. Often, however, that aversion comes from poor data that are even more poorly interpreted.

To defend their views, such managers typically make superheated efforts to prove that the old technology holds more promise than the new, in what might be called the "sailing ship phenomenon." Sailing-ship builders knew they had a problem when the first steamships were introduced. Initially, steamships were not as fast or reliable, so to sink the potential threat, conventional shipbuilders quickly set about designing more efficient sailing ships. But they could not get around the implications of the S-curve. Steamships improved far beyond the best of the sailing ships, and the latter were finally sunk.

Ironically, this phenomenon often works to a company's short-term benefit, further clouding the picture. Renewed efforts on old technology frequently bring significant improvements. Troubles begin, however, when management interprets this as a sign that the business has turned around and funds a technology that is running out of momentum. Competitors, meanwhile, put their resources into technologies with vastly greater potential and eventually get greater returns for smaller investments. Again, economic realities favor attackers.

RCA Corp. acutely exhibited the sailing ship syndrome when it devoted its resources to the vacuum-tube devices it had successfully developed and marketed over many years. It continued to pour effort and money into designing ever more sophisticated tubes even after solid-state technology appeared. Its early success gave the company false hopes. But by the late 1960s tubes could no longer counter transistors, and RCA's market, investment, and effort went for naught. And, because it had focused solely on the old technology, RCA had lost its chance to become a force in the new market.

Even when companies willingly accept technological change, they frequently are ill-equipped to manage it. Of all the corporate officers who can effect such change, the key is the R & D vice-president. But in many companies, this role is seen more as administrative, insuring smooth relations between the labs and the business side, than as strategic. To play the strategist, the vice-president needs a broader perspective and charter. His goal should be to reduce his involvement in project management and expand it in the areas of technological limits and pertinent families of technologies. He should be demanding R & D support tools from management and designing methods of bringing information to researchers more efficiently. He should also be aware of experts in the fields of the corporate research efforts and be able to recruit them when needed. Understanding the resistance to change, he might establish core research projects on new technologies separate from the support work on old ones.

Such a key role can be effective only when the R & D vice-president becomes a full member of strategic planning councils and has the support and promotion of the chief executive, who sets the initial technological horizons for the company. The CEO may or may not make the decision to reallocate resources from old to new technologies, but even if he does not, his attitude toward change will ultimately control its pace and effectiveness. Because decisions related to technological change affect everyone in the corporation, from those concerned with capital allocation to marketers and human resource personnel, the attitude of the CEO will vividly demonstrate his true feelings toward the change.

Exploiting technological potential is not an overnight exercise. It requires a strong technological heritage, which most companies do not possess. Traditions can be started, however, if a dedicated leader is determined to initiate them. George S. Dively, for one, began the arduous process of turning Harris-Intertype Corp., a Cleveland-based printing-equipment producer, into a manufacturer of electronic communications gear. Anticipating a declining future for mechanical typesetting equipment in the mid-1960s, Dively spent ten years siphoning money from existing operations to acquire electronics companies. Ultimately, he totally transformed Harris's business. By the late 1970s he even changed the company's name—to Harris Corp.—and moved its headquarters to Florida, closer to its new electronics operations. Meanwhile, most division managers were replaced with people who had started their careers in the acquired companies.

Dively provides a sterling example of effective technological transition. But there are few others. Typically, CEOs do not change their sights. Rather, companies change CEOs when technologies collapse or challenges are not met. Most often the challenges come not from entrenched market leaders, but from hungry competitors.

Successful corporate strategies are almost invariably guided by powerful corporate visions and realistic assessments of the company's ability to attain them. They come not only from careful analysis, but also from judgment, conviction, and even intuition, and they are grounded in the necessity for sustaining competitive advantages. Frequently, this means the ability to develop superior technologies on a continuing basis and to alter the company consistently to exploit them.

Establishing this vision imposes great demands on management, but meeting the demands can produce a corporate renaissance. Paradoxically, the more people understand about technical limits, the more they seem to expand the limits of technology. Such an expansion may provide the most effective way for a company to sustain itself and prosper in the future.

■ Hemingway: What Happened?

PETER G. GOSSELIN

Richard Edwards gives a visitor to his empty trucking company a tape cassette of the Hemingway Transport song. He wrote it himself.

To the tune of "The Green Berets," it goes, in part:

> Hustling freightmen of the road,
> Men who manage, drive and load,
> Men who mean just what they say,
> These are men of Hemingway.

Or they were until two weeks ago.

Then—in the midst of a strike by the Teamsters union—Edwards shut down the company he owns. The men, almost 1,000 of them, are out of work.

Richard Edwards is the kind of guy who takes things seriously, like a scout leader who considers it his highest calling to teach campcraft and the square knot.

He had a plaque installed outside company headquarters off Dartmouth Street that reads, "You are now entering the general offices of Hemingway Transport. Inside this building we think about, talk about and act to achieve excellence. . . ." He thought that up.

He gave the men hundreds of belt buckles, windbreakers, and wrist watches that carried the company motto, "A Whale of a Truckline." He thought that up, too.

He wrote the company song, "Wheels and Whales."

Even his competitors acknowledge Edwards could have saved Hemingway Transport.

The story of Hemingway is about what happens to a company when its industry changes. It is also about the International Brotherhood of Teamsters.

Edwards says he was trying to cope with the change when the end came. The Teamsters won't say what they were doing.

Hemingway was one of New England's largest regional truckers and one of the nation's oldest when Edwards took it over in May, 1976. It was also almost bankrupt.

It had lost $2.73 million the year before and was on its way to losing $5 million and then another $4 million in the two years to come.

Its newly purchased southern branch had not made a cent; its new computer didn't work; its vice-president of operations had a heart attack and died; its vice-president of sales contracted Parkinson's disease.

The company needed help.

Edwards's first move was to sell anything he could lay his hands on. Old trucks, surplus parts, freight terminals that he then leased back (it was cheaper), entire freight routes. He cut the number of drivers from 2,000 to 1,000.

His next move was to buy a new International Harvester truck fleet, 525 trucks, and 800 trailers, for $28 million, payable in seven years at $4 million a year.

He wrote a song on the occasion of the trucks' delivery: "The Big Red Harvey," to the tune of "Puff, the Magic Dragon."

His gamble started paying off. The company made a $320,000 profit in 1978, about $1 million in 1979, and more than $1.8 million in 1980. Not much by trucking standards, but still a profit.

Things were looking up for Hemingway.

For the industry as a whole, things had never looked otherwise.

Rising gas prices hurt some truckers in the mid-1970s, but most were prospering. They could hardly help themselves. The government, the companies, and the union had worked out an unbeatable system.

The government: Federal regulators had decided decades ago that the public interest was linked to stability, not competition, in the trucking industry. By the time Edwards got to Hemingway, the industry was deep in the lap of regulation.

The regulators devised a foolproof arrangement for discouraging competitors. They demanded that newcomers have "operating authority" before trucking across state lines. Then they asked established truckers whether the newcomers were needed.

The companies: For their part, established companies insured that the nation's freight business was neatly divided between them. Basically, they had only two kinds of business to handle, truckload and less-than-truckload. By insuring both were taken care of, they left little room for competitors.

Truckload freight involves shipments large enough to fill a trailer. A truck picks up the shipment and takes it directly to a receiver. Less-than-truckload involves loads that can't fill a trailer. It is picked up, taken to a terminal, packed with other loads, and carried to destination terminals, where the process is reversed.

While most companies handled both, smaller, regional companies, like Hemingway, handled the bulk of less-than-truckload freight. The big national carriers took care of the truckload business. It was a genteel arrangement and very profitable.

The union: The Teamsters have never been accused of being genteel, but they did wonders at keeping the industry orderly. They did it with the National Master Freight Agreement.

The agreement covered virtually every truck company in the nation with more than a pickup and local service. It made sure that everybody paid the same wages and minimum benefits.

It also made sure that national union officials had a hammerlock on their locals. They, not the local leaders, renegotiated the agreement every three years.

The arrangement did not leave much room for decisions by average union members. But then why did they need it? The average member was making more than $10 an hour and could expect that to go to almost $13. The system was working well.

Until July 1, 1980.

On that date, the federal government officially changed its mind about stability and competition. It deregulated the trucking industry: it said, in effect, that henceforth anybody could ship anything, anywhere.

For the industry, it was like announcing that anyone could now do brain surgery.

It took Richard Edwards some time to figure out what deregulation was doing to his business. He didn't realize it until a fall day several months after the government's about-face, when Preston Trucking Co. of Preston, Md., undercut Hemingway's price on a load of Sherwin-Williams paint from Newark, N.J., to Virginia.

Edwards couldn't understand how Preston could do the job for the price so he called up his colleague, Preston president Will Potter. Potter told him it was none of his damn business.

Other executives first saw the changes coming in other ways, for instance, in the lists of who was getting government operating authority. They didn't recognize any names.

With most regulations gone, almost anyone could enter the business. All one needed was $350 for a federal license, the down payment on a truck ($4,000 for the cab, you could always lease the trailer), and a customer.

In the eighteen months that followed deregulation, 5,122 new companies registered with the government, more than had registered in any comparable period since the 1930s. By the time the Hemingway men struck six months later, government officials estimated that the number of new companies was up to 7,800.

Many executives wrote off the new companies at first. The upstarts had the advantage of being non-union—their wages averaged 20 percent to 30 percent below Teamster scale. But most were one-truck shops with no cash on which to survive and grow. They seemed to collapse as fast as they appeared.

However, the newcomers found an entering wedge: the national carriers' truckload business. Since there was no need for terminals, they could handle the freight with only their trucks. Since they didn't have to pay for terminals—or the Teamsters—they could do it for less.

The scramble was on. The newcomers went after the big carriers' truckload business. The big carriers slashed prices and went after regional companies' less-than-truckload work. The regionals started failing.

According to industry figures, 144 companies closed; 47 were on the ropes. The unbeatable system was beginning to collapse.

By the beginning of last year, Hemingway's slim profits had evaporated. By the end of the year, it would lose $400,000.

Edwards decided it was time to act.

The Teamsters were, as usual, silent in the months after deregulation. Union members referred questions to local leaders. The local leaders passed them on to union representatives in Washington. The representatives were always in conference.

But it is impossible that the union did not notice what was happening. For one thing, its top national official had been indicted for trying to bribe government officials to block deregulation. For another, it was losing members in droves.

Teamster president Roy L. Williams and four other officials were charged by a federal grand jury with trying to give a senator a very good deal on some Nevada real estate in return for a promise he would derail deregulation before it became law.

Williams recently told an interviewer that the charge has not been distracting him from union business. "I spent less time on my legal problems this time than I ever spent," he said.

The few union insiders who talk say they doubt he will remain in office much longer.

Williams and other union officials always took pride in their assertion that the Teamsters were the biggest union in the nation. They continued to make the claim after deregulation.

But their own figures showed membership was plummeting. The 2.3 million members who were paying dues in the late 1970s had dropped to 1.9 million by 1980. The losses were worst among the truck drivers.

By the middle of last year, 120,000 Teamsters truckers—more than one in every five—were out of work.

On July 16, 1981, Edwards wrote a letter to his men. It started, "We will soon be faced with a serious crisis here at Hemingway."

He listed four possibilities for the company. The first three were to continue business as usual—and go bankrupt; sell out—if a buyer could be found; or shut down.

The fourth was to break with the National Master Freight Agreement and negotiate a cheaper contract with the union.

It was the company's only hope—and the drivers', Edwards said.

"We are all in this together," he wrote, "and we will either sink or swim together."

Sometime in late August or early September, Roy Williams and the Teamsters' sixteen vice-presidents met in a hotel room in Kansas City.

By then, representatives for the nation's biggest truckers had already said that something had to be done if they—and the union—were to survive the competition. The Teamsters had to make concessions.

By then, too, more than 200 companies had taken the same step as Hemingway and announced they could no longer afford the master freight agreement—not even for the six months before it expired on April 1 this year.

Williams emerged from the meeting to pledge the union would be "as reasonable as conditions will permit."

What that would turn out to mean was that the Teamsters were willing to make some concessions. But they were not going to let go of the master freight agreement.

Edwards called for negotiations between Hemingway and the Teamsters to start in late July or early August. He didn't get his first negotiating session until eight months later on March 18. The old master agreement was due to expire in only thirteen days.

In the eight-month interim, the union and the big truckers had worked out a new agreement. It included some concessions. For example, it provided what amounted to a freeze on drivers' pay and on some fringe benefits.

But the freeze was for the future. Before it took effect, the agreement provided a cost-of-living increase. Pay went up forty-seven cents an hour. Benefit payments went up twenty-five cents. A union driver now made hourly wages of $13.26. The nation's fifth-largest trucker, Spector-Red Ball, collapsed.

Looking back on the settlement, Williams recently told an interviewer that the union had saved the master freight agreement.

"It did try to fall apart," he said, but "we put it back together."

Edwards flew into Washington at mid-day March 18 to meet the union at the Hospitality Inn, five minutes from National Airport. The two sides met in a windowless room. Edwards started the session by making his contract proposal.

The union would have to waive the forty-seven cent raise and the twenty-five cent benefit increase. That would save Hemingway $1 million. It would also have to give up running its health and welfare program. Edwards said he could provide the same benefits as the program's and do it for $1 million less.

For its part, Hemingway would try to survive.

The union was polite. Another meeting was scheduled.

The old agreement expired. The meetings continued through April. Then Edwards stopped hearing from the union.

May passed without a word. The men kept working. The company turned its first profit in more than a year.

Finally, the word came. Another meeting had been called for June 10 at the Hospitality Inn. This time it turned out to be in a room with a window.

The union opened the session: Will Hemingway compromise? Edwards said no.

The company had to make a $1-million payment on its trucks by the end of the month. It only had $400,000 and was going to have to borrow the rest. Even if it had wanted to cut a deal, Edwards said, it could not: the bank was demanding a lean contract as a condition of the loan.

Would the Teamsters compromise? Edwards asked.

No. They couldn't agree to the business with the health and welfare program. And even if they could have, they still could not have settled. There were the other companies to think of, the ones that had already signed with the union. They were putting on an awful lot of heat. Making a lot of noise about what would happen if a competitor got a better deal than the one they got.

There was really no choice: Hemingway must sign the new master freight agreement or be struck.

Men on both sides were silent.

Shortly before the first negotiating session had been called back in March, Edwards had written to the men.

He had told them that Hemingway could not afford a strike and that if one occurred the company would fold. He had asked them to cross picket lines if it came to that. He had quoted former President Kennedy: "The courage we desire is not the courage to die decently but the courage to live manfully."

After it was over, most of the men would not talk. But a few, who refused to be identified, tried to explain why they had walked off their jobs.

One man, a 20-year veteran of the company, recited a long list of complaints. There was no reason he should have trusted Edwards on the health benefits. The guy probably wanted the company to close so he could re-open as a non-union shop under a different name.

Then he said, "You have to remember that the men have to stick with the union because the union's got their retirement. If I got in dutch with the union that would go out the window."

Teamster negotiators ended the June 10 meeting by telling Edwards he could expect a strike sometime late the following week. Union pickets shut the company at six the next morning.

Edwards rushed off another letter. Again, he asked the men to cross the lines. Again, he quoted Kennedy: "Courage is an opportunity that sooner or later is presented to us all." A few listened, but not enough.

Hemingway went out of business within a week.

The teamsters had defended the master freight agreement. Companies that had signed it were assured that a competitor would not enjoy lower labor costs.

It is widely conceded that the agreement will not survive beyond its current term. When it expires on March 31, 1985, the Teamsters will have to cope with the change.

On Saturday, June 19, two days before the public would hear, Edwards flew to Newark to tell his terminal managers the company was closing. As the plane swung out over the coast, he wrote a finale to "Wheels and Whales."

To the Tune of "The Green Berets," it goes:

Wheels and Whales upon their chests,
These are men, America's best,
Two thousand men will roll no more.
Perhaps in heaven we'll do an encore.

■ Personal Touch Pulls SAS Out of Its Stall

ROY HILL

In a small, bright conference room at the old domestic airport in Stockholm, a blond-haired, blue-eyed man who calls himself an itinerant preacher stabs at a blackboard with a piece of chalk to drive home a key point. Jan Carlzon, age 41, the stylish new president of Scandinavian Airlines System (SAS) has a straightforward message to sell—making profits in the airline business today means operating like a first-line service company. By comparison, the dirty work of calculating fuel economy, choosing types of aircraft, or scheduling take-offs is just so much routine, he says.

The twenty SAS managers in the room sit riveted to their seats, impressed by this smooth talker who has needed only a year to pull their airline out of a financial stall.

Carlzon, whose mature good looks suggest a matinee idol or a film star, has dropped in at the managers' meeting to deliver a pep talk. "I have been travelling around and preaching ever since I took this job," he tells a visitor.

A communicator to his fingertips, he paints a picture of a marketer's heaven, in which the customer is always right and always happy, costs are trimmed at the head office while more is spent on service, business people are pampered without paying any extra on the standard fares, tourists fly for the price of second-class rail travel, and

profits flow in like clear water from a mountain stream.

But the heaven that Carlzon sketches is no distant vision. It appears to be happening now, in an organization he has transformed in a year from one that suffered its biggest loss to one that made its biggest profit.

Turnaround is no novelty to this man who became a public figure in Sweden after joining Linjeflyg, the Swedish domestic airline, in 1978. In his first year there, he introduced a number of low-fare innovations that increased passenger traffic by forty-four percent and turned a deficit of $4 million into a profit of some $1.35 million.

The gospel Carlzon preaches at SAS is that customer services and relations come first, second, and third, and everything else practically nowhere. He has also brought a refreshingly original approach to employee communications, fare structures, and cost reduction, confining the latter to those areas where any cuts will not affect passenger service and comfort.

According to John A. Herbert, SAS's American director of external information, who has been with SAS for twenty years, Carlzon has put the airline through a cultural revolution. "Previously," he says, "executives liked to play their cards close to their chests. Now everything is wide open."

SAS employees used to act on instructions handed down from above, Carlzon reminded the middle managers at the Stockholm meeting. For example, the cabin crews, when welcoming passengers on board, were not allowed to use their own words. Greetings were programmed from headquarters. The airline seemed to exist for the sake of its eighty-odd aircraft, its technical facilities, and the administrative machinery.

When those at the bottom of the management pyramid, who were in contact with the passengers, tried to communicate upwards, there were so many filters in the hierarchy that by the time a decision was made, and got back to the bottom, there was little left of the original impulse from the market.

Standing at the blackboard, Carlzon rubbed out the pyramid he had drawn and substituted a wheel, with operating departments revolving around a hub at which he sat, like an airport traffic controller in a centrally located tower.

"I am the manager in the middle," Carlzon said. "I give a vision of the future of the company and formulate business strategy. But I delegate responsibility. I give everyone full authority to use his own initiative when dealing with passengers.

"We have eight million passengers a year," he added, "and each one of them makes personal contact with at least five SAS people. That means forty million contact points a year—forty million occasions on which the personal relationship with our customers can go wrong."

He told the managers that he appreciated their problems. It was easier to run the company using top-down instructions than to act as an advisor and consultant. "Instructions, however, only succeed in providing employees with knowledge of their own limitations. Information, on the other hand, provides them with a knowledge of their opportunities and possibilities."

Notably informal himself, Carlzon approves of the pilot who opened his address to a plane-load of business people bound for Copenhagen with the word "Comrades!"—which evoked a lot of laughter from the passengers. Another pilot reacted to a sit-down strike, which blocked the runway at Kastrup, Copenhagen's international airport, by opening the bar and taking his passengers on a guided tour of the airport

perimeter pointing out places of interest. Such initiatives are encouraged at SAS.

The airline has two directors of information on the same level, each acting as the other's deputy and handling internal and external communications respectively. Both have instant access to Carlzon.

Internal information ranges from talks delivered by Carlzon and staff parties in aircraft hangars, which he attends, to company publications, including a broadsheet that reprints articles about SAS that appear in Swedish and foreign publications.

"Carlzon feels very strongly about the importance of feedback," says Christina Edler, director of internal information, who had been planning to leave the airline in some frustration before he arrived.

It was she who was partly responsible for Carlzon's unusual "red book" entitled *Let's Get in There and Fight,* a 52-page compilation of statistics, exhortations, and simple cartoon drawings, which was issued to all staff and which some managers thought was "talking down" to them. But it wasn't aimed at managers. Rather it was aimed at what Carlzon calls "the people in the front line"—about 7,500 of them, ranging from reservation clerks to pilots.

External writings about SAS, facilitated by Herbert, often polarize around Carlzon himself, who is no shrinking violet where personal publicity is concerned. He welcomes the publicity so long as it contributes to SAS's image as a progressive airline that puts people first.

Carlzon can react very personally to any public attacks upon SAS. For instance, while driving to the office recently he dictated a rebuttal of a highly critical article, by an ex-SAS hostess, which had appeared in *Dagens Nyheter,* Sweden's largest newspaper, alleging that the airline's service course was full of sexist innuendo. The rebuttal, published under Carlzon's name, ran longer than the offending item.

Inevitably, in Scandinavia, there are some who disparage Carlzon for his extrovert image. Many Swedes refuse to believe that a man they see as a playboy, and larger than life, can also be a good and successful manager.

When Carlzon joined the airline as chief executive in November, 1980—he was appointed group president nine months later—he found an outfit that was over-staffed, under-motivated, and suffering from productivity problems.

The instinct of most managers on taking over an ailing company in a debt-ridden industry probably would be to make drastic cuts. But Carlzon says he tries to look at costs as resources, as future possibilities, rather than as dead wood to be pruned.

"I would never, as a first move, work on hard cost-reduction programmes," he says, "When there is no competition in the market—and remember, we didn't have any competition, really, at SAS for thirty years—you could work with general cost-cutting, because your revenue side was always given. Every year, you came in with a budget and management said, 'This is not enough.' So you cut by 5 percent. It didn't matter much if they reduced on functions where people were prepared to pay for services.

"But when you enter into a competitive situation, and you are competing for revenue when the market is standing still, it is more important than ever to decide what kind of person you are trying to do business with. When you have decided on that, you must adjust and develop your resources to this specific market. You must go out and invest in the market, which means that you take away resources which are not profitable and develop ones that are."

Of course, SAS does have cost problems. Some are built into the tripartite nature of its ownership. For instance, aircraft overhaul facilities are spread over four bases in the different countries. Carlzon would like to have them centralized. He also says that the costs of civil aviation, in a Scandinavian tax and regulatory environment, are very high compared with those of competitors.

There have been some redundancies but not many. Currently SAS has 16,400 employees, compared with 17,100 two years ago.

Carlzon says that when he joined SAS, replacing Carl-Olov Munkberg, who became head of the Swedish parent company, he realized that, because the old culture and traditions were so strong, it would be difficult for him to use only those senior managers already in place. "I had to create a certain turbulence. One way of doing it was to appoint new people."

Even so, there was no wholesale axing. Managers already in the company were promoted.

Carlzon has approached costs with an open mind. One of his first moves was to launch about 150 project study groups that put the entire company under a microscope. "We went through every single function within the company," he says, "from my desk down to the service within the cabins. We asked ourselves whether we really needed that function in order to satisfy the needs of the frequent traveler."

One result was that, at headquarters, many statistics that used to be supplied monthly are now provided only quarterly, and statistics and research in some departments have been eliminated entirely. Wherever possible, headquarters staff has been moved out to jobs "up front." But at the same time Carlzon spent money brightening up the headquarters offices, on the grounds that dingy surroundings are bad for morale.

In pursuit of his marketing aims he is prepared to try new things and, if they don't work, get rid of them. "It is much better to try, and make something that is not 100 percent correct, than not to do anything," he says. "We want to be 1 percent better in 100 details rather than 100 percent better in a single detail."

Less understandable to competitors in the airline industry is why Carlzon proposes to dispose of his four Airbus A300s—a highly successful wide-bodied jet with efficient operating costs—when other airlines are buying them. But for him the reasoning is simple. Scandinavian travelers like more frequent services, for which SAS's DC9s are ideally suited. For Carlzon, it is the market that decides the aircraft, and not a question of purchasing aircraft on technical merit, then trying to fill the seats.

This point of view will be driven home when shareholders receive the latest annual report, at the end of January next year. They will find it completely reorganized, with the emphasis on the market, on competition, on objectives, strategies, and organization, in that order. There will be no aircraft pictured in the entire publication.

The 150 study projects initiated by Carlzon looked at operating efficiency, as well as costs.

Announcing that he wanted SAS to be the most punctual airline, he installed a terminal in his office so that he could monitor personally any improvements or failings in arrival and departure times. Now SAS *is* the number one in punctuality, in Europe and the North and South Atlantic, according to the Association of European Airlines.

Carlzon's biggest and boldest innovation on which his entire business strategy is based, is aimed at motivating the frequent traveler to pay the full economy price while, at the same time, pursuing flexible pricing in the tourist market, to get new clients into the aircraft.

"We want to be the company of free choice for the customer," Carlzon says. "High service, relatively high price. Low service, low price." By doing this, average revenue would climb comfortably. "I want SAS to be in a situation where if, for example, there was deregulation in Europe in two years' time, we could reduce our prices by 25 percent without losing our shirt."

Carlzon's introduction of EuroClass travel, in the autumn of 1981, which offered frequent travelers in Europe many advantages in comfort, better food, and free drinks, infuriated some rival airlines because it was done at normal economy fares and without a surcharge.

They are responding in different ways. British Airways offers Club Class with free drinks, but the knee-room in its seating doesn't match that of SAS and generally speaking it costs more. Iberia is offering what it calls Preference Class as a cheaper alternative to first class on some of its European routes. Lufthansa and Swissair say that they will stick with first class, thank you very much.

Rolf Hoehn, deputy director, U.K. and Ireland, for Lufthansa, says their figures prove there is a continuing demand for first class in Europe with enough people prepared to pay first-class prices.

A Swissair representative says that their policy is to upgrade the service for everybody in economy. "We think that demand on most routes varies so much that whatever way you divide the cabin you will get it wrong somehow," he says. "If you move an economy passenger up to a first-class seat, you are giving him a discount. If you offer an inferior seat to a first-class passenger, you are turning him away from using you again."

But Carlzon sticks to his guns. "I have no interest whatsoever in what a passenger is paying me," he says. "The only interest I have is how much revenue did I get from each specific aircraft before it left the ground. I am working, if you like, in the fresh food business. Each time the aircraft takes off every empty seat in it is 'rotten,' like the unsold tomatoes on a market stall. So if I get one cent for the last seat, if it would otherwise be empty, that is fair enough, because it is one cent more."

Perhaps both approaches are defensible, but it could be significant that while SAS has attracted 8 percent more passengers to its EuroClass, and is making a record profit, Swissair showed an uncharacteristic loss in the first half of this year.

Carlzon acknowledges that many people in the industry, and in Scandinavia, regard his marketing dedication as superficial and not to be taken too seriously. He is aware that between 10 percent and 20 percent of his own employees do not think he has been doing the right things. "The difficult thing," he says, without looking too concerned, "is to convince these people that this is actually a much more serious, much more long-term way than to work very hard on the cost side.

"If you achieve a profitable situation by reducing costs, even more than we have done before, it would be a very short-term profit because it would only be achieved with more dissatisfied clients and more un-motivated personnel. Such a profit would only be worth the interest we would get from it when we put it into the bank account. But if we could achieve the same profit with more satisfied clients, and more satisfied employees, that is real substance. That is of real value for the future."

■ Eye Need Help—Now!

I had trouble reading in the afternoon. My left eye couldn't quite focus on the letters, but I assumed it was a simple case of eye strain. Probably caused by driving from Connecticut to San Francisco. Three thousand miles of highway glare. All the way to the edge of America.

By evening I knew something was wrong with me. My eye felt all right when I stared out across the bay, but it hurt when I tried to look around the Cliff House lounge. I could see Ann and Kim at the bar ordering an Irish Coffee for me, but their images were blurred. I blinked my eyes several times, and then the pain started. It felt like someone had stuck a hot knife into my eye. I wanted to scream, but I didn't. Kim must have turned and saw me clutching my face. It was exactly 11:34 P.M., June 27, 1974. . . .

A Chinese woman was screaming. She was sitting in a seat to my left. She was ahead of me, which was a relief. Her screaming bothered me. She wasn't bleed-

ing or anything. I never found out what her problem was. God, my eye hurt. Waiting in the emergency room of·San Francisco General Hospital at two o'clock in the morning wasn't my idea of a fun night in 'Frisco. We'd been sitting there since midnight and there were still five people ahead of me.

"Steve, I'm going to see if one of these doctors can tell me how much longer we'll have to wait." Ann was gone before I could say a word. I would have preferred it if Kim went. Only the empty seat Ann had occupied was between me and the screaming woman. It was exactly 2:07 A.M.

"Hi. I'm Dr. Vargas. Your friend Ann tells me something is wrong with your eye." I couldn't believe he was a doctor. He had hair to his waist!

"Yes. My left eye's been ·sore for two days and now it feels like something is in it."

"Have you been hammering metal or doing any welding without safety glasses?"

"No. I just drove here from Connecticut."

"Oh. You probably sunburned your eyes on the way across. Regardless of what the problem is, the eye clinic isn't open until seven o'clock. Why don't you come back then?"

READER NOTE: This account is a personal journal written by Steven J. Montaperto about an incident that occurred in a hospital. The writer uses some language that may be offensive to you. However, we felt it best not to edit the journal so that the full flavor of the experience could be understood.

"It hurts. Can't you do anything?"

"Not until the morning. Go to the admitting desk and tell the nurse I want you sent to the eye clinic. I've got to take care of that Chinese woman. Her screaming is driving all of us nuts. Later, Steve. . . ."

The hospital was fifteen minutes away, so we left at exactly 6:30. We wanted time to park the car. Ann didn't have to be at work until 9:00, so we figured she could drive me to the eye clinic and wait while they treated me. Even if it took an hour we would be out at 8:00 and back at her apartment at 8:30. She could catch the subway, or take my car, and be at work by 9:30. Since she and Kim worked for the same company, Kim was going to tell her boss that Ann might be late.

We arrived at the admitting desk at exactly 6:51 A.M. The admitting nurse wore a neatly pressed, white, starched, uniform with a collar turned up. Her name tag read . . . Carla B. Smith. Her blond hair was in a bun under her cap. She looked about twenty-five years old and very firm—large breasts and slender legs. I would have invited her to lunch if my eye didn't hurt so much. All things considered, I preferred seeing the eye doctor over her naked flesh. Which is indicative of just how much pain I was in.

"Good morning. I've got to go to the eye clinic. Can you please tell me how to get there?" I decided to try to be calm and polite. No point in screaming in pain. It didn't do much for the Chinese woman.

"Sir, you have to see a doctor to be admitted. I can't send you to the eye clinic until a member of our emergency staff has seen you."

"That's no problem. I saw Dr. Vargas last night. He told me to go to the eye clinic first thing in the morning."

"You already saw Mike Vargas. No problem. Give me your blue slip and you can go straight to the eye clinic."

"I don't have a blue slip." I didn't like the expression on her face when I told her I didn't have a slip."

"Then you'll have to see a doctor."

"But I already saw Mike Vargas. Isn't he considered a doctor around here? He walks around in a white coat and has a stethoscope."

"Yes, but you couldn't have seen Dr. Vargas."

"Why not?"

"Because if you'd seen Dr. Vargas you would have a blue slip signed by him!"

"He didn't have time to give me a slip, damn it! He examined me in the hall. There was a hysterical Chinese woman in here last night. He had to take care of her."

"I'm sorry sir, but you must see a doctor."

"You mean I waited for two hours last night for nothing!"

"Yes."

"But Vargas told me I'd have to go to the eye clinic anyway and my eye hurts like hell. Can't I go to the clinic first and then be admitted?"

"No. Also, we have to determine who is going to pay for your treatment."

"Screw that. I've got health insurance and two hundred dollars in American Express travelers checks in my pocket. I'll pay you right now, just direct me to the eye clinic."

"I'm sorry but your ability to pay has to be analyzed so we can determine your admission status."

"What if I were bleeding or my chest were caved in? What would you do then?"

"We'd treat you immediately, of course. But you aren't an emergency case. Just a sore eye."

"Sore eye! It feels like the goddamn thing is falling out of my head."

"I'm sorry, you must be processed. Follow the yellow line." A six-inch thick yellow line was painted on the floor and led down the hall. Ann and I followed it.

There were four people ahead of me. Most of them were dressed in ragged clothes and looked like they were suffering from malnutrition and scurvy. Winos! It was exactly 9:41 A.M. when I sat down at his desk.

"Now sir, I'm your social worker. My name is Jim Lee. It's our job to evaluate just how much of your hospital bill you can afford to pay. Of course an installment payment schedule can be arranged. How much money do you feel you can spare?"

"Mr. Lee, I have hospital insurance, two hundred dollars in my pocket, two thousand dollars in a bank in Connecticut and six thousand dollars in marketable securities. My father has three cars, a one-hundred-thousand-dollar house, several hundred thousand dollars in stocks and bonds and earns thirty thousand dollars a year. And that's in a bad year. Does that answer your question?"

"What are you doing here?"

"The admitting nurse sent me!"

"I'm sorry for the mix-up. Follow the red line." There was a six-inch thick red line that led down a second hall and around a corner. Ann and I followed it.

There were thirteen people ahead of me. Ann called her office and told them she'd be late. At exactly 12:47 I was led into a curtained-off area and Jim Price examined me.

"Hi, I'm Dr. Price. What's the problem?"

"Aside from the hospital administration, it's my left eye. It hurts like hell."

"When did it start bothering you?"

"Things began to get blurry two days ago. It didn't hurt until last night."

"Have you been doing any chemicals?"

"Just some speed I picked up for the drive. I got in from Connecticut on Tuesday."

"That's interesting. I'm from Old Saybrook. I began my residency here last month."

"Marvelous. What can you do for my eye?"

"It looks sunburned, but it also could be irritated by a piece of foreign matter. I can see a small speck on the right side. Regardless, I'll have to send you to the eye clinic. Just follow the green line." There was a six-inch thick green line that led to a staircase.

"Don't I need a blue slip?"

"No, that's just for readmittance. If I wanted you to come back tomorrow I'd have to give you a blue slip so you could get past the admitting nurse."

"Why?"

"Who knows? I imagine that's the way it's always been done around here."

There were only two people ahead of me at the eye clinic. At exactly 1:59 P.M. I walked into the clinic and sat down in the examination chair. It reminded me of a dentist's office. There was a head rest and head clamps oral surgeons use to steady your head for full mouth X-rays. The doctor's name was Victoria Lee. A beautiful Oriental lady who was no relation to the social worker downstairs. She was every bit as beautiful as the admitting nurse, dark eyes and blue-black shoulder-length hair, but in a maternal way. My eye still hurt like hell, so it was irrelevant anyway.

"Rest your head against the cushion. I'm going to put the clamps on your head so you don't move. There appears to be a very small speck in your eye and I want to cut it out." Jim Price had been right. I had a piece of metal in my eye. A credit to Old Saybrook, Connecticut.

"Keep the patch on your eye for two days, Steve, and come back to see me if it still hurts after that. And here's some eye wash you can use after the patch comes off. Enjoy your stay in San Francisco."

"Thanks, Victoria. It will certainly be more enjoyable without that metal in my eye. It's feeling better already." And it did!

At exactly 2:18 P.M., nineteen minutes after entering the eye clinic, Ann and I walked past the admitting desk and out the door of San Francisco General Hospital.

. . .

At exactly 3:04 P.M. on October 4, 1974, a bill arrived from San Francisco General Hospital. Thirty-five dollars for services rendered. I threw it in the garbage.

It's exactly 11:26 P.M. on March 1, 1978. I'm waiting for a second notice of balance due!

Exercises

■ Common Target Game

It is often assumed that to gain a perspective of the total organization and how it develops one must be in a top management position. Whether a person be a top manager or a new recruit, the human (cognitive) process used in gaining such an understanding remains essentially the same. It is truly unfortunate that most managers do not seem to develop insights into how an organization develops until they are at or near the top of the organization. By not having this macro perspective, people at lower levels of the organization often cannot be of value and may even be a hindrance in the organization's attempts to develop strategy and future organizational structure.

This exercise is designed to make its participants aware of the process by which organizations develop and in particular the analogous human problem-solving process that decision-makers use when organizations face uncertainty. It is believed that such an awareness could lead to the development of managers who, over years of having this perspective, might sharpen and refine their view of the total organization, thereby making a more effective contribution to their organization's survival and growth efforts.

Directions

1. Your instructor will put the class into groups of four and assign each group a game coordinator.
2. Once in your groups, you will be seated back-to-back and will *not* be allowed to communicate in any way.
3. The game coordinator will give you all the materials needed for the exercise.
4. Do *not* read the Instructions to Game Players until told to do so by the instructor.
5. Each game player should have three sheets of paper and a pencil for use during the game.
6. At the end of the game, the group should talk quietly until other groups are finished. Once all groups have completed the task, your instructor will give you further directions.

■ DO NOT READ UNTIL INSTRUCTED TO DO SO.

Instructions to Game Players

The Common Target Game is played by four people in a group. The participants are *not* allowed to communicate with each other in any way. You must be seated back-to-back so that you cannot observe other members in your group.

Alex Bavelas of Stanford University originally developed the experiment upon which this exercise is based.

The Game Coordinator will announce to your group a target number between zero and forty. Each of you has been given a set of cards from zero through ten. At the Coordinator's command, each member of the group will be instructed to raise a card displaying the amount he or she wishes to contribute to help the group reach its target number. Only *one* card may be held up by a group member.

The Game Coordinator will total all of the cards displayed and announce the total to your group. The Game Coordinator will not tell you who has contributed what amounts or anything else; only the total contributed will be revealed. The group will repeat this process until the target number is achieved. Once the target is achieved, a new target will be announced. Your group's objective is to minimize the number of trials the group takes to achieve each of several targets.

From time to time the Game Coordinator will ask you to make some notes. You will be told what to write about. If you have any questions on how the game is played, raise your hand and the instructor will answer your question privately.

■ DO NOT READ UNTIL INSTRUCTED TO DO SO.

Rules to Remember for Game Coordinators

1. *Allow no communication between group members.*

2. Be sure to total *accurately* all cards shown by group members.

3. *Very important:* Do not make any comments on how the group is doing with respect to reaching its target. Just announce whatever the total is. For example, *don't* say: "You missed it by one," or "If one person would learn how to divide this would go much faster." *Just announce* the target and the total shown.

4. Be sure to allow time for group members to think *after* you announce the target and before you ask them to put the cards up. Allow plenty of time between each trial for the participants to think about their next contribution.

5. Groups should follow your commands of "cards up" and "cards down" after each attempt. Don't allow anyone to keep a card up in the air; this will make each participant consciously evaluate each move.

6. Continue on the same target until it is achieved, moving down the left column and then down the right column stopping at the places noted "stop" and directing the participants to do the following: "Write a few sentences describing the procedure you think your group is following." Also, ask each person to answer the question, "What are you trying to accomplish?" Allow enough time for everyone to complete this task. (Collect these each time and keep them in separate piles.)

7. After your group has achieved all its targets, ask the members to talk quietly until all the other groups have completed their targets.

8. When your group is finished, tally up the total number of trials required by your group to achieve all the targets and report that information to the instructor.

▪ DO NOT READ UNTIL INSTRUCTED TO DO SO.

COMMON TARGET COORDINATOR RECORDING FORM

Target	Number of Trials	Target	Number of Trials
19	_____	9	_____
3	_____	18	_____
31	_____	35	_____
13	_____	24	_____
25	_____	34	_____
6	_____	29	_____
20	_____	17	_____
12	_____	30	_____
28	_____	*Stop	▓▓▓▓▓▓▓▓▓▓▓▓▓▓
36	_____	38	_____
26	_____	33	_____
37	_____	8	_____
39	_____	4	_____
21	▓▓▓▓▓▓▓▓▓▓▓▓▓▓	32	_____
*Stop		11	_____
14	_____	27	_____
15	_____	23	_____
16	_____	22	_____
1	_____	10	_____
2	_____	5	_____
7	_____	40	▓▓▓▓▓▓▓▓▓▓▓▓▓▓
		*Stop	

Total Trials _____

■ The Football Pool

Often the official goals of an organization are vague and subject to wide interpretation. In addition, such goals do not reflect the various alternative ways of reaching the same goal. As members of an organization go about the business of operationalizing the official goals, their actions implicitly reflect a variety of operative or subunit goals that can complement or subvert the official goals. In the following role-play situation, the official goals of the organization are not spelled out; however, they are below the surface of its members' behaviors. The intent of the role play is to confront some of the organizational dynamics that occur as official goals and operative goals become misaligned.

Directions

1. Your instructor will assign class members to the role of Mo Holihan or Bill Sanner. You will be asked to study your role carefully for about five minutes and then the meeting between Mo and Bill will take place.
2. The setting for this meeting will be outside the classroom in the hallway or near a coffee machine. You will be paired with another participant and sent to a location of your choice for about 20–25 minutes. Your instructor may assign some observers to the role-playing pairs.
3. Your instructor will indicate at what time you should return to the classroom.
4. Read *only* the role you have been assigned.

■ READ ONLY IF INSTRUCTED TO DO SO.

Mo Holihan Role

Moira Holihan was the sales manager for Steel Products Inc. "Mo" had demonstrated by a very successful sales career with Steel Products that a woman engineer could sell industrial products in a market dominated by tool and die makers. The sales department consisted of seven men who had worked their way up from the manufacturing division. These men "spoke the language" of the tool and die makers and provided useful insights about customers. In addition, the sales department had three graduate engineers who provided technical expertise and who helped develop new customers much as Mo had done.

Bill Sanner, one of the graduate engineers, had some trouble making friends when he first joined the sales department. However, when he began running a weekly football pool he seemed to begin to find his niche. At his first performance evaluation he noted that he was beginning to really enjoy his job and that the pool had provided him an excellent opportunity to talk with people in all departments. Mo was pleased that Bill fit in. She had recruited all the department's engineers and had purposely looked for individuals who had interpersonal skills that would help them work more effectively with the members of the department who did not have formal training. In fact, she had made it very clear in her interviewing efforts that getting along with other members of the department was crucial.

One day during a department heads meeting, Jim Krans, the plant manager, said, "Say, Mo, how's that new guy Bill Sanner doing? He seems like an amiable sort. He catches me every Monday morning and lets me in on his football pool. He's always ready to advise me on what teams to back."

"Well, Jim," Mo said, "I'm pleased with his progress. His sales record has been fairly good and he seems to be fitting in well."

Samuel Cooke, the controller, interjected. "That Sanner, what a character. He tried to convince me to bet on the Packers last week. I should have. On Tuesday, after the Packers won by twenty-one points, he must have spent the whole morning getting members of my department to come in and kid me about my choice. Boy, he's something else."

"Well, Sam, he made a side bet with me that all the people in the Personnel Department who invested in the pool would lose," said Art Walker, supervisor of personnel. "Naturally I came to the rescue of my people and made him a $25 bet. You should have heard the ruckus he made Friday when he paid off."

After the meeting, Mo headed back to her office a little concerned over what she had heard. Along the way she ran into Bill Sanner who was just completing a football pool sale and decided to discuss her concerns with Bill informally.

▪ READ ONLY IF INSTRUCTED TO DO SO.

Bill Sanner Role

Moira Holihan was the sales manager for Steel Products Inc. "Mo" had demonstrated by a very successful sales career with Steel Products that a woman engineer could sell industrial products in a market dominated by tool and die makers. The sales department consisted of seven men who had worked their way up from the manufacturing division. These men "spoke the language" of the tool and die makers and provided useful insights about customers. In addition, the sales department had three graduate engineers who provided technical expertise and who helped develop new customers much as Mo had done.

As one of the graduate engineers who works for Mo, you had some trouble making friends when you first joined the sales department. However, you really found your niche when you started running a weekly football pool. You told Mo at your first performance evaluation session that you were really beginning to enjoy your job and that the pool had provided you with an excellent opportunity to talk with people in all departments. In fact, by getting to know department heads informally, you discovered that you were able to get information and action a lot faster than the other sales engineers, which helped your sales record. Mo told you she was pleased that you fit in, especially since she had made a point during recruiting of stressing the need for interpersonal skills. You remember her saying, "Getting along with other members of the department, especially the tool and die makers, is crucial."

In your rounds with the football pool you have become friends with the plant manager, Jim Krans. He always asks you for detailed advice on what teams to bet on. The plant controller, Sam Cooke, never wants your advice on the pool and just last week you tried to convince him to go with the Packers. When the Packers won by twenty-one points, you made sure several members of his department went in and kidded Sam for not taking your advice. Of course, sometimes your advice can backfire. A few weeks ago Art Walker, who supervises the personnel department, convinced his department members to disregard your advice. You kiddingly told Art in front of several of his people that you would bet him $25 that all his department would lose in the pool. Art took you up on the bet and you took quite a razzing when you paid off. You are just now finishing collecting some money for next week's pool and have spotted Mo coming over to join you. Maybe she will want to get in on this week's pool?

■ Organizational Prognosis

Often we are surprised to hear of the demise of a well-known organization. When W.T. Grant Co. declared bankruptcy in 1976 many people were surprised. "Grant City" had become a well-established part of many large cities and towns. The complacency with which we assume that such organizations are stable and effective ignores the true nature of their environments. In this exercise, your group is asked to brainstorm sources of environmental turbulence that could endanger the survival of some well-known organizations. You are also asked to consider possible strategies that might aid in reducing the severity of the impact of such potential turbulence.

Directions

1. Below is a suggested list of organizations that your group can consider. Your instructor may want to add to or delete from this list.

   a. McDonald's
   b. NBC
   c. U.S. Post Office
   d. Xerox Corporation
   e. General Motors Corporation
   f. _____ University

   g. The Catholic Church
   h. Trans World Airlines
   i. Levi-Strauss Co.
   j. Blue Cross/Blue Shield
   k. New York Mets Baseball Club
   l. Other _____

2. The class as a whole should go through the following process as a warm-up with the instructor. Select an organization from the list provided and discuss the following questions:
   a. *Event(s)*—What events can you envision that might endanger the survival of this organization? Try not to focus solely on external factors. Using your knowledge of the organization, speculate on some possible existing organizational factors (e.g., policies, procedures, practices, current strategy, or structure) that might lead to problems.
   b. *Probability*—What is your estimate of the probability of occurrence of each event? (Use 0 to 100%.)
   c. *Possible Strategy*—What might the organization do to reduce the severity of the impact of this event?

3. Now, in your group, select another organization to work on and respond to the questions posed in Step 2 using the *Individual Worksheet*. Members should then share prognosis, having someone keep records on the *Group Worksheet*.

4. Each group presents its prognosis and the class discusses each group's predictions.

ORGANIZATIONAL PROGNOSIS—INDIVIDUAL WORKSHEET

Name of Organization: _____

Event(s)	*Probability*	*Possible Strategy*
1. _____	1. _____	1. _____
_____		_____
_____		_____
2. _____	2. _____	2. _____
_____		_____
_____		_____
3. _____	3. _____	3. _____
_____		_____
_____		_____
4. _____	4. _____	4. _____
_____		_____
_____		_____
5. _____	5. _____	5. _____
_____		_____
_____		_____

ORGANIZATIONAL PROGNOSIS—GROUP WORKSHEET

Name of Organization: _____

Event(s)	*Probability*	*Possible Strategy*
1. _____	1. _____	1. _____
_____		_____
_____		_____
2. _____	2. _____	2. _____
_____		_____
_____		_____
3. _____	3. _____	3. _____
_____		_____
_____		_____

4. _____

_____

_____

5. _____

_____

_____

6. _____

_____

_____

7. _____

_____

_____

8. _____

_____

_____

9. _____

_____

_____

10. _____

_____

_____

4. _____

_____

5. _____

_____

6. _____

_____

7. _____

_____

8. _____

9. _____

10. _____

_____

4. _____

_____

_____

5. _____

_____

6. _____

_____

7. _____

_____

8. _____

_____

9. _____

_____

10. _____

_____

_____

■ Odds

When Parker Brothers lost several million dollars on a new toy line because two small children swallowed parts and choked to death, the probability of such an event occurring was in the realm of *objective* uncertainty—no one knew and no one could have known such an event would happen. Conversely, when U.S. automakers were delivered a severe blow to the sales of their large, gas-guzzling cars the event was in the realm of *subjective* uncertain-

Inspired by an article in *The New Yorker* (December 11, 1978) by S. Lem. Based on a book review of Kouska's *De Impossibilitate Prognoscendi* and *De Impossibilitate Vitae.*

ty—because of incomplete or faulty information or a misreading of what information was available or because they chose to ignore what they or others knew.

Objectively uncertain events take management by surprise—no warning signs are evident. Subjectively uncertain events may take management by surprise, but the surprise is more a reaction to underestimating the speed with which an event occurred or the extent of impact the event had.

While events in either realm can do permanent, irreparable damage, it is for those in the realm of subjective uncertainty that management is held personally accountable. Producing a product that ultimately loses a lot of money because of a freak accident is *not* management's fault. Producing a product that consumers don't wish to buy because of continued high fuel costs over a period of several years is just plain stupid. As one reporter wrote in *Business Week:*

> For an industry that has always prided itself most on its marketing skills, nothing could be more humiliating than the prospect that it may have to cede nearly a third of its home market. But much more than Detroit's wounded pride is at stake. Indeed, what may be at stake is Detroit itself—at least in its present form. (March 24, 1980, p. 79)

Assignment

Go to any recent source of news about the business world (e.g., *Wall Street Journal, New York Times, Business Week, Forbes, Fortune,* your local newspaper) and find a story about a company that is currently experiencing some difficulty because of an *objectively* uncertain event and a story representing a *subjectively* uncertain event. Bring a copy of both stories to class.

2 Environmental Fit

■ LEARNING OBJECTIVES

1. To increase the participant's awareness of the effects of turbulent environments on organizational performance

2. To provide the participants with an opportunity to gain insights into the functional and dysfunctional aspects of organic and mechanistic management systems

3. To acquaint the participants with some of the major factors to consider in prescribing management systems

4. To examine some ways an organization can scan the environment and analyze it

■ OVERVIEW

Every organization functions within an environment that is somewhat unique. Because of this uniqueness, understanding the nature of the organization's environment becomes a key management function. Unfortunately, managers often lack the needed sensitivity to react to forces in the environment that threaten their organization's survival until after the impact has been felt and a costly toll exacted. Why this insensitivity exists can be understood in part by examining the nature of the management system.

If an organization is in a stable environment facing little or no uncertainty, the management system most likely to evolve will be a well-defined, highly structured (mechanistic) one. On the other hand, where the environment is turbulent, i.e., highly uncertain and constantly changing, a more loosely structured, less-defined (organic) system would seem to be the most appropriate. But this may not evolve. If the management system that evolves is inappropriate, given environmental conditions, organizational friction and inefficiency will result. This friction is often caused by attempts to alter the existing system while the inefficiency usually results from attempts to accommodate the existing system. A more serious problem arises when an organization faces a shifting environment that fluctuates, from periods of stability to turbulence and back again. During these transitional periods, individuals within an organization, and especially management, are likely to experience excessive amounts of anxiety and frustration with the system. And during this time the greatest threat to organizational survival, an inability to adapt rapidly enough to environmental demands, is experienced.

From a manager's perspective, what is at issue is the dilemma of optimizing, through the management system, organizational adaptability while at the same time providing organizational stability. In Part 2, we will examine the relationship between an organization's design and its environment and the factors involved in the selection and design of a management system. In addition, we will attempt to gain an understanding of what an organization can do to scan the environment and analyze it.

Readings

Environmental Analysis and Forecasting

JAMES M. UTTERBACK

This paper focuses on the firm's environment, the economic, technological, social, political, and institutional context within which the firm operates, and on the ways in which firms have attempted to analyze their environments as an input to the process of accommodation between the firm and change in the world outside. To explore the topic fully, several questions are addressed in turn.

- What can be known about changes in the environment, and how can such knowledge about change be acquired as an aid in strategy formulation and planning?
- What methods have been used to forecast environmental changes?
- Are particular methods of analysis and forecasting better suited for some types of environments than others?
- How should the firm integrate environmental assessments into its strategic planning process?
- What topics are suggested for further research in this area?

James M. Utterback, "Environmental Analysis and Forecasting" from Dan E. Schendel and Charles W. Hofer, eds., *Strategic Management: A New View of Business Policy and Planning.* Copyright © 1979 by Little Brown and Company (Inc.). Reprinted by permission. References deleted. See original work.

WHAT CAN BE KNOWN ABOUT CHANGES IN THE ENVIRONMENT, AND HOW CAN SUCH KNOWLEDGE ABOUT CHANGE AS AN AID IN STRATEGY FORMULATION AND PLANNING BE ACQUIRED?

Remarkably, our ability to assess single future trends and changes is quite accurate and comprehensive. Methods for generating forecasts are growing rapidly in number, and projections of specific trends and events are growing even more rapidly. The expansion of the futures field has been characterized as a new discipline striving for professional recognition on the one hand and as a social movement, attracting a degree of involvement similar to that of the civil rights movement, ecology, or consumerism on the other.

Despite the burgeoning popularity and growth of environmental analysis and forecasting and its enthusiastic reception by policy makers in business and government, both in the United States and abroad, its usefulness is severely constrained in practice. The reason is that predictions of the effects of trends and events are much more difficult than foreseeing the primary changes themselves. This is even more problematic in an organizational context of limited resources and established interests and programs, where potential changes and effects must be linked to corporate, agency, or institutional strategy and plans. And there are also some general problems noted below with the use of popular methods for environmental analysis and forecasting.

For instance, forecasts of future trends and potentials are seldom value free. Indeed, forecasts are often meant to be self-fulfilling—to marshal resources and efforts toward some goal—or self-defeating—to create action to avoid some negative consequences of continuing the status quo. In some cases, it is appropriate to look for a converging set of forces or trends, but in others conflict over alternative assumptions and their consequences may be crucial. Often the underlying philosophy of a method of analysis is unrecognized, and it is generalized to too great an extent or is misapplied. But futures research has tended to ignore the intellectual roots of systematic conjecture, concentrating instead on specific techniques and specific forecasts. Application of the principles of value-free science to forecasting may at best be a self-deception and at worst a limitation of the range of human possibility.

Another problem arises in the fact that attempts to forecast often involve rich and diverse collection of data with little attempt made to relate them in a formal way, or they involve elaborate manipulation of narrow and subjectively derived data. There is also a tendency to be sophisticated about model building without being equally sophisticated about data gathering or the use of results. This can be particularly limiting since peripheral information and data from diverse sources are often crucial to the validity of a forecast. Development of measurements and means for gathering data may make the most significant contribution to futures research according to Miles.

Lorange points out the danger that arises when a firm behaves as though it can dominate its environment and completely predict outside developments. The consequence is an attempt to "plan" uncertainty away, re-ducing the firm's sensitivity to unexpected developments and its flexibility to deal with them. A related problem is that the firm may selectively perceive much of the environmental information available to it. But as noted above, environmental change often comes from unexpected directions, and the "peripheral" information that is discarded may be the very information that is most crucial. Klein has addressed this problem by devising a prescriptive method for directing management's attention to a broader range of interactions with the environment as they are related to a particular firm's products and resources.

With these concerns in mind, the basic techniques that are widely used for environmental analysis and forecasting will be summarized briefly. Then it will be argued that different approaches for analysis and forecasting will be better suited to different environments. The integration and use of forecasts in corporate strategic planning, and the effectiveness with which information is obtained for analysis are key concerns, and research in these areas will then be treated briefly.

WHAT METHODS HAVE BEEN USED TO FORECAST ENVIRONMENTAL CHANGES?

A number of methods and approaches have been developed in attempts to anticipate the nature and direction of change and its impact on the firm. These include various means for quantification of expert opinion, constrained extrapolation of past trends, scanning or monitoring the environment, and simulation of the interaction of changes in environmental variables and constraints.

Quantification of expert opinion is usually based on questions either about the estimated probability of the occurrence of a given event before some time or, conversely, about the estimated time by which the expert thinks the event may have occurred with a given (usually 0.50) probability. Fusfeld and Foster review the elements of the *learn*

"Delphi" technique in which such questions are asked of an anonymous panel of experts. Each member of the panel is given several opportunities to revise his estimate after being given feedback on the distribution of the panel's estimates and individuals' reasons for extreme positions. Versions using a computer to increase interaction and feedback among the panelists have been developed, and research has been done on the reliability and validity of this concept. Recent research and applications have focused on the interpersonal dynamics of the Delphi approach and on ways to improve the process through discussion with other members of the panel while still raising and resolving conflicting points of view. Delphi has been widely used to highlight social demographic and political shifts that may affect the firms, though reading these studies leaves the strong impression that the panels reflect business's views of the changing environment rather than more diverse views. The use of the Delphi technique, which originated at RAND, for policy and strategy analysis has been sharply criticized in a recent extensive study from the same source, and the popularity of this approach has resulted in many poorly designed and inappropriate studies.

Extrapolation of trends in technological parameters and capabilities was one of the earliest methods attempted to forecast technological change. Various equations based on both theoretical and empirical results have been used to derive projections from available data. A recent example is provided by efforts to determine the future course of substitution of one product for another based on the current proportion and rate of substitution. Terleckyj has recently made near term estimates of possibilities for improvements in the quality of life in the United States, while Robinson and others have conducted a broader, international extrapolation of trends in the business environment over the coming decade.

Monitoring or scanning the environment is closely related to the ideas of statistical decision theory in that the prior probabilities assigned to a set of competing hypotheses are revised as more tangible early evidence of changes becomes available. The idea of monitoring different dimensions of the environment and its relationship to the process of innovation has been stated by Bright. Monitoring involves searching the environment for signals that may be the forerunners of significant change, identifying the possible consequences assuming that the indications persist, and choosing the events and decisions that should be observed and followed in order to verify the speed and timing of the anticipated change. This method is predicated on the idea that change will be visible in increasingly tangible forms over a period of time before it assumes economic, social, or strategic importance. One of the most interesting monitoring applications is the Trend Analysis Program of the Institute of Life Insurance. Members of the Institute monitor different areas of change and contribute to a series of occasional reports on trends that might affect the industry, but that are of much more general interest as well.

Simulation of the interactions of environmental variables and constraints has been attempted at the level of the firm and its products for housing choices in an urban area, at the level of a region and its resources and industries, and on a global basis for particular resources and pollutants. To date, the use of simulation for forecasting has been largely an exploratory effort, due to measurement problems and a lack of understanding of underlying relationships. An application of great interest is Forrester's attempt to model the dynamics of the United States economy. With relationships and data being reasonably well known and available, he has shown that the economy may be less responsive to monetary and fiscal policies than currently assumed, with the underlying structure of the system of production having a greater long-term influence on its dynamics than is generally expected.

While each of the basic approaches to anticipating change has been treated separately, they are logically related in the order presented. For example, expert opinion has been used to establish "confidence" intervals for projected trends. Both expert opinion and trend extrapolation provide useful data for establishing hypotheses in monitoring, while developing a simulation model requires each of the preceding types of inputs to establish relationships, initial conditions, reasonable ranges for the variables, and so forth.

Two fascinating papers have recently examined how well past forecasts passed the test of time. Most of the forecasts examined were based essentially on expert opinion, but often were quite detailed, comprehensive, and sophisticated in their approach. Wise constructed a sample of more than 1,500 specific predictions made in eighteen specified areas of technology from 1890 to 1940, and predictions of the economic, social, or political effects to be expected from changes in these fields. Forty percent of these predictions were either fulfilled or in progress, while one third (33 percent) have been refuted. Experts had a better record of prediction, but not significantly so, and batting averages appeared to improve with increases in the experts' age and experience. No individuals were remarkably better than average, but a number had success rates of better than half. Predictions of continuation of the status quo were no more accurate than were predictions of change. Most interesting from our point of view is that predictions of the effects of the changes that were accurately foreseen were woefully inadequate. This point is strongly emphasized in a study by Farmer, who examined forecasts published in *Fortune* from 1933 to 1950. He found that authors were not only able to hit the mark more often than they missed, but they were able to predict in considerable detail. Gilfillan, in a seminal study, also reports a better than average success rate for forecasts of major technical change. Forecasts of general trends, structural change, and performance of the economy reviewed by Farmer were also quite accurate. However, he reports that

changes in key political and legal constraints were most difficult to anticipate and also strongly affected accuracy in other areas. While the economic trends were clear, their impacts on individual choices were not. Nor were the impacts of technological change foreseen. Farmer concludes that even the most radical of *Fortune*'s forecasts were too conservative when compared with the actual trends that have occurred.

ARE PARTICULAR METHODS OF ANALYSIS AND FORECASTING BETTER SUITED FOR SOME TYPES OF ENVIRONMENTS THAN OTHERS?

Based on the above analysis, one can hypothesize that the emergence of formal efforts to forecast change will depend on the degree of uncertainty and complexity of the firm's environment and on the differing salience of economic, technological, social, and political factors in the firm's strategy for competition and growth. The effectiveness of a firm's forecasting effort in terms of integration of its outputs into the planning process is expected to be mainly related to internal factors such as formal and informal communication, the organization's structure, and support given to the forecasting and planning functions. One could further hypothesize that those firms with formal forecasting efforts will experience greater sales growth and profitability than comparable firms that carry on these activities on an informal or ad hoc basis.

Gerstenfeld reported results from 162 responding firms that are compatible with these hypotheses. He found that there was a positive relationship between an industry's growth rate and its use of technology forecasting techniques. Five of six higher growth industries also had a majority of firms using some technology forecasting techniques, while this was true of only one industry with a lower rate of growth. Gerstenfeld speculated that more rapidly growing industries "are faced with such rapid technological change that they are forced to use forecasting techniques." One would expect this hypothesis to hold for other types of changes as well.

The essence of the argument to follow is that a firm's environment largely determines its strategy and other responses such as policy, organization structure, and planning process. The appropriateness of these responses, both in the context of the environment and with respect to one another largely determines the effectiveness of its performance. Formal environmental analysis and forecasting efforts are one possible response to more complex and changing environments.

Firms in a simple-static environment will probably not use formal methods in forecasting, or will use the simpler (expert opinion) of the approaches outlined above as shown in exhibit 2.1. Those facing a complex-static environment could be expected to use monitoring, perhaps in a less formal manner than described above, because it seems well suited to handling complexity and is based on the premise that change will occur gradually with increasingly tangible and unambiguous signals. Firms in a simple-dynamic environment would probably use trend-extrapolation, computer-based interaction of expert panels, and other means suited to a limited, but rapidly changing, data base. Only those firms in the most complex and dynamic environments would be expected to undertake simulation, quantification of environmental scanning, or other approaches designed to deal with both a large and rapidly chang-

ing set of variables. Further, the planning process may be expected to be more dynamic (to involve more iterations and more frequent iterations) in this type of environment than in the less difficult ones. A firm using any of the forecasting approaches that are more complex and require more data and computation would probably also use some of the simpler approaches to developing forecasts.

Environmental uncertainties are likely to transcend firm and often traditional industry boundaries. But our particular interest here is in predicting differences in the use of forecasting models among firms in differing environments. It seems logical to propose that a given firm's approach to its environment, that is, its competitive strategy, is likely to have a major influence on differences between it and other firms with which it competes. For example, Ayres has suggested that explicit competitive strategy probably has as great an impact on the types of accommodations to environmental changes undertaken by a firm as the types of opportunities and needs available have on the evolution of strategy. He suggests that three distinct strategies can be described as "performance-maximizing," "sales-maximizing," and "cost-minimizing." Simmonds has developed this idea further and provided a gross classification of industries by dominant strategy.

These categories of types of strategies are highly oversimplified and surely need to be differentiated into more dimensions than performance, sales, and cost. Nor is there any empirical basis for such a taxonomy. It

EXHIBIT 2.1 Types of Environment Related to Forecasting Methods

Complexity	Change	
	Static	Dynamic
Simple	No formal methods, or expert opinion	Expert opinion, monitoring, and trend extrapolation
Complex	Expert opinion, monitoring	As above and simulation, quantitative models, probabilistic information processing

is simply suggested here as an exploratory hypothesis that does have appeal because of its tie to characteristics of the environment as noted below.

The importance of a firm's competitive strategy is that we expect that performance-maximizing firms will clearly be more likely to employ formal and sophisticated models for forecasting and planning than will those with other strategies, as shown in exhibit 2.2. Sales-maximizing firms would likely concentrate on product improvements and components and perhaps use extrapolation or monitoring with respect to these. Cost-minimizing firms would be least likely to adopt technology forecasting effects or techniques, with the exception of attempts to anticipate changes in a few variables or technologies that might lead to major cost reductions in competitors' operations.

There is some evidence for these hypotheses from previous research. Litschert, in a study of 35 firms in the paint industry, noted that the fourteen that were research (product performance) oriented used the most sophisticated planning techniques of those in the sample. The twenty-one firms that were market-oriented focused on existing products and were generally less sophisticated in their planning approaches. He also found that the greater the change in the firm's area of product technology, the greater the focus on research-oriented strategies, while the more stable the technological environment, the greater the use of market-oriented strategies.

A complex-dynamic environment as described above would be characterized by diverse products and rapid product change. One would expect a majority of firms in this type of environment to follow a performance-maximizing strategy and to emphasize product technical performance. Flexible, uncoordinated types of production technology would be typical. Conversely, a simple-static environment would be characterized by few highly standardized products and relatively slow, incremental product change. One would expect a majority of firms in this type of environment to follow a cost-minimizing strategy and to emphasize highly automated, large-scale production facilities, minimum factory and transportation costs. Firms in environments with intermediate levels of uncertainty and complexity might follow sales-maximizing and mixed strategies with emphasis on product differentiation and using varying degrees of automation and subcontracting in the production process. It follows that a firm in a complex-dynamic environment with a performance-maximizing strategy for competition would be most likely to use formal methods to anticipate change, and firms in a simple-static environment following a cost-minimizing strategy would be least likely to do so, as shown in exhibit 2.2.

Complexity may be viewed as a function of both the number of environmental variables and constraints of importance to the firm and as a function of the diversity, or number of different components of the envi-

EXHIBIT 2.2   Environmental Characteristics and Firm Strategy Related to Forecasting Methods

Environmental change	Environmental complexity	Type of strategy	Forecasting methods
Static	Simple	Cost-minimizing	No methods, or expert opinion
Static	Complex	Mixed and sales-maximizing	Expert opinion, monitoring, and trend extrapolation
Dynamic	Simple	Mixed and sales-maximizing	Expert opinion, monitoring, and trend extrapolation
Dynamic	Complex	Performance-maximizing	Above and simulation, quantitative and probabilistic models

ronment (technological, political, legal, etc.) containing important variables or constraints. One might extend this view to argue that it is not simply the number or diversity of variables and constraints that contributes to complexity, but fundamentally the number of relationships that exist among important variables. For example, the formation of organized groups to contest utilities' decisions on the location of nuclear generating plants poses a new relationship, but not additional variables in the environments of these firms. An extreme case of the complex-dynamic type of environment is one in which *relationships* among different variables and sets of variables are changing. That is to say, cases in which the structure of the environment is changing. The term "turbulent" was used earlier to apply to this special case.

None of the approaches for environmental analysis and forecasting discussed above seems suited for dealing with turbulent environments. Current mathematics and ways of formal thinking about the environment may be reasonably well tailored to deal with change and complexity, but not with moving structure and relationships. Systems for this setting will need to be adaptive and to be flexible in their approach. Means must be available to include crucial informal communication and seemingly peripheral information. One idea that might prove a fruitful avenue for development has been originated by Edwards. It essentially takes a rigorous approach to the monitoring concept already discussed. A panel of judges establishes the hypotheses to be tested, while a similar panel estimates the impacts of individual data on the prior probabilities for each hypothesis. A computer display is used to revise and graphically portray the resulting probabilities of different potential threats for the panel. Such a probabilistic information-processing system can deal with a changing structure of relationships and includes informal and subjective information in a rigorous manner. But on the whole, if we are ill equipped to anticipate change in

changing and complex environments, we are even less well equipped to do so in turbulent ones.

In sum, we are suggesting that a firm's environment largely conditions its strategy and that its use of formal methods in anticipating change is largely a response to both its environment and its strategy.

HOW SHOULD THE FIRM INTEGRATE ENVIRONMENTAL ASSESSMENTS INTO ITS STRATEGIC PLANNING PROCESS?

Studies of the actual use of formal methods for environmental analysis and forecasting show that few firms are using the methods discussed and fewer still to the degree suggested in the previous section. Aguilar stresses the essentially informal nature of environmental scanning. Keegan concluded from a study of executives responsible for multinational operations headquartered in the United States that they rely little on systematic monitoring methods. It is clearly not sufficient for a firm simply to adopt such techniques. To be used effectively the techniques must be integrated into the normal routine of the firm's planning and decision-making processes. In general, we hypothesize that integration requires development of a network of informal communications both inside and outside the organization.

The difficult problem of integration in uncertain environments may be met in several ways. It requires among other things more fully developed informal relationships, boundary roles, and lateral relationships, or a more "organic" form of organization. Additional alternatives include increasing slack resources, simplifying organization structure, or increasing the amount of redundancy in the structure, and greater definition of formal integrative devices such as staff groups and management information systems. Our argument is that the use of formal methods or procedures for forecasting will be one of the types of specialization encountered under conditions of increasing environmental uncertainty and complexity, and effective use of forecasting will require integration with the firm's strategic planning effort.

In some respects, an environmental analysis and forecasting department might be thought of as an integrating unit. Respondents in Utterback and Burack's study stressed the role of forecasting in stimulating ideas and communication among management and technical personnel. Lawrence and Lorsch claimed that, to be successful, integrating units must be viewed as legitimate in terms of both formal and informal criteria. This requires a position in the formal organization intermediate between the functions to be integrated and a broad base of technical and managerial skills to assist in developing informal relationships.

Similarly, we expect that analogous formal linkages between groups and the formal status and support given the firm's forecasting effort will influence its integration into the planning and decision-making process. Recent evidence on this point has been reported by Regan. His study involved comparison of seven successful and seven less successful (in terms of their exploration efforts) metals mining firms. Regan found that the more successful companies considered long-range corporate and exploration planning (including the coordination of exploration with total corporate goals and objectives) of greater importance than did less successful firms. Long-range plans had a greater effect on the size of the exploration budget in more successful companies, while short-range factors had more influence in the less successful firms. Regan also notes that five of the more successful firms had a formal integrating group functioning to transfer discoveries from exploration to operations, while this was true in only one of the less successful cases.

Environmental uncertainty may be expected to affect patterns of informal communication, and firms' competitive strategy may be expected to affect formal relationships and the support given the use of forecasting. The finding that firms in less certain environments tend to have more extensive informal and lateral relationships was mentioned above. Most of the critical information for strategy formulation comes to the firm from informal and unstructured contacts with its environment. Litschert has reported a finding for planning groups in four industries ranging from two with numerous product changes and innovations (electronics, chemicals) to two with few such changes (oil refining, utilities). He concluded that groups operating under conditions of rapid technological change possessed little formal structure, while in the more stable environments planning groups were formally structured and divided into subunits. Most recently, Brown has shown from a study of technical communication in six firms in three industries that those in more complex and changing environments had a greater degree of external communication than those in more simple and static contexts. He also showed that some individuals mediated the flow of outside information and thus served to buffer others from high levels of perceived uncertainty.

In sum, we expect that formal efforts for environmental analysis and forecasting will be less frequently encountered in simple and static environments. When such efforts are undertaken, we would expect them to be highly structured, more centralized, and more formally integrated into the existing line organization. Simple techniques would be used on a relatively continuous basis to reveal possibly disruptive longer run trends. In contrast, we expect conscious efforts by firms to analyze and forecast outside changes will be more necessary and much more frequently encountered in complex and changing environments. But to be effective such efforts would involve a more decentralized structure, greater participation by various elements of management including top management, a more informal and flexible organization, and greater use of informal integrating devices such as liaison groups, parallel assignments, and so on. More diverse techniques might be used, but on an ad hoc basis to detect immediate opportunities and threats.

WHAT TOPICS ARE SUGGESTED FOR FURTHER RESEARCH IN THIS AREA?

The findings and hypotheses above suggest many topics for research, the majority of which and the most important of which link various topics discussed in this volume rather than falling strictly within the area of environmental analysis and forecasting. For example, the most critical issue, at least in the author's view, is understanding the process through which organizations can accommodate themselves to changes in their environment. Various ideas about constraints to change and flexibility to allow change were mentioned at the outset. If a firm clearly knows that it is threatened by change, will it have the resources, perception and creativity to respond? Aren't its incentives and options quite different from those, say, of others invading its business? What of the conflicts and power shifts that such knowledge would generate? How can needs for productivity and efficiency be balanced against needs for slack resources in order to respond flexibly? How can a highly structured and previously successful firm change to meet an unexpected threat resulting from change in its environment? Conversely, if presented with a major opportunity, would such a firm recognize it, and if so would it respond rapidly enough to realize its full potential?

Another class of problems centers on environmental analysis and forecasting as a problem of information and communication. How can information about change in the environment be presented in ways that facilitate accommodation? How can the problem of selective perception of too narrow a

part of the environment be overcome? What ways can be devised to avoid the pitfall of treating forecasts as deterministic? How can "peripheral" and subjective sources of information critical for successful accommodation to change be captured? How can consistent sets of measurements and data about the environment be generated, especially about the more general or non-proximate aspects of the environment such as political, social, and institutional changes? How can the firm create and maintain a viable network of contacts and channels of communication with its environment?

Clearly, designing new techniques for forecasting and adding nuances to existing techniques are research directions with little potential. Nor will another Delphi study, extrapolated trend, etc., add much of any value. Research on the reliability, validity, and generalizability of different methods might be productive. More comprehensive approaches to environmental analysis that are compatible with the regular activities of management would offer real promise. This lends importance to processes that creatively draw on the resources of groups of managers, such as the nominal group technique and probabilistic information processing. Research on the usefulness of monitoring approaches such as that of the Institute of Life Insurance would be of immediate interest for the same reason. A more differentiated approach for selecting techniques that fit the demands of given environments and corporate strategies should hold promise. This might be extended to the case where different divisions of the same firm require quite different approaches to their different arenas of business. And much needs to be done to better understand the ways in which environmental analysis and forecasting can be implemented and linked to firms' strategic planning processes.

Finally, the idea that predictions of the effects of trends and events are much more difficult than seeing the primary changes themselves was repeatedly stressed above.

Perhaps the reason for this finding is that there are so many influences shaping outcomes for a particular firm. Other environmental changes, internal resources and capabilities, established interests, and so on, must be considered as they interact. How can we understand the implications of important interactions? How can we deal with the difficulties involved in accommodations to structural changes in the firm's environment? Surely the above agenda is incomplete and represents the author's biases, but it includes many of the important and immediate challenges for research.

Mechanistic and Organic Systems of Management

T. BURNS AND G.M. STALKER

Recently, with G.M. Stalker, I made an attempt to elucidate the situation of firms in the electronics industry that were confronted with rapidly changing commercial circumstances and a much faster rate of technical progress. I found it necessary to posit two "ideal types" of working organization, the one mechanistic, adapted to relatively stable conditions, the other organic, adapted to conditions of change.

In mechanistic systems, the problems and tasks that face the firm are, typically, broken down into specialties. Each individual carries out his or her assigned task apart from the overall purpose of the company as a whole. "Somebody at the top" is responsible for seeing that each individual's work is relevant to that of others. The technical methods, duties, and powers attached to each post are precisely defined, and a high value is placed on precision and demarcation. Interaction within the working organization follows vertical lines—i.e., between superiors and subordinates. How people operate and what they do is prescribed by their functional roles and governed by instructions and decisions issued from superiors. This hierarchy is maintained by the assumption that the only person who knows—or should know—all about the company is the boss at the top. This person is the only one, therefore, who knows exactly how the human resources should be properly disposed. The management system, usually visualized as the complex hierarchy familiar in organization charts, operates as a simple control system, with information flowing upwards through a succession of filters, and decisions and instructions flowing downwards through a succession of amplifiers.

Mechanistic systems are, in fact, the "rational bureaucracy" of an earlier generation

Combined excerpts taken from T. Burns, "Industry in a New Age," *New Society, London, The Weekly Review of the Social Sciences,* 31 January 1963, London: New Science Publications; and T. Burns and G.M. Stalker, "Mechanistic and Organic Systems of Management," *The Management of Innovation,* London: Associated Book Publishers Ltd., 1961. Both used with permission of publisher.

of students of organization. For the individual, it provides an ordered world of work in which decisions and actions occur within a stable constellation of jobs, skills, specialized knowledge, and sectional responsibilities. In a textile mill, or in any factory that sees itself turning out any standardized product for a familiar and steady market, one finds decision-making at all levels prescribed by the familiar.

As one descends through the levels of management, one finds more limited information and less understanding of the human capacities of other members of the firm. One also finds each person's task more and more clearly defined by a superior. Beyond a certain limit the individual has insufficient authority, insufficient information, and usually insufficient technical ability to be able to make decisions. He or she is informed quite clearly when this limit occurs; beyond it, there is one course open—report to one's superior.

Organic systems are adapted to unstable conditions, when new and unfamiliar problems and requirements continually arise that cannot be broken down and distributed among specialist roles within a hierarchy. Jobs lose much of their formal definition. The definitive and enduring demarcation of functions becomes impossible. Responsibilities and functions, and even methods and powers, have to be constantly redefined through interaction with others participating in common tasks or in the solution of common problems. Members have to do their jobs with knowledge of overall purpose and the situation of the company as a whole. Interaction runs laterally as much as vertically, and communication between people of different rank tends to resemble lateral consultation rather than vertical command. Omniscience can no longer be imputed to the boss at the top.

The head of one successful electronics concern, at the very beginning of the first interview of the whole study, attacked the idea of the organization chart as inapplicable in his concern and as a dangerous method of thinking. The first requirement of management, according to him, was that it should make the fullest use of the capacities of its members; any individual's job should be as little defined as possible, so that it would "shape itself" to his or her special abilities and initiative.

In this company, insistence on the least possible specification for managerial positions was much more in evidence than devices for insuring adequate interaction within the system. This did occur, but it was often due to physical conditions rather than to order by top management. A single-storeyed building housed the entire company, two thousand strong, from laboratories to canteen. Access to anyone was therefore physically simple and direct; it was easier to walk across to the laboratory door, the office door, or the factory door and look for the person one wanted than even to telephone. Written communication inside the factory was actively discouraged. More important than the physical set-up however was the need of all managers for interaction with others in order to get their functions defined, since these were not specified from above.

For the individuals, the important part of the difference between the mechanistic and the organic is in the degree of commitment to the working organization. Mechanistic systems tell individuals what has to be attended to, and how, and also what does *not* have to be bothered with, what is not their affair, what is *not* expected of them—what is the responsibility of others. In organic systems, such boundaries disappear. Individuals are expected to regard themselves as fully implicated in the discharge of any task appearing over their horizon. They have not merely to exercise a special competence, but to commit themselves to the success of the concern's undertakings as a whole.

We are now at the point at which we may set down the outline of the two management systems that represent for us the two polar extremities of the forms that such systems can take when they are adapted to a specific rate of technical and commercial change.

Both types represent a "rational" form of organization, in that they may both, in our experience, be explicitly and deliberately created and maintained to exploit the human resources of a concern in the most efficient manner feasible in the circumstances of the firm.

A *mechanistic* management system is appropriate to stable conditions. It is characterized by:

1. The specialized differentiation of functional tasks into which the problems and tasks facing the concern as a whole are broken down;

2. The abstract nature of each individual task, which is pursued with techniques and purposes more or less distinct from those of the concern as a whole, i.e., the functionaries tend to pursue the technical improvement of means, rather than the accomplishment of the ends of the concern;

3. The reconciliation, for each level in the hierarchy, of these distinct performances by immediate superiors, who are in turn responsible for seeing that each is relevant in his or her own special part of the main task;

4. The precise definition of rights and obligations and technical methods attached to each functional role;

5. The translation of rights and obligations and methods into the responsibilities of a functional position;

6. Hierarchic structure of control, authority, and communication;

7. A reinforcement of the hierarchic structure by the location of knowledge of actualities exclusively at the top of the hierarchy, where the final reconciliation of distinct tasks and assessment of relevance is made;

8. A tendency for interaction between members of the concern to be vertical, i.e., between superior and subordinate;

9. A tendency for operations and working behavior to be governed by the instructions and decisions issued by superiors;

10. Insistence on loyalty to the firm and obedience to superiors as a condition of membership;

11. A greater importance and prestige attaching to internal (local) than to general (cosmopolitan) knowledge, experience and skill.

The *organic* form is appropriate to changing conditions, which give rise constantly to fresh problems and unforeseen requirements for action that cannot be broken down or distributed automatically, arising from the functional roles defined within a hierarchic structure. It is characterized by:

1. The contributive nature of special knowledge and experience to the common task of the firm;

2. The "realistic" nature of the individual task, which is seen as set by the total situation of the firm;

3. The adjustment and continual redefinition of individual tasks through interaction with others;

4. The shedding of "responsibility" as a limited field of rights, obligations, and methods (problems may not be posted upwards, downwards, or sideways as being someone else's responsibility);

5. The spread of commitment to the firm beyond any technical definition;

6. A network structure of control, authority, and communication. The sanctions that apply to the individual's conduct in his or her working role derive more from presumed community of interest with the rest of the working organization in the survival and growth of the firm and less from a contractual relationship between the individual and a nonpersonal corporation, represented by an immediate superior;

7. Omniscience no longer imputed to the head of the company; knowledge about the technical or commercial nature of the here and now task may be located anywhere in the network, this location becoming the ad hoc center of control, authority, and communication;

8. A lateral rather than a vertical direction of communication through the organization, communication between people of different rank, also, resembling consultation rather than command;

9. A content of communication that consists of information and advice rather than instructions and decisions;

10. Commitment to the concern's tasks and to the "technological ethos" of material progress and expansion is more highly valued than loyalty and obedience;

11. Importance and prestige attach to affiliations and expertise valid in the industrial and technical and commercial milieu external to the firm.

One important corollary to be attached to this account is that while organic systems are not hierarchic in the same sense as are mechanistic systems, they remain stratified. Positions are differentiated according to seniority, i.e., greater expertise. The lead in joint decisions is frequently taken by seniors, but it is an essential presumption of the organic system that the lead, i.e., authority, is taken by whoever is the most informed and capable, i.e., the "best authority." The location of authority is settled by consensus.

A second observation is that the area of commitment to the firm—the extent to which individuals yield themselves as resources to be used by the working organization—is far more extensive in organic than in mechanistic systems. Commitment, in fact, is expected to approach that of professional scientists to their work, and frequently does. One further consequence of this is that it becomes far less feasible to distinguish informal from formal organization.

Thirdly, the emptying out of significance from the hierarchic command system, by which cooperation is insured and that serves to monitor the working organization under a mechanistic system, is countered by the development of shared beliefs about the values and goals of the company. The growth and accretion of institutionalized values, beliefs, and conduct, in the form of commitments, ideology, and manners, around an image of the firm in its industrial and commercial setting make good the loss of formal structure.

Finally, the two forms of system represent a polarity, not a dichotomy; there are, as we have tried to show, intermediate stages between the extremities empirically known to us. Also, the relation of one form to the other is elastic, so that a firm oscillating between relative stability and relative change may also oscillate between the two forms. A company may (and frequently does) operate with a management system that includes both types.

The organic form, by departing from the familiar clarity and fixity of the hierarchic structure, is often experienced by the individual manager as an uneasy, embarrassed, or chronically anxious quest for knowledge about what should be done, or what is expected, and similar apprehensiveness about what others are doing. Indeed, as we shall see later, this kind of response is necessary if the organic form of organization is to work effectively. Understandably, such anxiety finds expression in resentment when the apparent confusion besetting the manager is not explained. In these situations, all managers some of the time, and many managers all the time, yearn for more definition and structure.

On the other hand, some managers recognize a rationale of non-definition, a reasoned basis for the practice of those successful firms in which designation of status, function, and line of responsibility and authority has been vague or even avoided.

The desire for more definition is often in effect a wish to have the limits of one's task more neatly defined—to know what and when one doesn't have to bother about, as much as to know what one does have to. It follows that the more definition is given, the more omniscient the management must be, so that no functions are left wholly or partly undischarged, no persons are overburdened with undelegated responsibility, or left without the authority to do their jobs properly. To do this, to have all the separate functions attached to individual roles fitting together and comprehensively, to have communication between persons constantly maintained on a level adequate to the needs of each functional role, requires rules or traditions of behavior proved over a long time and an equally fixed, stable task. The omniscience that may then be credited to the head of the firm is expected throughout its body through the lines of command, extending in a clear, explicitly titled hierarchy of officers and subordinates.

The whole mechanistic form is instinct with this twofold principle of definition and dependence that acts as the frame within which action is conceived and carried out. It works, unconsciously, almost in the smallest minutiae of daily activity. "How late is late?" The answer to this question is not to be found in the rule book, but in the superior. Late is when the boss thinks it is late. Is the boss the kind of person who thinks 8:00 is the time, and 8:01 is late? Does the boss think 8:15 is all right occasionally if it is not a regular thing or that everyone should be allowed five minutes' grace after 8:00 but after that they are late?

One other feature of mechanistic organization needs emphasis. It is a necessary condition of its operation that individuals "work on their own," functionally isolated, that they "know their jobs," "and are responsible for seeing them done." They work at jobs that are in a sense artificially abstracted from the realities of the situation the company is dealing with, the accountant dealing with the cost side, the works manager pushing production, and so on. In practice, the rest of the organization becomes part of the problem situation the individual has to deal with in order to perform successfully, i.e., difficulties and problems arising from work or information that has been handed over the "responsibility barrier" between two jobs or departments are regarded as "really" the responsibility of the person from whom they were received. As a

design engineer put it, "When you get designers handing over designs completely to production, it's 'their responsibility' now. And you get tennis games played with the responsibility for anything that goes wrong. What happens is that you're constantly getting unsuspected faults arising from characteristics which you didn't think important in the design. If you get to hear of these through a sales person, or a production person, or somebody to whom the design was handed over to in the dim past, then, instead of being a design problem, it's an annoyance caused by that particular person, who can't do the job—because you'd thought you were finished with that one, and you're on to something else now."

When the assumptions of the form of organization make for preoccupation with specialized tasks, the chances of career success, or of greater influence, depend rather on the relative importance that may be attached to each special function by the superior whose task it is to reconcile and control a number of them. And, indeed, to press the claims of one's job or department for a bigger share of the firm's resources is in many cases regarded as a mark of initiative, of effectiveness, and even of loyalty to the firm's interests. This state of affairs thus engenders an aloof detachment similar to a court of appeal. The ordinary relationship prevailing between individual managers "in charge of" different functions is one of rivalry, a rivalry that may be rendered innocuous to the persons involved by personal friendship or the norms of sociability, but that turns discussion about the situations that constitute the real problems of the firm— how to make products more cheaply, how to sell more, how to allocate resources, whether to curtail activity in one sector, whether to risk expansion in another, and so on—into an arena of conflicting interests.

The distinctive feature of the second, organic system is the pervasiveness of the working organization as an institution. In concrete terms, this makes itself felt in a preparedness to combine with others in serving the general aims of the company. Proportionate to the rate and extent of change, the less can the omniscience appropriate to command organizations be ascribed to the head of the organization; for executives, and even operatives, in a changing firm it is always theirs to reason why. Furthermore, the less definition can be given to status, roles, and modes of communication, the more do the activities of each member of the organization become determined by the real tasks of the firm than by instruction and routine. The individual's job ceases to be self-contained; the only way in which one's job can be done is by participating continually with others in the solution of problems that are real to the firm,

and put in a language of requirements and activities meaningful to them all. Such methods of working place much heavier demands on the individual.

We have endeavored to stress the appropriateness of each system to its own specific set of conditions. Equally, we desire to avoid the suggestion that either system is superior under all circumstances to the other. In particular, nothing in our experience justifies the assumption that mechanistic systems should be superseded by organic systems in conditions of stability. The beginning of administrative wisdom is the awareness that there is no one optimum type of management system.

■ Technological Determinism

Factors influencing the structure of an organization, that is, design of work and arrangement among people to get work done, have received much attention. Several theorists, notably Charles Perrow, emphasize the important impact of technology upon organization structure and management.

This view called *technological determinism*, argues that technology determines organization structure. Technology is defined by Perrow as the actions that an individual performs upon an object, with or without the aid of tools or mechanical devices in order

to make some change in that object. The objects of change can be human beings, symbols, or inanimate materials.

TECHNOLOGY AND PROBLEM–SOLVING PATTERNS

According to Perrow, there are two important characteristics in the process of getting work done: (1) the number of exceptional cases encountered in work and (2) the type of search required to solve problems that arise. The number of exceptions can range from "few" to "many." The type of search or the analyzability of problems involves the search process that is undertaken when exceptions are encountered. Structured or analyzable problems involve the use of a

---

This article, while containing departures from Perrow's work, is based on Charles Perrow, "A Framework for the Comparative Analysis of Organizations," *American Sociological Review*, vol. 22, no. 2 (April 1967), pp. 194–208.

logical, systematic search that lends itself to some known form of analysis such as routine engineering problems. Unstructured unanalyzable problems call for unique searches based on the problem-solver's experience, intuition, and guesswork.

These two problem-solving dimensions create a two-dimensional matrix composed of four technology categories (exhibit 2.3). The matrix also indicates some industries that correspond to each technology.

TECHNOLOGY AND STRUCTURE

In order to demonstrate the connection between technology and organization structure Perrow examined how each technology relates to four structural dimensions—discretion, power, coordination, and interdependence. See exhibit 2.4 for a definition of these dimensions.

In addition to the above dimensions, Perrow also differentiated the management function involved with technology into two levels: (1) technical support and control of production and marketing; and (2) supervision of production and marketing operations. Technical support and control involves such functions as quality control, product research, engineering, accounting, and customer service.

The model in exhibit 2.4 superimposes on each cell parallel to the cells of exhibit 2.3 the structure and management that can be expected. Cells 2 and 4 are extreme cases and resemble the mechanistic and organic structures.

In Cell 4, the few exceptions that occur are handled through an analytical search process. The routinized search means that both technical and supervisory management are likely to exercise a low amount of discretion. The production and marketing processes are programmed in great detail. At the technical level, such functions as engineering, product and process research, and quality control are likely to exercise a high amount of power because they direct the activities of the supervisors. The interdependence between the technical personnel and supervisors is likely to be low and the little amount of interaction is probably of a "directive" form. The organization is likely to be characterized generally as "formal and centralized."

Cell 2 represents a situation in which routine means are not available for analyzing

EXHIBIT 2.3   Technology and Industry Matrix

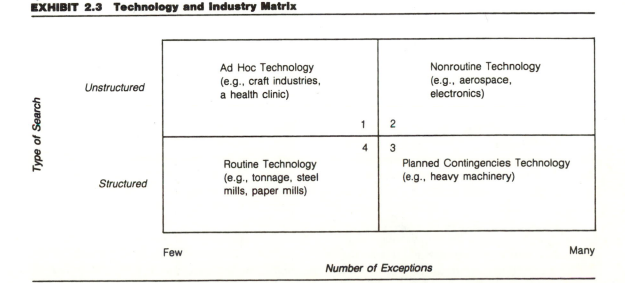

EXHIBIT 2.4   Technology and Structure

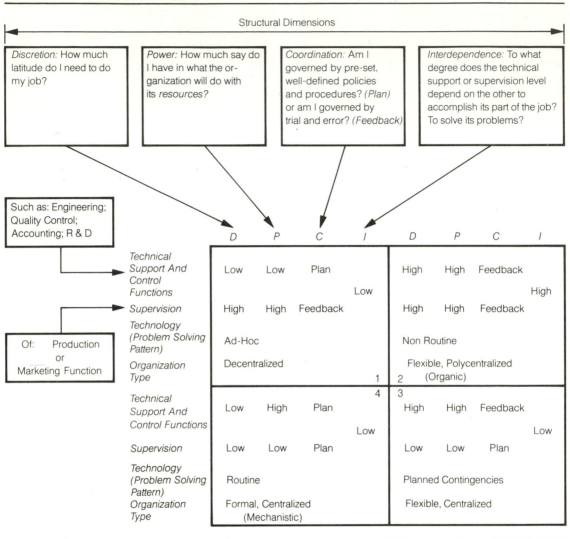

the many exceptions that occur. Both technical and supervisory functions use much discretion and power to solve vague and ambiguous problems. Programmed planning techniques must give way to feedback as the primary method of coordination. Both groups depend on each other to solve the unstructured problems. To such a technological situation, organizations respond with transient forms such as team management, project management, product managers, and matrix arrangements. These forms of organization are flexible with multiple centers of decision-making and activity.

Cell 3 depicts a situation in which the many exceptions can be handled by using the available *canned* solution techniques. Planned contingencies exist and they are kept on a shelf until needed. Technical groups rather than supervisors exercise discretion and power in selecting canned solutions for the many problems that arise. Supervisors receive from the technical groups solutions in terms of plans, which they in turn implement. Supervisors are placed in a situation of responding to the results of the technical group's search for a solution rather than initiate their own search. As in the case of Cell 1, the interdependence between the two groups is low and the interactions are of a "directive" form. While some flexibility must exist, most of the decisions and the search for solutions are centralized.

Cell 1 represents a situation where supervisors, who are in close proximity to the production process, rather than technical people, exercise discretion and power in solving the few unstructured problems that arise. Supervisors under these conditions rely on feedback for coordination (e.g., a trial-and-error approach) and have a low dependence on technical support groups for the solution of problems. Problems are so infrequent that they are handled on an ad hoc (trial-and-error) basis, often by a skilled craftsman or professional. The organization can operate in a decentralized mode.

■ Organization Design: Fashion or Fit?

HENRY MINTZBERG

■ A conglomerate takes over a small manufacturer and tries to impose budgets, plans, organizational charts, and untold systems on it. The result: declining sales and product innovation—and near bankruptcy—until the division managers buy back the company and promptly turn it around.

■ Consultants make constant offers to introduce the latest management techniques. Years ago PERT and MBO were in style, later it was LRP and OD, and now it's QWL and ZBB.

■ A government sends in its analysts to rationalize, standardize, and formalize citywide school systems, hospitals, and welfare agencies. The results are devastating.

These incidents suggest that a great many problems in organizational design stem from the assumption that organizations are all alike: mere collections of component parts to which elements of structure can be added and deleted at will, a sort of organizational bazaar.

The opposite assumption is that effective organizations achieve a coherence among their component parts, that they do not change one element without considering the consequences to all the others. Spans of control, degrees of job enlargement, forms of decentralization, planning systems, and matrix structure should not be picked and chosen at random. Rather, they should be selected according to internally consistent groupings. And these groupings should be consistent with the situation of the organization—its age and size, the conditions of the industry in which it operates, and its production technology. In essence, my argument is that—like all phenomena from atoms to stars—the characteristics of organizations fall into natural clusters, or *configurations*. When these characteristics are mismatched—when the wrong ones are put together—the organization does not function effectively, does not achieve a natural harmony. If managers are to design effective organizations, they need to pay attention to the fit.

If we look at the enormous amount of research on organizational structuring in light of this idea, a lot of the confusion falls away and a striking convergence is revealed. Specifically, five clear configurations emerge that are distinct in their structures, in the situations in which they are found, and even in the periods of history in which they first developed. I call them the simple structure, machine bureaucracy, professional bureaucracy, divisionalized form, and adhocracy. In this article, I describe these configurations and consider the messages they contain for managers.

DERIVING THE CONFIGURATIONS

In order to describe and distinguish the five configurations, I designed an adaptable picture of five component parts (see top half, exhibit 2.5). An organization begins with a person who has an idea. This person forms the *strategic apex*, top management if you like. He or she hires people to do the basic work of the organization, in what can be called the *operating core*. As the organization grows, it acquires intermediate managers between the chief executive and the workers. These managers form the *middle line*. The organization may also find that it

EXHIBIT 2.5   The Five Basic Parts of the Organization

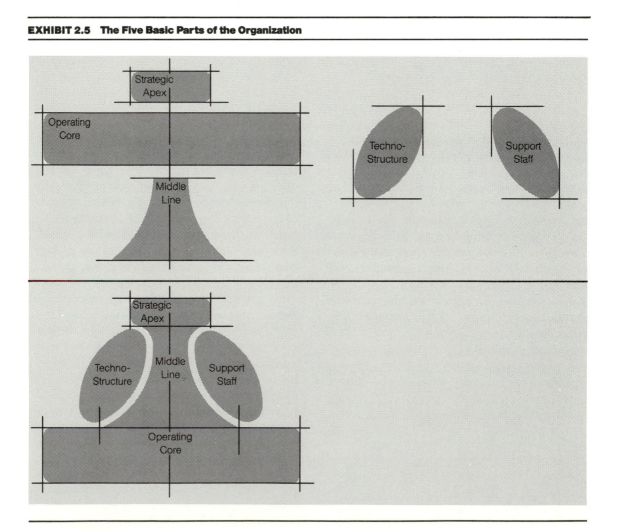

needs two kinds of staff personnel. First are the analysts who design systems concerned with the formal planning and control of the work; they form the *technostructure*. Second is the *support staff*, providing indirect services to the rest of the organization—everything from the cafeteria and the mail room to the public relations department and the legal counsel.

Put these five parts together and you get the whole organization (see bottom half, exhibit 2.5). Now not all organizations need all these parts. Some use few and are simple, others combine all in rather complex ways. The central purpose of structure is to coordinate the work divided in a variety of ways; how that coordination is achieved— by whom and with what—dictates what the organization will look like (see exhibit 2.6):

■ In the simplest case, coordination is achieved at the strategic apex by *direct supervision*—the chief executive officer gives the orders. The configuration called *simple structure* emerges, with a minimum of staff and middle line.

■ When coordination depends on the *standardization of work*, an organization's entire administrative structure—especially its technostructure, which designs the standards—needs to be elaborated. This gives rise to the configuration called *machine bureaucracy*.

■ When, instead, coordination is through the *standardization of skills* of its employees, the organization needs highly trained professionals in its operating core and considerable support staff to back them up. Neither its technostructure nor its middle line is very elaborate. As a result, we get the configuration called *professional bureaucracy*.

■ Organizations will sometimes be divided into parallel operating units, allowing autonomy to the middle-line managers of each, with coordination achieved through the *standardization of outputs* (including performance) of these units. The configuration called the *divisionalized form* emerges.

■ Finally, the most complex organizations engage sophisticated specialists, especially in their support staffs, and require them to combine their efforts in project teams coordinated by *mutual adjustment*. This results in the *adhocracy* configuration, in which line and staff as well as a number of other distinctions tend to break down.

I shall describe each of these five configurations in terms of structure and situation. But first let me list the elements of structure, which are described in more detail in the appendix. These include the following:

■ Specialization of tasks.
■ Formalization of procedures (job descriptions, rules, and so forth).
■ Formal training and indoctrination required for the job.
■ Grouping of units (notably by function performed or market served).
■ Size of each of the units (that is, the span of control of its manager).
■ Action planning and performance control systems.
■ Liaison devices, such as task forces, integrating managers, and matrix structure.
■ Delegation of power down the chain of authority (called *vertical decentralization*).
■ Delegation of power out from that chain of authority to nonmanagers (called *horizontal decentralization*).

Also included in the appendix, together with their impact on these elements of structure, are the situational factors—namely, the age and size of the organization, its technical system of production, and various characteristics of its environment (e.g., how stable or complex it is) and of its power system (e.g., how tightly it is controlled externally).

Our job now is to see how all these elements cluster into the five configurations. I describe each in the sections that follow and summarize these descriptions in exhibit 2.7, where all the elements are displayed in relation to the configurations. In the discussion of each configuration, it should become evident how all its elements of structure and situation form themselves into a tightly knit, highly cohesive package. No one element determines the others; rather, all are locked together to form an integrated system.

Simple Structure

The name tells all, and exhibit 2.6 shows all. The structure is simple—not much more

---

Exhibit 2.6   The Five Configurations

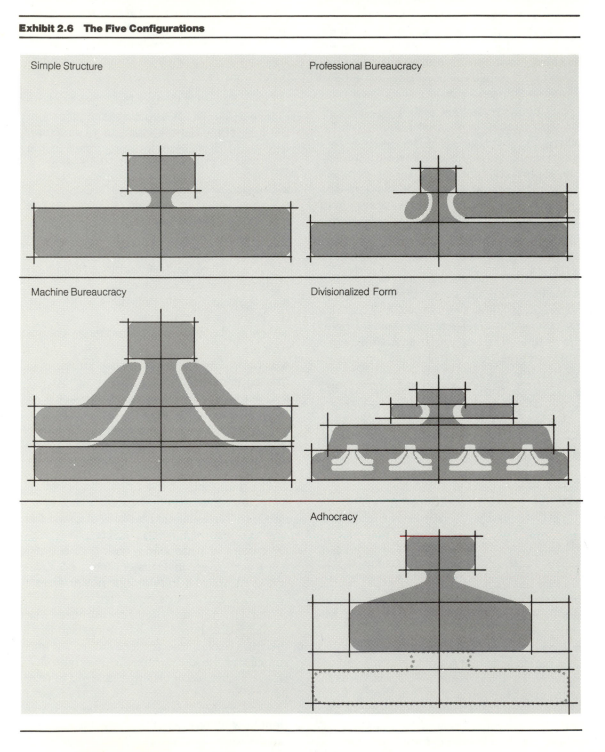

Simple Structure

Professional Bureaucracy

Machine Bureaucracy

Divisionalized Form

Adhocracy

than one large unit consisting of one or a few top managers and a group of operators who do the basic work. The most common simple structure is, of course, the classic entrepreneurial company.

What characterizes this configuration above all is what is missing. Little of its behavior is standardized or formalized, and minimal use is made of planning, training, or the liaison devices. The absence of standardization means that the organization has little need for staff analysts. Few middle-line managers are hired because so much of the coordination is achieved at the strategic apex by direct supervision. That is where the real power in this configuration lies. Even the support staff is minimized to keep the structure lean and flexible—simple structures would rather buy than make.

EXHIBIT 2.7   **Dimensions of the Five Configurations**

	Simple Structure	Machine Bureaucracy	Professional Bureaucracy	Divisionalized Form	Adhocracy
Key Means of Coordination	Direct supervision	Standardization of work	Standardization of skills	Standardization of outputs	Mutual adjustment
Key Part of Organization	Strategic apex	Technostructure	Operating core	Middle line	Support staff (with operating core in operating adhocracy)
Structural Elements					
Specialization of Jobs	Little specialization	**Much horizontal and vertical specialization**	**Much horizontal specialization**	Some horizontal and vertical specialization (between divisions and headquarters)	**Much horizontal specialization**
Training and Indoctrination	Little training and indoctrination	Little training and indoctrination	**Much training and indoctrination**	Some training and indoctrination (of division managers)	Much training
Formalization of Behavior — Bureaucratic/ Organic	**Little formalization organic**	**Much formalization bureaucratic**	**Little formalization bureaucratic**	Much formalization (within divisions) — bureaucratic	**Little formalization organic**
Grouping	Usually functional	**Usually functional**	Functional and market	**Market**	Functional and market
Unit Size	Wide	Wide at bottom, narrow elsewhere	Wide at bottom, narrow elsewhere	Wide at top	Narrow throughout
Planning and Control Systems	Little planning and control	Action planning	Little planning and control	**Much performance control**	Limited action planning (esp. in administrative adhocracy)
Liaison Devices	Few liaison devices	Few liaison devices	Liaison devices in administration	Few liaison devices	**Many liaison devices throughout**
Decentralization	**Centralization**	**Limited horizontal decentralization**	**Horizontal and vertical decentralization**	**Limited vertical decentralization**	**Selective decentralization**
Situational Elements					
Age and Size	Typically young and small	Typically old and large	Varies	Typically old and very large	Typically young (operating adhocracy)
Technical System	Simple, not regulating	Regulating but not automated, not very complex	Not regulating or complex	Divisible, otherwise like machine bureaucracy	Very complex, often automated (in administrative adhocracy). not regulating or complex (in operating adhocracy)
Environment	Simple and dynamic; sometimes hostile	Simple and stable	Complex and stable	Relatively simple and stable; diversified markets (esp. products and services)	Complex and dynamic; sometimes disparate (in administrative adhocracy)
Power	Chief executive control; often owner managed; not fashionable	Technocratic and external control; not fashionable	Professional operator control; fashionable	Middle-line control; fashionable (esp. in industry)	Expert control; very fashionable

Note:
Bold italic type indicates key design parameters.

The organization must be flexible because it operates in a dynamic environment, often by choice because that is the one place it can outmaneuver the bureaucracies. And that environment must be simple, as must the organization's system of production, so that the chief executive can retain highly centralized control. In turn, centralized control makes the simple structure ideal for rapid, flexible innovation, at least of the simple kind. With the right chief executive, the organization can turn on a dime and run circles around the slower-moving bureaucracies. That is why so much innovation comes not from the giant mass-producers but from small entrepreneurial companies. But where complex forms of innovation are required, the simple structure falters because of its centralization. As we shall see, that kind of innovation requires another configuration, one that engages highly trained specialists and gives them considerable power.

Simple structures are often young and small, in part because aging and growth encourage them to bureaucratize but also because their vulnerability causes many of them to fail. They never get a chance to grow old and large. One heart attack can wipe them out—as can a chief executive so obsessed with innovation that he or she forgets about the operations, or vice versa. The corporate landscape is littered with the wrecks of entrepreneurial companies whose leaders encouraged growth and mass-production yet could never accept the transition to bureaucratic forms of structure that these changes required. Yet some simple structures have managed to grow very large under the tight control of clever, autocratic leaders, the most famous example being the Ford Motor Co. in the later years of its founder.

Almost all organizations begin their lives as simple structures, granting their founding chief executives considerable latitude to set them up. And most revert to simple structure—no matter how large or what other configuration normally fits their needs—

when they face extreme pressure or hostility in their environment. In other words, systems and procedures are suspended as power reverts to the chief executive to give him or her a chance to set things right.

The heyday of the simple structure probably occurred during the period of the great American trusts, late in the nineteenth century. Although today less in fashion and to many a relic of more autocratic times, the simple structure remains a widespread and necessary configuration—for building up most new organizations and for operating those in simple, dynamic environments and those facing extreme, hostile pressures.

Machine Bureaucracy

Just as the simple structure is prevalent in pre-Industrial Revolution industries such as agriculture, the machine bureaucracy is the offspring of industrialization, with its emphasis on the standardization of work for coordination and its resulting low-skilled, highly specialized jobs. Exhibit 2.6 shows that, in contrast to simple structure, the machine bureaucracy elaborates its administration. First, it requires many analysts to design and maintain its systems of standardization—notably those that formalize its behaviors and plan its actions. And by virtue of the organization's dependence on these systems, these analysts gain a degree of informal power, which results in a certain amount of horizontal decentralization.

A large hierarchy emerges in the middle line to oversee the specialized work of the operating core and to keep the lid on conflicts that inevitably result from the rigid departmentalization, as well as from the alienation that often goes with routine, circumscribed jobs. That middle-line hierarchy is usually structured on a functional basis all the way up to the top, where the real power of coordination lies. In other words, machine bureaucracy tends to be centralized in the vertical sense—formal power is concentrated at the top.

And why the large support staff shown in exhibit 2.6? Because machine bureaucracies depend on stability to function (change interrupts the smooth functioning of the system), they tend not only to seek out stable environments in which to function but also to stabilize the environments they find themselves in. One way they do this is to envelop within their structures all the support services possible, ones that simple structures prefer to buy. For the same reason they also tend to integrate vertically—to become their own suppliers and customers. And that of course causes many machine bureaucracies to grow very large. So we see the two-sided effect of size here: size drives the organization to bureaucratize ("we do that every day; let's standardize it"), but bureaucracy also encourages the organization to grow larger. Aging also encourages this configuration; the organization standardizes its work because "we've done that before."

To enable the top managers to maintain centralized control, both the environment and the production system of the machine bureaucracy must be fairly simple. In fact, machine bureaucracies fit most naturally with mass-production, where the products, processes, and distribution systems are usually rationalized and thus easy to comprehend. And so machine bureaucracy is most common among large, mature mass-production companies, such as automobile manufacturers, as well as the largest of the established providers of mass services, such as insurance companies and railroads. Thus McDonald's is a classic example of this configuration—achieving enormous success in its simple industry through meticulous standardization.

Because external controls encourage bureaucratization and centralization (as discussed in the appendix), this configuration is often assumed by organizations that are tightly controlled from the outside. That is why government agencies, which are subject to many such controls, tend to be driven toward the machine bureaucracy structure regardless of their other conditions.

The problems of the machine bureaucracy are legendary—dull and repetitive work, alienated employees, obsession with control (of markets as well as workers), massive size, and inadaptability. These are machines suited to specific purposes, not to adapting to new ones. For all these reasons, the machine bureaucracy is no longer fashionable. Bureaucracy has become a dirty word. Yet this is the configuration that gets the products out cheaply and efficiently. And here too there can be a sense of harmony, as in the Swiss railroad system whose trains depart as the second hand sweeps past the twelve.

In a society consumed by its appetite for mass-produced goods, dependent on consistency in so many spheres (how else to deliver millions of pieces of mail every day?) and unable to automate a great many of its routine jobs, machine bureaucracy remains indispensable—and probably the most prevalent of the five configurations today.

Professional Bureaucracy

This bureaucratic configuration relies on the standardization of skills rather than work processes or outputs for its coordination and so emerges as dramatically different from the machine bureaucracy. It is the structure hospitals, universities, and accounting firms tend most often to favor. Most important, because it relies for its operating tasks on trained professionals—skilled people who must be given considerable control over their own work—the organization surrenders a good deal of its power not only to the professionals themselves but also to the associations and institutions that select and train them in the first place. As a result, the structure emerges as very decentralized; power over many decisions, both operating and strategic, flows all the way down the hierarchy to the professionals of the operating core. For them this is the most democratic structure of all.

Because the operating procedures, although complex, are rather standardized—

taking out appendixes in a hospital, teaching the American Motors case in a business school, doing an audit in an accounting firm—each professional can work independently of his or her colleagues, with the assurance that much of the necessary coordination will be effected automatically through standardization of skills. Thus a colleague of mine observed a five-hour open heart operation in which the surgeon and anesthesiologist never exchanged a word!

As can be seen in exhibit 2.6, above the operating core we find a unique structure. Since the main standardization occurs as a result of training that takes place outside the professional bureaucracy, a technostructure is hardly needed. And because the professionals work independently, the size of operating units can be very large, and so few first-line managers are needed. (I work in a business school where fifty-five professors report directly to one dean.) Yet even those few managers, and those above them, do little direct supervision; much of their time is spent linking their units to the broader environment, notably to insure adequate financing. Thus to become a top manager in a consulting firm is to become a salesperson.

On the other hand, the support staff is typically very large in order to back up the high-priced professionals. But that staff does a very different kind of work—much of it the simple and routine jobs that the professionals shed. As a result, parallel hierarchies emerge in the professional bureaucracy—one democratic with bottom-up power for the professionals, a second autocratic with top-down control for the support staff.

Professional bureaucracy is most effective for organizations that find themselves in stable yet complex environments. Complexity requires that decision-making power be decentralized to highly trained individuals, and stability enables these individuals to apply standardized skills and so to work with a good deal of autonomy. To further insure that autonomy, the production system must be neither highly regulating, complex, nor

automated. Surgeons use their scalpels and editors their pencils; both must be sharp but are otherwise simple instruments that allow their users considerable freedom in performing their complex work.

Standardization is the great strength as well as the great weakness of professional bureaucracy. That is what enables the professionals to perfect their skills and so achieve great efficiency and effectiveness. But that same standardization raises problems of adaptability. This is not a structure to innovate but one to perfect what is already known. Thus, so long as the environment is stable, the professional bureaucracy does its job well. It identifies the needs of its clients and offers a set of standardized programs to serve them. In other words, pigeonholing is its great forte; change messes up the pigeonholes. New needs arise that fall between or across the slots, and the standard programs no longer apply. Another configuration is required.

Professional bureaucracy, a product of the middle years of this century, is a highly fashionable structure today for two reasons. First, it is very democratic, at least for its professional workers. And second, it offers them considerable autonomy, freeing the professionals even from the need to coordinate closely with each other. To release themselves from the close control of administrators and analysts, not to mention their own colleagues, many people today seek to have themselves declared "professional"— and thereby turn their organizations into professional bureaucracies.

Divisionalized Form
Like the professional bureaucracy, the divisionalized form is not so much an integrated organization as a set of rather independent entities joined together by a loose administrative overlay. But whereas those entities of the professional bureaucracy are individuals—professionals in the operating core— in the divisionalized form they are units in the middle line, called divisions.

The divisionalized form differs from the other four configurations in one central respect: it is not a complete but a partial structure, superimposed on others. Those others are in the divisions, each of which I shall be arguing is driven toward machine bureaucracy.

An organization divisionalizes for one reason above all—because its product lines are diversified. (And that tends to happen most often in the largest and most mature organizations, those that have run out of opportunities or become stalled in their traditional markets.) Such diversification encourages the organization to create a market-based unit, or division, for each distinct product line (as indicated in exhibit 2.6) and to grant considerable autonomy to each division to run its own business.

That autonomy notwithstanding, divisionalization does *not* amount to decentralization, although the terms are often equated with each other. Decentralization is an expression of the dispersal of decision-making power in an organization. Divisionalization refers to a structure of semiautonomous market-based units. A divisionalized structure in which the managers at the heads of these units retain the lion's share of the power is far more centralized than many functional structures where large numbers of specialists get involved in the making of important decisions.

In fact, the most famous example of divisionalization involved centralization. Alfred Sloan adopted the divisionalized form at General Motors to *reduce* the power of the different units, to integrate the holding company William Durant had put together. That kind of centralization appears to have continued to the point where the automotive units in some ways seem closer to functional marketing departments than true divisions.

But how does top management maintain a semblance of control over the divisions? Some direct supervision is used—headquarters managers visit the divisions periodically and authorize some of their more important decisions. But too much of that interferes

with the necessary autonomy of the divisions. So headquarters relies on performance control systems or, in other words, on the standardization of outputs. It leaves the operating details to the divisions and exercises control by measuring their performance periodically. And to design these control systems, headquarters creates a small technostructure. It also establishes a small central support staff to provide certain services common to the divisions (such as legal counsel and external relations).

This performance control system has an interesting effect on the internal structure of the division. First, the division is treated as a single integrated entity with one consistent, standardized, and quantifiable set of goals. Those goals tend to get translated down the line into more and more specific subgoals and, eventually, work standards. In other words, they encourage the bureaucratization of structure. And second, headquarters tends to impose its standards through the managers of the divisions, whom it holds responsible for divisional performance. That tends to result in centralization within the divisions. And centralization coupled with bureaucratization gives machine bureaucracy. That is the structure that works best in the divisions.

Simple structures and adhocracies make poor divisions because they abhor standards—they operate in dynamic environments where standards of any kind are difficult to establish. (This might partly explain why Alan Ladd, Jr., felt he had to leave the film division of Twentieth-Century Fox.) And professional bureaucracies are not logically treated as integrated entities, nor can their goals be easily quantified. (How does one measure cure in a psychiatric ward or knowledge generated in a university?)

This conclusion is, of course, consistent with the earlier argument that external control (in this case, from headquarters) pushes an organization toward machine bureaucracy. The point is invariably illustrated when a conglomerate takes over an entrepreneurial company and imposes a lot of bureaucratic systems and standards on its simple structure.

The divisionalized form was created to solve the problem of adaptability in machine bureaucracy. By overlaying another level of administration that could add and subtract divisions, the organization found a way to adapt itself to new conditions and to spread its risk. But there is another side to these arguments. Some evidence suggests that the control systems of these structures discourage risk-taking and innovation, that the division head who must justify his or her performance every month is not free to experiment the way the independent entrepreneur is.

Moreover, to spread risk is to spread the consequences of that risk; a disaster in one division can pull down the entire organization. Indeed, the fear of this is what elicits the direct control of major new investments, which is what often discourages ambitious innovation. Finally, the divisionalized form does not solve the problem of adaptability of machine bureaucracy, it merely deflects it. When a division goes sour, all that headquarters seems able to do is change the management (as an independent board of directors would do) or divest it. From society's point of view, the problem remains.

Finally, from a social perspective, the divisionalized form raises a number of serious issues. By enabling organizations to grow very large, it leads to the concentration of a great deal of economic power in a few hands. And there is some evidence that it sometimes encourages that power to be used irresponsibly. By emphasizing the measurement of performance as its means of control, a bias arises in favor of those divisional goals that can be operationalized, which usually means the economic ones, not the social ones. That the division is driven by such measures to be socially unresponsive would not seem inappropriate—for the business of the corporation is, after all, economic.

The problem is that in big businesses (where the divisionalized form is prevalent)

every strategic decision has social as well as economic consequences. When the screws of the performance control system are turned tight, the division managers, in order to achieve the results expected of them, are driven to ignore the social consequences of their decisions. At that point, *un*responsive behavior becomes *ir*responsible.

The divisionalized structure has become very fashionable in the past few decades, having spread in pure or modified form through most of the *Fortune* "500" in a series of waves and then into European companies. It has also become fashionable in the nonbusiness sector in the guise of "multiversities," large hospital systems, unions, and government itself. And yet it seems fundamentally ill suited to these sectors for two reasons.

First, the success of the divisionalized form depends on goals that can be measured. But outside the business sector, goals are often social in nature and nonquantifiable. The result of performance control, then, is an inappropriate displacement of social goals by economic ones.

Second, the divisions often require structures other than machine bureaucracy. The professionals in the multiversities, for example, often balk at the technocratic controls and the top-down decision-making that tends to accompany external control of their campuses. In other words, the divisionalized form can be a misfit just as can any of the other configurations.

Adhocracy

None of the structures discussed so far suits the industries of our age—industries such as aerospace, petrochemicals, think-tank consulting, and film-making. These organizations need above all to innovate in complex ways. The bureaucratic structures are too inflexible, and the simple structure is too centralized. These industries require "project structures" that fuse experts drawn from different specialties into smoothly functioning creative teams. Hence they tend to favor our fifth configuration, adhocracy, a structure of interacting project teams.

Adhocracy is the most difficult of the five configurations to describe because it is both complex and nonstandardized. Indeed, adhocracy contradicts much of what we accept on faith in organizations—consistency in output, control by administrators, unity of command, strategy emanating from the top. It is a tremendously fluid structure, in which power is constantly shifting and coordination and control are by mutual adjustment through the informal communication and interaction of competent experts. Moreover, adhocracy is the newest of the five configurations, the one researchers have had the least chance to study. Yet it is emerging as a key structural configuration, one that deserves a good deal of consideration.

These comments notwithstanding, adhocracy is a no less coherent configuration than any of the others. Like the professional bureaucracy, adhocracy relies on trained and specialized experts to get the bulk of its work done. But in its case, the experts must work together to create new things instead of working apart to perfect established skills. Hence, for coordination adhocracy must rely extensively on mutual adjustment, which it encourages by the use of the liaison devices—integrating managers, task forces, and matrix structure.

In professional bureaucracy, the experts are concentrated in the operating core, where much of the power lies. But in adhocracy, they tend to be dispersed throughout the structure according to the decisions they make—in the operating core, middle line, technostructure, strategic apex, and especially support staff. Thus, whereas in each of the other configurations power is more or less concentrated, in adhocracy it is distributed unevenly. It flows, not according to authority or status but to wherever the experts needed for a particular decision happen to be found.

Managers abound in the adhocracy— functional managers, project managers, integrating managers. This results in narrow "spans of control" by conventional measures. That is not a reflection of control but of the small size of the project teams. The managers of adhocracy do not control in the conventional sense of direct supervision; typically, they are experts too who take their place alongside the others in the teams, concerned especially with linking the different teams together.

As can be seen in exhibit 2.6, many of the distinctions of conventional structure disappear in the adhocracy. With power based on expertise instead of authority, the line/staff distinction evaporates. And with power distributed throughout the structure, the distinction between the strategic apex and the rest of the structure also blurs. In a project structure, strategy is not formulated from above and then implemented lower down; rather, it evolves by virtue of the multitude of decisions made for the projects themselves. In other words, the adhocracy is continually developing its strategy as it accepts and works out new projects, the creative results of which can never be predicted. And so everyone who gets involved in the project work—and in the adhocracy that can mean virtually everyone— becomes a strategy maker.

To describe what happens to the distinction between operating core and administrative structure, I need to introduce two basic types of adhocracy. The *operating* adhocracy carries out innovative projects directly on behalf of its clients, usually under contract, as in a creative advertising agency, a think-tank consulting firm, a manufacturer of engineering prototypes. Professional bureaucracies work in some of these industries too, but with a different orientation. The operating adhocracy treats each client problem as a unique one to be solved in creative fashion; the professional bureaucracy pigeonholes it so that it can provide a standard skill.

For example, there are some consulting firms that tailor their solutions to the client's order and others that sell standard packages off the rack. When the latter fits, it proves much cheaper. When it does not, the money is wasted. In one case, the experts must cooperate with each other in organic structures to innovate; in the other, they can apply their standard skills autonomously in bureaucratic structures.

In the operating adhocracy, the operating and administrative work blend into a single effort. That is, the organization cannot easily separate the planning and design of the operating work—in other words, the project—from its actual execution. So another classic distinction disappears. As shown above the dotted lines in exhibit 2.6, the organization emerges as an organic mass in which line managers, staff, and operating experts all work together on project teams in ever-shifting relationships.

The *administrative* adhocracy undertakes projects on its own behalf, as in a space agency or a producer of electronic components. NASA, for example, as described during the Apollo era by Margaret K. Chandler and Leonard R. Sayles, seems to be a perfect example of administrative adhocracy. In this type of adhocracy, in contrast to the other, we find a sharp separation of the administrative from the operating work—the latter shown by the dotted lines in exhibit 2.6. This results in a two-part structure. The administrative component carries out the innovative design work, combining line managers and staff experts in project teams. And the operating component, which puts the results into production, is separated or "truncated" so that its need for standardization will not interfere with the project work.

Sometimes the operations are contracted out altogether. Other times, they are set up in independent structures, as in the printing function in newspapers. And when the operations of an organization are highly automated, the same effect takes place naturally. The operations essentially run themselves, while the administrative component tends to adopt a project orientation concerned with change and innovation, with bringing new facilities on line. Note also the effects of automation—a reduction in the need for rules, since these are built right into the machinery, and a blurring of the line/staff distinction, since control becomes a question more of expertise than authority. What does it mean to supervise a machine? Thus the effect of automation is to reduce the degree of machine bureaucracy in the administration and to drive it toward administrative adhocracy.

Both kinds of adhocracy are commonly found in environments that are complex as well as dynamic. These are the two conditions that call for sophisticated innovation, which requires the cooperative efforts of many different kinds of experts. In the case of administrative adhocracy, the production system is also typically complex and, as noted, often automated. These production systems create the need for highly skilled support staffers, who must be given a good deal of power over technical decisions.

For its part, the operating adhocracy is often associated with young organizations. For one thing, with no standard products or services, organizations that use it tend to be highly vulnerable, and many of them disappear at an early age. For another, age drives these organizations toward bureaucracy, as the employees themselves age and tend to seek an escape from the instability of the structure and its environment. The innovative consulting firm converges on a few of its most successful projects, packages them into standard skills, and settles down to life as a professional bureaucracy; the manufacturer of prototypes hits on a hot product and becomes a machine bureaucracy to mass-produce it.

But not all adhocracies make such a transition. Some endure as they are, continuing to innovate over long periods of time. We see this, for example, in studies of the National Film Board of Canada, famous since the 1940s for its creativity in both films and the techniques of filmmaking.

Finally, fashion is a factor associated with adhocracy. This is clearly the structure of our age, prevalent in almost every industry that has grown up since World War II (and none I can think of established before that time). Every characteristic of adhocracy is very much in vogue today—expertise, organic structure, project teams and task forces, diffused power, matrix structure, sophisticated and often automated production systems, youth, and dynamic, complex environments. Adhocracy is the only one of the five configurations that combines some sense of democracy with an absence of bureaucracy.

Yet, like all the others, this configuration too has its limitations. Adhocracy in some sense achieves its effectiveness through inefficiency. It is inundated with managers and costly liaison devices for communication; nothing ever seems to get done without everyone talking to everyone else. Ambiguity abounds, giving rise to all sorts of conflicts and political pressures. Adhocracy can do no *ordinary* thing well. But it is extraordinary at innovation.

CONFIGURATIONS AS A DIAGNOSTIC TOOL

What in fact are these configurations? Are they (1) abstract ideals, (2) real-life structures, one of which an organization had better use if it is to survive, or (3) building blocks for more complex structures? In some sense, the answer is a qualified yes in all three cases. They are certainly abstract ideals, simplifications of the complex world of structure. Yet the abstract ideal can come to life too. Every organization experiences the five pulls that underlie these configurations: the pull to centralize by the top management, the pull to formalize by the technostructure, the pull to professionalize by the operators, the pull to balkanize by the managers of the middle line, and the pull to collaborate by the support staff.

Where one pull dominates—where the conditions favor it above all—then the organization will tend to organize itself close to one of the configurations. I have cited examples of this throughout my discussion— the entrepreneurial company, the hamburger chain, the university, the conglomerate, the space agency.

But one pull does not always dominate; two may have to exist in balance. Symphony orchestras engage highly trained specialists who perfect their skills, as do the operators in professional bureaucracy. But their efforts must be tightly coordinated; hence the reliance on the direct supervision of a leader—a conductor—as in simple structure. Thus a hybrid of the two configurations emerges that is eminently sensible for the symphony orchestra (even if it does generate a good deal of conflict between leader and operators).

Likewise, we have companies that are diversified around a central theme that creates linkages among their different product lines. As a result, they continually experience the pull to separate, as in the divisionalized form, and also to integrate, as in machine bureaucracy or perhaps adhocracy. And what configuration should we impute to an IBM? Clearly, there is too much going on in many giant organizations to describe them as one configuration or another. But the framework of the five configurations can still help us understand how their different parts are organized and fit together—or refuse to.

The point is that managers can improve their organizational designs by considering the different pulls their organizations experience and the configurations toward which they are drawn. In other words, this set of five configurations can serve as an effective tool in diagnosing the problems of organizational design, especially those of the *fit* among component parts. Let us consider four basic forms of misfit to show how managers can use the set of configurations as a diagnostic tool.

Are the Internal Elements Consistent?

Management that grabs at every structural innovation that comes along may be doing its organization great harm. It risks going off in all directions: today long-range planning to pin managers down, tomorrow Outward Bound to open them up. Quality of working life programs as well as all those fashionable features of adhocracy—integrating managers, matrix structure, and the like—have exemplary aims: to create more satisfying work conditions and to increase the flexibility of the organization. But are they appropriate for a machine bureaucracy? Do enlarged jobs really fit with the requirements of the mass-production of automobiles? Can the jobs ever be made large enough to really satisfy the workers—and the cost-conscious customers?

I believe that in the fashionable world of organizational design, fit remains an important characteristic. The *hautes structurières* of New York—the consulting firms that seek to bring the latest in structural fashion to their clients—would do well to pay a great deal more attention to that fit. Machine bureaucracy functions best when its reporting relationships are sharply defined and its operating core staffed with workers who prefer routine and stability. The nature of the work in this configuration—managerial as well as operating—is rooted in the reality of mass-production, in the costs of manual labor compared with those of automated machines, and in the size and age of the organization.

Until we are prepared to change our whole way of living—for example, to pay more for handcrafted instead of mass-produced products and so to consume less—we would do better to spend our time trying not to convert our machine bureaucracies into something else but to insure that they work as effectively as the bureaucracies they are meant to be. Organizations, like individuals, can avoid identity crises by deciding what it is they wish to be and then pursuing it with a healthy obsession.

Are the External Controls Functional?

An organization may achieve its own internal consistency and then have it destroyed by the imposition of external controls. The typical effect of those controls is to drive the organization toward machine bureaucracy.

In other words, it is the simple structures, professional bureaucracies, and adhocracies that suffer most from such controls. Two cases of this seem rampant in our society: one is the takeover of small, private companies by larger divisionalized ones, making bureaucracies of entrepreneurial ventures; the other is the tendency for governments to assume increasingly direct control of what used to be more independent organizations—public school systems, hospitals, universities, and social welfare agencies.

As organizations are taken over in these ways—brought into the hierarchies of other organizations—two things happen. They become centralized and formalized. In other words, they are driven toward machine bureaucracy. Government administrators assume that just a little more formal control will bring this callous hospital or that weak school in line. Yet the cure—even when the symptoms are understood—is often worse than the disease. The worst way to correct deficiencies in professional work is through control by technocratic standards. Professional bureaucracies cannot be managed like machines.

In the school system, such standards imposed from outside the classroom serve only to discourage the competent teachers, not to improve the weak ones. The performance of teachers—as that of all other professionals—depends primarily on their skills and training. Retraining or, more likely, replacing them is the basic means to improvement.

For almost a century now, the management literature—from time study through operations research to long-range planning—has promoted machine bureaucracy as the "one best way." That assumption is false; it is one way among a number suited to only certain conditions.

Is There a Part That Does Not Fit?

Sometimes an organization's management, recognizing the need for internal consistency, hives off a part in need of special treatment—establishes it in a pocket off in a corner to be left alone. But the problem all too often is that it is not left alone. The research laboratory may be built out in the country, far from the managers and analysts who run the machine bureaucracy back home. But the distance is only physical.

Standards have a long administrative reach: it is difficult to corner off a small component and pretend that it will not be influenced by the rest. Each organization, not to mention each configuration, develops its own norms, traditions, beliefs—in other words, its own ideology. And that permeates every part of it. Unless there is a rough balance among opposing forces—as in the symphony orchestra—the prevailing ideology will tend to dominate. That is why adhocracies need especially tolerant controllers, just as machine bureaucracies must usually scale down their expectations for their research laboratories.

Is the Right Structure in the Wrong Situation?

Some organizations do indeed achieve and maintain an internal consistency. But then they find that it is designed for an environment the organization is no longer in. To have a nice, neat machine bureaucracy in a dynamic industry calling for constant innovation or, alternately, a flexible adhocracy in a stable industry calling for minimum cost makes no sense. Remember that these are configurations of situation as well as structure. Indeed, the very notion of configuration is that all the elements interact in a system. One element does not cause another; instead, all influence each other interactively. Structure is no more designed to fit the situation than situation is selected to fit the structure.

The way to deal with the right structure in the wrong environment may be to change the environment, not the structure. Often, in fact, it is far easier to shift industries or retreat to a suitable niche in an industry than to undo a cohesive structure. Thus the entrepreneur goes after a new, dynamic en-

vironment when the old one stabilizes and the bureaucracies begin to move in. When a situation changes suddenly—as it did for oil companies some years ago—a rapid change in situation or structure would seem to be mandatory. But what of a gradual change in situation? How should the organization adapt, for example, when its long-stable markets slowly become dynamic?

Essentially, the organization has two choices. It can adapt continuously to the environment at the expense of internal consistency—that is, steadily redesign its structure to maintain external fit. Or it can maintain internal consistency at the expense of a gradually worsening fit with its environment, at least until the fit becomes so bad that it must undergo sudden structural redesign to achieve a new internally consistent configuration. In other words, the choice is between evolution and revolution, between perpetual mild adaptation, which favors external fit over time, and infrequent major realignment, which favors internal consistency over time.

In his research on configuration, Danny Miller finds that effective companies usually opt for revolution. Forced to decide whether to spend most of their time with a good external fit or with an established internal consistency, they choose consistency and put up with brief periods of severe disruption to realign the fit occasionally. It is better, apparently, to maintain at least partial configuration than none at all. Miller calls this process, appropriately enough, a "quantum" theory of structural change.

FIT OVER FASHION

To conclude, consistency, coherence, and fit—harmony—are critical factors in organization design, but they come at a price. An organization cannot be all things to all people. It should do what it does well and suffer the consequences. Be an efficient machine bureaucracy where that is appropriate and do not pretend to be highly adaptive. Or be an adaptive adhocracy and do not pretend to be highly efficient. Or create some new configuration to suit your own needs. The point is not really *which* configuration you have; it is *that* you achieve configuration.

■ APPENDIX: ELEMENTS OF THE CONFIGURATIONS

Elements of structure

Job specialization refers to the number of tasks in a given job and the worker's control over these tasks. A job is horizontally specialized to the extent that it encompasses few narrowly defined tasks, vertically specialized to the extent that the worker lacks control of the tasks he or she performs. Unskilled jobs are typically highly specialized in both dimensions, while skilled or professional jobs are typically specialized horizontally but not vertically. Job enrichment refers to the enlargement of jobs in both the vertical and horizontal dimensions.

Behavior formalization refers to the standardization of work processes by imposition of operating instructions, job descriptions, rules, regulations, and the like. Structures that rely on standardization for coordination are generally referred to as bureaucratic, those that do not as organic.

Training and indoctrination refer to the use of formal instructional programs to establish and standardize in people the requisite skills, knowledge, and norms to do particular jobs. Training is a key design parameter in all work we call professional. Training and formalization are basically substitutes for achieving the standardization (in effect, the bureaucratization) of behavior. In the one, the standards are internalized in formal training as skills or norms; in the other, they are imposed on the job as rules.

Unit grouping refers to the optional bases by which positions are grouped together into units and these units into higher-order units. Grouping encourages coordination by putting different jobs under common supervision, by requiring them to share common resources and achieve common measures of performance, and by facilitating mutual adjustment among them. The various bases for grouping—by work process, product, client, area, etc.—can be reduced to two fundamentals: the function performed or the market served.

Unit size refers to the number of positions (or units) contained in a single unit. The equivalent term "span of control" is not used here because sometimes units are kept small despite an absence of close supervisory control. For example, when experts coordinate extensively by mutual adjustment, as in an engineering team in a space agency, they will form into small teams. In this case, unit size is small and span of control is low despite a relative absence of direct supervision. In contrast, when work is highly standardized (because of either formalization or training), unit size can be very large because there is little need for direct supervision. One supervisor can supervise dozens of assemblers because they work according to very tight instructions.

Planning and control systems are used to standardize outputs. They may be divided into two types—action planning systems, which specify the results of specific actions before they are taken (for example, that holes should be drilled with diameters of three centimeters), and performance control systems, which specify the results of whole ranges of actions after the fact (for example, that sales of a division should grow by 10 percent in a given year).

Liaison devices refer to a whole set of mechanisms used to encourage mutual adjustment within and among units. They range from liaison positions (such as the purchasing engineer who stands between purchasing and engineering); through task forces, standing committees that bring together members of many departments, and integrating managers (such as brand managers); and finally to fully developed matrix structures.

Vertical decentralization describes the extent to which decision-making is delegated to managers down the middle line, while **horizontal decentralization** describes the extent to which non-managers (that is, people in the operating core, technostructure, and support staff) control decision processes. Moreover, decentralization may be selective, concerning only specific kinds of decisions, or parallel, concerning many kinds of decisions altogether. Five types of decentralization may be found: vertical and horizontal centralization, where all power rests at the strategic apex; limited horizontal decentralization (selective), where the strategic apex shares some power with the technostructure that standardizes everybody else's work; limited vertical decentralization (parallel), where managers of market-based units are delegated the power to control most of the decisions concerning their line units; vertical and horizontal decentralization, where most of the power rests in the operating core at the bottom of the structure; and selective vertical and horizontal decentralization, where the power over different decisions is dispersed widely in the organization—among managers, staff experts, and operators who work in groups at various levels in the hierarchy.

Elements of situation

The **age and size** of the organization affect particularly the extent to which its behavior is formalized and its administrative structure (technostructure and middle line) elaborated. As they age and grow, organizations appear to go through distinct structural transitions, much as insects metamorphose—for example, from simple organic to elaborate bureaucratic structure, from functional grouping to market-based grouping.

The **technical system** of the organization influences especial-ly the operating core and those staff units most clearly associated with it. When the technical system of the organization regulates the work of the operating core—as it typically does in mass production—it has the effect of bureaucratizing the organization by virtue of the standards it imposes on lower-level workers. Alternately, when the technical system succeeds in automating the operating work (as in much process production), it reduces the need for external rules and regulations: the necessary rules are automatically incorporated into the machines, enabling the structure to be organic. And when the technical system is complex, as is often the case in process production, the organization must create a significant professional support staff to deal with it and then must decentralize selectively to that staff many of the decisions concerned with the technical system.

The **environment** of the organization can vary in its degree of complexity, in how static or dynamic it is, in the diversity of its markets, and in the hostility it contains for the organization. The more complex the environment, the more difficulty central management has in comprehending it and the greater the need for decentralization. The more dynamic the environment, the greater the difficulty in standardizing work, outputs, or skills and so the less bureaucratic the structure. These relationships suggest four kinds of structures: two in stable environments (one simple, the other complex) leading, respectively, to a centralized and a decentralized bureaucra-cy; and two in dynamic environments (again, one simple, the other complex) leading, respectively, to a centralized and a decentralized organic structure. Market diversity, as noted earlier, encourages the organization to set up market-based divisions (instead of functional departments) to deal with each, while extreme hostility in the environment drives the organization to centralize power temporarily—no matter what its normal structure—to fight off the threat.

The **power** factors of the organization include external control, personal power needs, and fashion. The more an organization is controlled externally, the more centralized and bureaucratic it tends to become. This can be explained by the fact that the two most effective means to control an organization from the outside are to hold its most powerful decision-maker, the chief executive officer, responsible for its actions and to impose clearly defined standards on it (performance targets or rules and regulations).

Moreover, because the externally controlled organization must be especially careful about its actions—often having to justify these to outsiders—it tends to formalize much of its behavior and insist that its chief executive authorize key decisions. A second factor, individual power needs (especially by the chief executive), tend to generate excessively centralized structures. And fashion has been shown to be a factor in organization design, the structure of the day often being favored even by organizations for which it is inappropriate.

■ Organization Boundary Roles and Units

ROBERT H. MILES

Conventional employees usually spend the majority of their working day engaged in one or more of the following activities: the direct production of a product or service; the support of those who engage in production or the formal management of these direct and support activities. These internal functions may be generally categorized as the *technical* and *managerial* functions within complex organizations.

In contrast, persons occupying organization boundary roles are charged with the *institutional-adaptive* function. The activities required by this function include: (1) *representing* the organization to its external constituencies; (2) *scanning and monitoring* environmental events that are potentially relevant for the organization; (3) *protecting* the organization from environmental threats; (4) *information processing and gatekeeping*; (5) *transacting* with other organizations for the acquisition of inputs and the disposal of outputs; and (6) *linking and coordinating* activities between organizations. Each of these critical functions will be discussed below, along with its implications for the design and management of the organization boundary role.

REPRESENTING THE ORGANIZATION

Representation may be defined as the presentation of information about the organiza-

tion to its environment for the purpose of shaping the opinions and behavior of other organizations, groups, and individuals, in the service of the organization. Persons occupying representational boundary roles serve as the "face" of the organization, and to a very great extent outsiders form opinions about an organization on the basis of their observations of its representatives.

The effectiveness of the representative depends in large measure on credibility. Outsiders must be able to rely on the representative's information. Many factors contribute to the credibility of the representational role, including whether the representative is backed by a constituency that: (1) is not in disagreement; (2) communicates unambiguous and congruent expectations to the representative; and (3) can be depended upon to make good the "representations" the incumbent is obliged to convey to outsiders.

These delicate linkages are highlighted in the roles of peace and labor negotiators, but the representational function is also performed by individuals occupying more conventional boundary roles. The activities of public-relations executives, lobbyists, and press agents have a high representational component.

The ease with which an organization is able to deal with outside groups, to achieve legitimacy in their eyes, and consequently to win their support and goodwill, is directly related to the abilities of persons occupying representational boundary roles. However, "representations" may be calculated or accidental, deceptive or truthful, and "impression management" is often an important feature of the representational role and an essential skill of its incumbent.

For instance, in some cases a representative may wish to have his counterpart in another organization believe that his behavior is dictated by internal constituents over which he has no control. In other cases, the representative may wish to make his opponent believe that a concession made is attributable to his good faith, when in fact it is a "give-away" his constituents have instructed him to make. Here, the representative is capitalizing on the opponent's belief that he is offering a "social gift" of his own accord, in order to create an obligation to reciprocate.

In general, then, the representational function of boundary roles is intended to create and manage the image of the organization to its outside constituencies; to create impressions that will lead, at least indirectly, to the enhancement of the organization's power and autonomy in its environment. The role is often a source of esteem and recognition because of the power and visibility it causes the organization to share with the representative, but it is not without hazards. The representative is obliged to simultaneously present the preferred view of one group of itself to another while maintaining a bond of credibility between the two.

SCANNING AND MONITORING THE ENVIRONMENT

Distinctions may be made between the two basic types of information-gathering activities in organizations. *Scanning* is primarily a search for major discontinuities in the external environment that might provide opportunities or constraints to the organization. The emergence of new technologies that might leapfrog the organization's existing or planned production processes is an example of a major qualitative change induced by the environment. A case in point is the recent upheaval in the watch-making industry, which experienced a rapid technologi-

cal transformation from mechanical to electronic timekeeping devices.

Firms whose environmental scanning alerted them to developments in the electronics technology, which would eventually replace the age-old mechanical timepiece, were able to adapt. They were able to do so because of the lead time afforded by the early detection and subsequent monitoring of these events by scanning units. For example, the Hamilton Watch Company was able to develop an electronics watch division while selling its traditional mechanical watch-making operation to the Swiss. Indeed, many of the Swiss companies were so wedded to the traditional timepiece that they have witnessed a sharp decline in their share of the world market. It is alleged that the national pride of the Swiss prevented them from being able to "appreciate" the impact of the electronic revolution on their provincial industry. Thus, failure in scanning and monitoring potentially relevant changes in the external environment of the watchmaking industry resulted in an almost overnight conversion of the mechanical expertise of traditional watch makers into a liability.

By scanning the environment for new technological developments, innovations in organizational design, relevant trends in related fields, and so forth, boundary personnel can prevent organizations from becoming prematurely ossified and possibly no longer matched with their environments. . . .[1]

Monitoring, on the other hand, involves tracking continuous, sometimes gradual, changes in environmental indicators that have been established as strategic contingencies of the organization. Examples include the measuring and forecasting of demand for the organization's products or services, supply of essential raw materials, and changes in relevant legislation, public opinions, and economic conditions.

---

1. Howard Aldrich and Diane Herker, "Boundary Spanning Roles and Organization Structure," *The Academy of Management Review*, vol. 2, April 1977, p. 219.

A case in point is the behavior of R.J. Reynolds Tobacco Company, the leading producer of cigarettes in the U.S. domestic market, in response to the product innovations of its competitors. RJR had built a commanding share of the domestic cigarette market on the strength of two regular, nonfilter brands: Camel and Cavalier. With the growing environmental pressure during the early 1950s regarding the smoking and health issue, RJR's competitors had begun market testing innovative filter-tip cigarettes that were lower in harmful "tar" and nicotine content. RJR's annual reports during this time indicated that these innovations were being carefully monitored by its marketing-research staff. Their 1953 report noted that filter-tip brands had achieved a $1\frac{1}{4}$ percent share of the domestic market by 1952, which had risen to $3\frac{1}{4}$ by 1953, and that the company had for some time been internally developing its own filter-tip product for distribution should market demand develop. With this information and the lead time it provided, coupled with the Sloan-Kettering Report of 1953, linking cigarette smoking with heart and lung disease, RJR introduced the Winston filter-tip cigarette in 1954, which was to rapidly become and remain the leading filter-tip brand in the U.S. market.

Thus, organizations must develop the ability to obtain external information needed in current decision-making and policy formulation and to learn of unpredictable, relevant environmental events that *may* occur. For these purposes, organizations must develop two classes of boundary-scanning units: the kind that engages in highly specialized, focused monitoring, and the kind that engages in broad-gauged, general scanning. Both classes of boundary units must be differentiated from other parts of the organization as well as from each other.

Focused monitoring units include the affirmative-action office, the organization's formal instrumentality for coping with the impacts of civil rights legislation, and the office of the corporate legal counsel, which keeps tabs on changing precedents on issues of central concern to the organization.

More broad-gauged, environmental scanning units exist as parts of the "environmental analysis" and "corporate planning" units in large corporations. The great difficulty confronting these units is deciding what "out there" is potentially relevant for the organization and what is just noise. While the resolution of this dilemma must be responsible to cost-benefit tradeoffs, it is probably true that failing to obtain relevant information is more serious than acquiring irrelevant information. In general, however, the greater the decision-making uncertainty caused by features of the external environment, the more complex and differentiated must be the organization in terms of its scanning and monitoring functions.

PROTECTING THE ORGANIZATION

Protecting in this context refers to warding off environmental influences and noises that might otherwise disrupt the ongoing operations and structures of the focal organization. In a sense, boundary-role occupants must often act as shock absorbers. This condition places the protector or "flak catcher" in a position of high role conflict. The role expectation communicated by organizational superiors demands that protectors absorb external threats and pressures for change, particularly those judged to be unwarranted interventions into organizational life, and not transmit them to other parts of the organization, which depend on being buffered in order to maximize the efficiency of their activities. Juxtaposed against these expectations are the demands of outsiders to have the boundary-role occupant effectively transmit their pressures.

A variety of behavioral and structural strategies are available to the boundary-role incumbent for achieving this function. For example, the protector may *buffer* his organization or unit from unwarranted intrusions or threats to ongoing operations by stockpiling inventories or "goodwill" or by socializing new members before they enter the main body of the organization, as in "vestibule training" programs. The protector may rely on various scheduling and pricing strategies to *smooth* demands placed on the organization or on *forecasting* to give the organization lead time necessary for interpretation of, and reaction to, environmental threats. Finally, protectors may resort to *rationing* of organizational inputs or outputs when environmental demands exceed capacity.

Mau-mauing the flak catchers. The protecting function of boundary roles has been described in great detail for the poverty agencies of the "Great Society." To hear Tom Wolfe, a self-styled urban sociologist, tell it, the protecting function of organization boundary roles reached its apogee in the poverty program bureaus of the late 1960s and early 1970s. Apparently, a new art form emerged from the ghetto culture. Wolfe describes it as "mau-mauing the flak catchers." The idea was to confront the decision-maker, or more often his or her spokesperson, in the open in an attempt to make the agency more responsive to the needs of its local constituency.

The staging of a mau-mauing required elaborate planning. The desired effect was to have the bureaucrat or his flak catcher perceive the situation as out of control, in need of some decisive organizational response that was unavoidably associated with his person. Wolfe paints some scenarios of the detailed planning and creative genius underlying the apparently uncontrollable—wild—mau-mauing tactic:

There was one genius in the art of confrontation who had mau-mauing down to what you could term a laboratory science. He had it figured out so he didn't even have to bring his boys downtown in person. He would just show up with a crocus sack full of revolvers, ice picks, fish knives, switchblades, hatchets, blackjacks, gravity knives, straight razors, hand grenades, blow guns, bazookas, Molotov

cocktails, tank rippers, unbelievable stuff, and he'd dump it all out on somebody's shiny walnut table. He'd say, "These are some of the things I took off my boys last night . . . ." And they would lay money on this man's ghetto youth patrol like it was now or never. . . .[2]

When actually taking "the boys" downtown, elaborate dress rehearsals were required, with roles carefully synchronized with the predictable stages of mau-mauing; predictable, at least, to the brothers.

Here is how Wolfe described the function of the flak catcher. His job is to catch the flak for the No. 1 man. It doesn't matter what bureau they put him in. It's all the same. Poverty, Japanese imports, valley fever, tomato-crop parity, partial disability, home loans, second-probate accounting, the Interstate 90 detour change order, lockouts, secondary boycotts, G.I. alimony, the Pakistani quota, cinch mites, Tularemic Loa loa, veteran's dental benefits, workman's compensation, suspended excise rebates—whatever you're angry about, it doesn't matter, *he's there to catch the flak.*[3]

Flak catchers, of course, are not limited to poverty agencies, and mau-mauing takes many forms. Recall the famous encounters between White House press secretaries and the demands placed on them by newspaper reporters in recent years, or the humble complaints-department clerk in your local retail store. Yet, Wolfe's study does reveal several of the key features of the protective function of organization boundary roles.

Protecting by coding boundaries. In contrast to the extreme example of the flak catcher, much of the protective function is achieved through relatively routine operations in well-defined roles with established decision rules, standard procedures, and contingency plans, and with some provision

2. Tom Wolfe, *Radical Chic and Mau-Mauing the Flak Catchers,* N.Y.: Bantam Books, 1970, pp. 118–119.

3. Ibid., pp. 132–33.

for exceptions and discretion. The procedures for "qualifying" a food-stamps applicant or candidate for social security, or for deciding whether to grant an early release from active duty to an armed-services inductee for "family reasons," fall into this functional category, as do procurement, final quality control, and hiring operations in most complex organizations. These aspects of protection are performed by people who *code* the organization's boundary with a set of criteria in order to limit the quality and quantity of inputs entering the organization.

The personnel department represents a common element in most all organizations that serves as a protector, in their case, of unwanted, potentially threatening human-resource inputs. An interesting case study of this function in a hospital setting has revealed the important boundary functions performed in managing the flow of employees into the organization and the coding of successive filters used to select job applicants.

The hospital's personnel department was responsible for providing qualified personnel to staff 2,500 positions in over 200 job classifications throughout the hospital. To provide the required quality and quantity of employees, the department had to interact with units both internal and external to the hospital. The principal links were between the various departments within the hospital, potential employees, and the state's personnel office, an outside regulatory agency. An important secondary link was with the various advertising and employment agencies.

The hospital personnel unit accomplished its mission by coding that portion of the organization's boundary through which new employees pass. The coding schemes it employed were designed to maximize the probability that the correct number of individuals, and only those who would make successful hospital employees, were admitted into the system. Data from the year preceding the study indicated that this filtering or protecting process was quite intense. Of the 67,000 individuals who submitted application forms that year, 2,500 passed this filter and were interviewed by personnel officers. Only about 25 percent of them were actually offered a job. An understanding of how this selection process was managed provides insight into the protective function of organization boundary-spanning units.

A variety of protecting functions may be performed in boundary-spanning units, and they may range from routine to nonroutine in nature, as demonstrated in the hospital example. However, judging just how much protection is appropriate may be difficult. Certainly, "overprotection" may cause the organization to lose touch with its external environment and create a situation in which mau-mauing becomes an outsider's only avenue for expressing grievances.

INFORMATION PROCESSING AND GATEKEEPING

Persons occupying boundary roles must also (1) *interpret* the meaning of environmental information in terms of the opportunities, constraints, and contingencies they pose for the organization; (2) *translate* these implications into terms comprehensible to organizational decision-makers; and (3) make choices about *what* and *when* to communicate to internal managers. The interpretation and translation activities are the information-processing part of this boundary-role function; the choices made regarding what and when to communicate and to whom are the gatekeeping activities. All these activities require special skills, the effectiveness of which will surely vary with the personalities involved as well as with the decision issues and contexts.

The importance of information processors and gatekeepers has been emphasized by many contemporary organizational theorists. The critical nature of this boundary-spanning activity has been summarized as follows:

As organizations are forced to operate in increasingly complex environments, the ability to gather, analyze, and act on the best information available becomes critical. It is not the full and free flow of information per se which is necessary for the accomplishment of organizational goals. Consequently gatekeeping mechanisms are required at the organizational boundaries to filter, condense, and interpret volumes of raw data . . . however . . . there is a potential error component to gatekeeping activities. Improper application of coding rules, omissions, exaggerations, and selective biases in information transmission represent breakdowns in the gatekeeping process. Reliance on information gatekeepers may leave organizational policy makers vulnerable to acting on incomplete or distorted information. Since the successful or unsuccessful execution of information transmission from the environment to internal decision centers has significant consequences for organizational adaptation, the entire process of information flow from gatekeeper to policy maker deserves systematic examination.[4]

Once information has been filtered through the initial boundary of an organization, it is usually processed in a unit or by a person occupying a role designed specifically for that purpose. Information available to the organization frequently does not consist of simple, immutable facts; therefore, this processing activity includes interpretation, analysis, and translation. Together, these activities have been called "uncertainty absorption," the process by which inferences are drawn from perceived facts, and only the inferences passed on to others.

Information imputs may be *solicited* or *unsolicited*. Solicited information represents data purposely sought by specialized boundary-role occupants whose constituents have decided that the data are particularly relevant to organizational goals or process-es. Solicited information for private-sector organizations usually includes marketing, technological, and general economic developments and trends; for public-sector organizations, it would certainly include funding prospects and political contingencies.

Unsolicited-information inputs usually encounter much more resistance at the boundaries of complex organizations because, unlike solicited information, they are often inconsistent with established policy and operations. They frequently take the form of pressures for change from elements of the environment reacting against organizational objectives or operations. Antitrust and malpractice suits, pressures for recall of defective or dangerous products, chastisement for violation of equal employment opportunity guidelines, demands for pollution abatement, public disclosure, or greater organizational "responsiveness," all fall into this category. Therefore, unsolicited information is much more likely to become ignored, misinterpreted, and distorted in its path to the ultimate decision-maker for whom it is intended.

The personalities and role relations of the people involved in the gatekeeping process also influence the processing of new information by the boundary spanner as well as the exchange of information between organization boundary positions or units and internal decision-making centers. Defensive decision makers give off cues that indicate that they are not receptive to various kinds of negative feedback, thereby encouraging gatekeepers to withhold conflicting opinions and unpopular data. A decision maker who prefers to be kept isolated from the information sources may be encouraging information distortion. Gatekeepers who must submit reports or briefs with the knowledge that there will be no independent checks of their accuracy may be more inclined to "manage" the information flow to the decision maker.

Gatekeepers who have very strong "upward mobility" aspirations seem to be more reluctant to communicate negative, particu-

---

4. For a more comprehensive review of these findings on information processing and gatekeeping, see Benson Rosen, "Organization Boundary Roles." Paper presented at 84th Convention of American Psychological Association, Washington, DC, 1976.

larly personally derogatory, information to their superiors. Gatekeepers also seem to be especially reluctant to communicate negative information to decision makers who they believe are very defensive and who exercise high "fate control" over them, that is, who are the major sources of rewards and sanctions for the gatekeeper. Much freer and accurate transmission of negative information occurs when the decision maker is believed to be low in defensiveness but high in fate control.

In order to maintain good relations with outside constituencies, whether they be sources or targets of information, the gatekeeper must meet certain of their expectations, expectations that are at least partially incongruent with those of the gatekeeper's internal constituencies. Often, gatekeepers of information inputs must guarantee minimal distortion and maximal transmission of information they receive from sources, the identity or status of which they must attempt to "protect." Yet, gatekeepers face the potential wrath of the uninformed decision maker, whose primary charge is to maintain, not change, the status quo of the organization, a decision maker, who, at the very least, needs to know the nature and quality of the information source in order to decide what weight to give the data received.

Credibility is also important at both ends of the information-transmission continuum. Although gatekeepers of information outputs are charged by their internal constituents with the creation of organizational images to the public, the public demands authenticity and honesty in reporting. Organizational superiors may ask the output gatekeeper to "buy us time." They may solicit the help of the output gatekeeper in order to pursue an operating strategy designed to confuse or throw off competitors. These demands for impression management often come into conflict with both the personal values and expectations of gatekeepers and those of outsiders who rely upon their communications. This condition is just another example of the conflict inherent in

all organization boundary-spanning activities.

TRANSACTING

Transacting refers to the activities necessary for the acquisition of inputs and the disposal of outputs, both of which are essential to organizational survival. On the input boundary, purchasing agents and "grantspeople" are employed to insure a constant flow of needed resources. On the output boundary, the activities of salespersons and social workers maintain effective outputting of the organization's goods or services—including not only products, but byproducts and wastes as well. Like most boundary-spanning functions, transacting is usually set apart from internal activities, involves a heavy influence component, and exposes the agent to conflicting pressures and episodes of suspicion resulting from the lack of appreciation of the boundary-role requirements by organizational internals or externals.

As a boundary-role person, the outside salesperson has a role set extending outward into customer organizations. The sales task is to reconcile partially conflicting goals and expectations of supplying and purchasing organizations in an exchange relationship. Thus, the salesperson is placed in a position of serving two masters, customer and supervisor, each representing different organizations and each having goals that may be conflicting.

One study revealed that the sources of salesperson performance and job satisfaction might depend on factors that are at odds in the context in which the role is performed. Sales performance was shown to increase as a result of the salesperson achieving some independence from the employing organization, such as by controlling delivery times or credit approvals. However, these tactics also served to intensify the cross-pressures and tensions created by the distrust they created in sales supervisors and by the incongruity between supervisor and client demands. The input counterpart of the salesperson, the purchasing agent, also provides some insight into the transacting function of organization boundary roles.

Purchasing agents perform two general functions on behalf of their employing organization. They negotiate and place orders for resource materials at the best possible terms, but typically in accordance with specifications set by others, and they expedite orders, checking with suppliers to make sure that deliveries are made on time. Under normal conditions, this arrangement gives the agent broad power in dealing with outside salespersons but reduces the agent to little more than a clerk in terms of company status or power.

One study revealed that purchasing agents receive little attention from organizational superiors. They have to act on their own, being given support of top management only in exceptional circumstances. At the same time, they are delegated relatively wide latitude in defining their roles and appear to be controlled chiefly by their client departments in the organization—such as engineering, where a typical conflict involves the specifications provided by the latter for the agents' purchases. If the specifications were too tight, or particularly if they called for one brand only, agents would have little or no freedom to choose among suppliers, thus reducing their social status within the organization and their bargaining power externally with potential suppliers. Moreover, engineers look first for quality and reliability, but agents are charged to insure low cost and quick delivery. These seeds of conflict are aggravated by the "completion barrier," which results when the agent seeks to change specifications *after* the engineer has gone on record by reducing them to final blueprints. Any attempt by the agent to return the specifications to the engineer for revision in light of purchasing opportunities is likely to be hardily resisted because of its threat to the engineer's status.

LINKING AND COORDINATING

Organization boundary roles also serve as links between two or more systems. At least three general levels of linkage may be distinguished. The first deals with establishing and maintaining relationships between the organization as a whole and other individuals, groups, or organizations. Despite the fact that these linkages are crucial for organizational survival, they often have to be maintained on a delicate, informal basis. It is under these conditions that the organization boundary role assumes great importance relative to more conventional, internal roles.

For example, social-service agencies must often rely on a host of public- and private-sector organizations to obtain the necessary resources for continued operations. This dependency requires them to develop and maintain a delicate set of linkages with a variety of potential sources of funds and other forms of needed support. These sources include not only federal and state granting agencies but also local interest groups, community foundations, and sometimes wealthy individuals. They must "stay in touch" with the local juvenile authority and court system, the police department, schools, hospitals, newspapers, and other community agencies providing complementary services in order to accomplish their mission. In order to make it possible for the agency to accomplish its primary tasks, boundary roles are created to develop these bonds, which typically lack the certainty of formalized, contractual relations.

Linking and coordinating also take place between specific units within the organization and outside elements. The development of complex missile systems by the federal government is accomplished through the joint activities of public-sector laboratories and private-sector contractors. Often, a project office will be established in one of the government commands, and individuals occupying roles labeled "lead systems engineer" or "advanced research projects manager" may be assigned the task of coordinating the interdependent activities of departments located in organizations outside as well as inside the command.

Relations may be partially governed by legal contract or standard operating procedures, but these formal coordinative devices seldom apply to all parts of the puzzle. When they do apply, they frequently get in the way of the coordinative process, especially when the project is complex and interdependent, requiring mutual adjustments in service of an uncertain, state-of-the-art objective. The boundary-role person is needed to provide the essential function of facilitating communications and responsiveness between the project units.

Before leaving the *functions* of organization boundary roles, it is important to emphasize that, although each function is conceptually distinct, boundary spanners are likely to perform more than one function. *Gatekeepers* must maintain *linkages* between information sources and targets; *representatives* often *protect* the organizations. Yet, although boundary roles are probably best treated as various mixes of some of these functions, the functions themselves will be related to different individual outcomes and require different staffing criteria. Moreover, different functions will be required depending on the nature of the context in which the organization must operate.

SOME FACTORS INFLUENCING THE NUMBER AND NATURE OF BOUNDARY ROLES AND UNITS

What factors cause organizational decision-makers to create boundary-spanning units and roles? What environmental and organizational conditions are sources of variation that must be considered in the design and management of organization boundary units and roles?

Although all organizations engage to some degree in boundary-spanning activities, if only at the level of chief executive of-

ficer or small enterprise entrepreneur, these activities may be formalized into full-time positions and permanent units or they may exist in conjunction with more conventional internal organizational activities on an informal, ad hoc basis.

ORGANIZATIONAL SIZE

A small organization is able to survive with a fairly simple formal structure so long as essential functions—technical, managerial, and institutional-adaptive—are performed informally. In fact, one may observe the gradual elaboration of formal structure as an owner-founder of a small enterprise begins to "shed" some responsibilities for technical, managerial, or institutional-adaptive activities with firm growth. The important point is that, although informal in nature, boundary-spanning functions must nonetheless be performed as required, and the neglect of these functions is dramatically illustrated in the high attrition rate of new businesses.

ORGANIZATIONAL ENVIRONMENT

Features of the external environment of the organization or unit obviously exert an important influence on the types of boundary-spanning activities and structures that are required. Organizations confronted with external environments high in complexity and turbulence, especially when coupled with low environmental "receptivity," will tend to have a higher proportion of boundary roles to successfully adapt than will those operating in more stable, simple, and receptive environments. Moreover, the more critical these contingencies, the more attention will be devoted to the explicit formalization and staffing of the boundary role.

The structures of boundary-spanning units should correspond to the complexity of the external environment. An organization deals with environmental complexity—the number of different, important environmental components or segments—by functionally differentiating its overall structure and, hence, its boundary-spanning structure. Complexity demands complexity.

★THE PARADOX OF ROUTINENESS

A paradox of routineness appears to govern boundary-spanning activities. Those activities that are structured nonroutinely to deal with unpredictable environments or technologies offer boundary spanners the benefits of enhanced power, autonomy, and upward and outward job mobility; however, they also expose them to high levels of job conflict and stress. Therefore, attempts to reduce conflicts and stresses of the boundary role by routinizing its activities paradoxically serve to reduce the power and autonomy that usually accompany nonroutine activities. As a consequence, both the design and staffing of organization boundary roles must take into account the needs of the personnel involved and the nature of the contingencies that they are asked to manage on behalf of the organization.

Management Practice

■ The Paradoxical Twins: Acme and Omega Electronics

PART I

In 1955, Technological Products of Erie, Pa., was bought out by a Cleveland manufacturer. The Cleveland firm had no interest in the electronics division of Technological Products and subsequently sold to different investors two plants which manufactured printed circuit boards. One of the plants, located in nearby Waterford, Pa., was renamed Acme Electronics and the other plant, within the city limits of Erie, was renamed Omega Electronics Inc. Acme retained its original management and upgraded its general manager to president. Omega hired a new president, who had been a director of a large electronics research laboratory, and upgraded several of the existing personnel within the plant.

Acme and Omega often competed for the same contracts. As subcontractors both firms benefited from the electronics boom of the early 1960s and both looked forward to future growth and expansion. Acme had annual sales of $10 million and employed 550 people. Omega had annual sales of $8 million and employed 480 people. Acme was consistently more effective than Omega and regularly achieved greater net profits, much to the chagrin of Omega's management.

Inside Acme

The president of Acme, John Tyler, credited his firm's greater effectiveness to his manag-

---

This case was developed with material gathered from the two firms by Dr. John F. Veiga. All names and places have been disguised.

er's abilities to run a "tight ship." He explained that he had retained the basic structure developed by Technological Products because it was most efficient for high volume manufacture of printed circuits and their subsequent assembly. Tyler was confident that had the demand not been so great, its competitor would not have survived. "In fact," he said, "we have been able to beat Omega regularly for the most profitable contracts thereby increasing our profits." Acme's basic organization structure is shown in exhibit 2.8. People were generally satisfied with their work at Acme; however, some of the managers voiced the desire to have a little more latitude in their jobs. One manager characterized the president as a "one-man band." He said, "While I respect John's ability, there are times when I wish I had a little more information about what is going on."

Inside Omega

Omega's president, Jim Rawls, did not believe in organization charts. He felt that his organization had departments similar to Acme's but he thought the plant was small enough that things such as organization charts just put artificial barriers between specialists who should be working together. Written memos were not allowed since, as Jim expressed it, "The plant is small enough that if people want to communicate they can just drop by and talk things over." Other members of Omega complained that too much time was wasted "filling in" people who could not contribute to problems and

EXHIBIT 2.8   Acme Electronics Organization Chart

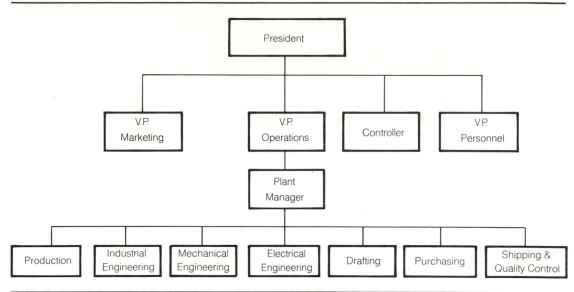

solutions. As the Head of the Mechanical Engineering Department expressed it, "Jim spends too much of his time and mine making sure everyone understands what we're doing and listening to suggestions." A newer member of the Industrial Engineering Department said, "When I first got here, I wasn't sure what I was supposed to do.

One day I worked with some mechanical engineers and the next day I helped the shipping department design some packing cartons. The first months on the job were hectic but at least I got a real feel for what makes Omega tick." Most decisions of any significance were made by the management team at Omega.

■ ANALYSIS QUESTIONS

1. How would you describe the management systems utilized by Omega and Acme? What factors led you to this conclusion?

2. How can you explain Acme's effectiveness in contrast to Omega's? What factors might change it?

PART II

In 1966, the integrated circuits began to cut deeply into the demand for printed circuit boards. The integrated circuits (IC) or "chips" were the first step into micro-miniaturization in the electronics industry. Be-

cause the manufacturing process for ICs was a closely guarded secret, both Acme and Omega realized the potential threat to their futures and both began to seek new customers aggressively. In July 1966, one of the major photocopy manufacturers was looking for a subcontractor to assemble the memory unit for their new experimental copier. The projected contract for the job was estimated to be $5 to $7 million in annual sales. Both Acme and Omega were geographically close to this manufacturer and both had submitted highly competitive bids for the production of one hundred prototypes. Acme's bid was slightly lower than Omega's; however, both firms were asked to produce one hundred units. The photocopy manufacturer told both firms that speed was critical because their president had boasted to other manufacturers that they would have a finished copier available by Christmas. This boast, much to the designer's dismay, required pressure on all subcontractors to begin prototype production before final design of the copier was complete. This meant that Acme and Omega would have at most two weeks to produce the prototypes or delay the final copier production.

■ ANALYSIS QUESTION

Which firm do you think will produce the best results? Why?

PART III

Inside Acme

As soon as John Tyler was given the blueprints (Monday, July 11, 1966), he sent a memo to the Purchasing Department requesting them to move forward on the purchase of all necessary materials. At the same time, he sent the blueprints to the Drafting Department and asked that they prepare manufacturing prints. The Industrial Engineering Department was told to begin methods design work for use by the Production Department supervisors. Tyler also sent a memo to all department heads and executives indicating the critical time constraints of this job and how he expected that everyone would perform as efficiently as they had in the past. On Wednesday, July 13, Purchasing discovered that a particular component used in the memory unit could not be purchased or shipped for two weeks because the manufacturer had shut down for summer vacations. The Head of Purchasing was not overly concerned by this obstacle because he knew that Omega would face the same problem. He advised Tyler of this predicament who in turn decided that Acme would build the memory unit except for the one component and then add that component in two weeks. Industrial Engineering was told to build this constraint into their assembly methods. On Friday, July 15, Industrial Engineering notified Tyler that the missing component would substantially increase the assembly time if it was not available from the start of assembly. Mr. Tyler, anxious to get started, suggested he would live with that problem and gave the signal to go forward on the assembly plans. Mechanical Engineering received manufacturing prints on Tuesday, July 12, and evaluated their capabilities for making the chassis required for the memory unit. Because their procedure for prototypes was to get estimates from outside vendors on all sheet metal work before they authorized in-house personnel to do the job, the Head of Mechanical Engineering sent a memo to the Head of Drafting requesting vendor prints be drawn up on the chassis and that these prints then be forwarded to Purchasing who would obtain vendor bids. On Friday, July 15, Mr. Tyler called the Head of Mechanical Engineering and asked for a progress report on the chassis. He was advised that Mechanical Engineering was waiting for vendor estimates before they moved forward.

Mr. Tyler was shocked by the lack of progress and demanded that Mechanical Engineering begin building those "damn chassis." On Monday, July 18, Mr. Tyler received word from the Shipping Department that most of the components had arrived. The first chassis were sent to the Head of Production who began immediately to set up an assembly area. On Tuesday, July 19, two Methods Engineers from Industrial Engineering went out to the production floor to set up the methods to be used in assembly. In his haste to get things going, the Production Foreman ignored the normal procedure of contacting the Methods Engineers and set up what he thought would be an efficient assembly process. The Methods Engineers were very upset to see assembly begin before they had a chance to do a proper layout. They told the foreman they had spent the entire weekend analyzing the motions needed and that his process was very inefficient and not well-balanced. The Methods Engineers ordered that work be stopped until they could rearrange the assembly process. The Production Foreman refused to stop work. He said, "I have to have these units produced by Friday and already I'm behind schedule."

The Methods Engineers reported back to the Head of Industrial Engineering who immediately complained to the plant manager. The Plant Manager sided with the Production Foreman and said, "John Tyler wants these units by Friday. Don't bother me with methods details now. Once we get the prototypes out and go into full production then your boys can do their thing." As the Head of Industrial Engineering got off the phone with the Plant Manager, he turned to his subordinates and said, "If my boss doesn't think our output is needed, to hell with him! You fellows must have other jobs to worry about, forget this one." As the two Methods Engineers left the Head Industrial Engineer's office, one of them said to the other, "Just wait until they try to install those missing components. Without our methods, they'll have to tear down the units almost completely."

On Thursday, July 21, the final units were being assembled although the process was delayed several times as Production waited for chassis from Mechanical Engineering to be completed. On Friday, July 22, the last units were finished while John Tyler paced around the plant. Late that afternoon, Tyler received a phone call from the head designer of the photocopier manufacturer who told Tyler that he had received a call on Wednesday from Jim Rawls of Omega. He explained that Rawls' boys had found an error in the design of the connector cable and had taken corrective action on their prototypes. He told Tyler that he checked out the design error and that Omega was right. Tyler, a bit overwhelmed by this information, told the designer that he had all the memory units ready for shipment and that as soon as they received the missing component, on Monday or Tuesday, they would be able to deliver the final units. The designer explained that the design error would be rectified in a new blueprint he was sending over by messenger and that he would hold Acme to the delivery date on Tuesday.

When the blueprint arrived, Tyler called the Production Foreman in to assess the damages. The alterations in the design would call for total disassembly and the unsoldering of several connections. Tyler told the foreman to put extra people on the alterations first thing on Monday morning and try to finish the job by Tuesday. Late Tuesday afternoon the alterations were finished and the missing components were delivered. Wednesday morning, the Production Foreman discovered that the units would have to be torn apart again to install the missing components. When John Tyler was told this, he "hit the roof." He called Industrial Engineering and asked if they could help out. The Head of Industrial Engineering told Tyler that his people would study the situation and get back to him first thing in the morning. Tyler decided to wait for their study because he was concerned that tearing apart the units again could weaken several of the soldered contacts and increase their potential rejection. Thursday, after several heated debates between the

Production Foreman and the Methods Engineers, John Tyler settled the argument by ordering that all units be taken apart again and the missing component installed. He told Shipping to prepare cartons for delivery on Friday afternoon. On Friday, July 29, fifty prototypes were shipped from Acme without final inspection. John Tyler was concerned about his firm's reputation so he waived the final inspection after he personally tested one unit and found it operational. On Tuesday, August 2, Acme shipped the last fifty units.

Inside Omega

Jim Rawls called a meeting on Friday, July 8, that included department heads to tell them about the potential contract they were to receive. He told them that as soon as he received the blueprints, work could begin. On Monday, July 11, the prints arrived and again the department heads met to discuss the project. At the end of the meeting, Drafting had agreed to prepare manufacturing prints while Industrial Engineering and Production would begin methods design. On Wednesday, July 13, at a progress report session, Purchasing indicated a particular component would not be available for two weeks until the manufacturer reopened from summer vacation shutdown. The Head of Electrical Engineering suggested using a possible substitute component, which was made in Japan, containing all the necessary characteristics. The Head of Industrial Engineering promised to have the Methods Engineers study the assembly methods to see if the unit could be produced in such a way that the missing component could be installed last.

The Head of Mechanical Engineering raised the concern that the chassis would be an obstacle if they waited for vendor estimates and advised the group that his people would begin production even though it might cost more. On Friday, July 15, at a progress report session, Industrial Engineering reported that the missing component would increase the assembly time substantially. The Head of Electrical Engineering offered to have one of his engineers examine the missing component specifications and said he was confident that the Japanese component would work. At the end of the meeting, Purchasing was told to order the Japanese components.

On Monday, July 18, a Methods Engineer and the production foreman formulated the assembly plans and production was set to begin on Tuesday morning. On Monday afternoon, people from Mechanical Engineering, Electrical Engineering, Production, and Industrial Engineering got together to produce a prototype just to insure that there would be no snags in production. While they were building the unit, they discovered an error in the connector cable design. All the engineers agreed, after checking and rechecking the blueprints, that the cable was erroneously designed. People from Mechanical Engineering and Electrical Engineering spent Monday night redesigning the cable and on Tuesday morning the Drafting Department finalized the changes in the manufacturing prints. On Tuesday morning, Jim Rawls was a bit apprehensive about the design changes and decided to get formal approval. Rawls received word on Wednesday from the head designer of the photocopier firm that he could proceed with the design changes as discussed on the phone. On Friday, July 22, the final units were inspected by Quality Control and then they were shipped.

■ ANALYSIS QUESTIONS

1. How can you explain the differences between what happened at Acme and Omega?

2. What do you predict will happen to the final contract? Why?

PART IV

Retrospect

Ten of Acme's final memory units were ultimately defective while all of Omega's units passed the photocopier firm's tests. The photocopier firm was disappointed with Acme's delivery delay and incurred further delays in repairing the defective Acme units. However, rather than give the entire contract to one firm, the final contract was split between Acme and Omega with two directives added: (1) maintain zero defects and (2) reduce final cost. In 1967, through extensive cost-cutting efforts, Acme reduced its unit cost by 20 percent and was ultimately awarded the total contract.

■ ANALYSIS QUESTIONS

1. How can this turn-about be explained?

2. If you were to counsel the presidents of Acme and Omega, what advice would you give each one concerning future survival?

■ The Power Brokers

JAMES M. PERRY

The local lobbyists for General Electric Co. call their rival in the manufacture of aircraft engines, United Technologies Corp., "Brand X." United Technologies lobbyists call GE the "lightbulb company." They don't like each other much.

It's hardly surprising. Their companies are locked in a battle over which will produce some $10 billion in military jet engines during the next decade. United Technologies, through its Pratt & Whitney division, has most of the fighter-engine business now; GE wants to steal it away.

Heading United Technologies' save-the-engines team is the man in charge of its capital office, 59-year-old Clark MacGregor, the prototypical Washington insider. A burly, good-natured figure, he was a Republican Congressman from Minnesota for a decade, served in the Nixon White House as a Capitol Hill lobbyist and then directed President Nixon's 1972 campaign (in which, participants agree, he was kept in blissful ignorance of the Watergate activities).

He and his United Technologies colleagues have assumed the role of underdog.

"They [GE] would like to wipe us out," Mr. MacGregor says. His deputy adds, partly in jest, "We're just a little company trying to get along."

In fact, these are both giant corporations; GE is No. 10 on the *Fortune* "500" list with $25 billion of annual sales, United Technologies No. 21 with more than $12 billion in sales.

The great engine fight is a typical three-ring circus—the contractors, the military, the Congress—different only in that the stakes are unusually large. It is what Washington corporate offices were created for—to listen, to evangelize, finally to bring the big guns to bear in support of the company's interest.

More than 500 corporate offices—little two-man shops and huge outfits with 100 or more professional employes—are in Washington. United Technologies, with forty-one professionals, is somewhere in the middle.

"Generally," says Larry Smith, a veteran Capitol Hill staffer, "Washington offices are a mess. Much of what they do is simply gross. They tend to be excited, ignorant, hysterical. They live by rumor."

United Technologies' office, Mr. Smith says (and others agree), is better than that. "They are mean and lean," adds Gordon Adams, the author of *The Iron Triangle*, a book about defense contracting.

Mr. MacGregor is the star.

"He's our contact man, he's out front for us," says Francis Murphy, United Technologies' vice-president for public relations. (Mr. MacGregor, officially, is the senior vice-president for external affairs.)

Like Robert Gray, president of Gray & Co., the Washington public-relations firm, Mr. MacGregor is a man about town, though in a somewhat more subdued and purposeful way. Critics say he is a little pompous, but he belies that by the poster on the door of his office. It shows the back of an attractive lady tennis player. Her skirt is hitched up over her hip. She is wearing nothing under it.

Mr. MacGregor explains how he operates on the job: "I see high-ranking people at the White House, in the Congress, and at the Defense Department. I see [White House Chief of Staff] Jim Baker and his wife a lot. I go to a campaign fundraiser for [Sen.] Dick Lugar [of Indiana], and I see [Sen.] John Tower [of Texas]. We remember things. I remember he came to Minnesota to campaign for me. He remembers I went to Texas to campaign for him." Sen.

Tower is the chairman of the Armed Services Committee.

"I might find myself sitting next to Ursula Meese [the wife of White House Counselor Edwin Meese] at a concert at Wolf Trap. When these occasions arise, I talk about the need for competition in the industry. I talk about the money that will be saved by multiyear contracts."

In case Mrs. Meese should wonder, "competition in the industry" means that Pratt & Whitney should continue to make those engines. And "multiyear contracts" means that the Sikorsky group's Black Hawk helicopter should be financed over a period of several years, not, as it is now, one year at a time. These are the company's two principal lobbying goals.

Mr. MacGregor entertains quietly at home. "A few old comrades from Congress will drop by," he says. He also entertains more lavishly at larger dinner parties in places like the East Wing of the National Gallery of Art. His boss, Harry Gray, the company chairman, will often show up for those affairs.

"Our goal," Mr. MacGregor says, "is to make sure no decision-maker should ever cast a vote without knowing where we stand." That goal was reinforced when Mr. Gray encountered a Congressman who said he was surprised to hear that United Technologies was interested in the government work under discussion. "Harry Gray let it be known in no uncertain terms he never wanted to hear anything like that again," Mr. MacGregor says.

"Access" is a big word in Washington. Mr. MacGregor is important to the company because, with his contacts, he can supply access to important people when the company wants to deliver a message. It is unspoken, but not forgotten, that Secretary of State Alexander Haig is the former president of United Technologies and that sometime he might be back at headquarters in Hartford, Conn. United Technologies' rivals suggest, churlishly, that Secretary Haig continues to put in a good word for the old company. But there isn't any evidence of that.

From time to time, Mr. MacGregor also plays hard-ball politics. He directs his own company's political-action committee, which distributed $140,200 to candidates in 1980—$108,750 to 165 Republicans, $31,450 to 64 Democrats. He is also the principal adviser for the U.S. Chamber of Commerce's PAC. "He's too partisan," grumbles a political adviser for a Democratic Congressman who was burned by a low rating from the chamber's PAC.

Mr. MacGregor played a political role, too, in the intense lobbying for the sale of Awacs planes—powered by Pratt & Whitney engines—to Saudi Arabia. He sent telegrams to wavering Republicans saying that failure to deliver for the Saudis would bring defeat for the Republicans in 1982.

Leading the parade. So Mr. MacGregor leads the parade, waves the flag, entertains the guests and hands out the good-conduct badges. The heavy day-to-day detail work is done by the troops back in the ranks.

A Washington office for a large diversified corporation—and United Technologies fits that bill—is a peculiar creature. At United Technologies, Mr. MacGregor is at the top, but only three other people on the corporate payroll report directly to him. The other thirty-seven professionals work for the various corporate divisions, called groups, that include Pratt & Whitney engines, Sikorsky helicopters, Carrier air conditioning, Otis elevators and Essex wire. They report directly to the heads of their individual groups. "A dotted line runs between these people and me," Mr. MacGregor explains.

"It is typical of these large corporations," a Senate staffer says, "that lines of authority are often unclear. Sometimes that causes tension and even chaos."

Mr. MacGregor's right-hand man, reporting directly to him, is Hugh Witt, the kind of expert technician that is filling up more and more Washington corporate offices. Mr.

Witt served eighteen years as a civilian specialist in logistics and procurement for the Air Force and the Navy, then worked for the Office of Management and Budget, setting up the first Office of Federal Procurement Policy.

Indemnification issue. Mr. Witt worries about things that affect the entire corporation, things such as indemnification and strategic minerals.

Indemnification—who pays if the space shuttle falls down in the middle of New York, for instance—"is dull as hell," Mr. Witt says, "but we're talking about what could be billions of dollars. All contractors (and United Technologies is one of them) aren't very well indemnified on the Space Shuttle" with the National Aeronautics and Space Administration, he adds. Indemnification is better with the Defense Department. Contractors wouldn't be nearly so desperate if a flight of F16 fighters crashed in Manhattan.

United Technologies, in a common tactic, joined a coalition to push legislation through Congress to change the indemnification procedure and bring NASA into line. Allies include the Chamber of Commerce and the Aerospace Industries Association.

Asked what role Mr. MacGregor takes in these detailed negotiations, Mr. Witt says, "Oh, hell, that's too technical for him."

But everything pales into insignificance in comparison to United Technologies' trouble with its F100 jet engine, which powers the Air Force's front-line F15 and F16 fighter planes.

When the engine works, it's a marvel. The F15, with two of the engines, can climb straight up and streak horizontally at two and a half times the speed of sound. The problem is, the engines sometimes stall, even break apart. Planes occasionally crash.

Central figure. The crucial man for the engine in Washington is Eugene Tallia, vice-president of the Pratt & Whitney group. He doesn't report directly to Mr. MacGregor and conceivably could refuse to take instructions from him. He reports directly to Robert Carlson, the head of the Power Group, with offices in East Hartford.

"We say flatly we have fixed the engine with the design changes now going into production," Mr. Tallia says.

But the Air Force remains skeptical. To cover its bet, it asked GE to develop an alternative engine, the F101DFE. This is the engine that GE hopes will wipe Pratt & Whitney out as far as the fighter market goes (18 percent of United Technologies' business).

"When we began developing the F100 for the F15," said Gen. Alton Slay when he ran the Air Force's Air Systems Command, "we were in a high-performance frame of mind. We wanted the flashiest, best fighter in the world. So we made Pratt & Whitney push the state of the art."

Says United Technologies' Mr. Witt, "They demanded the last 5 percent we could give them." Pratt & Whitney's Mr. Tallia adds, "We traded off durability for performance."

Experts' role grows. The technology of weapons systems has become so complicated that members of Congress lean more and more on the expertise of their professional staffs. "What happens when the Senate and House committees go into conference is extraordinary," says Democratic Sen. Gary Hart of Colorado. "The Senate staffers will argue the merits of one weapons system. The House staffers will argue the other side. We just sit there and watch the argument like it was a Ping-Pong ball."

GE lobbyists pursue their strategy by taking not-so-sly digs at the Pratt & Whitney engine. They call it "the Turkey." They roll out press releases extolling the performance of their own engine, which is a fighter version of the engine that they designed for the B1 bomber. It is simpler, it may be more durable, and it has more power.

The Air Force will decide in the next few weeks how—and when—it should run a competition between the engines.

United Technologies wants no part of that. "That's no competition," Mr. Witt says. "They'd win."

Back-and-forth debate. United Technologies' lobbyists grumble that GE has received $150 million for its engine—and there's another $54.5 million for it in the new 1983 budget. Ominously for United Technologies, the Air Force says the new money will bring the engine into "full-scale" production. GE people say the government has spent more than $500 million to fix the Pratt & Whitney engine—and there's $48 million in the new budget for more fixes.

Just wait, says United Technologies; it will ultimately cost $650 million to develop the new GE engine, and it will have bugs, too. "There never was an engine without a problem," Mr. Tallia says, adding that he prefers to call them "service-revealed difficulties" when they show up in a Pratt & Whitney product.

United Technologies' strategy seems to be to delay the competition a year or more while it develops, with government funds that it doesn't have yet, a new and more powerful engine that would stack up with GE's.

Getting the money will require congressional help, and, again, United Technologies contends that GE has the upper hand. "We're only big in maybe twenty congressional districts," Mr. Tallia says. "GE is big in 200 congressional districts. That's what we're up against."

One recent coup. United Technologies isn't exactly helpless, though. GE admits that its rival pulled a coup last year when it won $17.5 million in government money to start designing that more powerful engine.

But folks at United Technologies were disappointed when they were unable to find anything in the new fiscal 1983 budget to continue the work. It is no wonder, then, that they breathed a sigh of relief when a Pentagon official, Richard Delauer, told a

House subcommittee on March 4 that efforts to ''upgrade'' the Pratt & Whitney engine ''will proceed.''

And they were delighted to be told that $8 million for the work was actually squirreled away in an obscure corner of the budget.

Mr. MacGregor modestly attributes the victory to Pratt & Whitney's engineers. He admits, though, he might have had a minor role in convincing members of Congress that a prototype of the new engine should be built.

Next step: to convince the Congress and the Air Force that the more powerful engine should go into production and that it should be the one tested against the GE engine. A lobbyist's work is never done.

■ Managing by Mystique at Tandem Computers

MYRON MAGNET

It's 4:30 on Friday afternoon, and the weekly beer bust is in full swing at Tandem Computers' Cupertino, California, headquarters. Sun shines on the basketball court beyond the corporate patio and sparkles on the company swimming pool. Programmer A, bearded like a mountain man, is discussing stock options and tax-law changes while dancing in place to the secret music he hears in his own conversation. Earnest Programmer B, clinching his point about Silicon Valley culture by noting that the Programmer Bs have more married than single friends, turns to greet with a soulful kiss a convivial employee his visitor mistakes for Mrs. B.

Five hundred cheerfully bibulous souls, mostly young and casual-looking, are talking animatedly, glass in hand; and the same genial scene is being reenacted on a smaller scale at Tandem offices as far afield as Omaha or Kowloon. Every week 60 percent of the company drops in at the beer bust for an hour, joined sometimes by visiting customers or suppliers, who take away indelible memories. Says the representative of one satisfied user, a stately major bank, ''When the president comes down in a cowboy hat and boots and swills beer—that's different!''

The fun's not confined to Fridays. Take the company's last Halloween costume party, which filled most of a gigantic warehouse. The merriment was heightened by the granting of a 100-share stock option to every employee. Another big event has left its mark, too, on a sunny, modest office belonging to the vice-president of software development, who's one of Tandem's phalanx of mid-thirtyish millionaires. With nondescript steel furniture and a humid display of potted plants, it's indistinguishable from any other Tandem executive's office, including the president's—except for the red satin sash on the wall, bearing the legend ''Incredible Hunk,'' won a while ago by the vice-president himself. He and another Tandemite outshone thirty-odd gym-shorts-

Reprinted from June 28, 1982 issue of *Fortune Magazine,* by special permission. Copyright © 1982 Time Inc.

clad male opponents in a headquarters-wide beauty contest sponsored by the company's female employees.

Growth Without a Hiccup

Can this company be serious? Meteoric growth and surging profits say it is. Only 7½ years old and already a more than $300-million-a-year operation, it's one of the bright stars of the *Fortune* "Second 500" list and seems inexorably growing to "First 500" magnitude. This isn't only because its Nonstop II system—the computer that's never down—is an estimable machine, commanding a market only recently contested. As Ulric Weil, a Morgan Stanley security analyst, puts it, "No company could be as successful as Tandem is—without a hiccup—unless its management were gifted and kept its finger on the tiller."

Indeed, all the corporate high jinks play their part in an elaborate management scheme conceived largely by Tandem's founder-president, James G. Treybig (pronounced *Try*-big), a 41-year-old Texan whose hands-in-pockets slouch and untucked shirttail give him the incongruous air of a teenager hanging out on Main Street. Freewheeling theorizing comes naturally to Jimmy T., as Tandemites call him. Yet he's no idle daydreamer. Before he started Tandem he fleshed out his engineering BS and Stanford MBA with several years in sales and marketing at Texas Instruments and Hewlett-Packard and in venture capital at San Francisco's high-flying Kleiner Perkins Caufield & Byers partnership. He speaks, in his lovingly preserved Texas twang, from experience.

"Jim Treybig sometimes likes to shock people," says Samuel Wiegand, 50, Tandem's former marketing VP. The result, according to software-development VP Dennis McEvoy (the aforementioned Hunk), is that "a lot of people when they meet Jim for the first time think he's a bullshitter, just shuckin' and jivin'." Certainly getting to the heart of his management theory requires pushing through an exotic tangle of rhetoric about how the company represents "the conver-

gence of capitalism and humanism" or how it tries to foster not just its employees but also their spouses and "spouse equivalents." What's more, Treybig (himself married and the father of three) is given to reducing complexity to a simplicity more elegant than true, as in his five cardinal points for running a company, beginning with the at least debatable assertion that "all people are good".

Is there anything in this provocative talk that other CEOs should be listening to? The answer comes down to yes, but. Behind the verbiage is a cluster of hard-headed policies, many of them familiar in high-tech companies, especially in the Bay Area, and some of them applicable to other businesses. But the swaggering tone also points to something in Tandem that's far out, even for California, and that every company wouldn't want.

Generous stock options aimed at riveting employees' attention on the business's success are nothing new in high-tech companies, though perhaps none has gone so far as Tandem, where *every* employee gets gift options. This can mean real money: Tandem's stock has risen steeply from the start, and each employee with the company since it went public in 1977 has drawn options theoretically worth almost $100,000. So raptly attentive to corporate performance have employees become that Tandem now posts the stock price three times a day on its work-station screens; formerly too many people were monopolizing the telex machines to find out. A forceful promotion-from-within policy, so diligently observed that three out of five new managers have risen from the ranks, similarly concentrates the mind.

Unrevolutionary too is Tandem's easy-going flexibility about working hours. As Michael Green, a company founder, puts it, "We don't want to pay people for attendance but for output." So time clocks are out, and managers often don't know just how long their subordinates toil, though indicators like the position of an employee's car in the democratically first-come, first-served parking lot speak volumes to the discerning. As for jogging trails, space for dance-exercise, and yoga classes, and periodic company-supplied weekend barbecues for employees working overtime—amenities like these are not unheard of in other companies.

Treybig argues that the swimming pool, to take one example, improves productivity by giving single parents an agreeable place to park their kids, thus enabling them to work on weekends. Perhaps so—if only because all such appurtenances help spark the so-called Hawthorne effect, an increase in productivity that appears to result from *any* new attention paid to employees' working conditions or amenities. Even the beer bust, in terms of the current fashion for fostering unstructured communication across an institution's vertical and horizontal boundaries, is arguably a productivity ploy.

The Tandem Gospel

Also hardly novel is soaking employees in an endless stream of company-boosting propaganda urging loyalty, hard work, self-esteem, and respect for co-workers. But Tandem's indoctrination effort goes so far beyond the ordinary as to make clear how radical a departure the company's managerial style, taken as a whole, really is. First, there's its sheer quantity—from orientation lectures and breakfasts, newsletters, and a glossy magazine that some Tandemites call "Propaganda Quarterly" to a fat tome (standard issue to all employees) called *Understanding Our Philosophy*, supplemented by a two-day course on its finer points. This is mandatory for all employees, notes James Katzman, a company founder, though mandatory is a taboo word, for it "goes against the culture." A lavish facility to house these so-called philosophy seminars and other programs is in the planning stage.

Then there's the content, in which conventional pieties, by their vehemence of expression, take on new meaning. For instance, here's "all employees should be

treated with respect" rendered in Treybigese: "You never have the right at Tandem to screw a person or to mistreat them. It's not allowed . . . . No manager mistreats a human without a fear of their job." An aggrieved employee's ready access to anyone in the company gives this provision teeth: managers have been fired. Or take the idea that everyone in a company is essential to its success. In the Tandem ideology this platitude takes on a more egalitarian tinge than usual: Treybig dismisses with indulgent but characteristic sarcasm some German productivity experts who "had never danced with an assembly worker."

Yet the indoctrination goes further, for Tandem, in its "philosophy" book and seminars, takes pains to give each employee an understanding of the essence of the company's business and five-year plan. Folded into the philosophy book is a labyrinthine chart the size of a road map—it took two weeks of Treybig's time to draft—showing how a push on this spot of the complex system will have repercussions everywhere else. Several computers shipped late, for instance, can drop quarterly profits enough to lower the stock price, which makes raising capital more expensive, which leaves less money for research and incentives, which . . . You get the idea.

The Once-a-Month Manager

Letting employees see the big picture and peek at strategic secrets boosts loyalty. "People really get a great kick out of being part of the team and trusted with the corporate jewels," as Jim Katzman says. But the deeper purpose is to lessen the need for management by pointing everybody in the right direction and explaining what's happening on all sides of him. "Most companies are overmanaged," Treybig believes. "Most people need less management than you think." Thus at Tandem, says marketing director Gerald Peterson, stating the company's fundamental managerial principle, "the controls are not a lot of reviews or meetings or reports, but rather the control is understanding the basic concept and philosophy.'' What this means in practice, says one software designer, is that ''I speak to my manager about once a month—that's how often my manager manages me.''

Not everyone can work this way, so hiring is crucial at Tandem. The philosophy, aiming to curb the all-too-human tendency of institutions to clog themselves with unthreatening mediocrities and yes-men, nags managers to choose smarter or more qualified people than themselves and not to ''hire in their own image.'' Normally, only proved and experienced applicants get considered—which incidentally insures Tandem a steady flow of new ideas from other companies—and grueling interviews, sometimes twenty hours of them, put candidates through the wringer. Tandem's managers, not its essentially administrative personnel office, do all the hiring; prospective co-workers interview applicants too. ''A manager will never hire somebody his people don't think is good,'' says a programmer. ''Basically, he says will you work with this person, and you say yes or no.'' As a result, new employees are on their way to integration into the community even before their first day on the job.

Without question this system works. Tandem's productivity figures are among the highest in the industry; even shipping clerks don't seem just to go through the motions by rote. As to imbuing employees with zeal for the company's success—one satisfied customer speaks of a service technician who gladly gave out his home phone number, cheerfully took an emergency call at 2:30 in the morning, and turned up, toolbox in hand, at 6 A.M.

Yet this managerial style can't be applied indiscriminately to all businesses. What makes it work at Tandem is its close fit to that company's special circumstances. For instance, aiming everybody in the same direction and keeping supervision light makes sense in a company with one basic product and one clearly defined market, but it could spell chaos in a complex, diversified corporation. Lean management works well, too, in an operation with so many functions farmed out. Tandem buys most of its components from subcontractors and gets cleaned by a contract janitorial service. For all its talk about equality, the whole company is an elite, leaving the lowest functions to others.

What manufacturing Tandem does itself—in quiet, airy rooms more like labs than factories—is high-level assembly and massive testing. This requires skilled workers, self-disciplined and intelligent enough to dispense with a supervisor over each shoulder. Rare everywhere, such workers are especially hard to hire in Silicon Valley, where demand is so high that ''assembly people and operators can literally walk across the street and find work the next day,'' as Gordon Campbell, president of neighboring Seeq Technology, puts it. Stoking employee loyalty with every conceivable amenity thus becomes a matter of urgency, particularly when sky-high Valley housing costs make an influx of new assembly workers most unlikely.

But the real competition is the battle for engineering talent among the Valley's high-tech companies, all constantly making passes at each other's technical staffs. ''Once you have one of these guys,'' says Stanford computer-science Professor Edward Feigenbaum, ''you don't want to lose him. You have to coddle these people.'' Hence the Tandem swimming pool (which competes with the health clubs and hot tubs of nearby companies), the six-week sabbaticals every four years that have sent Tandemites up the mountains of Nepal or into London's Cordon Bleu cooking school, and the stock options, some of them carefully calibrated to make leaving the company before four years very expensive. Such emoluments not only stay the footloose; they've also largely kept unions out of Silicon Valley.

''The most creative computer people are the semi-freakies,'' Feigenbaum notes, and—especially in the case of the software designers who breathe the soul into Tandem's machines—they need freedom and solitude to perform their occult art. After all, the continual refining and extending of the system's intelligence, not the bolting together of components, is the essence of Tandem's business and the key to its future. "When you have a good systems-development shop, things always look to the outside observer as if they're out of control—and to some extent they are," explains John Boddie, a software consultant who writes programs for some of Tandem's customers. "It's semi-channeled chaos." Tandem's loose, flexible style reflects this industry reality.

It reflects, too, the youth of its staff, many of whom went to college in the Sixties and early Seventies, when they were at least touched by the values of the counter-culture. "I used to call those development people down at Tandem pseudo-hippies," ex-VP Wiegand says with a chuckle, "but they were terribly hard workers." That statement sums up a tension common enough in people of that generation, especially in northern California, between the claims of openness, spontaneity, non-judgmental acceptance, brotherhood, freedom, and expressiveness on the one hand, and technical proficiency coupled with personal ambition on the other. Tandem, with its youthful style, beer-bust rap sessions, high-flown egalitarianism, engineering excellence, and hefty financial incentives, resolves that conflict.

Asked if this is the right way to run a company, one personnel officer, not quite 30, sounds the authentic Tandem tone: "It's progressive. It's ahead of the times. I don't know that it's right. I don't know what's right or wrong. I know that it's very unique. It sure feels right to me: it fits in with the way I like to see people treated."

Tandemites do have a way of growing vague when they try to make sense of the company mystique. Often enough, they are reduced to quoting *Understanding Our Philosophy* as if it were Chairman Mao's Little Red Book. "Some people might call it brainwashing," says corporate-materials VP Jerald Reaugh, "but I don't think it is. I

don't think it's immoral or illegal." Treybig himself, half jokingly, makes a different analogy. "I know this sounds like religion or something," he says, adding, "It's almost like religion."

The Boss Likes That Noise

Certainly it resembles religion, at least of the sect or cult variety, in the premium it puts on inner dedication. As a programmer remarks, "I don't think someone who thought Tandem was just a job would work out, because Tandem expects commitment." Accordingly, ordeals like the prolonged interviews serve not just to hire good people but also to build loyalty by making employees feel tried and specially chosen by an exacting community. And such initiations boost dedication simply by being ordeals, for, in the economy of the emotions, people value what has cost them a lot.

All sects need a charismatic leader, and Tandem's is, of course, Treybig. "Jimmy gets almost like an evangelist when he talks about the basic people issues of running a company," says marketing director Peterson, and McEvoy allows that seeing Treybig address the Tandem staff in a huge tent in the parking lot brings unwelcome thoughts of religion to his mind. Venture capitalist Franklin "Pitch" Johnson, Jr., a Tandem director, describes the "muttering that builds up into a roar of approval" that greets Treybig at such events. "It's an acknowledgment that they believe in him and they support him," Johnson says. "Jimmy likes it when he stands up there and hears that noise—that Tandem noise—of approval." Says Yale management professor Rosabeth Moss Kanter of companies like these, "Their success makes it feel magical." Their employees, she says, feel that "we must be touched by some special gift."

Tandemites explain how all this has affected them by endless talk about how the company has helped them "grow." Like many Tandem values, this one, much emphasized in the corporate creed, is a little vague. "I can't describe it," says Richard Bixler, the company's engineering-operations manager, "but it feels pretty good. I feel like I'm accomplishing something with myself." Certainly the rich opportunities for promotion, learning, and initiative, added to the corporate culture's hold on the self-image of employees, gives them a sense of moving toward the full development of all their human potentialities. To convince employees that they are amply filling their innermost goals of self-realization as they advance the company's interest is almost a miraculous feat in itself. But the sense of self-realization Tandem's mystique produces may prove illusory, for the radiance of mystiques is, like the glow of moonshine, notoriously liable to fade.

It's on a less ineffable kind of growth—explosive corporate growth—that Tandem's system ultimately rests. This creates not only the big profits and lavish benefits, but also the acute need for new managers, rapid promotion, and the ability of employees to manage themselves that gives Tandemites

their sense of personal growth and freedom. With nearly half the employees at the company for less than six months, hierarchies are not fully defined, roles are relatively unfixed, and there's potential power and opportunity for all.

"The haunting question," says Johnson, "is, if we have a hickey on our growth rate, will this fantastic morale we've built hold up?" He foresees no such blemish, but Tandem management is working to institutionalize and codify the magic. Such devices as those philosophy seminars are preparation for the fast-approaching day when the company is too big for Treybig to dance with every employee and the day, sometime after that, when the amazing growth inevitably starts to slow. Meanwhile Treybig, by announcing plans to expand a $300-million-a-year company with 3,000-odd employees into a $1-billion one with 11,000 employees over the next three years, has promised his next faith-inspiring wonder.

■ A Japanese in the Works

The Japanese ability to take American production techniques and use them to outproduce us has baffled some industrialists. The incursion of Japanese companies on American soil confounded the issue. The Sony Corporation's plant in San Diego, for example, employs American workers under Japanese management and still outproduces American companies at the same level as similar plants that are in Japan.

The secret seems to be Japanese management techniques, judging from the work of Stanford University business professors Richard Tanner Johnson and William G. Ouchi, who undertook a comparative study of Japanese and United States businesses for the National Commission on Productivity. Based on interviews at twenty Japanese companies, Johnson and Ouchi outline several characteristics that may help explain why the Japanese methods are both more humane and, when it comes to cash, more productive.

Upward Flow

Management in Japanese companies follows a "bottom up" process, the researchers believe, in which information and ideas originate with low-level personnel close to the problems and rise through the ranks. Middle-level managers help shape and facilitate decisions as they pass them on to those above. Japanese managers expect employees to communicate laterally as well as with officials of similar rank in other functional areas of the company. Eventually, consensus on important business decisions is reached.

An example of the clash between Western and Eastern means of operations is the case of a major Japanese automotive firm that brought in several Americans as department heads. The Americans, in the American way, sat back awaiting statements of direction, objectives, and priorities from the Japanese executives above. The Japanese stood ready to respond to initiatives from below. Finally, the Americans, sensing the stall in the system, drew up an elaborate diagram outlining the hierarchy of command with neat boxes showing the complex theoretical connections between the various departments of the company and where the authority and responsibility for various decisions lay.

Flummoxed by this awesomely American document, the Japanese watched as the Americans then proceeded to concentrate on their respective functional roles, expecting the top executives to coordinate their efforts from above, as is usual in American companies. To the Japanese, it seemed "as if the various departments were separate companies, all competing against each other," as one Japanese executive described the Americans' efforts in corporations.

Fewer Barriers

In most Japanese firms, there are few private offices, the symbols of status and authority from which most American industry is commanded. Managers and subordinates work in the same areas without walls to keep them from questioning one anothers' methods and talking over any problems that arise. Another distinctive difference is that the Japanese handle their employees with an almost paternalistic concern for their personal problems, which American bosses believe workers should leave at home. Perhaps as a result, absenteeism and turnover rates are low in most Japanese-owned firms.

American companies could learn much from the ways of the Japanese, the researchers believe. Some of our pioneer cultural emphasis on independence, competition, and ambition may at times be inappropriate in the complex organizations in which most modern Americans work. "The West could accommodate ten thousand John Waynes spread over the vast landscape," say Johnson and Ouchi. "But millions of John Waynes employed under ten thousand roofs may not, in the long run, prove workable."

■ Coaxing a Broiler to Fly

HICKS B. WALDRON

In considering how to approach what to say to you this morning, I could have gone a couple ways. As a CEO who is and has been very personally and very deeply involved in the strategic planning process, I could have discussed the theory, the process, skimmed over a few examples—and left you with a typical "Here's how we do it in our company" message. Or I could get into the guts and nuts and bolts of a single real-life situation in which everything we know about strategic planning was brought into play—to turn around a business—and succeeded. I selected the latter, partly because I suspect you're exposed to about all the theory you can handle, and partly because I'm proud of the accomplishment, and proud of the role that strategic planning played in one of the most significant turn-arounds in U.S. business history—Kentucky Fried Chicken. I warn you in advance, I'll be throwing nuts and bolts at you—and some feathers and eggs—for the next twenty minutes or so.

Kentucky Fried Chicken, one of Heublein's biggest groups, wasn't doing too well late in 1976. Wall Street analysts and all the business publications were talking about the fact that we had a sick chick on our hands. Actually, it was really a pretty big bird that was ailing. KFC had 842 company-owned stores and 3,230 franchised units in the United States with

Remarks given by Hicks B. Waldron, Chief Executive Officer, Heublein, Inc., on May 14, 1982, at the Eastern Academy of Management Annual Meeting (Baltimore, MD). Reprinted by permission of Heublein, Inc.

sales of $1.1 billion. In addition, we had 295 company and 416 franchised stores abroad with sales of $240 million. Outsiders didn't agree on the root causes of the problems, but they did agree that KFC's problems were terminal. However, one fellow knew exactly what the problems were. KFC's founder, 86-year-old Colonel Sanders, said that the chicken was awful, and the cole slaw, mashed potatoes, and gravy were worse. The Colonel announced his findings to a reporter of the *New York Times*, which was unfortunate, because the Colonel's shot was heard 'round the world. More unfortunate, however, was the fact that, with regard to our company-owned operations, he was right.

In defense of our subsidiary, I should point out that we had purchased a sickly system in 1971. We didn't realize how sick it was at the time, nor did we fully appreciate that it wasn't getting better, because it appeared to be growing. Total sales and profits from the system increased, lulling us into a belief that we were moving. But when the effects of inflation were stripped away, we found that KFC's per-store sales had been flat before we bought the chain in 1971. That disheartening performance had been masked by the addition of new outlets, both franchised and company, and by the revenues of some new products.

To find out why we weren't growing in real terms at the store level, we had commissioned a study in the fall of 1976. It was the most comprehensive consumer research study ever conducted by us. When it was completed later that year, it confirmed everything the Colonel had said—and more.

Our service wasn't fast, and it was frequently surly. Our chicken wasn't consistent—sometimes old and dry, sometimes overcooked and greasy, and only sometimes "Finger-lickin' Good." Our cole slaw, mashed potatoes, and gravy and even our dinner roll all got poor marks. Frequently our hot foods weren't very hot and our cold foods weren't very cold. Our prices were also too high. Nobody could remember what our advertising theme was, but they did remember that we had frequent discounts. Our facilities were perceived as being out of date, with too much plastic and not enough cleaning. In virtually every respect, our competitors outscored us by a wide margin. Other than that, things were pretty good, thank you.

How do you go about a top-to-bottom overhaul of a system with some 5,000 stores? We started by developing a strategic plan, which had its base in the research study that had identified our problems. That consumer and competitive orientation is critical. It's one of the characteristics that differentiate a strategic plan from an old-fashioned business plan. There are at least six of these characteristics that you should keep in mind as I tell you the saga of the Kentucky Fried Chicken turnaround:

1. External orientation. In a strategic plan, all changes, all programs and actions are made in the context of consumers, competitors, the economy, and other external environmental factors.

2. Critical issues. A strategic plan carefully identifies critical issues, or success factors, which are derived from an in-depth analysis of the industry and what it takes to succeed.

3. Comprehensive. Strategic planning isn't a single great idea, but a comprehensive identification of sound programs that are multi-disciplinary and mutually reinforcing.

4. Implementation. Strategic planning provides for the translation of strategic concepts into implemented action plans.

5. Administration. Strategic planning provides for administrative systems that force and monitor action plans.

6. Resource allocation. Another tenet of strategic planning is that enough resources must be provided to win.

With these six points in mind, let's get on with the story.

We needed to move quickly to develop and implement our plan, because by the time the marketing research study was completed, our sales—which had been flat—were now declining. Indeed many industry observers had decided that KFC was a dead bird, beyond saving. I shouldn't leave you with the impression that KFC had been running without a plan. But, unfortunately, planning had been viewed as a once-a-year chore, an interruption to the job of running the business that could be forgotten once the plan was drafted. It should have been—as it is now—a tool for managing the business on a day-to-day basis.

Starting in January 1977, a strategic plan was developed. We reemphasized our mission at KFC: It was to become the strongest, most profitable, and fastest growing chain in its segment of the quick-service restaurant industry. Our objective was—and is—to satisfy our customers better than our competitors could and to reach specific share and financial goals.

Setting objectives and goals was easy. Achieving them was obviously going to be something else. The first thing that the new KFC management did was to identify the critical issues. Critical issues have been defined as those things that—if you don't do them right—will kill you. There were ten of these: Quality, Service, Cleanliness, Value, Facilities, something we called Other Operating Factors, which I'll explain in a minute, Advertising, Merchandising, Promotion and franchise relations. They came to be known by the acronym QSCVFOOFAMPF. For each of these critical issues, we developed a strategy. In the area of food quality, for instance, our strategy was simply to provide our customers with better quality products than any of our competitors could. We were going to give them the best chicken, the best mashed potatoes and gravy, and the best cole slaw anyone could get anywhere.

When you get to strategies, plans have to get specific. You keep asking and answering questions until there aren't any questions left, only answers. For instance, question: How are we going to offer the best possible chicken? We're going to cook it the Colonel's way. Question: How are we going to get our employees to do that? We're going to train them better. How are we going to do that? We'll develop an in-store, audio-visual training tool, so everyone will be taught exactly the right procedures. Who's going to develop this tool? Our training department. When will it be done? Within six months. (An impossible schedule, incidentally, which they met.) Then, how will we know if and when we've succeeded? Sales would be an uncertain indicator, so we decided to institute a program of inspections by mystery shoppers, who would visit the store and anonymously rate product quality.

If I've made strategic planning sound like unromantic, hard work with almost infinite attention to detail, I've described it properly. It carefully identifies who's going to do the jobs, when they're going to be done, and quantifies goals. Monthly reviews of plans, which numbered in the hundreds, often took two days. Six- and seven-day weeks at KFC were the rule. In some areas we took what we recognized were temporary, emergency measures. The whole area of food quality was one of them. We simply could not afford to wait for the training program to be installed in every store. We needed to start seeing improvement immediately. The same was true of service and store cleanliness. We had store personnel who had been trained. Obviously not as well trained as they needed to be, but they knew at least the rudiments. We decided that field bonuses—that is, bonuses for store

managers and assistants, their supervisors, and all the way up to operation vice-presidents—would be based heavily on their QSC (Quality, Service, and Cleanliness) performance. These ratings came from mystery shoppers, who visited all the stores every month and rated them. A perfect store could get a score as high as 103. When we started the program, scores averaged in the 70s, and it took a while for the program to catch on. At first, managers didn't believe us when we said that our emphasis on QSC was going to continue forever. It was a switch. We'd talked about sales goals for so long, some managers had trouble changing. It took a while to persuade them that falling sales were not the problem, merely the symptom. The fundamental problem was poor QSC. But missing a quarterly bonus tended to drive home the point that we were truly serious about making QSC a religion. And those agnostics that we couldn't convert, we fired. As we moved into the summer of 1977, QSC average scores inched up into the 80s. We now average in the mid 90s.

Not at all incidentally, our mystery shoppers also visited our competitors' stores and ranked them. We needed to see how we were doing not only in absolute terms but also in terms of our competitors. We were beginning to close the gap, but ever so slowly. Sales were still going down, although the rate of decline had slowed, and profits had plummeted. Our marketing research studies showed that our prices were generally far too high. The solution was apparent: we were going to have to reduce prices, which would drive sales and profits down further, at least in the short term. We simply had no choice. On average, our product wasn't as good as our competitors, but our prices were higher. So we bit the bullet. We reduced prices to parity with our competitors. Sales dropped directly in proportion to the price reduction and profits fell through the floor. In company operations, the ink was red. This was a gutsy move, but we had faith in our plans. So we were gaining ground on QSC and V. At the same time we took on the problem of facilities. In many ways, this was the toughest task we faced.

As a pioneer of the quick-service restaurants, KFC's facilities were the oldest in the industry. Because the concept was originally take-out only, our stores were small and without seats. The design was 1960 ugly, topped off with what the Colonel characterized as "those damned red-and-white circus tent roofs." Plastic predominated. In some cases, the neighborhoods or the traffic patterns had changed, so we were in secondary locations. Remodeling was expensive and relocating stores was even more expensive. But, again, our consumer research clearly showed that we had no choice. We'd been aware of the need and had, in fact, begun studies in 1972 of a design for the new generation of stores. Not satisfied with the results, we hired another consultant to design our stores again in 1975. But you see what happens when a plan doesn't have firm completion dates. The job is never completed. In January 1977, we directed our real estate department to have a new store designed within three months and a prototype open three months after that. We began remodeling stores that summer, refining plans and figuring ways to optimize costs as we went. The changes were more than just cosmetic. Often they involved shrinking the kitchens so that we could add seating, because many of our customers wanted to eat in our stores.

We also added drive-thru windows to our stores, wherever possible, because there were any number of people who didn't want to come into our stores. They weren't dressed up. Or they had kids, whom they didn't want to bring in the store or leave in the car. Or it was raining or snowing. Whatever the reason, and our marketing research said there were a lot of them, consumers liked the convenience of drive-thru windows. So we added them.

At the same time we were remodeling our stores, we also were working on the other operating factors, which deals with running stores effectively, efficiently, and profitably. Among other things, it means having enough people in the stores to maintain outstanding QSC, but none extra. It means having all the hot, fresh chicken the customers want, but none extra. It means having all the inventory the stores need, but none extra. One of the first things that was developed was a labor matrix, to help the manager schedule employees on an hour-by-hour basis. You can't provide QSC without enough employees. And you can't make a profit with too many.

The labor matrix became just part of a management system, which included inventory sales and purchasing data. With this new system, the store manager had a mini, store-level P & L at the end of the week. This system made our managers in name managers in fact. Probably for the first time, they understood *why* they were doing what they did. This was another of those emergency steps we took because we needed information quickly about what was going on in each of our stores. By the time the store P & Ls were pulled together by the accounting department, it was three weeks or more after the end of a month. By then we were talking about history, not a tool to help operators manage the business. Even as we were installing our management system we were studying the installation of computerized cash registers in all our stores. These were finally put in all stores a year later, and we now know each night what happened in every store in our company system. Our master computer polls each store each night for complete information on the day's transactions.

Managers can look at their report and spot problems or opportunities. Area managers use their reports to identify problems that need to be fixed or training that needs to be given. Instead of telling the manager that he or she needs to improve the bottom line, the area manager and store manager know *exactly* what needs to be done to improve profitability—or quality, for that matter. A manager who doesn't schedule enough people is just as derelict as one who has too many. There are also daily district level reports, regional reports, and a company-wide report that goes to each level of management. These reports are enabling us to design better in-store operating procedures. In fact, they have application to every aspect of our business, including advertising, promotion, and merchandising.

If we have a new advertising campaign, featuring chicken sandwiches, for instance, our computerized cash register system enables us to measure its effectiveness immediately and make adjustments, if necessary. But we knew even back in the summer of 1977 that our advertising was ineffective. Our customers couldn't remember it. As a result we changed advertising agencies and developed a new campaign. The old campaign had been "A Bucket of Chicken is a Barrel of Fun," and the commercials showed people having fun with chicken in the background. At the time we were in a recession, so people weren't having much fun—with or without Kentucky Fried Chicken. The advertising didn't give the consumer any reason to buy our products.

After substantial marketing research, the new advertising agency developed a campaign around the theme: "It's Nice to Feel So Good About A Meal." The campaign capitalized on the fact that consumers recognized that chicken was a healthy, wholesome, nutritious food. It was properly perceived as having significant advantages over hamburger and other fast-food competitors. That campaign has been succeeded by one with the theme: "We Do Chicken Right," a pre-emptive claim of superiority we can make now that our Quality, Service, and Cleanliness are right, and one we needed to make, as all the hamburger chains discovered the tremendous economic advantages of chicken and began to add chicken to their menus.

Even as we were working to improve all aspects of our QSCVFOOFAMP, we had a hostile franchisee family to contend with.

To say that they were livid over the way the company stores had been operated would be a gross understatement. They generally had been running their stores well, so their businesses were still growing. They were understandably angry. Our strategy here was simply to survive. We wanted them to postpone their plans to kill us all until we had a chance to demonstrate that our QSCVFOOFAMP program would work. The action plan involved intensive communications with franchisees of our plans and our results. We were concerned about class-action suits that could have torn the system asunder. We were concerned about individual franchisees going off on their own and ending up with thousands of units offering different products, turning our system into a loose confederation of only distantly related operations. I took on the responsibility for this communications chore, moving my headquarters down to Louisville. I was on the road for most of the next year, speaking at franchisee seminars, advertising co-op meetings, regional association meetings and conventions, and one-on-one meetings with some of our larger and more influential franchisees. Supporting this were letters, bulletins, company magazines and newspapers, which candidly talked about the problems and the programs. I also got support from KFC's founder, the Colonel. Quality, Service, Cleanliness, and Value had always been part of the Colonel's creed.

In spite of all these efforts by so many talented and hard-working people, in spite of our masterful strategic plan, in spite of great new advertising, in spite of my efforts and those of the Colonel, sales continued to run behind the depressed levels of the year before. They bounced up once in the fall of 1977, but then settled down again—until the following spring.

During those dark days of '76 through '78, KFC's key indicators declined steadily. Per store average sales fell at an average annual rate of 3 percent. And real sales, that is, the actual number of meals served, were down 3 percent. The number of chickens sold per store declined 2 percent. For the three-year period, earnings plummeted 43 percent. Sales finally turned around in May 1978. And they have continued to go up. We've had real growth in every quarter since then, flying in the face of a declining economy and tough times generally for the retail food service business.

Since then, average sales per store have increased at a compound annual rate of 14.5 percent. Store level pre-tax profits have grown 24 percent, compounded annually. Real sales growth, adjusted for pricing, has been up an average of 6 percent a year, compounded. Incidentally, this is four times faster than the industry has been growing. And total earnings from the KFC system have increased 309 percent.

From being a drag on Heublein, KFC has become the star in our portfolio, and our biggest growth opportunity for the future. KFC has written probably the most dramatic turnaround in the annals of American business. But I want to make it clear that strategic planning wasn't the silver bullet or some kind of voodoo.

Our strategic plan did not turn the business around. The actions that derived from the plan did, however, and our turnaround would not have been possible without the plan. The cliche is true that plans are nothing, but planning is everything. Planning continues at KFC. Our mission, our objectives, and our strategies are unchanged from those of five years ago. Of course, our action plans change each year. As old problems are solved, new ones emerge, or old ones take on new importance. What is evolving from these strategic-plan-driven programs is a total store management system that is improving quality, service, and cleanliness, and reducing costs. This is enabling us to keep prices down even as we fund record-level advertising programs, build and remodel stores. At the same time KFC is producing continually improving profits. What we have is the opposite of the vicious circle; I guess you could call it the delightful cycle.

It did not happen by magic. It happened by planning and executing more programs, plans, and projects than ever accomplished by a chain in a similar period since the Colonel invented the quick-service restaurant industry thirty years ago. Instead of dying, as predicted five years ago, KFC is growing. Instead of competition taking our business, we are regaining what we lost. Instead of franchisee discontent, we have the closest, most cooperative, and most constructive relationship we've ever had. Instead of declining sales, we have new sales records. Instead of poor QSC, we have the best QSC in the industry. Instead of high prices, we offer the best value in food service today. Instead of old facilities, we have new ones. Instead of profits falling, they are rising to new heights. And instead of being a bird with a crippled wing, we have taught Kentucky Fried Chicken to fly like an eagle. And the best is yet to come.

Exercises

■ Alpha/Beta Space Technology, Inc.

The space race of the 1960s proved to the world that a highly sophisticated and experimental technology could be harnessed effectively by human organization. While the resulting organizational structure and management of NASA may not have been as publicized a feat as its space achievements were, the implications for organization design are clear. It is possible to organize highly specialized and sophisticated talent in such a way as to insure maximal individual effort and contribution and create synergistic outcomes in a highly turbulent and uncertain environment. To ignore the uncertainties and turbulence of the environment is, in the words of James E. Webb, former Administrator of NASA, "courting disaster."[1] Webb suggests that much of NASA's success was due to its "adaptive organizational structure," and points out that:

> . . . they [executives] must be fully adaptive in their approach . . . they must apply what I have called an "administrative discount" to assumptions . . . they must also organize and conduct their operations so as to make possible similar allowances . . . they must avoid rigidities in the organizational structure . . . they must leave areas of choice to other key executives . . . they must allow opportunities for them to innovate. . . . More than that, they must keep their associates under a judicious level of pressure to develop and employ their capabilities for acting on their own.[2]

In this exercise, the participants can become more aware of the effects of a turbulent environment upon organizational effectiveness and some of the problems associated with harnessing and coordinating human efforts to produce desired results.

Directions

1. Each team will be required to engage in some phase of designing and/or constructing a model space tower made of plastic parts and tubes.
2. Materials will be available for the development of a design for the space tower. About ninety minutes will be allotted for this phase of the exercise.
3. After the space tower has been designed, each person will be asked to complete the *Alpha/Beta Analysis Questionnaire* and record personal assessments of what happened during the exercise.
4. The construction of the space tower will be done competitively between selected teams and a winner will be decided based on the best performance.
5. Your instructor will give you all the additional information you will need.

---

1. James E. Webb, *Space Age Management* (New York: McGraw-Hill Book Co., 1969), p. 150.
2. Ibid., p. 151.

ALPHA/BETA ANALYSIS QUESTIONNAIRE

Alpha Company _____

Beta Company _____

Group Designation _____

This questionnaire deals with your experiences in your company. Please try to answer as honestly as you can.

1. To what degree did you feel frustrated during the exercise?   (Circle one)

Low				*High*
1	2	3	4	5

2. How committed were you to your company's objectives?

Low				*High*
1	2	3	4	5

3. How effective was your group in designing a tower?

Low				*High*
1	2	3	4	5

4. To what degree did you feel you knew what was going on in your company?

Low				*High*
1	2	3	4	5

5. How involved did you feel in your company's efforts?

Low				*High*
1	2	3	4	5

6. How much confidence did you have in your company's leadership?

Low				*High*
1	2	3	4	5

■ Alpha/Beta: Option A—Post Exercise Analysis

Each of you has been through the Alpha/Beta Space Technology Exercise and you have been asked to think about your experiences and to read the Burns and Stalker article on organizational design. In this exercise each of you is asked to "re-live" the experience and to record some conclusions about the functional and dysfunctional aspects of the mechanistic and organic management systems.

Directions

1. Each person records on the *Alpha/Beta Post Analysis Form* statements that describe his or her experiences in the Space Tower Exercise.

2. Form groups composed of members from both Alpha and Beta to discuss the exercise.

3. Each member should share with the others the statements recorded on his or her *Alpha/Beta Post Analysis* form. From all these statements the group should reach some conclusions about the functional and dysfunctional aspects of both mechanistic and organic organizations. Record these conclusions on the *Group Inventory* form.

4. Each group will be asked to present its conclusions to the entire class on newsprint. Each group should select and prepare a spokesperson for this task.

ALPHA/BETA POST ANALYSIS FORM

In this exercise we are interested in reviewing your experience in the Alpha/Beta space technology exercise. Below you are asked to think over the entire exercise in your mind's eye and then quickly jot down words or statements that describe the experience you had. Try to list feelings, reactions, thoughts, or even dialogue that you can recall.

Words or statements that describe my experience in the Alpha/Beta space technology exercise . . .

_____

_____

_____

_____

_____

_____

_____

_____

_____

Now that you have reviewed your experience, the next step is to share your ideas with the other members of your group. The group should try to draw conclusions from each member's reactions about the nature of organic and mechanistic systems. Focus particularly on functional (factors that increase effectiveness) and dysfunctional (factors that decrease effectiveness) aspects of each system.

GROUP INVENTORY

On page 145 you are asked to inventory your group's conclusions. Also, the group should be prepared to present its conclusions to the other participants.

Mechanistic Systems

Functional Aspects	*Dysfunctional Aspects*

Organic Systems

Functional Aspects	*Dysfunctional Aspects*

■ Boundary Spasms

Organizations facing turbulence in their environments have several ways to deal with it. Relying on New England tradition, the President of the Haliconn Company decided to go directly to the ordinary citizens of the community to present the story on what the company was doing to control toxic wastes disposal into the river. Proud of the role the Company had played in the town, the President wanted to span the gulf that was developing between the Company and the community. Using the most direct way—the peculiar New England forum of the town meeting—the President was set to perform the boundary role function for Haliconn.

Directions

1. Read the background data on the Haliconn Company.
2. Individuals will be assigned roles to study and prepare.
3. The remaining participants will be asked to observe what happens during the role-played town meeting.
4. The role players will play their parts at a town meeting called by the President of the Haliconn Company. The meeting is open to the public. The meeting will begin after a twenty-minute coffee reception during which role players are free to get to know other attendees.

Background

Haliconn is a large producer of organic chemicals used for dye additives and drug products. About 75 percent of its products are prescription medicines and the other 25 percent are over-the-counter medications.

The company has three manufacturing plants in the United States and three in other parts of the world. Its largest organic chemical plant is located in a rural area ten miles from Duxbury, Connecticut. The original plant built in 1909 in Duxbury was closed and sold when the company relocated to a rural area in 1965 with plenty of room for growth, parking lots, and open spaces. Since then, suburban residential areas of Duxbury have expanded and now there is a sizable residential park three miles from the Haliconn plant. At one time Haliconn was the principal industry of the Duxbury area but now there are several other firms. Yet, Haliconn still employs over 1,100 people, close to 10 percent of the local labor force.

Over the years Haliconn has played a key role in the growth and development of the community and it has made a determined effort to maintain a respectable public image, a task that has become progressively more difficult in recent years. As various protectionist groups emerged and began to make more demands for consumer and environmental protection, the company has preferred to disperse its manufacturing operations. With the opening of world markets and emergence of the sunbelt in the United States, Haliconn has opened plants in Spain, Brazil, and the Philippines as well as in the sunbelt states of South Carolina and Louisiana. The protectionist laws in these foreign countries and sunbelt states are not as restrictive, as laws in northeastern states.

The growth and change in organic chemical products requiring frequent changes in product line, about 10 percent each year, is accompanied by constant changes in raw materials used in the manufacturing process. The company has used the Quinnibaug River for the disposal of wastewaters generated from organic chemical manufacturing operations at its Duxbury plant since 1965. The wastewaters have received increased levels of treatment as treatment technology has improved and federal and state regulations have been tightened. Local residents have often voiced concern over the foul odors released from the Haliconn plant, but now they, along with other groups in Duxbury, are complaining about the dumping of toxic chemical wastes into the Quinnibaug River. These complaints and concerns are affecting the company's public image. Under the present wastewater discharge permit issued by the Connecticut EPA, Haliconn is in compliance with all regulations. Haliconn is also presently in compliance with all air pollution regulations by default (i.e., the substances being emitted by Haliconn cannot be controlled by current promulgated state and federal air pollution regulations). However, the permit, which is renewable every five years, will expire in six months. Preliminary discussions between representatives of Haliconn and the Connecticut EPA have revealed the following:

1. The reissued wastewater discharge permit will require tighter effluent limitations and therefore construction of additional treatment facilities to meet current state and federal discharge limitations. Current levels of toxic compounds such as dichlorobenzidine and metals are not acceptable.

2. Haliconn President Oli Towers feels that this company has spent enough already on pollution control facilities. He has threatened to move production to other Haliconn facilities or open a new plant in West Palm Beach, Florida, if the EPA demands too much.

3. The source of the odors emanating from Haliconn is the wastewater treatment system. Existing air pollution regulations do not address these emissions. If these emissions are to be controlled by existing statutes Connecticut EPA water regulatory people will have to "buffalo" Haliconn to control these emissions through the reissued wastewater permit by stretching existing statutory authorities. Connecticut EPA water regulatory people are reluctant to do so.

In an effort to defuse these complaints, Oli Towers decided to hold an old-fashioned New England town meeting. Oli wants to settle this problem but believes the people of the community are being misled by various environmental protection groups such as the Connecticut Environmental Guard (CEG) and the Duxbury Citizens for the Environment (DCE).

Oli was born and raised in a small town in Connecticut and wants to talk directly with the people. He believes that once he presents the facts of this matter, many of the people will support Haliconn. The meeting has been widely publicized in the local newspaper and radio, and invitations have been extended to all the citizens of the area who are interested in hearing about the issue and speaking openly about it. Time will be made available to speak and be heard.

The Haliconn Company

The Roles

1. Oliver Towers, President of the Haliconn Company
2. Pat Hiller, Vice-President of Community Relations, Haliconn Co.
3. President, Connecticut Environmental Guard (CEG)
4. Chairperson, Duxbury Citizens for the Environment (DCE)
5. Chairperson, Senior Citizens Association
6. President of Quinnibaug Valley Sportsman's Association
7. President, Rollo Swimming Pools Company
8. Fire Chief, Duxbury Volunteer Fire Company
9. Newspaper reporter for the Duxbury Evening Reporter
10. Resident of Quinnibaug Valley
11. Mayor of Duxbury
12. Member of CALPA, Citizens Anti-Lead Poisoning Association
13. Personal Attorney of Oliver Towers
14. Vice-President of Community Affairs, Constitution National Bank
15. Student in a course on "Organization Theory"

The role plays are numbered in order of importance. The size of the "town meeting" can be varied in accordance with the number of people available. Roles 1 through 8 are major roles that should be used in the exercise, Roles 9 through 15 are auxiliary roles.

■ Organizational Preference Inventory

People differ in their organizational and work setting preferences. Debates on how the organization should be run consume untold hours around the water cooler. While such debates very often involve specific personalities and policies, they also tend to reflect the general biases or preferences of the individuals involved. The inventory below is designed to help you survey your own preferences. There are no right or wrong answers and each is open to debate. The inventory may be scored (see the analysis at the end of the inventory after you've filled it out); however, the score has no real evaluative significance. The inventory is designed to stimulate debate and discussion. After you have filled out the inventory, your instructor may want to put you in a group to discuss the different preferences.

Directions

Your preferences are to be expressed by circling a response using the following key:

SA — Strongly Agree
A — Agree Somewhat
U — Undecided
D — Disagree Somewhat
SD — Strongly Disagree

Your first reaction to each statement is probably the best. Spending too much time debating your feelings with yourself will only result in your rationalizing no answer or an undecided response. The debate should take place after you've done the inventory.

I prefer to work in an organization where . . .

1. goals are defined by those in higher level positions.	SA	A	U	D	SD
2. methods and procedures for achieving goals are specified for me.	SA	A	U	D	SD
3. top management makes important decisions.	SA	A	U	D	SD
4. my loyalty counts as much as my ability to do the job.	SA	A	U	D	SD
5. clear lines of authority and responsibility are established.	SA	A	U	D	SD
6. top management is decisive and firm.	SA	A	U	D	SD
7. my career is pretty well planned out for me.	SA	A	U	D	SD
8. I can specialize.	SA	A	U	D	SD
9. my length of service is almost as important as my level of performance.	SA	A	U	D	SD
10. management is able to provide the information I need to do my job well.	SA	A	U	D	SD
11. a chain of command is well established.	SA	A	U	D	SD
12. rules and procedures are adhered to equally by everyone.	SA	A	U	D	SD
13. people accept the authority of the leader's position.	SA	A	U	D	SD
14. people are loyal to their boss.	SA	A	U	D	SD
15. people do as they have been instructed.	SA	A	U	D	SD
16. people clear things with their boss before going over his or her head.	SA	A	U	D	SD

■ DON'T READ THIS UNTIL AFTER YOU HAVE DONE THE INVENTORY.

Scoring

Each question attempts to assess your preference for a mechanistic or bureaucratic work environment. The more you agree with each statement, the more you prefer such an environment. By assigning a 5 to each strongly agree response (SA), a 4 to each agree response (A) on down to a 1 for each strongly disagree response (SD) you can score the strength of your preferences.   The following "tongue-in-cheek" evaluation is for debate only.

Total Score	Preference Type
66–80	Dyed-in-the-wool Bureaucrat
56–65	Organization Person
48–55	Ambivalent Idealist
32–47	Organizational Malcontent
Less than 32	Latent Anarchist

Remember, the important issue is to discuss your preferences, *not* to evaluate yourself.

3 Structure and Design

■ **LEARNING OBJECTIVES**

1. To examine the obstacles in designing an organizational structure with a capacity for adaptation

2. To demonstrate the impact of organizational structure on performance and behavior

3. To provide participants an opportunity to assess the advantages and disadvantages of different types of structures

4. To examine structural issues faced by multinational and foreign firms

■ OVERVIEW

Designing an organization capable of adaptation is still more of an art than a science. In the past, the organization designer was more likely to seek a solution by conducting a search for a model to imitate. Today's organization designer, confronted with a changing and turbulent environment, can no longer rely on patterning after the historical models. The designer must explore and innovate forms of organization that are appropriate for the circumstances. This architect must attempt to answer questions such as: "How should the work of this organization be divided up?" "How should efforts be coordinated?" "How precisely should roles and duties be specified?" Beyond such fundamental questions as these, the designer must also grapple with a complex set of trade-offs associated with each alternative design principle. To this end the manager may need to invent, develop, and analyze new hybrid forms that provide the best possible fit between the people, the task, and the organization's environment.

While some theorists have readily concluded that there is no one best way to organize, organizational research has begun to provide some guidelines that will be explored in this part.

An organization's structure, to some degree, emerges as the result of the behavior and needs of its members. What is depicted on the organizational chart is often quite different from reality. Nevertheless, it is the purpose of structure to provide reinforcement for consistent and reliable member behavior. Hence, even though the state of the art in organizational design is somewhat primitive, a designer's lack of awareness of these basic design principles could severely limit organizational effectiveness. Additionally, managers today need to be aware of the cross-cultural implications of structure as multi-national firms become more common. As we shall see, designing an organization involves several complex variables over which the manager can have substantial influence.

Readings

■ Strategy and Management Structure

WILLIAM H. NEWMAN

The matching of strategy and management design presents a challenging opportunity to scholars of management. It calls for skill in building a viable, integrated system, it draws upon insights on many facets of management, and it plunges us into a highly dynamic set of relationships. Both synthesis and refinement of theory are involved.

Moreover, as A.D. Chandler demonstrates in his classic study, *Strategy and Structure*, keeping managerial arrangements in tune with strategy plays a vital role in enterprise survival and growth. The accelerating pace of change in economic, technological, political, and social forces will lead companies to adjust their strategies more often in the future than has been typical in the past. And with each shift in strategy the appropriateness of existing management design should be examined anew. Consequently, the issues we explore in this paper hold practical as well as theoretical significance.

Our discussion is divided into four parts: (1) Strategy is defined. (2) The concept of a coherent management design is set forth, with particular attention to those features most likely to be affected by strategy. (3) An analytical approach for matching strategy and management design is examined. (4) Implications for heterogeneous as well as homogeneous enterprises are identified.

SCOPE OF MASTER STRATEGY

Strategy, as the term is used in this paper, sets the basic purposes of an enterprise in terms of the services it will render to society and the way it will create these services. More specifically, master strategy involves (a) picking particular product market niches that are propitious in view of society's needs and the company's resources, (b) selecting the underlying technologies and the ways of attracting inputs, (c) combining the various niches and resource bases to obtain synergistic effects, (d) expressing these plans in terms of targets, and (e) setting up sequences and timing of steps toward these objectives that reflect company capabilities and external conditions.

Obviously, the formulation of strategy calls for diagnostic skills and keen judgment. A great deal of analysis and theorizing remains to be done on this frontier. It is an area of study in itself, especially since it provides the major opportunity for the enterprise to adapt to an ever-shifting environment. The present paper, however, focuses on another task of central management—the interrelation between master strategy and management design. Here we assume that strategy does get formulated and periodically revised. Such strategy will become effective only when it is linked to a mutually supporting management design.

Academy of Management Proceedings, August 1971. A revised version of this paper also appears in W.H. Newman and E.K. Warren, *The Process of Management*, 4th ed., ch. 29 (Prentice-Hall, Inc., 1977). References deleted. See original work.

INTEGRATED MANAGEMENT DESIGN

Discussions of "strategy and structure" often focus on only organization structure. If the match between strategy and management design is to be fully effective, however, more than organization must be harmonized. The nature of the planning process, the leadership style, and the form and location of control mechanisms are also intimately involved. This more inclusive view of management arrangements—planning, organizing, leading, and controlling—we call management design.

Management designs differ. Every university is, and should be, managed in ways that are different from those used to manage the bus system that brings students to its doors. Likewise, within the university, the managerial design best suited to research laboratories is inappropriate to the cafeteria. To be sure, several common processes—organizing, planning, leading, and controlling—are essential for each of these units, but as we adapt various concepts to the unique needs of each venture refinement is vital. Management sophistication is revealed in this adapting and refining of the design.

NEED FOR COHERENT MANAGEMENT DESIGN

In each particular situation the phases of management should be synergistic. That is, organization structure should facilitate control, control should generate useful data for planning, planning should be conducted in a way that assists in leading, and so forth. These mutually supporting effects are a vital feature of a good management design. Yet in practice a surprising number of instances arise where just the opposite pull occurs. Tensions mount instead of reinforcements.

A striking lack of synergy arose when one of the nation's leading railroads undertook a sweeping decentralization. According to the plan, regional managers were to replace a highly centralized headquarters as the focus for operating decisions, and these regional managers were given significantly increased authority. Unfortunately, the control mechanisms did not change with the organization design. Detailed reports continued to flow to the vice-presidents at headquarters, and these men continued their previous practice of stepping into trouble spots and issuing orders. Confusion resulted. The fact that legal and technological reasons prevented regional managers from making their own plans regarding prices, train schedules, new equipment, wage rates, and other important matters merely aggravated the situation. So the actual planning mechanism did not line up with the announced organization. It soon became obvious that the total management design had not been thought through.

The chief executive of a computer company, to cite another example, decided that participative leadership would stimulate the engineers and other technical people in his firm. He arranged for all managers from vice-presidents to first-line supervisors to have T-group training so that everyone would understand the new leadership style. The results were not entirely happy. Competition forced the president himself to make several key decisions, specifications had to be frozen, pressure was placed on production people to meet tough deadlines, and budgetary-control limits were stipulated by headquarters. This top-down planning was a well-established pattern within the company. But to many managers who had just gotten the message about participative leadership, the former planning procedures suddenly became oppressive. Their morale was hurt rather than helped because their expectations, which had been raised by the leadership training, were soon undermined by use of the old planning mechanisms. Here again we see that a change in one phase of management was not matched by necessary adjustments in other phases.

Prominent Features of a Management Design

Recognition of need for a coherent management design raises a question of what is embraced in such a design. What features do we need to consider?

It is not very helpful to suggest that elements in the management design for a particular situation can be selected from the many concepts covered in management literature, even though this statement is true. Such guidance is too broad. In order to narrow the focus a bit, let us concentrate on those managerial arrangements most likely to be affected by choice of strategy. In other words, which features probably will need adjustment when we fit a structure to new requirements?

Analysis of a wide variety of management designs points to the elements listed in the accompanying tables as distinguishing features. In any single design only a few of these features will dominate, and others may be insignificant. In addition, for unusual circumstances a feature not listed here may be critical. Nevertheless, careful consideration of the features listed will enable us to comprehend and to deal with the management designs of most enterprises.

Distinguishing organizational features. Organization is widely acknowledged as a prime vehicle for adapting a management design to new needs. In fact, organization is often overemphasized. Some managers make a change in their formal organization and then assume everything else will fall in place. To be fully effective, however, several compatible changes in formal organization are frequently necessary. These changes must be incorporated into informal behavior, and supporting adjustments must be made in other facets of management.

Key personnel, the last feature listed in exhibit 3.1, warrants special emphasis. It is always involved in a change in management design, and it may be as vital to the success of a change as any other feature.

EXHIBIT 3.1 Organizational Features that Are Likely to Vary with a Change in Strategy

Centralization versus decentralization

Degree of division of labor

Size of self-sufficient operating units

Mechanisms for coordination

Nature and location of staff

Management information system

Characteristics of key personnel

Personnel capable of functioning in the new jobs should be carefully selected and should be given time to learn new patterns of behavior.

Distinguishing forms of plans. The need to think carefully about forms of plans is illustrated sharply in any international airline. Preparation of tickets in Vienna that will be understood in Nairobi and Seattle, that can be reissued in Baghdad and canceled in Tahiti, and that provide the basis for allocating the fare collected among a dozen different airlines requires an impressive use of standing operating procedures. Nor can equipment maintenance be left to local ingenuity. On the other hand, companywide policies relating to sales promotion and payrates for baggage handlers must be cast in broad terms or shunned entirely. Then if the airline enters the local hotel business in several countries, the appropriateness of worldwide policies and procedures must be examined anew. For each subject, either too little or too much planning can lead to great confusion.

Questions about the kinds of plans suitable for a specific situation typically center around the topics listed in exhibit 3.2.

Planning, in contrast to organizing, often receives scant attention during the preparation of a management design. This disregard of planning arises from two confusions. First, the substance of specific plans may be so engrossing that little thought is given to the more basic issue of the form in which guidance will be most useful. Second, the process of arriving at a decision is confused with the mechanisms introduced to guide decision-making activities throughout the enterprise. When shaping a management design, we are primarily concerned with these mechanisms (standing plans, project planning, intermediate objectives, and the like) because they help pull the entire managerial effort into a coherent thrust.

Distinguishing elements in leadership style. The leadership features listed in exhibit 3.3 are aspects of leading that should be adjusted to fit the total management design. Many guides to good leadership practice that emerge from behavioral research apply to virtually all settings, and so they are not included in this particular list.

Leadership style is intimately tied to the temperament and beliefs of each manager. Consequently, this style is more difficult to change than, say, departmentation or control reports. Nevertheless, all of us can modify our behavior to some degree, especially when the environment in which we work reinforces our new behavior. If a manager cannot provide the kind of leadership needed in a given situation, replacing him is an alternative. So even though leadership style is not easy to change, it should be included in the total process of matching management design to strategy.

Distinguishing features of the control process. The design of controls all too often lags behind shifts in other aspects of management. The railroad reorganization mentioned earlier revealed a failure to revise controls so that they would reinforce major moves in related areas. Over-reliance on short-run, quantitative measurements shows a similar tendency to pay too little attention to control structure. Yet controls can provide the synergy we seek in an effective management design.

The features of control most likely to need adjustment when changes are made in other phases of management are listed in exhibit 3.4. Closely associated with changes in these features should be a refinement of the management information system, which has already been listed under organization. Although the preparation of a total management design rarely starts with control, no plan is complete until provision is made for control.

Weaving the various features of organizing, planning, leading, and controlling that have been singled out in this section into a coherent management design calls for great skill. Each enterprise needs its own unique system. Fortunately, synergistic benefits are usually possible if we are ingenious enough to make reinforcing combinations, such as those suggested under Nature of Technology in exhibit 3.7. A company's design is effective, however, only when it fits neatly with the company strategy, as pointed out in the next section.

INFLUENCE OF STRATEGY ON DESIGN

The idea of a management design is a useful concept because it turns our focus from analytical refinements to reinforcing integration. The preceding section identified an array of variable features that should be considered in building such an integrated design, and indicated how some combinations of these features tend to be destructive whereas other combinations promote coherence. We can now tackle the tougher task—relating management design and company strategy.

Technology: The Intervening Variable

The best bridge between strategy and design is "technology." Here we use technology in a very broad sense to include all sorts of methods for converting resource inputs into products and service for consumers. The inputs can be labor, knowledge,

and capital as well as raw materials. Thus an insurance company has its technology for converting money, ideas, and labor into insurance service just as an oil company has its technology for converting crude oil and other resources into petroleum products. By extending our thinking from strategy to the technology necessary to execute that strategy, we move to *work to be done*. Once we comprehend the work to be done—both managerial and operating work—we are on familiar ground. Most of our management concepts relate directly to getting work done, and so preparing a management design to fit a particular kind of work falls within the recognized "state of the art."

The use of technology as an intervening variable produces the arrangement shown in exhibit 3.5. To maintain perspective and to highlight key influences, strategy should focus only on a few basic ideas. Its formulation is by necessity in broad terms. We cannot jump directly from strategy to management design because we have not yet classified the array of actions that will be necessary to execute the strategy. Thinking of technology helps us to elaborate the work implications of the strategy and thereby provides us with the inputs for shaping a management design.

EXHIBIT 3.5   Outlook to Design

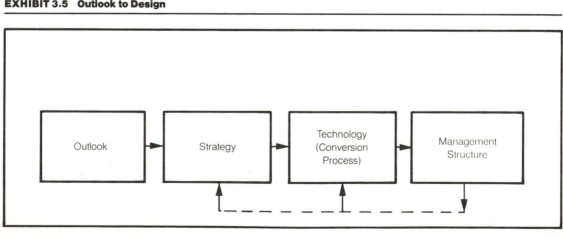

Types of technology. Technology, especially in the broad sense in which we are using the term here, deals with all sorts of situations and methods. For purposes of relating technology to management, however, we can concentrate on only a few characteristics of the technology. For instance, the way a technology deals with change is very significant for our purpose.

In a company with a given strategy and technology, the need for change will fall somewhere along a continuum of infrequent to frequent. Similarly, the kinds of changes the company typically faces will fall somewhere along another continuum ranging from brand new, unprecedented problems to familiar, precedented problems; in the case of the familiar problems, the company will have a well-established pattern for resolving them.

Using these two characteristics of a firm's technology, we can set up the matrix shown in exhibit 3.6. Of course, many technologies will fit around the middle of one or both dimensions, but by thinking about technologies toward the ends of the scales we arrive at three well-known types of businesses.

Enterprises confronted with familiar problems rather infrequently are basically *stable*. Paper mills and other firms processing large volumes of raw materials fall into this category. When the need for change moves from infrequent to frequent, and the problems remain precedented, we encounter businesses that display *regulated flexibility*.

EXHIBIT 3.6 Change Matrix

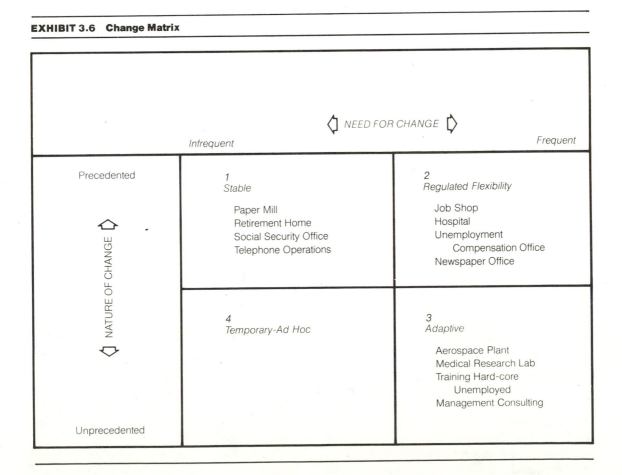

Job shops—used by management writers since Frederick Taylor to illustrate management concepts—fit this category. But when the need for change is frequent and the problems are unprecedented, as often occurs in the aerospace industry, we face a sharply different situation. Here technology requires an *adaptive* structure.

These three technology types—stable, regulated flexibility, and adaptive—are found in many lines of endeavor. In the health field there are retirement homes, hospitals, and medical research labs. In government, offices for Social Security (old-age pensions), for unemployment compensation, and for the training of hard-core unemployed illustrate the types. In the service industries, examples are telephone operations, newspaper publications, and management consulting.

In contrast to the first three types, the fourth division in the change matrix does not point to a clear type of technology or management design. Unprecedented problems that arise only infrequently are handled by some temporary arrangement. This ad hoc setup does not exist long enough to modify the underlying structure.

From Technology To Management Design

An intriguing aspect of the three technology types just identified is that each leads to a well-known management design. The usual relationships between technology and design are shown in exhibit 3.7. For each of the distinguishing features of a management design, discussed earlier in this paper, we can see the typical response to a stable technology, a regulated-flexibility technology, and an adaptive technology.

The primary features of each design remain substantially the same even though the companies come from different industries. For instance, when the work situation is stable as it usually is in a paper mill, retirement home, Social Security office, and telephone exchange, planning tends to be comprehensive and detailed, intermediate goals are sharply defined, decision-making is centralized, and central staff is strong. In addition, we find limited participation and close supervision. Controls are focused on dependability and efficiency, checks are made frequently, and few mistakes are tolerated. These and other management features indicated in exhibit 3.7 enable an executive working in a stable situation to convert resource inputs into the maximum output of consumer services.

Actually, in our modern world, regulated flexibility is much more common than the stable technology just described. A job shop, hospital, unemployment compensation office, and newspaper all face a continuing procession of new situations, most of which can be handled by well-developed techniques for resolving such problems. For this kind of technology, the typical management design introduces flexibility by the use of craftsmen and professionals, by separate scheduling units, by careful programming of workloads, by close control of work passing from one stage to the next, by prompt information on the status of work at each stage, and so on. The kind of flexibility needed is anticipated, and provisions for dealing with it are built into the system. Each person understands the limits of his discretion, and other conditions are fully planned and controlled so that reliability of the total system is not lost.

Adaptive technology calls for quite a different management design. The research lab, consulting firm, and hard-core unemployed training project all face unprecedented problems frequently. Here operating units become smaller, greater reliance is placed on face-to-face contacts, authority is decentralized, planning tends to focus on objectives and broad programs, leaders use participation and expect high personal involvement, control checks are less frequent and concern results rather than methods. These and other features listed in exhibit 3.7 are often called "organic" or sometimes "democratic."

This adaptive type of situation is what many human relations advocates dream

EXHIBIT 3.7   Typical Features of Management Structures for Three Types of Technology

	Features That Distinguish Management Structures	Nature of Technology		
		Stable	Regulated Flexibility	Adaptive
Organizing	Centralization versus decentralization	Centralized	Mostly centralized	Decentralized
	Degree of division of labor	Narrow specialization	Specialized, or crafts	Scope may vary
	Size of self-sufficient operating units	Large	Medium	Small, if equipment permits
	Mechanisms for coordination	Built-in, programmed	Separate planning unit	Face-to-face within unit
	Nature and location of staff	Narrow functions; headquarters	Narrow functions; headquarters and operating unit	Generalists at headquarters; specialists in operating units
	Management information system	Heavy upward flow	Flow to headquarters and to operating unit	Flow mostly to, and within, operating unit
	Characteristics of key personnel	Strong operators	Functional experts in line and staff	Analytical, adaptive
Planning	Use of standing plans; Comprehensiveness of coverage	Broad coverage	All main areas covered	Mostly "local," self-imposed
	Specificity	Detail specified	Detail in interlocking activities	Main points only
	Use of single-use plans; Comprehensiveness of coverage	Fully planned	Fully planned	Main steps covered
	Specificity	Detail specified	Schedules and specs detailed	Adjusted to feedback
	Planning horizon	Weekly to quarterly	Weekly to annually	Monthly to three years or more
	Intermediate versus final objectives	Intermediate goals sharp	Intermediate goals sharp	Emphasis on objectives
	"How" versus results	"How" is specified	Results at each step specified	End results stressed
Leading	Participation in planning	Very limited	Restricted to own tasks	High participation
	Permissiveness	Stick to instructions	Variation in own tasks only	High permissiveness if results OK
	Closeness of supervision	Follow operations closely	Output and quality closely watched	General supervision
	Sharing of information	Circumspect	Job information shared	Full project information shared
	Emphasis on on-the-job satisfactions	Limited scope	Craftsmanship and professionalism encouraged	Opportunity for involvement
Controlling	Performance criteria emphasized	Efficiency, dependability	Quality, punctuality, efficiency	Results, within resource limits

Controlling (Cont.)	Location of control points	Within process; intermediate stages	Focus on each processing unit	Overall "milestones"
	Frequency of checks	Frequent	Frequent	Infrequent
	Who initiates corrective action	Often central managers	"Production control" and other staff	Personnel in operating unit
	Stress on reliability versus learning	Reliability stressed	Reliability stressed	Learning stressed
	Punitive versus reward motivation	Few mistakes tolerated	Few mistakes tolerated	High reward for success

about. It provides ample opportunity for employee participation and self-actualization. However, the fact that only a small portion of all work involves frequent, unprecedented problems explains why a lot of human relations training has failed to find practical application.

Of course, no company will fit exactly into any one of the technology-management design types we have described. But the examples do suggest how thoughtful analysis of technology provides a basis for designing a suitable structure.

Related Influences on Design

Although the analysis of technology in terms of the frequency and uniqueness of the problems it faces is a fruitful first step, we should not overlook other influences. For instance, technology will also be affected by complexity and the need for speed. When several interrelated variables affect the work, as in building a communications satellite, more thorough planning and control will be necessary. The need for speedy action usually has an opposite effect. Here the urgency to get prompt action reduces the opportunity for thorough planning and control; quick results now may have a higher value than somewhat improved results a month later.

Size and uncertainty should also be taken into account. A larger volume of work will support the expense of more division of labor, mechanization, and specialized staff, and greater size complicates communication

and coordination. For both these reasons an increase in size tends to add to the planning and control.

Uncertainty permeates many activities. Because of an unknown environment or unpredictable responses to our own actions, we are confronted with uncertainty. If time permits we may try to reduce this uncertainty by further tests and experiments, and this will probably add staff to our organization and reduce the permissiveness in the structure. On the other hand, if such attempts to reduce uncertainty are impractical we may hire people with the best intuitive judgment we can find, get rid of our staff, and decentralize authority to the experts. This latter response to uncertainty, which is favored by the managers of some conglomerates, creates a simple, lean management design.

Management design, then, must be developed in light of a variety of influences. However, the added dimensions just cited still fit into our basic proposal of moving first from strategy to character of work, and then from work to management design.

COMPOUND DESIGN WITHIN A COMPANY

Thus far we have discussed the management design for a whole company. We have assumed that one technology and one design predominates, and for a single-function company this holds true. Most enterprises, however, are more complex. Within the corporate scope quite different activities may take place. So if we are correct in urging that management design reflect technology, the concepts should be applied to parts of a complex company as well as to the whole.

Diverse Technologies of Department

Consider the Greenfield Company, which has a strategy of performing the complete job of providing new, low-cost housing, from land acquisition to planting shrubbery in the play yard. Separate departments deal with architecture, real estate and finance, component manufacture, and building. The architects are the planners who conceive of types of construction, space utilization, layouts, and specifications that will create good housing at low cost; their work ranges from the highly unique and creative to the painstaking preparation of specifications for actual construction. The real estate and finance people spend a lot of their time negotiating with government agencies and other outsiders; their problems are technical and often unique. In contrast, manufacture of components (standard wall-sections, bathroom and kitchen modules, and the like) is standardized, routinized, and mechanized as much as possible. Actual building construction necessarily is "job order" in character and requires the synchronization of various craftsmen.

In this one company, two of the major departments, architecture and real estate and finance, come close to the adaptive type described in the preceding section. The building department clearly displays regulated flexibility, and the component manufacturing department is moving as close to the stable type as volume permits.

A university is as heterogeneous as the Greenfield Company. Although the suitability of the same technique for teaching biology, logic, and fine arts is debatable, everyone will agree that managing a controller's office and the buildings and grounds department is in a different category. Other enterprises may not have as much diversity as the Greenfield Company or a university, but mixed activities are very common.

This diversity has serious implications for management design. Many executives who have had successful careers in one type of design believe their style of managing should be extended to all parts of the company. We often find that the managerial practices that are well suited to the dominant department of a company are automatically applied throughout. Such consistency in managerial methods does have benefits, but the astute manager will at least consider the possibility of using different administrative styles for diverse departments.

Composite Design

Generally, when a department is both large and important to the strategy of the company it should be managed with a design suited to its own activity. This means that companies embracing diverse technologies should use several different managerial styles. The justification for this mixture of managerial styles lies, of course, in the improved performance of the respective departments.

Such diversity has its costs.

Cooperation between departments becomes increasingly difficult. Voluntary cooperation between groups with different values, time orientations, and willingness to take risks is inevitably strained. Divergent management designs add to this "cultural barrier." Because the departments are so different, we may even separate them geographically—remove research labs from the plants, separate mills designed for long production runs from those for short runs, and so on.

When management designs of departments differ sharply, special liaison staff or other formal means for coordination is often needed. Having deliberately accentuated the difference between departments, we then add a "diplomatic corps" to serve as a communication link between them.

Companywide services drop in value. With a composite design, the rotation of key personnel is impeded, budgeting is complicated, training programs fit only parts of the company, capital allocation procedures have to be tailored to different inputs and criteria. In other words, synergy arising from pooled services and reinforcing features of a management design is lacking for the company as a whole.

The task of central managers is complicated. Understanding the subtleties of the several management designs and personally adjusting one's leadership style to each calls for unusual skill and sophistication. Most managers, often unconsciously, favor departments whose management design they find congenial.

Blended Designs

Because of the drawbacks of a composite design and because dissimilar departments may be too small to support their own distinct management structure, we often try to blend two or more systems.

Some types of designs are compatible. For instance, both the stable and the regulated-flexibility designs used as examples earlier call for a high degree of central planning, strong staff, limited permissiveness, and control at intermediate points. The chief difference lies in frequent adjustment by one system to variations in client requirements; nevertheless, these adjustments normally occur within anticipated limits and often follow rules. Consequently, a combined arrangement that accommodates both technologies (for example, the component manufacturer and building construction in the Greenfield Company) can be devised. The blended design is not just what each department would do for its own purposes, but the modification can be tolerated.

Another common arrangement is to build one strong structure and then recognize that exceptions must be made for some segments of the total operation. For instance, accounting usually gets special treatment in a research laboratory, just as members of the advertising group are accepted as "oddballs" in a manufacturing firm. If the people in the exception spots have enough missionary zeal for their specialty to withstand the normal pressure to conform with the majority, the mismatch can function reasonably well.

The fact that many companies need a composite, or blended, management design does not detract from the major theme of this paper. Coherence in each management design is vital whether the design be simple or complex. The springboard for shaping each design is the character of the work to be managed; the character of the work, in turn, is a function of the company strategy. Diversity of work and the resulting complexity of designs only multiply the components that we have to take into account. The combined result, of course, is a whole mosaic of planning instruments, organizational relationships, leadership influences, and control mechanisms.

A final check, after arranging the many parts, involves going back to the master strategy of the enterprise, identifying the elements that are keys to success, and then asking whether the management design promises to emphasize these elements. In thinking through the necessary refinements of a design we are always in danger of losing perspective on the major mission.

SUMMARY

1. The interaction of two areas of management thought—master strategy and management design—offers an unusual opportunity for fruitful synthesis.

2. The "strategy and structure" approach to this synthesis should be expanded. More than organization structure is involved. Adjustments in planning, leading, and controlling, as well as in organizing, are

often needed to execute a new strategy; and the integration of these sub-processes into a total *management design* is vital.

3. Of course, a particular change in strategy will affect some facets of management more than others. Several facets likely to need adjustment are listed in exhibits 3.1 to 3.4. Note that controllable variables are identified within each of the sub-processes of management.

4. Matching management design and strategy directly is difficult. A useful bridge is to focus on "technology" as the intervening variable. Here technology is used broadly to embrace the conversion of all sorts of resources—human and financial as well as physical—into services and goods for consumers. Fortunately, we can relate technology both to *strategy* and to *manageable* tasks.

5. One characteristic of a technology is its accommodation to changes. A matrix based on frequency of changes and their novelty helps us understand three common types of technologies: stable, regulated flexibility, and adaptive. Exhibit 3.6 gives both business and nonbusiness examples of each type. And for each type we can identify likely features of an appropriate management design. For instance:

Stable technology fits well with detailed planning, intermediate goals, centralization, close supervision, tight control.

Regulated flexibility fits well with separate planning and scheduling staff, controlled information flows, circumscribed decentralization, limited use of participative and permissive leadership.

Adaptive technology fits well with planning by objective, decentralization, high personal involvement, control focused on results.

For further elaboration see exhibit 3.7.

6. A corollary of the proposition that management design should be varied so that it is (a) integrated within its parts and (b) matched to specific company strategy is that no single management design is ideal for all circumstances. We cannot say, for example, that management by objectives, decentralization, participative management, or tight control are desirable in all situations. Company strategy is one of the important factors determining what managerial arrangement is optimal.

7. Turning from a total company to its constituent parts, if the preferred technologies of various departments *within* the company differ sharply, their optimal management structure will also differ. Central management is then confronted with a dilemma of either having a mismatch of technology and management design in some departments or coordinating diverse management designs.

While much refinement and amplification remains to be done, the foregoing approach to synthesizing diverse management concepts has exciting possibilities: it provides a vehicle for putting content into a "total systems" treatment of management; it helps reconcile conflicting research findings and experience about particular managerial techniques; and it suggests some very practical guidance for managers who wish to implement changes in their company strategy.

■ Strategy, Mechanisms of Integration, and Integrating Roles

JAY R. GALBRAITH

Organizations have created a number of information-sharing and decision-making processes to integrate or coordinate activities, particularly those activities that cut across divisional and departmental boundaries. These processes vary from simple spontaneous meetings to complicated matrix forms. Our task here is to identify these processes, to order them in a way that will allow them to be related to strategy, and to identify the conditions under which the different processes should be chosen for implementing strategy.

INTEGRATION MECHANISMS

Organization theorists had occasionally performed studies that examined interdepartmental contact and communication. However, the results were not very operational, because it was not clear what were the mechanisms that produced the contact. Lawrence and Lorsch made a significant step toward giving us a language for talking about these lateral processes. They postulated two dimensions that were important for organizational effectiveness. First, organizations had to differentiate their functions so that each functional department could deal with its different subenvironment. Second, it had to integrate the differentiated functions around the interdependencies brought on by the key competitive requirements of the industry. For those firms where new product introduction was the key competitive issue, the integration problem was one of coordinating marketing and research and development. Where on-time delivery was the key competitive issue, the integration problem was one of coordinating marketing and production. The Lawrence and Lorsch thesis was that the most effective firms would be those that had differentiated their functions to the extent needed to adapt to functional subenvironments and had simultaneously found mechanisms to integrate the differentiated functions in order to deal with the competitive issue of the overall corporate environment. The results for the mechanisms of integration are shown in exhibit 3.8.

This exhibit shows the integration mechanisms used by the *most effective* firms in three different industries. That is, the exhibit shows the variation across industries, as shown by those firms that have successfully adapted to that industry. There are two main implications of this exhibit. First, it shows the different kinds of mechanisms used to integrate interdepartmental activities. Four of the mechanisms are used by all the firms. The hierarchy of authority is the principal mechanism used to resolve interdepartmental problems. The problem is referred upward into the heirarchy to a common superior who oversees all depart-

From *Strategy Implementation: The Role of Structure and Process* (St. Paul, MN: West Publishing Co., 1978), ch. 5, reprinted by permission of the author and West Publishing Co. References deleted, see original work.

EXHIBIT 3.8 Integrating Mechanisms Used in Three Different Industries

	Plastics	Food	Container
% New products in last 20 years	35%	15%	0%
Integrating devices	Rules	Rules	Rules
	Hierarchy	Hierarchy	Heirarchy
	Goal-setting	Goal-setting	Goal-setting
	Direct contact	Direct contact	Direct contact
	Teams at 3 levels	Task forces	
	Integrating dept.	Integrators	
% Integrators/ managers	22%	17%	0%

ments affected by the problem. When a problem arises frequently, a rule or procedure is devised for it as a substitute for hierarchical referral. Other problems are best solved on the spot, so goals are set by way of planning processes like scheduling and budgeting. Organizational control shifts from control over behavior to control over results, and discretion over actions to achieve results is decentralized. Exceptions to goals and rules are either referred to the hierarchy, or are resolved on the spot through direct contact between affected parties. The informal, spontaneous processes serve as another substitute for hierarchical referral. These four processes constitute standard practice for all three industries.

The second feature illustrated in exhibit 3.8 is the requirement of some firms for more mechanisms for coordination. The food processing firms and plastics firms need more than the standard practices, for example. In contrast to the effective container firm, they have evolved cross-functional teams and task forces to manage the activity associated with the introduction of new products. These group mechanisms are actually substitutes for the general manager. The general manager would make these decisions under less variable and less diverse conditions. Also, new roles were created to help integrate the cross-depart-

mental new-product activities. Product managers were created to cope with diverse product lines and new-product creation. These too are general manager equivalents. Pieces of general management work needed to coordinate interfunctional work when introducing new products are delegated to groups and integrating roles. But this delegation occurs only under conditions of diversity and uncertainty. The added managerial effort was not needed for the more predictable and less diverse container industry.

In summary, there are a number of specific mechanisms that are used to achieve interdepartmental coordination. These mechanisms vary from hierarchical referral to the addition of integrating departments such as product management departments. An enlarged list of mechanisms is shown below:

- Hierarchy
- Rules
- Goal-setting (planning)
- Direct contact
- Interdepartmental liaison roles
- Temporary task forces
- Permanent teams
- Integrating roles
- Integrating departments

Organizations select from the list those mechanisms that will permit them to implement their strategy. The selection is not random, however; choice makes a difference.

The list of coordination mechanisms is an ordered list. Each step down the list represents the commitment to a more complicated and more expensive mechanism of coordination. The increasing expenditure of resources for coordination results, first, because integrating departments is more expensive than temporary task forces using line managers. But expenditures increase also, because mechanisms at the bottom of the list are added to, not substituted for, those high on the list. They are not direct substitutes. The plastics organization uses all coordination mechanisms. Therefore, an organization should select from the list starting at the top and going down only as far as is necessary in order to implement its strategy. The successful container firm stopped at direct contact, the successful food processor stopped with integrators (product managers), and the plastics firm adopted all of them in order to be successful. The costs of these mechanisms can be seen by comparing the percentage of managers who play integrating, as opposed to line, roles. These figures are shown at the bottom of the exhibit. In the plastics organization, 22 percent of the managers work in product management activities, yet they have a functional organization. In contrast, the container firm has no managers working in integrating roles. The difference is attributable to the amount of new-product introduction that must be undertaken to remain competitive in the industry, and the level of technology required to support the new products. The more new-product activity, the higher the level of technology and uncertainty, the more the hierarchy needs to be buttressed with cross-departmental coordination mechanisms. Therefore, those organizations pursuing strategies characterized by interdepartmental activity, high uncertainty, and high diversity will select mechanisms farther down on the list than those organizations pursuing strategies characterized by low uncertainty and diversity.

The hypothesis that strategies characterized by uncertainty and diversity lead to cross-departmental processes (teams) and integrating roles is supported and elaborated by the work of Corey and Star. They studied various types and responsibilities of integrating roles (program structures, in their terminology) in functional business structures. First, they identified more complex integrating role combinations. For example, they showed the Monsanto Organic Chemicals Division structure (1967) as illustrating the type of integrating role that characterized the Lawrence and Lorsch plastics firms. The chart is shown in exhibit 3.9. It illustrates product management departments (directorates), which are overlaid on a basic functional structure. This structure is a response to product diversification strategies designed when size limits the creation of multi-divisional structures, sometimes in the presence of significant economies of scale in one or more functions as well. However, they also note that some organizations experience diversity in markets as well as in products. Some organizations then adopted market-based integrating departments. An example was IBM meeting the need to tailor the same product lines to government and commercial markets and to distinguish between manufacturing, retailing, and banking submarket applications within commercial markets. And, finally, they presented some organizations like IBM and Du Pont, who have experienced both market and product diversity. The response of these organizations has been to organize simultaneously by markets, products, and functions. The Du Pont Fibers organization of 1956 is shown in exhibit 3.10. The integrating departments are located in marketing in order to coordinate with the regional sales force and to take a marketing focus. The geographic sales force is concerned with the short-run approach to clients in their area. The industry market groups are concerned with intermediate-term issues such as market strategy, forecasts, promotions, and coordination with field sales. The product managers are concerned with longer-run issues of product strategy, new-product development, product scheduling, and coordination with manufacturing and research. Thus, diversity is handled within functional organizations by developing integrating roles around the sources of diversity.

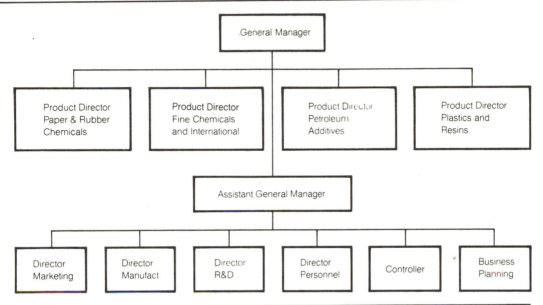

Adopted from E. Raymond Corey and Steven H. Starr, *Organization Strategy: a Marketing Approach.* Boston: Division of Research, Harvard University, Graduate School of Business Administration, 1971, p. 346 with permission, as cited in Jay R. Galbraith and Daniel A. Nathanson; *Strategy Implementation: The Role of Structure and Process.*

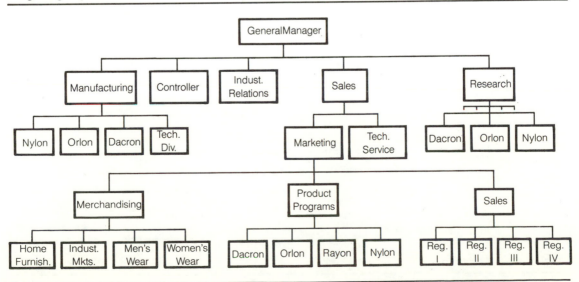

The second point made by Corey and Star was that the greater the diversity and the greater the amount of new-product introduction, the greater the likelihood of integrating roles and departments and the greater was their influence. Thus, integrating roles represents one of the principal means with which to implement diversification strategies *without reorganizing* into a product divisionalized structure.

In summary, it has been shown that organizations create integrating mechanisms in order to cope with general management problems of interdepartmental coordination caused by product and market diversity. The mechanisms, such as product task forces, are information and decision processes that are general manager substitutes but are less than full-time equivalents that result from product divisionalized structures. These mechanisms vary in their cost and their ability to cope with uncertainty and diversity. The more diversity in the business strategy, the greater the number of mechanisms adopted. For diverse and uncertain strategies, separate roles are created around the sources of diversity. These roles, such as product management roles, represent the move to simultaneous structures, which are structures in which the organization is simultaneously product and functional, or any other combination.

SIMULTANEOUS OR MATRIX STRUCTURES

The adoption of coordination mechanisms with which functional organizations can manage diversity suggests that there are a number of transition phases between the functional and multi-divisional structures. Indeed, each step down the list of coordination mechanisms represents a step toward more product-oriented decision making. Thus, the change from functional to product structures need not be a major discrete alteration but can be an evolutionary movement. There is a continuous range of distribution of influence between product and functional orientations. This description is shown in exhibit 3.11.

EXHIBIT 3.11   The Range of Alternatives

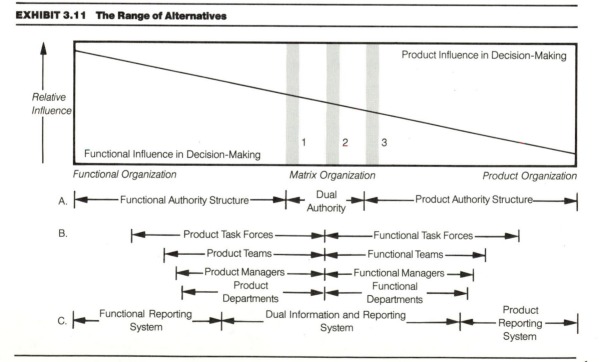

One moves along the distribution of influence by adding additional coordination mechanisms and adding power to integrating roles. The point at which product and function are of equal power is called the matrix organization. At that point, there are simultaneously two line organizations of equal power. The organization is simultaneously functional and product. Equal power is obtained through multiple authority relations. The chart for such a company is shown in exhibit 3.12. It shows a matrix organization for a geographically organized bank that is pursuing a strategy of segmenting markets and creating new financial services for those markets. The resulting market diversity forces the bank into a simultaneous structure built around markets and geography. At some point, the two

structures must intersect. In exhibit 3.12 the market organization and geographic organization intersect at the country level. The individual who manages multi-national corporate banking has two bosses—the country manager and the market manager. The task of that individual is to integrate the two perspectives for that business in that country.

One could also move to the right-hand side of the diagram in exhibit 3.11 where the product divisions are dominant and the functional managers play integrating roles. Thus, organizers are not faced with a choice of function versus product (or market or geography) divisions, but with a choice of whether to give priority to product or function. Organizations nowadays are simultaneous structures (simply a generalization of

EXHIBIT 3.12   Worldwide Matrix for a Banking Firm

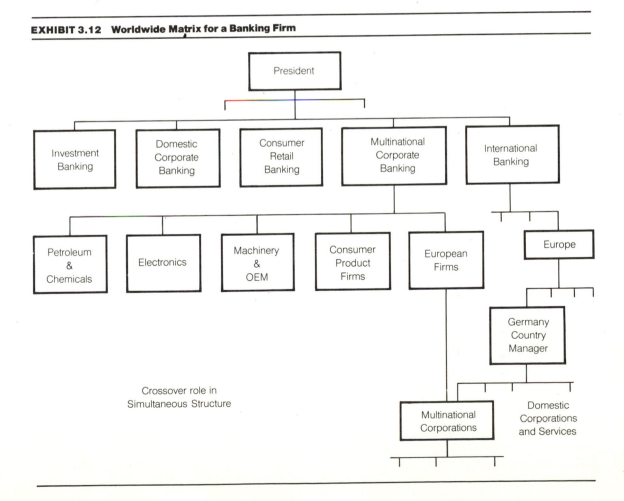

line staff models), with product and functional managers reporting to the general manager. Multi-national firms add a third geographic dimension. Which dimension is more influential and has higher priority depends upon several factors, including the strategy and the business environment.

Several factors favor emphasizing the product side. As already mentioned, diversity and new-product introductions are best managed through product-oriented structures. One would move to the right of the diagram as a result. Also, increasing interdependence among functional departments and increased need for responsiveness to the market favor a product or project orientation. However, these generalizations must be qualified by considerations of size. Self-contained product divisions may be too small to have their own sales force or to achieve size economies in production. Therefore, the larger the organization, the more likely the establishment of product or project divisions. The smaller the organization, the more likely the establishment of product or project integrating departments. The longer the life cycle of the product or project, the more likely it is that a self-contained division will be created.

A couple of factors favor the functional organization. Economies of scale in the functions mitigate against breaking them up and distributing the pieces among the product divisions. The need for special expertise and career paths for specialists are facilitated by the functional form. Therefore, firms pursuing state-of-the-art technology should have strong technical functions. The uncertainty connected with high technology also argues for a coordination capability across functions. It is usually the high-technology firms that adopt some form of the matrix, which simultaneously gives them high technology and high coordination.

The general business environment also influences the organization's strategy. Galbraith describes how the business environment has shifted in the aerospace industry and how organization structures have been adopted in order for the firms to remain competitive. These changes are independent of considerations based on size, product diversity, technology, and so on.

In the late 1950s and early 1960s, technical performance was the critical dimension. The environment was characterized by Sputnik, the space race, and the missile gap. It was deemed imperative by the government to produce technical accomplishments and to do so rapidly. The priorities placed technical performance first, schedule second, and cost a poor third. Data on actual performance during this time period reflect this order of priorities. All projects met or exceeded technical specifications, but completion times were 1.5 times as great as projected, and costs exceeded targets by a factor of 3.2. In aerospace firms performing these projects, the functional managers dominated the joint decisions, but project managers were also influential because of time pressures. Since technical performance dominated other considerations, the influence distribution was approximated by the shaded line marked "1" in exhibit 3.11.

In the early and middle 1960s, the environment changed. This was the McNamara era. McNamara believed that technical performance could be achieved, but at less cost. The contracts changed from cost plus fixed fee to various incentive contracts and fixed-price contracts. Defense Department officials demanded that aerospace firms use PERT, then PERT/Cost information systems. The effect of these changes was to make the project manager more influential in the decision process. In exhibit 3.11 the influence distribution was represented by the shaded line marked "2".

Still another change occurred in the late 1960s. Strong pressures to reduce defense costs began to operate. First, there was the publicity concerning cost overruns on the giant C–5A aircraft. Senator Proxmire began hearings on contractor efficiency practices. Finally, inflation and shifting national priorities combined to make cost the top priority, as opposed to technical performance and schedule completion. In the internal workings of aerospace firms, the project managers began to dominate the joint decision processes. The pattern of influence was explicit. Project managers held vice-presidential status, whereas laboratory and functional managers had the title of "director." The influence distribution moved to the shaded line marked "3" in exhibit 3.11.

Currently, still another change is occurring. The federal government is shifting spending away from aerospace projects. The effect is to reduce the size of the aerospace industry and of firms in it. The firms must retain specialized personnel to create the technology while meeting demands to reduce costs and size. Thus, the effective utilization of specialized resources across a number of projects has increased in importance. Firms must avoid duplication of personnel or fractional utilization of shared resources. Internally, the need to increase utilization is causing the functional managers to regain some of their previous strengths. Reduced size increased the importance of the utilization of resources and of its champion, the resource manager.

This brief account of the aerospace industry demonstrates the effect of environmental influences upon internal decision processes. Normally, the general manager would watch these trends and alter decision-making behavior accordingly. When decisions

are decentralized, however, the general managers must change internal power bases as well as their own decision behavior. It becomes the task of the general manager to see that the distribution of internal influence reflects the external realities faced by the organization. The general manager must therefore take an open-system view of the organization.

Several implications can be derived from the scenario. First, the matrix is not the ultimate structure but, like all structures, is a transitional one that should be adopted when conditions merit and discarded when conditions no longer pertain. Second, simultaneous structures are flexible structures that can be adjusted and fine-tuned by altering the power distribution of the existing roles as strategy and environment change. Third, the task of the chief executive is one of power balancing. The power balance among the roles needs to be adjusted continually with regard to assignments, salary, physical location, titles, and other factors. Thus, as technological changes such as minicomputers reduce economies of scale and promote power shifts to self-contained product divisions, the chief executive needs to plan the organization as he or she plans strategy and investments. The internal power distribution must produce decisions consistent with external reality and strategy.

■ What Is the Right Organization Structure?

ROBERT DUNCAN

Organization design is a central problem for managers. What is the "best" structure for the organization? What are the criteria for selecting the "best" structure? What signals indicate that the organization's existing structure may not be appropriate to its tasks and its environment? This article discusses the purposes of organization structure and presents a decision tree analysis approach to help managers pick the right organization structure.

THE OBJECTIVES OF ORGANIZATIONAL DESIGN

What is organization structure and what is it supposed to accomplish? Organization structure is more than boxes on a chart; it is a pattern of interactions and coordination that links the technology, tasks, and human components of the organization to insure that the organization accomplishes its purpose.

An organization's structure has essentially two objectives: First, it facilitates the flow of information within the organization in order to reduce the uncertainty in decision-making. The design of the organization should facilitate the collection of the information managers need for decision-making. When managers experience a high degree of un-

certainty—that is, when their information needs are great—the structure of the organization should not be so rigid as to inhibit managers from seeking new sources of information or developing new procedures or methods for doing their jobs. For example, in developing a new product, a manufacturing department may need to seek direct feedback from customers on how the new product is being accepted; the need to react quickly to customer response makes waiting for this information to come through normal marketing and sales channels unacceptable.

The second objective of organization design is to achieve effective coordination—integration. The structure of the organization should integrate organizational behavior across the parts of the organization so it is coordinated. This is particularly important when the units in the organization are interdependent. As James Thompson has indicated, the level of interdependence can vary.

In *pooled interdependence* the parts of the organization are independent and are linked together only in contributing something to the same overall organization. In many conglomerates, the divisions are really separate organizations linked only in that they contribute profits to the overall organization. Simple rules—procedures—can be developed to specify what the various units have to do.

In *sequential interdependence*, however, there is an ordering of activities, that is, one organizational unit has to perform its function before the next unit can perform its. For example, in an automobile plant manufacturing has to produce the automobiles before quality control can inspect them. Now such organizations have to develop plans to coordinate activities; quality control needs to know when and how many cars to expect for inspection.

Reciprocal interdependence is the most complex type of organizational interdependence. Reciprocal interdependence is present when the outputs of Unit A become the inputs of Unit B and the outputs of B cycle back to become the inputs of Unit A. The relationship between the operations and maintenance in an airline is a good example of this type of interdependence. Operations produces "sick" airplanes that need repair by maintenance. Maintenance repairs these planes and the repaired planes become inputs to the operations division to be reassigned to routes. When reciprocal interdependence between organization units is present, a more complex type of coordination is required. This is coordination by feedback. Airline operations and maintenance must communicate with one another so each one will know when the planes will be coming to them so they can carry out their respective functions.

Organizational design, then, is the allocation of resources and people to a specified mission or purpose and the structuring of these resources to achieve the mission. Ideally, the organization is designed to fit its environment and to provide the information and coordination needed.

It is useful to think of organization structure from an information-processing view. The key characteristic of organizational structure is that it links the elements of the organization by providing the channels of communication through which information flows. My research has indicated that when organizational structure is formalized and centralized, information flows are restricted and, as a consequence, the organization is not able to gather and process the information it needs when faced with uncertainty.

For example, when an organization's structure is highly centralized, decisions are made at the top and information tends to be filtered as it moves up the chain of command. When a decision involves a great deal of uncertainty, it is unlikely therefore that the few individuals at the top of the organization will have the information they require to make the best decision. So decentralization, that is, having more subordinates participate in the decision-making process, may generate the information needed to help reduce the uncertainty and thereby facilitate a better decision.

ALTERNATIVE ORGANIZATIONAL DESIGNS

The key question for the manager concerned with organization design is what are the different structures available to choose from. Contingency theories of organization have shown that there is no one best structure. However, organization theorists have been less clear in elaborating the decision process managers can follow in deciding which structure to implement.

In discussing organization design, organization theorists describe structure differently from the way managers responsible for organization design do. Organizational theorists describe structure as more or less formalized, centralized, specialized, or hierarchical. However, managers tend to think of organizational structure in terms of two general types, the *functional* and the *decentralized*. (The most common form of decentralization is the *product* organization.) Most organizations today are either functional or decentralized or some modification or combination of these two general types. Therefore, if we are to develop a heuristic for helping managers make decisions about organization structure, we need to think of structures as functional or decentralized and not in terms of the more abstract dimensions of formalization, centralization, and so on, that organizational theorists tend to use.

ORGANIZATIONAL ENVIRONMENT AND DESIGN: A CRITICAL INTERACTION

In deciding what kind of organization structure to use, managers need to first understand the characteristics of the environment they are in and the demands this environment makes on the organization in terms of information and coordination. Once the environment is understood, the manager can proceed with the design process.

The first step in designing an organization structure, therefore, is to identify the organization's environment. The task environment constitutes that part of the environment defined by managers as relevant or potentially relevant for organizational decision making. Exhibit 3.13 presents a list of environmental components managers might encounter. Clearly, no one organization would encounter all these components in decision-making, but this is the master list from which organizational decision-makers would identify the appropriate task environments. For example, a manager in a manufacturing division could define an environment consisting of certain personnel, certain staff units and suppliers, and perhaps certain technological components. The usefulness of the list in exhibit 3.13 is that it provides a guide for decision-makers, alerting them to the elements in the environment they might consider in decision-making.

Once managers have defined the task environment, the next step is to understand the state of that environment. What are its key characteristics? In describing organizational environments, we emphasize two dimensions: simple–complex and static–dynamic.

The simple–complex dimension of the environment focuses on whether the factors in the environment considered for decision

---

EXHIBIT 3.13   Environmental Components List

Internal Environment	*External Environment*
Organizational personnel component	*Customer component*
■ Educational and technological background and skills	■ Distributors of product or service
■ Previous technological and managerial skill	■ Actual users of product or service
■ Individual member's involvement and commitment to attaining system's goals	*Suppliers component*
■ Interpersonal behavior styles	■ New materials suppliers
■ Availability of human resources for utilization within the system	■ Equipment suppliers
	■ Product parts suppliers
Organizational functional and staff units component	■ Labor supply
■ Technological characteristics of organizational units	*Competitor component*
■ Interdependence of organizational units in carrying out their objectives	■ Competitors for suppliers
■ Conflicts among organizational functional and staff units	■ Competitors for customers
	Sociopolitical component
Organizational level component	■ Government regulatory control over the industry
■ Organizational objectives and goals	■ Public political attitude toward industry and its particular product
■ Integrative process integrating individuals and groups into contributing maximally to attaining organizational goals	■ Relationship with trade unions with jurisdiction in the organization
■ Nature of the organization's product service	*Technological component*
	■ Meeting new technological requirements of own industry and related industries in production of product or service
	■ Improving and developing new products by implementing new technological advances in the industry

making are few in number and similar or many in number and different. An example of a *simple* unit would be a lower-level production unit whose decisions are affected only by the parts department and materials department, on which it is dependent for supplies, and the marketing department, on which it is dependent for output. An example of a *complex* environment would be a programming and planning department. This group must consider a wide variety of environmental factors when making a decision. It may focus on the marketing and materials department, on customers, on suppliers, and so on. Thus this organizational unit has a much more heterogeneous group of environmental factors to deal with in decision-making—its environment is more complex than that of the production unit.

The static–dynamic dimension of the environment is concerned with whether the factors of the environment remain the same over time or change. A *static* environment, for example, might be a production unit that has to deal with a marketing department whose requests for output remain the same and a materials department that is able to supply a steady rate of inputs to the produc-

tion unit. However, if the marketing department were continually changing its requests and the materials department were inconsistent in its ability to supply parts, the production unit would be operating in a more *dynamic* environment.

Exhibit 3.14 provides a four-way classification of organizational environments and some examples of organizations in each of these environments. Complex–dynamic (Cell 4) environments are probably the most characteristic type today. These environments involve rapid change and create high uncertainty for managers. The proper organizational structure is critical in such environments if managers are to have the information necessary for decision-making. Also, as organizations move into this turbulent environment, it may be necessary for them to modify their structures. For example, AT & T has moved from a functional organization to a decentralized structure organized around different markets to enable it to cope with more competition in the telephone market and in communications. This change in structure was a response to the need for more information and for a quicker response time to competitive moves.

EXHIBIT 3.14   Classification of Organizational Environments

	Simple		Complex
Static	*Low perceived uncertainty* Small number of factors and components in the environment Factors and components are somewhat similar to one another Factors and components remain basically the same and are not changing *Example*: Soft-drink industry — 1	2 —	*Moderately low perceived uncertainty* Large number of factors and components in the environment Factors and components are not similar to one another Factors and components remain basically the same *Example*: Food products
Dynamic	*Moderately high perceived uncertainty* Small number of factors and components in the environment Factors and components are somewhat similar to one another Factors and components of the environment are in continual process of change *Example*: Fast-food industry — 3	4 —	*High perceived uncertainty* Large number of factors and components in the environment Factors and components are not similar to one another Factors and components of environment are in a continual process of change *Examples*: Commercial airline industry Telephone communications (AT&T)

STRATEGIES FOR ORGANIZATIONAL DESIGN

Once the organization's environment has been diagnosed, what type of structure the organization should have becomes the key question.

Simple Design Strategy

When the organization's environment is relatively simple, that is, there are not many factors to consider in decision-making, and stable, that is, neither the make-up of the environment nor the demands made by environmental components are changing, the information and coordination needs for the organization are low. In such circumstances, a *functional organization structure* is most appropriate.

A key characteristic of the functional organization is specialization by functional areas. Exhibit 3.15 presents a summary of this structure's strengths and weaknesses. The key strengths of the functional organization are that it supports in-depth skill development and a simple decision-communication network. However, when disputes or uncertainty arises among managers about a decision, they get pushed up the hierarchy to be resolved. A primary weakness of the functional organization, therefore, is that when the organization's environment becomes more dynamic and uncertainty tends to increase, many decisions move to the top of the organization. Lower-level managers do not have the information required for decision-making so they push decisions upward. Top-level managers become overloaded and are thus slow to respond to the environment.

Organizational Design Dilemma

The organizational designer faces a dilemma in such situations. Designs can be instituted that *reduce* the amount of information required for decision-making. Decentralization is the principal strategy indicated. Or organizations can develop more lateral relations to *increase* the amount of information available for decision-making.

A decentralized organization is possible whenever an organization's tasks are self-contained. Decentralized organizations are typically designed around products, projects, or markets. The decentralized healthcare organization in exhibit 3.16 is or-

---

EXHIBIT 3.15 Characteristics of the Functional Organization

Organizational Functions	*Accomplished in Functional Organization*
Goals	Functional subgoal emphasis (projects lag)
Influence	Functional heads
Promotion	By special function
Budgeting	By function or department
Rewards	For special capability

Strengths	*Weaknesses*
1. Best in *stable* environment	1. Slow response time
2. Colleagueship ("home") for technical specialists	2. Bottlenecks caused by sequential tasks
3. Supports in-depth skill development	3. Decisions pile at top
4. Specialists freed from administrative/coordinating work	4. If multiproduct, product priority conflict
5. Simple decision/communication network excellent in small, limited-output organizations	5. Poor interunit coordination
	6. Stability paid for in less innovation
	7. Restricted view of whole

EXHIBIT 3.16   Decentralized Organization

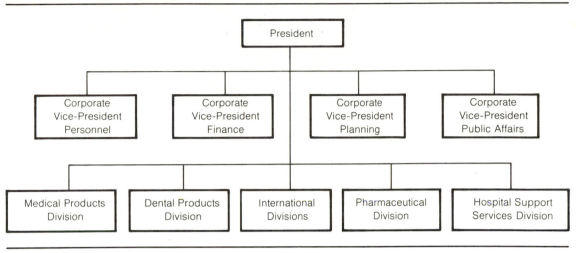

ganized around product areas (Medical and Dental) and market area (International). Each division has all the resources needed to perform its particular task. For example, Medical Products (exhibit 3.16) has its own functional organization consisting of production, marketing, and R & D to carry out its mission. The information needed by Medical Products Division's managers is reduced because they have organized around a set of common medical products, and they don't have to worry about dental, pharmaceutical, or hospital support services or products.

In the decentralized organization, managers have to worry only about their own products or services; they have the resources to carry out these activities, and they don't have to compete for shared resources or schedule shared resources. There is also a full-time commitment to a particular product line. The decentralized structure is particularly effective when the organization's environment is very complex, that is, there is a large number of factors to be considered in decision-making, and the environment can be segmented or broken down into product or market areas around which the organization can structure itself. For example, the health products organization (exhibit 3.16) probably started out as a

functional organization. However, as its product line increased, it undoubtedly became more difficult for one manufacturing unit to have the expertise to produce such a wide range of products efficiently and to handle the diversity of information needed to do it. It would also be difficult for one marketing unit to market such a diverse group of products; different kinds of information and skills would be required to sell the different products. Segmenting this complex environment into product areas facilitates increased specialization. As a result, divisional managers need less information than if they had to deal with all the products and services of the corporation.

Exhibit 3.17 summarizes the characteristics and the strengths and weaknesses of the decentralized organization. Decentralized organizations face several problems. For example, it is sometimes difficult to decide what resources are to be pooled in a corporate staff to be used to service the entire organization. If the divisions are very different from one another in terms of products, customers, technology, and so on, however, it becomes very difficult to staff a corporate services unit with the diverse knowledge needed to be able to help the divisions. A restricted approach to innovation is another problem decentralized organizations may

EXHIBIT 3.17 Characteristics of the Decentralized Organization

Organizational Functions	Accomplished in Decentralized Organization
Goals	Special product emphasis (technologies lag)
Influence	Product, project heads
Promotion	By product management
Budgeting	By product, project, program
Rewards	For integrative capability

Strengths	Weaknesses
1. Suited to fast change	1. Innovation/growth restricted to existing project areas
2. High product, project, or program visibility	2. Tough to allocate pooled resources (i.e., computer, lab)
3. Full-time task orientation (i.e., dollars, schedules, profits)	3. Shared functions hard to coordinate (i.e., purchasing)
4. Task responsibility, contact points clear to customers or clients	4. Deterioration of in-depth competence—hard to attract technical specialists
5. Processes multiple tasks in parallel, easy to cross functional lines	5. Possible internal task conflicts, priority conflicts
	6. May neglect high level of integration required in organization

encounter. Because each division is organized around a particular product or geographic area, each manager's attention is focused on his or her special area. As a result, their innovations focus on their particular specialties. Managers don't have the diverse information needed to produce radical innovations.

One major liability of decentralized organizations is their relative inability to provide integration—coordination among the divisions, even when their interdependence increases. When divisions are relatively autonomous and have only pooled interdependence, there is not much need for coordination. However, when uncertainty increases and the divisions have to work together because of increased sequential or reciprocal interdependence between the units, decentralized organizations have no formal mechanisms to coordinate and resolve the increased needs for information.

Since today's organizational environments are becoming more complex and interdependent, large decentralized corporations are finding that the need to integrate has increased for at least five reasons:

1. The increased level of regulation organizations face requires more and more coordination across divisions to be sure that all regulatory requirements are being met. For example, crackdowns by the SEC on illegal foreign payments and the increased liabilities of boards of directors have required organizations to have better control systems and information sources to enable their headquarters staff groups to know what's going on in the divisions. Affirmative action requirements have required that divisions share information on how they are doing and where possible pools of affirmative action candidates may be found.

2. Organizational environments are changing, and this can lead to a requirement of more coordination across divisions. New customer demands may require what were previously autonomous divisions to coordinate their activities. For example, if the International Group in the health products company mentioned earlier faces a demand to develop some new products for overseas, it may be necessary to provide a means by which the Medical Products and Pharmaceutical Divisions can work in a coordinated and integrated way with International to develop these new products.

3. Technological changes are placing more emphasis on increased interaction among divisions. More and more, computer systems and R & D services are being shared, thus compelling the divisions to interact more with one another.

4. The cost of making "wrong" strategic decisions is increasing in terms of both sunk costs and losses because of failure to get market share. Since such "wrong" decisions sometimes result from a lack of contact between divisions, it emphasizes the need to have more coordination across divisions and more sharing of information. For example, AT & T has just recently begun to market telephone and support equipment to counter the competition of other suppliers of this equipment that have entered the market. To do this AT & T has organized around markets. It has also increased the opportunities for interaction among these market managers so they can share information, build on one another's expertise and competence, and insure required coordination.

5. Scarce resources—for example, capital and raw materials—will require more interaction among divisions to set overall priorities. Is a university, for example, going to emphasize its undergraduate arts program or its professional schools? By setting up task forces of the deans of the schools, the university might be able to identify opportunities for new innovative programs that could benefit the entire organization. New programs in management of the arts—museums, orchestras, and so on—could draw on the expertise of the arts department and the business school and would not require a lot of new venture capital.

For a number of reasons, then, there is a need for increased coordination among divisions in decentralized organizations. Given the decentralized organization's weakness, organizational designers need to implement the second general design strate-

gy, increasing the information flow to reduce uncertainty and facilitate coordination.

Lateral Relations: Increasing Information Available for Decision-making

Lateral relations is really a process that is overlaid on an existing functional or decentralized structure. Lateral relations as a process moves decision-making down to where the problem is in the organization. It differs from decentralization in that no self-contained tasks are created.

Jay Galbraith has identified various types of lateral relations. *Direct contact*, for example, can be used by managers of diverse groups as a mechanism to coordinate their different activities. With direct contact, managers can meet informally to discuss their common problems. *Liaison roles* are a formal communication link between two units. Engineering liaison with the manufacturing department is an excellent example of the liaison role. The engineer serving in the liaison role may be located in the production organization as a way of coordinating engineering and production activities.

When coordination between units becomes more complex, an *integrator role* may be established. Paul Lawrence and Jay Lorsch have indicated that the integrator role is particularly useful when organizational units that must be coordinated are differentiated from one another in terms of their structure, subgoals, time, orientation, and so on. In such situations, there is the possibility of conflict between the various units. For example, production, marketing, and R & D units in an organization may be highly differentiated from one another. Marketing, for example, is primarily concerned with having products to sell that are responsive to customer needs. R & D, on the other hand, may be concerned with developing innovative products that shape customer needs. Production, for its part, may want products to remain unchanged so that manufacturing set-ups don't have to be modified. Obviously there are differences among the three units in terms of their subgoals. The integrator role is instituted to coordinate and moderate such diverse orientations. The integrator could be a materials manager or a group executive whose additional function would be to coordinate and integrate the diverse units in ways that meet the organization's common objectives.

To be effective as an integrator, a manager needs to have certain characteristics. First, he needs wide contacts in the organization so that he possesses the relevant information about the different units he is attempting to integrate. Second, the integrator needs to understand and share, at least to a degree, the goals and orientations of the different groups. He cannot be seen as being a partisan of one particular group's perspective. Third, the integrator has to be rather broadly trained technically, so that he can talk the language of the different groups. By being able to demonstrate that he has some expertise in each area, he will be viewed as more credible by each group and will also be better able to facilitate information exchange between the units. The integrator can in effect become an interpreter of each group's position to the others. Fourth, the groups that the integrator is working with must trust him. Again, the integrator is trying to facilitate information flow and cooperation between the groups and thus the groups must believe that he is working toward a solution acceptable to all the groups. Fifth, the integrator needs to exert influence on the basis of his expertise rather than through formal power. The integrator can provide information and identify alternative courses of action for the different units as they attempt to coordinate their activities. The more he can get them to agree on solutions and courses of action rather than having to use his formal power, the more committed they will be to implementing the solution. Last, the integrator's conflict-resolution skills are important. Because differentiation between the units exists, conflict and disagreement are inevitable. It is important, therefore, that confrontation is used as the conflict-resolution style. By confrontation we mean that parties to the conflict identify the causes of conflict and are committed to adopting a problem-solving approach to finding a mutually acceptable solution to the conflict. The parties must also be committed, of course, to work to implement that solution.

When coordination involves working with six or seven different units, task forces or teams can be established. Task forces involve a group of managers working together on the coordination problems of their diverse groups. For example, in a manufacturing organization, the marketing, production, R & D, finance, and engineering managers may meet twice a week (or more often when required) to discuss problems of coordination that they may be having that require their cooperation to solve. In this use a task force is a problem-solving group formed to facilitate coordination.

The matrix type of structure is the most complex form of lateral relations. The matrix is typically a formal structure in the organization; it is not a structure that is often added temporarily to an existing functional or decentralized structure. As Lawrence, Kolodny, and Davis have indicated, there are certain key characteristics of a matrix structure. The most salient is that there is dual authority, that is, both the heads of the functions and the matrix manager have authority over those working in the matrix unit.

The matrix was initially developed in the aerospace industry where the organization had to be responsive to products/markets as well as technology. Because the matrix focuses on a specific product or market, it can generate the information and concentrate the resources needed to respond to changes in that product or market rapidly. The matrix is now being used in a variety of business, public, and health organizations. Exhibit 3.18 provides a summary of the characteristics and strengths and weaknesses of the matrix form of organization.

EXHIBIT 3.18 Characteristics of the Matrix Organization

Organizational Functions	Accomplished in Matrix Organization
Goals	Emphasis on product/market
Influence	Matrix manager and functional heads
Promotion	By function or into matrix manager job
Budgeting	By matrix organization project
Rewards	By special functional skills and performance in matrix

Strengths	Weaknesses
1. Full-time focus of personnel on project of matrix	1. Costly to maintain personnel pool to staff matrix
2. Matrix manager is coordinator of functions for single project	2. Participants experience dual authority of matrix manager and functional area managers
3. Reduces information requirements as focus is on single product/market	3. Little interchange with functional groups outside the matrix so there may be duplication of effort, "reinvention of the wheel"
4. Masses specialized technical skills to the product/market	4. Participants in matrix need to have good interpersonal skills in order for it to work

The matrix structure is particularly useful when an organization wants to focus resources on producing a particular product or service. The use of the matrix in the aerospace industry, for example, allowed these organizations to build manufacturing units to produce particular airplanes, thus allowing in-depth attention and specialization of skills.

Matrix organizations, however, are complicated to manage. Because both project managers and traditional functional area managers are involved in matrix organizations, personnel in the matrix have two bosses, and there is an inherent potential for conflict under such circumstances. As a result, the matrix form of lateral relations should be used only in those situations where an organization faces a unique problem in a particular market area or in the technological requirements of a product. When the information and technological requirements are such that a full-time focus on the market or product is needed, a matrix organization can be helpful. Citibank, for example, has used a matrix structure in its international activity to concentrate on geographic areas. Boeing Commercial Airplane has used the matrix to focus resources on a particular product.

Lateral relations require a certain organizational design and special interpersonal skills if this process for reducing uncertainty by increasing the information available for improving coordination is going to be effective. From a design perspective, four factors are required:

1. The organization's reward structure must support and reward cooperative problem-solving that leads to coordination and integration. Will a manager's performance appraisal, for example, reflect his or her participation in efforts to achieve coordination and integration? If the organization's reward system does not recognize joint problem-solving efforts, then lateral relations will not be effective.

2. In assigning managers to participate in some form of lateral relations, it is important that they have responsibility for implementation. Line managers should be involved since they understand the problems more intimately than staff personnel and, more important, they are concerned about implementation. Staff members can be used, but line managers should be dominant since this will lead to more commitment on their part to implementing solutions that come out of lateral relations problem-solving efforts.

3. Participants must have the authority to commit their units to action. Managers who are participating in an effort to resolve problems of coordination must be able to indicate what particular action their units might take in trying to improve coordination. For example, in the manufacturing company task force example mentioned earlier, the marketing manager should be able to commit his group to increasing the lead time for providing information to production on deadlines for delivering new products to customers.

4. Lateral processes must be integrated into the vertical information flow. In the concern for increasing information exchange *across* the units in the organization there must be no loss of concern for vertical information exchange so that the top levels in the organization are aware of coordination efforts.

Certain skills are also required on the part of participants for lateral relations to work:

1. Individuals must deal with conflict effectively, in the sense of identifying the sources of conflict and then engaging in problem-solving to reach a mutually acceptable solution to the conflict situation.

2. Participants need good interpersonal skills. They must be able to communicate effectively with one another and avoid making other participants feel defensive. The more they can learn to communicate with others in a descriptive, nonevaluative manner, the more open the communication process will be.

3. Participants in lateral relations need to understand that influence and power should be based on expertise rather than on formal power. Because of the problem-solving nature of lateral relations, an individual's power and influence will change based on the particular problem at hand and the individual's ability to provide key information to solve the problem. At various times different members will have more influence because of their particular expertise.

Lateral relations, then, is a process that is overlaid onto the existing functional or de-centralized organization structure. Lateral relations requires various skills, so it is imperative that an organization never adopt this approach without training the people involved. Before implementing lateral relations, team building might be used to develop the interpersonal skills of the participating managers. These managers might spend time learning how to operate more effectively in groups, how to improve communication skills, and how to deal with conflict in a positive way so that it does not become disruptive to the organization.

The Organizational Design Decision Tree

We have discussed the different kinds of organization structure that managers can implement. We are now prepared to identify the decision-making process the manager can use in selecting the appropriate structure to "fit" the demands of the environment. Exhibit 3.19 presents a decision tree analysis for selecting either the functional or decentralized organization structure. This decision analysis also indicates when the existing functional or decentralized organization structure should be supplemented with some form of lateral relations in the form of a task force or team or a matrix. In general, an organization should use one of the simpler forms of lateral relations rather than the more complex and expensive matrix. In using this decision tree, there are a number of questions that the designer needs to ask.

The first question is whether the organization's environment is *simple*, that is, there are few factors to consider in the environment, or *complex*, that is, there are a number of different environmental factors to be considered in decision-making. If the environment is defined as simple, the next question focuses on whether the environmental factors are *static*, that is, remain the same over time, or are *dynamic*, that is, change over time. If we define the environment as static, there is likely to be little uncertainty associated with decision-making. In turn, information requirements for decision-mak-

EXHIBIT 3.19   Organizational Design Decision Tree Heuristic

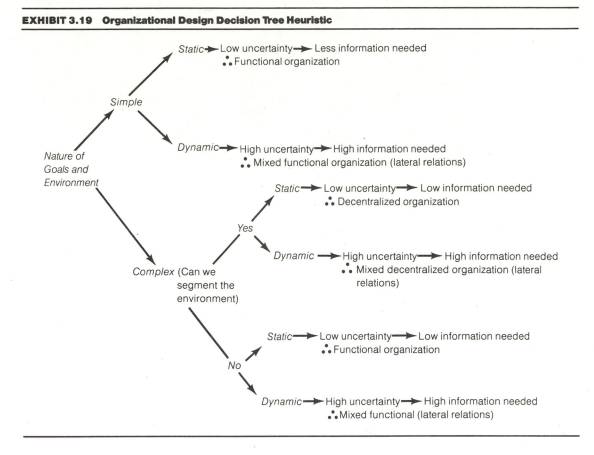

ing are low. In this simple-static environment, the functional organization is most efficient. It can most quickly gather and process the information required to deal with this type of environment.

At this point a question might be raised: Are there any organizational environments that are in fact both simple and static or is this a misperception on the part of the managers that oversimplifies the environment? There may be environments like this, but the key is that these environments may change, that is, they may become more dynamic as the marketplace changes, as resources become scarce, or the organization's domain is challenged. For example, the motor home/recreational vehicle industry was very successful in the early 1970s. Its market was relatively homogeneous (simple) and there was a constantly high demand (static) for its products. Then the oil

embargo of 1973 hit, and the environment suddenly became dynamic. The industry had a very difficult time changing because it had done no contingency planning about "what would happen if" demand shifted, resources became scarce, and so on. The important point is that an organization's environment may be simple and static today but change tomorrow. Managers should continually scan the environment and be sensitive to the fact that things can change and contingency planning may be useful.

If this simple environment is defined as dynamic, with some components in the environment changing, some uncertainty may be experienced by decision-makers. Thus information needs will be greater than when the environment was static. Therefore, in this simple-dynamic environment the mixed functional organization with lateral relations is likely to be the most effective in gathering and processing the information required for decision-making. Because the organization's environment is simple, the creation of self-contained units would not be efficient. It is more economical to have central functional areas responsible for all products and markets as these products and markets are relatively similar to one another. However, when uncertainty arises and there is need for more information, some form of lateral relations can be added to the existing functional organization.

Exhibit 3.20 shows the functional organization of a manufacturing organization. The organization may suddenly face a problem with its principal product. Competitors may have developed an attractive replacement. As a result of this unique problem, the president of the firm may set up a task force chaired by the vice-president of sales to develop new products. The task force consists of members from manufacturing, sales, research, and engineering services. Its function, obviously, will be to develop and evaluate suggestions for new products.

If the organization's environment is defined by the managers as complex, that is, there is a large number of factors and components that needs to be considered in decision-making, the next question to ask is, can the organization *segment* its environment into geographic areas, market, or product areas? If the environment is defined as segmentable, the next question focuses on whether the environment is static or dynamic. If the environment is defined

EXHIBIT 3.20   Functional Organization with Task Force

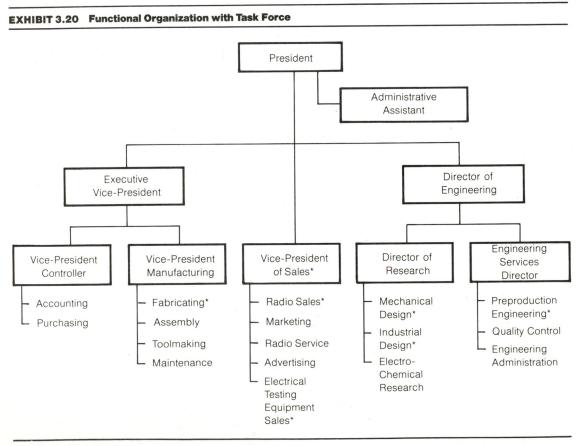

*Members of task force

as static, there is going to be low uncertainty and thus information needs for decision-making are not going to be high. Thus, in the complex-segmentable-static environment, the decentralized organization is most appropriate, and the health products organization discussed earlier is a good example of this. The organization can break the environment apart in the sense that it can organize around products or markets, for example, and thus information, resources, and so forth, are only required to produce and market these more homogeneous outputs of the organization.

In the complex-segmentable-dynamic environment there is a change in the components of the environment and the demands they are making on the organization, or else the organization has to consider different factors in the environment that it had not previously considered in decision-making. Uncertainty and coordination needs may be higher. The result is that decision-makers need more information to reduce uncertainty and provide information to facilitate coordination. The mixed decentralized organization with lateral relations is the appropriate structure here.

Exhibit 3.21 presents the design of a multidivision decentralized health products or-

ganization. Some form of lateral relations may be added to this structure to help generate more information. For example, the International Division may be attempting to develop new products but may be encountering problems, with the result that the entire organization, stimulated by the president's concern, may be experiencing uncertainty about how to proceed. In such a situation, a task force of the manager of the International Group and the Dental Group and the Pharmaceutical Group might work together in developing ideas for new products in the International Division. The lateral relations mechanism of the task force facilitates information exchange *across* the organization to reduce uncertainty and increase coordination of the efforts of the divisions that should be mutually supportive. By working together in the task force, the division managers will be exchanging information and will be gaining a better understanding of their common problems and how they need to work and coordinate with one another in order to solve these problems.

If the organization's complex environment is defined by managers as nonsegmentable, the functional organization will be appropriate because it is not possible to break the

---

EXHIBIT 3.21   Decentralized Organization with Lateral Relations

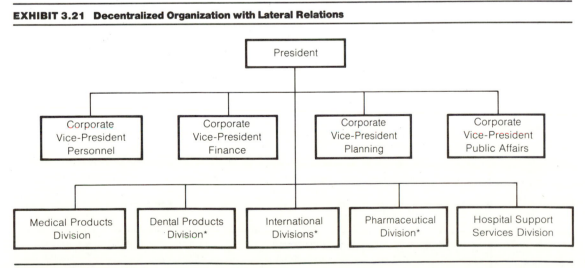

*Members of task force

environment up into geographic or product/service areas.

In effect, there simply might be too much interdependence among environmental components, or the technology of the organization may be so interlinked that it is not possible to create self-contained units organized around components of the environment.

A hospital is a good example of this organization type. The environment is clearly complex. There are numerous and diverse environmental components that have to be considered in decision-making (for example, patients, regulatory groups, medical societies, third-party payers, and suppliers). In the complex-nonsegmentable-static environment, environmental components are rather constant in their demands. Thus here the functional organization is most appropriate.

However, the functional organization, through its very specific rules, procedures, and channels of communication, will likely be too slow in generating the required infor-

mation. Therefore, some form of lateral relations may be added to the functional organization. Exhibit 3.22 presents an example of an aerospace functional organization that uses a matrix structure for its airplane and missile products divisions. The matrix structure provides in-depth concentration of personnel and resources on these different product areas, each of which has its own very unique information and technological requirements.

SYMPTOMS OF INAPPROPRIATE ORGANIZATIONAL STRUCTURE

The key question at this point is: So what? What are the costs to an organization if it is using the wrong structure, given its product/service and the environment in which it operates? In order to be effective, an organization needs to attain its goals and objectives, it needs to adapt to the environment, and, last, it should be designed in such a

EXHIBIT 3.22   Functional Organization with Matrix

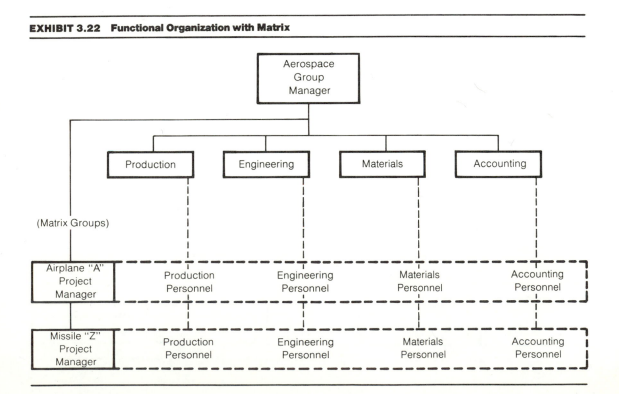

way that its managers experience low role conflict and ambiguity.

Therefore, there are certain kinds of information the manager responsible for organizational design should be sensitive to in monitoring whether the appropriate structure is being used. While using the appropriate structure may have some direct impact on the organization's ability to attain its goals, its biggest impact will probably be on the adaptability of the organization and the role behavior of its managers.

Certain kinds of symptoms regarding ineffective adaptability may occur. For example:

■ Organizational decision-makers may not be able to anticipate problems before they occur. There may be a tendency in the organization to wait until problems occur and then react to them because the organization simply does not have enough information to develop contingency plans.

■ Decision-makers may err in trying to predict trends in their decision environment. Without proper coordination across divisions, the organization may lose control over the relationship between its internal functioning and its environment.

■ The organization may not be able to get key information for decision-making to the right place for effective decision-making. For example, division managers from different product groups may have information that quality and liability standards on their respective products are unrealistically high. However, because of decentralization and lack of effective coordination through some form of lateral relations, this information may not get to the staff groups in the organization that are responsible for setting corporate policy in this area.

■ The organization, having identified a problem vis-à-vis its environment, may simply not be able to take corrective action quickly enough.

Symptoms of poor fit between structure and environment may also show at the level of the individual in terms of some increase in either role conflict or role ambiguity. It is important, therefore, that the organization monitor the level of role conflict and role ambiguity among its managers and the resulting stress they experience so the system has a baseline for comparison. If there is a significant increase from this baseline in conflict and ambiguity and stress, then the organization may consider that the increase is a symptom of an organizational design problem. For example:

■ Individuals may be experiencing increased role conflict. This may occur when the organization is implementing a functional organization in a dynamic environment. The environment may be changing and the individuals may be required to make quick responses to this changing environment. Having to wait for new policy changes to come down the hierarchy may delay the organization from responding appropriately. Decision-makers at the top of the organization will also suffer from role conflict when the environment is changing rapidly. In the functional organization, when new situations occur they are referred to higher levels of the organization for decision and action. The result is that top-level decision-makers become overloaded and the organization's response to the environment slows down. In a dynamic environment, the functional organization constrains the decision-making adaptation process.

■ Individuals in the organization also may experience increased role ambiguity—they may be unclear as to what is expected of them in their roles. For example, role ambiguity is likely to occur when the decentralized organization is implemented without some effective use of lateral relations. Individuals may feel they don't have the information needed for decision-making. Divisional managers may not know what the corporate staff's policy is on various issues, and corporate staff may have lost touch with the divisions.

These are the kinds of information managers should be aware of as indicators of dysfunctional organization design. These data can be collected in organizational diagnosis surveys that we have developed so that a more systemic monitoring of structure exists just as we monitor organizational climate. As fine tuning the organization's design to its environment becomes more critical, organizations will begin to monitor their organizational design more systematically.

SUMMARY

What are the advantages to managers in using the design decision tree? There appear to be several:

1. It provides a *broad framework* for identifying the key factors a manager should think about in considering an organizational design. For example: What is our environment? What different structural options do we have?

2. It forces the manager to *diagnose* the decision environment. What is our environment like? How stable is it? How complex is it? Is it possible to reduce complexity by segmenting the environment into product or geographical subgroups?

3. It causes managers to think about *how much interdependence* there is among seg-ments of the organization. How dependent on one another are different parts of the organization in terms of technology, services, support, help in getting their tasks completed? The decision points in the heuristic force managers to question themselves about what other parts of the organization they need to coordinate their activities with, and then to think about how to do it.

4. Once the organization is in either a functional or decentralized structure, the decision tree points out what can be done to meet *the increased needs for information* through the use of lateral relations. Lateral relations provide a mechanism for supplementing the existing structure to facilitate dealing with the organization's increased needs for information and coordination.

Managers in a variety of organizations have commented that the decision tree gives them "a handle for thinking about organizational design so we can tinker with it, fine tune it and make it work better. We don't have to be coerced by structure. We now have a better feel for when certain structures should be used and for the specific steps we can take to make a given structure work."

■ Managing in a Matrix

HARVEY F. KOLODNY

Before its demise, for a lot of different reasons, the Applied Devices Center of Northern Electric was considered to be one of the most impressive examples of a comprehensive matrix organization. Conceived from the beginning as "The Factory of the Future," its design was based on the latest behavioral science concepts. As with so many who followed in its footsteps, the Applied Devices Center wrestled daily with the difficulties of implementing its complex matrix design. Team management, specialists who reported to two or more bosses, decision-making by consensus, elimination of or reductions in traditional hierarchical status devices—all demanded new behaviors from those who formed the central core of the matrix.

However, changes in behavior take time to learn. New cultures in old climates are always fragile. Other economic, marketing, and organizational woes set in before the learning was complete or the culture well established. Some eight years after it began, the Applied Devices Center was terminated. The complex processes associated with introducing the matrix design may have accelerated that unfortunate end. We will never really know. We just know that implementing a matrix organization design is tough.

Harvey F. Kolodny, *Business Horizons*, March/April 1981. Copyright © 1981, by the Foundation for the School of Business at Indiana University. Reprinted by permission. References deleted. See original work.

Some organizations have managed to survive the difficulties. The TRW Systems Group initiated its matrix design as far back as 1959. Led by NASA, a large number of aerospace organizations followed suit soon after. Most are still going strong today. By the mid-1960s, matrix organization designs had been adopted by some of the largest domestic organizations, and towards the end of that decade "global matrix" structures were almost de rigueur for multinational companies. By the mid-seventies, usage of the matrix form had spread to government labs, hospitals and health agencies, professional firms, and a wide variety of service sector organizations.

Although the ranks of matrix adopters have swelled rapidly, there have also been some dissenters. The giant Dutch-based Philips has pulled back from matrix because of a concern for the negative impact of the design on entrepreneurship. And at the same time that the Chase Manhattan Bank decided to embark on a matrix organization design, Citibank has chosen to withdraw from its elaborate matrix structure. In a recent issue of *Business Horizons*, one author has suggested that the complexity of matrix designs and the effects of that complexity on behavior, particularly strategic behavior, may be the root cause of some of those defections.

Why do so many organizations continue to adopt a design that appears so difficult to manage even under the best of conditions? This article addresses this question and some of the relevant issues, namely, what are the benefits of matrix organization? what new behaviors are required? what are the difficulties of implementation? The answers to these questions suggest that interested managers must recognize the evolutionary process involved in implementing a matrix design. Managers must realize that ultimately matrix is as much or more a change in the behavior of the organization's members as it is a new structural design. Changes in behavior can take place only at a measured pace.

CONDITIONS FOR MATRIX

The question "Why adopt a matrix organization design?" is best answered by examining some current concepts of the conditions that justify moving to a matrix. Recent research points to three such conditions:

- Outside pressure for a dual focus;
- A need to process large amounts of information simultaneously;
- Pressure for shared resources.

The first condition, multiple orientation, recognizes that more than one orientation may be critical to managing an organization given its particular environment. A high-technology manufacturing organization may have to maintain its scientific and technical knowledge or its manufacturing know-how at the state of the art while being equally responsive to changes in its market sector and product mix. An insurance company may have to respond simultaneously to product line competition (life, fire, marine, automobile) and to area differences (for example, urban vs. rural or west vs. east). A human services department operating out of a central facility must continue to be effective in developing rehabilitation, corrections, social work, and psychological skills while it provides services to a variety of towns, villages, and "catchment" areas. Hence the matrix duality may be function-product, product-

area, or function-area, as in each of these examples.

The second condition is a recognition of the increased amounts of information an organization must process when it tries to respond simultaneously to two critical subenvironments. The human services example is an illustration. To provide effective services to a town, a "contact person," one of the interfaces between the town and the organization, must get to know all the local ways of getting help for the individuals being served. This includes knowing the local priest or minister, police, service clubs, community agencies, and business leaders if the problem is finding a job for a juvenile, qualified private homes if the problem is finding a room for a pensioner, or nursing homes if the client needs constant attention.

At the same time the contact person must know the resource capabilities of the organization: which doctors in the psychiatric group have shown a concern for teenagers in trouble; which social workers will take the time to acquire a sympathetic understanding for an older person who must be displaced from the home his or her family has lived in for generations.

With the social fabric in the town changing constantly, with new professionals coming in and out of the different functional groups, with new knowledge generated every day about problems of the young and the old, and with such knowledge showing up in all areas—rehabilitation, corrections, social work, and psychiatry, with a wide variety of contact persons with an even wider variety of clients, it is just not possible for the organization to develop and maintain an administrative system capable of matching all the different resources to all the sources of need. Nevertheless, the organization must develop the capacity to process all this information if its task of service is to be accomplished. Given this requirement, the justification for a matrix design continues to build.

Two illustrations will explore the concept of pressure for shared resources, the third condition that determines the need for a matrix organization design. In a typical industrial organization, product or business teams make up one side of the matrix (see exhibit 3.23). At different stages in the life cycle of a product or business (product development, prototype testing, market testing, production tooling, marketing programs, product introduction, and so on) different resources are needed: design engineers,

EXHIBIT 3.23   General Form of a Matrix Organization

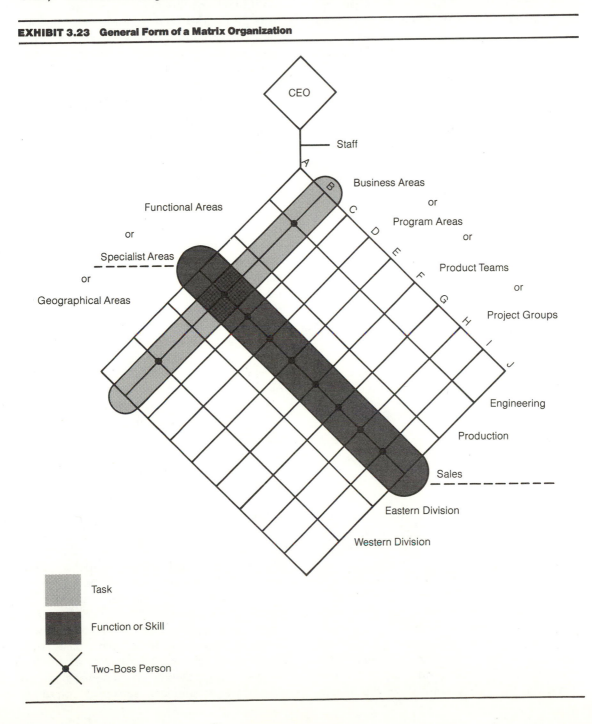

Task

Function or Skill

Two-Boss Person

market research analysts, advertising experts, salespersons, and others.

Apart from the sequential demands, some resources may be required in quantities that are rarely large enough to justify their full-time application for even short periods (such as media experts, materials specialists, packaging consultants). Their justification for a place in the organization only comes about through shared usage. Where even sharing cannot provide that justification, product business team managers contract out for those services.

Another illustration is a government agency involved in the evaluation of many different projects. Such evaluation calls for the occasional expertise of a wide variety of specialists. To carry out its assessment of a particular project, the project leader may call on in-house economists, technical experts from a local university, and financial consultants from an international development agency. Budgetary constraints prevent the agency from hiring full-time resources as long as a continuously varying evaluation workload promises that the kinds of skills and talents needed will constantly change. Sharing and contracting out for resources is the only way the agency can respond effectively to the variety in its project tasks and still stay within its budget constraints.

BENEFITS OF MATRIX

Some obvious benefits of matrix organization design flow directly from the conditions that drive organizations to adopt the form. The organization can respond simultaneously to sectors of the environment that are critical to its success. The external or environmental importance of one sector is not made secondary to the traditional arrangement (such as functional organization), since each side of the matrix has direct access to the chief executive officer and each is represented in the policy councils of the organization. There is a voice to speak directly for the importance of each of the environmental sectors, a voice that also serves as an identifiable point of contact for the constituents of that sector (customers, clients, suppliers, outside experts).

With a wide range of information to process, the organization can decentralize decision-making to the level where the relevant knowledge to process that information properly and make the appropriate decision resides. This decentralization of responsibility to a particular manager provides the organization with confidence that individual "chunks" of the total organization are being managed and cared for.

While the business or product manager has the responsibility for a task, more often than not he or she has less than the required authority to carry it out. Resources are incomplete and must be shared, borrowed, or bargained for. Amongst themselves, product managers compete for capital funds and budget allocations. Functional managers negotiate for preferred people, the best facilities, and the newest equipment. Where their negotiated outcomes are unsatisfactory, they search outside the organization and its constituencies of outsiders (clients, suppliers); as a result, they transact heavily with that external world. The reality of their situation drives them into an extensive network of lateral communication—they have far more horizontal interactions than vertical contacts with their bosses. This is the way that matrix organization's capacity to process large amounts of information manifests itself.

With so much of the management decentralized, the upper level of the organization is not overloaded with operational decisions. The span of control of the CEO can be large because he or she is freed from day-to-day decisions. The CEO's information is good because it comes through fewer levels of hierarchy, fewer filters to absorb and distort relevant information about the markets, competitors, and changes in the relevant environmental sectors. Conversely, policy decisions are made in concert with those most in control of the relevant information, most capable of transmitting them with a minimum of distortion, and most responsible for making them happen.

The benefits from the third condition are clear. Resource utilization is efficient. With everyone double-counted, the matrix allows no place to hide. Key resources can be shared across several important programs or products at the same time. The organization can flexibly accommodate the different phases through which its products and programs pass. Information transfers easily from the program side to the functional through the shared personnel.

NEW BEHAVIORS IN THE MATRIX

Four particular roles are significantly changed as an organization moves to a matrix design. The chief executive officer or person heading up the matrix organization (at the apex of the diamond in exhibit 3.23) must learn to balance power between the dual orientations. The product or program managers become mini-general managers and must learn the functions of general management. Most of all they must learn to stop being their own specialists. The functional managers must learn an entirely new style of behavior: proactive rather than reactive. Finally, the two-boss persons must learn to live with ambiguity.

The person at the apex of the matrix is the CEO, if the entire organization is the unit under consideration. The matrix organization succeeds or fails according to how well that CEO understands how it works. A key element of that understanding is the importance of the appropriate balance of power.

Power must shift as the environment does. When economic times are tough, the power must swing to the product side. It is the product managers who have the short-term profit-and-loss orientation necessary for survival. When the environment is benevolent

or generous, it is the functions that must have the resources to advance the state-of-the-art in their specialties. During such economic times, the organization's competitors will also be investing in their functional areas. The organization cannot afford to lag too far behind if it is to maintain its competitive position. The functional competencies are, in the end, what the organization "is about"—in other words, what it brings to bear against the environment in order to give itself a justification for existing, for carving out a niche or domain in the larger society. Functional competence can occasionally be diminished when short-run survival is the issue, but in the long run it must be carefully guarded. Power balancing in the matrix is a matter of the *appropriate* balance for the particular situation.

To maintain the appropriate balance the CEO needs tools—organization mechanisms or support systems or processes—that can help shift the emphasis, when it needs to be shifted. However, it is not a single organizational issue that establishes an appropriate balance. It isn't even several. It is many. Understanding them and knowing how to manipulate them is what gives the CEO the ability to adjust the balance. Exhibit 3.24 illustrates a typical set of organizational issues (processes, systems, even concepts) that balance power in a product-function matrix structure. For the CEO who understands how to manipulate them, they are the levers for change.

Product or program managers (PMs) are usually chosen from the ranks of the particular functional area that is dominant for that organization. Hence, in engineering companies, engineers become PMs; in consumer marketing companies it is the marketers who get the job; in insurance companies it is actuaries, and in hospitals it is doctors. There are many reasons why: (1) PMs must be from the dominant specialty if they are to acquire credibility in the organization, where most of the power lies with the dominant function or functions; (2) they must be able to order the problems, but not necessa-

EXHIBIT 3.24 The Balance of Power in a Matrix Organization

Function	Product/Project
	←— *Gestalt authority*
	Product managers are responsible for something whole that, no matter how small, is a type of perceived authority no functional manager obtains.
Sell outside —→	←— *Contract outside*
The right to sell resources outside the organization, making the functional manager who does so also a product manager.	The right to buy/access resources outside the organization, even when same are available inside.
	←— *Profit and loss responsibility*
	A measure of performance congruent with the way the organization itself is measured, suggesting high importance.
Control over technological uncertainty —→	←— *Control over market or customer uncertainty*
Control over important environmental uncertainties for the specialist areas gives off significant perceptions of power.	Control over important environmental uncertainties for the market segments of the different product lines gives off significant perceptions of power.
Non-substitutability (of unique resources) —→	
Control over the availability and development of resources not available elsewhere gives off significant real and perceived power.	←— *Rewards*
	Rewarding product managers more than functional managers and signaling same to the organization shifts power to the product side.
People management —→	
Hiring, firing, training, promoting, career trajectory decisions belong to the functional managers.	←— *Job titles*
	A fictitious perception of power accruing to the seemingly large group of similarly titled program managers, whose different goals rarely cause them to cooperate.
Reporting level —→	←— *Access to leader*
Functional managers report directly to the CEO, a relationship obvious to the organization.	Product managers usually report to managers of product managers who serve as their functional bosses (of how to manage products and programs) while the CEO is their product boss and, as such, always provides them with direct access to himself or herself.
Career evaluation —→	←— *Performance evaluation*
The functional managers exercise a powerful influence over the career trajectories of most people in the organization.	The product managers provide crucial inputs to the short-run appraisal of product/program people, particularly when such people are physically located with the product group.
Top management meetings —→	←— *Control over budget*
Frequent (often weekly) operations meeting to manage the organization include the CEO and the first-level functional managers, but usually not the product managers.	Product managers often have control over the budgeted dollars and negotiate with functional managers for needed resources.

rily solve them; (3) they can determine a good fit between the requirements of the subenvironment they face, e.g., market sector and the resources or technical strengths the organization possesses; and (4) the clients and subenvironments expect that it is just that type of person with whom they will interact.

Just because the PMs are so often drawn from the ranks of the dominant specialist function, there are problems created for that office. The PMs can be effective only if they *do not* become their own specialists—for example, their own project managers. It is hard for them not to want to do so. If they do, however, they will not tend to the particular external world they were explicitly established to manage. In effect, they must become general management oriented. They must be wise enough in their knowledge of how the dominant specialty works to put priorities on problems, but they must be broad enough to see themselves in charge of a total program or product line, not merely its specialist aspects.

Functional managers, long the repository of their particular skills within their organizations, must stop functioning like librarians, that is, waiting for people to come to them because they control the source of a particular skill or knowledge or discipline for the organization. If PMs are to truly manage their subenvironments, they need functional managers to take care of their backside, by managing the people and other internal aspects of the product team. Functional managers are equipped to do so because they normally have a long-run view of the organization. They should be able to anticipate a product manager's functional needs.

However, this requires a *proactive* stance from functional managers. Learning to say to PMs who are frequently much younger and have much less seniority than the functional managers, "How can I help you?" is difficult for functional managers to learn to do. If they don't learn to do it, however, the matrix often degenerates into acrimonious "we-they" squabbles as the product managers, overloaded with managing both internal and external issues, fault the functions for not being sufficiently supportive. To forestall this, functional managers must learn to go to the product managers. For some functional managers, this entails radically new behavior and may take a long while to learn. The CEO must often intervene to keep the peace while the new roles are being learned and understood. The personal stress can get quite high.

Last, but not least, in the list of those who must learn new behaviors are the two-boss persons. For some, the ambiguity of the job is a re-awakening, an opportunity to flower and bloom, to carve out a role that

fits better than anything hierarchical organizations ever offered them. For others, it is a disaster. It is not just a complex role that they cannot learn. It is more than the clear career trajectory they once viewed has been suddenly truncated, and just above the place where they are currently positioned. The dyadic superior-subordinate behaviors of bureaucracies die hard. They take a while to learn and we have no idea how long they take to unlearn. Unfortunately, organizations often have less tolerance for the time that it takes supervisors to learn to become "coordinators" in their new two-boss roles than they do for the higher level functional managers who must learn to become proactive. For some would-be two-boss persons, the coming of matrix spells the end of a career.

Can people learn the needed new behaviors? Some can and can even do so themselves. Others cannot. Even the retraining skills of many organizations are not adequate to help the second group. Many of them would be better off continuing their careers in a more traditional form of organization.

The personnel implications of the preceding paragraph are frequently not as frightening as they at first appear. Not everyone need be involved in the new matrix behaviors. In a manufacturing organization, those actively involved in the dual functional orientations may be as few as five percent of the organization's members. They will comprise the product and functional managers and their next level of subordinates and not very many others. For the rest of the people, the organization will continue to function quite traditionally. For example, a two-boss person may be both a manufacturing manager for a program and a member of the functional manufacturing group. He or she may have several or several hundred subordinates reporting through a traditional hierarchical structure. The vast majority of those people might go on about their work quite oblivious to the existence of a matrix structure at the top.

Alternatively, if the matrix is in a professional organization, for example, a consulting firm where planners, architects, and engineers are shared across different projects, everyone, including the office secretaries, may feel the effects of the matrix design.

IMPLEMENTATION

For those who can learn the requisite new behaviors there is much to learn: conflict-resolution, confrontation skills, negotiation skills, meeting management. Most organizations can work out the new needs. These issues are important to the individuals involved and they must be addressed. But they won't make or break the matrix. Because the anxieties of individuals are concerned, the organization must pay some attention to the two-boss roles, but it must pay much more attention to how the rest of the matrix works and not be seduced into believing that the "bottom cross-over points" are the dominant areas of concern. The two-boss roles will work out well if the CEO and the product and functional managers understand and carry out their required roles. They will never work out well if these high-level roles are not well performed.

Getting started is difficult. If the organization has been a functional one, where do the product bosses come from? If they are capable but low-level younger managers, will it take too long before they can swing the balance of power even a little bit away from the entrenched positions of strong functional managers? If the new product managers come from the ranks of the senior functional managers, will they be capable of acquiring a general management orientation? How long can the organization operate with the confusion of whether the ex-functional managers are exercising the new roles appropriately and of whether subordinate managers are able to cast off their deference to the historic roles these managers held? If the new product managers come from outside, will it be too much to expect them to both gain credibility and make a possibly unpopular structural change work?

Starting up is indeed difficult. It is best if everyone is clear in their understanding that it is going to be a very different way of working. If the organization has had considerable lateral communication and has begun to be familiar with interpersonal methods of information processing, the transition should be easier. (As an aside, if the organization hasn't had a lot of such experience, there is a real question about whether it is an environment that truly demands a matrix design.) There must be mechanisms to allow people to raise their concerns about (1) how the matrix works and (2) what impact it might have on their individual jobs.

There are stages towards the development of an effective matrix organization design. The process demands a significant amount of behavioral, structural, and cultural change and will necessarily take a long time. It will be costly. The organization that chooses to adopt a matrix design had first better be certain it cannot possibly manage its tasks in a simpler way before embarking on a matrix journey.

■ Productivity: The Japanese Approach

YOSHI TSURUMI

Five years ago, when my first book in English, *The Japanese Are Coming*, came out, one critic observed, "It is not that the Japanese are coming, but that they are already here . . . and we wish them to go away." Now, the recent fascination among North American business and government circles with the high degree of productivity and quality achieved in Japanese manufacturing and service industries has touched off a new episode in the "Japanese-are-coming" syndrome.

Employees in Japanese factories, from top management to rank-and-file workers, are dedicated to producing "zero-defect" products. Trains in Japan run on time to such an extent that you can almost set your watch by them. In small and large stores alike, the customer is treated like royalty. Japanese taxi drivers wear white gloves, and appear to be programmed to avoid hitting each other on the street by a matter of inches. And Canadian tourists have been known to say, "In Japan, when they say the tour bus leaves your hotel at 7:35 A.M., they *mean* 7:35 A.M. You'd better be on it a few seconds beforehand if you want to go on the tour."

Many observers of these small wonders of Japan have tried to credit them to some sort of cultural mystique, as though politeness, hard work, an orientation toward group ac-

tivity, and loyalty to management were inborn traits. Nothing, however, is further from the truth. Some Japanese are lazy, some bright, and some are careless, as the recent accident at the Tsuruga Nuclear Power Plant in Japan demonstrated. Many are considerate. But most of us are ordinary people, searching for economic security and personal recognition, with our own share of greed, anger, and other very human feelings. We are not very different from people in Canada and the United States.

DEBUNKING THE JAPANESE MYSTIQUE

My task here is to debunk these myths about Japan. I will try to explain as rationally as possible how corporate culture and the relationship between business and government have led to the conscious development of a complex economic system, which so far has been effective in coping with the rapid post-war industrial growth in that country from the 1950s to the early 1970s and most capable in handling the knotty issues of inflation, unemployment, and balance of payment disequilibrium that ensued in the wake of the first oil crisis in 1973.

Contrary to popular belief, Japanese industries do not outperform American, Canadian, and other foreign counterparts in every area of industrial endeavor. Japanese industries, for example, are out-

Reprinted from the *Pacific Basin Quarterly*, no. 6, Summer, 1981, with the permission of the Pacific Basin Center Foundation.

performed by America and Canada in agriculture, aircraft, nonferrous metals, and some advanced telecommunications equipment. In the fields of organic and non-organic chemicals, pharmaceuticals, large-scale computers, and large earthmoving equipment, American firms lead the Japanese by a substantial margin.

Compared with their international competitors, however, Japanese firms have come to excel in the mass-production of quality products ranging from automobiles, household appliances, steel, compact word processors, compact computers, precision machinery, and optical equipment to semiconductors and integrated circuitry. To support their impetus in the mass-production of quality products, Japanese firms now lead North American and European competitors in installing industrial robots in their factories and expanding the use of robotic techniques. Of the approximately 40,000 sophisticated industrial robots in operation in the world today, about three-quarters are in Japan.

What one sees today in Japanese manufacturing and service industries is the result of conscious, cumulative efforts since World War II on the part of business, labor, and government to rebuild a war-torn economy and reverse the shoddy image of goods "made-in-Japan." Products of superior quality and their acceptance in the world market have become the two key elements in the business strategy of Japanese firms. The rest has followed from these strategic postures. In the more than one hundred years since Japan began to industrialize in the 1870s, this "quality-first" approach is rather new. It is only during the last thirty years or so that Japanese firms have come to embrace this new philosophy.

In the celebrated U.S.-Japan debate over productivity in the automobile industry, it was noted that Ford Motor Co.'s most productive assembly plant is its subsidiary in Spain. This plant, however, barely achieves one-half the level of efficiency recorded daily by Toyota's comparable plant in Japan. The General Motors' Lordstown assembly plant in Ohio and Honda's assembly plant in Suzuka, Japan, are both equally modern and automated. Yet, Honda's plant easily exceeds an assembly rate of 100 cars per hour with impeccable workmanship, while GM's Lordstown plant barely reaches a rate of 75 cars an hour, many of which may have to be recalled to repair defects.

Americans and Canadians often contend that the Japanese work ethic, and the resulting high productivity and quality, could happen only in Japan. But is that really true? I use as one example the Sony Corporation's San Diego plant in the United States, which records productivity and product reliability figures just as high as its closest rival in Japan. In another instance, Sanyo, after taking over a Warwick color television assembly plant in Arkansas, cut its product defect rate from about 30 percent to less than 5 percent in about two months without making any substantial changes in the factory's manufacturing equipment. What causes such a turnaround in plant performance? Management, of course.

In this regard, I find the comments of Soichiro Honda, the founder of Honda Motors in Japan, to be particularly informative. In a recent book on the Honda company by Tetsuo Sakitani entitled *Honda Cho-Hasso Keiei* ("Honda's Supra-Creative Management"), Honda was heard to observe after a visit to an automobile plant in Detroit, "One thing that struck me was how the worst workers were in jobs like casting. Casting shops have poor working conditions. They're hot and dusty, so none of the better workers wanted to go near them. Traditionally, only workers who had no other choice, such as disadvantaged blacks, would take these jobs. But metal castings and other basic materials are really the most important elements. If these materials are poorly made, there is no way that you can produce a good product. Take engine blocks, for example. If the metal isn't cast properly, you have to add another process for drilling holes or filing. And that means you have to buy another expensive machine. Then, after that you discover that they still have pinholes and can't be used . . .."

In order to solve this problem at his own plant, Honda collected many ideas on casting and welding from his workers and other sources. As a result of this research Honda equipped his welding and casting shops with machine tools. He wanted his workers to be able to proceed directly to the next process as soon as the fittings were welded or cast. This scheme was a real challenge to common practice and conventional wisdom at the time, since the sand used in these shops, particularly in the casting process, leaked out of the machines. And sand is the greatest enemy of precision machine tools. Eventually, Honda and his workers developed a method for preventing the sand from escaping from casting and forging machines.

Along the same lines, Sanyo's Vice Chairman Takemoto once told of his immediate reaction to an inspection tour of a Warwick facility his company later acquired. He said, "The American managers were proudly pointing out to me the spacious, well-equipped, and well-staffed Quality Inspection Section at the end of the assembly line. I wondered why they needed such an elaborate Quality Inspection Section if they made their products properly in the first place. I told our workers to take as much time as they needed to properly and carefully complete the assigned job, and not to send any slipshod work down the assembly line. In this way we cut the product defect rate drastically. You can never inspect quality into products. You can only build it into them."

And lastly, Akio Morita, the chairman of Sony Corporation, at one time confided, "When we opened our San Diego plant, we really had some difficulty persuading our American engineers and managers to go onto the production floor and mingle with the foremen and workers to learn how things were really being made. Without knowing how things are made, how can you design quality into new products and design out product defects?"

CORPORATE PRODUCTIVITY

How do you measure productivity? In North America, no other term has been more misunderstood by managers, academics, and workers alike than the word "productivity." Workers hate it and fight it because, to them, productivity is synonymous with the layoff of some workers. Managers love it, but treat it as if there were an economic trade-off between productivity and product quality. Furthermore, many managers, economists, and engineers have developed an almost blind faith in automation and mechanization alone as the cure-alls for sagging productivity in their operations. Top management sees productivity and quality as technical and operational problems that should be delegated to some lower-rung supervisors or quality inspectors while they concern themselves with quarterly share earnings. In business schools, plant management is often reduced to numerical gamesmanship involving less than meaningful simulation models of inventory control and production flows. Sociological verbiage has replaced a basic comprehension of actual human behavior on production floors and inside corporate offices.

In Japan, at least, such misunderstandings and prejudices about productivity are largely absent. Productivity is singularly determined through top management's undivided attention to a "quality-first" approach. This type of approach works most effectively in a corporate environment in which the blame for such management errors as misreading market trends or designing poor products is not shifted to the rank-and-file workers in the form of layoffs.

I would now like to examine the relationship of productivity to industrial technology in some depth. First, we should understand clearly the three different kinds of technology and their inter-relationship with each other. These are: (1) product-related technology; (2) production process-related technology; and (3) institution-related technology. Product-related technology emanates from identifiable products that are new to the firm. It is often the proprietary possession of the inventing or innovative firm. Production process-related technology originates in identifiable manufacturing processes, and often is also a proprietary holding unique to the inventing firm. The technological advantage of these firms is that they possess unique manufacturing processes not held by other firms. Institution-related technology results from a firm's organizational expertise, developed through use of a specific technology related to products and production processes of the innovative firm. The firm's method of organizing and motivating its employees and managers to produce specific products and services of high quality is but one example of such a technology. Another example is the proper flow of management information within a given firm from one functional area to another. A firm's skill in evaluating global markets and technological developments and commercializing them is one form of institution-related technology.

Canada and the United States have often excelled in generating product-related technological innovations, while Japan has developed superior production process-related and institution-related technologies. The latter two types of technology appear to have great significance in determining a given firm's international competitive strength.

QUALITY AND PRODUCTIVITY AS A NON–DELEGABLE RESPONSIBILITY OF TOP MANAGEMENT

Most studies of quality control in industrial plants show that about 80 percent of the problems relating to poor quality and productivity can be remedied by management alone and that the remaining 20 percent can be solved by workers on the production floor with the means and resources available to them.

There are several possible causes for product defects and poor productivity within the manufacturing processes of a firm. These factors are often depicted schematically in what is known as an Ishikawa diagram.

Workers on the production floor of a plant are severely limited in what they are able to do to alleviate problems without having the input of top management. Consequently, the full support by top management of the production workers, entailing a total commitment to high quality and productivity, is required. This is the non-delegable responsibility that I mentioned earlier. Actual operational authority exercised in the management of quality may be delegated to others, but not management's ultimate responsibility for it. Inferior quality and poor productivity, therefore, are merely symptoms of poor management.

THE MANAGEMENT ETHIC (QUALITY DETERMINES PRODUCTIVITY)

Terms such as planned obsolescence and acceptable quality level (AQL) are a copout on the part of management. Once managers develop the attitude that a trade-off can be made between quality and productivity, they invite rampant defects in their products.

To compare corporate organizations in North America and Japan, we should first identify some of the major contrasts between the types of organizations predominantly found in those two regions. They are summarized in exhibit 3.25. Another useful tool for comparing the differences in internal hierarchy and long-term commitment to the goals of the firm between Model A and Model J firms requires that you visualize the corporate structures of these two types of firms in terms of geometric figures. The Model J firm may be imagined as a

EXHIBIT 3.25 Typical Japanese and North American Corporations

	Model J	Model A
Key Characteristics	Japanese Firms	American Firms
Business orientation	Global; toward long-term growth	Domestic; toward short-term growth
Business target	Market share at home & abroad	Quarterly profits
Management attitude toward job security of rank-and-file employees	Seen as efficient means for insuring long-term commitment of employees to growth and technological innovation	Considered inefficient and an obstacle to growth
Staffing of executive positions	Promotion from within	Hiring from outside
Internal control of organization	Through implicit rules and shared goals among managers & employees	Through explicit rules & management by objective

square-shaped figure, indicating by its equal width at both top and bottom that the same degree and breadth of long-term commitment to the goals of the firm exists from top to bottom within the Model J firm's internal hierarchy. Conversely, the broad commitment to the long-term goals of the Model A firm indicated at the top echelon of its internal hierarchy diminishes sharply as you descend through the hierarchy to rank-and-file production workers, and might be depicted as an inverted isosceles triangle.

The Model J type is also to be found among American firms, notably IBM, Texas Instruments, and ITT. There are also many small- to medium-size manufacturing firms in the U.S. that have successfully adopted the total-quality approach by involving their rank-and-file workers in management's total commitment to raising productivity through improved quality.

This would seem to indicate that Japanese production process-related technology may be "transplanted" to other nations. More important, however, is that what mistakenly has been called a "uniquely Japanese management style" appears to be a common feature of almost any well-managed firm, be it Japanese or North American. In recent months, a flashy name—the Type Z firm—has been coined by one observer and applied to certain American firms thought to possess a propitious combination of Ameri-

can and Japanese characteristics.[1] This Type Z category is not only logically redundant, but is based in large part on his tenuous interpretation of another observer's accounts of the internal workings of Japanese firms. An excellent study of Japanese management styles and methods is the recently published book *The Art of Japanese Management* (Simon & Schuster) by Pascale and Athos. The work is based on actual on-site research done at American and Japanese firms in the U.S. While Theory Z would have us believe that all Japanese subsidiaries in the United States are outperforming their American counterparts, a closer look at the comparative performance of Japanese and American firms reveals that some Japanese firms do outperform their American counterparts while others face serious management problems. This finding is far more pertinent to a serious examination of the transferability of Japanese management systems to North America.

The management ethic that engenders the highest possible quality and fewest possible defects is a reflection of the overall corporate culture embodied in the Model J

---

1. Both the name and the conceptualization of Theory Z appear to have been taken, without attribution, from a lesser known work of a famous psychologist, Abraham Maslow. See ch. 22, Theory Z, in *The Farther Reaches of Human Nature* (Viking Press, 1971) by Abraham Maslow.

type firm. As a consequence of that, production of high quality products having considerably lower incidence of defects—one of the more noteworthy accomplishments of a Type J firm—is possible, due in large measure to the way in which the production lines commonly found in Type J firms are set up. The best example of this can be found in the automobile industry. The Honda Motor Company's automobile assembly plant in Japan is set up according to the standard practices used in that country. In the United States, its closest equivalent is the General Motors' Lordstown plant, which is a reflection of what have now become typical American standards of operation in that industry. How are they different?

For the sake of simplicity, assume that the assembly lines in both plants consist of five separate, mechanically similar substations. Products "flow" from the first station through the fifth before they are moved to the final quality control (QC) inspection station. The GM facility, like other American industrial plants, has a large QC staff whose function it is to either pass or fail the assembled products that come before them, using primarily visual or other simple testing procedures. To insure that the workers on the production line pay close attention to product quality, the QC department often positions sub-QC inspection personnel at points between the various production stations. These sub-QC personnel supervise production workers along the production line. The Honda plant, on the other hand, has few if any QC inspectors stationed at the end of the assembly line. What QC staff there is merely attaches an "OK (Passed)" label to each already-completed product. And no special sub-QC inspectors are scattered along the assembly line to look over the shoulders of production workers.

Management at the GM plant, through its QC inspectors, emphasizes the notion of acceptable quality level (AQL) in dealing with the question of quality control. Just how a particular level of defects is judged to be

"acceptable" is not entirely clear to me. For in reality, the concept of an AQL is essentially a euphemism for tolerating product defects at each station along the production line of up to a level of 2 percent (or 98 percent reliability).

Since there is no real certainty that the five different production workers at stations one through five will build the permissible 2 percent of defects into the same product on a cumulative basis, it is highly likely we will discover that by the time a given product passes station five, as many as 31 products out of 100 will contain some sort of product flaw—a defect rate of 31 percent!

At the Honda plant, each and every worker assigned to a production station is trained to strive to eliminate product defects. A slight one-percentage-point reduction in the defect rate at each station lowers the maximum overall defect rate dramatically, from 10 to 30 percent down to a mere 5 percent. Obviously, the total productivity of a Honda-style plant will also be greater than that of a GM-style plant. To make matters worse, the preoccupation of management in Model A-type plants with productivity—in terms of mere physical output per worker—often puts pressure on the QC staff to approve and ship almost anything that is produced. In Model J factories the product defect that is detected will be repaired before it is shipped to outside customers.

THE BUSINESS–GOVERNMENT RELATIONSHIP IN JAPAN

The last myth I would like to lay to rest is that government subsidies to Japanese firms are somehow responsible for Japanese productivity and industrial vitality. If government subsidies were the answer, we should expect to see Chrysler leading the American automobile industry and British industries at the apex of their industrial might.

A variation on this notion has also emerged in the form of allegations that Japan's industrial productivity in steel, automobiles, and other fields was possible only because over the years the U.S. defensive umbrella has protected, or subsidized, if you will, Japan's defense, freeing resources for the civilian economy. The proponent of this fallacious assumption seems to be implying that Japan's worldwide defense commitment should somehow equal that of the United States, and that American industry has been drained of necessary investment funds because of the nation's high defense burden. This is but another diversion from the central issue: the sagging productivity of the American economy.

Contrary to popular belief, the role of government in the Japanese economy is to promote the survival of the fittest of many competing private firms in each industry. Government policies, in the form of tax incentives and other assistance, are geared specifically toward rewarding only those firms meeting publicly stated goals that contribute to the industrial growth and stability of the nation as well.

Japanese firms do pay lower corporate income taxes than their American counterparts. But at the same time, Japanese companies will carry many of their employees without laying them off when the company encounters economic hard times. The choice for the Japanese nation as a whole is either to let private firms take care of their own employees or to jettison them in times of hardship because of mistakes made by top management. If the Japanese nation were to choose the latter, corporations and individuals would also have to be taxed at higher levels in order for the State to be able to carry those laid-off workers at public expense.

The Japanese government's role is to develop, through consultations with business, labor, and academic circles, broad national goals for industrial growth. This is why economic planning in Japan is called indicative economic planning. Economic plans formulated by the government merely "indicate" the desirable directions of the Japanese economy. Actual implementation of the plans is accomplished through competition for the survival of the fittest among the private firms. Once private firms are in accord with the economic policies of the government, you will find that there is less uncertainty regarding the specific objectives in the long-range planning of each firm.

As the international competitiveness of these firms grows, they are in the process forced to prove their prowess, first abroad and then in Japan, by competing with foreign firms. This is why during Mazda's near collapse and bankruptcy in the period from 1974 to 1978—the Japanese version of Chrysler—import tariffs on automobiles entering Japan were cut even further and were eventually abolished in 1978. The principle of "the survival of the fittest," as it applies in the Japanese context, demands that private parties, consisting of the manufacturing firm and its suppliers and banks, pool their resources and exercise self-discipline in order to cope with the economic downturns likely to befall them from time to time.

The phrase "supply management" has long been used to characterize the way in which the Japanese government and businesses manage the national economy. If the experience of the Japanese can be useful to the governments of Canada and the United States, it will be by showing that so-called supply side economics works only when the microscopic actors in the economy—the individual firms—are taught to exercise self-discipline in pursuing the expansion of their worldwide market share.

As a result of the self-discipline of the private parties involved in protecting their collective interests—namely, that of the firms—the "income policy" à la Japonaise usually functions effectively (general wage rises are contained within the level of increase in productivity by business and labor, at the suggestion of the government). In this way, Japan managed to bring its domestic inflation rate of over 30 percent during the period from 1974 to 1975 after the oil crisis down to a single-digit rate within one year's time.

The congruency between the goals of private firms and the goals of the nation must be the guiding principle of business-government relations. But this does not mean that what is good for General Motors is also always good for the country. Only when companies are fully dedicated to the goals of (1) exporting and other international activities, (2) R & D efforts and constant retraining of workers, managers, and engineers, and (3) stable growth in employment and job security for the rank-and-file are the objectives of private companies and those of the nation most likely to converge.

■ Trends in the Organization of Multinational Corporations

STANLEY M. DAVIS

Methods of organizing and managing multinational industrial corporations have matured considerably in the last five years, and the basic rules are now rather well understood. Changes in the external environment, however, together with new complexities that arise from corporate responses to these changes, continually reduce the effectiveness of these basic structures and practices. The result is that new methods and forms evolve in response to the new exigencies. Basic design involves three different organizing units: *functions*, *products*, and *geography*. Neat distinctions between the three, however, have been found inadequate because they only optimize along one of these dimensions.

Reprinted with permission from the Summer 1976 issue of the *Columbia Journal of World Business*. Copyright © 1976 by the Trustees of Columbia University in the City of New York. References deleted. See original work.

THE BASIC PATTERNS

There are many variations in organizational design of an international business, but the general tendency among U.S.-based industrial corporations is quite clear.

When a corporation has four or more foreign manufacturing operations it is likely to place them all into an international division, reporting to a single executive. While the structure of the domestic company is laid out along product and/or functional lines, the international division is organized around geographical interests. The head of the division is on a hierarchical par with the heads of the domestic product groups, and all report directly to the president. General managers of each foreign unit report up to the boss of the international division, sometimes through an intermediary regional level, and the units themselves reflect the same functional organization as exists in the domestic product divisions. For the foreign units, the creation of the international division provides guidance and support, but it also increases the control of headquarters over the subsidiaries and reduces some of their previously enjoyed autonomy.

PRODUCT VERSUS GEOGRAPHY

Once the international division grows large enough to rival the largest domestic product division, pressures to create a new organization design that bridges the domestic-international split become irresistible. The two dominant choices involve maximizing either the product or the geographic dimension.

In the global product structure, the international division is carved up, and its products are fed back into the rest while domestic units become worldwide product groups. Products that require different technologies and that have dissimilar end-users are logically grouped into separate categories, and the transfer of products into various world markets is best managed within each distinctive product classification.

To create a global structure based on geography, the domestic business is labeled as the North American area and the regional pieces in the international division are elevated to similar status. In contrast to the diversity and renewing growth phases of the product-structured firms, companies that elect an area mold tend to have a mature product line that serves common end-user markets. They generally place great reliance on lowering manufacturing costs by concentrating and specializing production through long runs, in large plants, using stable technology. They also emphasize marketing techniques as the competitive basis for price and product differentiation. Industries with these characteristics that favored the area structure include food, beverage, container, automotive, farm equipment, pharmaceuticals, and cosmetics.

The worldwide area structure is highly suited to mature businesses with narrow product lines, because their growth potential is greater abroad than in the domestic market where the products and brands are in later phases of their life cycles. Since they derive a high proportion of their total sales from abroad, intimate knowledge of local conditions, constraints, and preferences is essential. Many of these firms rely heavily on advertising and benefit from standardizing their marketing as well as production techniques worldwide. But standardization and area variegation are sometimes incompatible. In one classical gaffe, for example, advertisement for a major U.S.-based banking firm used a picture of a squirrel hoarding nuts. The idea was to convey an image of thrift, preparedness, and security. When the same advertisement appeared in Caracas, however, it brought a derisive reaction, since Venezuela has neither winters nor squirrels as we know them. Instead, the image evoked a thieving and destructive rat. The major advantage of a worldwide area structure, then, is its ability to differentiate regional and local markets and to determine variations in each appropriate market mix. Its disadvantage as a form of organization is its inability to coordinate different product lines and their logistics of flow from source to markets across areas.

ELIMINATING THE INTERNATIONAL DIVISION

Through time, the disjunction between a corporation's product structure in its domestic divisions and a geographic basis for organizing its overseas activities creates difficulty. Ironically, the more successful the international division, the more rapidly these difficulties occur. Strategically, the posture shifts from that of a domestic firm with international activities to that of a global corporation. Structurally, the pressures build to reflect this new unity. Although the emergent design is rather predictable in rational economic terms, the speed, clarity, and success with which it is accomplished depends mainly on history, power, and personalities in the firm. The major players are bound to have different structural priorities:

Domestic Priorities
- Products
- Functions
- Areas

International Priorities
- Areas
- Products
- Functions

Central staff may compound the conflict by its predominantly functional orientation. While managers are looking for ways to maximize the advantages of all three dimensions simultaneously, resolution is delayed by the need to defend their interests and perspectives. In the process, the existing organization lags behind the evolving strategy, usually catching up in a large quantum jump known as a "shake up," only to begin lagging behind again.

GIVEN: GEOGRAPHIC ORGANIZATION NEEDED: GLOBAL PRODUCT MANAGEMENT

The international division, and the extension of the geographic basis to a worldwide area structure, improves the coordination of all product lines within each zone, but at the expense of reduced coordination between areas for any one product line. IBM's office products division diversification effort is an example of this phenomenon.

IBM

IBM was one of the last holdouts for the international division (IBM World Trade Corporation) structure long after its international sales suggested that a dichotomous structure of "here and abroad" was inadequate. Shortly after it broke up its international division and created a worldwide area structure, it began to differentiate the global structure for its office products (OP) business. OP is a substantially different business than the very large data processing (DP) operations, and the head of this division wanted it to be one profit center independent of the geographic profit centers for data processing. In less than three years, between 1972–75, the locus of OP in the IBM hierarchy moved upward from a role subordinate to DP in each country unit, to that of a product division with worldwide responsibility.

Until 1972, there was a single composite sales and profit objective at the country level for both DP and OP. Since as much as 90 percent of a country's business was DP, OP usually would be slighted in any trade-off. Also, staff at World Trade Headquarters were shared and, on critical functions like pricing, OP did not get the support it needed. Steps were taken in 1972 to correct this problem when the country manager was no longer allowed to make OP–DP trade-off decisions; they were to be made at the group (Europe, Americas/Far East) level. For a brief while the OP country managers reported to the OP group managers, but then the reporting line was further centralized and they reported directly to World Trade Headquarters. Under that arrangement OP became a separate profit center within the international side of IBM, and the reporting lines effectively bypassed the area and country levels of the old structure. In what must have been read as a moderate challenge to the hegemony of the country managers, who were generally DP types, the OP country manager now had to rely on him only for non-marketing staff support on a dotted line basis.

The third structural change in three years took place in mid-1975 when OP was centralized once again. It was taken out of the geographic groups (United States, and Americas/Far East) and set up with the new minicomputers and software as part of a worldwide General Business Group. The General Business Group, an almost $4 billion unit, then set up its own international division based on country management units.

The lessons of IBM are repeated in other firms that move outside their original, narrow product base:

1. Pure geographic structures do not permit sufficient integration of any one different product line.

2. The more differentiated a new product line is from the main business the more centrally (globally) it should be managed.

3. The need to introduce product differentiation into a geographically specialized hierarchy increases the managerial and the structural complexity by geometric proportions.

GIVEN: GLOBAL PRODUCT MANAGEMENT NEEDED: GEOGRAPHIC COORDINATION

Global corporations that are organized along product lines have the opposite problem: how to coordinate their diverse business activities within any one geographic area. Having made the strategic choices to carry a diversity of products to new areas, their structures reflect the need to maximize technological linkages among the far-flung plants in each business unit. This has been done, however, at the cost of duplicating management and organization in each area. To cope with problems of coordinating and simplifying these parallel managements, firms must reach through their existing product structure and weave an additional dimension across the organizational pattern. In the language of this metaphor, those who do it successfully will have a blend rather than a plaid fabric as the result. Eaton Corporation offers one example of a global firm that has successfully woven a few threads across the straight grain.

Eaton

Eaton is a highly diversified company in the capital goods and automotive industries. It has sales of over $1.5 billion, employs over 50,000 people and operates over 140 facilities in more than twenty countries. In 1974 each of its four worldwide product groups had a Managing Director for European operations. Each of the firm's twenty-nine manufacturing facilities and six associate companies in Europe reported to one of these four people. In addition, eighteen service operations, a finance operation, and an R & D center in Europe reported to their functional counterparts in the parent company. Senior management was concerned about how well it was coordinating these activities in Europe.

It was important for Eaton to be able to evaluate and respond to significant trends and developments in European countries, such as tariffs, tax matters, duties, government legislation, currency fluctuations, environmental controls and energy conservation, co-determination and industrial democracy, labor matters, nationalization, and government participation in ownership. Its current organization structure did not provide a regular and convenient means of communication among its European units, either for exchanging information, for building a positive corporate identity, or for assessing corporate needs and coordinating programs and procedures to meet them.

Rejecting the notion of country managers, and/or of one Vice-President for Europe, they instituted a European Coordinating Committee (ECC) together with coordinating committees in each country where they had major involvement. The four European Managing Directors were permanent members of the ECC and each served as a coordinator for one or more of the country committees. Europeans representing various functions were appointed to one-year terms, and the firm's Executive Vice-Presidents and Group Vice-Presidents were all made ex-officio members, with one being present at each ECC meeting on a rotating basis.

Meetings are held monthly, midway between the monthly meetings of the corporate Operating Committee, and minutes are sent to world headquarters within five working days. Attendance is required, the chair rotates periodically, and the location rotates among the major facilities.

The President and the four Group Vice-Presidents flew to Europe to formally launch the new coordinating committees, and the corporate newsletter devoted an entire issue to the new developments.

Six months later Eaton formed a Latin American Coordinating Committee, and about a year after that they created a U.S. and Canadian Division Managers' Council, using the same model. The same attention was paid to details of the committees' operations and to their implementation. The European committee, then, served as a model for realizing better coordination across business lines in each of the firm's major geographic concentrations, and it is probable that the capstone in the future will be a council of councils that will take the form of annual or semi-annual worldwide coordinating committee meetings.

This example is a moderate step, in structural terms, towards complementing the warp of a traditional product line organization with the woof of geographic coordinates. The fabric of the organization is not significantly altered, rather it is reinforced. Little is done to increase the complexity of the global design or management practices. Success depends on thorough implementation of a plan that least disturbs the existing managerial style and corporate culture. The change is supplementary, rather than radical, and it has the desired effect of managing *both* product and country diversity.

Firms that are organized along global product lines will probably experience similar needs to coordinate their activities within a foreign country when:

1. They have at least two significant but organizationally independent business units there.

2. There are economies to be gained from pooled information.

3. There are benefits derivable from a more unified corporate identity.

4. There is a discernible need for assessing and coordinating corporate programs and their implementation.

THE FUNCTIONAL DIMENSION IN GLOBAL TERMS

The product and area structures, and any combinations, all treat the functional dimension in tertiary fashion, locating it in the various parts of the structure after the deck already has been cut twice. Extractive raw material ventures are an exception to this rule.

Functional activities play a critical role, for example, in the petroleum industry because of the scale required for economy, the technological complexity involved, and the importance of captive markets for the sale of crude. All major petroleum companies encompass exploration, crude production, tanker and pipeline transportation, manufacturing (refining), and marketing, in addition to the logistics of worldwide supply and distribution at each step in these process and product flows. These may be managed directly through centralized functional departments acting with worldwide line responsibility, and supplemented by corporate staff who coordinate the functions within areas, or, conversely, through area management, with staff coordination for the functions. In any one petroleum company, the structure is either a mixture of the two or else it shifts back and forth. Conoco, for example, dropped its area division and returned to a functional structure in 1975. It reasoned that environmental changes, such as the oil import program and the Arab oil embargo, no longer made it feasible to think of domestic and foreign markets separately.

The aluminum industry is another example in which functional activities continue to play a primary role in fixing the structure. Alcan, for example, organized their activities in 1970 around the three major steps in the making and selling of their single product line. Reporting directly to the president were three executive vice-presidents for raw materials, smelting, and fabricating sales; within each of these functional divisions, foreign subsidiaries then grouped around area managers. Where a national subsidiary is itself vertically integrated, as in Brazil and India, they report up the fabricating line. A worldwide functional structure, however, is not very stable and in 1973 Alcan subsumed its ore activities under the executive vice-president—smelting. Their concern was with the vulnerability of their sources of supply. This left the company with a global dichotomy between production and sales in line operations, which continues to drift to an area format with problems of integration for supply and distribution on a global basis.

The lesson is, don't organize global structures around business functions unless you are in extractive raw materials industries, and even then you will find that they are unstable and will have to share primacy with geographic factors and, in some instances, with product differences. For global industrial corporations, basic functions such as manufacturing and marketing are and should be subsumed under product or geographic units. Even European-based companies, who have tended to emphasize functional structures in their domestic activities far more than U.S.-based ones, give this dimension lesser importance in their multinational design.

ORGANIZING AROUND MARKETS, NOT GEOGRAPHY

Although the basic organizing dimensions for multinational corporations are functions, products, and geographic areas, some firms have begun to think in terms of market differences as a more important basis for determining their global structure. A market is conceived as an identifiable and homogeneous group that has a similar pattern of need, purchasing behavior, and product use. Taking this definition and applying it to the nations of the world, companies are less likely to divide the globe on the basis of physical proximity than on the basis of needs and abilities to satisfy them. The traditional categories of Latin America, Far East, Europe, and the like lose their power, and the new categorization is derived from development economics. Here, the oversimplified dichotomy between developed and less-developed has yielded to the current preference for dividing the globe into five "worlds." The first world includes the familiar capitalist economies of the industrialized world, and the second world includes the 1.3 billion people in the centrally planned communist economies. The third world comprises developing countries that have a modern infrastructure and/or have exceptional wealth in natural resources. Able to attract foreign investment and to borrow on commercial terms, they need time and technology more than foreign aid. They include OPEC members, Brazil, Mexico, South Korea, Taiwan, and Turkey. The fourth world countries have similar characteristics but in much less generous amounts and therefore need injections of both trade and aid. The fifth world countries are the complete have-nots, without resources or the likelihood of ever improving their lot.

The basic principle in this approach is that geography is an obfuscation for conceptualizing global growth strategy and for organizing and managing the multinational corporations' response. This avenue is far from new as regards market segmentation for domestic activities. A common differentiation in a domestic structure, for example, is between a government sector, an industrial sector, and a consumer sector. Organizing around markets, rather than geography, is recent, however, as applied to worldwide corporate structuring. The country, or nation-state, is kept as the basic unit of analysis, but the grouping together of countries is done on the basis of a different set of questions and assumptions—not on the assumption that understanding management in Mexico helps one to start a business next door to Guatemala, but that demographic, income, natural resource data, and the like are more relevant criteria, and also are ones that lend themselves to country cluster analysis and hence to market-determined organization design.

The market-center concept is useful to all firms, though few thus far have actually structured their worldwide activities around it. Companies might want to do so when:

1. Operations in neighboring countries are totally independent of each other.

2. Communication networks are good, and the technology for processing information rapidly and accurately is present or is not important.

3. There already exists a marketing orientation with the parent company.

4. A set of markets can be identified that have more managerial validity than do sets of countries with geographic regions.

5. The concept is already familiar to managers through the planning process.

6. Management is not locked in to defense of territories.

GLOBAL MATRIX ORGANIZATION

Dow Chemical Company is perhaps one of the first industrial corporations to use the matrix form in its global macro-structure. Although Dow does not publish organization charts, for internal or external consumption, its 1968 annual report nevertheless did publish a matrix diagram of sorts in the form of a photo cube. Along each dimension of the cube were photos of the key managers for the various functions, product groups, and geographic areas in the Dow organization. At that time the Dow organizational philosophy was that they managed with a three-dimensional matrix. Shortly after that, in fact, one of Dow's senior managers, William Goggin, became President of Dow Corning and introduced what he called a four-dimensional matrix, by adding "time" into the sense of structure.

While these ambitious notions of multidimensional structuring grappled with managing global complexities simultaneously, they proved exceedingly difficult to keep in balance. By 1970, it was apparent that Dow Chemical's matrix was effectively two-dimensional, a worldwide grid of product and geography with functions variously located at different levels in the grid hierarchies. In 1972 the matrix became further imbalanced when the product dimension lost line authority and was kicked upstairs in the form of three Business Group Managers who reported to Corporate Product Development. They were to be separate channels of communication for their product group across the areas, and their clout came from their control over capital expenditures. Life Sciences was the only product division that maintained worldwide reporting control.

Around 1974 Dow Chemical held a meeting of its senior managers worldwide. During an anonymous question-and-answer period with the Chairman, Carl Gerstaker, the question was asked: Which dimension of the matrix do you consider to be most important? The very fact that the question was asked demonstrates that the matrix had deteriorated significantly. Gerstaker's answer was to the point: The most important dimension in a matrix organization is the weakest and/or the most threatened. Despite the Chairman's understanding of multidimensional structures, however, the matrix continued to decompose. In 1975, the Life Sciences Division lost its worldwide reporting line and was subsumed under each of the geographic "operating units." Whereas each product used to have an identifiable team linking its business through the areas, the basic locus of these teams now exists within each area. Today, Dow Chemical would be described more appropriately as using a geographically-based structure. In retrospect, it should be noted that, with the exception of Life Sciences, only these areas ever had their own letterhead stationery. Although the ideology of global matrix management still exists in some corners of Dow, the ethos and spirit of it is not to be found.

The example of Dow is not to be read as a failure. As Peter Drucker says, the matrix structure "will never be a preferred form of organization; it is fiendishly difficult." He concludes, nevertheless, that "any manager in a multinational business will have to learn to understand it if he wants to function effectively himself." Dow's global matrix was a valiant and creative effort, a radical approach to structuring a multinational corporation. Some European firms, such as Phillips, with a matrix organization for years, and some U.S.-based non-industrial corporations have also relied on the matrix form. Global construction and engineering firms, such as Bechtel Corporation, and one bank, Citibank, are companies that have been more successful than Dow Chemical.

Dow Corning, one twentieth the size of Dow Chemical, has been more successful in maintaining its global matrix. A relatively smaller size may be one reason, but far more important is that Dow Corning pays great attention to the behavioral requirements of matrix management in addition to the structural ones. The Chairman is an overt enthusiast of the matrix, amiably stressing to his managers that they will be democratic and share power. The balance of power and shared decision-making is translated into non-concrete form, for example, by the elimination of walls and corridors in favor of office landscaping around family groupings. Since the organization is purposefully built around a paradox of competing claims, stability rests in managers' behavior more than in structural form. Matrix is a verb.

Management Practice

▪ Aquarius Advertising Agency

▪ DO NOT READ THIS CASE UNTIL DIRECTED TO DO SO BY YOUR INSTRUCTOR.

PART I

The Aquarius Advertising Agency is a middle-sized firm that offered two basic professional services to its clients—customized plans for the content of an advertising campaign, e.g., slogans, layouts, etc., and complete plans for media such as radio, TV, newspapers, billboards, magazines. Additional services included aid in marketing and distribution of products and marketing research to test advertising effectiveness.

Its activities were organized in a traditional manner. The formal organization is shown in exhibit 3.26. Each of the functions includes similar activities, and on top of that each client account was coordinated by an account executive who acted as a liaison between the client and the various specialists on the professional staff of the Operations and Marketing Divisions. The amount of direct communications and contacts between clients and Aquarius specialists, client and account executives, and Aquarius specialists and account executives is indicated in exhibit 3.27. These sociometric data were gathered by a consultant who conducted a study of the patterns of formal and informal communications. Each intersecting cell of Aquarius personnel and the clients contains an index of the direct contacts between them.

Although an Account Executive was designated to be the liaison between the client and agency specialists among various specialists within the agency, frequently communications occurred directly among parties bypassing the Account Executive. These direct contacts involved a wide range of interactions such as meetings, telephone calls, and letters. A large number of direct communications occurred between agency specialists and their counterparts in the client organization. For example, an art specialist working as one member of a team on a particular client account often would be contacted directly by the client's in-house art specialist, and agency research personnel had direct communication with research people of the client firm. Also, some of the unstructured contacts often led to more formal meetings with clients in which agency personnel made presentations, interpreted and defended agency policy, and committed the agency to certain courses of action.

Both a hierarchical and professional system operated within the departments of the Operations and Marketing Divisions. Each department was organized hierarchically with a director, an assistant director, and several levels of authority. Professional communications were widespread and mainly concerned with sharing knowledge and techniques, technical evaluation of work, and development of professional interests. Control in each professional department was exercised mainly through control of promotions and supervision of work done by subordinates.

EXHIBIT 3.26   Aquarius Advertising Agency Organization Chart

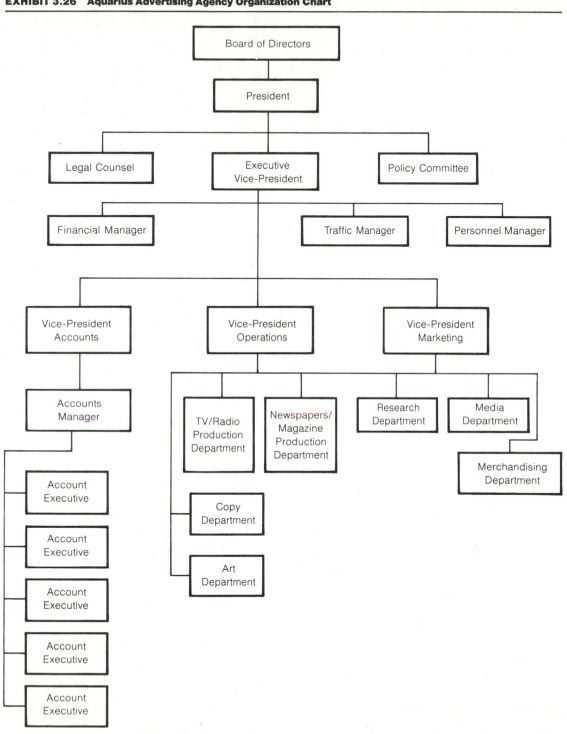

EXHIBIT 3.27   Sociometric Index of Contacts of Aquarius Personnel and Clients

	Clients	Account Manager	Account Executives	TV/Radio Specialists	Newspaper/Magazine Specialists	Copy Specialists	Art Specialists	Merchandising Specialists	Media Specialists	Research Specialists	Traffic
Clients	X	F	F	N	N	O	O	O	O	O	N
Account Manager		X	F	N	N	N	N	N	N	N	N
Account Executives			X	F	F	F	F	F	F	F	F
TV/Radio Specialists				X	N	O	O	N	N	O	N
Newspaper/Magazine Specialists					X	O	O	N	O	O	N
Copy Specialists						X	N	O	O	O	N
Art Specialists							X	O	O	O	N
Merchandising Specialists								X	F	F	N
Media Specialists									X	F	N
Research Specialists										X	N
Traffic											X

F = Frequent—daily
O = Occasional—once or twice per project
N = None

■ ANALYSIS QUESTIONS

1. Characterize the type of organization that exists at the Aquarius Advertising Agency (Galbraith reading).

2. Speculate on what you think are the functional and dysfunctional consequences of the organization of Aquarius.

3. Design an organization that you think could overcome the dysfunctional consequences of the Aquarius organization (Galbraith reading).

■ DO NOT READ UNTIL INSTRUCTED TO DO SO BY YOUR INSTRUCTOR.

PART II

The Aquarius Advertising Agency underwent a reorganization that had a marked effect upon internal communication among its 200 employees and the degree of control and coordination.

The occurrence of short-cut direct communications solved some problems but created others. Account executives complained about being bypassed and in some instances they were unaware of the commitments made by the specialists. Many account executives felt the need for more control and one commented:

> Creativity and art. That's all I hear around here. It is hard as hell to effectively manage six or seven hot shots who claim that they have to do their own thing. Each of them tries to sell his or her idea to the client and most of the time I don't know what has happened until a week later. If I were a despot I would make all of them check with me first to get approval first. Things would sure change around here.

The need for reorganization was made more acute by the changes in the environment. Within a short period of time there was a rapid turnover in the major accounts

handled by the agency. It was not atypical for advertising agencies to gain or lose clients quickly, often with no advance warning as consumer behavior and lifestyle changes emerged and product innovations occurred.

An agency reorganization was one of the solutions proposed by top management to increase flexibility in this subtle and unpredictable environment. The reorganization was aimed at reducing the agency's response time to environmental changes and at increasing cooperation and communications among specialists of different types.

The Operations Division was the first one to be reorganized. The various departments, i.e., Art, Copy, etc., were dissolved and replaced by several composite groups. Each composite group became client-centered and was assigned the work of one or more specific clients.

Shortly after the change in the Operations Division, a similar reorganization occured in the Aquarius Marketing Division. Exhibit 3.28 shows the reorganization. Each client-centered group was managed by a Client Group Vice-President who was responsible

EXHIBIT 3.28 Reorganization of Aquarius Advertising Agency

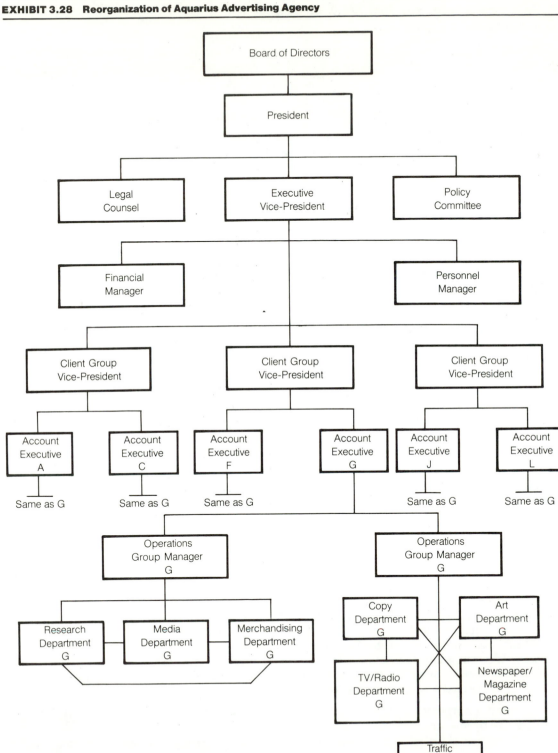

for both internal coordination of work in his or her group and external coordination of contacts and communications with clients and other client-centered groups within Aquarius.

The reorganization necessitated physical relocation of offices. Personnel of each client-centered group were assigned offices that were contiguous and clustered. This new clustering tended to facilitate supervision and intragroup communications. In effect, Aquarius was converted into several semiautonomous, small advertising agencies that were coordinated and connected only at the higher levels of management.

■ ANALYSIS QUESTIONS

1. Characterize the type of organization structure that was implemented at the Aquarius Advertising Agency in its reorganization (Galbraith reading).

2. How has the reorganization affected the flow of information and the interpersonal relationships at Aquarius (Galbraith reading)?

3. How does your proposed reorganization plan compare to the one adopted by the Aquarius Advertising Agency?

4. What are the likely dysfunctional consequences of your organization design?

■ A New Strategy for No. 2 in Computers

Back in 1957, when a computer was a room-sized behemoth that cost millions of dollars and needed a sterile, air-conditioned chamber, Kenneth H. Olsen set out to make a smaller, cheaper, and easier-to-use computer for the mass market. His company, Digital Equipment Corp., gave birth to a revolution by developing the first mass-produced minicomputer. By the 1970s companies were distributing minicomputers throughout their operations rather than concentrating their data processing in one large mainframe machine. DEC rode the trend to become the second-largest computer maker in the world, after giant International Business Machines Corp. Over the past decade, its annual revenues grew fourteenfold, to nearly $4 billion.

Now revolution is sweeping the computer industry again. Personal computers and office automation systems are putting computer power directly onto the desks of managers and executives. But this time, instead of leading the trend. Olsen has found himself having to play catch-up. "DEC for a period of time seemed to lose strategic direction—which markets it would go after and what its targets were," says Aaron C. Goldberg, a researcher at International Data Corp. in Framingham, Mass.

To get the Maynard (Mass.) company back on track, the 57-year-old Olsen has again moved into the company's day-to-day operations and launched a massive—and risky—corporate overhaul. Olsen's goal: a

radical transformation of his engineering-oriented company into a tough, market-driven competitor. "The issues [that led to this overhaul] are not technical but have to do with products and marketing," Olsen says. "The key strategy of the corporation," he adds, is making the new low-end desk-top products work together with DEC's bread-and-butter minicomputer line, then selling them together.

Three key pieces of this restructuring are only now falling into place:

■ Products. Olsen's new-product strategy calls for a broad range of computers—from small desk-top machines to large office minicomputers—that can communicate easily with one another.

■ Marketing. DEC is adopting aggressive new marketing tactics for office automation, personal computers, and small-business users. It is working hard to develop closer ties with customers, organize new distribution channels, and launch more innovative promotions.

■ Management. Olsen is streamlining an overgrown corporate bureaucracy and decentralizing decision-making.

The corporate overhaul will amount to "a vast transformation that ranks as one of the most critical periods in the company's history," says Frederic G. Withington, an industry analyst at Arthur D. Little Inc., a Cambridge (Mass.) consulting company. If the computer maker does not succeed in realigning itself for the fast-growing personal computer and office automation markets of the 1980s, it could be relegated to the older and slower-growing minicomputer market.

DEC has always been recognized by data processing professionals for its technical virtuosity. The company has been extremely successful at selling its minicomputers to sophisticated data processing managers, scientists, engineers, and the original-equipment makers (OEMs) who buy its computers and customize them for end-users. But DEC's traditional minicomputer business has been whittled away by a growing number of competitors. Microcomputer companies—replacing the mini's chip-laden circuit boards with a simpler design using a microprocessor, or computer-on-a-chip—have introduced compact units that do much of what DEC's more powerful machines can but sell for only a fraction of their price.

DEC's delay in developing its own family of easy-to-use desk-top and office computers gave the microcomputer makers a headstart in attracting the horde of neophyte end-users who will be buying these products in the 1980s. The company was also hindered because its name has never become a household word among these new customers.

These fundamental problems are now showing up on the bottom line. Olsen and his management team, however, did not need the recent poor financial results to alert them to the problem: They had already begun to institute major changes. To compete in the new low-cost desk-top arena—with its falling prices, short product cycles, and high-volume manufacturing—"we knew we had to cut costs, simplify, streamline, delegate, and establish short communication lines inside and outside to be competitive," says John J. Shields, vice-president in charge of field operations, who is one of Olsen's two chief lieutenants.

Although Olsen denies that the company has suffered delays in product development, insiders maintain that attempts to develop desk-top computers, office automation gear, and a new high-performance super-minicomputer foundered in DEC's bureau-cracy. "Some parts of the company were not doing a good job of reacting quickly," concedes Winston R. Hindle Jr., vice-president for corporate operations, who was also instrumental in directing the reorganization.

"Puritan father." Olsen, a plain-talking engineer trained at the Massachusetts Institute of Technology, recognized as early as 1980 that shifting markets would mean trouble for DEC. "Ken played the role of Puritan father, getting people to drive themselves. But he was always the glue that held the company together," says one former manager. Adds another, "Ken had to step in," because the company's management process had become increasingly contentious and had stalled any decision on how to enter the new markets. Olsen says as much himself: "It was my job to direct the overall change. There is no question the general's job is to understand the issues."

Olsen's new strategy is to insure that DEC's current minicomputer products work together with its new desk-top computers and office automation gear. The approach is fundamentally different from that of arch-rival IBM. To get an early jump on the market, IBM introduced several stand-alone desk-top units that did not work together. They included the Datamaster small-business computer, the Displaywriter word processor, and the IBM Personal Computer.

Olsen is gambling that if DEC can get all its new products to work together effectively, it can enter the growth markets late and still succeed. "The personal computer will fall flat on its face in business because users want to share files and want more than one user on the system," he asserts. "Under those circumstances, the minicomputer becomes more important than ever. Our strategy emphasizes the mini."

DEC's new strategy is inherently risky. The company is pursuing broad-based markets where it will run head-to-head with such established contenders as IBM and Wang Laboratories Inc. and also such new competitors as American Telephone & Telegraph Co. and the Japanese. DEC had always managed to coexist with IBM by serving the large minicomputer markets that the industry leader had mostly ignored. "In the past, DEC and IBM existed in largely separate spheres, but now they are going after similar [market] niches, and IBM presents a serious threat," says Goldberg of International Data.

But not all the challenges to DEC will come from outside. Olsen's realignment is fundamentally altering the company's power structure, and it could take years for the new organization to settle in.

DEC's previous power structure was built around eighteen separate product-line groups that concentrated on selling to specific industries, such as engineering, education, and commercial OEMs. Originally this structure was one of DEC's strong points because it enabled the company to respond quickly to the special demands of each kind of customer. Although most of the product-line groups used the same products and components, each had discretionary funds for product development, and each handled its own market strategies, forecasting, product pricing, order processing, and even inventories. Each group had to contract with a central department for any job it needed done in manufacturing, sales, field service, or engineering.

Fiefdoms. Eventually, the product–line groups became headquarters-bound fiefdoms that grew more and more protective of their own interests and lost sight of the company's long-range goals. Strategic planning mechanisms broke down because the narrowly focused groups were not anticipating new market demands that fell beyond their immediate purview. "The product-line groups were too short-term-oriented to look at major new markets and set strategic goals," says Arthur D. Little's Withington.

The DEC bureaucracy not only stymied product planning but also gummed up operations and hindered the sales force. Salespeople had no flexibility to bid com-

petitively on contracts because prices could not be changed without the approval of the product groups. Worse, the product-line groups began fighting among themselves for limited central engineering and manufacturing resources. If a group wanted to develop a new product, it had to build a consensus among some of the four central departments and the product groups. The process got so complex that it soon became difficult for DEC to move decisively.

Sabotage? This internal squabbling stalled DEC's personal computer efforts. In the mid-1970s, Stanley C. Olsen, Ken Olsen's brother and one of DEC's founders, became convinced that word processing could become DEC's stepping-stone into the low-cost end of the computer market. He sold his brother on the idea and spearheaded a major development project. But when the word processor was finally introduced in 1976 it was "a flop because they had no idea how to sell, support, or provide software for it," asserts Thomas R. Billadeau, president of the Office Systems Consulting Group Inc., a Boston firm.

Since DEC hands out development money in proportion to sales, Stan Olsen had difficulty pushing ahead with an improved word processor or a personal computer. Furthermore, insiders say that his efforts were sabotaged by other groups in the company. Andrew C. Knowles, then head of the terminals product-line group, "fought Stan because he saw the projects potentially cutting into terminal sales and because he wanted to head the low-end efforts himself," says one former manager. C. Gordon Bell, head of engineering, supported a low-end effort but insisted on building a more sophisticated machine. "It was a four-ring circus," the former manager recalls.

Stan Olsen, frustrated by his inability to get a consensus among engineering and other departments, finally resigned. And Ken Olsen stepped in to ramrod a project that turned out to be a compromise between Bell's advanced machine and personal computers then on the market. The result: the

Professional 325 and 350, priced at $4,000 and $5,000 respectively, and aimed at white-collar managers. At the same time, two other personal computers were built: the Rainbow, at $3,500 the least expensive machine, which was targeted mainly at the customers of the terminals group, and the DECmate II word processor, the machine Stan Olsen had persuaded his brother to build.

Consensus. With Stan Olsen's departure, the management of the low-end effort was up for grabs. Into the breach stepped Knowles, described by several insiders as a ''vicious infighter,'' who won control of DEC's three personal computers and was named last year to head a new Small Systems Group, which was given its own sales, marketing, and development resources.

A similar drama, say insiders, was played out in office automation. Julius L. Marcus, then manager of the commercial product-line group, was excited about Stan Olsen's word processing project and became the internal champion of higher-priced office automation systems. But he did not have the engineering resources to design office automation products within his own group. Like Stan Olsen, he had to build a consensus among DEC's in-house departments before he could move. ''As Julius made OA more visible, the same group of people were working him over,'' remembers one insider. ''Gordon Bell wanted a next-generation system; the technical group supported OA but wanted to control it. Friction built up between them.''

As a result, Marcus failed to marshal the needed resources, and the products were not developed on time or to specifications. Finally, to speed up the drive into the office, Olsen gave Marcus his own engineering staff to design office automation systems. At the same time, Robert C. Hughes, who had sixteen years of marketing experience at both IBM and DEC, was named to head office systems marketing.

To restore DEC's fighting trim and speed up product development, Olsen placed the main engineering and manufacturing operations under one umbrella organization. Then he consolidated the operations of twelve U.S. product groups into three regional management centers, leaving the product groups with only marketing duties. Each center has profit-and-loss responsibility and gives administrative support to the sales force. They also act as the direct link from the field to manufacturing, a job formerly done by the product groups at headquarters.

By consolidating administrative tasks in the management centers, DEC has dismantled its headquarters bureaucracy and begun to slash its staff. Already, 110 people in the U.S. now process orders once handled by 270 people. In Europe, the results have been even more promising. The company cut its central product-line operations in Geneva to 100 employees, from 350.

The final piece of Olsen's reorganization fell into place when DEC's thirteen-member Operations Committee was replaced by three committees in charge of product strategy, marketing and sales, and management. Olsen was concerned that decision-making had become too centralized at headquarters.

A hydra. By adding thirty middle managers and line executives to the original thirteen, the new structure ''spreads the decision-making to a larger number of people who have expertise in those areas,'' says Olsen. A similar move was also made by IBM, which added ten senior operating managers to its six-man corporate management structure.

As a result of DEC's reorganization, the sales force will now be assigned to accounts rather than to specific markets. Before, as many as six salespeople, each from a different product line, could have called on one large customer. Customers sometimes got no response from DEC to their requests for bids, or they got multiple bids from several different product groups. ''DEC was a multiheaded Hydra, each head with its own identity,'' recalls one large customer. For example, when Fidelity Management & Research Inc. bought a DEC system, it was besieged by two groups selling the same training courses at different prices.

Potential customers often walked away from the company in utter frustration. DEC lost out on a bid for a $40-million office automation contract from E.F. Hutton Group Inc. because "the marketing effort was chaotic," says Bernard Weinstein, Hutton's first vice-president for communications and branch information. Now, with just one salesperson calling on a large customer, DEC should be able to do a better job of capturing such business as the Hutton account, according to Naomi O. Seligman, senior partner at the Research Board Inc., a New York computer consulting firm.

DEC's reorganization faces other hurdles as well. Shifting operations from product lines to regional management centers, and reassigning salespeople, will be disruptive at first. Some former managers wonder if the management centers will push down decision-making, as they are supposed to do, or instead become new bottlenecks themselves. "If they don't work, selling, forecasting, delivery, and capacity will be screwed up," says a former manager. Salespeople will need extensive training, and the transition to an effective sales force could take as long as four years, predicts Wang's Cunningham.

DEC's basic strengths will no doubt help soften the transition, however. Having installed some 400,000 computers—more than any other minicomputer manufactur-

er—the company can make significant sales of new products to its present customers alone. Still, the biggest challenge that DEC will face will be "to participate successfully both in the explosive [new] markets and to continue to be a front-runner in the supermini sweepstakes," says Ulric Weil, an analyst for Morgan Stanley & Co.

The company's strong balance sheet will also help ease the strains of reorganization. DEC has $765 million in cash and only $92 million in long-term debt. "Their cash position is the envy of the industry—they're a small bank," says Morgan Stanley's Weil. "There's no reasonable storm they couldn't weather with that cash balance." Even a competitor agrees: "Given DEC's other strengths, it has time to make the transition."

DEC executives are confident they can make the transition without severe disruption. The company has adapted well to change in the past, they say. This is the fourth major overhaul since DEC's founding, and it has been accomplished without massive turnover, layoffs, or firings. "We're used to it," notes one middle manager.

Olsen, whose genial public demeanor throughout the two-year reorganization has concealed a frenetic, hard-driving management style, refuses to be as sanguine about DEC's prospects as his executives and shareholders. "I'm never satisfied—when you get satisfied, you're in trouble," he says. However he acknowledges with a grin, "Well, maybe fleetingly—for just a moment. I do think we are exactly where I'd like us to be."

■ A U.S. Concept Revives Oki

Japanese executives are often amused when Americans ask about the secrets of their managerial successes. For decades, the Japanese have studied Peter Drucker's books on managerial organization, have attended U.S. business schools, and have successfully implemented made-in-America concepts. Now another purebred U.S. concept has made it to Japan's shores, where it is reshaping the management structures of such companies as Hitachi, Toshiba, and Oki Electric Industry.

That concept is to reorganize companies into strategic business units, or SBUs—self-contained businesses that meet three criteria: They have a set of clearly defined external competitors, their managers are responsible for developing and implementing their own strategies, and their profitability can be measured in real income, rather than in artificial dollars posted as transfer payments between divisions. The SBU structure, pioneered by General Electric Co. more than a decade ago, helps a corporation pinpoint which products have the best growth potential.

A stumbling block. Until 1973, when soaring oil prices put the brakes on Japan's economic growth, "plant managers didn't care what product was making money so long as the company overall made a profit," notes Kenichi Ohmae, managing director of McKinsey & Co.'s Tokyo and Osaka offices. But since then, GE sources say that many

Japanese companies have asked for special GE seminars on strategic business planning and have sent managers to GE in the U.S. to learn how to implement SBUs.

Adopting the SBU concept has not been easy for Japanese companies. The name itself has been a stumbling block, says Masao Miyake, Oki's president, who notes that "Japanese people don't like the word 'strategy'" because it connotes "war" or "fight" to them. Furthermore, Japanese companies often fall into the same trap as U.S. companies in trying to set up SBUs—carving out so many units that each one is so small as to be meaningless from a marketing and planning viewpoint.

For example, Toshiba Corp. started in 1976 with 104 separate SBUs, only to discover that this many units made the process of allocating corporate resources unwieldly. Today the company is down to 43 SBUs, and Sadao Okano, Toshiba's general manager of corporate planning, says the SBU structure has enabled his company to boost sales from $3 billion in 1975 to an estimated $8 billion in 1981 while reducing its overall payroll by 6 percent. The leaner costs came in part from divesting such lackluster profit performers as sealed-beam lights for automobiles, fluorescent display units, small motor-operated cranes, and desk-top calculators.

Dramatic turnaround. At Oki Electric Industry Co., the move to an SBU structure in 1978 represented a last-ditch attempt to survive. Today, Oki is healthy: Its sales increased last year by 12 percent to $880 million and its net earnings, although still a meager $19 million, were boosted nearly 28 percent over the previous year's level. Most important, those sales and profits are coming from a varied group of products and markets.

Until 1973, Oki had made a healthy profit almost entirely by selling telecommunications equipment to Japanese government agencies. But then the energy crisis caused production costs to soar, and the government started using multiple suppliers instead of just Oki. Unprepared to compete in the private sector, the 100-year-old company suffered flat sales of some $440 million annually for five years. Its profits steadily eroded, culminating in a $7 million loss in 1978.

President Miyake—until 1977, executive managing director of Nippon Telegraph & Telephone Public Corp., Oki's largest customer—remembers trying to warn Oki about the coming downturn in NTT business. Although other Japanese companies heeded his warnings, "Oki continued to rely heavily on NTT," Miyake recalls. He retired from NTT in 1977 and assumed Oki's presidency a year later. "My mission," he says, "was to change the management of this company. It was too conservative, and it lacked a decisive marketing policy."

New markets. By July, 1978, Miyake had made his decision to adopt General Electric's SBU structure. He set up fifteen units, all centered on high-profit, high-technology products such as computer terminal peripherals, facsimile machines, integrated circuits, and electronic switching systems. The company either eliminated or deemphasized such products as crossbar telephone switching systems, marine radar, and numerical control systems. One result has been that Oki last year reduced its reliance on NTT to just 20 percent of sales, and Miyake hopes to get that down a few more percentage points by the end of the year. Moreover, the company now boasts of being Japan's primary maker of Kanji (Chinese character) printers for computers, a status that was underlined in October when Oki

concluded a large deal to sell such printers to IBM Japan.

Indeed, Oki's quick rise in the computer printer market provides an excellent case history of how the SBU structure has helped the company get its act together. Prior to the reorganization, the company not only sold primarily to government agencies but also developed products according to requests from each agency. Company engineers would be assigned to a customer team. The teams could be working on similar products for different agencies without the duplication ever becoming apparent.

After the reorganization, Oki assigned engineers in each SBU to product planning teams, which were expected to seek markets for new products rather than simply to fill existing customers' needs. And Oki personnel were encouraged to look not only to Japan's private sector for sales but also to overseas markets. Akinobu Yoshida, general manager of Oki's data products business unit, recalls that it was this new orientation that led his group to develop matrix printers with "near-letter" quality—high-speed computer printers that could generate the typewriter-like Roman letters needed for markets outside Japan. Adds Heihachiro Murota, corporate planning manager, "The SBUs have reinforced product planning strategy. Previously a customer team would be thinking only of its own customer and not of potential printer sales overall."

The combination of the Kanji matrix printer's overseas sales with its wider domestic sales to the private sector has boosted Oki's total computer printer sales more than threefold in three years. The product orientation has also provided economies of scale. Yoshida notes that before the reorganization, numerous customer teams were designing computer printers for different customers, with the result that each printer needed its own assembly line. Now similar printers are grouped together, allowing for mass-production and "substantially lower" production costs.

Oki has had similar success with its facsimile equipment. In the past, customer teams had developed numerous facsimile machines for NTT and other government offices. Today all Oki's facsimile research and marketing rests under the umbrella of a facsimile SBU, and Murota says that the attendant "shift in marketing strategy toward the private sector" brought about a tenfold increase in sales, to $26 million, in three years.

More exports. Oki is actively seeking to expand its international horizons, both in sales and manufacturing facilities. Miyake hopes to boost the company's exports to 25 percent of sales this year, up from 15 percent two years ago. Oki is getting ready to sell computer printers to Britain's ICL Ltd., and is negotiating a hefty contract with American Telephone & Telegraph Co. for automobile telephone and radio receiver systems.

Oki has also increased its production of personal computers by 50 percent, to 3,000 a month. And the company is investing in semiconductors and integrated circuits, items that Miyake hope to sell as well as use in its own products.

Presumably, the SBU structure, with its built-in emphasis on marketing, will help Oki achieve these goals, provided the company does not fall into the trap that Toshiba encountered—creating too many SBU units. Indeed, a senior GE planner notes that even his company, although it officially has about forty SBUs, in actuality has closer to seventy. "The SBU is a good tool to decide how to deconglomerate and to maximize growth in remaining divisions," he sums up. "But if you start creating SBUs around little $10 million products, they get lost in the shuffle, and you're back where you started in terms of lack of control."

■ An About-Face in TI's Culture

For years, Texas Instruments Inc. managed innovation brilliantly with a corporate planning system that many observers considered one of the best—and most complex— in existence. But the Dallas electronics giant began losing control. Now, after more than a year of soul-searching over whether to change its vaunted matrix management system, TI has uncorked a massive overhaul.

First TI created several new profit centers and delegated unprecedented responsibili-

Reprinted from the July 5, 1982, issue of *Business Week* by special permission. Copyright © 1982 by McGraw-Hill, Inc., New York, NY 10020. All rights reserved.

ty to the managers of these businesses. This spring's stunning reorganization was capped in mid-June by the election of a new cadre of executive vice-presidents, setting up for the first time a clear mechanism to choose successors to Chairman Mark Shepherd, Jr. and President J. Fred Bucy.

TI must reverse a record that of late has been spotted by delayed product introductions and missed opportunities—problems highlighted by the current economic crunch. Profits have declined for the past six quarters and last year the Dallas company lost its longtime No. 1 spot in sales in the key U.S. semiconductor market to archrival Motorola Inc.

Mistakes. "In essence, TI is doing nothing short of changing its corporate culture," says John J. Lazlo, Jr., an analyst at San Francisco's Hambrecht & Quist. "It has no choice but to decentralize, to structure its businesses so they can play in the same ball park as their smaller competitors." But while TI may waste little time in reasserting itself, an heir apparent is unlikely to emerge soon. Shepherd, 59, has so far indicated no intention of relinquishing control of the $4-billion semiconductor giant. And it is clear that, before he steps aside, Shepherd wants to return TI to the preeminence it enjoyed in the early 1970s.

Even TI executives now admit that the company's problems are the result of a turgid management system that has become increasingly inept at coping with TI's 25 percent compound annual growth rate of the past decade. In an unprecedented recital of mistakes at the company's April shareholders' meeting, Bucy laid the blame squarely on TI's matrix structure, a cumbersome overlapping of operating and strategic managements. To correct the ills, TI is according new respect to marketing and making renewed efforts to decentralize— changes that strike at the heart of the company's lifelong technology orientation and a planning system that tended to push all decisions into the board room.

TI's restructuring actually began a year ago, when it started shedding such unprofitable product lines as digital watches and some electronic components. Further, TI began focusing development efforts more narrowly killing a $50-million magnetic-bubble memory program, for example, that it figured would cost too much to bring to market.

The company continues to pare. It has essentially given up on multichip microprocessors—one of the most important and fastest growing semiconductor product lines—redirecting its effort instead toward versions that pack all the elements of a computer onto a single chip. And in the past year it has reduced its worldwide work force by more than 10,000 or 10 percent, mainly through layoffs.

Promotions. The most dramatic changes came this spring, when TI completely reorganized its two sickest operating groups, semiconductors and distributed computing. For both, TI redefined its basic profit-and-loss unit, the product customer center (PCC), to encompass a complete business. And it gave each PCC manager control of the resources—people, capital, and facilities—needed to run the business. Previously, PCC managers in the semiconductor group had been reduced to begging for those resources from huge central support entities, while the PCC structure in computers had fragmented into a series of individual product lines that were difficult to team together for a system sale.

The PCC management structure was also brought in line with TI's strategic planning organization, so that PCC managers will be responsible for making and marketing their products as well as for developing extensions to their product families. And an advanced-development activity was set up in the semiconductor group so that products and processes that leapfrog the state of the art do not get diffused among managers concerned with day-to-day operations.

The aftermath of that streamlining was a series of far-reaching changes in senior management and the election of the new executive vice-presidents. William N. Sick, Jr., widely credited with turning around TI's consumer operations, added the semiconductor group to his responsibilities. He replaces James L. Fischer, who became chief financial officer. Also named to senior posts were Jerry R. Junkins, who took over TI's computer business last fall, and Grant A. Dove, who runs the company's government, geophysical exploration, and materials and controls businesses.

Executive vice-president Stewart Carrell, a widely experienced TI manager has the new job of coordinating technology, marketing, and planning. That move signals TI's new commitment to its customer. "The company has always developed products from a technology point of view, as opposed to what the market wanted," says Michael J. Krasko, a vice-president at Merrill Lynch, Pierce, Fenner & Smith Inc. "What we see happening now is a corporate determination to match technology prowess with what will sell."

Too early. Nowhere is that more apparent than in consumer businesses, where TI uncharacteristically named William J. Turner, a marketer with a scant two-year tenure at the company, as the group's new head. And the experience of Sick, the new semiconductor chief, "will bring that business a di-

mension of marketing awareness and strategies that we badly need," admits one TI officer.

It is still too early to tell whether TI's new attitude toward marketing will help it shed its reputation as an arrogant, middle-aged company. And some outsiders still question whether top management will ever really give up enough authority to let individual managers run their own businesses. "On paper, the moves are very positive," says James L. Barlage, vice-president for research at Smith Barney, Harris Upham & Co. "But we'll be moving into a period of economic strength, and that will mask any improvements, just as the economy in the late '70s masked the problems."

■ State Drug Council

■ DO NOT READ THIS CASE UNTIL DIRECTED TO DO SO BY YOUR INSTRUCTOR.

PART I

The State Drug Council had to review, as one of its charges, a variety of proposals dealing with drug abuse in the state. Proposals and programs that the Council might be asked to review included requests for funding on such topics as drug treatment effectiveness, statewide educational programs, level and extent of drug abuse within the state, factors that lead to drug abuse, evaluation of various educational efforts, evaluation and study of law enforcement ef-

forts, support for new treatment facilities, etc. The head of the Drug Council, who readily admitted limited knowledge on the subject, decided to recruit a variety of professionals from the state to provide valid assessment of the proposals submitted.

Several professionals concerned with drug abuse were contacted by the head of the Drug Council and asked to come to a meeting at the capital city headquarters. At the first meeting people involved in drug treatment, law enforcement, drug-related research, and educators from all parts of the state were present. The head of the Drug Council chaired this meeting, which includ-

---

This case was written by John F. Veiga and it represents a real situation. All names and places have been disguised.

ed twenty-two professionals, and after calling the meeting to order told the group he did not want to impose any of his ideas on the group about how it might organize. He was sensitive to the fact that the people involved were donating their time and felt he would let the group decide.

After a few minutes, the meeting degenerated into several people talking at once, each proposing a different approach. The law enforcement people knew each other even though they were from different parts of the state and felt they should form a separate committee. The research methodology people felt it would be difficult to meet regularly as a separate committee because they came from different parts of the state and driving to the capital city took at least one hour each way. The educators, coming from different universities, expressed concern over driving time, while the psychologists and psychiatrists involved in treatment just wanted to be sure that adequate funds went into effective treatment programs. The first meeting was terminated with little resolved except that a second meeting time was set up.

At the second meeting the group continued to flounder as more and more individuals became frustrated and threatened to be absent from future meetings. At the third meeting the group demanded that the head of the Drug Council provide some direction. He told the group that he had some proposals for them to consider and suggested that they begin by looking at the proposal he had sent to them prior to the meeting, concerning a new free treatment clinic. The people involved in treatment suggested they go off by themselves and review the proposal since this was their bailiwick. As the discussion continued, a police chief stated that he perceived real problems with law enforcement officials accepting free and private clinics. He felt that police would see them merely as "crash pads." The educators expressed concern over having sufficient funding to provide adequate publicity in local schools. The research methodology people attacked the lack of effective assessment measures in the proposal and suggested it be sent back for revision. The meeting continued with accusations of "grandstanding," and several people departed early. Most people left this meeting angry and frustrated, and several members told the head of the Drug Council that something had to be done or they would not be returning. Prior to the next meeting, the head of the Drug Council sent out a memo detailing what he believed to be the objectives of the group and how he hoped to deal with the problems they had proposed (see exhibit 3.29).

■ ANALYSIS QUESTIONS

1. As a consultant to the head of the Drug Council, what organizational structure would you propose (Galbraith reading)? What problems can you anticipate with your proposal?

2. What other questions would you like to ask the Advisory Board members and/or the head of the Drug Council? Why?

EXHIBIT 3.29   State Memo

To: Members of Drug Council Advisory Board
From: Head of Drug Council
Subject: Council Objectives

The objective of the Advisory Board, as I see it, is to provide recommendations to the State Drug Council concerning various proposals involved with drug abuse. As I see it, some proposals may require specific expertise for evaluation such as those that deal with education. On the other hand, as we discovered last week, most proposals seem to overlap all our areas of expertise to some extent, and effective recommendations require several inputs. Therefore, it is imperative for all of you to contribute your ideas.

I have asked a management consultant to attend our next meeting and to propose to us how we might organize ourselves. I would appreciate it if everyone would come and cooperate with her.

■ DO NOT READ PART II UNTIL DIRECTED TO DO SO BY YOUR INSTRUCTOR.

PART II

After the consultant attended the next meeting of the board, she requested a list of the board members, their areas of expertise, and their geographic locations. In addition, after discussing the Board's objectives and past performance with the head of the Drug Council, she met privately with several members and listened to their complaints. Exhibit 3.30 represents the data she gathered.

■ COMPLAINT LIST

1. "A one-hour drive each way to a meeting is too much given the amount of time we waste at the meeting."
2. "You can't do a damn thing with twenty-two people all talking at once."
3. "Some of the proposals could really benefit from the people in my area (Treatment) getting together separately."
4. "Some of these people don't realize the value of sharing ideas with professionals outside their own area. They act as if they have the only answer."

EXHIBIT 3.30 Board Member List

	Member	Area of Expertise	Geographic Location*
1.	A. Alfred	Research Methodology	Central
2.	T. Brougham	Law Enforcement	Northeast
3.	N. Brown	Treatment	Central
4.	R.J. Crousee	Research Methodology	Northeast
5.	J.F. Donley	Treatment	Southern
6.	P.W. Everett	Education	Central
7.	J. Francis	Treatment	Northeast
8.	T. French	Research Methodology	Southern
9.	S. Gant	Education	Southern
10.	N. Hughes	Research Methodology	Southern
11.	J.L. Hughes	Research Methodology	Central
12.	S. Islay	Treatment	Central
13.	G. Jones	Treatment	Northeast
14.	H. Kronsel	Research Methodology	Northeast
15.	M. Listro	Law Enforcement	Central
16.	R. Nunes	Research Methodology	Southern
17.	L.M. Lacey	Treatment	Southern
18.	G. Turner	Research Methodology	Northeast
19.	P. Vail	Treatment	Northeast
20.	W. Walters	Education	Northeast
21.	J. Verna	Law Enforcement	Southern
22.	S. Yates	Research Methodology	Central

* Grouped by general location within the state.

■ ANALYSIS QUESTIONS

1. Based on the above information, how would you reorganize the Advisory Board? Why?

2. Do you still need additional information? If so, what?

■ DO NOT READ PART III UNTIL DIRECTED TO DO SO BY YOUR INSTRUCTOR.

PART III

Based on the data gathered, the counsultant advised the head of the Drug Council to organize the Advisory Board into a matrix organization. Functional specialties and geographic area were used to form task forces.

(Your instructor will provide you a drawing of the final organization chart.)

According to the design, task forces were set up by geographic location to reduce travel time for each board member. Task forces could then meet near their own state locations. The task force leaders rotated within their teams depending upon the nature of the proposal being evaluated. The functional coordinators (FC) were members of different task forces. These people had the responsibility of meeting regularly with the head of the Drug Council to review the proposals to be examined. After this group reviewed the proposals, one of the task forces would be assigned the evaluation task depending upon current work load with results fed back to the head of the Drug Council through the Functional Coordinators. When a proposal involved just one specialized area, a meeting of all members with that special expertise could be called and they could then make a recommendation. This proposal went into operation immediately after it was presented to the entire group.

■ ANALYSIS QUESTIONS

1. Do you think the consultant made a wise recommendation? Why? Why not?

2. Do you see some problems for the new organization? If so, what?

■ Starting at the Bottom

One method of organizing, and perhaps the most important one prescribed by traditional organization theory, is based on the functional approach. The principal criterion used for designing an organization by the functional method is the division of labor and specialization according to the function to be performed. For the sake of efficiency and economy, similar tasks and jobs are grouped into one functional department. At the work level, a functional organization would group together, for example, all the jobs involving sales—salespeople, sales records, and cashier. The same would be the case for all production tasks, engineering tasks, finance tasks, accounting tasks, and so on.

Functional organization can be used also at the managerial level, placing managers with similar tasks and activities together in one unit. The development of functional organization at the managerial level is usually secondary in the evolution of an organization. It is secondary to the work level because organizations generally evolve from the work that must be accomplished and because a large part of the efficiency of specialization is derived from the work level rather than from the managerial level. Yet

This article is based on the idea of a unit work flow presented in Eliot D. Chapple and Leonard R. Sayles, *The Measure of Management* (New York: The Macmillan Co., 1961), ch. 2.

most of the management literature about organization design focuses on the managerial level beginning at the top with the directors and president and down through the vice-president, division managers . . . First-line supervision is treated as a variable dependent on the way top management is organized. As appropriate as this top management emphasis may be, we should not lose sight of the need for emphasizing the bottom-up viewpoint of organizational design.

WORK AS THE BASIS FOR ORGANIZATION DESIGN

Organizing at the work level as opposed to the managerial level requires a distinctly different approach. This approach requires looking at how specific tasks should be grouped. For instance, should sales recordkeeping be grouped with other sales activities or with the accounting department? Should credit analysis be assigned to the

sales department or to the finance unit? There are many such problems to be solved at the work level. The following criterion is offered for use in solving such problems.

The Unit of Work Flow Criterion

The criterion proposed for the work-level approach is to group activities on the basis of a unit work flow. This requires studying the work process—when does the process begin; in what sequence is work to be done; and when does the process end. To understand the work process, it is necessary to examine the sequence of work activities required to produce some product, service, or end result. Interrelatedness among activities in the work process suggests that those tasks that are interrelated and dependent upon each other, even if they are functionally dissimilar, should be grouped into a *unit of work flow* and supervised by one person.

The following case illustrates the problem created when activities are grouped on the basis of similarity of functions. Exhibit 3.31

EXHIBIT 3.31 Putnam Plastics Co. Organization Chart

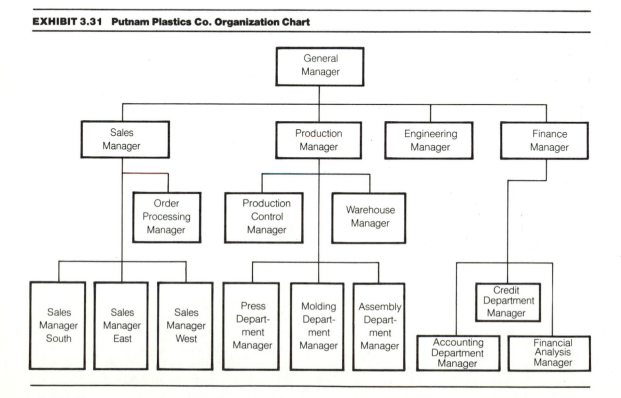

shows part of the organization chart of one division of the Putnam Plastics Co. and the functional departmentation of activities. Six months ago Putnam installed a computerized system that gave the sales managers an up-to-date readout of availability of goods. Sales personnel in the field can have their inquiries answered in a few minutes and this has stimulated sales. At the point of sale, the salesperson can place a telephone call to the salesclerk in the Sales Processing Department to obtain up-to-date information on prices and availability and delivery dates. The pricing information is provided by the salesclerk who obtains availability information from the order clerk in the Production Department. The order clerk interrogates the computer for a readout on the availability of the goods and probable delivery date. Salespeople can thus respond very quickly to customer inquiries about the availability and anticipated delivery date of an order. Salespeople like this quick access to information, but some customers have complained about subsequent treatment. Once the order is taken, the salesclerk in the Sales Department requests a credit clearance from the Finance Department. Most orders are then written up by the salesclerk and processed through to the warehouse clerk, while other orders have to be altered or cancelled because of credit limitations on a particular customer or unacceptable credit

ratings. This subsequent treatment occurs to about 10 percent of the orders and has resulted in bad relations with prospective customers. It has also created some internal tension between the Sales Manager and Credit Manager, as well as between the salesclerks and the credit analysis personnel.

Using a work flow approach to analyze Putnam's sales-credit problem, exhibit 3.32 shows how the work moves through the organization. Interactions numbered 1, 2, 3, and 4 show the initial inquiry to obtain pricing and availability of goods, interaction 5 involves the request for credit clearance, interaction 6 depicts those cases in which the credit check results in an alteration in or cancellation of a customer order, and interaction 7 indicates the processing of an order through to the warehouse. Three departments are involved in one unit of work, which includes order processing.

Using the work flow criterion, a reorganization of order processing would group all the activities and personnel involved in the ordering process into one unit with one supervisor. Exhibit 3.33 shows the work flow under the revised organization design. The Salesclerk, Credit Analysis Clerk, and Order Clerk functions are grouped into one work unit under the direction of an Order Process Supervisor. The broken lines connecting the functional manager to respec-

---

EXHIBIT 3.32   Putnam Plastics Co. Work Flow Chart

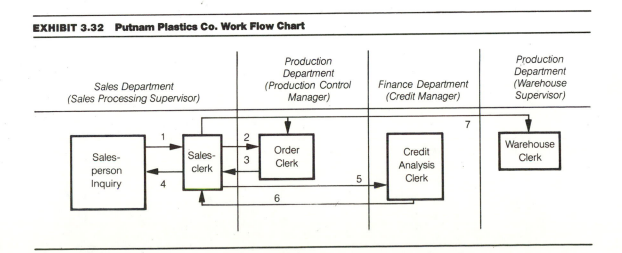

EXHIBIT 3.33   Putnam Plastics Co. Revised Work Flow Chart

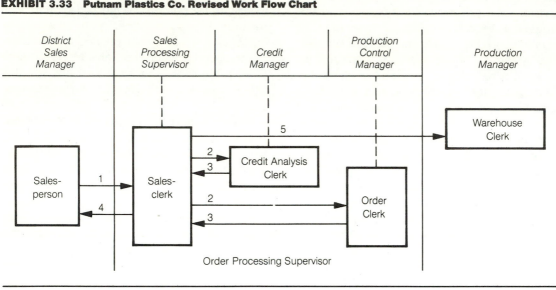

tive clerks represent functional relationships. The Sales Processing Supervisor still has to make inputs, such as pricing lists and other sales policies. The Production Control Manager also makes inputs concerning goods availability information and the Credit Manager inputs credit policies. All the necessary functions for order processing are handled in one unit supervised directly by one person.

Exercises

■ Pen Mark Creative Verses

Often the organization architects are too far removed from the actual work being performed to fully understand the effects of their design on members' behavior. For a manager, becoming aware of this cause-effect linkage is necessary if he or she wants to develop an effective organization. Even though top management may have the final say on the structure of the organization, every manager must take responsibility for its effectiveness. Hence, it is important that managers at all levels of the organization understand its structure and have some input into those decisions involving final design. Moreover, irrespective of their level in the organization, all managers must face these same basic design issues every time they attempt to organize their subordinates to accomplish subunit objectives effectively.

Unfortunately, what looks good on the drawing board may be disastrous in practice. While it is possible to provide the organization architects with some basic design principles and ideal design specifications, the final translation of organizational requirements and basic strategy remain the responsibility of the manager. It has already been conceded that there is no one best way to organize; however, the novice designer should recognize there are certainly better ways.

In this exercise, you will have to design an organization faced with changing market demand. You will have to evaluate various design logics and design specifications and, based on your capacity to translate the demands on the organization, design an organization structure that will be able to cope effectively with its environment.

Directions

In this exercise your group will be asked to design an organization capable of meeting several specified organization requirements and to prepare a formal presentation on your design. The instructor will indicate to you how much time is available for the design phase. All the groups will have an opportunity to critique each design presentation and select the final design to be implemented. Design groups should be willing to accept the final selection and participate as members in whatever design is chosen. The total size of the organization, in terms of number of employees, will be equal to the total number of participants involved in the exercise.

Task

The group will design and operate an organization that produces prototype creative verses. The positions in the organization are to be filled by members of the group. Be certain your organization can meet emergencies and shifting market demand since these will be introduced into the exercise.

According to Allen Zoll, the task used in this exercise was first developed by Dr. Richard W. Wallen for use in the Senior Management Seminar of the Boeing Aircraft Co.

The products are sheets of paper containing prototype creative verses such as those used in greeting cards. Products must conform to the specifications outlined on the *Product Specification Sheet*.

There will be three production periods of fifteen minutes each. Each period will have differing market conditions and product demands. You will be informed of those conditions and product demands before the start of each period and there will be no changes during each production period. A maximum of five card types (e.g., New Year, Easter, Birthday) will be demanded during any given period. You will need to work out some way of making sure that the specifications are met and that data are gathered on: (1) volume of output, (2) proper product mix, and (3) any other data you deem necessary for decision-making purposes. Your records should be current. In determining volume and product mix figures, you can count only finished products in inventory at the end of any production period. Goods in process are *not* to be counted. Thus you will need a place to store finished inventory. In meeting changes in market requirements, excess finished inventory may be carried over to the next production period, but work in process must be scrapped at the end of each period. You will also need someone to get market requirements from Veyan Creations, the *sole purchaser* of your product, and someone to make raw material purchase requests (ask your instructor).

Product Specification Sheet

1. Each verse card must contain two different two-line verses. Both must be on the same theme.

2. Every verse on each card must be different. Full lines must change. Single word changes are *not* acceptable.

3. The lines of each two-line verse must rhyme, but the two verses on each card need not rhyme with each other.

4. Grammar, spelling, punctuation, and capitalization must be correct. Lines should have approximately the same meter, but this is not a rigid requirement.

5. Verses may be serious or humorous, but slang is *not* acceptable.

6. Verse card dimensions will vary with market demand and verse type. You will be given raw material of $8^{1}/_{2}'' \times 11''$ paper that will have to be cut to size (plus or minus one-eighth inch) on a paper-cutting board. Purchased raw material will have about a 10 percent scrap rate. Faulty raw material will have a large X on its unusable side and can be returned for replacement only if done so *prior* to being cut. Verse cards made from faulty material will be rejected. Normally one full sheet of paper will yield two cards.

7. Each sheet must have a title at the top that indicates the kind of occasion (type) for which the verses are to be used, for example, New Year's Day, Get Well, Mother's Day. In addition, all cards must be printed and read from left to right along the largest dimension of the card. Each card should be laid out *exactly* like the example on page 237.

8. Inspection: Veyan Creations will utilize an AQL (Acceptable Quality Limit) of 10 percent, that is, from each batch of ten, if one defect is found, the entire lot of ten cards will be rejected automatically.

> *Valentine's Day*
> Don't Take this as a Line;
> Won't you be my Valentine?
>
> Cupid has done just fine,
> Making you my Valentine.

9. Verse cards should be delivered at the end of each production period. Cards should be grouped according to type and stapled together in stacks of ten (staple once at upper left corner). Veyan Creations' inspection will occur during the following production period. Therefore, final results will not be available until sometime during the following period. Hence, excess inventory data will *not* be available at the beginning of a production period.

Production Equipment

The following equipment will be available for the production of the products:

> One paper-cutting board
> One stapler

The equipment will be provided by the instructor and no other equipment can be used.

Market Mix

The market mix will determine what percentage of your total salable output will be actually purchased by Veyan for a given verse type. For example, assume you produce 200 units in a given period and 180 units pass Veyan inspection. The following represents an illustration of what can happen:

General Type of Verse	Delivered	Number of Units that Passed Veyan Inspection	Scrap	Specified Mix	Maximum Number of Units Veyan is Willing to Buy	Actual Units Purchased By Veyan	Excess Inventory *
A	40	40	0	20%	36 (20% of 180)	36	4
B	60	44	16	30%	54 (30% of 180)	44	–
C	20	20	0	10%	18 (10% of 180)	18	2
D	80	76	4	40%	72 (40% of 180)	72	4
	200 —	180 =	20	100%	180	170	10

* Units not purchased that exceed maximum

Delivery Requirement

Ten minutes after a production period begins, a company representative will have to estimate the total number of cards that Veyan will *actually* purchase for the period. For example, while 200 units were produced in the above illustration, only 170 were *actually* purchased by Veyan Creations. This estimate will be delivered to Veyan Creations as a formal delivery promise. Errors in delivery, the difference between actual and promised delivery units, will be penalized at the following rate:

Error in Delivery Promise	Penalty (Reduction in Profit)
± 10 units	No penalty
± 11 – 20 units	$ 50
± 21 – 30 units	$100
± 31 – 40 units	$150
± 41 or more units	$250

In the above illustration, if 200 units had been promised, the error would have been 30 units (200–170) and the penalty charged against profit for that period would have been $100.

Profit and Loss

Veyan will pay your company $10 for each prototype unit it *actually* purchases, i.e., those units that meet quality and mix requirements. Your only manufacturing cost will be $5 for each sheet of raw material you process. All raw materials must be purchased from the instructor. Full sheets of *unused* raw material may be returned for full credit at the end of each production period. Your organization's effectiveness will be measured by the total profit earned. Below is a sample profit and loss statement:

Profit and Loss Statement (3 Production Periods)

1st Production Period

a. Units *actually* sold to Veyan: 100 × $10	=	$ 1000.00
b. Raw material used: 60 sheets × $5	=	−300.00
c. Delivery Penalty (15-unit error)	=	−50.00
Net Profit		$ 650.00

2nd Production Period

a. Units actually sold to Veyan: 120 × $10	=	$ 1200.00
b. Raw material used: 80 sheets × $5	=	−400.00
c. Delivery Penalty (35-unit error)	=	−150.00
Net Profit		$ 650.00

3rd Production Period

a. Units actually sold to Veyan: 82 × $10	=	$ 820.00
b. Raw material used: 90 sheets × $5	=	−450.00
c. Delivery Penalty (100-unit error)	=	−250.00
Net Profit		$ 120.00
Total Production Period Profit		$1,420.00

Requirements for the Organization

1. Produce a large volume of verses that meet specifications and are of the type required to meet market demand.
2. Maximize profits and minimize raw material cost and delivery promise error.
3. Encourage maximum involvement and self-direction among all personnel.
4. Maximize the creativity of all personnel as they do their work.
5. Maintain flexibility needed to deal with changes in market demand or unexpected internal disturbances.
6. Provide assistance and consultation for personnel who are being blocked or hindered from doing a good job.

ORGANIZATION DESIGN WORKSHEET

1. What is the basic strategy behind your design? That is, in what business is your company? What are your company's primary objectives?

2. Below, draw a sketch of the final structure of your organization.

■ Evaluating Organizational Structures

In this exercise, you are asked to use what you know about organization design and structure. The task is to create questionnaire items that you feel would help assess the effectiveness of an organization's structure.

Directions

1. Each group will develop two or three questions to be included in a final questionnaire. The questions should be stated so that they can be answered using a five-point scale. Each statement should be posed in such a way that a higher level of agreement always represents a more positive assessment. For example: "In this organization, there is very little wasted motion because people are always aware of what to do and when to do it."

Strongly Disagree	Disagree	Neither Agree nor Disagree	Agree	Strongly Agree
1	2	3	4	5

2. For each question developed, try to determine what is the underlying attribute or quality you are attempting to evaluate. For instance, in the example just given, the quality being examined might be called "Coordination efficiency."

3. Given three organizational structures—function, product, and matrix—your group should hypothesize how employees in each of these structures might differ on their average response to each of your questions.

4. All groups share their questions and create a final questionnaire for use in Option A, B, or C (your instructor will indicate the option to follow).

5. Participants can compare their dimensions with the "Design Specifications" suggested by Peter Drucker on the last page of this exercise.

Option A

Discuss the various dimensions of structural effectiveness developed. Post each item on newsprint or chalkboard and have each group discuss how they felt each dimension might vary according to structure.

Option B

Develop a final questionnaire using two or three items from each group. Have copies made and have each participant administer the questionnaire to five employees in a particular organization structure. For example, one-third of the class gathers data from a functional organization, one-third from a product organization, and one-third from a matrix. Results are tabulated and shared, and each group reconciles its initial hypotheses with survey findings.

Option C

For participants who are to engage in the Penmark Creative Verses exercise, the survey can be done after each production round and quickly tabulated as a basis for discussion. The questionnaire can be constructed during the time the management team is making final preparation for implementing their design for Penmark. Each group should develop two questions. The final survey can be administered using the blank questionnaire provided. The group that proposes a question should be prepared to interpret the results during post-production analysis.

EXERCISE WORKSHEET

Question 1: _____

_____

Underlying attribute: _____

We expect this attribute to be rated as follows on the questionnaire:

	Low (1–2)	Moderate (3)	High (4–5)
In a functional organization	_____	_____	_____
In a product organization	_____	_____	_____
In a matrix organization	_____	_____	_____

Question 2: _____

_____

Underlying attribute: _____

We expect this attribute to be rated as follows on the questionnaire:

	Low (1–2)	Moderate (3)	High (4–5)
In a functional organization	_____	_____	_____
In a product organization	_____	_____	_____
In a matrix organization	_____	_____	_____

Question 3: _____

_____

Underlying attribute: _____

We expect this attribute to be rated as follows on the questionnaire:

	Low (1–2)	Moderate (3)	High (4–5)
In a functional organization	_____	_____	_____
In a product organization	_____	_____	_____
In a matrix organization	_____	_____	_____

ORGANIZATIONAL QUESTIONNAIRE

Below are several statements about your organization's structure. Please indicate the degree to which you agree or disagree with each statement using the following scale:

1 = Strongly Disagree
2 = Disagree
3 = Neither Agree nor Disagree
4 = Agree
5 = Strongly Agree

_____   1. _____

_____

_____   2. _____

_____

_____   3. _____

_____

_____   4. _____

_____

_____   5. _____

_____

_____   6. _____

_____

_____   7. _____

_____

_____   8. _____

_____

_____   9. _____

_____

_____   10. _____

_____

_____   11. _____

_____

_____   12. _____

_____

_____   13. _____

_____

_____   14. _____

_____

_____   15. _____

_____

Design Specifications

According to Peter Drucker, a well-known management consultant, organizational architects should strive to design organizations with certain key specifications in mind—much like the designer of a building. However, unlike the design of a concrete edifice, in which rigid, well-defined specifications can be identified, the specifications for the design of an organization must be more loosely defined. Nonetheless, striving to identify such specifications is a valuable step toward a more thorough understanding of the design process. Below are the seven design specifications that Drucker identified. As you review them you will probably notice that these specifications are somewhat conflicting if carried to an extreme. Thus, in the end, no organization structure can fully satisfy all specifications.

_____

Based on Peter Drucker, *Management: Tasks, Responsibilities and Practices*, ch. 44, Harper & Row, 1974.

1. Clarity.—Individuals, especially managers, need to know where they belong, where they have to go for whatever is needed (be it for information, cooperation, or decisions), and how to get there.
2. Economy.—Minimum effort should be needed to control, to supervise, and to coax people to perform. The smallest number of people possible should have to devote time and attention to "keeping the machinery going."
3. Direction of Vision.—Organization structure should direct the vision of individuals and of managerial units toward *performance* rather than toward *efforts*. It must not make *effort* more important than *results*.
4. Understanding one's own task and the common task.
   a. Own task. An organization should help all members and especially all managers and professionals *understand* their own task.
   b. Common task. At the same time, an organization should enable everyone to understand the common task, the task of the entire organization. Every member of the organization, in order to relate his or her efforts to the common good, needs to understand how his or her tasks fit in with the task of the whole.
5. Decision-making.—The design should be such that it strengthens the decision-making process. Design should focus decisions at the lowest possible level rather than forcing decisions to the top.
6. Stability and Adaptability.
   a. The design should provide enough certainty as possible for the individual so as to insure each person has a "niche" and not be constantly bombarded with turmoil and uncertainty.
   b. The design should allow for adaption to new situations, new demands, new conditions—and also to new faces and personalities.
7. Perpetuation and self-renewal.—An organization must be capable of producing from within tomorrow's leaders.
   a. Structure should help each person *learn* and *develop* in each job held. It should be designed for continuous learning.
   b. Structure should be *accessible to new ideas* and capable of responding to new situations.

■ Corrugated Paper Products, Inc.

Making decisions that involve organizational design and structure is becoming a more frequent occurrence for managers in the dynamic, changing environment that exists today. The manager must not only have the ability and skill for planning and implementing the work, but must also be able to diagnose problems created by a given work arrangement.

To the outsider, an organizational chart represents a neat and orderly arrangement of the tasks to be performed for the organization to produce an output (at least if it is drawn well). To the insider, the same organizational chart often appears an oversimplification of what really occurs in the organizational milieu. The designer of the organizational structure often finds himself or herself on the boundary between the two perspectives—recognizing the complexity and, at the same time, being aware of the need for simplicity. An organizational structure, like the foundation of a building, has a great deal of impact on the orderliness of the final edifice, but has little effect on what the observer sees. Herein lies the dilemma.

The structure must provide enough stability so that members' behaviors are predictable and reliable in terms of achieving the final goal of the organization. And yet, the structure is also invisible to, but felt by, those very same people. The designer, thus, should be guided by the maxim that a good organizational structure can be measured by the problems it does not create.

Directions

In this exercise you will be formed into mini-organizations with several other people. The success of your company will depend on (1) organizational structure, (2) quality control, and (3) efficient use of personnel. Each mini-organization should consider itself a separate company whose objective is to maximize profit.

Your company has been a successful manufacturer of various paper products including napkins, paper towels, and a variety of cardboard containers. Recently you received an order for the manufacture of a small paper container, which is used to display oriental jewelry. The container, made from hand-lettered parchment, has defied all attempts to be folded by existing equipment. The parchment rips very easily and the hand lettering is often marred by mechanical folding equipment. Therefore, the containers must be hand folded.

Your group should design as efficient an organization as you can to produce paper containers during a ten-minute production period. After your first production run, you will have an opportunity to reorganize your company, if you wish, and then start a second ten-minute production run. The basic folding procedure is shown in the *Paper Container-Blueprint* section. You will have thirty minutes to design your organization. Be sure to keep an accurate description of your initial organizational design.

Construction information

Your company has given a firm quotation of $0.50 per unit as the selling price. Your objective will be to try to organize to achieve the greatest margin of profit per unit as possible. The following table presents the material cost per unit.

Material Cost	
Number of Units Purchased	Cost per Unit
0–10	$0.35
11–20	0.34
21–30	0.33
31–40	0.32
41–50	0.31
over 50	0.30

At the beginning of each production period, you must purchase raw materials using the above cost schedule. You may purchase materials more than once during the period; however, the per unit cost will be based on the size of *each* order and *not* on the total units purchased for the entire period. Materials *cannot* be returned for credit. The cost of *all* materials purchased will be charged against the total cost of raw materials for that period. Unused materials from the first period may *not* be counted in the second period. Only containers that meet quality control requirements can be counted as output. The Quality Control Review Board will evaluate the quality of each final unit. In addition to material cost, the standard cost for labor (including overhead, fringe benefits, etc.) will be $0.10 per minute per employee or $1.00 per employee for the entire trial period. In both production periods, every member of your team must be employed at the standard cost for the entire period.

Quality control board

The Quality Control requirements for paper containers are listed under the *Paper Container Quality Control* section. A board of inspectors (one from each group) will be charged with determining acceptability. If there is disagreement among the board members, a coin toss will be used to settle the differences. During inspection, each group should prepare an organization chart to share with other participants.

Second production run

After the first production run has been completed and profit margin tabulated on the *Profit Margin Analysis Form*, the group will be given twenty to thirty minutes to discuss any changes in organization structure that are necessary to increase their company's effectiveness. At the end of this design period, a second ten-minute production period will be run.

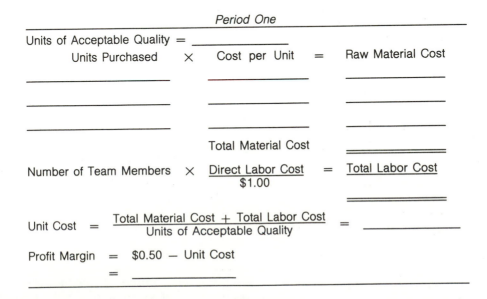

PROFIT MARGIN ANALYSIS

Period One

Units of Acceptable Quality = _____

| Units Purchased | × | Cost per Unit | = | Raw Material Cost |

_____ _____ _____

_____ _____ _____

_____ _____ _____

Total Material Cost _____

Number of Team Members × $\dfrac{\text{Direct Labor Cost}}{\$1.00}$ = Total Labor Cost _____

Unit Cost = $\dfrac{\text{Total Material Cost} + \text{Total Labor Cost}}{\text{Units of Acceptable Quality}}$ = _____

Profit Margin = $0.50 − Unit Cost

= _____

Period Two

Units of Acceptable Quality = _____

Units Purchased	×	Cost per Unit	=	Raw Material Cost
_____		_____		_____
_____		_____		_____
_____		_____		_____
		Total Material Cost		_____

Number of Team Members × $\dfrac{\text{Direct Labor Cost}}{\$1.00}$ = <u>Total Labor Cost</u>

$$\text{Unit Cost} = \frac{\text{Total Material Cost} + \text{Total Labor Cost}}{\text{Units of Acceptable Quality}} = \underline{\hspace{3cm}}$$

Profit Margin = $0.50 − Unit Cost

= _____

PAPER CONTAINER QUALITY CONTROL

1. Sides must be squared as shown below:

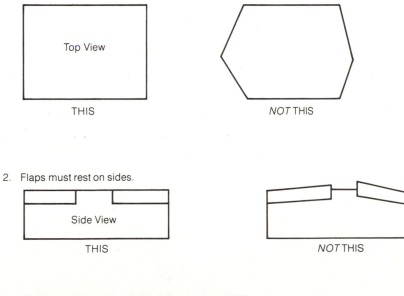

THIS   *NOT* THIS

2. Flaps must rest on sides.

Side View

THIS   *NOT* THIS

3. Flaps should be of equal size (plus or minus 1/8″).

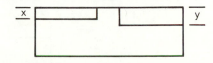

x = smaller flap
y = larger flap
The difference between x and y should not be greater than ⅛″.

PAPER CONTAINER BLUEPRINT

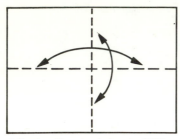

1. Begin with a sheet of paper 8½″ x 11″ and make creases for vertical and horizontal center lines.

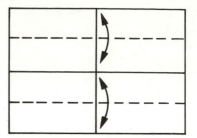

2. Fold the narrow sides up to the center line. Then unfold.

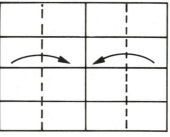

3. Now fold the wide sides to the vertical center line and unfold again.

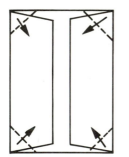

4. Fold each corner in as shown up to the first crease line.

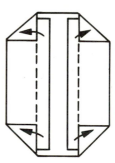

5. The excess left along the center line may be folded back over the folded corners.

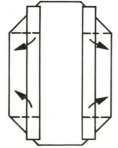

6. To open container, place thumbs under position **A** and **B** and pull in the direction of the arrows.

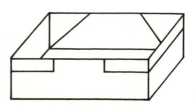

7. Finished container.

■ Creative Industries: Fun or Profit?

Directions

1. Everyone should read the background on Creative Industries, Inc.
2. Your instructor will assign you to one of four groups:
   a. Staff of Samuel Powell, Executive Vice-President
   b. Staff of Creative Unit
   c. Staff of Promotion Unit
   d. Staff of Production Unit
3. You should read the role and task description for your group. *DO NOT READ THE OTHERS.*
4. The instructor will tell you how much time each group has to prepare.
5. Select a member of the group to play the role and prepare him or her for the meeting.
6. The meeting will last approximately thirty minutes. During the meeting all staff members should observe and reflect on the arguments raised by all members.
7. Hold a general class discussion on what is needed in the way of reorganization at Creative Industries.

BACKGROUND ON CREATIVE INDUSTRIES, INC.

In Creative Industries Inc.'s modern New York City offices, Samuel E. Powell, a conservatively clad executive vice-president, rides up in an elevator with a woman wearing jeans, a sweatshirt, and a large button that reads, "I am woman." Powell, pointedly, says nothing. Later he explains that the woman was a motion picture executive. Powell goes on to discuss his problems with managing people in the creative fields of recording, movie making, and the like:

> . . . this industry requires different rules. My B-school training simply did not prepare me to deal with this environment. None of the sophisticated marketing or sales projection techniques really work. The best ideas are often a shot in the dark—a gut feeling. Moreover, the artists have, at best, peculiar work habits and outsized egos. The creative staff will not follow orders, constantly demand artistic freedom, and must be persuaded to follow a profitable path. If you push them too hard, there are plenty of other rivals ready to hire them, especially the really creative ones. Sometimes staff members

This case was inspired by "Mastering Management in Creative Industries" in *Business Week*, May 29, 1978, pp. 86–88.

will work on an idea until 2:00 A.M. and then not show up for work until 11. Sometimes they hit a creative roadblock and need a walk in Central Park.

The chances of success are very slim in this industry. Only one out of five movies ever makes a profit. For example, *The Godfather* pulled in $129 million and cost $6.8 million, while $8 million was spent on *The Great Gatsby* and it netted only $24 million. With this in mind, and some substantial losses being attributed to organizational inefficiencies, Powell was contemplating a reorganization of the movie-making unit.

The movie-making division was primarily organized into three units—promotion, production, and the creative group. All three units were extremely competent. The creative group was headed by a woman who was outspoken and preferred to have her staff working on new motion picture concepts, leaving only one or two staffers to finish up the routine details of present production efforts. The promotion unit head was very pleased with his staff and felt they had produced some of their best promotional schemes in a work climate that he described only as "far out." The production unit head and his staff were somewhat contemptuous of both the other units, feeling that their technical expertise saved many a picture from suffering huge losses due to production and distribution overruns. In general, costs were getting way out of line and friction between the three units seemed to be a prime factor. For example, the creative group often could never seem to find the time to give the promotion people the central theme of the film being shot to aid them in promotion design. "Such efforts," according to one creative group staffer, "would destroy the true essence and gestalt of the film." With such attitudes, it was not uncommon to hear a production staffer say "gestalt or no gestalt they are going to finish shooting today or we are going to cut off the lights."

Role and task for Samuel Powell and staff

You are Samuel Powell, Executive Vice-President at Creative Industries. You and your staff are to work on some ways to reorganize the movie-making unit. You should have your staff help you prepare a five to ten minute presentation for a meeting of the three unit heads—promotion, production, and the creative groups. (Your instructor will indicate how much time you will be allowed to prepare.) Your presentation should include your views of present organizational strengths and weaknesses as well as recommendations for reorganization.

Role and task for head of creative group and staff

As head of the creative group, you realize the value of autonomy for your unique department. You and your staff are to discuss the present advantages of remaining organized as you are at Creative Industries and what you believe is wrong with the other units. This discussion will aid you in preparing for a meeting at which Sam Powell is going to discuss reorganization. (Your instructor will indicate how much time you will be allowed to prepare.) You should be prepared to list *and* defend why you favor keeping Creative Industries as it is. Of course, you are willing to accept change—as long as it does not break up or otherwise destroy the "critical mass" you've developed in your unit.

Role and task for head of promotion and staff

As head of the promotional unit, you have fostered a fairly "organic," loosely structured department. You believe in minimum structure in order to get the creative juices flowing. You and your staff are to discuss the present advantages of remaining organized as you are at Creative Industries and what you believe to be wrong with the other units. This discussion is designed to help prepare you for a meeting with Sam Powell at which reorganization is going to be discussed. (Your instructor will indicate how much time you will be allowed to pre-pare.) While you aren't opposed to some minor modifications of the way things are (be sure you decide what these are), you generally resent formal meetings and would much prefer to brainstorm at the meeting. However, you will be prepared to defend your turf and fight to insure your unit is *not* infringed upon.

Role and task for head of production and staff

As head of production, you feel as if you are the only sane person in a room full of "whackos." You and your staff feel the upcoming meeting on reorganziation is your chance to expose the true inefficiencies that exist at Creative Industries. You are not opposed to reorganization, so long as production staff are given final authority on all film-making activity. You should ask your staff to help you brainstorm just how it would be possible to reorganize in order for more authority to reside in production's hands. Be prepared to make your cases. (Your instructor will indicate how much time you will be allowed to prepare.)

4 Power, Conflict and Politics

■ **LEARNING OBJECTIVES**

1. To develop an awareness of the functional and dysfunctional consequences of organizational conflict

2. To increase knowledge and understanding of the primary antecedents of organizational conflict and power

3. To develop skills in selecting and utilizing appropriate conflict-resolution or conflict-stimulation techniques

4. To develop an awareness of the organizational implications for political vs. trustful managerial behavior

■ OVERVIEW

The manager of the future must learn how to cope more effectively with intra-organizational conflict and gain a better understanding of its antecedents that are within his or her control. Coping does not necessarily mean eliminating or reducing the level of conflict. We are beginning to discover that conflict can be organizationally healthy and necessary for optimal performance. Whether or not a manager attempts to resolve conflict and work toward collaboration, or attempts to stimulate conflict, he or she should develop a deliberate strategy aimed at organizational effectiveness.

Surprisingly, while conflict has been traditionally viewed as something to avoid, it is difficult to identify many organizations that failed solely as the result of conflict, or those that have been highly successful because of total collaboration. A balance and an understanding of appropriate levels of conflict have to be reached. Unfortunately, the state of the art does not provide an exacting formula for the manager. Nevertheless, contingency models are beginning to help the manager diagnose strategic factors to consider.

One particularly important, but often overlooked, antecedent is the inherent conflict that results from organizational structure. Inevitably, structure will cause organizational friction, particularly at those points where parts are joined together. Such friction may be purposely intended by the organization's architect or may be the unintended consequences of an ill-conceived design. Understanding the consequences of organizational conflict as well as its antecedents provides the organizational architect with additional insights necessary to achieve optimal performance. However, even when the organization has been effectively designed, the manager needs a tool kit of techniques that can aid either in the resolution of unintended conflict or in the stimulation of needed conflict.

In this part you will deal with many of the organizational issues and dilemmas faced by a manager in the real world of power politics. While the solutions will always seem difficult, the real dilemma you have to face is that while conflict may produce optimal results for the organization, it may also come at an intolerably high human cost.

Readings

■ Power Failure in Management Circuits

ROSABETH MOSS KANTER

Power is America's last dirty word. It is easier to talk about money—and much easier to talk about sex—than it is to talk about power. People who have it deny it, people who want it do not want to appear to hunger for it, and people who engage in its machinations do so secretly.

Yet, because it turns out to be a critical element in effective managerial behavior, power should come out from undercover. Having searched for years for those styles or skills that would identify capable organization leaders, many analysts, like myself, are rejecting individual traits or situational appropriateness as key and finding the sources of a leader's real power.

Access to resources and information and the ability to act quickly make it possible to accomplish more and to pass on more resources and information to subordinates. For this reason, people tend to prefer bosses with "clout." When employees perceive their manager as influential upward and outward, their status is enhanced by association and they generally have high morale and feel less critical or resistant to their boss. More powerful leaders are also more likely to delegate (they are too busy to do it all themselves), to reward talent, and to build a team that places subordinates in significant positions.

Powerlessness, in contrast, tends to breed bossiness rather than true leadership. In large organizations, at least, it is powerlessness that often creates ineffective, desultory management and petty, dictatorial, rules-minded managerial styles. Accountability without power—responsibility for results without the resources to get them—creates frustration and failure. People who see themselves as weak and powerless, and who find their subordinates resisting or discounting them, tend to use more punishing forms of influence. If organizational power can "ennoble," then, recent research shows, organizational powerlessness can (with apologies to Lord Acton) "corrupt."

So perhaps power, in the organization at least, does not deserve such a bad reputation. Rather than connoting only dominance, control, and oppression, *power* can mean efficacy and capacity—something managers and executives need to move the organization toward its goals. Power in organizations is analogous in simple terms to physical power: it is the ability to mobilize resources (human and material) to get things done. The true sign of power, then, is accomplishment—not fear, terror, or tyranny. Where the power is "on," the system can be productive; where the power is "off," the system bogs down.

But saying that people need power to be effective in organizations does not tell us where it comes from or why some people, in some jobs, systematically seem to have more of it than others. In this article I want to show that to discover the sources of productive power, we have to look not at the *person*—as conventional classifications of effective managers and employees do—but at the *position* the person occupies in the organization.

WHERE DOES POWER COME FROM?

The effectiveness that power brings evolves from two kinds of capacities: first, access to the resources, information, and support necessary to carry out a task and, second, ability to get cooperation in doing what is necessary. (Exhibit 4.1 identifies some symbols of an individual manager's power.)

Both capacities derive not so much from a leader's style and skill as from his or her location in the formal and informal systems of the organization—in both job definition and connection to other important people in the company. Even the ability to get cooperation from subordinates is strongly defined by the manager's clout outward. People are more responsive to bosses who look as if they can get more for them from the organization.

We can regard the uniquely organizational sources of power as consisting of three "lines":

1. *Lines of supply.* Influence outward, over the environment, means that managers

have the capacity to bring in the things that their own organizational domain needs—materials, money, resources to distribute as rewards, and perhaps even prestige.

2. *Lines of information.* To be effective, managers need to be "in the know" in both the formal and the informal sense.

3. *Lines of support.* In a formal framework, a manager's job parameters need to allow for non-ordinary action, for a show of discretion or exercise of judgment. Thus managers need to know that they can assume innovative, risk-taking activities without having to go through the stifling multi-layered approval process. And, informally, managers need the backing of other important figures in the organization whose tacit approval becomes another resource they bring to their own work unit as well as a sign of the manager's being "in."

Note that productive power has to do with *connections* with other parts of a system. Such systemic aspects of power derive from two sources—job activities and political alliances:

1. Power is most easily accumulated when one has a job that is designed and located to allow *discretion* (nonroutinized action permitting flexible, adaptive, and creative contributions), *recognition* (visibility and notice), and *relevance* (being central to pressing organizational problems).

2. Power also comes when one has relatively close contact with *sponsors* (higher-level people who confer approval, prestige, or backing), *peer networks* (circles of acquaintanceship that provide reputation and information, the grapevine often being faster than formal communication channels), and *subordinates* (who can be developed to relieve managers of some of their burdens and to represent the manager's point of view).

When managers are in powerful situations, it is easier for them to accomplish more. Because the tools are there, they are likely to be highly motivated and, in turn, to

---

EXHIBIT 4.1 Some Common Symbols of a Manager's Organizational Power (Influence Upward and Outward)

To what extent a manager can—

Intercede favorably on behalf of someone in trouble with the organization

Get a desirable placement for a talented subordinate

Get approval for expenditures beyond the budget

Get above-average salary increases for subordinates

Get items on the agenda at policy meetings

Get fast access to top decision-makers

Get regular, frequent access to top decision-makers

Get early information about decisions and policy shifts

be able to motivate subordinates. Their activities are more likely to be on target and to net them successes. They can flexibly interpret or shape policy to meet the needs of particular areas, emergent situations, or sudden environmental shifts. They gain the respect and cooperation that attributed power brings. Subordinates' talents are resources rather than threats. And, because powerful managers have so many lines of connection and thus are oriented outward, they tend to let go of control downward, developing more independently functioning lieutenants.

The powerless live in a different world. Lacking the supplies, information, or support to make things happen easily, they may turn instead to the ultimate weapon of those who lack productive power—oppressive power: holding others back and punishing with whatever threats they can muster.

Exhibit 4.2 summarizes some of the major ways in which variables in the organization and in job design contribute to either power or powerlessness.

POSITIONS OF POWERLESSNESS

Understanding what it takes to have power and recognizing the classic behavior of the powerless can immediately help managers make sense out of a number of familiar organizational problems that are usually attributed to inadequate people:

■ The ineffectiveness of first-line supervisors.
■ The petty interest protection and conservatism of staff professionals.
■ The crises of leadership at the top.

Instead of blaming the individuals involved in organizational problems, let us look at the positions people occupy. Of course, power or powerlessness in a position may not be all of the problem. Sometimes incapable people *are* at fault and need to be retrained or replaced. Another case has been made for women managers, see pp. 257–258.

EXHIBIT 4.2 Ways Organizational Factors Contribute to Power or Powerlessness

Factors	Generates **power** when factor is	Generates **powerlessness** when factor is
Rules inherent in the job	few	many
Predecessors in the job	few	many
Established routines	few	many
Task variety	high	low
Rewards for reliability/predictability	few	many
Rewards for unusual performance/innovation	many	few
Flexibility around use of people	high	low
Approvals needed for nonroutine decisions	few	many
Physical locations	central	distant
Publicity about job activities	high	low
Relation of tasks to current problem areas	central	peripheral
Focus of tasks	outside work unit	inside work unit
Interpersonal contact in the job	high	low
Contact with senior officials	high	low
Participation in programs, conferences, meetings	high	low
Participation in problem-solving task forces	high	low
Advancement prospects of subordinates	high	low

■ Women managers experience special power failures

The traditional problems of women in management are illustrative of how formal and informal practices can combine to engender powerlessness. Historically, women in management have found their opportunities in more routine, low-profile jobs. In staff positions, where they serve in support capacities to line managers but have no line responsibilities of their own, or in supervisory jobs managing "stuck" subordinates, they are not in a position either to take the kinds of risks that build credibility or to develop their own team by pushing bright subordinates.

Such jobs which have few favors to trade, tend to keep women out of the mainstream of the organization. This lack of clout, coupled with the greater difficulty anyone who is "different" has in getting into the information and support networks, has meant that merely by organizational situation women in management have been more likely than men to be rendered structurally powerless. This is one reason those women who have achieved power have often had family connections that put them in the mainstream of the organization's social circles.

A disproportionate number of women managers are found among first-line supervisors or staff professionals; and they, like men in those circumstances, are likely to be organizationally powerless. But the behavior of other managers can contribute to the powerlessness of women in management in a number of less obvious ways.

One way other managers can make a woman powerless is by patronizingly overprotecting her:

putting her in "a safe job," not giving her enough to do to prove herself, and not suggesting her for high-risk, visible assignments. This protectiveness is sometimes born of "good" intentions to give her every chance to succeed (why stack the deck against her?). Out of managerial concerns, out of awareness that a woman may be up against situations that men simply do not have to face, some very well-meaning managers protect their female managers ("It's a jungle, so why send her into it?").

Overprotectiveness can also mask a manager's fear of association with a woman should she fail. One senior bank official at a level below vice-president told me about his concerns with respect to a high-performing, financially experienced woman reporting to him. Despite *his* overwhelmingly positive work experiences with her, he was still afraid to recommend her for other assignments because he felt it was a personal risk. "What if other managers are not as accepting of women as I am?" he asked. "I know I'd be sticking my neck out; they would take her more because of my endorsement than her qualifications. And what if she doesn't make it? My judgment will be on the line."

Overprotection is relatively benign compared with rendering a person powerless by providing obvious signs of lack of managerial support. For example, allowing someone supposedly in authority to be bypassed easily means that no one else has to take him or her seriously. If a woman's immediate supervisor or other managers listen willingly

to criticism of her and show they are concerned every time a negative comment comes up and assume she must be at fault, they are helping to undercut her. If managers let other people know that they have concerns about this person or that they are testing her to see how she does, they are inviting other people to look for signs of inadequacy or failure.

Furthermore, people assume they can afford to bypass women because they "must be uninformed" or "don't know the ropes." Even though women may be respected for their competence or expertise, they are not necessarily seen as being informed beyond the technical requirements of the job. There may be a grain of historical truth in this. Many women come to senior management positions as "outsiders" rather than up through the usual channels.

Also, because until very recently men have not felt comfortable seeing women as business-people (business clubs have traditionally excluded women), they have tended to seek each other out for informal socializing. Anyone, male or female, seen as organizationally naive and lacking sources of "inside dope" will find his or her own lines of information limited.

Finally, even when women are able to achieve some power on their own, they have not necessarily been able to translate such personal credibility into an organizational power base. To create a network of supporters out of individual clout requires that a person pass on and share power that subordinates and peers be empowered by virtue of their connection with that person. Traditionally, neither men nor women have seen women as capable of sponsoring others, even though they may be capable of achieving and succeeding on their own. Women have been viewed as the *recipients* of sponsorship rather than as the sponsors themselves.

(As more women prove themselves in organizations and think more self-consciously about bringing along young people, this situation may change. However, I still hear many more questions from women managers about how they can benefit from mentors, sponsors, or peer networks than about how they themselves can start to pass on favors and make use of their own resources to benefit others.)

Viewing managers in terms of power and powerlessness helps

explain two familiar stereotypes about women and leadership in organizations: that no one wants a woman boss (although studies show that anyone who has ever had a woman boss is likely to have had a positive experience), and that the reason no one wants a woman boss is that women are "too controlling, rules-minded, and petty."

The first stereotype simply makes clear that power is important to leadership. Underneath the preference for men is the assumption that, given the current distribution of people in organizational leadership positions, men are more likely than women to be in positions to achieve power and, therefore, to share their power with others. Similarly, the "bossy woman boss" stereotype is a perfect picture of powerlessness. All those traits

are just as characteristic of men who are powerless, but women are slightly more likely, because of circumstances I have mentioned, to find themselves powerless than are men. Women with power in the organization are just as effective—and preferred—as men.

Recent interviews conducted with about 600 bank managers show that, when a woman exhibits the petty traits of powerlessness, people assume that she does so "because she is a woman." A striking difference is that, when a man engages in the same behavior, people assume the behavior is a matter of his own individual style and characteristics and do not conclude that it reflects on the suitability of men for management.

But where patterns emerge, where the troubles associated with some units persist, organizational power failures could be the reason. Then, as Volvo President Pehr Gyllenhammar concludes, we should treat the powerless not as "villains" causing headaches for everyone else but as "victims."

First-line Supervisors

Because an employee's most important work relationship is with his or her supervisor, when many of them talk about "the company" they mean their immediate boss. Thus a supervisor's behavior is an important determinant of the average employee's relationship to work and is in itself a critical link in the production chain.

Yet I know of no U.S. corporate management entirely satisfied with the performance of its supervisors. Most see them as supervising too closely and not training their people. In one manufacturing company where direct laborers were asked on a survey how

they learned their job, on a list of seven possibilities "from my supervisor" ranked next to last. (Only company training programs ranked worse.) Also, it is said that supervisors do not translate company policies into practice—for instance, that they do not carry out the right of every employee to frequent performance reviews or to career counseling.

In court cases charging race or sex discrimination, first-line supervisors are frequently cited as the "discriminating official." And in studies of innovative work redesign and quality of work life projects, they often appear as the implied villains; they are the ones who are said to undermine the program or interfere with its effectiveness. In short, they are often seen as "not sufficiently managerial."

The problem affects white-collar as well as blue-collar supervisors. In one large government agency, supervisors in field offices were seen as the source of problems concerning morale and the flow of information to and from headquarters. "Their attitudes are negative," said a senior official. "They turn people against the agency; they put down senior management. They build themselves up by always complaining about headquarters, but prevent their staff from getting any information directly. We can't afford to have such attitudes communicated to field staff."

Is the problem that supervisors need more management training programs or that incompetent people are invariably attracted to the job? Neither explanation suffices. A large part of the problem lies in the position itself—one that almost universally creates powerlessness.

First-line supervisors are "people in the middle," and that has been seen as the source of many of their problems. But by recognizing that first-line supervisors are caught between higher management and workers, we only begin to skim the surface of the problem. There is practically no other organizational category as subject to powerlessness.

First, these supervisors may be at a virtual dead end in their careers. Even in companies where the job used to be a stepping stone to higher-level management jobs, it is now common practice to bring in MBAs from the outside for those positions. Thus moving from the ranks of direct labor into supervision may mean, essentially, getting "stuck" rather than moving upward. Because employees do not perceive supervisors as eventually joining the leadership circles of the organization, they may see them as lacking the high-level contacts needed to have clout. Indeed, sometimes turnover among supervisors is so high that workers feel they can outwait—and outwit—any boss.

Second, although they lack clout, with little in the way of support from above, supervisors are forced to administer programs or explain policies that they have no hand in shaping. In one company, as part of a new personnel program supervisors were required to conduct counseling interviews with employees. But supervisors were not trained to do this and were given no incentives to get involved. Counseling was just another obligation. Then managers suddenly encouraged the workers to bypass their supervisors or to put pressure on them. The personnel staff brought them together and told them to demand such interviews as a basic right. If supervisors had not felt powerless before, they did after that squeeze from below, engineered from above.

The people they supervise can also make life hard for them in numerous ways. This often happens when a supervisor has himself or herself risen up from the ranks. Peers who have not made it are resentful or derisive of their former colleague, whom they now see as trying to lord it over them. Often it is easy for workers to break rules and let a lot of things slip.

Yet first-line supervisors are frequently judged according to rules and regulations while being limited by other regulations in what disciplinary actions they can take. They often lack the resources to influence or reward people; after all, workers are guaranteed their pay and benefits by someone other than their supervisors. Supervisors cannot easily control events; rather, they must react to them.

In one factory, for instance, supervisors complained that performance of their job was out of their control: they could fill production quotas only if they had the supplies, but they had no way to influence the people controlling supplies.

The lack of support for many first-line managers, particularly in large organizations, was made dramatically clear in another company. When asked if contact with executives higher in the organization who had the potential for offering support, information, and alliances diminished their own feelings of career vulnerability and the number of headaches they experienced on the job, supervisors in five out of seven work units responded positively. For them *con-*

tact was indeed related to a greater feeling of acceptance at work and membership in the organization.

But in the two other work units where there was greater contact, people perceived more, not less, career vulnerability. Further investigation showed that supervisors in these business units got attention only when they were in trouble. Otherwise, no one bothered to talk to them. To these particular supervisors, hearing from a higher-level manager was a sign not of recognition or potential support but of danger.

It is not surprising, then, that supervisors frequently manifest symptoms of powerlessness: overly close supervision, rules-mindedness, and a tendency to do the job themselves rather than to train their people (since job skills may be one of the few remaining things they feel good about). Perhaps this is why they sometimes stand as roadblocks between their subordinates and the higher reaches of the company.

Staff Professionals

Also working under conditions that can lead to organizational powerlessness are the staff specialists. As advisers behind the scenes, staff people must sell their programs and bargain for resources, but unless they get themselves entrenched in organizational power networks, they have little in the way of favors to exchange. They are seen as useful adjuncts to the primary tasks of the organization but non-essential in a day-to-day operating sense. This disenfranchisement occurs particularly when staff jobs consist of easily routinized administrative functions that are out of the mainstream of the currently relevant areas and involve little innovative decision-making.

Furthermore, in some organizations, unless they have had previous line experience, staff people tend to be limited in the number of jobs into which they can move. Specialists' ladders are often very short, and professionals are just as likely to get "stuck" in such jobs as people are in less prestigious clerical or factory positions.

Staff people, unlike those who are being groomed for important line positions, may be hired because of a special expertise or particular background. But management rarely pays any attention to developing them into more general organizational resources. Lacking growth prospects themselves and working alone or in very small teams, they are not in a position to develop others or pass on power to them. They miss out on an important way that power can be accumulated.

Sometimes staff specialists, such as house counsel or organization development people, find their work being farmed out to consultants. Management considers them fine for the routine work, but the minute the activities involve risk or something problematic, they bring in outside experts. This treatment says something not only about their expertise but also about the status of their function. Since the company can always hire talent on a temporary basis, it is unclear that the management really needs to have or considers important its own staff for these functions.

And, because staff professionals are often seen as adjuncts to primary tasks, their effectiveness and therefore their contribution to the organization are often hard to measure. Thus visibility and recognition, as well as risk-taking and relevance, may be denied to people in staff jobs.

Staff people tend to act out their powerlessnesss by becoming turf-minded. They create islands within the organization. They set themselves up as the only ones who can control professional standards and judge their own work. They create sometimes false distinctions between themselves as experts (no one else could possibly do what they do) and lay people, and this continues to keep them out of the mainstream.

One form such distinctions take is a combination of disdain when line managers attempt to act in areas the professionals think are their preserve and of subtle refusal to support the managers' efforts. Or staff groups battle with each other for control of new "problem areas," with the result that no one really handles the issue at all. To cope with their essential powerlessness, staff groups may try to elevate their own status and draw boundaries between themselves and others.

When staff jobs are treated as final resting places for people who have reached their level of competence in the organization—a good shelf on which to dump managers who are too old to go anywhere but too young to retire—staff groups can also become pockets of conservatism, resistant to change. Their own exclusion from the risk-taking action may make them resist *anyone's* innovative proposals. In the past, personnel departments, for example, have sometimes been the last in their organization to know about innovations in human resource development or to be interested in applying them.

Top Executives

Despite the great resources and responsibilities concentrated at the top of an organization, leaders can be powerless for reasons that are not very different from those that affect staff and supervisors: lack of supplies, information, and support.

We have faith in leaders because of their ability to make things happen in the larger world, to create possibilities for everyone else, and to attract resources to the organization. These are their supplies. But influence outward—the source of much credibility downward—can diminish as environments change, setting terms and conditions out of the control of the leaders. Regardless of top management's grand plans for the organization, the environment presses. At the very least, things going on outside the organization can deflect a leader's attention and drain energy. And, more detrimental, decisions made elsewhere can have severe consequences for the organization and affect top management's sense of power and thus its operating style inside.

In the go-go years of the mid-1960s, for example, nearly every corporation officer or university president could look—and therefore feel—successful. Visible success gave leaders a great deal of credibility inside the organization, which in turn gave them the power to put new things in motion.

In the past few years, the environment has been strikingly different and the capacity of many organization leaders to do anything about it has been severely limited. New "players" have flexed their power muscles: the Arab oil bloc, government regulators, and congressional investigating committees. And managing economic decline is quite different from managing growth. It is no accident that when top leaders personally feel out of control, the control function in corporations grows.

As powerlessness in lower levels of organizations can manifest itself in overly routinized jobs where performance measures are oriented to rules and absence of change, so it can at upper levels as well. Routine work often drives out nonroutine work. Accomplishment becomes a question of nailing down details. Short-term results provide immediate gratifications and satisfy stockholders or other constituencies with limited interests.

It takes a powerful leader to be willing to risk short-term deprivations in order to bring about desired long-term outcomes. Much as first-line supervisors are tempted to focus on daily adherence to rules, leaders are tempted to focus on short-term fluctuations and lose sight of long-term objectives. The dynamics of such a situation are self-reinforcing. The more the long-term goals go unattended, the more a leader feels powerless and the greater the scramble to prove that he or she is in control of daily events at least. The more he is involved in the organization as a short-term Mr. Fix-it, the more out of control of long-term objectives he is, and the more ultimately powerless he is likely to be.

Credibility for top executives often comes from doing the exraordinary: exercising discretion, creating, inventing, planning, and acting in nonroutine ways. But since routine problems look easier and more manageable, require less change and consent on the part of anyone else, and lend themselves to instant solutions that can make any leader look good temporarily, leaders may avoid the risky by taking over what their subordinates should be doing. Ultimately, a leader may succeed in getting all the trivial problems dumped on his or her desk. This can establish expectations even for leaders attempting more challenging tasks. When Warren Bennis was president of the University of Cincinnati, a professor called him when the heat was down in a classroom. In writing about this incident, Bennis commented, "I suppose he expected me to grab a wrench and fix it."

People at the top need to insulate themselves from the routine operations of the organization in order to develop and exercise power. But this very insulation can lead to another source of powerlessness—lack of information. In one multinational corporation, top executives, who are sealed off in a large, distant office, flattered and virtually babied by aides, are frustrated by their distance from the real action.

At the top, the concern for secrecy and privacy is mixed with real loneliness. In one bank, organization members were so accustomed to never seeing the top leaders that when a new senior vice-president went to the branch offices to look around, they had suspicion, even fear, about his intentions.

Thus leaders who are cut out of an organization's information networks understand neither what is really going on at lower levels nor that their own isolation may be having negative effects. All too often top executives design "beneficial" new employee programs or declare a new humanitarian policy (e.g., "Participatory management is now our style") only to find the policy ignored or mistrusted because it is perceived as coming from uncaring bosses.

The information gap has more serious consequences when executives are so insulated from the rest of the organization or from other decision-makers that, as Nixon so dramatically did, they fail to see their own impending downfall. Such insulation is partly a matter of organizational position and, in some cases, of executive style.

For example, leaders may create closed inner circles consisting of "doppelgängers," people just like themselves, who are their principal sources of organizational information and tell them only what they want to know. The reasons for the distortions are varied: key aides want to relieve the leader of burdens, they think just like the leader, they want to protect their own positions of power, or the familiar "kill the messenger" syndrome makes people close to top executives reluctant to be the bearers of bad news.

Finally, just as supervisors and lower-level managers need their supporters in order to be and feel powerful, so do top executives. But for them sponsorship may not be so much a matter of individual endorsement as an issue of support by larger sources of legitimacy in the society. For top executives the problem is not to fit in among peers; rather, the question is whether the public at large and other organization members perceive a common interest that they see the executives as promoting.

If, however, public sources of support are withdrawn and leaders are open to public attack or if inside constituencies fragment and employees see their interests better aligned with pressure groups than with organizational leadership, powerlessness begins to set in.

When common purpose is lost, the system's own politics may reduce the capacity of those at the top to act. Just as managing decline seems to create a much more passive and reactive stance than managing growth, so does mediating among conflicting interests. When what is happening outside and inside their organizations is out of their control, many people at the top turn into decline managers and dispute mediators. Neither is a particularly empowering role.

Thus when top executives lose their own lines of supply, lines of information, and lines of support, they too suffer from a kind of powerlessness. The temptation for them then is to pull in every shred of power they can and to decrease the power available to other people to act. Innovation loses out in favor of control. Limits rather than targets are set. Financial goals are met by reducing "overhead" (people) rather than by giving people the tools and discretion to increase their own productive capacity. Dictatorial statements come down from the top, spreading the mentality of powerlessness farther until the whole organization becomes sluggish and people concentrate on protecting what they have rather than on producing what they can.

When everyone is playing "king of the mountain," guarding his or her turf jealously, then king of the mountain becomes the only game in town.

TO EXPAND POWER, SHARE IT

In no case am I saying that people in the three hierarchical levels described are always powerless, but they are susceptible to common conditions that can contribute to powerlessness. Exhibit 4.3 summarizes the most common symptoms of powerlessness for each level and some typical sources of that behavior.

I am also distinguishing the tremendous concentration of economic and political power in large corporations themselves from the powerlessness that can beset individuals even in the highest positions in such organizations. What grows with organizational position in hierarchical levels is not necessarily the power to accomplish—productive power—but the power to punish, to prevent, to sell off, to reduce, to fire, all without appropriate concern for consequences. It is that kind of power—oppressive power—that we often say corrupts.

The absence of ways to prevent individual and social harm causes the polity to feel it must surround people in power with constraints, regulations, and laws that limit the arbitrary use of their authority. But if oppressive power corrupts, then so does the absence of productive power. In large organizations, powerlessness can be a bigger problem than power.

EXHIBIT 4.3 Common Symptoms and Sources of Powerlessness for Three Key Organizational Positions

Position	Symptoms	Sources
First-line supervisors	Close, rules-minded supervision	Routine, rules-minded jobs with little control over lines of supply
	Tendency to do things oneself, blocking of subordinates, development, and information	Limited lines of information
	Resistant, underproducing subordinates	Limited advancement or involvement prospects for oneself/subordinates
Staff professionals	Turf protection, information control	Routine tasks seen as peripheral to "real tasks" of line organization
	Retreat into professionalism	Blocked careers
	Conservative resistance to change	Easy replacement by outside experts
Top executives	Focus on internal cutting, short-term results, "punishing"	Uncontrollable lines of supply because of environmental changes
	Dictatorial top-down communications	Limited or blocked lines of information about lower levels of organization
	Retreat to comfort of like-minded lieutenants	Diminished lines of support because of challenges to legitimacy (e.g., from the public or special-interest groups)

David C. McClelland makes a similar distinction between oppressive and productive power:

> The negative . . . face of power is characterized by the dominance-submission mode: if I win, you lose. . . . It leads to simple and direct means of feeling powerful [such as being aggressive]. It does not often lead to effective social leadership for the reason that such a person tends to treat other people as pawns. People who feel they are pawns tend to be passive and useless to the leader who gets his satisfaction from dominating them. Slaves are the most inefficient form of labor ever devised by man. If a leader wants to have far-reaching influence, he must make his followers feel powerful and able to accomplish things on their own. . . . Even the most dictatorial leader does not succeed if he has not instilled in at least some of his followers a sense of power and the strength to pursue the goals he has set.

Organizational power can grow, in part, by being shared. We do not yet know enough about new organizational forms to say whether productive power is infinitely expandable or where we reach the point of diminishing returns. But we do know that sharing power is different from giving or throwing it away. Delegation does not mean abdication.

Some basic lessons could be translated from the field of economics to the realm of organizations and management. Capital investment in plants and equipment is not the only key to productivity. The productive capacity of nations, like organizations, grows if the skill base is upgraded. People with the tools, information, and support to make more informed decisions and act more quickly can often accomplish more. By empowering others, a leader does not decrease his power; instead he may increase it—especially if the whole organization performs better.

This analysis leads to some counterintuitive conclusions. In a certain tautological sense, the principal problem of the powerless is that they lack power. Powerless peo-

ple are usually the last ones to whom anyone wants to entrust more power, for fear of its dissipation or abuse. But those people are precisely the ones who might benefit most from an injection of power and whose behavior is likely to change as new options open up to them.

Also, if powerless bosses could be encouraged to share some of the power they do have, their power would grow. Yet, of course, only those leaders who feel secure about their own power outward—their lines of supply, information, and support—can see empowering subordinates as a gain rather than as a loss. The two sides of power (getting it and giving it) are closely connected.

There are important lessons here for both subordinates and those who want to change organizations, whether executives or change agents. Instead of resisting or criticizing a powerless boss, which only increases the boss's feeling of powerlessness and need to control, subordinates instead might concentrate on helping the boss become more powerful. Managers might make pockets of ineffectiveness in the organization more productive not by training or replacing individuals but by structural solutions such as opening supply and support lines.

Similarly, organizational change agents who want a new program or policy to succeed should make sure that the change itself does not render any other level of the organization powerless. In making changes, it is wise to make sure that the key people in the level or two directly above and in neighboring functions are sufficiently involved, informed, and taken into account, so that the program can be used to build their own sense of power also. If such involvement is impossible, then it is better to move these people out of the territory altogether than to leave behind a group from whom some power has been removed and who might resist and undercut the program.

In part, of course, spreading power means educating people to this new definition of it. But words alone will not make the difference; managers will need the real experience of a new way of managing.

Here is how the associate director of a large corporate professional department phrased the lessons that he learned in the transition to a team-oriented, participatory, power-sharing management process:

> Get in the habit of involving your own managers in decision-making and approvals. But don't abdicate! Tell them what you want and where you're coming from. Don't go for a one-boss grass roots "democracy." Make the management hierarchy work for you in participation. . . .
> Hang in there, baby, and don't give up. Try not to "revert" just because everything seems to go sour on a particular day. Open up—talk to people and tell them how you feel. They'll want to get you back on track and will do things to make that happen—because they don't really want to go back to the way it was. . . . Subordinates will push you to "act more like a boss," but their interest is usually more in seeing someone else brought to heel than getting bossed themselves.

Naturally, people need to have power before they can learn to share it. Exhorting managers to change their leadership styles is rarely useful by itself. In one large plant of a major electronics company, first-line production supervisors were the source of numerous complaints from managers who saw them as major roadblocks to overall plant productivity and as insufficiently skilled supervisors. So the plant personnel staff undertook two pilot programs to increase the supervisors' effectiveness. The first program was based on a traditional competency and training model aimed at teaching the specific skills of successful supervisors. The second program, in contrast, was designed to empower the supervisors by directly affecting their flexibility, access to resources, connections with higher-level officials, and control over working conditions.

After an initial gathering of data from supervisors and their subordinates, the personnel staff held meetings where all the supervisors were given tools for developing action plans for sharing the data with their people and collaborating on solutions to perceived problems. But then, in a departure from common practice in this organization, task forces of supervisors were formed to develop new systems for handling job and career issues common to them and their people. These task forces were given budgets, consultants, representation on a plantwide project steering committee alongside managers at much higher levels, and wide latitude in defining the nature and scope of the changes they wished to make. In short, lines of supply, information, and support were opened to them.

As the task forces progressed in their activities, it became clear to the plant management that the hoped-for changes in supervisory effectiveness were taking place much more rapidly through these structural changes in power than through conventional management training, so the conventional training was dropped. Not only did the pilot groups design useful new procedures for the plant, astonishing senior management in several cases with their knowledge and capabilities, but also, significantly, they learned to manage their own people better.

Several groups decided to involve shop-floor workers in their task forces; they could now see from their own experience the benefits of involving subordinates in solving job-related problems. Other supervisors began to experiment with ways to implement "participatory management" by giving subordinates more control and influence without relinquishing their own authority.

Soon the "problem supervisors" in the "most troubled plant in the company" were getting the highest possible performance ratings and were considered models for direct production management. The sharing of organizational power from the top made possible the productive use of power below.

One might wonder why more organizations do not adopt such empowering strategies. There are standard answers: that giving up control is threatening to people who have fought for every shred of it; that people do not want to share power with those they look down on; that managers fear losing their own place and special privileges in the system; that "predictability" often rates higher than "flexibility" as an organizational value; and so forth.

But I would also put skepticism about employee abilities high on the list. Many modern bureaucratic systems are designed to minimize dependence on individual intelligence by making routine as many decisions as possible. So it often comes as a genuine surprise to top executives that people doing the more routine jobs could, indeed, make sophisticated decisions or use resources entrusted to them in intelligent ways.

In the same electronics company just mentioned, at the end of a quarter the pilot supervisory task forces were asked to report results and plans to senior management in order to have their new budget requests approved. The task forces made sure they were well prepared, and the high-level executives were duly impressed. In fact, they were *so* impressed that they kept interrupting the presentations with compliments, remarking that the supervisors could easily be doing sophisticated personnel work.

At first the supervisors were flattered. Such praise from upper management could only be taken well. But when the first glow wore off, several of them became very angry. They saw the excessive praise as patronizing and insulting. "Didn't they think we could think? Didn't they imagine we were capable of doing this kind of work?" one asked. "They must have seen us as just a bunch of animals. No wonder they gave us such limited jobs."

As far as these supervisors were concerned, their abilities had always been there, in latent form perhaps, but still there. They as individuals had not changed—just their organizational power.

■ The Management of Interdepartmental Conflict: Some Antecedents and a Model

RICHARD E. WALTON and JOHN M. DUTTON

Conflict can result from factors or antecedents that originate outside the particular relationship under consideration. Below are nine major types of such antecedents—mutual dependence, asymmetries, rewards, organizational differentiation, role dissatisfaction, ambiguities, common resources, communication obstacles, and personal skills and traits—which precede or antedate conflictual relationships.

Abridged from "The Management of Interdepartmental Conflict: A Model and Review," by Richard E. Walton and John M. Dutton, *Administrative Science Quarterly*, vol. 14, no. 1 (1969), pp. 73–82. References deleted. See original work.

Mutual Task Dependence
Task dependence is the extent to which two units depend upon each other for assistance, information, compliance, or other coordinative acts in the performance of their

respective tasks. It is assumed here that dependence is mutual and can range from low to high, although interdependence may be asymmetrical. Mutual task dependence is a key antecedent because of its impact on all other antecedents. Task interdependence not only provides an incentive for collaboration, but also presents an occasion for conflict and the means for bargaining over interdepartmental issues. A related factor, task overload, has similarly mixed potential for conflict and collaboration. Overload conditions may intensify the problem of scarce resources and lead to bargaining; may increase tension, frustration, and aggression; and may decrease the time available for the social interactions that would enable the units to contain their conflict. On the other hand, overload may place a premium on mutual assistance. The net directional effects of high task interdependence and overload are therefore uncertain.

Other implications of the extent of mutual task dependence are more predictable. High task interdependence and overload tend to heighten the intensity of either interunit antagonisms or friendliness, increase the magnitude of the consequences of unit conflict for organizational performance, and contribute to the difficulty of changing an ongoing pattern.

Task-Related Asymmetries

Symmetrical interdependence and symmetrical patterns of initiation between units promote collaboration; asymmetrical interdependence leads to conflict. For example, in a study by Dalton, a staff group resented the asymmetries in their relationship with line groups. The staff group had to understand the problems of the line groups, had to get along with them, promote their ideas, and justify their existence; but none of these relations were reciprocal requirements imposed on the line groups. Strauss reported that asymmetrical high dependence of puchasing agents on another group led them to make more attempts to influence the terms of requisition they received and thereby force interaction to flow both ways.

The adverse effects of asymmetrical conditions are sometimes related to the fact that one unit has little incentive to coordinate. The more dependent unit may try to increase the incentive of the more independent unit to cooperate by interfering with their task performance. The assumption is that once the independent unit is made aware of its need for the cooperation of the dependent unit (i.e., to desist from interfering acts), they will behave more cooperatively (supply the assistance necessary). This tactic may indeed achieve its purpose, and the conflict-interfering acts may cease, but frequently interference elicits a retaliatory response.

Conflict is also produced by differences in the way units are ranked along various dimensions of organizational status, namely direction of initiation of action, prestige, power, and knowledge. Seiler studied an organization in which it was generally agreed that research had more prestige than engineering and engineering had more prestige than production. When the sequential pattern of initiation and influence followed this status ordering, it was accepted. However, where a lower-status industrial engineering group needed to direct the higher-status research group to carry out routine tests, the result was a breakdown in relationships between the departments.

Performance Criteria and Rewards

Interunit conflict results when each of the interdependent departments has responsibility for only one side of a dilemma embedded in organizational tasks. Dutton and Walton noted that the preference of production units for long, economical runs conflicted with the preference of sales units for quick delivery to good customers. Dalton observed that staff units valued change, because that was one way they proved their worth, whereas line units valued stability, because change reflected unfavorably upon them or inconvenienced them. Also, staff units were strongly committed to preserving the integrity of control and rule systems, whereas line personnel believed they could be more effective by flexible reinterpretation of control and incentive schemes, and by ignoring many discipline and safety violations. A study by Strauss showed that engineers preferred to order brand items, whereas purchasing agents sought specifications suitable for several vendors. Similar instances abound. Landsberger postulated several basic dilemmas that probably underlie many interdepartmental differences: flexibility versus stability; criteria for short-run versus long-run performance; emphasis on measurable results versus attention to intangible results; maximizing organizational goals versus responding to other societal needs.

Although the dilemmas may be inherent in the total task, the reward system designed by management can serve either to sharpen or to blunt their divisive effect. Therefore, the more the evaluations and rewards of higher management emphasize the separate performance of each department rather than their combined performance, the more conflict.

Organizational Differentiation

In contemporary society, most large-scale organizations have to deal with both organic and mechanistic subunits and must combine these contradictory forms. Litwak regards the inclusions of these contradictory forms as a source of organizational conflict.

Lawrence and Lorsch emphasized the effects of differentiation. Where each unit (such as research, sales, or production) performs a different type of task and copes with a different segment of the environment, the units will develop significant internal differences. Such units may differ from each other (a) in the degree of structure, that is, tightness of rules, narrowness of span of supervisory control, frequency and specificity of performance review; (b) in the orienta-

tion of its members toward the environment, such as, new scientific knowledge versus customer problems and market opportunities versus costs of raw materials and processing; (c) in their orientation toward time, such as planning time perspective; and (d) in their orientation toward other people, such as, openness and permissiveness of interpersonal relationships.

Lawrence and Lorsch believe this fourfold differentiation is largely a response to the degree of uncertainty in the environments of the different departments. They use a notion of optimum degree of differentiation, which depends upon the task environments. Thus, either overdifferentiation or underdifferentiation has implications for the coordinative processes. Although greater differentiation apparently results in more *potential* for conflict, these authors do not assume that more conflict will automatically result.

Role Dissatisfaction

Role dissatisfaction, stemming from a variety of sources, can lead to conflict. Blocking status aspirations in purchasing agents and in staff members led to conflict with other units. In these cases, professionals felt they lacked recognition and opportunities for advancement. Similarly, White stated that members might feel that the growth of their units and their units' external status did not meet their needs, and therefore might enter another unit or withdraw from contacts that were painful reminders of the lack of status. Where one unit informally reports on the activities of another unit, resentment can occur, as with staff units reporting to management on production irregularities. Argyris and Dalton both argued that role dissatisfaction and conflict followed where one unit with the same or less status set standards for another.

Where there is role dissatisfaction, ambiguities in the definition of work responsibilities further increase the likelihood of interunit conflict. Landsberger pointed out that ambiguities tempted the dissatisfied unit to engage in offensive maneuvers so as to improve its lot, and thus induced other units to engage in defensive maneuvers.

Role dissatisfaction and ambiguity are related to more basic organizational variables, including growth rate, organizational level, and hierarchical differences. Organizational growth appears to have offsetting consequences. Slower rates of organizational growth and of opportunities for promotion increase role dissatisfaction, but are also accompanied by fewer ambiguities. Interfaces higher in the organization are more likely to be marked by conflict to redefine departmental responsibilities. At the higher levels, jurisdictional boundaries are less clear, and the participants perceive more opportunity to achieve some restructuring. Steep and heavily emphasized hierarchical differences in status, power, and rewards were seen by Thompson as responsible for some lateral conflict, because these factors tended to activate and to legitimate individual aspiration for increased status and power and tended to lead to increased upward orientation toward the desires of one's superiors, rather than to problem orientation and increased horizontal coordination.

Ambiguities

In addition to its interaction with role dissatisfaction, ambiguity contributes to interunit conflict in several other ways. Difficulty in assigning credit or blame between two departments increases the likelihood of conflict between units. Dalton attributed part of the staff-line conflict he observed to the fact that although improvements required collaboration between line and staff units, it was later difficult to assess the contribution of each unit. Similarly, disputes resulted between production and sales units, when it could not be determined which department made a mistake.

Low routinization and uncertainty of means to goals increase the potential for interunit conflict. Similarly, ambiguity in the criteria used to evaluate the performance of a unit may also create tension, frustration, and conflict.

Dependence on Common Resources

Conflict potential exists when two units depend upon a common pool of scarce organizational resources, such as physical space, equipment, personnel, operating funds, capital funds, central staff resources, and centralized services (e.g., typing and drafting). If the two units have interdependent tasks, the competition for scarce resources will tend to decrease interunit problem-solving and coordination. Also, if competition for scarce resources is not mediated by some third unit and they must agree on their allocation, they will come into direct conflict.

Communication Obstacles

Semantic difficulties can impede communications essential for cooperation. Strauss observed that differences in training of purchasing agents and engineers contributed to their conflicts. March and Simon stated that organizational channeling of information introduced bias.

Common experience reduces communication barriers and provides common referents. Miller proposed that the less units know about each other's job, the less collaboration and that lack of knowledge can lead to unreasonable interunit demands through ignorance. Cozer argued that accommodation is especially dependent on knowledge of the power of the other unit.

Personal Skills and Traits

Walton and McKersie, reviewing experimental studies, found that certain personality attributes, such as high authoritarianism, high dogmatism, and low self-esteem, increased conflict behavior. Kahn et al. found that in objective role conflict persons who scored lower on neurotic anxiety scales tended to depart more from "cordial, congenial, trusting, respecting, and understanding relations," and introverts tended to lose their confidence, trust, and respect for work associates more than extroverts.

Most interunit relationships are mixed-motive situations, which require high behavioral flexibility to manage optimally. A person with a narrower range of behavioral skills is less likely to exploit the integrative potential fully in an interunit relationship. He or she may either engage in bargaining to the exclusion of collaborative problem-solving, or withdraw or become passive, according to Walton and McKersie. Dalton and Thompson found that personal dissimilarities, such as background, values, education, age, and social patterns, lowered the probability of interpersonal rapport between unit representatives, and in turn decreased the amount of collaboration between their respective units. Personal status incongruities between departmental representatives, that is, the degree to which they differed in rank orderings in various status dimensions (such as length of service, age, education, ethnicity, esteem in eyes of superiors, pay, and so on) increase the tendency for conflict (Dutton and Walton).

Personal satisfaction with the internal climate of one's unit decreases the likelihood that a member will initiate interunit conflict. Seiler observed that in one firm constructive handling of interdepartmental differences occurred in part because the members of each department derived social satisfaction from their work associates, had high job interest and good opportunities for promotions, and were not in conflict with each other.

ONE MORE ANTECEDENT: THE NORM OF RECIPROCITY *

"There is no duty more indispensable than that of returning a kindness . . . all men distrust one forgetful of a benefit." (Cicero) Such a universal rule has governed social exchanges (including not only the tangibles

of money or concrete items but also love, friendship, support, advice, etc.) between individuals, groups, organizations, and countries in all cultures. In defining the norm we are told that generally "reciprocity is a mutually contingent exchange of benefits" between two or more parties. Reciprocity "connotes that *each* party has rights *and* duties." In effect, a right of A against B implies a duty of A to B and, in similar fashion, a duty of A to B implies a right of A against B. Put simply, if I do you a favor, I expect something in return. According to the norm, you "owe" me or should recognize the obligation. As Gouldner points out, what is involved is a "higher level moral norm: you should give benefits to those who give you benefits."

Though transactions are supposed to be roughly equivalent, there are conditions under which this may not happen. Generally, Gouldner suggests that "a group is more likely to contribute to another that provides it with benefits than to one that does not; nonetheless, there are certain general conditions under which one group may provide benefits for the other despite a *lack* of reciprocity. . . ."

If one group is more powerful than another, or not as dependent upon the other for achieving its goals, the stronger group may be able to coerce the weaker group. While the weaker group may expect benevolence or gratitude, such reciprocity need not follow for the pattern to stabilize. Gouldner calls such expectations the "Pollyanna Fallacy." He makes several observations worth noting here.

On the value of the benefit received . . . The value of the benefit received is a function of "the intensity of the recipient's need

* This section of the article on the norm of reciprocity is not part of the original work by Walton and Dutton. It is added for clarification and further refinement and is based on Alvin W. Gouldner, "The Norm of Reciprocity: A Preliminary Statement," *American Sociological Review* 25, no. 2, April 1960, pp. 161–178.

at the time the benefit was bestowed ("a friend in need . . ."), the resources of the donor ("he gave although he could ill afford it"), the motives imputed to the donor ("without thought of gain") and the nature of the constraints that are perceived to exist or to be absent ("he gave of his own free will"). When a party violates the norm, the value of the obligation it "owes" the other party is also a function of the above factors.

On obligations from past behavior . . .
"There are certain duties that people owe one another, not as human beings, or as fellow members of a group, or even as occupants of social statuses within the group but, rather, because of their prior actions. We owe others certain things because of what they have previously done for us, because of the history of previous interaction we had with them."

On "roughly equivalent" repayment . . .
This requirement "induces a certain amount of ambiguity as to whether indebtedness has been repaid and, over time, generates uncertainty about who is in whose debt." This requirement contributes to the stability of the social system because, "it is *morally* improper, under the norm of reciprocity, to break off relations or to launch hostilities against those to whom you are still indebted."

On the norm as a "starting mechanism" . . . Beside the norm operating to stabilize relationships, it can act as a "starting mechanism" for new relationships. For example, two people or groups each possesses valuables sought by the other and each feels that the only motive to interact is the anticipated gratification that will result. Each may then feel it would be to its advantage to obtain the other's valuables without relinquishing its own. "When internalized in both parties, the norm *obliges* the one

who has first received a benefit to repay it at some time; it thus provides some realistic grounds for confidence, in the one who first parts with his valuables, that he will be repaid."

Eliot added one caveat about the norm of reciprocity for each of us to ponder:

> The last temptation
> is the greatest treason;
> To do the right thing
> for the wrong reason.

A MODEL OF INTERUNIT CONFLICT

Organizational antecedents create conditions that can either influence perceptions or create ill feelings in individuals as well as in members of a unit or department in an organization (see exhibit 4.4). The feelings and perceptions cluster around two dimensions relevant to organization life: (1) the opportunity for one party to interfere with the other or (2) the incompatibility of goals between two or more parties. Once antecedents are perceived or felt in a conflictual manner by one party, that party engages in conflict-oriented behavior either at the overt or covert level. The conflict may range from passive resistance or blocking behavior to open warfare. Whether the antecedents are real or not is irrelevant since a party may engage in conflict-oriented behavior as long as he or she perceives them as real or feels they are real.

A move by one party often leads to a reaction or retaliation from the other party. Once conflict is manifested, there may be an attempt to resolve it. But even if there is no resolution reached by the parties, there is a conflict outcome—resolved or unresolved conflict. In the aftermath of most conflict, there is often a residue that can become added fodder in a future conflictual episode.

EXHIBIT 4.4   A Model of Interunit Conflict

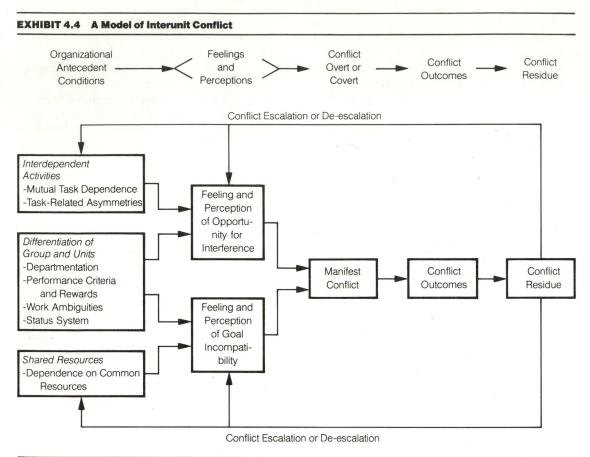

■ **Managing the Paradox of Organizational Trust**

LOUIS B. BARNES

Several years ago, the largest subsidiary in a giant international complex found itself with a new president, a bright young mar-

Reprinted by permission of the *Harvard Business Review*, "Managing the Paradox of Organizational Trust" by Louis B. Barnes (March-April 1981). Copyright © 1981 by the President and Fellows of Harvard College; all rights reserved. References deleted.

keting manager named Jones from one of the subsidiary's divisions. Jones soon let it be known that the old days of delegation were over and that he was going to create a strong, centralized head office with himself as its driving force. On more than one occasion, Jones made it clear that he had little respect for either the previous management or for some of the managers still in the company. He introduced specific cost, measurement, and reporting procedures; a number of managers and staff members were fired, took early retirement, or resigned. As Jones set his policies in motion, other old-timers were immobilized or bypassed.

Jones spent a good deal of time in the field, and every three months he took a team of headquarters staff with him to area plan-and-review sessions that cynics labeled "jump for Jonesie" shows, "rock 'em, sock 'em" binges, and "point the finger" days. Along with his periodic outbursts about the shortcomings of certain subordinates or reports, Jones's tough-spoken demands for tight budgets, detailed action plans, and short-term goals set the tone for management meetings.

As time went on, opposition to Jones appeared within both the company and the parent organization, but it remained underground because his company's measurable benefits seemed to outweigh the obvious costs of his behavior. The performance figures looked good. With increased inflation, cost cutting, and rising demand, the so-called bottom line showed the company to be very successful. Balanced against these positive indicators, high dissatisfaction, high turnover, postponed investments, and little evidence of succession planning all seemed negligible.

After several long, serious strikes in three of the subsidiary's key plants, however, top management finally became concerned with Jones's hard-line approach. Shortly after the last strike, senior managers in the parent company began to review their options—and about a year later replaced Jones with a senior manager from the parent company. No one within the subsidiary appeared capable of taking the job at that time.

This story may sound dramatic, but I suggest that the Manager Joneses of the world are legion. Sometimes the battle lines are more subtly drawn than in this case; sometimes managers are the masters and sometimes the victims, but almost invariably at

one time or another managers fall into Jones-like situations.

Like all people, managers behave according to their assumptions of how the world works—whether, for instance, it is a kind or a cruel place. Disastrous behavior such as Jones' follows when a manager's assumptions about the world establish a dangerous and self-defeating pattern.

The pattern develops, I believe, when managers hold three simple assumptions that, in combination, prevent trust from forming. Even though managers like Jones will state that it is trust more than either power or hierarchy that really makes an organization function effectively, these same managers all too often find themselves operating in and sometimes creating an atmosphere of pervasive *mis*trust in their companies.

Using Manager Jones as representative of all of us at times, I want to explore this mistrust—so subtle, so prevalent, and yet so unproductive—and then to describe how the three assumptions people make daily can create this destructive atmosphere.

I will briefly describe the three "harmless" assumptions, show how they appear in a managerial context, and then explore some alternative approaches and assumptions. In presenting these alternatives, I argue in favor of two fragile but important concepts—namely, tentative trust and paradoxical action.

Too often we fail to go beyond our initial reactions in order to look at an issue's deeper levels and thus avoid the time and the tension that such work entails. Then, as Manager Jones did, later on we pay the price. To see how this happens, let's begin with the assumptions as Manager Jones might have experienced them.

THREE HARMLESS ASSUMPTIONS

The three assumptions are, first, that important issues naturally fall into two opposing camps, exemplified by either/or thinking; second, that hard data and facts are better than what appear to be soft ideas and speculation, exemplified in the "hard drives out soft" rule; and finally, that the world in general is an unsafe place, exemplified by a person's having a pervasive mistrust of the universe around him or her. These assumptions can often be useful and necessary. Separately, they seem so natural that we don't see them as harmful. As a matter of fact, we often see them as healthy; in certain situations, for instance, we think only a fool would *not* be mistrustful.

Nevertheless, when managers combine all three assumptions at the same time, which we do very naturally as well, the assumptions may benefit us in the short run—but be very destructive in the long. Now let's look at them in turn.

Do or Die

A person holds assumption number one when *either/or* thinking dominates choices and decision-making. Like the rest of us, Manager Jones had to turn complex sets of alternatives into useful prime choices. Under conditions of uncertainty, Jones relied on experience and instinct to help him limit the alternatives, make choices, and then implement them. Using analysis and discussion, managers typically narrow their alternatives into such options as make or buy, act or react, centralize or decentralize, expand or retrench, and reward or punish.

But the problem with this way of thinking is more serious than that it limits options. People often become emotionally attached to a symbol or choice and see it as either good or bad. We set up the alternatives as adversaries and turn them into unions *versus* management, blacks *versus* whites, government *versus* business, theory *versus* practice, and us *versus* them (whoever they are). Despite Lincoln's reminder that a house divided against itself cannot stand, American tradition and history have taught us to separate issues into their two most obvious alternatives—and then to pronounce one of them "good" and the other "bad." It seems that part of what Manager Jones created in those around him was this either/or mentality. By his own definition, his choices were good. Others were to be criticized and attacked.

Even when it occurs, however, either/or thinking by itself is not destined for disaster. The real problem is that the assumption builds certain future expectations. For Manager Jones, these expectations prevented him from stepping outside of each either/or dichotomy to look again at the ingredients—to find an unseen paradoxical alternative or ingenious recombination. In Jones's case, for instance, he never sought to reintegrate the old-timers into his new management scheme. Because he saw them as having caused the problems, that would have seemed absurd at the time. Yet, paradoxically, they might have helped Jones overcome his subsequent turnover, morale, and strike problems.

Other examples of either/or ingredients illustrate the problem as well as a resolution. For example, for several generations now, people have viewed the management versus union dichotomy as a fact of life. One is good while the other is bad, depending on your perspective. If not enemies, the two have been at least antagonistic adversaries bound mainly by a legal contract. In many companies, this view leads to daily frictions between workers and supervisors. These can escalate into formal grievances. Under such conditions, even honest cooperative gestures are seen as dishonest or hostile. In one company, management tried to start some "improvement meetings" with workers. But because of past union-management experiences, the meetings were doomed before they started.

Yet in other companies, workers and managers have bargained hard on some issues and achieved shop floor cooperation on others, beyond the legalities of the contract. They were both bound to but not always limited by the contract.

Are these latter situations an exception to the rule? Probably they are, simply because the rule in most companies seems based on the more prevalent either/or assumption and its traditions. It is easier to take a firm position and act as if us or them, right or wrong, and good or bad were the major real-life options. But again, the villain here is not the either/or assumption itself. It is the distortion that occurs when people assume they need to defend their positions while also adopting the other two assumptions.

A Bird in the Hand . . .

Assumption number two is the principle that *hard is better than soft*, which means that hard drives out soft.[1] We saw it in Jones; we see it in ourselves. The idea goes as follows. Once Jones began to make either/or choices, he almost "had to" show their superiority and defend them; at least, that's the way he saw it. And to defend his position, he needed hard facts rather than soft feelings, hard numbers rather than soft words, and hard data and concrete steps rather than abstract possibilities. It meant short-term action-taking rather than long-term planning, "tell it like it is" statements rather than speculative explorations.

Consequently, Jones became a tough wheeler-dealer manager who needed to win out over the other side. As "they" became the opposition, having the best defense meant having a good offense. In Jones's case, as in many of our own situations, it is easy to see how the dangerous link between the first and second assumptions gets fused.

Holding this second assumption easily leads a person to a hard-nosed, buccaneer management style that turns doubt into ac-

tion and stirs the hearts of those who idolize such uncompromising figureheads as General George S. Patton, Harold Geneen of ITT, the Ayatollah Khomeini, or the late John Wayne's macho cowboy roles. Such leaders at least *act* as if they know what they're doing. And the shoot-from-the-hip style is not restricted to management; the hard/soft assumption shows up in the hard-nosed skepticism of science and in the lawyer's quest for hard evidence. In the best competitive tradition, people who hold this assumption "get things done," despite later consequences.

Yet both proponents and opponents of hard-is-better-than-soft can make profound mistakes in its name. Both can propel an either/or position a long way toward a disaster of the extremes, as the following example shows:

When John F. Kennedy took office in 1961, he was confronted with the CIA's plans for the Bay of Pigs invasion. Although Kennedy seemed to have early doubts about the invasion and even though a few advisers like Arthur Schlesinger, Jr., and Chester Bowles expressed reservations, Kennedy went along with the arguments for an attack as presented by Allan Dulles of the CIA, some joint chief of staff members, and other highly qualified advisers.

Schlesinger later wrote about the hard-drives-out-soft mood of those meetings in his book *A Thousand Days*—"Moreover, the advocates of the adventure had a rhetorical advantage. They could strike virile poses and talk of tangible things—fire power, air strikes, landing craft, and so on. To oppose this plan, one had to invoke intangibles— the moral position of the United States, the response of the United Nations, 'world public opinion,' and other such odious concepts.

"But just as the members of the White House Staff who sat in the Cabinet Room failed in their job of protecting the President, so the representatives of the State Department failed in protecting the diplomatic interests of the nation. I could not help feeling that the desire to prove to the CIA and

---

1. Author's note: George F.F. Lombard of the Harvard Business School first called my attention to this assumption some years ago as a variant on Gresham's Law that "bad money drives out good money." I have since heard of similar variations such as one coined by Warren Bennis, recent president of the University of Cincinnati, as Bennis's Principle: "Routine work drives out nonroutine work." In the same spirit, I suppose, "hard drives out soft" deserves to be known as Lombard's Law, which is what some of us have affectionately called it in recent years.

the Joint Chiefs that they were not soft-headed idealists but were really tough guys too influenced State's representatives at the Cabinet table.''

The Bay of Pigs example illustrates the power of the hard-is-better-than-soft assumption in combination with its either/or companion. When opposing sides are formed, people feel almost compelled to choose one or the other—and to find tangible ways of defending their choices. The side that usually seems most convincing is the one that is supported by hard evidence and defended by hard tactics, which have both an intellectual and an emotional appeal for the tough-minded and the would-be tough-minded, like Jones.

The danger with people's tendencies to make hard-nosed choices is that, as in the Bay of Pigs discussions, such choices quickly acquire their own momentum. To stop the snowball—to try to reexamine the options—means violating the either/or and hard/soft assumptions, while seeming, as Schlesinger says, to be a ''soft-headed idealist.'' As many managers know, in most tough-guy contexts it can be very hard to appear soft.

Pitting himself and his hard-line approach against both old-line practices and old-time managers, Jones exemplified the tough-guy manager. However, he personified a third assumption as well.

Nice Guys Finish Last

The third harmless assumption forms a basis for and helps contaminate the other two. It holds that the world is a dangerous place requiring that a person adopt a position of *pervasive mistrust* to survive. When held, this assumption dominates the atmosphere and blots out situational factors. Like the other two assumptions, mistrust can be very useful when our safety or well-being is at stake. On other occasions, however, our own mistrust helps set the stage for either/or thinking and hard-drives-out-soft behavior.

According to those who had known him in earlier years, Manager Jones had been taunted in childhood for being weak. To avoid the appearance of weakness, he adopted an aggressive posture and an air of superskepticism, which fit his view of the world. He was bright enough to be a rising star in a company where mutual trust among managers was considered important. Jones, himself, was considered trustworthy by his superiors in the sense of being a predictable producer.

As Jones set one subordinate faction against another, however, and as hard began to drive out soft, the parent company managers saw how destructive Jones's sense of mistrust was and how absent and important the softer, more caring side of trust had become. Not surprisingly, key subordinates reciprocated Jones's lack of caring, which led them to indulge in inconsistent and unpredictable behavior. As a result, any earlier bases for organizational trust disappeared.

Jones's assumption of pervasive mistrust was reinforced by his either/or and hard-drives-out-soft viewpoints. The situation deteriorated even more as Jones's subordinates took sides and added fuel to the fires of mistrust. It took the company more than five years to move out of what was by then commonly acknowledged to be a very difficult situation. This experience suggests how much harder it is to drive out hard with soft then vice versa, even though it can be done over time. It also suggests that we should examine the tenacious roots of trust and mistrust more closely. For this, the work of Erik H. Erikson is instructive.

Although Erikson's work rests on rich clinical evidence, it seems reasonable to ask, ''What do early trust-mistrust patterns have to do with managers like Jones?'' In response, researchers would generally agree that we never fully conquer old anxieties or doubts; when we encounter difficult new situations, we often reexperience old tensions. Thus the early major dilemmas of the human life cycle can often return in later years when we meet new tension-filled settings and experiences.

In addition—and most important for managers—even though our earliest and most basic assumptions about trust and mistrust are formed in early infancy, they are affected by new situations and by how a person feels about the immediate situation. Consequently, the trust versus mistrust dilemma constantly confronts us as we face new situations, new people, new adversities, and even new successes.

In this fashion, much of our initial behavior in these new situations is an effort to search for, test out, and initiate a tentative sense of trust or mistrust. When other people see this initial behavior as *both* predictable and caring, they develop an expectation of future hope, which accompanies trust. Such early search behavior also invites similar responses from others.

This exchange creates the giving and getting-in-return behavior that Erikson pictures and pervades all cultures in what sociologists call the norm of reciprocity. Its universal pattern gives us (and Jones) a way to check out and test for the presence of trust. When we try to give something, we have a chance to see what we get in return. If the exchange is unsuccessful, for whatever reason, we usually assume it is a situation in which mistrust prevails.

To further show how the trust/mistrust assumption works, though, let me briefly describe three studies by other behavioral scientists.

The first, by James Driscoll, shows how satisfaction in organizations is determined more by the degree of trust present than by either levels of particpation or people's inherent trust. In other words, Driscoll suggests that with trust, the immediate environment is more important than either one's background or one's participation in decisions.

The second study of trust and mistrust is Dale Zand's simulation of managerial problem-solving, and the third is R. Wayne Boss's replication of Zand's study done some years later. Both studies examine how high-trust and low-trust conditions af-

fect the quality of managerial problem-solving involving a company president and three vice-presidents. Each study set up teams with sets of instructions; some teams' instructions were filled with high-trust assumptions, others' had low-trust assumptions. The surprising thing in these studies is how easily the simple instructions given to each set created these trust differences. Zand's instructions for the high-trust teams, all of whom were managers attending a course, read as follows (note the words I have italicized):

"You have learned *from your experience* during the past two years that *you can trust* the other members of the top management team. You and the other top managers *openly express your differences and your feelings of encouragement or of disappointment.* You and the others *share all relevant information and freely explore ideas and feelings that may be in or out of your defined responsibility.* The result has been a *high level of give and take and mutual confidence in each other's support and ability.*"

According to Zand, the instructions given to the low-trust groups were "worded to induce a decrease in trust." This was epitomized by the president perceiving his or her vice-presidents as potentially competitive.

The key difference in the two sets may be the specific cues about the give-and-take reciprocity among managers. In the high-trust teams, the norms of reciprocity included expressing differences of opinion, stating feelings of encouragement and disappointment, sharing information, exploring ideas outside of one's own function, providing high give-and-take, and giving support. For the low-trust teams the opposite was implied.

Both the Zand and the Boss studies indicate that high trust was the key factor in problem-solving effectiveness. Moreover, in his replication study, Boss reports a surprising finding (italics mine):

"*The fact that trust was the overriding variable was not initially apparent to the sub-*

jects. When participants were asked to explain the reasons for the obvious differences in team effectiveness, they offered a number of plausible explanations. . . . When told of the different instructions, the group members reacted with amazement and relief. *They were amazed that they had not perceived what seemed to them after the fact to be obvious."*

What does all this tell us about the soft assumption of trust?

1. Our concerns about trust apparently begin very early and recur throughout our lives.

2. Trust seems important for both effective performance and high satisfaction.

3. Trust may be easier both to create and to destroy, under some conditions, than we have assumed (it depends on how norms of reciprocity develop and take hold).

4. Managers may gloss over the crucial role of trust-and-mistrust assumptions and fall back on more convenient explanations for behavior in their companies, such as personality differences and the boss's actions.

5. Perhaps most important, our assumptions of trust and mistrust come at us from both past and present situations.

We may not be able to do much about the past, but we do have some control over present and future actions. In new situations, once we question the inevitability of pervasive mistrust, then the either/or and hard/soft assumptions also stand on shakier ground. Indeed, if we question all three assumptions enough, it becomes apparent that they no longer need to combine to our detriment. But what can we use to replace them?

ALTERNATIVE APPROACHES

So far I've discussed how long-term problems arise when managers combine the three harmless assumptions. The same is true when we combine their most obvious alternatives, which, in good either/or fashion, happen to come from their exact opposites. Manager Jones would most likely reject the idea that pervasive trust (the obvious alternative to pervasive mistrust) could possibly replace his assumption. His experience has taught him otherwise. And he would surely (and with reason) reject the idea that a prolonged-tolerance-for-ambiguity or a soft-is-better-than-hard viewpoint is a suitable replacement for any more rigorous stance.

Even though Jones might reject these obvious alternatives, others do not. For some people, the concepts of pervasive trust, prolonged ambiguity, and soft-overwhelming-hard fit together and have great appeal. With almost religious fervor, like flower children or sensitivity training converts, they promote their causes to proclaim the new utopias. Typically, that fervor is all it takes for their more mistrustful adversaries to draw new lines and define new battlegrounds.

Ultimately, holders of opposing viewpoints emerge and throw loaded overstatements at the other side, as both parties get drawn into defending fixed positions.

Over the years the management pendulum swings back and forth from liberal to conservative, from centralization to decentralization, from harsh layoff periods to expensive benefit programs, and from severe survival controls to expanded product development and cries for creativity. A major problem is that early dialogue between the opposing viewpoints often triggers defensive thinking within each position, as happened in Jonestown, Watergate, and Iran. In each case, typically—and tragically—either/or, mistrust, and hard-drives-out-soft prevail in the short term.

At the same time, people in organizations can and do learn. What appears to be pendulum behavior isn't merely that. Opposites sometimes converge or change as they develop. Sometimes new managers and new situations phase new assumptions into old issues. Sometimes a wise, experienced manager can rise above a repeated false dichotomy and furnish the impetus for finding new approaches. Such approaches, however, require people adept at a third path, not just a middle way, as well as specific steps toward organizational trust and constructive reciprocities. To do this, managers need to abandon the three assumptions and their opposites in favor of less rigid, more creative combinations.

Things Aren't Always As They Seem

Another example, as follows, might help to illustrate how this third way can work:

The faculty and administration of a small college were torn by argument and dissension. The veteran president had recently resigned, and a search committee had chosen a woman with a distinguished academic record as the new president. Not long after the new president arrived, the dean of faculty also resigned.

After conferring with the executive committee of the faculty, the new president appointed a young, recently tenured faculty member as the acting dean of faculty. She also announced three short-term goals: improving the enrollment picture, improving the financial situation, and building new trust. She resisted strong pressures to produce a specific "mission" statement, saying that as soon as she did, it would polarize the college community into those who agreed with the statement and those who didn't. She also chose to keep the new dean of faculty as an acting dean so that he could be tested in his new role while she and the faculty learned to work with him and with each other.

During their first year of working together, the new president and the acting dean took supportive but active roles in faculty discussions, helped to pass legislation that greatly simplified the cumbersome committee structure, improved the enrollment and financial pictures, and tried to strengthen faculty work relationships.

Specifically, the new dean worked hard to reinvolve a number of senior faculty members who were described by others as "burned out" and "losers" of earlier faculty battles. He did this by going to them for advice on important matters, frequently seeking them out in their offices, refusing to let them withdraw, helping them get money for such mundane tasks as manuscript typing and library research, sending them to conferences on innovative practices in their own fields, asking them to chair short-term task forces, and seeking and finding financial help for them to start new research.

At the start of the second year of the acting dean's appointment, the president still refused to appoint him as the permanent dean until the official search committee was set up and made its own report and recommendation. The acting dean agreed: "I have everything to gain by not having the official title and authority. This way I can still get help from everyone and don't have to act like an official dean." Nevertheless, within a few months a search committee did recommend that his title be made official.

A number of knowledgeable sources have since reported that the college is progressing excellently.

As managers, the new president and her acting dean posed a puzzle to most of their constituents. She was new, an outsider, and wouldn't take a firm position on educational policy; he was young and had little administrative experience. In an institution where protocol, tradition, and gestures of strong leadership had been important, neither administrator leaned on them. Where mistrust had been rampant, she set out to assume and to build trust. In an effort to demonstrate that there was still leadership in the faculty ranks as well, he set out to revitalize burned-out faculty members.

In effect, the president and the dean refused to adopt either set of simple hard or soft assumptions. Instead they assumed a condition of tentative trust and worked toward a set of *and/also* rather than either/or expectations. They did this by behaving in ways that explored, listened, and confronted while exemplifying care for the school and its people. In effect they began reciprocities that could lead to organizational trust.

In doing so, the president and dean created a sense of shared hope for the future. Both gave ample evidence of caring for the school and its individual members. After identifying a set of crucial problems—enrollment, finances, trust, a demoralized faculty, little support for faculty projects, and low student and faculty initiative—both confronted them. As new leaders, they worked on old issues in new ways and surprised some people. They did not initially set forth a master plan or mission. She chose a relatively inexperienced person as dean. They both tried to build and rebuild faculty leadership instead of drawing attention to their own. And even after the acting dean had convinced the faculty of his competence, the president refused to push for his permanent appointment until the faculty also took responsibility for it.

As a result, the either/or power struggles that had existed between the previous administration and the faculty moved toward a set of and/also expectations. The new administration, the senior faculty, the junior faculty, the students, and the subfactions built a new leadership network where the quality of students rose, student turnover and attrition declined, programs expanded, and finances improved. Paradoxically, the president and dean accomplished the expected, or hoped-for, results by creatively pursuing the unexpected—at least in the eyes of many constituents.

These seemingly inappropriate about-faces are what I call paradoxical actions. In using the word *paradox* in this way, I'm borrowing from philosopher W.V. Quine's notion that paradox is "any conclusion that at first sounds absurd but that has an argument to sustain it," although these arguments are often buried, ignored, or brushed over quickly. Paradoxical actions are the "absurd" steps, such as listening hard to the

other person when one is trying to win an argument, that break up and bridge false dichotomies. They create working links toward trust where there were few or none before.

Paradoxical Actions . . .

The mysteriousness of paradox has fascinated poets, scientists, philosophers, and lay people for thousands of years. Paradoxical puzzles can both pose unanswerable questions and lead to insightful creative answers; Kierkegaard called paradox the "source of the thinker's passion." The reconciliation of apparent contradictions underlies some of the most truly creative discoveries of science, not to mention most religions, while the suggested unity of opposites permeates the works of great writers like O'Neill and Conrad. Most important, partly because it is based on an unfamiliar logic or rationale, a paradox's true workings always seem to be just beyond our understanding.

Once we see these same paradoxical situations as and/also propositions rather than either/or contradictions, the reconciliations seem relatively obvious. That awareness, though, doesn't always help us find the underlying unities the next time we face a set of apparent opposites. Manager Jones is not the only one who finds it difficult to break old reciprocities or the patterns that reinforce them. Sometimes, however, change requires the very opposite of what appears to be logically appropriate behavior.

At the same time, paradoxical actions are not foreign to many a modern manager. To buy when others are selling, to ask questions when others expect answers, or to give new autonomy when subordinates expect tighter controls are all actions that make sense under certain conditions. And, without highlighting it, some of the most popular management concepts of recent years have relied on paradox. The work of McGregor, Blake and Mouton, and Lawrence and Lorsch all entail paradoxes.

In a sense, these real and theoretical examples highlight the almost unnoticed role of paradox in organizational behavior. In similar fashion, I suspect, most readers overlook the crucial role that paradox plays in their own more creative actions. And yet, acting paradoxically constitutes one way to get beyond tentative trust rather than adopting the extremes of pervasive trust or pervasive mistrust.

Likewise, a manager who avoids either/or thinking or its mushy opposite, prolonged ambiguity, must consciously adopt an and/also viewpoint whereby ingredients are kept separate but are not assumed to be in conflict. Finally, and most difficult, managers need to replace the hard versus soft behavior with paradoxical actions that *cope* with new information, *confront* important discrepancies, and *care* for individual people and issues. The goal is not to do one or the other; it is to weave them into a pattern of separate behaviors that sets the basis for new reciprocal patterns.

. . . and Norms of Reciprocity

Earlier, I suggested that the fragile toughness of trust is a crucial factor in blending extremist hard- and soft-line assumptions into an organizational bonding that holds a company's disparate parts together. Trust that is too tentative, emotional, and fragile will fall back into pervasive mistrust. Trust that is too tenacious, impervious, and tough becomes inflexibly shaped into a pattern of pervasive trust. Organizations with too much mistrust become overly differentiated, with people succumbing to either/or expectations and hard-drives-out-soft behavior. Organizations with too much trust become overly integrated, with people lapsing into prolonged ambiguity and soft-is-better-than-hard behavior. Both extremist patterns depend on emotions more than on data and self-awareness. Both also build up ineffective reciprocity patterns.

The three-path diagram in exhibit 4.5 displays the points I've made so far plus another path that is based on the more modest assumption of tentative trust. The diagram also suggests that the patterns persist because people reinforce them, i.e., attack/defend/withdraw behavior follows from an assumption of pervasive mistrust and win/lose expectations. Such behavior begins a cycle that repeats itself until it becomes a norm of reciprocity and degenerates into a continuing self-oriented need pattern. Obeying a distorted golden rule, people do to others what they perceive is being done to them. Beginning with a pervasive sense of mistrust, they shift eventually into a set of destructive reciprocities and finally to even more divisive and self-oriented needs. As emotions run high, the cycle continues, engendering even more mistrust.

The three-path diagram also suggests that norms of reciprocity need not result in rigid patterns and structures. One way to break those norms, which are perceived as natural by the time they are frozen, is to seek for and initiate paradoxical actions. New norms cannot be set into motion unless the old ones are broken. And the old ones cannot be broken unless paradoxical insights and actions help break old patterns. Some of this paradoxical behavior is subtle and difficult to capture. It hinges on words, gestures, and maybe most of all on careful listening for new clues and knowledge.

But even more, paradoxical actions begin to set up new relationships and in that sense lead to the unexpected. Such actions suggest that, in Lewis Carroll's words, "things aren't always as they seem." Consider one final example where a major company president, reflecting on a turbulent year of employee relations, notes:

"Some of our problems are our own fault. We lost contact with our own employees. Managements in large companies say that they get too big to stay in personal contact with their employees. We swallowed that. Now, however, I think that the opposite is true. The larger we get, the *more* important it is for us to emphasize personal contact by top management down through all levels.

EXHIBIT 4.5 The Assumptions and the Patterns They Create

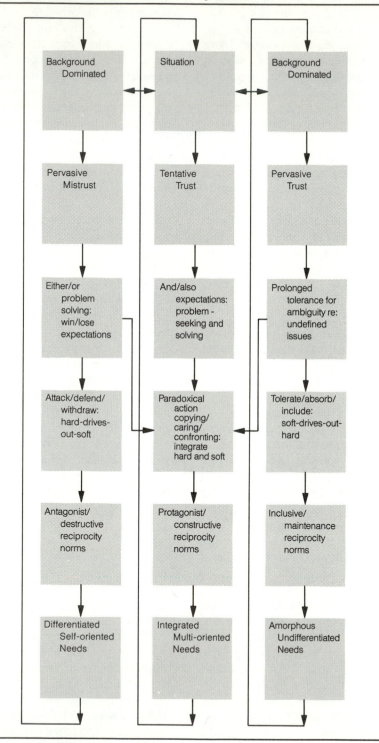

We've been doing it all wrong. We stumbled over our own assumptions."

In essence, to prevent mistrust beliefs or their extreme opposites from becoming frozen, we sometimes need, unlike our friend Manager Jones, to live and to create paradoxical actions. We need to know and act as though some things are both certain and uncertain. We need to polarize and synthesize, to see questions in answers, to be both inside and outside situations, to learn while teaching, and to find unity in opposites as well as opposites in unity. Interestingly enough, excellent managers, though they are not used to talking these ways, *are* used to thinking paradoxically. Our hope for dealing with an increasingly complex organizational future lies in understanding—and making more explicit—the implicit truth in this way of thinking.

■ Dynamics of Escalation/De-escalation

KENNETH THOMAS

During the course of negotiations with Other, Party's orientation, strategic objectives, and tactics may change as a reaction to Other's behavior. For example, Party's orientation may change when the stakes change or when Other's behavior alters Party's identification with him; Party's strategic objectives may change with his perceptions of Other's power and the degree of conflict of interest between them; and Party's tactics may change to reflect his trust and respect for Other.

Such changes are frequently described in terms of the escalation/de-escalation dimension. Escalation usually denotes an increase in the level of conflict, however that term is defined. Escalation might involve: increasing the number or the size of issues disputed, increasing hostility between par-

ties, increasing competitiveness, pursuing increasingly extreme demands or objectives, using increasingly coercive tactics, and decreasing trust.

This section will cover eleven dynamics that occur during negotiations. Most of these refer to the dynamics of escalation and de-escalation. As such, they have special relevance for mediators and for other third parties who are concerned with conflict management.

1. The first dynamic involves the concept of revaluation. Follett maintained that parties rarely actually give in to their opponents. Instead, agreements usually accompany changes in a party's conceptualization of an issue. Coming into conflict with Other and hearing Other's arguments may lead Party to "revaluate" his definition of the issue and his preferred alternative. For example, revaluation may occur when Party realizes that his preferred alternative has undesirable consequences for other important concerns. Marketing may stop pressing for short lead times on an order when they learn that such lead times would force Pro-

Kenneth Thomas, "Conflict and Conflict Management," in Marvin D. Dunnette (ed.), *Handbook of Industrial and Organizational Psychology*, Copyright © 1976 Rand McNally College Publishing Company, pp. 905–907. Reprinted by permission. References deleted. See original work.

duction to neglect other important orders; Management changes its position when it realizes that its preferences would be counter to existing regulations; and so on. While it may occur under any circumstances, revaluation is facilitated by open communication, trust, and the use of persuasive rather than coercive tactics—in short, by collaboration and problem-solving.

2. Self-fulfilling prophecies are common in conflict phenomena. The behavior Party receives from Other is to some extent a response to Party's *own* behavior. Walton and McKersie hypothesized that problem-solving tends to encourage problem-solving responses and that bargaining tends to elicit bargaining responses. Deutsch hypothesized the same for cooperation and competition. In the context of interdepartmental relations, Thomas and Walton found that managers reported using tactics that were similar to those they saw the other party using: forcing was related positively to Other's forcing, and negatively to Other's candor and accommodation; candor was related positively to Other's candor, and negatively to Other's forcing and avoiding. The upshot of this is that Party's orientation toward the other and his trust or distrust toward Other have some tendency to be reinforced by generating the predicted behavior in Other—regardless of the other's original orientation. For example, if a foreman sees a union steward as competitive and therefore fights him on every issue, he may actually prod the steward into fighting. Likewise, if a subordinate avoids confronting his boss because he believes the boss would not respond to his needs, the boss, in his ignorance of his subordinate's needs, will not respond to them.

3. A number of biases occur in Party's perceptions of Other. To begin with, Party is largely unaware of Other's motives. Party is familiar with the reasons behind his own actions, since he has planned them himself. But since he is not usually privy to Other's thinking, the reasons behind Other's behavior are often unknown. His own

actions, therefore, appear quite reasonable to him, while the behavior of Other often appears arbitrary. What he sees as a necessary move on his part might be seen as an arbitrary and unjustified attack if made by the other party. For example, Defense Department statements frequently contrast the enemy's "arbitrary acts of aggression" with our own "protective reactions." In addition, Party is selective in his perception of Other's behavior. Depending upon his level of trust or suspicion toward Other, he looks for different things. If suspicious, he is vigilant for signs of threat, competition, hostility, and conflict of interest—which he is then more likely to find. With this bias, he underestimates the commonalities between parties, according to Blake & Mouton, and may miss the other's cooperative overtures and signs of goodwill.

4. Another source of bias stems from cognitive simplification. We have already noted that cognitive simplification may result in a win/lose conceptualization of issues. Here, we are more concerned with Party's perception of himself and Other. Party's perceptions tend to become more black/white under stress, threat, and ego involvement; but some of these simplifications also fulfill Party's need for cognitive consistency or dissonance reduction. As these simplifications occur, Party is less able to simultaneously see good and bad qualities in himself or Other—Party becomes good in all respects while Other becomes bad. Blake and Mouton have demonstrated these distortions in intergroup conflict. To some extent these distortions increase the stakes for Party because he is defending good against evil, and he accordingly becomes more righteous. In addition, Party's identification with Other diminishes as Other becomes less likable. The extreme case of such distortions occurs in holy wars, where defenders of the faith righteously butcher infidels. But a significant number of these distortions also occurs across bargaining tables, between departments, and elsewhere in organizations.

5. Communication is the medium through which Party's misperceptions can be corrected: Other's communications may lead Party to revaluate his own position, to recognize Other's actual orientation, and to revise his stereotype of Other. However, communications tend to become distorted with perceived conflict of interest or with competitive behavior. Trust is diminished as either party uses communications to manipulate or coerce the other or as either party becomes suspicious that the other is doing so. With diminished trust, Other's communications cease to be believed or even listened to, and Party concentrates on getting his own message across. In the context of labor relations, Stagner and Rosen referred to such communication patterns as the "dialogue of the deaf." After a while, as communication attempts prove fruitless, communications channels cease to be used at all, and both parties may communicate only through their actions.

6. Breakdowns in communications enable both parties to develop and maintain their distorted views of each other and to feed their mutual hostility. Newcomb used the term "autistic hostility" to describe hostility that develops in the absence of communication, and went on to develop the thesis that persistent hostility varies with the degree to which a party's perception of a relationship "remains autistic, its privacy maintained by some sort of barriers to communication." At the extreme, political assassinations may be performed by parties whose autistic and withdrawn personalities enable them to fantasize their targets as devils and themselves as heroes and army morale (largely dependent upon hostility) is maintained by preventing fraternization with the enemy.

7. As hostility and distrust increase, Party's tactics tend to become coercive. Each of the remaining bases of Party's power tends to disappear with increasing hostility. Information power becomes ineffective as Other becomes suspicious of Party and ceases to listen to him. Expert power becomes ineffective with Other's mistrust and lack of respect. Party has no referent power, or has *negative* referent power when Other ceases to identify with him. Party's legitimate power becomes ineffective when Other sees him acting arbitrarily. Even reward power may become ineffective when Other views gifts from Party as tainted or as bribes. As Party perceives that these types of influence are ineffective, he tends to fall back upon coercive power—threatening various unfavorable consequences for Other if Other does not comply with Party's preferences: "I've tried to be reasonable with you, but that's over now. If you don't do *X* by Wednesday, you'll have to pay the consequences."

8. After competing with Other to satisfy his initial concern, Party may lose sight of his initial concern and simply compete with Other for its own sake. This phenomenon has been called goal substitution or goal displacement. Party's objective becomes beating Other, even if it means sacrificing some of his own concerns. Party may see himself as saving face, getting even, teaching Other a lesson, showing Other he can't get away with it, etc. Like the battered fighter, his satisfaction comes from being able to say, "You ought to see the other guy."

9. Competition between the parties may spread to other issues. This "proliferation" of issues is discussed by Walton and Deutsch. New issues (or revived old issues) become opportunities for Party to "seize the high ground" in his ongoing struggle with Other: "While we're on that subject, how about the time *you* did such and such." We may find that the parties bicker over issues that they would otherwise have no trouble resolving, and take apparently unreasonable positions merely to oppose the other.

10. As this competitiveness spreads and is accompanied by cognitive simplification, Party may perceive that the basic concerns of the two parties are generally incompatible. At this point, it may appear to Party that the relationship cannot continue: "This organization isn't big enough for both of us." And Party may try to drive Other away: Production tries to eliminate Maintenance as a separate department, one politician demands another's resignation, management tries to destroy a union, etc.

11. Where substantial hostility and cognitive simplification exist, Walton notes that the parties must ventilate their feelings to each other and state the issues that divide them before they can begin to seek an integrative solution. In his terms, a "differentiation" phase precedes the integration phase. Ventilating feelings, or "getting it off your chest," produces a catharsis for Party—a reduction in hostility toward Other.

In order for catharsis to occur, however, Other must listen to Party's negative feelings. If Other ignores them or counters with abuse toward Party, Party's hostility toward Other will increase. If both parties succeed in ventilating their feelings to each other, the reduced hostility will remove some of the tendencies toward cognitive simplification, allowing the parties to develop a more balanced perception of themselves and the issues. As the parties appreciate similar interests and positive characteristics in each other, the succeeding integration phase may even involve considerable positive feelings: "You know, he's not really such a bad guy."

■ Impression Management: The Politics of Bargaining in Organizations

SAMUEL B. BACHARACH and EDWARD J. LAWLER

Coalitions essentially partition organization members into distinct groups on the basis of common interests. While coalitions bind the members with the most common interests together, they also pit those with the most divergent interests in opposition to one another. Coalitions create and define the parameters of conflict by crystallizing the different interests of subgroups. In any organization, there are likely to be numerous differences among members and subgroups, and it is coalitions that highlight and make salient the most critical differences. In this sense, coalitions are not just

the principal units of political action but also the mechanisms for establishing and defining the political game. The political game, in turn, is manifested in bargaining between coalitions.

Coalitions are not ends in themselves; they are strategic devices to improve the power position of component interest groups vis-à-vis others with regard to some issue or set of issues. Thus, coalition mobilization gives rise to *inter*coalition bargaining. The goals underlying coalition formation require the maintenance of a strong coalition and bargaining with opposing coalitions. The bargaining in this case is not designed to develop a new coalition but to use the existing coalition to advantage. This intercoalition bargaining is the essence of con-

Excerpted from Samuel B. Bacharach and Edward J. Lawler, *Power and Politics in Organizations* (San Francisco: Jossey Bass, 1981), ch. 6, pp. 105–140.

flict in organizations. Coalitions define and crystallize the different interests, and intercoalition bargaining is the concrete manifestation of conflict. In this sense, bargaining and conflict in organizations are indistinguishable phenomena.

The coalition metaphor does not deny that there are positive-sum and zero-sum [1] elements within nearly any intraorganizational relationship, whether between individuals, interest groups, or coalitions. However, our coalition imagery does assume that these elements are typically not the dominant ones governing the interaction of subgroups. Instead, the coalition model implies that intraorganizational relations are mixed motive. A mixed-motive situation encompasses elements from both positive-sum and zero-sum situations. In other words, parties are simultaneously confronted with incentives to cooperate and incentives to compete. Such situations encompass greater complexity and uncertainty than either positive-sum or zero-sum situations.

Bargaining is a central element of any mixed-motive setting. Given simultaneous incentives to cooperate and compete, mixed-motive relationships are inherently unstable and inevitably involve some distrust. In this context, bargaining is the primary means for keeping the conflict within acceptable bounds and avoiding a complete bifurcation of the relationship. Through bargaining, parties "resolve" the competition versus cooperation dilemma, maintain or improve their positions, and protect themselves from other groups or individuals. However, a mixed-motive situation further implies that any resolution of the conflict is likely to be temporary, with the danger of conflict emerging repeatedly over time. Bargaining is a never-ending aspect of mixed-motive contexts. Thus, we expect persistent bargaining over time, and there ap-

pears to be no way to separate or distinguish conflict from bargaining in organizations.

NATURE OF BARGAINING RELATIONSHIPS

Bargaining is the give-and-take that occurs when two or more interdependent parties experience a conflict of interest. The degree of interdependence or conflict of interest can vary considerably across social settings. The point is that some minimal level of each is necessary to engender or maintain a bargaining relationship.

Bargaining is the action component of conflict. The central elements of bargaining are the tactical moves and countermoves by which parties attempt to achieve dual, often conflicting, objectives: to resolve the conflict, but to do it in a way that is advantageous to their own interests. The dilemma is that parties wish to give as little as possible and take as much as possible, yet conflict-resolution may necessitate more giving and less taking than they expect or desire. Resolution of the current issue or problem may also affect future bargaining and bear on the long-term maintenance of good relations.

By now, it is undoubtedly obvious that we view bargaining processes as ubiquitous aspects of complex organizations. The specific nature or form of bargaining can vary almost infinitely across different sectors, subgroups, issues, and other factors within a given organization. For example, bargaining may be tacit and involve little direct communication between parties, or it may be explicit and involve substantial contact, or it may lie somewhere between these two extremes. Bargaining may also be informal or formal. Informal bargaining usually is not officially recognized or sanctioned. Formal bargaining implies not only official sanctioning but also that parties accord recognition and legitimacy to one another and to the bargaining relationship.

---

1. Positive sum refers to situations in which both parties stand to gain *more* by working together; zero-sum refers to essentially a win/lose situation. If A wins, B *must* lose or vice versa.

Given the variability of bargaining in organizational contexts, our first task is to identify the basic dimensions of any bargaining relationship. In order to understand the tactical action that constitutes the essence of bargaining, we must have some sense of the relational context within which that tactical action takes place.

The literature on bargaining emphasizes the formal, explicit, or conscious manifestation of bargaining. Specifically, the give-and-take is conceptualized as an explicit exchange of offers and counteroffers, as action consciously designed to find a mutually acceptable solution to the conflict. While collective bargaining and international negotiations often fit this conceptualization, many instances of less explicit or less conscious bargaining are excluded by this approach. It is especially important to consider more subtle forms of negotiation when dealing with intraorganizational relations, because coalitions in this context may be hesitant to admit or confront conflict. Instead, they may try to handle issues in a less visible way. Intraorganizational relations provide a context within which highly explicit bargaining is likely to exist side-by-side with less explicit bargaining.

The conditions that affect the explicitness of the bargaining can be elaborated by considering Schelling's contrast between explicit and tacit bargaining. Explicit bargaining is essentially what nations, corporations, and unions do when they sit at the bargaining table, that is, they exchange offers and counteroffers. In such settings, the parties have relatively open lines of communication, define the relationship as a bargaining one, and consent to consider compromise. In this context, the most critical aspect of the give-and-take is concession behavior (the nature of the offers and counteroffers). Tacit bargaining, on the other hand, implies that the parties have obstructed communication lines and may not even define the relationship as a bargaining one or be conscious of the fact that they are in a bargaining relationship. At a minimum, tac-

it bargaining implies that the parties do not publicly acknowledge the bargaining relationship. The give-and-take involves few explicit offers or counteroffers; instead, parties attempt to outmaneuver and manipulate each other, often using subtle influence tactics or rewards and punishments. Tacit bargaining often precedes and is transformed into explicit bargaining.

Given this distinction, it is important to consider how or when bargaining is likely to become more explicit and formal. This is an extremely important question, because the labor-management literature assumes that an explicit, formal bargaining relationship provides the most effective way both to reduce immediate conflicts and to maintain harmonious relations over time while keeping conflict within acceptable or manageable bounds. From this standpoint, one of the key problems of conflict-resolution is getting parties to recognize each other as legitimate and enter a formal, explicit bargaining relationship. Yet, the explicitness and formality of the bargaining vary substantially across sectors within an organization. For example, committees that contain representatives of different subgroups or coalitions can be construed as bargaining settings, but there is substantial variation in the degree to which parties treat such settings as arenas for explicit bargaining.

Unfortunately, there is little literature on the establishment of explicit bargaining relationships outside of research on unionization. However, Schelling's distinction between tacit and explicit bargaining does suggest a number of basic conditions that facilitate or are necessary for explicit bargaining, and these provide a worthwhile starting point.

Lines of communication. Explicit bargaining implies free-flowing communication, typically face-to-face, allowing coalitions to examine, discuss, debate, and make proposals regarding all areas or issues in the conflict. Tacit bargaining implies that either the opportunities to communicate are constrained by the social setting or the existing opportunities are used ineffectively (to communicate aggression rather than conciliation).

The effect of communication on conflict-resolution is not a simple matter. The common-sense notion that getting the parties to communicate will eventually resolve the conflict is not clearly supported by the social psychological literature. Specifically, that research indicates that the mere opportunity to communicate does not have a consistent effect on conflict-resolution. Sometimes parties use lines of communication to express hostility, instead of conciliation, or simply do not use the lines of communication at all. Furthermore, open lines of communication may be more effective as a preventive than as a corrective measure. Marwell and Schmitt found that there was little conflict in a mixed-motive setting when communication was possible from the beginning to the end of the experiment; when the communication was delayed or was possible only after conflict developed, it did not restore full cooperation. Once conflict is established, therefore, an expansion in communication opportunity is insufficient to produce conciliation.

Overall, it is the content of the communication, not the opportunity to communicate, that is critical. To the extent that coalitions use lines of communication to transmit conciliatory messages, those lines will enhance conflict resolution; if the lines of communication are used for messages of aggression, communication may exacerbate the conflict. In sum, lines of communication are a necessary, but not a sufficient, condition for explicit bargaining. An increase in explicit bargaining requires opportunity plus conciliatory use.

Potential for compromise. Explicit bargaining implies that the issues underlying the conflict allow some room for compromise. In other words, there are intermediate positions or agreements that lie somewhere on a continuum between the preferred positions of the two coalitions.

Tacit bargaining is more likely when there are undeveloped or relatively few intermediate positions, in part because coalitions are likely to perceive the situation as a win/lose choice. To the extent that coalitions can and do identify a range of intermediate positions, explicit bargaining becomes a more attractive alternative. Thus, explicit bargaining should increase with the number of viable intermediate positions between complete winning and complete losing.

Mutual consent. The transformation of tacit to explicit bargaining requires the opening of lines of communication, a willingness to use the communication lines to search for the solution, and the ability to transform or redefine dichotomous win/lose issues into continuums with a number of intermediate positions. These conditions set the stage for an increase in the explicitness of bargaining, but fully developed explicit bargaining also requires a shift in the orientation of the parties. Specifically, it requires that coalitions consent to treat the relationship publicly as a bargaining one and consider the possibility of making concessions.

The conditions that give rise to explicit bargaining make it apparent why explicit bargaining should be a more effective mode of conflict-resolution than tacit bargaining. As noted earlier, merely getting to the bargaining table is often a significant problem for coalitions in conflict. Some of the most basic obstacles to conflict-resolution are related to the tacit/explicit distinction. Issues allowing few intermediate positions, the failure to develop or use communication lines, lack of willingness to recognize the claims of the opposing coalition, or unwillingness to make concessions will render it difficult for coalitions to establish an explicit bargaining relationship.

Furthermore, agreements established through explicit rather than tacit bargaining are likely to be more stable. Tacit agreements are likely to be more ambiguous, nonbinding, and unenforceable in a strict sense. Such agreements can be broken with relative impunity and typically require more trust than is likely to be present under conditions of tacit bargaining. On the other hand, agreements from explicit bargaining tend to be more specific and unambiguous. Unlike tacit agreements, explicit ones are likely to include some safeguards against a breach by either party. These safeguards may be a part of the formal agreement itself or a function of the public character of the negotiations and agreement.

TACTICAL DIMENSION OF BARGAINING

Parties in a bargaining relationship face a delicate tactical issue. Given uncertainty and incomplete information about each other's goals, aspirations, and intentions, they are faced with the task of gaining information about the other's situation while giving little information about their own. Bargaining should be viewed as an information-manipulation game in which parties fake, bluff, lie, and so forth, in an attempt to create certain impressions, to test or evaluate the impressions given by the opposing coalition, and, most important, to assess the resolve or commitment of the opponent. This view places strong emphasis on the cognitive aspects of bargaining.

While this image of bargaining appears to have substantial credibility, it is surprising how little attention has been given to the cognitive features of bargaining.

First of all, conflicting parties do not have complete information about each other's inputs and outputs. Secondly, bargaining nearly always involves heteromorphic exchange, that is, the exchange of qualitatively different commodities. This means that the equivalence of the exchange is inherently indeterminate, and coalitions are likely to disagree with each other regarding the location and criteria for evaluating equity. At best, equity theory provides a very rough, imperfect foundation for predicting the outcome of conflicts in organizations. In the context of limited information and heteromorphic exchange, the bargaining process becomes the major determinant of the bargaining outcome.

We are concerned with the social psychology aspects of bargaining that are generally neglected or assumed away by game theory. Game theorists are typically concerned with situations in which parties have complete information on each other's payoffs at a variety of potential solution points. The precise nature of this complete information assumption varies somewhat across different game-theory models, yet some variant of complete or perfect information remains a key premise underlying nearly all game-theory models. On the other hand, social psychological approaches are more suitable to an organizational analysis, because relations within organizations are unlikely to provide coalitions with such information. Given the ambiguity that characterizes organizational relations, coalitions can only infer the preferences of the opposing coalitions from the actual process of negotiation, and such inferences are inherently tenuous, because deception and manipulation are intrinsic aspects of the political game.

In addition, while game theory would examine how the actual solution (agreement) arrived at by the actors compares with the optimal one (for rational actors) predicted by formal models, the present work is concerned with the maneuvering and influence processes that lead a party to yield more or less. One of the key elements of this influence process is bargaining stance or posture.

Bargaining stance or posture is one of the prime means that parties use to manipulate information and interpret each other's intentions, orientations, and aspirations in the context of ambiguous information on payoffs, subjective utilities, and other factors. In sum, the focus departs from game theory and falls squarely in the social psychological tradition, which is crucial to an understanding of bargaining between coalitions in an organizational context.

If, as the equity theory and game-theory approaches imply, the outcome or result of bargaining is governed by a priori rules (such as equity), the bargaining process is important only with respect to how these rules are applied to the specific issues by the bargainers, and bargaining tactics are of relatively little importance. The only purpose of tactical action would be to prevent a divergence from equity by one side or to retaliate against the other for attempting to force an inequitable settlement. Tactics become merely protective mechanisms for assuring that the equilibrium point specified by equity or game theory is achieved, maintained, or at least approximated in the bargaining. This equilibrium point is essentially the reference point for making tactical decisions.

An alternative approach is implied by Siegel and Fouraker's level-of-aspiration theory. This theory makes no assumptions about an equilibrium point and cannot be used as a means to specify a determinate solution. It implicitly assumes that the outcome of a bargaining encounter is indeterminate, primarily because of the limited information available to the parties and their willingness to use deception and manipulation. In brief, level-of-aspiration theory emphasizes the impression-management aspects of bargaining.

Based on level-of-aspiration theory, the key point to which coalitions will direct their impression-management tactics is each other's *aspirations*. Each coalition in a bargaining setting has an aspiration level, that is, a goal or set of goals about the ultimate agreement, and each coalition will adopt a concession tactic or level based on its aspirations. The most basic assumption of the theory is that each coalition's aspiration level will be inversely related to its concession level: Higher aspirations will produce tougher bargaining. The theory suggests that tactically a coalition can extract more concessions from an opponent by manipulating the opponent's aspirations; and a key way to do this is by creating the impression that it has very high aspirations itself and is irrevocably committed to them. Exhibit 4.6 delineates the dynamics underlying this impression management process. In Exhibit 4.6, A_1 and C_1 represent the aspiration and concession levels of coalition 1; A_2 and C_2 represent the aspirations and concessions of coalition 2. The basic assumptions are that each party's aspirations (A_1 or A_2) will determine their own concessions (C_1 or C_2). The tactical implications are indicated by the links between each party's concessions and the opponent's aspirations, for example, the effect of C_1 on A_2. The key implication is that the tactics (concessions) of each coalition can convey high aspirations for itself and reduce the aspiration level of the other. That is, the effect of one coalition's *aspirations* on the other's *aspirations* is affected by the coalition's concession behavior; similarly, the effect of one coalition's *concessions* on the other's *concessions* is affected by the other's aspiration levels, based on the theory that "it pays to be tough."

To summarize, level-of-aspiration theory stipulates that a bargainer's concessions will affect the opponent's aspirations, which, in turn, will determine the opponent's concessions. Soft tactics in the bargaining, therefore, will raise the opponent's aspiration level and reduce the opponent's yielding, while tough tactics will decrease the opponent's level of aspiration and thereby increase the opponent's yielding. The theory recommends a tough stance in bargaining. The best overall stance is to make no or only very small concessions or conciliatory

EXHIBIT 4.6 Relationship of Aspirations and Concessions

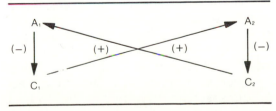

gestures early in the bargaining or until the opponent stops making concessions. Then, relatively small, infrequent conciliatory actions will ostensibly prevent a deadlock while inducing the greatest yield from the opponent.

It is probably evident that the theory is concerned primarily with concession behavior and emphasizes the inferences parties are likely to draw from different patterns or types of concession tactics. However, tactical behavior is not limited to concession behavior; any verbal or nonverbal behavior can convey greater or less toughness. The specific behaviors that connote toughness will vary with the context and the type of bargaining relationship. The important point is that tactics of bargaining can be arrayed on a tough/soft continuum. Furthermore, regardless of whether coalitions group their tactics together or use them singly, and regardless of the nature of the tactic, level-of-aspiration theory indicates that behavior that conveys greater toughness is more likely to increase or maximize the yielding by an opposing coalition.

The basic problem with level-of-aspiration theory is the potential for an impasse. Toughness may indeed work, that is, produce an agreement that distinctly favors the coalition with the tougher posture, but it can also backfire and exacerbate the conflict. There are two interrelated reasons for this. First, as many theorists and researchers in the bargaining field note, bargaining often implies an expectation of reciprocal yielding. To the extent that parties recognize the rights of each other and consent to consider compromise, some reciprocity is likely to be not only expected but also demanded. The salience and strength of these reciprocity expectations should be closely related to the explicitness of the bargaining: greater explicitness should produce more pressure to reciprocate concessions. The failure to live up to these expectations, or a substantial departure from them, should heighten the opponent's inclination to meet toughness with toughness. Second, if

toughness appears too aggressive, it is likely to arouse a loss of face issue. Yielding in response to excessive toughness is tantamount to accepting an inferior status and conveying a willingness to demean oneself, that is, conciliation in response to toughness could produce a loss of face. To avert a loss of face or restore already lost face, a coalition may counter excessive toughness with toughness.

Social psychological research tends to document the risks of following the advice of level-of-aspiration theory strictly. While substantial research indicates that toughness does extract more concessions than softer strategies, other research indicates that the most effective strategy is a tough but conciliatory one. In a review of this literature, Chertkoff and Esser indicate that bargainers must consider the impressions they give not only in terms of toughness but also in terms of reasonableness. The optimum image is toughness moderated by reasonableness. This implies a modification of the practical implications suggested by level-of-aspiration theory. It is important for a coalition to be tough or firm enough to avoid exploitation by others and to demonstrate its resolve while remaining reasonable enough so that opponents feel it has some willingness to resolve the conflict.

Despite the foregoing modification of level-of-aspiration theory, the basic ideas underlying the theory remain sound. Toughness has been found to be effective (1) in the early stages of the bargaining, when parties' aspirations are not fully crystallized and are subject to greater manipulation; (2) when parties have little information on each other's priorities or utilities—the bluffing that is intrinsic to the theory becomes transparent if the opponent has complete information; (3) when parties are not under severe time constraints—sufficient time makes a tough stance less of a surprise and also makes it appear less aggressive; (4) when the user of tough tactics has greater power than the target of toughness. The theory provides a sound starting point for analyzing intercoalition bargaining in organizations just as it provides a foundation for actors making tactical decisions.

From the standpoint of the organization, the major difficulty is that the theory applies only when just one of the coalitions follows its dictates. If both (or all) coalitions adopt tough tactics in bargaining, the likely result is an impasse. If this occurs across a multitude of intercoalition conflicts, the organization could become riddled with many seemingly unresolvable conflicts. Level-of-aspiration theory, therefore, points to a major dilemma for organizations: how to establish structural conditions that encourage coalitions to resolve conflicts effectively. One way to do this, of course, is by the forceful intervention of third parties. However, such efforts can be costly and lead to an expansion of conflicts beyond their prior scope by involving even more coalitions in each conflict. Another approach is to structure the relationship between two coalitions so that conflict will be resolved by the parties themselves before it becomes too damaging to the organization as a whole.

The latter approach implies that the organization or its representatives create conditions that minimize the toughness of the tactics adopted by conflicting coalitions. Based on our earlier discussion of bargaining relationships, one possibility is to move the bargaining relationship in the direction of an explicit integrative one. Any shift toward explicit or integrative bargaining should reduce the use of tough tactics in the bargaining. This may be a major reason why explicit integrative relationships produce the greatest likelihood of conflict-resolution.

The conditions under which toughness is more or less effective also have implications for minimizing impasses in organizational contexts. First of all, time limits will inhibit toughness, because coalitions will have less room to maneuver and should foresee the deleterious effects of tough tactics. In an organizational context, outside parties or subgroups (such as superiors) can apply

time pressure by establishing explicit time limits. Another approach is to pressure one or more of the conflicting coalitions to accomplish other tasks that just happen to be contingent on quick and effective resolution of the conflict.

Aside from setting time constraints, the organization or its representatives may manipulate the availability and flow of information between conflicting coalitions. Simply requiring more information exchange could enable both coalitions to infer each other's intentions, aspirations, and so forth more accurately and confidently. Such information would enable both parties to identify deception and bluffs more clearly and would thereby inhibit the inclination of the coalitions to maintain tough tactics. The information issue is very complex, however. The organization must consider the type of information, how it is communicated, from whom it comes, and other aspects of it. In addition, a coalition or subgroup could undermine their areas of control within the organization if they released information that serves as one basis for regulation of an opposing coalition's activities.

Finally, an organization might mitigate impasses by creating conditions of mutual dependence between key coalitions within it. Dependence is a major dimension of power, and it affects the costs of not reaching agreement. When a coalition has only minimal or narrow dependence on its opponent, it can adopt and maintain a tough stance in bargaining. In this context, the basic dilemma of bargaining (to yield as little as possible but still reach agreement) is less of a dilemma. The optimum stance for a coalition with little dependence on its opponent is to maintain toughness and see what the opponent does. If the opponent yields substantially, then conflict-resolution may produce more benefit (or fewer costs) than an impasse; otherwise, an impasse might be perceived as the best option. High levels of mutual dependence, on the other hand, should make it difficult for coalitions to maintain toughness over time as the prospect of an impasse becomes more real. The bargaining dilemma is increased when there are higher levels of dependence because an impasse entails significant costs.

Thus, one way to alter the costs of an impasse to the coalitions is to alter their dependence or interdependence.

■ Managing Organizational Conflict

C. BROOKLYN DERR

Conflicts are normal and natural consequences of human interaction in organizational settings. But they are also complex. Conflicts may occur for multiple reasons, for example, internal stress coming from the person and overlapping into the workplace, incompatible expectations among workers and work groups, differences over task procedures, values, orientations, and desired outcomes, increasing interdependencies and work loads, and external pressures and crises. This is an article for conflict managers who want to try a variety of methods to manage serious disputes that may have multiple and complex causes. A contingency approach to conflict management is suggested to provide managers with a conceptual framework for knowing what to do when.

This article emphasizes the costs and feasibility issues of successful conflict management implementation. While others emphasize either the desirability of a particular mode of dispute settlement or an optimal level of conflict, this contingency approach stresses the realistic constraints and complexities that are important for practical and workable conflict management methods.

THREE CONFLICT MANAGEMENT MODES

This article focuses on three major conflict management modes from which one can draw to formulate a situational theory. These are collaboration, bargaining, and power-play. Walton has already outlined the differences between collaboration and bargaining approaches. Exhibit 4.7 presents a modification of his ideas, with the addition of power-play, which serves to contrast the three conflict management approaches. Tabular schemes such as that in Exhibit 4.7 inevitably fail to account for overlaps. In reality, much of what is listed as collaboration also occurs in bargaining, and power-play also overlaps with bargaining. The exhibit does serve to highlight basic differences, however.

None of these three conflict modes is appropriate for every contingency; neither is any one used without consequence. Following is a brief description of each mode with its possible cost, benefits, and requirements.

Collaboration

Collaborative theory maintains that people should surface their differences (get them out in the open) and then work on the prob-

EXHIBIT 4.7 Conflict Management Characteristics: Collaboration, Bargaining, Power-Play

Characteristic	Collaboration	Bargaining	Power-Play
Overall Objective	1. Seeking win/win position	1. Seeking compromise or win/lose position	1. Seeking win/lose
Strategic Objective	2. Emphasis on problem-solving conflicts and using energy effectively	2. Emphasis on inducing and using conflicts for better bargaining positions	2. Emphasis on coping with and using conflicts to better one's power position
Assumptions about People	3. People are open, honest, trusting, collaborative	3. People are united in the face of a common good	3. People act primarily in own self-interest
Type of Settlement	4. Psychological contracts	4. Legal contracts	4. Informal or unstated contracts
Individual's Relationship to Organization	5. Overall improvement orientation for the common good	5. Purposeful in pursuing goals of the group	5. Pure self-interest with a sense of limits
Efficiency/ Effectiveness	6. Effective but inefficient use of conflict energy	6. Periodically ineffective and inefficient use of energy	6. Efficient but ineffective use of energy
Information Use	7. Information openly shared	7. Information strategically shared	7. Secrecy or distortion
Problem-Solving Mechanism	8. Joint problem-solving	8. Trade-offs on positions to which there is apparent commitment	8. Unilateral, reciprocal manipulations to maximize self-interests
Power Relationship	9. Power parity	9. Struggle for parity	9. Power inequalities accepted
Parties' Support of Organizational Decisions	10. Voluntary (Internal commitment)	10. Voluntary support (Legal agreement)	10. Contractual support (Free to subvert)

lems until they have attained mutually satisfactory solutions. The approach assumes the people will be motivated to expend the time and energy for such problem-solving activity. It tries to maximize the possible mutual gains of the parties in the dispute and views the conflict as a creative force pushing them to achieve an improved state of affairs to which both sides are fully committed. Information is openly and willingly exchanged. When the parties stagnate because they are too close to the situation to perceive viable alternatives or are too protective of their own positions, a third-party consultant may be used to help clarify the problem, sharpen the issues, find commonalities, and, in general, help them to discover a win/win position.

Essentially, the collaborationists argue that theirs is the most preferred strategy for the good of the enterprise because: (1) open and honest interaction promotes authentic interpersonal relations; (2) conflict is used as a creative force for innovation and improvement; (3) this process enhances feedback and information flow; and (4) the solving of disputes has a way of improving the climate of the organization so that there is more openness, trust, risk-taking, and feelings of integrity.

In my consulting experience, however, I have found that collaboration is not always useful or feasible. Collaboration seems best employed when there is a combination of factors that assures the method some reasonable degree of success. Four major conditions help to determine the practicality of the collaborative mode.

First, a moderately high degree of *required interdependence* is important to force parties to expend the time and energy necessary to work out their differences.

Openly confronting the issues is hard work and not likely to occur unless there is a long-term stake in developing and preserving the relationship.

Second, seeking collaborative solutions to conflicts involves more than simply acting together in various roles to accomplish a task and reach an objective. It also requires feeling free enough to interact openly, including conflicting, in the collaborative relationship. A kind of *power parity* must exist that allows the parties to feel free to interact candidly and to use all their resources to further their beliefs and concerns (regardless of their superior/subordinate status).

Third, there must be potential for *mutual benefits* as a result of solving the specific dispute. The person or group in conflict should "feel" a need that leads to a desire to work on the issue. This is related to the two requisites cited above. But in addition to a compelling reason and feeling enough parity to be able to collaborate, the parties themselves must perceive some significant motivation concerning the issue at hand. Their motivation often depends on whether the mutual gains are self-evident.

When there is required interdependence, power parity, and a felt need provoking the will to engage in the process, the fourth factor comes into play. It is the extent to which there is *organizational support* for such behavior. Considerable organizational resources are needed to effectively manage conflict using the collaborative strategy. Such a program often requires a commitment of time, money, and energy. For example, the organization (including top executives) should engage in a collaborative mode systemwide, so that the norms, rewards, and punishments of the enterprise will encourage such behavior. Most people are unaccustomed to open disagreement, especially with someone of higher organizational rank, and need assurance that such behavior will not draw reprisals.

To confront one another effectively and emerge having resolved a problem also requires numerous personal skills. Learning how to communicate effectively, how to synchronize the process, when and how to use a third party, how to engage in effective problem-solving, and how to keep the tension level moderate for optimal results requires skills that can be taught but may not have already been learned. Indeed, many organizations would view such constructive openness as deviant. The enterprise should be sufficiently committed to fund training for building skills to manage conflicts via collaboration.

Thus, it has become apparent to me that the implementation of collaboration is often either infeasible (that is, the right conditions do not exist for it to work) or too costly to be justifiable. Accordingly, it becomes important to reexamine other alternative modes from the viewpoint of their benefits, costs, and feasibilities as they are related to the desired outcomes.

Power-Play

Collaborationists often view power-play as diametrically opposed to their own values and theory. Power-play, they say, will harm both the individual and the enterprise. They argue that it: (1) unleashes aggressive behaviors and hostile feelings between those involved in the power struggle, shutting off communication and interaction; (2) promotes vicious gossip, which in turn distorts the valid information needed to manage successfully; (3) drives needed information underground, where it is not used for feedback and learning from experience; (4) sometimes subverts the corporate mission through acts of sabotage and non-compliance; and (5) displaces goals because much of the energy employed in the power struggle is diverted from more productive purposes—in fact, winning the struggle can become a more important end than achieving an organizational goal.

Much of the fear of power-play is connected with what Rapoport calls the "cataclysmic" view of conflict—that power struggles are necessarily unmanageable, irrational, and destructive. Although some escalated power struggles fit this description, Rapoport reminds us that the use of power strategies is often "strategic"—characterized by both rational self-interest and control.

Four sets of considerations suggest that power-play is an appropriate method of conflict management in many situations. First, there is a view of individuals that says that *they act first and foremost in their own self-interest* and play an active power game to protect that interest. This view is growing in popularity, reflected in the increased frequency of books on power in both the professional and popular literature. Many people perceive that they can win more by competing than by collaborating. Or, they do not feel comfortable or skilled at problem-solving, while they may feel particularly good, given their social experience, at power-play. Additionally, some individuals have primary outside-the-organization interests and do not want to be highly involved in or committed to their work; hence it is not in their interest to get highly involved in collaborating.

Individuals typically play one or a combination of three different power games that strive for different types of power.

■ *Authority* is the power that is delegated by the organization to the holder of a certain position. Formal authority results in the ability to use rewards, punishments, and other organizational resources in order to impact on persons and to affect behavior. Much has been written about positional power or authority.

■ *Informal influence* is normally defined as being able to affect behavior or gain compliance without holding a position of authority. Not everyone in authority has influence. Some persons have little or no authority but much influence. Some have influence far greater than that normally associated with their official role. It is possible to become influential in the enterprise without necessarily ascending the formal hierarchy.

■ *Autonomy*. Unlike the other power intents described above, autonomy power derives from the need to be in control of one-self and to minimize unwanted influence by others. It is manifested in one's ability to resist formal authority (control) and informal influence (normative demands) and to have ample "space" to accomplish prescribed ends using unrestricted means. Highly trained professionals, for example, seek autonomy, are little supervised, and are accountable for the quality of their end products (such as a surgical operation, a scholarly book, an architectural plan).

Individuals who strive for autonomy power may be very interested in building and protecting a piece of organizational territory. They try to become indispensable so they will be the experts, have the information, and hold unquestioned power. Autonomy-oriented persons may also have extraorganizational interests (such as a civic or religious organization) or parallel organizational interests (such as a professional association) and wish to remain "free" from organizational commitments or constraints in order to devote more time to those activities.

Power-play, it is hypothesized, will be the dominant conflict-management strategy for those who seek autonomy. It has been pointed out elsewhere that it is unpolitical in organizations to appear uncooperative and "anti-system." One must appear to act in the best interest of the enterprise. Those endeavors that are most self-interest-oriented, in which the interests of the worker and the organization are least congruent, require the most covert means. To be discovered as being aloof or free from the rules could cause a very negative, career-damaging impression. Autonomy is an unpopular intent in most organizations because marginality is discouraged and total commitment is rewarded. Power-play is a secretive mode that could work in the best interests of those whose covert objective is autonomy and whose desired impression is that of being committed. In contrast, collaboration requires the open sharing of personal intents and of preferred means for achieving them in the process of finding a mutually satisfactory solution.

A second set of arguments for power-play centers on the strategic reality that collaborating can increase one's vulnerability in competitive external environments. There are significant aspects of conflict of interest between firms that transact business directly or compete for resources, just as there are aspects of conflict of interest between managers within a firm over promotion and resources. Collaboration, and even bargaining, assumes the *exchange of information* necessary to resolve a problem. This information may apprise competitors of weaknesses and give them an unfair advantage. For example, disclosing strategic information (a key power-play resource) might provide another organization with data for increasing its efficiency, and therefore its competitive advantage.

Third, in some situations power-play strategies can contribute to the *joint welfare* of two adversary parties. Under conditions of routine and certainty, for example, the self-interests of the individual and the enterprise may be incompatible to a considerable degree. To maximize its objectives, the enterprise may tend to increase its efficiency through elaborate planning and control systems. The employees may likewise attempt to improve their working conditions through inclusive union contracts. In this way, power-play is the mechanism of flexibility used by both sides to cope within the confines of the rules (which are never so tightly delineated as to disallow some manipulation). Employees can use power-play to resist machine-like control; employers can use power-play to cope with union contracts during periods of uncertainty (such as rearranging work and calling for a common response to a crisis). Under this procedure, there exists a sort of dynamic equilibrium that works to the advantage of both within the rules. It is the dynamic interaction of finding compatible self-interests that is the substance of power-play conflict management. Such a mode allows multiple motives and various methods to eventually find a satisfactory equilibrium. Some activities are temporarily blocked as the power struggles are waged. Yet these are normally periods of realignment, reform, and adjustment. In the long term, they may be effective ways to manage differences for the greatest number of persons and for the enterprise.

Fourth, power-play is often best suited to decide *ideological disputes*. When values or philosophies clash, the parties are usually intransigent in their conflicting positions. They refuse to problem-solve or even to negotiate. The only recourse is for one to try to win at the expense of the other, and although neither may emerge victorious, both may emerge saving some face and being "right" for having taken their stand.

Bargaining

While neither party may emerge completely satisfied and one party may be clearly dissatisfied under this mode, both will at least come to terms openly about how to best resolve the most immediate issues. Bargaining can be a more or less elaborate mode of conflict management depending on the situation (from interpersonal trading to collective negotiation). The important point is that, like collaboration, a common solution to a problem can be found. The actual act of trading and compromise highlights the assumed strength and influence of each party. In this process, the power position of each side is clearly defined in direct ratio to the information it reveals to the other, the concessions it makes, the punishment or penalties it can impose.

Bargaining, while remaining unique, contains elements that overlap with both collaboration and power. It resembles the collaborative process because it is a systematic method that, in some of its forms, allows for collaboration between negotiators. Bargaining also contains many aspects of the strategic win/lose power struggles more typical in power-play. Exhibit 4.8 illustrates this point. Bargaining, therefore, can be viewed as a connecting bridge between the collaborative and power strategies of conflict management.

Bargaining employs some of the methods, values, and motivational forces used in each

EXHIBIT 4.8   Relationship Among Strategies

Collaboration
- shared information (open)
- requires consensus
- collaborative ethic
- power parity assumed
- theory and method explicit
- voluntary organizational support
- win/win

Bargaining
- shared information (strategic)
- requires agreement
- often collaborative between
  negotiators
- theory and method is explicit
- -
- adversary ethic (initially)
- self-interest assumed
- forced organizational support
- compromise, win/lose

Power-Play
- adversary ethic
- self-interest assumed
- no organizational support
- strategic use of information
- win/lose
- power-oriented ethic
- recognized power inequalities
- theory and method intuitive

of the other modes. Bargaining is therefore a middle-ground orientation in which both power-players and collaborationists may feel somewhat comfortable. There is little hope that a power-player and a collaborationist could deal effectively with one another while using their own incongruent approaches. Bargaining can serve to neutralize the values of conflict managers so that they do not impose one set of assumptions (such as collaboration) on a very different situation (such as power-play). In the Organization Development movement, for example, many instances of failure have been reported when collaborative values and methods of dispute settlement were superimposed on power settings. It is proposed herein that bargaining would have better matched the intervention situation.

Bargaining might also be viewed as an intervention bridge to either elevate a stalemated power-play situation from a covert "lose/lose" condition to a situation in which

both parties have at least made an explicit—albeit "hard" or power-based—agreement in their mutual interest. Or, using this bridge concept, it is a realistic alternative to fall back on when the conditions are not present for collaboration. Exhibit 4.9 illustrates this last point.

Those who favor the collaborative approach would argue that bargaining is of limited value because (1) it often creates new interpersonal-organizational conflicts by virtue of the win/lose strategies employed; (2) the commitments to resolutions adopted are formal (based on having to prove that an agreement has been violated) rather than intrinsic and are therefore often carried out only according to the letter of the law; and (3) no more than one, perhaps neither, of the parties emerges fully satisfied.

On the other hand, bargaining seems to work well in many situations. In addition to its middle-ground value, it is, for example, a good way to establish *power parity* so that more collaboration can follow. Just getting into a trading position assumes some equality, as each side recognizes that the other has something of value to offer or withhold.

Additionally, scarce resources can often be bargained according to the strategies of important interest groups, whereas they are not easily distributed using the collaborative method. Bargaining trade-offs, where some win and some lose according to a criterion

EXHIBIT 4.9   An Intervention Bridge

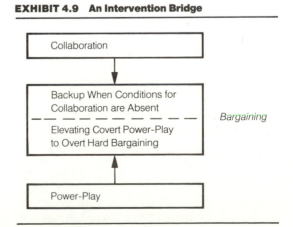

Collaboration

Backup When Conditions for
Collaboration are Absent
- - - - - - - - - - - - - - - -
Elevating Covert Power-Play
to Overt Hard Bargaining

Bargaining

Power-Play

of importance, seem optimally suited *to deal with conditions of scarcity*.

Some persons or groups also feel skillful at and comfortable with bargaining. It fits their *personal style*. Finally, bargaining is somewhat *economical* in that parties meet only periodically to review the old contract and to recontract.

CONCLUSIONS

It is assumed that a wide variety of organizational conflicts will occur quite naturally. Many of them will promote creative tensions that lead to system improvement. Some will serve the interests of various parties and groups without disrupting the organization itself. Others will be of such import that they must be effectively managed.

This article attempts to make the point that there is no one-best-way to manage organizational conflicts. The collaborative approach has been in vogue during the past few years but has proven inadequate on numerous occasions. This article has outlined three very different modes, one of which (power-play) is in sharp contrast with collaboration but optimal under some conditions.

In considering the use of these three modes, it is vital to separate our appreciation of organizational realities from the humanistic and sometimes utopian values that have affected the field. Conflict modes must be tailored to the actual motives, issues, and organizational circumstances of the conflict parties. Inappropriate application of collaboration or other modes by a conflict manager, however well intentioned, is apt to be ineffective at best—and destructive to one or both parties or to the organization at worst.

The following conclusions have been drawn:

■ Collaboration may be best employed when work relationships, which must be interdependent, would be substantially damaged by a given unresolved conflict, when the parties in conflict can openly confront

their differences and state their preferences without fear of reprisal (there exists power parity in the relationship), when there is evident mutual interest in solving the dispute, and when the organization supports the open surfacing and working of disagreements.

■ Bargaining seems to work best to establish power parity (usually between competing people or groups), as a means of distributing scarce resources, and as a somewhat efficient option for achieving a formal agreement to a common dispute. Bargaining may also be the most effective way to manage a dispute between two parties who each use one of the two other modes (collaboration, power-play) and are, therefore, unable to reach a common solution due to the disparity between them. Bargaining is often a midway or bridge strategy.

■ Power-play, on the other hand, is an important way to cope with conflicts for the autonomous, advantages those who are most adept at this mode, is a means for achieving a dynamic balance of competing forces, and is often the only feasible way to resolve ideological disputes.

Of these three modes, there is perhaps the greatest need to know more about power-play. Very few empirical studies document the dynamics of power-play. One major problem has been to find an appropriate method for studying it. Since information is power and power is secretive, few will divulge their power game to researchers. Also, being "political" or "selfish" is usually a negative organizational image that requires covert rather than overt methods of power-play, and an objective is to not be discovered and badly viewed. However, it is also very probable that the collaborative ethic in our field has discouraged research efforts on the uses of power-play in organizations, despite the fact that it appears to be the method most frequently used to resolve a number of kinds of differences. It is clear that more accurate descriptive theories of conflict management will require more extensive studies of the realities of power-play.

Management Practice

■ The 4 Horsemen

The four-way takeover battle launched with Bendix Corp.'s unfriendly offer for Martin Marietta Corp. has come to be dominated by the very different personalities of the four major executives involved.

Participants and observers say individual cunning, determination, and, above all, personal egos—rather than business or financial considerations—play a striking role in the takeover fight, which has grown to include Allied Corp. and United Technologies Corp. and at one time spawned seven simultaneous court actions.

"Believe me, this one was Original Amateur Hour," says one disgusted investment banker involved in the battle. He charges that the companies committed basic errors such as bidding against themselves, neglecting to remember and meet crucial deadlines, and failing to think out moves adequately before plunging in. Other Wall Street takeover experts also complain bitterly that the executives let personal considerations overshadow sound business judgment.

Much Sharp Criticism

"The underlying story," says a businessman who is a former Bendix director, "is that this epic struggle involving four big companies and more than four investment bankers and hordes of lawyers is not about economics, is not about using assets wisely, is not about economic growth. It's a struggle between a few ambitious men."

This businessman particularly singles out William M. Agee, the chairman and chief executive officer of Bendix, whom he describes as "a guy who isn't building a company that will contribute to the economy, who is maneuvering for his own personal glory."

Another former Bendix director says of Agee, "He has a big ego problem. He got into this thing, and now he's doing everything he can to get out of it with his ego intact."

Asked for comment, Agee replies that he is "proud of every decision I have made" throughout the takeover fight, and although he acknowledges that there are things he could have done differently, he says that on the whole he is "very pleased with the end product." He adds, "People who have leadership roles have to have a certain amount of ego and a certain amount of balance and a certain amount of courage. Obviously, I, like others in similar positions, have an ego. But I worry constantly about how I use it and that I not abuse it. People who have very big egos tend to abuse it."

Eager Shopper

Armed with Bendix's cash hoard and a big line of credit, Mr. Agee has long been eager to make a major acquisition. For some years, Bendix strategies had been drawing up "hit lists" of target companies. Marietta's name began turning up on these lists, Bendix insiders say, during the tenure of Mary Cunningham as Bendix's chief strategic planner. Miss Cunningham, who left Bendix amid rumors of possible romantic links with Agee, later married her former boss and now works as a Seagram Co. executive.

Despite her new job, Cunningham was one of her husband's main advisers at crucial moments in the Marietta takeover fight. She was present at negotiations between top Bendix and Marietta executives earlier this week, and she was active in advising the Bendix camp in strategy huddles during those sessions. "Agee depends on her counsel to a really remarkable degree," says a takeover adviser who has seen them together in numerous business situations.

Agee's overtures to Martin Marietta began before the Aug. 25 announcement of the $43-a-share tender offer. A Bendix adviser says Mr. Agee "made at least two overtures to Martin Marietta" and its president, Thomas Pownall, but "both were rebuffed." The adviser says Agee tried to telephone Pownall "as a courtesy" a few minutes before the hand-delivered notification of the tender offer arrived at Marietta's headquarters in Bethesda, Md., but Pownall, having "a pretty good idea what the call was about," refused to take it, the adviser adds.

Determined Fighter

That isn't untypical of Pownall's style, acquaintances say. Always determined to keep Marietta independent, Pownall is said to be particularly leery of Bendix because of his perception of Mr. Agee's personality and methods.

Pownall is described by one friend as "the business equivalent of urbane" but also stubborn once he makes up his mind. Another friend, a Marietta director since 1967, says Pownall's strong personality earns loyalty among the company's employees.

This director cites a recent incident in the thick of the fight with Bendix. Pownall, the director says, "made a little talk on a tape and sent it around to the company's major

installations" for employees to hear. The director says employees in a company plant in Denver who heard the tape told him "the experience was like being at a football game. For the last three or four minutes of the tape, it was getting so noisy it was hard to hear because people were cheering and applauding Pownall."

The personality differences between Mr. Agee and Mr. Pownall deeply affected the two men's strategies.

Pownall adopted the currently popular "Pac-Man" defense, which, in this case, involved a rival takeover bid for Bendix. He later enlisted United Technologies Corp. as an ally, but not in the usual role of a "white knight," which would buy his company at a higher price. Instead, United Technologies began a separate bid for Bendix.

Bendix's most crucial mistake, says Martin A. Siegel of Kidder, Peabody & Co., an investment-banking firm that represented Marietta, "was in coming after Marietta in the first place. They critically misjudged the Marietta board's willingness to fight."

As a result of that misjudgment—the first of several by Agee—the Bendix chief executive suddenly found himself faced with two tough, experienced rivals, Pownall and Harry Gray of United Technologies. Mr. Gray, who masterminded acquisition after acquisition to build United into a $14-billion conglomerate, is one of the most feared takeover fighters.

Gray saw an opportunity to take a big step toward his goal of making United a $20-billion company before he retires. Because of the structure of the complicated deal, investment bankers say, Gray stood to take over Bendix or, at the very least, to gain more than $100 million in cash for his company without much risk.

As the battle intensified, Agee, Pownall, or their aides huddled periodically to try to reach a settlement. Again, Marietta's tenacity was crucial. "We'd begin by agreeing what a mess we'd got ourselves into," says an investment banker on the Bendix team, "but it was always [Marietta's] position that we'd started it."

With no settlement possible, the executives headed toward the intolerable situation of each owning a big chunk of the other's stock. Bendix's offer became effective first, and the company proceeded to buy 70 percent of Martin Marietta's shares. But, says a Marietta adviser, by buying those shares Agee "pulled the trigger and shot himself in the foot."

The Bendix purchase made Marietta determined to buy as much of Bendix as it could when its offer became effective Wednesday night, before Bendix could use its 70 percent stake to oust Marietta's board. Marietta bought nearly half of Bendix. Faced with a possible stalemate dragging on in the courts for years and sapping his company of cash, Agee turned to a new ally, Allied Corp.

Merger Announcement

Last Wednesday, just before Marietta bought its shares in Bendix, Allied announced it was planning a merger with Bendix, under terms of which Bendix would become an Allied subsidiary, and Mr. Agee would become president—and No. 2 man—of Allied.

The attractions of the fight for Allied and its chairman, Edward L. Hennessy, Jr., are many. Allied has tried and failed in several publicized merger attempts in recent years. They "needed to do a deal," an investment banker says, lest they gain an image as the constantly frustrated suitor.

And for Mr. Hennessy, there was another, perhaps sweeter temptation—an opportunity to gain a measure of revenge from an old adversary, Gray of United Technologies. From 1972 to 1979, Hennessy worked for Mr. Gray as senior vice-president for finance and administration and later executive vice-president at United. He was once considered Gray's likely successor as chairman.

But both men have big egos, colleagues say, and they clashed repeatedly. Hennessy often privately took credit for many of United's spectacular string of acquisitions,

including Otis Elevator and Carrier, the air-conditioning company—the very acquisitions of which Gray is so proud. "In Ed's view, Ed put those deals together," an associate of Hennessy's says.

Personal Differences

There were also personal differences. Hennessy, a former Roman Catholic seminarian, is involved in raising scholarship funds for church schools and is still married to his first wife. Gray has been divorced twice and recently married for the third time.

Gray's style is said to have soured the relationship with Hennessy. And at the office Gray was said to be getting close to firing Hennessy just before Hennessy left to join Allied in 1979. "The two were fast approaching a knock-down, drag-out fight," says an observer who worked for both men.

"There wasn't any love lost between [them], and it was only a question of time before they met in the merger wars," a Wall Street analyst says. That happened last week, when, at Agee's request, Mr. Hennessy began considering a merger with Bendix. In addition to wanting Bendix's aerospace business, Hennessy relished the opportunity to beat Gray in a merger fight, associates say.

From Agee's point of view, however, the proposed merger with Allied is far from ideal. Although he would become president of a mammoth company, gain financially under the merger terms, and, less important, wouldn't have to commute between his job in Detroit and his wife's in New York, there's more than a hint of sadness in the proposed outcome.

Broken Dream?

"His dream and Mary's for the past couple of years was to build Bendix into a high-technology company through acquisitions," a takeover expert says. "It's too bad they've become a scalp on somebody else's belt instead."

But it could have been worse, says a former Bendix director. "Being the president of a big company and the chairman of one of its subsidiaries isn't as good as being the chairman of an independent company, but it's a hell of a lot better than being acquired [by Marietta] and being flushed down the drain."

Agee replies, "I have said all my business life that I would act to maximize shareholder value before I would do anything as far as the maintenance of management positions" is concerned. "I have said in speeches that I'm not respectful at all of managements who will go to unreasonable lengths to protect their own positions in the company." He adds that he has "felt very strongly from the very beginning that I would try my very best never to make a decision that would be at the significant . . . expense of the company and at the same time for the greater enhancement of myself individually."

There is a possibility, some observers say, that the strong egos of Hennessy at Allied and his potential new president, Mr. Agee, will soon clash. Both men are known as strong-willed executives, and Mr. Hennessy hasn't been in a hurry to name an eventual successor. "Frankly, I'd be surprised if [Agee] is still [at Allied] two years from now," a Wall Street merger specialist says. An associate of both men adds, "I really doubt that, after this latest fiasco, Hennessy is going to let Agee make a lot of decisions about acquisition strategy."

Agee says that "if that does transpire—I become a No. 2 person or a No. 3 person of whatever it may be in another organization—my job will be to serve those shareholders so long as I feel I have a contribution to make." He also says he rejected the Martin Marietta and United Technologies offers partly because "their strategy was to totally dismember the corporation. I didn't want to see Bendix dismembered. We have 60,000 people who are outstanding employees."

However, Agee may well have lost the support of some formerly loyal employees.

On Monday, they had celebrated "Unity Day" with rallies at Bendix plants around the country to demonstrate their support for the boss. "If you gave a Unity Day celebration today, no one would show up," says Virginia Hanadel, a word-processor operator at Bendix headquarters. "The mood around here is unbelievably depressing. Everyone thinks that Agee just sold us right down the river."

An organizer of the Unity Day celebration in Southfield, Michigan, showed up for work in a black mourning dress. On Unity Day, she had worn red, white, and blue.

Three Alleged Errors

Acquisition experts say Agee probably made three major errors, apart from possibly picking the wrong target.

The first occurred early this month. Worried that perhaps he hadn't bid high enough to lure Marietta stock, he raised his bid from $43 a share to $48. But because nobody else was bidding for Marietta at that time, he was in the position of bidding against himself.

The second error occurred at an eleventh-hour negotiating session earlier this week in Bethesda, where Agee and Pownall were trying to make peace. The fact that Agee brought Cunningham to the session as an adviser "infuriated the guys at Marietta," according to a Wall Street banker who later spoke to Marietta directors. "Just the thought of losing their company to a guy who is being advised or guided by Mary Cunningham was more than they could stand," the banker says.

The third error occurred Wednesday, as the midnight deadline approached for Marietta's purchase of Bendix stock. Under federal law, if Allied and Bendix had been prepared to make a formal offer on Wednesday, Marietta couldn't have bought the shares for ten days—thus giving Bendix breathing room.

But, say sources close to the negotiations, Mr. Agee didn't agree to the deal until midday Wednesday, after having explored various other options. That didn't leave enough time for the board to consider the merger, and for the appropriate documents to be prepared and filed. Bendix missed the deadline, and Marietta was able to buy nearly half of Bendix early yesterday morning.

Four Directors Quit

The rushed decision-making Wednesday also cost Agee and Bendix four outside directors. William P. Tavoulareas, president of Mobil Corp. and one of the Bendix directors who quit, is said to have raised a number of questions about the proposed transaction and to have objected to Agee's demand for a quick decision. In addition to Tavoulareas, the other directors who quit over the matter were Wilbur J. Cohen, Donald H. Rumsfeld, and Hugo E.R.

Uyterhoeven. None of them could be reached for comment.

Robert W. Purcell, a retired business adviser who quit the Bendix board last year saying he had "lost confidence" in the company's management, calls the quick Allied deal "desperation" on Agee's part. Purcell says the complex deal to, in effect, sell the company popped up without any study. "I applaud the directors who quit," he says. "They should have quit earlier." Adds Purcell, "It's a dreadful thing that's happening. Who's paying attention to the business" at Bendix?

Indeed, many are wondering who was minding the store at all four of the companies involved in the continuing fight. But one Wall Street analyst says that, given the egos involved, it isn't really that surprising: "It isn't very often that corporate executives get a chance to strut in the glare of publicity," and besides, takeover battles tend to distract from nagging problems like the recession.

■ Saint Vincent's Hospital

St. Vincent's Hospital serves the northern outskirts of a large metropolitan area. The hospital's recent request for a rate increase was rejected by the state's hospital board primarily because some patients had complained about the inadequate service offered by the hospital. Many of the complaints were aimed at nursing care. The nursing department, headed by the director of nursing, is made up of two subunits: Reg-

istered Nurses (RNs) and Licensed Practical Nurses (LPNs). The nurses are assigned by the director of nursing to various stations on the six floors of the hospital for each of three shifts.

Each station has a supervising nurse who is in most cases an RN. Both the RNs and LPNs assigned to each station report to the supervising nurse. While there are enough LPNs for each station, there is a shortage of

RNs. At some of the stations the only RN on duty is the supervising nurse.

According to hospital procedure, the RNs are supposed to receive orders from the attending physicians concerning medication and therapy for patients, obtain medicines, therapeutic supplies, and devices from the pharmacy, prepare them for use, and oversee the LPNs who help in administering the medication and/or therapy. Since some stations are understaffed in terms of RNs, the LPNs often help by performing some of the RN functions. For example, LPNs often go to the pharmacy to obtain medicines and other therapeutic supplies, while the RNs are occupied with patient treatment. On some occasions, LPNs take the physician's orders concerning patient care, medicines, special diets, time schedules for administering medicines, etc.

This type of cooperation had been going on for many years until recently when some of the LPNs refused to do any of the RNs' work. These LPNs felt that hospital policy on such factors as work schedules, parking privileges, and work breaks was too preferential and favored the RNs. RNs had the privilege of making work schedule changes to fit personal needs. The RNs were permitted flexible time scheduling as long as the work schedule provided the proper coverage at all times. For example, if three RNs working on successive shifts agreed to begin each shift one-half hour after the regular starting time, thus changing the shift starting times to 8:30 A.M., 4:30 P.M., and 12:30 A.M., it was permitted for RNs but not for LPNs.

LPNs also claimed that RNs were given preferred parking locations, while LPNs were required to park in the lot farthest from the hospital—a parking lot that was not paved and was poorly lighted.

The LPNs complained to the director of nursing, but the director indicated that these privileges had existed for several years and were designed to recognize the more professional nature of the RN's job. Since the nurses were not unionized, the LPNs felt that the only recourse they had was to perform their duties exactly as hospital procedures were developed until a union could be organized. Moreover, many LPNs had begun to express some concern over the legality of their performing the RNs' tasks, since they were not given the same professional training. As a result, some LPNs refused to go to the pharmacy for the RNs to obtain medicines and/or other therapy supplies. RNs now are taking time away from patient treatment to run errands like going to the pharmacy to get medicines.

Supervising nurses made attempts to get LPNs to help the RNs, but the LPNs refused to do work that was not included in their explicit training and hospital procedure. Consequently, RNs waste much time in doing work that could be done by LPNs at the expense of reducing the quality of patient care. This "play it by the rules" tactic has created additional friction between the physicians and nurses. Physicians complain that they waste too much of their time waiting and looking for RNs to give them new orders on patient care and treatment.

The pressure from the physicians caused the RNs to complain to the director of nursing about understaffing. Supervising nurses are demanding the employment of more RNs. The hospital administrator claims that since the state hospital board refused the requested rate increase, the budget does not have any funds in it to hire more RNs.

The ill feelings existing among nurses, between nurses and physicians, and between the director of nursing and the hospital administrators are resulting in a reduction of the quality of patient care and treatment as well as a loss of morale.

■ The Loyalty Mystique at IBM

At IBM, the rules and discipline, stiff white collars and gray suits, and positive attitudes and loyalty appeared to be waning after the death of Thomas J. Watson, Jr., in 1956. The Watson legacy of proper decorum and behavior is still alive and strong at International Business Machines Corporation, but marrying it to contemporary mores and norms does create some anachronisms.

Take the case of a California IBMer who insisted on wearing his three-piece suit in a hot tub instead of swimwear or a birthday suit. IBM seems to be concerned with more than making computer innovations and sales for it succeeds in socializing its employees with respect to their behavior, appearance, and attitudes even after hours. A person employed by the firm is a full time IBMer. This is poignantly reflected in a recent witness-stand exchange in San Francisco involving an IBM employee concerning an after-hours liaison with a competitor:

Question: "Were you in the hot tub with the XYZ regional manager?"
Answer: "Yes, the party adjourned to a hot tub, but fully clothed, I would add."

Adherence to propriety and decorum is based on Watson's fundamental principle: Employees must embrace the value of loyalty and fidelity to IBM in all matters, big and small. For Watson this was not just lip service to the IBM ethic, for he insisted on so-cializing employees from beginning to end. The regimen begins at the induction point and continues through close supervising of employees concerning values and behavior, repeated evaluation of performance, goal-setting and rewarding, through peer pressure and camaraderie. All of it is aimed at developing the IBM attitude and esprit de corps, a key component of the IBM culture. While this corporate culture is not internalized in the same degree by all IBM employees, it is so pervasive that as one former IBM employee saw it upon leaving the corporation, "Leaving IBM is like emigrating." And in return, for those who do not leave, IBM rewards loyal employees with lifetime success and security. But sometimes along the way to lifetime success and security there are conflicts between personal needs and values and what the corporation wants from its employees.

One such situation involved Alice Bradley, a self-described IBM "lifer" whose separation from IBM ended in the California Supreme Court. Alice went to work for IBM in 1967 at the age of nineteen as a receptionist and in twelve years, some five moves, and several training sessions later, she found herself as marketing manager in San Francisco. She supervised a sales force that sold IBM equipment to such well-known firms as Standard Oil of California and Pacific Telephone & Telegraph. This success story ended rather abruptly in June 1979 when her boss confronted her about a relationship she had with Ted Bentley, formerly a super salesman with IBM who had gone to work for a competing office products firm. As a result, Alice was reassigned to a non-management position without a sal-

---

Inspired by a story on life at IBM reported in the *Wall Street Journal*, April 8, 1982. All factual information and quotes are taken from the *Wall Street Journal* article. However, the names of the employees and some of their comments have been somewhat modified to protect anonymity.

ary reduction. Being "dead-ended" like this was equivalent to discharge. After leaving IBM, she sued the firm alleging wrongful dismissal.

Perceived Conflict?

That Alice Bradley was a loyal employee was never contested by IBM at the trial, but the main thrust of the defense was conflict of interest. IBM claimed that even if she did not disclose any secrets to the competitor, the existence of such a relationship represented a conflict of interest. Company witnesses could not agree on the motives of the move. Some claimed it was not an act of discipline but, rather, by moving Alice out of management, a way to accommodate her relationship with Ted Bentley. It also became clear that IBM does not have written rules prohibiting employees from fraternizing with the employees of its competitors.

Alice claimed her performance record was excellent and that she in no way deserved the demotion. At IBM she was a "10": her file was full of recommendations. The *Wall Street Journal* reported some of them: "Congratulations for qualifying for your third 100% club! . . . May the force be with you"; "Your performance in purchase and new equipment placements has been tremendous"; "Dear Alice, thank you . . . for the excellent job you did in setting up our case studies at your branch last month." The jury agreed that this was not the record of a below-average employee and awarded her $300,000 in compensation and punitive damages. Moreover, Alice's lawyers claimed that the demotion was aimed at discouraging her and other IBM employees from defecting to competitive firms. Yet, neither the jury's award nor IBM's punitive action, which resulted in the loss of her boyfriend and her job, has dimmed Alice's nostalgia for a company that created her as a professional. What is the mystique that creates such loyalty?

At IBM most agree that there is no mystique, it is simply a basic formula first pro-

nounced by Watson—systematic prodding of people toward excellence, combined with constant supervision and frequent rewards. Translated into management practices it means periodic reassignments and reorganizations, annual performance plans and goals for everyone, acceptance of personal responsibility for achieving challenging goals, a reward system yielding good monetary payoffs and promotions, and tight supervision in terms of close observation and evaluation. The performance plan is the key to the formula. People are graded based on the performance plan, they are supervised closely in terms of meeting periodic goals, turning in reports, attending meetings and training programs, etc., and they are given rewards for good performance.

Whether it is mystique or just sound management, it seems not only to inspire people to work hard but also to "pull together." Alice's brother, Max Bradley, who also works at IBM, believes that the work pressure encourages the creation of close cliques that spill over into social life. There is plenty of after-hour camaraderie that blends fun, relaxation, and business talk. They drink together and form softball, golf, tennis, sailing, and camping groups, etc.

So strong is the camaraderie, that even when employees leave IBM some of them retain the social relationships. It was such camaraderie that made Mr. Bentley share his beer as well as his hot tub with the fully clothed IBMers. Perhaps it was this same urge that kept him in contact with Alice.

Regardless of IBM's contentions or the jury's decision, the question still remains: Should IBM's jurisdiction, written or tacitly understood, extend into the personal lives of its employees? A California court says "no," but will this decision make any corporations change their management style? For every case that comes to court, there are thousands of others that do not. The clash between corporate expectations and individual behavior and values is most often resolved without the fanfare of the Alice Bradley case.

■ Angels or Demons at ABC

Reader Note: The following is a story compiled from various *allegations* made about ABC originally reported in the *New York Times*, August 17 and 18, 1980, and in *Fortune Magazine*, November 17, 1980.

Since Watergate, the word coverup stirs up much anguish and energy on the part of organizations to flush out suspected hanky-panky. Recently at ABC, there were rumors about some bookkeeping hanky-panky being covered-up at its Century City operation in Los Angeles. Steve Jacobs, an ABC News producer, was sent to investigate bookkeeping coverups running into the millions of dollars. The doors at Century City were slammed shut quickly on the ABC News camera crew. Security guards ejected the intruders, but the young producer adamantly refused to leave. Even the Los Angeles police saw the irony of the request to arrest Steve Jacobs for trespassing on ABC property. The confrontation ended with Steve Jacobs apologizing and departing voluntarily. The next morning, however, the ABC entertainment vice-president, Ron Sunderland, was confronted by another ABC camera crew as it staked out his house.

The confrontation, according to the *New York Times*, occurred as a result of an alleged coverup in the so-called *Charlie's Angels'* scandal, which included "allegations of criminal fraud, conspiracy, and conflict of interest."[1] Even though corporations do not like this kind of publicity, the temptation was too great for ABC News to pass up. Anyway, somebody else had disclosed the coverup first. *New York Times* reporter Jeff Gerth cited many examples of ABC's lax accounting practices for payments to Spelling-Goldberg Productions, the creators of *Charlie's Angels*. *Fortune Magazine* reported improper payments amounting to about $75 million in 1979 involving everything from "a damaged ocean liner to conflict-of-interest real estate ventures made by ABC President Elton Rule and Leonard Goldberg of Spelling-Goldberg Productions."[2]

It seemed that ABC News felt obligated to investigate a *New York Times* story involving "inflammatory memos written by a former ABC contract lawyer, Jennifer Martin." The *Fortune* story reported, "Martin's memo described a scheme to divert some $320,000 from the 'profit participants' in *Charlie's Angels* through some creative accounting."[3] The late Natalie Wood and her husband, Robert Wagner, were reported to be among the profit participants. Martin objected to shifting $30,000 per week of "exclusivity" fees from *Charlie's Angels* to *Starsky and Hutch*, a series in which Spelling-Goldberg retained most of the profits. Martin alleged, according to *Fortune*, that when she questioned the payments, Vice-President Sunderland told her, "Okay. So you want to know what it's really for? They're f---ing the Wagners out of their money."[4] The coverup seemed to be ordered from the top of ABC since there was a strong bond between ABC president, Elton Rule, and Aaron Spelling. Spelling-

---

[1] *New York Times*, op. cit.

[2] *Fortune Magazine*, op. cit.
[3] *Ibid.*
[4] *Ibid.*

Goldberg, known in Hollywood as the "hit factory," was a key supplier to ABC for as many as five hours per week of top-rated productions. The PR people at ABC attempted to deal with the stories of coverup by saying that an investigation done by outside counsel found no improprieties. Nonetheless, ABC refused to release the full report to ABC News. Interunit conflict ensued.

Conflict Escalation

The first stage of conflict resulted in ABC lawyers from New York ordering ABC Los Angeles Bureau Chief, Don Dunkel, to "call off your dogs"[5] from hounding Martin about the memos. Dunkel responded by asking ABC for copies of the Martin memos. ABC's refusal to share the Martin memos with Dunkel did not stop him, for he obtained copies from an "outside source."[6] The conflict escalated when ABC News in New York tried to get a camera interview, for "World News Tonight", from Sunderland, who was attending a company meeting in New York. When Sunderland refused to be interviewed, a camera chase occurred through the corridors at ABC. Before the day ended, as reported by *Fortune*, the message from topside to ABC news president Roone Arledge was, "Try that again and your boys will be arrested."[7] The doors were slammed shut to ABC News in Los Angeles and Sunderland played hide-and-seek in New York. It appeared that the coverup was sanctioned by ABC's top management.

Soon after the "hallway caper," the SEC launched an investigation of the scandal, the Los Angeles DA's office prepared for grand jury hearings, and the FCC became involved as part of the investigation for license renewal of KABC–TV in Los Angeles.

Power Struggle

Insiders at ABC believe that the conflict over improper payments at Century City was seized upon and used to strengthen positions of some parties in the never-ending power struggle going on among top executives. The *Fortune* story suggests that, on the surface, it seemed that the integrity of news coverage was the main stake, but conjectures produced by the corporate rumor mill hypothesized that the aggressive coverage of this scandal was directed by Roone Arledge and aimed at dethroning Elton Rule.

On August 25 at 6:13 P.M., for four minutes and twenty seconds, ABC's "World News Tonight" exposed the coverup. Correspondent Charles Gibson, standing at the entrance of the SEC headquarters in Washington, D.C., reported the story: articles of incorporation of 73 TIC, Inc.—the Rule-Goldberg joint venture, and a helicopter view of a 73 TIC, Inc., warehouse and shopping center. Gibson reported:

> Spelling-Goldberg at one point last season received over $4 million a week from ABC, from deals predicated on oral contracts. There exists, as one Spelling-Goldberg employee told ABC News, a "very cozy relationship between the network and the producers." For example, producer Goldberg and ABC President Elton Rule . . . are partners in a California land deal, which includes purchase of a shopping center.[8]

This is conflict at its glamorous best, on national television and in vivid color. While some see it as a triumph of truth and ethics, ABC's chairman complained that it was a "rough treatment,"[9] and insiders see it as part of the saga of power struggles in the corporation. Did Roone Arledge fall prey to the simplifying assumption of either/ or thinking? Is the "hard approach" better

---

[5] *Ibid.*
[6] *Ibid.*
[7] *Ibid.*

[8] ABC News program, The World Tonight, August 25, 1980.
[9] *Fortune Magazine*, op. cit.

for the corporation than "soft cozy relationships"? Is the corporate world such a dangerous place to live that its inhabitants must embrace the "nice guys finish last" assumptions?

Just when the corporation needed some favorable news coverage and PR help, Arledge decided that news media integrity was more important. The corporate world is full of such paradoxes.

Office Politics Is Inevitable

CLAUDIA M. CHRISTIE

The term office politics usually implies the nasties, the cutthroat things—sometimes subtle, sometimes not so subtle—that people do as they jockey for power within a company. Everybody knows most of them. People undercut their peers and competitors, they curry favors with their bosses, betray trusts, take credit for the achievements of others, find scapegoats to blame for mistakes. Toady . . . backbite . . . grovel . . . snake and snivel . . . At its nastiest, office politics is one of the most destructive and counterproductive forces at work in a company.

So the wise manager should stamp it out?

Well, it's not that simple. Experts say a *certain* amount and a *certain* kind of competition and strategy can be productive. Just as other kinds can be devastating.

Are office politics always vicious? Is there an inherent conflict between individual strategies and goals that are self-interested, and corporate strategies and goals that require cooperative effort? Was Machiavelli right, after all, when he wrote that people are basically bad and given any opportunity they will readily "display their vicious nature?"

Establishing Cultures

With office politics, the players are only one part of the calculation. People in office environments don't operate in a vacuum; the nature and intensity of game playing not only varies from company to company, but reflects the specific company's managerial culture. Antics that are everyday (and maybe productive) at one company might swamp the boat across the street. By and large, the experts seem to agree, the nature and likelihood of office politics comes down from the top. How people vie for recognition and power is directly tied to the "culture" and social organization of a compa-

From *New England Business*, April 4, 1983, pp. 15–19. Reprinted by permission of the author and associate editor, Claudia M. Christie.

ny—or any institution, for that matter. The academic world nearly prides itself on the variety and subtleties of its machinations.

Terrence E. Deal, a professor at Harvard's Graduate School of Education, calls one approach to office politics "the velvet fang." That's a specialty of the academic world, but it's in favor elsewhere, too. "The style has developed because people spend so much time trying to figure out how to 'off' someone in a nice way," he says. "Once it happened to me during a committee meeting," he recalls. Deal, no small game player himself, says, "I just grabbed my chest and fell off my chair. That very quickly called it up. Then you have the opportunity for some kind of shared cultural event. You can't have someone lying on the floor—and everyone knew what was being said—and not begin to talk about it a little bit."

The politics of business seems to be most intense in fields where it's hard to measure results, when there are no specific sales goals to target, no production triumphs or disasters that jump out of the worksheets.

According to one accountant, his field is such a beast. Describing the office politics at a Big Eight firm in Boston, this senior accountant (who is no longer with the firm) explains, "There are different kinds of politics that go on. To have power at that firm you have to be in the in-crowd. If you're Irish, Catholic, and an ex-Marine, you're in the in-crowd. If you're not, you're in the out-crowd. What really gets subtle is the politics of the in-crowd. To succeed once you're there requires a lot of shrewdness. You have to get the right people to go to bat for you, and you have to know how to manipulate your boss.

"The games in the accounting world are different, depending on the ballpark. In the big firms the players are sophisticated and professional; the game is more subtle, not so obviously ruthless and cutthroat. In a three- or four-person accounting department in a private company, it's a different story."

A Way of Working

Although social scientists, management experts, and consultants seem to agree that office politics is unavoidable, they also agree that it *isn't* always cutthroat and *doesn't* always run contrary to corporate objectives. In her recent book, *Office Politics*, Marilyn Moats Kennedy views office politics as a way of getting things done that is an integral part of every organization.

"Office politics is to the office what power politics is to any level of government—a process for getting things done," she writes. "It contains many of the same elements and maneuvers. Executives compete for power, responsibility, resources, and money. Secretaries jockey for position, using intricate methods of backstabbing and backbiting. Managers struggle to curry favor higher up while placating the troops below. And everyone barters for favors with a great deal of relish, push, and shove."

Although the elements and maneuvers Kennedy highlights in her definition seem to emphasize the negative, she insists that office politics is neither inherently good nor bad. "Anyone can use any part of the process to hurt or help anyone else. That it's occasionally used for evil purposes has no effect on the value of the process, or on the workings of the process."

Experts also agree that playing office politics is an essential, but not necessarily evil, part of getting ahead in the company. "A person who is doing good work can't assume that the work will speak for itself," says Harry Levinson, head of the Levinson Institute in Belmont, Massachusetts. "All organizations are political by their nature. If you're doing good work but nobody knows it, that's not much help. People who think that their work will speak for itself are dead wrong. It has to speak to somebody. Good work is a necessary, but not a sufficient, condition for making it."

The question of the quality of work aside, the question of how people compete for position and recognition is the basic political and ethical issue. "Politics is the informal communication that goes on in any organization; it's a fact of life," says Allan A. Kennedy, president of Selkirk Associates Inc., a Boston software development and consulting firm. "It becomes negative if, in fact, the climate of the organization is negative. It can be very constructive if the climate of the organization is positive."

The Boss' Fault

Harvard's Deal, who co-authored a book on *Corporate Culture* with Allan Kennedy last year, says "office politics takes place in a particularly weak corporate culture. It assumes much more importance there. In a stronger culture, what you are calling office politics I'd call office drama. Office drama is very productive; office politics can be very counterproductive. One is playing to win. The other is playing to express something of value or worth."

The item at the top of most analysts' lists when they explain what creates negative or positive corporate environments is the style of leadership at the top. "The less strong the leadership, the greater the struggle among people to try to get footholds in positions of power," says Levinson.

"A second kind of environment that promotes conflict is one where the boss manipulates people," he says. "People then have to manipulate back and try to manipulate other people. A third environment is one where people have to curry favor with the boss. Because the boss is autocratic, they have to work around him somehow."

How employees perceive the boss determines to a great extent how they feel about nepotism at a company, for example. The meteoric rise of the son of the boss through the company ranks might seem likely to create resentment among employees. Perhaps at some companies it does, but not at Wang Laboratories Inc. in Lowell, Massachusetts. Frederick A. Wang, the son of the founder and chairman, An Wang, was promoted to senior vice-president in charge of research

and development in 1981 at the young age of 31. "Certainly if An Wang weren't the founder, Fred wouldn't have come so far so fast," says one middle-level manager at the company.

"But people here respect Dr. Wang so much," says the Wang employee. "And they respect Fred too. He's intelligent, and he works hard. We don't think of him as a little Dr. Wang, Jr. He's his own person. There really isn't any resentment about Fred's promotion."

Kennedy cites three other companies in which the top leaders set a tone that he believes promotes a positive working environment. He mentions David B. Perini, president of Perini Corp. in Framingham, Massachusetts, whose open leadership style promotes an open and constructive working environment in his company and the turnaround of Gen-Rad Inc. in Concord, Massachusetts, under the leadership of William R. Thurston, chairman.

"My absolute favorite in the region is Zymark Corp., a startup company in Hopkinton, Masachusetts," says Kennedy. "It's a unique organization. When I visit there, I'll be having a cup of coffee in the cafeteria with Burleigh Hutchins, the chairman, and one of the plant workers might come in and say, 'We're having a problem with such and such.' They'll walk out to the factory floor and deal with the problem. Or a salesman might come over and talk about what happened on a call he just made. It's an open and hard-working environment where people want to get on with their jobs."

The formal systems of management and type of leadership on the middle levels are also significant elements in how politics are conducted in the office. Laurence J. Stybel, assistant professor of management at Babson College and general partner of Stybel Peabody & Associates, a Boston consulting firm, warns of the political pitfalls for middle managers who assume that their primary allegiance is to their boss and who see their role as essentially transmitting information from their boss to their subordinates.

Stybel calls that the "pipe school of management. Middle managers think that if they do a good job for their boss, everything is going to be OK," he says.

"But middle managers have different constituency groups they've got to please," Stybel says. "One obviously is the boss. Another group is the colleagues that they need to get the work done. A third group is their subordinates. If you please one group and alienate the others, you're dead." The more politically savvy style—being aware there are a number of constituency groups whose support is needed to get things done—Stybel labels the "umbrella school of management."

"Sometimes you have to get a bloody nose for your subordinates, so they know your job is to protect them," he says. "The pipe school of management assumes there's no conflict between the needs of the organization and the needs of the individual. My view says of course there is. And sometimes the needs of the employees are different from the needs of the organization. If a manager takes the view that the needs of the organization always take precedence over individual needs, then you're a good organization man, but long-term you don't have much of a future because subordinates will begin to mistrust you and begin to work around you."

How formal management systems operate also shape the various styles of informal politicking. Within the high-tech industry, "Digital Equipment is probably at one end of the spectrum, Data General may be at the other, and Prime might be somewhat in the middle," says Stybel. "And because companies have personalities, they attract certain kinds of people."

Stybel describes a "family" atmosphere at Digital, one that Kenneth H. Olsen, the company's founder and president, has tried to retain despite Digital's incredible growth. "Things can get chaotic at the company because of its matrix management structure"— where essentially one reports to many bosses and responsibilities overlap—"but

that's deliberate," says Stybel. He believes it is also healthy politically.

"When you have more than one boss, you can't play one against the other too often," he says. "It forces people to accept responsibility. In a traditional, hierarchical structure, it's easier to be a fox—to achieve your goals through manipulation, secrecy and betrayal." He describes the style at Data General as more autocratic and politically charged, "heads get chopped all the time," Stybel says.

But a former Digital employee, now at Wang, doesn't completely agree with Stybel's assessment. "Under the matrix structure, with all the levels of management at Digital, a lot of ineffective types continue managing," said the employee. "I was appalled at the company's reluctance to push those people into other staff functions. At Wang if someone isn't a good manager, they try to find a different niche for the person. They won't necessarily take away someone's title; it's just that the person won't be managing people. I like that better. I think it's more realistic.

"Also, with so many bosses, you never really knew who was in charge. At Wang you do. I think at Digital there was actually more jockeying for approval, and more political game-playing, because there were so many bosses you had to please."

Another crucial element in any discussion of office politics is the financial condition of a company, says Stybel. "Whether the financial pie is a stable or a shrinking one versus a growing one is very important," he says. "When you're talking about an expanding financial pie, you're in a potential win/win situation for everybody concerned. The flavor of the politics will be one thing. When you're talking about a situation where the pie is shrinking, now you're in a win/lose situation. One department gains, but only at the expense of another, and the flavor of the politics changes quite dramatically."

Stybel also thinks that the flavor of office politics is directly related to the degree to

■ OFFICE POLITICS AND CORPORATE CULTURE

United Technologies Corp. is one of the biggest and most carefully structured corporations in New England, and insiders say playing the game at UTC requires considerable dexterity.

First of all, if it's a game, it's a game that's won: UTC and UTC's stockholders have seen a decade of victories since Chairman Harry J. Gray took over.

But there *are* careful controls. A new employee in the corporation defined it succinctly: "They're making me over in their image."

It's a game with losers, and the outsiders feel really out.

This from a middle manager at Pratt & Whitney Aircraft, UTC's biggest unit: "At Pratt & Whitney the trick is don't make waves." (The manager's own game requires confidentiality.) "You have to be a yes man to make it to the upper levels."

"You've definitely got to conform. You've got to look like the guys who come over from the Gold Building [UTC's corporate headquarters]. They all wear blue pinstriped or gray suits, button-down white shirts, striped ties; even their attaché cases all look the same. They're all uniform height, no mustaches or beards or long hair; they all play racquetball . . . If you haven't made it by age 40, you might as well forget it, although that's not written down anywhere."

But within the culture, the trick is to stand out through achievement or by being a part of the winning team. The company carefully targets goals, and carefully tracks achievement, overachievement, and failure. Within the ranks, victory comes first, the appearance of victory second, and failure falls off the chart. Employees say the absoluteness of the third makes the second alternative sometimes seem reasonable.

A fast-growing company leaves a lot of room for perceptions. Since Gray took the helm in the early 1970s, Pratt & Whitney and other UTC divisions have seen a proliferation of managerial levels. With more niches to be filled, "everybody's scrambling even more," says the Pratt & Whitney manager.

There's an old wartime saying that confusion in battle is normal. So in a fast-growing company, "the objective seems to be play it safe, and to be safe you try not to make any decisions on your own. It's decision-making by committee, not by individuals. If you're up high enough, you don't go out on a limb; you can have the decisions made at a lower level.

"If something goes wrong, you can always point the finger or blame someone else at a lower level. So the guy on the middle level gets the black mark against him, and that follows him around.

Maybe it's a different situation at corporate headquarters. I think it's probably more sophisticated, but essentially the same thing."

It's also true that when Gray came to the company—it was then the old United Aircraft Corp.—it was about to suffer the only loss year in its history. Fast growth and tough goal-setting has rarely been known for establishing lasting morale among the middle ranks.

Competitive strategies are more clean cut and probably tougher in the top ranks. Over a series of years, Gray has made it a public guessing game who will succeed him upon his (scheduled) retirement in 1985.

Gray brought this competition into the open at one point. Edward L. Hennessey, his right-hand man and heir apparent, had just left to take the big job at Allied Corp. During a press conference, Gray clearly defined the head-to-head struggle between his executive vice presidents, Pratt & Whitney chief Robert J. Carlson and Peter L. Scott, head of UTC's electronics operations.

There are some pretty strong contenders right in the company, Gray explained, almost winking. Both men were standing nearby. Of course, Gray quickly hinted, an outsider might also sweep in and pick up the plum.

---

which a company stands for something—whether or not there exists an organizing theme or principle that everyone understands. When employees know what corporate priorities are, politics are then put in a context.

"At Babson College, for example, we stand for management education," he says.

"When someone comes to Babson, they know what they're getting. When you have an organizing theme, it puts budgetary battles in some kind of context. Everyone knows what the pecking order is."

By contrast, Stybel says, when a company has no organizing theme, "all hell breaks loose. And if you're dealing with a static pie on top of that, things can really blow up on you."

What about the impact of office politics on a company's overall game plan? While an organization is busy planning strategies for achieving corporate goals, people in the organization are busily figuring out how to advance their own careers—mapping out their own individual strategic plans for getting power and recognition.

The idea that the conflict is built-in is one he rejects, says Richard J. Hermon-Taylor, vice-president at the Boston Consulting Group. Hermon-Taylor cites one study that suggests people in organizations have a variety of different routines by which they govern their work lives. The first set are task routines, the things people do in order to get their jobs done. "These tend to be quite out in the open and free from politics," he says.

The second set of routines, however, is not. "These can be called survival routines," Hermon-Taylor says. "These are the things people do to cover their ass, to make sure that they look good and prevent them from falling foul of any of the written or unwritten corporate guidelines."

The third set is what Hermon-Taylor calls camouflage routines. These are things people do to disguise their use of survival routines.

To illustrate a camouflage routine, Hermon-Taylor describes a situation in which a manager is at a meeting where a decision is made that, when it is implemented, will mean a reduction in the size of his department. "The manager feels threatened by that, but his camouflage routine is essentially to say, 'Well, what's most important to me is the good of the company. I'm behind

this program and will do what I can to make sure it works.' Now that's a camouflage routine. It camouflages the fact that he would very much like to see if he couldn't hamstring this particular program in some way or other to see it didn't mean the reduction of his department size."

But the motivations behind survival and camouflage routines are many and varied—and complicated, Hermon-Taylor cautions. Some people will knowingly do things that are ineffective and that are not personally motivated in the belief they are accomplishing something appropriate and good for the company. And the activities may seem perfectly good from the viewpoint of the corporation's objectives, he says.

"We're working with a client now where there's such strong conflict-avoidance at the very top of the company, that at the next level down they basically get together to agree on what turn out to be the most inappropriate compromises in order that their bosses don't have to get into any kind of fight," he says.

"The lower-level managers have been at meetings where they were literally thrown out of the room because the senior guys didn't want to experience conflict. The meetings were called to a halt. Just like that. By trying to avoid conflict, the company is promoting dysfunctional activities."

In this company, personal backstabbing politics are not the destructive force. What is proving counterproductive are the things people are doing in the interests of the company, or in terms of balancing the interests as they perceive them. And that, Hermon-Taylor says, "is a complicated can of worms to deal with."

In a situation where office politics have become especially vicious and counterproductive, Kennedy advises managers to "intervene and intervene aggressively. In the jargon, the answer is you try to design a whole set of new rituals whose primary focus is getting away from politics. For example, you might launch a planning process that involves a lot of people and say, 'We're going to get away from short-term politics and interpersonal things, and we're going to talk about where this place is headed in the future.' "

A simpler suggestion for managers that Kennedy makes is, "You come out of your office and go out there to people and keep repeating over and over a message about how we don't want to be political here and stress what needs to be done. In other words, lots and lots of communication."

Stybel thinks that senior managers too often just accept the office environment as a given. "They don't spend enough time analyzing what exists, or think in terms of what kind of corporate culture they really need. In the rare cases when they do, they usually don't plan a long enough time frame for change. The process of changing a corporate culture can take anywhere from five to seven years," he says.

Et Tu, Jack

Do the nastiest players, whatever the company's climate, usually win? "I don't want to sound naive, but most often they don't," says Morgan W. McCall, Jr., project manager at the Center for Creative Leadership in Greensboro, North Carolina. McCall and Michael M. Lombardo, also at the center, recently completed a study on how *Fortune* "500" executives made it to the top.

"People say politics are ruining corporations, but I don't think so," McCall says. "After we did our study, I came out feeling a lot better about top management in corporations." Top executives focused on problem-solving and building the organization. "The ones who lose sight of that run into trouble," McCall says.

"Those who play cutthroat politics get away with it for a while," he says.

"Power can be heady. Executives can maybe find scapegoats for a while, but sooner or later it catches up with them. It becomes blatant. Sooner or later someone looks back and says, 'There are a lot of people out there who don't trust him.' Management requires trust, and executives have to work with a broad range of people. If someone can't be trusted, people stop talking to him. He gets no support. Friends come and go, but enemies accumulate."

McCall says that the managers who make it to the top are the ones who learn that politics are a part of any organization, but that instead of putting a value judgment on it, they learn to work through it. "They learned to accept different points of view. Instead of saying, 'Hey, that's terrible,' they say, 'Hey, that's the way it is, and if you want to get anything done, you learn to work with it.' Change what you can, accept what you can't. Go with it, don't fight it. I think that's a remarkable finding."

Exercises

■ Magna Inc.—Operation Expansion

In a survey of business executives, Argyris found that 65 percent of them believed that the most important unsolved problem of their organization was that top management was unable to help overcome intergroup rivalries.[1] To many this statistic is shocking, but to others it is perceived as a *low* estimate of the true nature and extent of conflict that exists in today's organizations.

In this exercise, your group will have to choose how it wishes to approach a situation of potential conflict. In planning you will have to weigh the advantages and the disadvantages of each strategy. You will want to be thinking about what factors led up to the situation you are faced with, and if the consequences (which you will experience) were intended and predictable.

Magna Inc.—Operation Expansion Instructions

Magna, Inc. is a growing conglomerate that comprises four major subsidiary companies, each of which is well regarded in its industry.[2] Each subsidiary is established as a separate company and the president of each sits on the Board of Directors of Magna, Inc. The four subsidiary companies and their respective industry are:

Delta Company	Nuclear research for domestic application, e.g., smoke alarms, heating systems.
Key Company	Manufacturing of large precision machined industrial parts, e.g., diesel crankshafts, submarine and ship parts.
Valco Company	High-technology precision etching and plating, e.g., gold and platinum plating of sensing devices on spacecraft and most major aircraft.
Excel Company	Consumer products, e.g., microwave ovens, minicomputers, kits for hobbyists.

Each subsidiary has experienced continuous growth over the years. This growth has already overtaxed the present facilities of each subsidiary company and anticipated future growth has made urgent the need for immediate building of new facilities.

Some years ago Magna located a large tract of land that was judged to be ideal for subsidiary expansion when their growth required new facilities. The tract was not available for purchase in total, so plots of land within it were acquired over time as they became available. The actual purchase of these plots was made by the subsidiary company that was in the most favorable cash position when the plot became available for sale.

---

1. C. Argyris, "Interpersonal Barriers to Decision-Making," *Harvard Business Review*, March-April 1966, p. 23.

2. Based on an exercise originally developed by Dr. Robert F. Maddocks, Staff Vice-President, Organization Planning, RCA Corp. Used with permission.

Last year, the final plot was purchased, so at this time the entire tract is owned by the various subsidiaries. Acquiring the land in this fashion has resulted in plot ownership being somewhat random insofar as each subsidiary is concerned. The attached map of Magna's Land Tract describes the tract in terms of current plot ownership by subsidiary company.

Subsidiary expansion plans that have been approved by Magna will require a different plot configuration than present ownership. Each subsidiary has carefully surveyed the site and has developed specific plans for the plots needed to accommodate its unique expansion requirements.

Following the decentralization policy that has been characteristic of Magna, the task of proper plot rearrangement has been delegated to the subsidiaries for solution. Consequently, the president of each subsidiary has appointed a key staff group and has chartered them with the responsibility of working out required land transactions. The Board has made it clear, however, that it expects the *most effective possible utilization of the land*.

Your group will assume the role of the special staff group of one of the subsidiary companies appointed by its president to obtain the particular land required for your expansion. You will be given the particular plot configuration you desire. Your task will be to conduct the required transactions with the other three subsidiary staff groups. A general meeting will be called shortly to facilitate these transactions.

Certain rules for the transactions have been established. These are:

1. Each staff group will have to decide before the meeting how it will approve transactions and then advise the instructor of its criteria, e.g., appoint one person to make all final decisions, require a majority vote then authorize a representative. Whatever approach is selected, it must be adhered to throughout the meeting.

2. Your instructor (or someone appointed by the instructor) will place in the front of the room the official map showing all plots and current ownership of each. As properly executed transactions take place, the official map will be changed to show new ownership. Only transactions signed off by duly authorized staff members of each party will be officially entered and once entered become legally binding.

3. Plots of land may be purchased, sold, or traded (evenly or with cash incentive).

4. All plots are nominally priced at $100,000 each. This is purely a nominal figure based on the average purchase price actually paid over the last ten years for separate plots. Each plot owner is free to establish true value. It is expected that one or more of the plots each subsidiary owns may be desired by one or more of the other subsidiaries making the plot considerably more valuable than its nominal price.

5. The Board of Directors of Magna has made it clear that it will *not* approve selling or leasing this land to any outside firms. Thus it is not possible to sell or trade lots with outside organizations now or in the future.

Your company has been authorized to spend a given sum of money for the procurement of needed land if you must do so. The amount varies with the profit picture of each company. In the past, all the companies have maintained fairly equal profit pictures, with the exception of Excel, which regularly turns in higher earnings. Each company will be told by the instructor how much money it will be authorized to spend. A company *cannot* operate in a deficit cash position. You may, of course, obtain cash by selling the plots you own. Your instructor will maintain a running balance for each company and will not authorize transactions that result in a deficit. Your group should keep its own records as well.

The instructor will give each staff group information about the plots of land desired.

Map of Magna's Land Tract

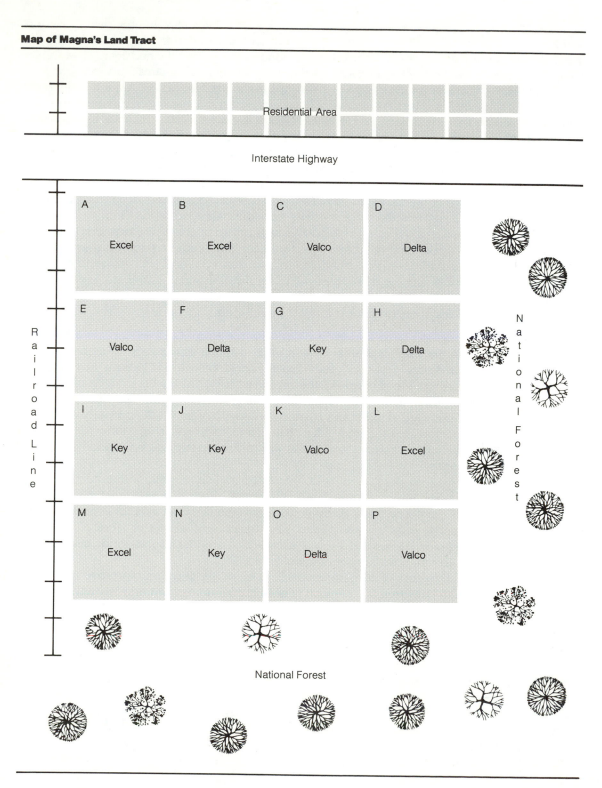

Meeting Schedule

1. Prior to the general meeting, your staff group will be given twenty minutes to:
   a. determine how your group will approve all land transactions and prepare a short statement of this process for the instructor. Be sure to indicate who will have the authority to sign off properties and close deals for your group. (Remember this must be adhered to throughout the meeting).
   b. determine your strategy and a specific plan of action for achieving your objectives.

2. At the end of the above planning session, the instructor will signal the beginning of the general meeting. Groups may interact in any way they desire, within the ground rules provided, in order to achieve their objectives. The framework for transactions and decisions will be an open meeting with all companies represented. Each company will have an area designated for any conferences it desires. The format of the meeting is up to the staff members present, and may change as the meeting progresses from open discussion to individual negotiations, etc. Companies may negotiate privately if they wish, however all final decisions must be made in the general meeting. The meeting will last no more than ninety minutes.

OBSERVER GUIDE: (PRE-GENERAL MEETING)

Company Observed _____

1. Does your group have a basic strategy for attaining its objectives? If yes, explain what you think it is. If no, what effect do you think the lack of strategy will have?

2. How do you think members of your group will behave during the general meeting? Check those that apply.

   a. _____ Every man/woman for himself/herself

   b. _____ Bargaining agents

   c. _____ Peacemakers

   d. _____ "Cautious" trust

   e. _____ Total honesty—get all the cards on the table

   f. _____ Other (describe)

   _____

3. Do you think your group will achieve its objectives? Why, or why not?

4. Who has the most influence in the group? What effect will his/her influence have?

OBSERVER GUIDE DURING MEETING

1. Did the group hold back, or in any way distort information during the general meeting?

2. If your group had a strategy, was it followed once the meeting began? Why, or why not?

3. How much influence over the other groups did your group seem to exert during the general meeting? How can you explain this?

4. If private meetings were called for by each group or between groups, how did they attempt to solve their differences?

5. Any other observations?

MAGNA INC., OPERATION EXPANSION—POST ANALYSIS

1. Quality of solution reached:

    Low   *High*
    1   2   3   4   5

2. Acceptability of solution to *all* teams:

    Low   *High*
    1   2   3   4   5

3. What kinds of feelings and reactions do you have about your team? Complete the following sentences.

    My team is _____

    My team is _____

    My team is _____

    My team is _____

    My team is _____

4. Do other team members feel the same?

    _____ yes   _____ no   _____ don't know

5. What kinds of behavior (yours or other's) *facilitated* reaching a solution?

6. What kinds of behavior *hindered* reaching a solution?

7. Below you are asked to classify your team and the other teams' conflict management mode using the following code:

N = Never observed
S = Sometimes used
R = Regularly used

Conflict Management Mode	Valco	Excel	Delta	Key
Collaboration	_____	_____	_____	_____
Bargaining	_____	_____	_____	_____
Power-Play	_____	_____	_____	_____

8. Which team seemed to have the most influence? Why?

■ Trimming the Fat at Delphi

Conflict in organizations is often precipitated by a written memo. Existing conflict may be smoothed over or exacerbated by the tactful or less than tactful memo. In this exercise, each person is asked to engage in the artful practice of memo writing.

Directions

1. Each person in the class will be assigned to either the role of Manager of the Management Consulting Group or Manager of the Printing Department.
2. The instructor will pair off participants who will be required to communicate with each other only through written memos during a designated period of time.
3. The instructor will distribute role information to each of the two parties.
4. The first memo will be sent by the Manager of the Consulting Group. The Manager of the Printing Department must then respond to this first memo.
5. A mailbox will be set up to facilitate the exchange of memos. Each party will be required to respond to a memo within twenty-four hours of receipt and no later than noon of the day after receiving the memo. Responses must be in the mailbox by noon.
6. Each party should send at least two memos and the memos must be typed (or legibly printed).

Delphi Organizational Services, Inc.

Delphi Organizational Services, Inc. (DOS) was founded in 1955 as a management consulting firm by its present president, Lee Otis. Its current name was adopted in 1971 after the firm had expanded beyond the original consulting services into training and publishing management literature. The current organization includes a Consulting Department, a Publications Department, a Training Department, an Administrative Services Department, and a Controller (see exhibit 4.10).

Each of the three line departments is headed by a vice-president who along with the President forms an Executive Committee. The President has withdrawn from the daily operations of the company and channels his efforts largely into developing and maintaining external relations. He is involved in developing better relations with several trade associations, he does some public speaking, he solicits articles for the company's journal, *Management Today*, he writes for the *Current Trends Newsletter*, and presides over the Executive Committee, which makes policy decisions and formulates strategy. All members of the Executive Committee are senior partners who have ownership in the firm.

The most recent organization change occurred in 1977 when the Consulting Department was divided into two subunits—Management Consulting and Technical Consulting. The Manager of the Management Consulting Group, Len Keller, became the Vice-President of Consulting, a Senior Associate, Roy Erving, was promoted to Manager of the Management Consulting Group, and Eli Bloomstein was brought in to head the Technical Consulting Group. In the past two years, the management consulting business has fallen off sharply and accordingly there have been some layoffs of associates. But the technical consulting business has been growing steadily, largely due to the increased pressure experienced by manufacturing businesses to improve the control of waste disposal. The Technical Consulting Group has specialized in toxic-waste disposal.

The economic recession has also affected other areas of the firm's business. While in-house training has held its own, conference training that involves one- to three-day seminars has required a 25 percent cutback in programs offered. The counts in seminars of two- and three-day duration have fallen from an average of thirty-four to seventeen but the one-day seminars, especially the series on Programming Your Personal Computer, have grown in demand. Accordingly, some trainers have been released and a few new ones in computer programming have been hired.

EXHIBIT 4.10   Delphi Organization Chart

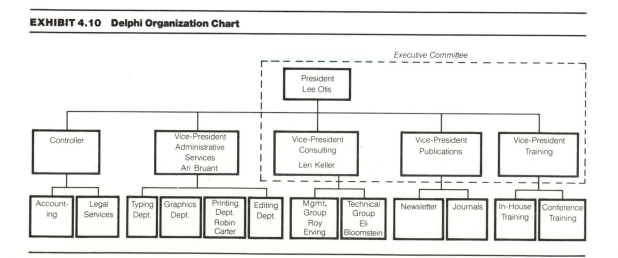

This slow-down in business has also affected the Administrative Services Department. Personnel has been laid off in the Graphics and Editing Department and a few new people hired who can do editing, graphics, and typing. The Vice-President of Administrative Services, Ari Bruant, is convinced that flexibility is needed in the personnel employed in administrative services. The economic benefits of having multiple-skilled personnel in graphics, editing, and typing is apparent but it creates management problems. People keep getting shifted back and forth, employees are somewhat confused, and the managers of the departments feel they are losing control. Rumors abound about possibly combining the three departments and having only one manager in charge of them. Because of the specialized skills involved in the Printing Department, the personnel in that department have not been affected by the consolidation efforts occurring in the other three departments; however, a few people in word processing have been released. The Manager of the Printing Department, Robin Carter, relies on some part-time people to work during periods of high demand. Some efforts have also been made to reduce the rigidity of the criteria used for scheduling printing jobs for the three line departments—Consulting, Publications, and Training.

It seems that the cost savings efforts are paying off; costs have been reduced by close to 10 percent for the last two quarters. The President has been encouraged by the efforts of all those involved and has urged everyone in management to continue looking for more ways to reduce costs.

■ Power Play

Every group or subunit within an organization has a certain amount of power at its disposal that it can utilize to achieve its own objective. Some managers view conflict as the natural outcome of the exercise of such power where only the strong survive. In support of this view, Kelly suggests that, "Contrary to conventional wisdom, the most important single thing about conflict is that it is good for you." [1] In contrast, other managers would strive to define all situations as collaborative attempts and avoid conflict at all cost. Such a view is supported by the hindsight produced by many negotiation sessions. In reality, neither view is acceptable. The former is perhaps too cynical, while the latter is too naive.

Whether the exercise of power involves joining forces with another group in support of a mutual point of view or a mere tie-breaking vote, the fact remains that the use of power often precedes conflict.

In this exercise, your group will have to develop its strategy regarding the exercise of power. You may well be confronted with the interdependence of power and trust no matter what the outcome. The exercise can symbolically illustrate this relationship and demonstrate the dilemma faced daily by a manager.

---

[1] Joe Kelly, "Make Conflict Work for You," *Harvard Business Review*, July-August 1970.

Power-Play Directions

Your group represents a department in a large organization. You are going to interact with another department in your organization. The two departments are in competition for increased budgetary funds. Your department's objective is to maximize its budget. In the past, budgetary funds have been closely tied to a department's power and influence in the organization. You will have to develop a strategy to influence the other department's decision-making. You will *not* be able to interact with the other department on an informal basis; however, you will be allowed to negotiate with them from time to time to make your position perfectly clear. Each department has been given *identical* instructions.

In order to maximize your department's influence, and subsequent budget, you have to decide on a strategy that will involve (a) increasing or decreasing your department's level of *power* in relation to the other department and (b) increasing or decreasing your department's level of *trust* in relation to the other department. Each department will begin with the same amount of power and trust.

The Exercise

1. Each department will be given twenty power/trust cards. Each card will be marked "power" on one side and "trust" on the other side. To begin the exercise, each department will place ten cards in a power position and ten cards in a trust position. During the course of the exercise, these cards will remain in your possession and out of sight of the other department.

2. There will be rounds and moves. Each round consists of up to five moves by each department. The number of rounds will depend on time. Payoffs will be made at the end of each round.

3. A move consists of turning two, one, or none of the department's power/trust cards from a power position to a trust position *or* from a trust position to a power position.

4. Each department will have three minutes to make each move-decision and one minute between moves. At the end of each move-decision period, a department must have moved two, one, or none of the department's power/trust cards. If the department fails to move in the allotted time, it will forfeit the move and no change will be permitted until the next move period.

5. Each new round of the exercise begins with a return of power and trust back to equal levels of ten and ten.

Payoffs

1. Departments will have an equal number of members. Before the exercise begins, each member will give 75¢ to their organization's controller (designated by the instructor) as their contribution to the president's "slush fund." They will also provide $1.50 each for their department's budget. Each department's remaining budget at the end of the exercise will be divided equally among its members.

2. Power Struggle
   a. Either department may call for a "power struggle" immediately *after* any move (during the one-minute period between moves) by notifying the controller. A power struggle may not be called for between moves in which negotiations have already taken place. A power struggle may be called after the last move.

b. If there is a power struggle, the round ends. The department with the most power will win five cents per member for each power card they have turned up over and above the power cards turned up by the other department. This money will be transferred directly from the budget of the losing department to the winning department's budget. In addition, power struggles cost both departments five cents per member payable to the president's slush fund. The controller will manage all transfer of funds.

c. If there is no power struggle, at the end of each round (five moves), each department's budget will receive two cents per member from the president's slush fund, for each trust card turned up. In addition, the controller will collect from each department's budget two cents per member for each power card turned up.

Negotiations

1. Between moves (not before a move) each department will have the opportunity to communicate with the other department through negotiators.

2. Either department may call for negotiations by notifying the controller during the one-minute period between any decision period. The other department may accept or reject the request.

3. Negotiations can last up to three minutes. When negotiators return to their departments, the three-minute decision period for the next move will start again. Negotiations will take place in private, away from both departmental areas.

4. Negotiators are free to say whatever is necessary to benefit themselves or their departments. The departments are not bound by agreements made by their negotiators, even when made in good faith.

5. Negotiators from both departments are *required* to meet after the second and fourth move (after the one-minute period following that move, if there is no power struggle). The controller will set up these negotiations and will call for the negotiators when it is appropriate.

Exercise Flow: See exhibit 4.11 for a flow chart showing the various moves and alternatives available to each department.

Special Roles

You will have twenty minutes to discuss your department's strategy and organize your department. During this time, the group must select a department head and two negotiators. These persons may be changed at any time by a majority vote of the department. You should also decide how your group will make each move decision. The role assignments are:

1. Two *negotiators*—activities stated above.
2. A *department head*—to communicate all department decisions to the controller.
   a. The controller will listen *only* to the department head.
   b. The department head cannot be a negotiator.
   c. The department head has tie-breaking power if a vote is used.
3. A *recorder/accountant*—to record department decisions and budget status.

EXHIBIT 4.11   Exercise Flow Chart

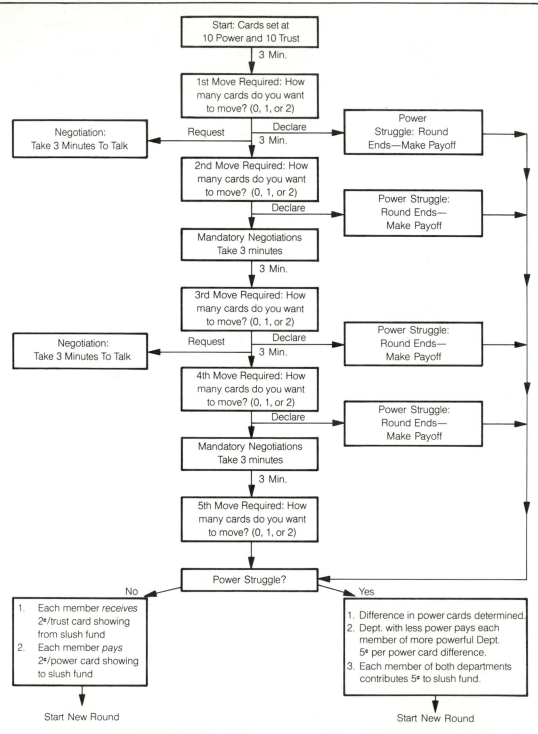

CONTROLLER RECORDING FORM

Department A			Department B		
Location _____			Location _____		
Head _____			Head _____		
Negotiator _____			Negotiator _____		
Negotiator _____			Negotiator _____		

Round 1

	Dept A		Dept B		
Move	*#Power*	*#Trust*	*#Power*	*#Trust*	*Action Taken (Remarks)*
Start	10	10	10	10	
1	_____	_____	_____	_____	
2	_____	_____	_____	_____	
3	_____	_____	_____	_____	
4	_____	_____	_____	_____	
5	_____	_____	_____	_____	
Payoffs					

Round 2

	Dept A		Dept B		
Move	*#Power*	*#Trust*	*#Power*	*#Trust*	*Action Taken (Remarks)*
Start	10	10	10	10	
1	_____	_____	_____	_____	
2	_____	_____	_____	_____	
3	_____	_____	_____	_____	
4	_____	_____	_____	_____	
5	_____	_____	_____	_____	
Payoffs					

Round 3

	Dept A		Dept B		
Move	*#Power*	*#Trust*	*#Power*	*#Trust*	*Action Taken (Remarks)*
Start	10	10	10	10	
1	_____	_____	_____	_____	
2	_____	_____	_____	_____	
3	_____	_____	_____	_____	
4	_____	_____	_____	_____	
5	_____	_____	_____	_____	
Payoffs					

Round 4

Move	Dept A		Dept B		Action Taken (Remarks)
	# Power	*# Trust*	*# Power*	*# Trust*	
Start	10	10	10	10	
1	_____	_____	_____	_____	
2	_____	_____	_____	_____	
3	_____	_____	_____	_____	
4	_____	_____	_____	_____	
5	_____	_____	_____	_____	

Payoffs

Power-Play Post Analysis

1. In the space provided, quickly jot down words or phrases in response to the following statements.

   a. Feelings I have about my department . . .

   b. Feelings I have about the other department . . .

2. Try to think of factors inherent in the situation (antecedents) that could heighten or reduce the potential for conflict, regardless of the groups involved. Also try to think of factors that *emerged*, as the groups interacted, which heightened or reduced the conflict potential. List them below.

Antecedent Factors

Heightened Potential	*Reduced Potential*
_____	_____
_____	_____
_____	_____
_____	_____

Emergent Factors

Heightened Potential	*Reduced Potential*
_____	_____
_____	_____
_____	_____
_____	_____

■ Rules and Knots

Once a new employee enters an organization and is "broken in," he or she must resolve conflicts between work life and personal values and beliefs. Often the conflicts between work life and personal values revolve around the rules and regulations formulated by the organization aimed at the member's behavior both on and off the job. The following role-playing affords you an opportunity to experience some of the organizational issues that enter into the conflict.

As you act out your role, it is important that you accept the facts as they are given, as well as assume the values, attitudes, and feelings supplied in your specific role. From this point on, let your feelings develop in accordance with the events that transpire while you play these roles. When facts or events arise that are not covered by the role description, make up things that are consistent with the way it might have been in the actual situation.

Read your role description several times and try to envision the type of person you will be role-playing. Try to figure out the values, attitudes, and feelings of the person you are to play. From then on you should try to be yourself, make up your own lines, adapt and innovate when necessary, and use your imagination. Do *not* read the role descriptions of the others in the role play and try not to consult your role description while playing your part. A good role player need not be an actor. Become familiar with the given facts and attitudes and then be yourself.

Directions

1. Your instructor will assign you a role. Carefully study your role. (Observers read all three roles.)

2. You will be assigned a place to enact this situation for about twenty to twenty-five minutes.

3. Your instructor will lead a class discussion regarding outcomes of the role play.

■ DO NOT READ UNLESS ASSIGNED THIS ROLE.

Role of Jan, Industrial Engineer

You are a young industrial engineer who was recently hired by the Industrial Engineering Department of the forge plant of a major manufacturer of aluminum products. The department is composed of one senior industrial engineer, two industrial engineers, eight time-study analysts, one secretary, and the head of the department. You have worked hard at completing several important projects assigned to you since being hired. Even though you often come to work ten to fifteen minutes late (which bugs a few of the time-study people), you also on occasion come to work on Saturdays and evenings. One of the projects you feel good about is an employee-incentive system that you designed, after the senior industrial engineer, Bob, had failed to do it to the satisfaction of Corporate Headquarters.

Your Department Head, Francis, seems to be pleased with your performance and your relationship with him (her) is good.   The time-study analysts, who have worked their way up from the shop and have not had any formal training in industrial engineering, seem to accept you as an industrial engineer even though some of them resent your youth and the status you have over them.   You feel you deserve this status becuse of your college training and competence; moreover, you work much harder than they do.   The other industrial engineer treats you as an equal.   The senior industrial engineer, Bob Marshall, has been friendly and fatherly, and he seems to be reserving his judgment about your technical ability.   You suspect that he may be harboring some resentment over the way you took over his project on the incentive system after his plan was rejected.

Last week you had a run-in with Bob over the dress code.   For the last two weeks you had been removing your necktie (not wearing hose if you are female) on days the temperature reading in the office was ninety degrees.   The Plant Manager (Pat) has implemented a policy that prohibits air conditioning or fans in the offices.   Pat expects that if the workers in the forge shop must work in high temperatures, all the others should tolerate it also.

Your boss, Francis, made a comment to you about not wearing a necktie (hose), but seemed to be satisfied with your reasons.   You feel that the necktie (hose) is an excessive burden that chafes your neck (legs) on very hot days.   Others in the plant offices also started to remove their neckties (hose), and this matter is becoming the main topic of discussion as you meet others around the plant.

When you arrived at the office this morning, the secretary gave you the following message, "The plant manager wants you in his (her) office at 10:30 A.M., sharp."   At 10:40 A.M. you are on your way to the plant manager's office, after being unavoidably detained in the plant because of a problem involving a major cost-saving project of yours.   You are entering Pat's office with your boss, Francis, at 10:45 A.M. to start the meeting.   Francis told you he (she) had been waiting for you since 10:30.

■ DO NOT READ UNLESS ASSIGNED THIS ROLE.

Role of Francis, Head of Industrial Engineering

You have been the head of the Industrial Engineering Department in the forge plant of a large manufacturer of aluminum products for a little over five years.   You were brought in from another division to replace Bob Marshall, Senior Industrial Engineer, who is close to retirement.

Recruiting and retaining competent industrial engineers has been a problem in your department.   With the exception of Bob Marshall, you've had close to 100 percent turnover of industrial engineers, while there has been no turnover of the eight time-study analysts in the department in the last three years.   All the time-study analysts have worked their way up to office work from the plant and none of them have had much formal training in industrial engineering.   In the past you thought Bob Marshall had been their informal leader and they were trying to model their behavior after his.   He is a steadying influence in the department, but recently he has been complaining to you about the young industrial engineer, Jan, that you hired recently.   Young Jan has many good ideas; he (she) has performed very well in the assignments you gave him (her) and recently rescued you from further criticism by designing an employee-incentive system that was accepted by Corporate Headquarters after Bob Marshall failed to produce an acceptable plan.   You're wondering what is going on between Bob and Jan.

Only last week Bob complained to you that Jan is coming to work late three to four times a week, and two days ago he expressed his chagrin at Jan's removing his necktie (not wearing hose if Jan is a female) at work. Bob feels that this is unprofessional conduct and sets up a bad example for the time-study analysts and others. You talked to Jan about both these matters but did not press him (her) for a commitment to refrain from such violations because you feel Jan's performance is superior, and Jan seems to be very sensitive about conforming on some matters. It is true that Jan comes in late sometimes but he (she) accomplishes more work than the others who are punctual. Jan even works during some weekends, while Bob and the time-study analysts never take the initiative to come to work on Saturday. You allow Jan a little extra latitude on some company rules, but you feel it can be justified by his (her) extra effort and good performance and, furthermore, you would not like to lose him (her).

Your tolerance in bending the rules for Jan has been noticed by the Plant Manager, Pat, who has mentioned it to you after one of the weekly staff meetings. Pat has asked you to come to his (her) office with Jan at 10:30 A.M. to discuss the dress code. You arrived promptly at 10:30 but had to wait for Jan. You are now walking into Pat's office with Jan who arrived for the meeting fifteen minutes late.

■ DO NOT READ UNLESS ASSIGNED THIS ROLE.

Role of Pat, Plant Manager

You are the Plant Manager of a forge plant of a large manufacturer of aluminum products. You are a college graduate with a degree in mechanical engineering and have worked your way up to this position. You aspire to be promoted to corporate headquarters at the level of vice-president and your success at this plant is an important stepping stone in your career plan.

However, you feel you must solve some personnel problems that have been brought to your attention. You have heard complaints that some plant workers have been violating the safety rules by not wearing hard hats, safety shoes, and goggles. You have also heard that some of the office personnel are violating the dress code—some men are wearing loud sportcoats, others are not wearing neckties, and some women are coming in without hose. Just yesterday one of the old-timers in the Industrial Engineering Department, Bob Marshall, confided to you that a young engineer no longer wears a necktie to work (hose if the engineer is a female) and that others in the Sales Department are adopting this behavior.

You want to be fair about any punitive action you take so you have decided to talk to the new industrial engineer, Jan. From all reports, Jan has been doing a good job. His (her) boss, Francis, and Jan have been told to be in your office at 10:30 A.M. Francis arrived on time and he (she) is waiting in the outer office for Jan before they come in. At this point you are disturbed about the violation of the dress code, but you are also angry at Jan's tardiness. They are walking into your office at 10:45 A.M.

Suggestions for the Process Observer

Your task is to observe and listen to the role-play as carefully as you can. Try to remain inconspicuous and do not interfere in the role-play. During the feedback session, present your remarks, comment briefly on what you think was taking place, and talk about your specific observations.

Questions to Ask Yourself While Observing:

1. What is going on between the boss and the subordinate? Is one trying to influence or convince the other?

2. Do they seem to be really trying to understand the other person in the way the other wants to be understood?

3. What factors (antecedents) in this situation seem to be increasing or decreasing conflict? What modes of conflict management can you identify?

5 Revitalization

■ **LEARNING OBJECTIVES**

1. To provide opportunities to utilize organization theory in gaining and developing a macro perspective of organizations

2. To gain insights into the behavioral and organizational factors that inhibit organizational revitalization efforts

3. To explore and build organizational diagnosis and action-planning skills

4. To gain a better understanding of the transitional dynamics underlying organizational mergers

■ OVERVIEW

The process of fine tuning and revitalizing an organization has become complex, and for those who accept responsibility for this process, it is a numbing one. Part of the numbness is rooted in the organizational resistance a manager often encounters when attempting to implement change. As a manager's numbness increases over time, the temptation to avoid such experiences is enhanced and the critical mass necessary for revitalization is gradually destroyed. Such a phenomenon necessitates the build-up of powerful internal and external forces for change, resulting in costly and painful organizational upheavals. Such occurrences are rarely tidy even though they are often associated with terms such as "house cleaning," and "reorganization." More important, they produce wasted resources and deep individual and organizational scars. It is often most painful for managers who lack an awareness of the organizational dynamics in which they function. In addition, today with mergers becoming commonplace,

it is essential for a manager to be more aware of the complex processes involved in organizational transitions.

Throughout this book, an effort has been made to raise your awareness by providing insight into the key organizational dimensions that help us understand and develop a macro perspective. These dimensions include, for example, environmental forces, organizational strategy and structure, organizational climate, the nature of work flow, and relationships between subunits. In this part we want to provide opportunities for you to test your newly gained conceptual skills in a variety of organizational settings.

An organization becomes more understandable only after one attempts to change it. We hope that in this part of the book you will get a chance not only to test and refine your conceptual skills and understanding of *Organization Theory*, but also to begin developing an appreciation for the skills necessary to implement organizational change.

Readings

■ Common Syndromes of Business Failure

DANNY MILLER

Business failures and near failures are frequent occurrences. Often, the plight of a failing firm comes as a great surprise to managers and shareholders alike. The business press solemnly points out that a competitor "got the jump" on the firm with a new product or technology, or that adverse economic or regulatory conditions proved too much to bear. Attributing failure to singular or predominantly external causes is popular but not always realistic. A recent study of over forty business failures indicates that such failures are often caused from within the company and by intrinsically interrelated factors that frequently are rooted in the behavior of managers. "Failure," for the purposes of this article, means protracted periods of poor profits and eroding market share but not necessarily bankruptcy.

Surprisingly few distinct failure syndromes recurred with frequency in our sample. Just as psychoanalysts and physicians see the same types of neuroses and diseases cropping up again and again, we witnessed extremely popular paths to corporate failure. In fact, the four failure syndromes that will be discussed account for over 80 percent of our sample of companies. We use the clinical word "syndrome" in analyzing organizational failure because, just as with organic illness, the symptoms must be distinguished from the fundamental causes of the disease.

Danny Miller, *Business Horizons*, November 1977. Copyright © 1977, by the Foundation for School of Business at Indiana University. Reprinted by permission.

Our studies showed that in all instances what occurred was not merely a random or haphazard clustering of symptoms, but rather a logical scenario in which various primary factors played a vital role in causing secondary symptoms to develop. For example, a jealous and power-hoarding executive became so busy meddling with the routine functions of his subordinates that he had time only for a "seat of the pants" management style when it came to major issues. The result was an unclear conception of corporate strategy and an unrealistically short planning horizon. A firm of consultants entered the picture and set up a remarkably sophisticated, long-term planning system. Because the top man still refused to delegate a line of authority, the project bombed. The consultants addressed one of the symptoms of the problem but neglected to deal with its primary cause.

The intent of this article is to enhance the perspective of managers by illustrating the logical internal structure of some very common organizational problems. We hope to leave managers in a better position to attack the *ultimate roots* of serious corporate weaknesses in their own firms.

DESCRIPTION OF THE RESEARCH

Our starting point in studying corporate failure was an analogy between a biological organism and a formal organization. An organism survives because it has an internal set of mediating capacities that enable it to behave in a manner consistent with survival in the environment. Problems may thus come from the nature of the environment, an internal "structural" inadequacy, or an inappropriate mode of response. Therefore, we decided to study three aspects of an organization: its environment, its structure, and the nature of its strategy-making behavior. In the environment category we were interested in such variables as the nature and severity of competition, the rates of technological change, the stability of consumer tastes, and the diversity of target markets. Organization and structural variables of interest included the following: the nature of the firm's intelligence system, that is, its methods of scanning the environment, as well as the sophistication of internal controls and information mechanisms; the degree to which power for making routine and strategic decisions is delegated to lower levels of management; the scarcity of human, material, and financial resources; the extent to which departments or divisions differ in their operating techniques, goals, and decision-making styles; the amount of conflict among executives; the length of tenure of top executives; and the percentage of professional people on the staff. Strategy-making characteristics studied included the proclivity toward product-market innovation and risk-taking, the intensity of analysis of key decisions, planning time horizons, the awareness of an explicit strategy, and the complementarity of decisions made in different units.

In order to obtain information about how companies encountered serious strategic and operating problems, we decided to employ as descriptive and rich a data base as possible. We used undisguised cases published in *Fortune* magazine, the Harvard Case Clearing House series, and several textbooks on management policy. Cases supply vivid and detailed accounts of strategy making. They also provide a time perspective, which gives insight into the evolutionary sequence that terminates in failure. Cases are generally written by a third party, an objective professional who is likely to

provide more accurate and detailed information than a harried and perhaps biased executive might supply. A case-study data base does pose some very real problems, however. For example, different cases provide different information and thereby cause scoring problems. Also, some types of information are simply not available in cases. Finally, cases may represent a biased sample because they portray unusually dramatic situations that occur most often in large companies.

To overcome some of these disadvantages, we tried to choose cases that contained data on nearly all our variables of interest and to choose variables that could be reliably scored, given the case data base. To faciliate quantitative analysis, we constructed gross seven-point scales for each of the thirty-one variables. Two of our raters, who had been exposed to a broad variety of case studies and were familiar with the meaning of each of the variables, scored one-third of the cases separately from one another. They agreed remarkably well on the ratings to be assigned where, for example, 1 represents a score on the variable such that other firms scored much higher, 7 represents the opposite, 4 is average, and so forth. (The inter-rater consistency or "reliability" coefficient was .85.) In order to check the accuracy of case information, letters were sent to executives of firms that were the subjects of the most recently written cases. Again the results were favorable.

The raw data took the form of thirty-one variable scores for each of forty-two cases of organizations in trouble. Our objective was to group these cases into internally homogeneous categories in order to identify any oft-recurring forms of organizational maladjustment. The grouping task was impossible to accomplish by eye because of the large volume of information contained in each case profile and because of the number of cases used. Therefore, an inverse or Q-type factor analysis procedure was used on a random one-half of the cases. Our intent was to put into the same groups those cases having similar score patterns for the thirty-one variables. Factor loadings revealed four such groups. Cases in each group were then reread to discern the essential similarities and differences among firms within the group. In this way we were able to construct four "regions," defined in terms of ranges of scores most probable for each variable, for each group. The four regions corresponded to the four factors. To insure that groups were not merely a statistical artifact of the factor analysis, a program was written to sort the remaining cases into the regions. It was shown that a much greater proportion of cases fell into the regions than could be expected by chance. These statistically significant regions are called "archetypes." About 85 percent of the cases fell into one of the four archetypes described in the next section.

The presentation is structured as follows: First, the most popular syndromes discovered by the research are discussed. A representative quote ("famous last words") from the chief executive officer (CEO) is given, a description of the problem syndrome is presented, a visual cause-effect diagram of the syndrome is displayed, and some disguised anecdotes are given to make the difficulties in each syndrome more concrete. Some general conclusions on all four syndromes are then presented, followed by a checklist of warning signs that will enable managers to detect if and how their own firms are threatened, followed by some tentative remedial suggestions for firms that currently may be facing one of the four most popular syndromes.

FOUR COMMON FAILURE SYNDROMES

F_1: The Impulsive Syndrome: Running Blind

Famous Last Words   This business of ours must be defined in the broadest possible terms if we are to continue to break our past growth

records. We must take risks in order to grow. Seize opportunities first, consolidate later.

The F_1 firms fail because they are dominated by a power-hoarding chief executive and because their strategies are overambitious, incautious, and oblivious to some very important features in their environment.

Typically, these firms are run by a very powerful chief executive who has ambitious plans and a strong tendency to make very bold decisions. As a consequence, F_1 companies are often involved in a process of rapid expansion. Many of them pursue a strategy of internal growth by developing new product lines and broaching new markets. The majority, however, attempt to grow via acquisitions. Not surprisingly, the pace of growth overtaxes the firm's financial and managerial resources.

A corollary weakness is that growth and increased diversity in the markets of a firm usually create the need for more broad-based and comprehensive information systems. As the firm grows, the intelligence system often lags behind and becomes increasingly inadequate with the passage of time.

Finally, the chief executives of the F_1 firms are used to running their own show. They are loath to delegate meaningful degrees of authority to, and to consult with, their middle managers. The need for delegation becomes more pressing as expansion escalates the complexity of operations. The failure to delegate results in an overburdened CEO who is forced to run the firm by a "seat of the pants" style. Inadequate attention is paid to the development of long-term plans and strategies, and the firm loses control over new subsidiaries or divisions.

A schematic representation of the problem syndrome of the F_1 firms is contained in exhibit 5.1 The arrows represent the direction of hypothesized cause-effect relationships. The roots of the problem generally are found on the left-hand side of the diagram and the symptoms are on the right-hand side. It is usually necessary to remove as many as possible of the former to

EXHIBIT 5.1   The F₁ Syndrome

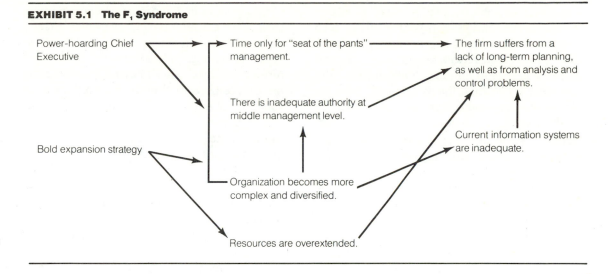

achieve a lasting turnaround. The following disguised anecdotes, taken from case histories of firms experiencing the F_1 syndrome, should help demonstrate the sources of the principal weaknesses.

■ Jackson Fire Plug Company was run by an aggressive entrepreneur who bought controlling interest in the firm with the intent of having it serve as a basis for a conglomerate. The CEO, Henry Grabbe, acquired new companies so quickly that careful scrutiny was impossible and unpleasant surprises were inevitable.

Sales increased fourteenfold in five years and most of the merger partners were in unrelated fields of endeavor. Grabbe consistently ignored the warnings of his accountants that financial resources were being depleted, that the firm was becoming dangerously leveraged, and that there appeared to be more problems than met the eye with the new acquisitions. Inadequate data made it impossible to discern the health of new subsidiaries.

■ Large Pot Corporation, an industrial boiler maker, had as its Chief Executive Burton Severe. Severe's control over the firm was absolute. In a bold departure from the past, Severe, without consulting managers better experienced in these matters than himself, ventured into the market for nuclear pressure vessels. The technologies required to produce such vessels and the characteristics of the market that purchased these products were completely different from LPC's old lines. In fact, neither Severe nor his staff knew very much at all about the potential difficulties surrounding the new venture. Important mistakes were made in constructing inappropriate new plant and equipment, recruiting inadequately skilled labor, delegating insufficient operating authority to those "in charge" of the new venture, and signing long-term sales and delivery contracts that were unrealistically ambitious and financially dangerous. What is more, a great deal of capital was spent upon the new venture. Eventually, the company's survival was seriously threatened.

F_2: The Stagnant Bureaucracy

Famous Last Words   Well, our methods and product lines were fine in the past and we'll be damned if we're going to change a successful strategy just because of some temporary fad.

The F_2 firm is also dominated by a power-hoarding chief executive. Yet it is very different from the F_1 company. The F_2 firms fail in part because they ignore their customers, competitors, and relevant developments in operating technologies. They also have a strong aversion to change. Even when low- and middle-level managers alert top executives to an important threat or a lucrative opportunity, this is ignored. The rationale for the status quo usually involves a reaffirmation of the soundness of past "successful" strategies and the merits of a conservative resource management program.

F_2 firms have existed in an unchanging and tranquil environment for long periods of time. In the past, any costly efforts at change could indeed be safely viewed as superfluous. Typically, the executive in charge has become acclimatized to operating under stable conditions over the years, and he refuses to recognize that these conditions have changed.

The great amount of power that the chief executive wields and his reluctance to condone change make it hard for his managers to institute required reforms. Problems of poor manager morale sometimes result. Much more often, however, lower levels of managers are not even sufficiently aware of the need for change. The firm's structure does not encourage scanning and analysis of the marketplace. Also, the dissemination of information that is gathered can be rather restricted since interdepartmental discussions about problems are rare. In contrast, such discussions in healthy firms can trigger further analysis and information-gathering on problems and thus may result in pressures for change and adaptation.

It is common for F_2 firms to be run in a bureaucratic manner. That is, much of the firm's functioning is automatic. It is conditioned by past policies, formal rules and regulations, and standard operating procedures and programs. Also, much attention is paid to the formal hierarchical reporting relationships, which are considered inviolate.

In summary, two basic obstacles thwart necessary change in the F_2 firm: first, a CEO who is convinced of the merits of the modus operandi of bygone days; second, a bureaucratic automaticity in the way the firm is run—that is, the emphasis is upon performing routine functions, and what is not covered by the established programs is ignored. The firm has effectively cut itself off from its surroundings—it marches to the beat of an "internal" drum. Exhibit 5.2 and the following anecdotes represent the F_2 syndrome.

EXHIBIT 5.2   The F$_2$ Syndrome

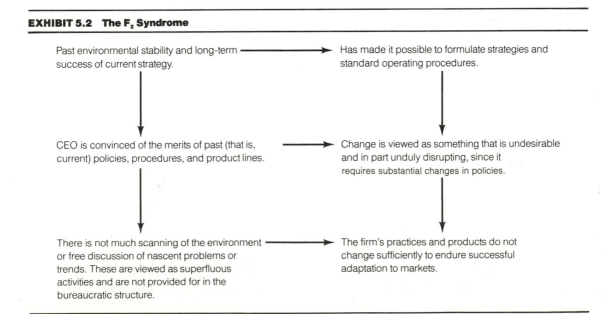

Past environmental stability and long-term success of current strategy. → Has made it possible to formulate strategies and standard operating procedures.

CEO is convinced of the merits of past (that is, current) policies, procedures, and product lines. → Change is viewed as something that is undesirable and in part unduly disrupting, since it requires substantial changes in policies.

There is not much scanning of the environment or free discussion of nascent problems or trends. These are viewed as superfluous activities and are not provided for in the bureaucratic structure. → The firm's practices and products do not change sufficiently to endure successful adaptation to markets.

■ The Old Shoe Company had for many years produced a narrow and traditional product line. Its motto was "any color you want as long as it's black"—although, to be fair, they always sold brown models as well. Competitors were introducing more stylish lines, and customers were becoming much more fashion-conscious. Still, the CEO, Tim Fuddy, insisted on producing a rather bland, proletarian line of products. Also, many of the company's models were aimed at the dwindling rural-agrarian markets, and little attempt was made to tailor products to the expanding urban sector.

■ Creaky Airlines was a pioneer in the industry. Earl Save, its founder and domineering chief, had the cautious soul of a greengrocer when it came to spending money, and his frugality became an industry legend. While Save's cost-consciousness helped profits during the monopoly years, it became a problem when Creaky had to compete. It was difficult to avoid losing customers while economizing ruthlessly on equipment and service. Much tardiness characterized the decision to order new jet aircraft, and substantial market share was lost as a result.

F_3: The Headless Firm

Famous Last Words We pride ourselves on the amount of autonomy that we leave to our divisions and departments. We control the finances, they make all the key strategies.

The F_3 firm suffers from a leadership vacuum and the consequent absence of a clearly defined strategy. The firm is expected to run itself—it is placed on "automatic pilot." The chief executive usually plays a predominantly figurehead role and is not actively engaged in setting long-term objectives. Nor does he bother to adapt the firm to combat threats or to capitalize upon opportunities. More important, the CEO fails to coordinate the efforts of the various corporate divisions and departments. The leadership gap results not only in an overly

vague strategy, but also in a decline in the effectiveness of everyday operations.

The F_3 firm has two interesting "context" features. Companies are usually large and quite diversified, and important changes in markets have occurred recently. For example, the amount of competition and the buying practices of consumers have become more challenging—features that make the absence of leadership particularly painful. Large firms, because of their diversity and complexity, tend to drift aimlessly unless there is a powerful rudder. Naturally, such an undirected orientation is doubly dangerous where there are important new threats that must be met with a cohesive and integrated strategy.

Personality factors play an important role in company leadership. When the top manager is not an expert on the company's major lines of business, some strong-willed middle managers may have parcelled the firm into quasi-independent fiefdoms. However, a tranquil environment may allow the need for a strong leader to go unnoticed. Also, the information systems often do not feed the top management the type of data needed for insight into, and effective control over, operations. Finally, a diverse and large enterprise requires a particularly strong leader to serve as an effective unifying force. Such persons have always been rare.

The repercussions of weak leadership are easy to pinpoint. Product-market innovation tends to be quite low. The firm is slow to adapt to changing conditions. There are no clear plans or strategies, and decisions made in different areas of the firm may conflict with one another. Exhibit 5.3 and the following anecdotes illustrate the F_3 syndrome.

■ Octopus Corporation is a widely diversified enterprise. The firm's continuing presence in more and more industries made it difficult to keep track of all the parts. The management group had nobody looking over its shoulder. Each division head focused his attention on his own industry, and

EXHIBIT 5.3 The F₃ Syndrome

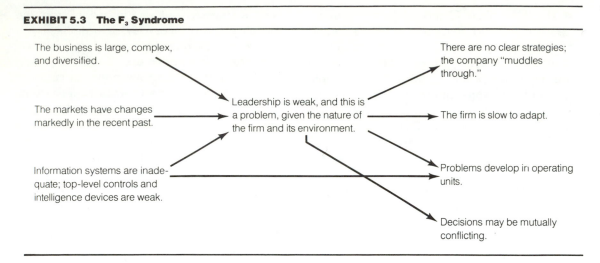

rarely saw reason to divert assets under his command into an entirely different, though more profitable, Octopus business run by a "rival" manager. Without question Octopus has failed to move with the times. It rarely abandons an original business even when it proves to be a great and costly burden.

■ Allied Machinery Corporation became a conglomerate long before the sophisticated techniques for managing such diverse and far-flung enterprises evolved, and for years it has failed to come to grips with that fact. The CEO, Mr. Meekly, has a view of management that is largely passive. He was overheard comparing Allied to a log floating down a stream, which represented the economy; its executives, he said, were ants trying to cling to that log. In this situation, management has no "concept of the business," and product-line diversity is actually a disadvantage because the firm competes with specialists who have larger volume and lower costs.

F₄: Swimming Upstream: The Aftermath

Famous Last Words In order to turn this company around, we have to take sizable risks. We've got to move quickly to plug up the weaknesses of our operations and go after greener pastures with new blood.

In some situations, such an orientation would be salutary. Where a firm is strong, has abundant financial resources and managerial talent, and is in need of a new product line, the strategy might be useful. Unfortunately, F₄ firms have been ravaged, usually over a considerable period of time, by past failures. Resources have been badly depleted, the market position substantially eroded, and plant and equipment may be outdated due to neglect. For such a firm, the "swimming upstream" strategy is usually devastating.

Typically, F₄ companies are already in great trouble, perhaps from being in an F₁, F₂, or F₃ mode for an extended period. The individual attempting to turn the company around is aware of the key problems but, generally, is inept in dealing with these problems. The CEO is usually new on the job, and his knowledge of the firm and its industry is not what it should be. Also, he has a tendency to try to effect a turnaround by himself or with the help of several "lieutenants" who joined the firm when he did. The new group often carries an implicit distrust of the older managers who may have contributed to past failures. Therefore, they have difficulty gaining the staff cooperation necessary for organizational improvement, and employees withhold the information needed to produce informed decisions at the top.

The CEO pushes the company a bit too much, trying to do too many things at once and overtaxing the already depleted resources of the firm. What is more, decisions tend to be impulsive and misdirected. The inexperience of top management, the lack of cooperation from other managers, and the desire to undertake projects of a rather major and risky nature often cause irreparable damage. In fact, the rate of bankruptcies was higher for F_4 companies than for any other failure syndrome. Exhibit 5.4 and the following examples summarize the problem.

■ Wildman Bank had for years been run by a hard-driving autocrat who made a lot of risky loans. When the loans went bad, he turned to bonds and when these fell in value, they could not be sold because of the loan losses. The bank was then trapped with a wad of low-yielding assets that had to be financed with progressively higher-cost money. When the new management took over, they found they didn't know how to run a healthy bank, much less a sick one. In a last-ditch effort to save the firm, they took grave risks by gambling heavily on the bond and foreign exchange markets. The bank eventually went into receivership.

■ Wobbly Steel was far behind the industry in terms of its facilities, operating efficiency, quality of products, costs, and personnel practices, when a financier took control of the firm and installed a new management team. The team was short of personnel with steel experience since only five of the top fourteen executives had any background in the business. The new CEO was direct, forceful, and impatient, and wasted no time before he started dictating ambitious plans. Unfortunately, the chief's behavior alienated the "old guard" managers, and he made his plans without understanding the constraints of the situation. The old guard was just standing at the sidelines waiting for the new fellow to fall flat on his face. They were not disappointed.

FINDINGS ON CORPORATE FAILURE

The failure studies suggest several general observations:

Organizational failure resembles organic illness. The symptoms are to be distinguished from the disease. Often tactical errors are confused with the more fundamental weaknesses that gave rise to such errors. In all instances, failure syndromes could be interpreted not only as a clustering of symptoms, but also as a scenario in which various primary factors led to the development of these symptoms.

EXHIBIT 5.4   The F₄ Syndrome

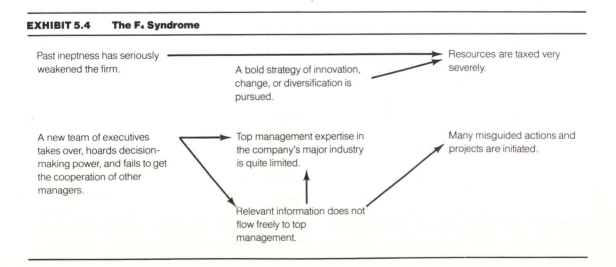

Past ineptness has seriously weakened the firm.

A bold strategy of innovation, change, or diversification is pursued.

Resources are taxed very severely.

A new team of executives takes over, hoards decision-making power, and fails to get the cooperation of other managers.

Top management expertise in the company's major industry is quite limited.

Many misguided actions and projects are initiated.

Relevant information does not flow freely to top management.

Organizational failure in many companies can be traced to a multitude of factors. Generally, no single mistake or weakness is the sole culprit. Managers and consultants often oversimplify in analyzing the difficulties or weaknesses of a company. There is usually a strong psychic reward in pinpointing the problem so that it becomes narrowly defined and appears amenable to a simple, stopgap solution. Unfortunately, our findings show that organizational problems may have many roots and manifestations requiring a program or multi-pronged attack that may involve fundamental corporate changes.

A number of quite diverse failure syndromes recur frequently in our sample; all are integrally related to the general nature of the firm. Conglomerates do not have the same problems as simple, functionally organized companies. High-technology firms do not face the same threats as those in stable environments. For example, large, highly diversified companies often suffer from problems in controlling their divisions and insuring that new acquisitions are profitable. Firms in stable industries may suffer from an unadaptive, counterinnovative, bureaucratic orientation. High-technology firms encounter most of their problems in the form of ill-conceived product-market innovations.

Failure is the result of three types of extremes. Too much product-market innovation or too little, too much emphasis on controls or too few controls, and an overly powerful chief executive or one who is a mere figurehead are the three types of extremes which cause corporate failure. Organizations are complex organisms, and excesses in particular areas may lead to imbalances in others. For example, a bold acquisition strategy may result in a depletion of resources and a state of administrative complexity that is too challenging for current procedures and personnel.

"Critical mass" is a concept as relevant to business as it is to physics. Some weaknesses are too trifling to be of serious consequence to firms, or are offset by important strengths. Sometimes, however, weaknesses have a multiplicative effect. An aggressively innovative product-market strategy coupled with an entrepreneurial chief executive whose power remains unchecked is a dangerous combination. A rule-bound, bureaucratic method of operating, coupled with a poor management information system, may also be deadly. On the other hand, a poor, formal management information system apparently may not have serious negative repercussions where there are relatively unchanging operations and markets, or when managers possess extensive expertise in their industry. Power-hoarding may also be far less threatening under such circumstances.

WARNING SIGNS TO LOOK FOR

Now that we have discussed the most popular failure syndromes that plague corporations, it may be useful to highlight some of the warning signs that indicate when a firm might be heading towards serious trouble. Executives can go through the following checklist, answering "yes" or "no" to the questions. The paragraphs following some of the sequences of questions can help the manager diagnose his firm. Tentative recommendations for corrective action are then suggested.

1. Is the firm run by a power-hoarding chief executive? Are all the decisions essentially being made by one or two people who are afraid to delegate?

2. Does the firm's growth strategy appear to be overly ambitious? That is, are sales and the array of businesses growing very rapidly? Is the administrative complexity of the firm rapidly accelerating as the result of acquisitions or extensive diversification of the product-market strategy?

3. Does there appear to be an overextension of financial resources because of excessive leverage and bank debt? Is existing managerial talent being stretched too thin because of the rapid expansion?

4. Is there increasing evidence that top managers' decisions reflect ignorance of what is going on in the field? Are crises that crop up in divisions and subsidiaries taking top managers by complete surprise? Are these occurring with notable frequency? Is the CEO extremely busy putting out fires and running from one crisis to another?

5. Is there almost no strategic planning being done? Does the company have a poorly defined product-market strategy and appear to be "riding off in all directions?"

If there are a significant number of affirmative responses to the questions in each of the first five categories, there may be a danger of succumbing to the F_1 "impulsive" or "running blind" syndrome. Should this be the case, the firm may have to set up better information systems, slow down the rate of expansion, clarify strategies, and get the top man to delegate more authority and to use middle management talent.

6. Is there a tendency to be very committed to old products, markets, and ways of doing things? Is the product-market scope so explicitly defined that it does not allow sufficient scope for innovation and adaptation? Do competitors appear to be gaining market share because of more novel products, services, production technologies, or merchandising techniques?

7. Are there elaborate standard operating procedures and extensively documented formal policies? Is a great deal of attention paid to formal reporting relationships, hierarchy, and symbols of status? Are policies, programs, and procedures notably resistant to change?

If the questions in categories 1, 4, 6, and 7 receive a significant number of affirmative responses, the F_2 "stagnant bureaucracy" syndrome may be encroaching. Some re-

lief may result from gathering explicit information on competitors' strategies and customer tastes to check whether the firm is in tune with its environment. If not, it might be useful to embark upon projects to seek the most profitable niche in the market, introduce new products or services, employ new technologies, and so on. But most important, management should be more receptive to suggestions for change and should make an effort to adapt to the markets on a continuous basis by setting up better internal communications networks. In this way, information on key trends may flow to the relevant decision-making parties.

The flow of information is facilitated by delegation of authority to middle management (information has to flow less far if lower-level managers are allowed to act on it). Also helpful is a process of informal communications in which parties may get together to make decisions on short notice and may speak frankly to one another. It should also be recognized that policies and programs, while they have a vital role to play, often can and must be changed. Finally, sometimes overprescription of tasks stifles the creativity of those assigned to carry them out, and suggestions for improvements are not generated.

8. Are there any signs of a leadership vacuum? For example, are all decisions made at the lower levels of management? Are strategies all "implicit," so that the firm muddles through instead of having a clear direction? Does the CEO play mainly a figurehead role and ignore key decision-making responsibilities?

9. Do decisions in one part of the firm conflict with those in other parts? For example, do new products of different divisions compete with one another? Is there evidence that departments or divisions are making decisions that make them look good at the expense of the firm as a whole?

If a good number of the responses to categories 4, 5, 8, and 9 are in the affirmative, the F_3 "headless firm" syndrome may be present. The critical need here is for leadership to knit together the diverse orientations of the subunits. A strong executive who has some direct familiarity with the company's key businesses would be very useful. He should probably be aided by a corporate staff whose task it would be to help control divisional operations. Also, corporate management needs to formulate overall strategies in combination with the divisional managers so that subunits of the firm work together in harmony toward mutually valued goals that are of benefit to the whole company.

10. Has the firm been subject to any of the above syndromes for a substantial length of time? Is there a very serious shortage of financial, managerial, or material resources?

11. Is there a relatively new and inexperienced team of managers that is attempting to turn the company around? Are there problems in getting the cooperation of more experienced managers?

12. Is the turnaround strategy relatively taxing to the firm's resources? Does it appear to involve too many changes too soon?

Affirmative answers to the questions in 10, 11, and 12 may signal the F_4 "swimming upstream" syndrome. This situation is perhaps the most difficult one to handle because of the often acute resource shortages.

Where possible, a "go slow" approach that builds on strength should be attempted. The first emphasis should be on dealing only with the most extreme crises. Then firms should get out of money-losing operations and should hire more expert managers. To identify the situations requiring immediate attention, the new managers should solicit help from the old guard who may have surprising insights into what is needed. The stress should be on open communications and a concerted effort to discover the most pressing items requiring change.

It is important to note that affirmative responses to several questions do not necessarily indicate serious trouble. Only when the affirmative responses are arrayed in the pattern of one of the major problem syndromes should there be concern. Such a situation indicates that weaknesses are mutually reinforcing or are occurring with the wrong types of contextual factors, thus causing a serious threat. Obviously, the remedial recommendations made in a brief article can only be gross and tentative. It is important that managers who find their firm exhibiting the danger signals attempt to diagnose their own syndrome in order to find its *roots* and to embark upon a sufficiently broad-based remedial program to eradicate not only the symptoms of the problem, but the underlying factors as well.

■ Neurotic Organizations: Symptoms, Causes, and Treatment

JERRY B. HARVEY and D. RICHARD ALBERTSON

Organizations, like individuals, develop neuroses. The toll on an organization's behavior, measured in terms of production, efficiency, absenteeism, turnover, overhead, and morale, is tremendous. And, since each of these organization variables has personal antecedents, the price paid by individual organization members, measured in terms of misery and loss of self-esteem and confidence, is inestimable. But organizations, like people, can be cured of neurotic behavior and returned to a state of healthy functioning. The purpose of this article is to describe the symptoms of organization neurosis, to identify some of its causes, and to define a course of treatment for restoring neurotic organizations to health. Implicit throughout are descriptions of the role and function of an organization consultant in the process of diagnosis and treatment.

SYMPTOMS OF ORGANIZATION NEUROSIS

Perhaps the most effective way to get a feel for the symptoms of organization neurosis is to read summaries of interviews with several employees including the head of one neurotic organization.

"Neurotic Organizations: Symptoms, Causes, and Treatment" Parts I and II by Jerry B. Harvey and D. Richard Albertson. Abridged with permission from *Personnel Journal*, copyright September and October 1971. References deleted. See original work.

Interview I

Consultant: How are things going on the job?

Employee A: Terrible, I hate to come to work. And once I'm here, I don't get anything done. We just sit around and gripe. The only thing I look forward to is vacation.

Consultant: What's the problem? What's causing the trouble?

Employee A: We have a couple of problems. First, we have a lousy boss. He never holds up our end with the higher-ups. And second, at least two of the five units making up this division should not be reporting to him. Putting Sales and Research under the same man is absurd. In a lot of ways they are competitive. There is no reason for them to work together. They never have and never will.

Consultant: Have you ever confronted your boss with his failure to "carry the flag?"

Employee A: Hell, no. Do you think I'm crazy or something?

Consultant: What about the problem with Sales and Research? What are you doing to solve that?

Employee A: Just last week we met and agreed to operate under a combined budget.

Interview II

Consultant: How are things going on the job?

Employee B: Pretty bad. This is a frustrating place to work. Right now I'm looking for another job. I take as much vacation and sick leave as I can. And I don't get anything done when I'm here. Really, I'm just marking time, hoping things will get better.

Consultant: What's causing all the frustration?

Employee B: Well, for one thing our organization set-up doesn't make sense. Whoever designed it must have been crazy. Having Sales and Research report to the same man is unworkable. We spend half our time fighting one another. In addition, our boss doesn't represent our viewpoint to the top.

Consultant: Are you taking any steps to deal with the problems you just described?

Employee B: Yes, just last week the president instructed my boss to get us together to solve the morale problem. It's beginning to cut into everyone's production. The last quarter was very poor from a profit standpoint. And two of our best researchers took jobs with another company.

Consultant: What did you do?

Employee B: We had an all-day meeting and agreed to operate under a combined budget. That should force us to work together more effectively.

Consultant: One other question. What about your boss? Has he ever asked whether he is doing an adequate job of carrying the division's viewpoint to the top?

Employee B: Yes, just the other day, he said he had heard by the grapevine that we thought he wasn't giving us good representation with the president and his staff.

Consultant: What did you say?

Employee B: I said I thought he was doing a good job.

Interview III

Consultant: What problems and issues are facing your division at the present time?

Boss: Well, morale is at an all-time low. We have had a couple of good people quit and go to other companies. And production is down. The heat is on me and everyone else. I've about given up.

Consultant: What's the cause of it?

Boss: One big problem is the way we are organized. My boss gave me several units that don't have any reason to work together. In fact, two of the units are actually competitive in a functional sense. With that kind of arrangement, it's impossible to build teamwork among the staff.

Consultant: What have you done about it?

Boss: Well, last week I gave a pep talk to the staff at our weekly meeting and said we have to work together more effectively. And to insure that we do, we developed a unit budget that ties each subgroup's performance into the overall performance of the division.

Consultant: Have you ever thought about telling your boss that the way you are organized does not make sense?

Boss: I've tried, but I can't seem to make him understand.

Consultant: Have you really pushed him hard?

Boss: I'm not about to do that. He might think I am not an effective manager.

As can be seen by the interviews, the neurotic organization exhibits a number of specific symptoms that are collectively expressed by its members.

Its members complain of frustration, worry, backbiting, loss of self-esteem, and a general sense of impotence. They do not feel their skills are being adequately used. As a result, they become less efficient and look for ways to avoid the job, such as taking vacation, taking sick leave, and "giving up" or "opting out" of trying to solve the problems they see as causing the pain.

1. Blaming others for the problems. Its members attempt to place much of the blame for the dilemma on others, particularly the boss. In "backroom" conversations among subordinates, he is termed incompetent, ineffective, "out of touch," or as a candidate for transfer or early retirement. To his face nothing is said or, at best, oblique or misleading information is given concerning his impact on the organization.

2. Subgroup formation. As pain and frustration become more intense, the personnel form into identifiable subgroups. These subgroups may develop on the basis of friendship with trusted acquaintances, meeting during coffee or over lunch to share rumors, complaints, fantasies, or strategies for dealing with the problems at hand. The most important effect of such meetings is to heighten the overall anxiety level in the organization rather than to help realistically cope with its problems.

3. Agreement as to problems. Its members generally agree as to the character of problems causing the pain. For example, in the interviews related above, organization members agree that the organization has two basic problems: (1) The composition of the units reporting to the same superior is inappropriate and (2) There is a failure to communicate the urgency of the composition issue to upper levels of management. The first problem reflects an important *task* issue, i.e., how to organize effectively. The second reflects an equally important *maintenance* concern, i.e., how to work together in such a way that the organization functions effectively. That agreement as to task and maintenance issues bridges both hierarchical and functional lines. Stated differently, the boss and his subordinates see the problems in the same way as do employees from Sales and Research. Although organization members may be unaware of the degree to which they agree with one another, the reality is they do agree.

4. Members act contrary to data and information they possess. Perhaps the most unique characteristic of neurotic organizations is that its members act in ways contrary to the data and information they possess. In analogous terms, it would be as if an outside observer viewed the following vignette involving twenty people from a neurotic organization:

Observer (approaching a group sitting around a camp fire): How are things going?
Organization Members (who are holding their hands over an open fire): Awful. It's too hot. We are burning up. The pain is excruciating. Our heads are too close to the coals.
Observer: What do you intend to do about it?
Organization Members: Move our hands closer to the fire, what else?

Although the analogy may sound absurd on the surface, it is certainly no more absurd than the following conversation that occurred in an actual organization:

Consultant: You say there is no possible functional relationship among the groups reporting to your boss and it is impossible to build one.
Organization Members: Yes, that's right.

Consultant: What do you propose to do about it?
Organization Members: Meet more often so we will have more opportunities to learn to work together.

It is this characteristic that really defines neurotic organization behavior the same way it defines neurotic individual behavior. The individual who consistently acts contrary to his best "internal signals" becomes neurotic, and if he acts in concert with a variety of others, the organization as an entity develops neurotic symptoms. Stated conversely, any human system must act congruently with reality if it is to function effectively.

5. Members behave differently outside the organization. Finally, the key to the diagnosis of organization neurosis is the fact that outside the organization context, members do not either suffer the pain nor demonstrate the irrational behavior (such as behaving contrary to their own views of reality) that they demonstrate in their day-to-day work. Outside the organization, individual members get along better, are happier, and perform more effectively then they do within it, a fact that heightens their discomfort when living and working within the organization.

CAUSES OF NEUROTIC ORGANIZATION BEHAVIOR

Given a description of organization neurosis, the question is then: Why do organization members engage in behavior that is both individually and organizationally destructive? Basically, there are two reasons: (1) lack of awareness and (2) fantasies about consequences of alternative actions.

Lack of Awareness
First, organization members are unaware of their behavior and the consequences it has

for them as individuals and for the organization as an entity. Such lack of awareness may involve any of three levels. At the most superficial level, an organization member may be unaware of the degree to which the information and feelings he possesses are shared by others in the organization. Thus, he may feel as if he is alone in his diagnosis of the organization's problems. Or, he may feel that, at most, the subgroup to which he belongs agrees as to the character of the organization's problems. He seldom realizes that his understandings and beliefs are widely shared across functional and hierarchical lines and that he is not an isolate.

Consultant: Do you think people other than yourself believe that the unit needs to be reorganized?

Employee: Well, several guys that work with me agree on that issue, but I doubt if any others do.

Consultant: What would you say if I told you that virtually everyone in the division feels the same as you do about that issue?

Employee: I'd say you must be kidding.

Since that lack of agreement reflects a simple information gap, it is the simplest form of unawareness to correct.

At the second level, organization members may be unaware of the dysfunctional group norms and standards that inhibit or prevent their coping with the problems at hand. It is at the normative level that the difference between individual and organizational neurosis is most clearly articulated. Individual neurosis stems from *personal* dynamics unique to the individual. Organization neurosis stems from *collective* dynamics unique to the organization. Thus, organizations develop social norms and standards, neurotic in character, the breaking of which by individual members results in the application of social pressure to conform. For example, some organizations develop dysfunctional norms mitigating against open discussion of important organization issues.

Organization Member A: I think we ought to confront the issue of whether we are appropri-

ately organized. I personally don't think these units belong together.

Organization Member B: Oh, knock it off! Let's not get involved in something like that.

Organization Member C: What are you trying to do? We don't need things stirred up any more than they already are.

Organization Member D: Yes, the problems aren't as bad as you crack them up to be. We really work together rather well. I move we change the subject.

As one consultant put it, "fish are the last to know that they are in water." So it is with organization members. They are frequently the last to know of the dysfunctional norms that govern and occasionally consume them. However, as Lewin has demonstrated, behavior rooted in group standards and norms is easier to change than behavior rooted in individual character structure. Because of this principle, organization neurosis is potentially more amenable to change than is the individual variety.

Finally, a third level relates to the degree to which organization members are unaware of the manner in which they contribute to maintaining the problems. For example, some members may see the part others, particularly the boss, play in maintaining destructive organization norms and standards, but few sense their own roles in the process.

Consultant: You say your boss is at fault, that he should demand of his superior that the situation be changed.

Employee A: Absolutely. He is doing a lousy job.

Employee B: You can say that again.

Consultant: Have you or any other members of your division ever demanded of your boss that he do a better job of representing your group to the President?

Employee A: No. That's not what I'm around here for.

Employee B: Me neither.

Employee C: I think it would be foolish and disrespectful to do something like that.

Consultant: It seems to me as if you may be doing exactly the same thing you don't want your boss to do.

Employee C (lamely): We are?

It is as if the identification with superiors, other peers, or the organization itself is so great that employees lose their capacities to understand either their individual or collective contributions to the dysfunctional organization process. Since the dynamics supporting such lack of awareness tend to be so deep within the individual and group psyche they are the hardest to identify, make explicit, and change.

Fantasies About Consequences of Alternative Actions

Second, even when organization members are aware of the degree to which they agree as to the substance of the problems, are knowledgeable about the group norms and standards that prevent their coping effectively with those problems, and are cognizant of their own unique ways of maintaining those dysfunctional norms and standards, they still may be unable to take effective problem-solving action. Again, the question is: Why?

In most cases, the inaction relates to rich and varied fantasies organization members have about possible negative consequences that may befall them if they do act. The fantasies have a myth-like quality and are frequently unrelated to reality.

Consultant: Each of you seems to agree this division needs to be reorganized and that the present format is unworkable. Why don't you suggest to your boss that you reorganize?

Employee A: He might fire us for treading on his territory. He's supposed to think of that, not us.

Employee B: The new organization might be worse than the present one. It's not worth taking the chance.

Employee C: I'm sure things will get better if we just wait it out. Life isn't as bad as we make it out to be.

Employee D: I've got a mortgage payment on the house. I can't afford to do anything that rocks the boat.

Consultant: Is there any possibility that things might get better if you do something other than wait?

Various Employees: We doubt it.

The fantasy-like quality comes from the fact that the projected outcomes are seldom if ever tested for reality. In general, such fantasies reflect a tremendous amount of underlying anxiety and concern that has to be taken into account in any process designed to treat the "neurosis."

The symptoms of a neurotic organization described above serve, in effect, as a diagnostic checklist for identifying organization neurosis.

PROCEDURES FOR TREATING NEUROSIS

In this part of the article, procedures for treating organization neurosis will be discussed. Like individual neurosis, it can be treated and, like the individual variety, the treatment is complex.

Collect Data

The first step is to collect data from a representative sample of organization members. It is particularly important that more than one level of the organization be represented in the data collection, since issues of hierarchy and authority are generally central to the kinds of problems identified. On the basis of their experiences with a variety of organizations, the authors have found that open-ended interviews conducted around three basic questions produce the data required. These questions are:

1. What issues and problems are facing the organization at the present time?

2. What is causing these problems?

3. What strengths are available in the organization to solve the problems?

Interviews last forty-five minutes to an hour. Basic to their success is that they be conducted by someone who can view the organization from an essentially objective standpoint. Although it is possible that an inside consultant with enough functional autonomy can achieve and maintain the kind of objective detachment required, an outside consultant is generally preferred.

An outsider is less likely to be caught up in the dysfunctional processes underlying the neurosis and therefore is less likely to have distorted perspectives of the organization and its problems.

Essentially, verbatim notes are taken by the consultant. When all interviews are completed, the data from interviewees are sorted into themes that are identified with nonevaluative titles. Actual statements of organization members are grouped under each theme. A typical set of themes and supporting statements are shown in Exhibit 5.5.

It should be stressed that the data must be verbatim accounts of what the organization members said relative to each theme. The data must not be a summary of what the

---

EXHIBIT 5.5   Examples of Themes, Supporting Data, and Summary Statements

Theme 1: Division Composition

1. The composition of this division does not make sense.
2. This division is a group of independent units operating under an umbrella.
3. It is not a group. It is a collection of units just thrown together.
4. Research does not belong in the division.
5. The way the division is constituted is inappropriate.
6. The division needs to be subdivided.
7. It is a mixture of apples and oranges.
8. The division is made up of remnants of an earlier era. There is not much logic to it.
9. What we have is a variety of subgroups.
10. Units do not have much in common.
11. It is not a group in any sense.

Summary Statement

The present composition and/or structure of the division is inappropriate, out of step with the opportunity to accomplish our purposes, and should be changed.

Theme 2: Collaboration within the Division

1. Some staff members do not communicate with anyone.
2. No communication within division.
3. Staff share few common goals—the exception is survival.
4. There's no relationship between some units, like Sales and Research.
5. There's too much time talking as a group. The subjects talked about are not perceived as making much difference.
6. There is no support. I occasionally feel close to harassment. We frequently talk to other staff members rather than confront the person we should talk to.
7. Within the division some are more willing to jump unit lines than others.
8. Other units in the division fight each other for stature.
9. Some units in the division are pro-active while others sit around waiting to be told what to do.
10. Each unit is a kingdom unto itself.

Summary Statement

In general, units within the division do not work together.

Theme 3: Pain

1. We are suffering from . . .
2. I feel no support and occasionally feel close to harassment.
3. People who are committed are frustrated as well.
4. Nothing feeds failure like failure.
5. Creativity is squelched.
6. Joe Smith is being stifled.
7. We want to contribute in a positive way, but can't.
8. There is a lot of insecurity and morale is very low.
9. The division is not conducive to good mental health and working conditions.

Summary Statement

Most division personnel are frustrated, worried, and feel insecure; morale is low.

consultant would like organization members to say or believe. Throughout the process of consultation, the actual data contributed by organization members, not the consultant's biases and prejudices, must be the topic of exploration.

Data Feedback to Organization Members

After data are collected and sorted into themes, the consultant presents both the themes and supporting statements to the interviewees in a modified version of a confrontation session. During this session, which usually requires several hours, organization members are encouraged to discuss, clarify, and modify both the themes and the supporting statements. Whenever organization members are satisfied that the themes and the supporting data are accurate reflections of their own feelings and knowledge, they are asked to develop a single summary statement that adequately summarizes the data contributed under each theme. (A theme is arbitrarily defined as an issue or concern that is spontaneously mentioned by at least 50 percent of the organization members interviewed). Examples of summary statements are also contained in Exhibit 5.5.

After each theme has been discussed and a summary statement developed, organization members are asked to vote publicly as to whether they agree or disagree with the content of the summary statement.

Votes are counted, and if a clear majority do not agree with the summary statement, the consultant works with the group to clarify the reasons for the disagreement. Discussion continues until the statement is modified so that most organization members can agree with it, or until the statement is eliminated because it does not actually reflect their feelings and attitudes.

Taking a public vote is important because it transfers ownership of the themes and the supporting data from the consultant to the organization members themselves. Stated differently, the vote forces the organization members to accept responsibility for the validity or lack of validity of the data they contributed.

Once the data are identified as belonging to organization members rather than to the consultants, the next step is to ask each member to "own up" to his individual contribution to each issue represented by the various themes.

Thus, each organization member is asked to produce a series of written statements according to the following directions:

> For each of the summary statements, write a few sentences describing the way in which you contribute to the issue that is summarized. Your descriptions will belong to you. Although you may want to share your thoughts with others later on, there will be no requirement to do so.

Here, the purpose is to help each organization member focus on his possible contribution to maintaining the processes causing the problems. It also helps to set a norm of examining one's own contribution to the organization's problems rather than blaming others.

Sharing the Theory

One of the most important steps in the treatment process involves the sharing of the consultant's theory with organization members. Again, organization members' own views of reality, which they have affirmed through a public vote, is central to the presentation process. The rationale for presenting the model is that theory itself is a powerful intervention. In brief, it helps organization members diagnose and understand organization problems and plan action steps that do not foster the continuation of those problems.

Basically, the theory is presented by the consultant as follows:

When organization members (1) experience pain and frustration, (2) agree with one another as to the problems and causes, and (3) act in ways contrary to their own thoughts, feelings, and information, the following assumptions should be tested: (1) Organization members are implicitly or explicitly collaborating with one another to maintain the status quo and (2) Organization members have fantasies about the disastrous consequences of confronting those issues and concerns they know and agree cause the pain and frustration.

At this point, the consultant helps organization members apply the model to their own lives by "walking them through" an actual case involving their own organization.

Consultant: In this organization you agree that you are unhappy and frustrated (theme 3), that the organization is inappropriately constituted (theme 1), and that units do not work well together (theme 2). Yet, when asked by top management to make a proposal for solving the problems of the organization, what happened?

Organization Member: We made a proposal.

Consultant: What did you say in the proposal?

Organization Member: That we develop a matrix organization and operate under a combined budget.

Consultant: What will that decision require?

Organization Member: Well, for one thing, a lot more teamwork.

Consultant: Is that decision congruent with the reality that everyone feels the organization is inappropriately constituted and that the various subparts do not work well together?

Organization Member: Oh, hell! We've done it again, haven't we?

Using members' own data forces them to become aware of the discrepancy between their own views of reality (we don't work well together) and the actions they take that, in effect, deny that reality (making decisions that require working more closely together). This new awareness confronts them with the necessity of making a conscious choice to explore alternatives based on their views of reality (for example, dissolving the division and reorganizing, a solution that may require painful shifts in job, status, and location) or continuing to act on the basis of irrational fantasies that are individually and organizationally destructive (organizing in a way that denies their beliefs that the composition of the division is inappropriate).

If the consultant is to be effective in helping the organization alter its destructive patterns, he must continue to help members confront the basic discrepancy that exists between their views of reality and the decisions they make.

CONSULTANT FUNCTIONS IN CHANGE PROCESS

Throughout the data feedback session, and in other encounters within the organization, events occur that mirror the problems organization members have in working during their day-to-day activities. In these encounters, the consultant has a variety of functions, all of which require his being sensitive to underlying emotional and process issues. Examples of these include the following.

Building Awareness of Dysfunctional Group Standards and Norms

The process of presenting data to the persons who contribute it helps organization members become aware of the degree to which they agree with one another about the character of the organization's problems. In effect, the sharing of data assists in solving problems stemming from an "information gap." However, the consultant must also help organization members become aware of dysfunctional norms and group standards that inhibit their capacity to cope with problems identified in the data sharing stage.

Organization Member (to consultant): I did not like being forced by you to fill out the questionnaire regarding my contribution to maintaining the problems. When you asked me to do that, I felt very manipulated. I didn't think the process would lead to anything and still don't. I just filled it out to suit you. It sure didn't suit any need of mine.

Consultant: I wonder how many others felt that way.

Various Members: I did.

Consultant: In some ways, that is similar to the tendency of members of this organization to act contrary to their own best views of reality.

Organization Member: I don't understand that either. We just did as we were told. What's wrong with that?

Consultant: Well, it looks as if most of you did not want to respond to the questionnaire because you didn't think it was relevant. Yet everyone responded and nothing was said at the time. That's very similar to not confronting the problem of reorganization even though there is uniform agreement that reorganization is needed.

Organization Member: You got us again.

Consultant: I didn't get you.

Organization Member: Yeah. We got ourselves. We contributed to the problem again.

Previous Member: Yes, but he still makes me mad, catching us.

Coping with Feelings

As the previous vignette indicates, the members of a neurotic organization, like neurotic individuals, demonstrate extreme difficulty in the area of learning new behavior. They find it difficult to appraise the past in the light of the present. As a consequence, they find it hard to assimilate and utilize new knowledge, although it may be all around them and clearly apparent to an outsider. They seem to be restricted to coping responses rooted in history. Although these responses may be inadequate and dysfunctional, organization members persist in using them and even exert a tremendous amount of collective energy in trying to maintain them.

Much of that energy in a change process may be directed against the consultant in the form of anger and resentment or lavish praise.

Organization Member: He makes me mad, catching us that way.

Organization Member: He doesn't make me mad. He sees things none of the rest of us see. He's doing a great job.

The feelings of ambivalence are understandable, for the consultant, in ways similar to the individual therapist, represents both a threat and a promise to organization members.

It is important for the change process that the consultant understand this and be prepared to cope with such feelings when they arise, because in any organization change process, as in an individual therapeutic process, there is an initial period of disorganization and anxiety before new, more functional norms and standards are developed.

The coping can take two forms. One is to help members learn from their feelings.

Consultant: Both comments may reflect some reality and some fantasy. For example, I don't think I "caught" anyone. And I also doubt that I'm the only one who sees what I reported. I would like to check that out with others here.

The other form of coping is more pragmatic. The authors suspect that it is around this issue that many organization change processes are terminated. Thus, organization members must be informed in advance of the possible turmoil they may feel and of the potential positive consequences. Otherwise, a change process may be stopped at the very time constructive change takes place. In short, just as it is with a neurotic individual, the neurotic organization is its own worst enemy.

Encouraging Fantasy and Reality Testing

One of the basic reasons for acting contrary to one's own view of reality is fantasies about the consequences for alternative actions. Again, underlying these fantasies is a great deal of emotionality and concern that must be dealt with if organization members are to clearly differentiate between fantasy and reality. One way to facilitate the process of clarification is to encourage the process of fantasizing.

Consultant: One of the reasons people sometimes act contrary to what they really know is that they have notions about what will happen if they actually do what needs to be done.

Organization Member: What do you mean?

Consultant: Well, one of the reasons people may not want to question whether Jim (the boss) is confronting enough in upholding the viewpoint of this organization to top management is that they don't know what he might do to those who question his actions.

Organization Member: Damn right. He might fire me. (nervous laughter)

Another Member: Or send me back to the production line.

Another Member: Or get back at me when annual reviews come along.

Interviewer: Has anyone in this group ever questioned Jim's actions before?

Organization Member: I have.

Consultant: What did he say?

Organization Member: He said "thanks" and that he was unaware of what he was doing.

Another Member: Same thing happened to me.

Consultant: I wonder if all the worries you have voiced are justified? Do they have any reality?

Organization Member: It doesn't sound like they do.

COACHING

Although organization members may (1) have full access to information, (2) be aware of dysfunctional norms and standards, (3) understand the way they contribute to maintaining these norms, and (4) be able to distinguish between fantasized consequences and reality, they still may not be able to develop new ways of coping. Therefore, another function of a consultant in a change process is to "coach" organization members in new behaviors. Such coaching can take place in group meetings, in private conversations, and in various subgroup configurations.

Organization Member: Okay, I want to tell Jim (the boss) that I don't think he is holding up our end with the President. What do I say? Do I say, "Jim, you are a lousy manager?" That doesn't seem to make much sense.

Consultant: One alternative would be to admit your own feelings about Jim and what he is doing.

Organization Member: What do you mean?

Consultant: Well, you might say, "When I don't feel you represent us at the top it makes it a lot harder for me to do my job in addition to making me downright angry." That way you're not saying that Jim is personally incompetent. You're saying what his actions do to you.

Organization Member: Hmm. I've never thought of that approach before.

In summary, the treatment of organization neurosis involves the use of consultants who help members (1) collect reality-centered information about the organization, (2) gain understanding of the dysfunctional norms and standards that keep them from using whatever information is available, (3) help them in differentiating reality from fantasy when assessing alternative solutions to the problems that are identified, and (4) assist them in developing the skills necessary to implement realistic alternatives. Although organization neurosis involves complex long-term treatment, change is possible and well worth the effort in terms of both economic and humanistic savings.

■ Patterns of Organization Change

LARRY E. GREINER

Today many top managers are attempting to introduce sweeping and basic changes in the behavior and practices of the supervisors and the subordinates throughout their organizations. Whereas only a few years ago the target of organization change was limited to a small work group or a single department, especially at lower levels, the focus is now converging on the organization as a whole, reaching out to include many divisions and levels at once, and even the top managers themselves. There is a critical need at this time to understand better this complex process, especially in terms of which approaches lead to successful changes and which actions fail to achieve the desired results.

REVOLUTIONARY PROCESS

The shifting emphasis from small- to large-scale organization change represents a significant departure from past managerial thinking. For many years, change was regarded more as an evolutionary than a revolutionary process. The evolutionary assumption reflected the view that change is a product of one minor adjustment after another, fueled by time and subtle environmental forces largely outside the direct control of management. This relatively passive

philosophy of managing change is typically expressed in words like these:

> Our company is continuing to benefit from a dynamically expanding market. While our share of the market has remained the same, our sales have increased 15 percent over the past year. In order to handle this increased business, we have added a new marketing vice-president and may have to double our sales force in the next two years.

Such an optimistic statement frequently belies an unbounding faith in a beneficent environment. Perhaps this philosophy was adequate in less competitive times, when small patchwork changes, such as replacing a manager here and there, were sufficient to maintain profitability. But now the environments around organizations are changing rapidly and are challenging managements to become far more alert and inventive than they ever were before.

Management Awakening

In recent years more and more top managements have begun to realize that fragmented changes are seldom effective in stemming the underlying tides of stagnation and complacency that can subtly creep into a profitable and growing organization. While rigid and uncreative attitudes are slow to develop, they are also slow to disappear, even in the face of frequent personnel changes. Most often these signs of decay can be recognized in managerial behavior that (1) is oriented more to the past than to the future, (2) recognizes the obligations of ritual more than the challenges of current problems, and (3) owes allegiance more to department goals than to overall company objectives.

Management's recent awakening to these danger signs has been stimulated largely by the rapidly changing tempo and quality of its environment. Consider:

■ Computer technology has narrowed the decision time span.
■ Mass communication has heightened public awareness of consumer products.
■ New management knowledge and techniques have come into being.
■ Technological discoveries have multiplied.
■ New world markets have opened up.
■ Social drives for equality have intensified.
■ Governmental demands and regulations have increased.

As a result, many organizations are currently being challenged to shift, or even reverse, gears in order to survive, let alone prosper.

A number of top managements have come around to adopting a revolutionary attitude toward change, in order to bridge the gap between a dynamic environment and a stagnant organization. They feel that they can no longer sit back and condone organizational self-indulgence, waiting for time to heal all wounds. So, through a number of means, revolutionary attempts are now being made to transform their organizations rapidly by altering the behavior and attitudes of their line and staff personnel at all levels of management. While each organization obviously varies in its approach, the overarching goal seems to be the same: to get everyone psychologically redirected toward solving the problems and challenges of today's business environment. Here, for example, is how one company president describes his current goal for change:

> I've got to get this organization moving, and soon. Many of our managers act as if we were still selling the products that used to be our bread and butter. We're in a different

business now, and I'm not sure that they realize it. Somehow we've got to start recognizing our problems, and then become more competent in solving them. This applies to everyone here, including me and the janitor. I'm starting with a massive reorganization that I hope will get us pulling together instead of in fifty separate directions.

Striking Similarities

Although there still are not many studies of organization change, the number is growing, and a survey of them shows that it is already possible to detect some striking similarities running throughout their findings. I shall report some of these similarities, under two headings.

1. *Common approaches* being used to initiate organization change.

2. *Reported results*—what happened in a number of cases of actual organization change.

I shall begin with the approaches, and then attempt to place them within the perspective of what has happened when these approaches were applied. As we shall see, only a few of the approaches used tend to facilitate successful change, but even here we find that each is aided by unplanned forces preceding and following its use. Finally, I shall conclude with some tentative interpretations as to what I think is actually taking place when an organization change occurs.

COMMON APPROACHES

In looking at the various major approaches being used to *introduce* organization change, one is immediately struck by their position along a "power distribution" continuum. At one extreme are those that rely on *unilateral* authority. More toward the middle of the continuum are the *shared* approaches. Finally, at the opposite extreme are the *delegated* approaches.

As we shall see later, the *shared* approaches tend to be emphasized in the more successful organization changes. Just why this is so is an important question we will consider in the concluding section. For now, though, let us gain a clearer picture of the various approaches as they appear most frequently in the literature of organization change.

Unilateral Action

At this extreme on the power distribution continuum, the organization change is implemented through an emphasis on the authority of a manager's hierarchical position in the company. Here, the definition and solution to the problem at hand tend to be specified by the upper echelons and directed downward through formal and impersonal control mechanisms. The use of unilateral authority to introduce organization change appears in three forms.

By decree. This is probably the most commonly used approach, having its roots in centuries of practice within military and government bureaucracies and taking its authority from the formal position of the person introducing the change. It is essentially a "one-way" announcement that is directed downward to the lower levels in the organization. The spirit of the communication reads something like "today we are this way—tomorrow we must be that way."

In its concrete form it may appear as a memorandum, lecture, policy statement, or verbal command. The general nature of the decree approach is impersonal, formal, and task-oriented. It assumes that people are highly rational and best motivated by authoritative directions. Its expectation is that people will comply in their outward behavior and that this compliance will lead to more effective results.

By replacement. Often resorted to when the decree approach fails, this involves the replacement of key persons. It is based on the assumption that organization problems tend to reside in a few strategically located individuals, and that replacing these people will bring about sweeping and basic changes. As in the decree form, this change is usually initiated at the top and directed downward by a high authority figure. At the same time, however, it tends to be somewhat more personal, since particular individuals are singled out for replacement. Nevertheless, it retains much of the formality and explicit concern for task accomplishment that is common to the decree approach. Similarly, it holds no false optimism about the ability of individuals to change their own behavior without clear outside direction.

By structure. This old and familiar change approach is currently receiving much reevaluation by behavioral scientists. In its earlier form, it involved a highly rational approach to the design of formal organization and to the layout of technology. The basic assumption here was that people behaved in close agreement with the structure and technology governing them. However, it tended to have serious drawbacks, since what seemed logical on paper was not necessarily logical for human goals.

Recently attempts have been made to alter the organizational structure in line with what is becoming known about both the logics and nonlogics of human behavior, such as engineering the job to fit the manager, on the one hand, or adjusting formal authority to match informal authority, on the other hand. These attempts, however, still rely heavily on mechanisms for change that tend to be relatively formal, impersonal, and located outside the individual. At the same time, however, because of greater concern for the effects of structure on people, they can probably be characterized as more personal, subtle, and less directive than either the decree or replacement approaches.

Sharing of Power

More toward the middle of the power distribution continuum, as noted earlier, are the shared approaches, where authority is still present and used, yet there is also interaction and sharing of power. This approach to change is utilized in two forms.

By group decision-making. Here the problems still tend to be defined unilaterally from above, but lower-level groups are usually left free to develop alternative solutions and to choose among them. The main assumption tends to be that individuals develop more commitment to action when they have a voice in the decisions that affect them. The net result is that power is shared between bosses and subordinates, though there is a division of labor between those who define the problems and those who develop the solutions.

By group problem-solving. This form emphasizes both the definition and the solution of problems within the context of group discussion. Here power is shared throughout the decision process, but, unlike group decision-making, there is an added opportunity for lower-level subordinates to define the problem. The assumption underlying this approach is not only that people gain greater commitment from being exposed to a wider decision-making role, but also that they have significant knowledge to contribute to the definition of the problem.

Delegated Authority

At the other extreme from unilateral authority are found the delegated approaches, where almost complete responsibility for defining and acting on problems is turned over to the subordinates. These also appear in two forms.

By case discussion. This method focuses more on the acquisition of knowledge and skills than on the solution of specific problems at hand. An authority figure, usually a teacher or boss, uses his power only to guide a general discussion of information describing a problem situation, such as a case or a report of research results. The "teacher" refrains from imposing his own analysis or solutions on the group. Instead, he encourages individual members to arrive at their own insights, and they are left to use them as they see fit. The implicit assumption here is that individuals, through the medium of discussion about concrete situations, will develop general problem-solving skills to aid them in carrying out subsequent individual and organization changes.

By T-group sessions. These sessions, once conducted mainly in outside courses for representatives of many different organizations, have also been used inside individual companies for effecting change. Usually, they are confined to top management, with the hope that beneficial "spill-over" will result for the rest of the organization. The primary emphasis of the T-group tends to be on increasing an individual's self-awareness and sensitivity to group social processes. Compared to the previously discussed approaches, the T-group places much less emphasis on the discussion and solution of task-related problems. Instead, the data for discussion are typically the interpersonal actions of individuals in the group; no specific task is assigned to the group.

The basic assumption underlying this approach is that exposure to a structureless situation will release unconscious emotional energies within individuals, which, in turn, will lead to self-analysis, insight, and behavioral change. The authority figure in the group, usually a professional trainer, avoids asserting his own authority in structuring the group. Instead, he often attempts to become an accepted and influential member of the group. Thus, in comparison to the other approaches, much more authority is turned over to the group, from which position it is expected to chart its own course of change in an atmosphere of great informality and highly personal exchanges.

REPORTED RESULTS

As we have seen, each of the major approaches, as well as the various forms within them, rests on certain assumptions about what *should* happen when it is applied to initiate change. Now let us step back and consider what actually *does* happen—before, during, and after a particular approach is introduced.

To discover whether there are certain dimensions of organization change that might stand out against the background of characteristics unique to one company, we conducted a survey of eighteen studies of organization change. Specifically, we were looking for the existence of dominant patterns of similarity and/or difference running across all these studies. As we went along, relevant information was written down and compared with the other studies in regard to (1) the conditions leading up to an attempted change, (2) the manner in which the change was introduced, (3) the critical blocks, the facilitators encountered during implementation, and (4) the more lasting results that appeared over a period of time.

The survey findings show some intriguing similarities and differences between those studies reporting "successful" change patterns and those disclosing "less successful" changes, i.e., failure to achieve the desired results. The successful changes generally appear as those that:

■ Spread throughout the organization to include and affect many people.
■ Produce positive changes in line and staff attitudes.
■ Prompt people to behave more effectively in solving problems and in relating to others.
■ Result in improved organization performance.

Significantly, the less successful changes fall short on all these dimensions.

"Success" Patterns

Using the category breakdown just cited as the baseline for "success," the survey reveals some very distinct patterns in the evolution of change. In all, eight major patterns are identifiable in five studies reporting successful change, and six other success studies show quite similar characteristics, although the information contained in each is somewhat less complete. Consider:

1. The organization, and especially top management, is under considerable external and internal pressure for improvement long before an explicit organization change is contemplated. Performance and/or morale are low. Top management seems to be groping for a solution to its problems.

2. A new person, known for the ability to introduce improvements, enters the organization, either as the official head of the organization, or as a consultant who deals directly with the head of the organization.

3. An initial act of the new person is to encourage a reexamination of past practices and current problems within the organization.

4. The head of the organization and immediate subordinates assume a direct and highly involved role in conducting this reexamination.

5. The new person, with top management support, engages several levels of the organization in collaborative, fact-finding, problem-solving discussions to identify and diagnose current organization problems.

6. The new person provides others with new ideas and methods for developing solutions to problems, again at many levels of the organization.

7. The solutions and decisions are developed, tested, and found creditable for solving problems on a small scale before an attempt is made to widen the scope of change to larger problems and the entire organization.

8. The change effort spreads with each success experience and, as management support grows, it is gradually absorbed permanently into the organization's way of life.

The likely significance of these similarities becomes more apparent when we consider the patterns found in the less successful organization changes. Let us briefly make this contrast before speculating further about why the successful changes seem to unfold as they do.

"Failure" Forms

Apart from their common "failure" to achieve the desired results, the most striking overall characteristic of seven less successful change studies is a singular lack of consistency—not just between studies, but within studies. Where each of the successful changes follows a similar and highly consistent route of one step building on another, the less successful changes are much less orderly.

There are three interesting patterns of inconsistency:

1. The less successful changes begin from a variety of starting points. This is in contrast to the successful changes, which begin from a common point, i.e., strong pressure both externally and internally. Only one less successful change, for example, began with outside pressure on the organization; another originated with the hiring of a consultant; and a third started with the presence of internal pressure, but without outside pressure.

2. Another pattern of inconsistency is found in the sequence of change steps. In the successful change patterns, we observe some degree of logical consistency between steps, as each seems to make possible the next. But in the less successful changes, there are wide and seemingly illogical gaps in sequence. One study, for instance, described a big jump from the reaction to outside pressure to the installation of an unskilled newcomer who immediately at-tempted large-scale changes. In another case, the company lacked the presence of a newcomer to provide new methods and ideas to the organization. A third failed to achieve the cooperation and involvement of top management. And a fourth missed the step of obtaining early successes while experimenting with new change methods.

3. A final pattern of inconsistency is evident in the major approaches used to introduce change. In the successful cases, it seems fairly clear that *shared* approaches are used, i.e., authority figures seek the participation of subordinates in joint decision-making. In the less successful attempts, however, the approaches used lie closer to the extreme ends of the power distribution continuum. Thus, in five less successful change studies, a *unilateral* approach (decree, replacement, structural) was used, while in two other studies a *delegated* approach (data discussion, T-group) was applied. None of the less successful change studies reported the use of a *shared* approach.

How can we use this lack of consistency in the sequence of change steps and this absence of shared power to explain the less successful change attempts? In the next section, I shall examine in greater depth the successful changes, which, unlike the less successful ones, are marked by a high degree of consistency and the use of shared power. My intent here will be not only to develop a tentative explanation of the more successful changes, but in so doing to explain the less successful attempts within the same framework.

POWER REDISTRIBUTION

Keeping in mind that the survey evidence on which both the successful and the less successful patterns are based is quite limited, I would like to propose a tentative explanatory scheme for viewing the change process as a whole, and also for considering specific managerial action steps within this overall process. The framework for this scheme hinges on two key notions:

1. Successful change depends basically on a *redistribution of power* within the structure of an organization. (By *power*, I mean the locus for formal authority and influence that typically is top management. By *redistribution*, I mean a significant alteration in the traditional practices that the power structure uses in making decisions. I propose that this redistribution move toward the greater use of *shared* power.)

2. Power redistribution occurs through a *developmental process of change*. (This implies that organization change is not a black to white affair occurring overnight through a single causal mechanism. Rather, as we shall see, it involves a number of phases, each containing specific elements and multiple causes that provoke a needed *reaction* from the power structure, which, in turn, sets the stage for the next phase in the process.)

Using the survey evidence from the successful patterns, I have divided the change process into six phases, each of them broken down into the particular stimulus and reaction that appear critical for moving the power structure from one phase to another. Exhibit 5.6 represents an abstract view of these two key notions in operation.

Let us now consider how each of these phases and their specific elements make themselves evident in the patterns of successful change, as well as how their absence contributes to the less successful changes.

I. Pressure and Arousal

This initial stage indicates a need to shake the power structure at its very foundation. Until the ground under the top managers begins to shift, it seems unlikely that they will be sufficiently aroused to see the need for change, both in themselves and in the rest of the organization.

The success patterns suggest that strong pressures in areas of top management responsibility are likely to provoke the greatest concern for organization change. These pressures seem to come from two broad sources: (1) serious environmental factors, such as lower sales, stockholder discontent, or competitor breakthroughs and (2) internal events, such as a union strike, low productivity, high costs, or interdepartmental conflict. These pressures fall into responsibility areas that top managers can readily see as reflecting on their own capability. An excerpt from one successful change study shows how this pressure and arousal process began:

> "Pressure" was the common expression used at all levels. Urgent telephone calls, telegrams, letters, and memoranda were being received by the plant from central headquarters . . . Faced with an increase in directives from above and cognizant of Plant Y's low performance position, the manager knew that he was, as he put it, "on the spot."

As this example points out, it is probably significant when both environmental and internal pressures exist simultaneously. When only one is present, or when the two are offsetting (e.g., high profits despite low morale), it is easier for top management to excuse the pressure as only temporary or inconsequential. However, when both are present at once, it is easier to see that the organization is not performing effectively.

The presence of severe pressure is not so clearly evident in the less successful changes. In one case, there was internal pressure for more effective working relations between top management and lower levels; yet the company was doing reasonably well from a profit standpoint. In another case, there was environmental pressure for a centralized purchasing system, but little pressure from within for such a change.

II. Intervention and Reorientation

While strong pressure may arouse the power structure, this does not provide automatic

EXHIBIT 5.6   Dynamics of Successful Organization Change

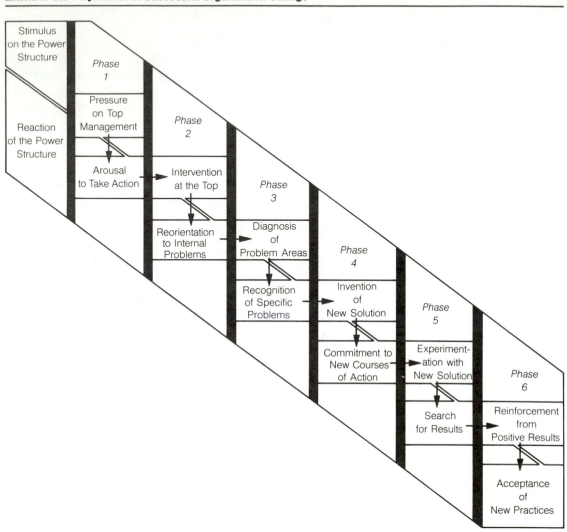

assurance that top management will see its problems or take the correct action to solve them. Quite likely, top management, when under severe pressure, may be inclined to rationalize its problems by blaming them on a group other than itself, such as "that lousy union" or "that meddling government."

As a result, we find a second stage in the successful change patterns—namely, intervention by an outsider. Important here seems to be the combination of the fact that the newcomer enters at the top of the organization and the fact that the newcomer is respected for possessing skills at improving organization practices. Being a newcomer probably allows a relatively objective appraisal of the organization; entering at the top gives the newcomer ready access to those people who make decisions affecting the entire organization; and being respected is likely to give added weight to the newcomer's initial comments about the organization.

Thus we find the newcomer in an ideal position to reorient the power structure to its own internal problems. This occurs in the successful changes as the newcomer encourages the top managers to reexamine their past practices and current problems. The effect appears to be one of causing the power structure to suspend, at least temporarily, its traditional habit of presuming beforehand where the "real" problems reside. Otherwise, we would not find top management undertaking the third stage—identifying and diagnosing organization problems. We can see how an outsider was accomplishing this reorientation in the following comment by the plant manager in one successful change study:

> I didn't like what the consultant told me about our problems being inside the organization instead of outside. But he was an outsider, supposedly an expert at this sort of thing. So maybe he could see our problems better than we could. I asked him what we ought to do, and he said that we should begin to identify our specific problems.

Three of the less successful changes missed this step. Two of the three attempted large-scale changes without the assistance of an outsider, while the third relied on an outsider who lacked the necessary expertise for reorienting top management.

III. Diagnosis and Recognition

Here, we find the power structure, from top to bottom, as well as the newcomer, joining in to assemble information and collaborate in seeking the location and causes of problems. This process begins at the top, then moves gradually down through the organizational hierarchy. Most often, this occurs in meetings attended by people from various organization levels.

A *shared* approach to power and change makes itself evident during this stage. Through consulting with subordinates on the nature of problems, the top managers are seen as indicating a willingness to involve others in the decision-making process. Discussion topics, which formerly may have been regarded as taboo, are now treated as legitimate areas for further inquiry. We see the diagnosis and recognition process tak-

ing place in this example from one successful change study:

> The manager's role in the first few months, as he saw it, was to ask questions and to find out what ideas for improvement would emerge from the group as a whole. The process of information gathering took several forms, the principal one being face-to-face conversations between the manager and his subordinates, supervisors on the lower levels, hourly workers, and union representatives. Ideas were then listed for the agenda of weekly planning sessions.

The significance of this step seems to go beyond the possible intellectual benefits derived from a thorough diagnosis of organization problems. This is due to the fact that in front of every subordinate there is evidence that (1) top management is willing to change, (2) important problems are being acknowledged and faced up to, and (3) ideas from lower levels are being valued by upper levels.

The less successful changes all seem to avoid this step. For example, on the one hand, those top managements that took a *unilateral* approach seemed to presume ahead of time that they knew what the real problems were and how to fix them. On the other hand, those that took a *delegated* approach tended to abdicate responsibility by turning over authority to lower levels in such a nondirective way that subordinates seemed to question the sincerity and real interest of top management.

IV. Invention and Commitment

Once problems are recognized, it is another matter to develop effective solutions and to obtain full commitment for implementing them. Traditional practices and solutions within an organization often maintain a hold that is difficult to shed. The temptation is always there, especially for the power structure, to apply old solutions to new problems. Thus, a fourth phase—the invention of new and unique solutions that have high commitment from the power structure— seems to be necessary.

The successful changes disclose widespread and intensive searches for creative solutions, with the newcomer again playing an active role. In each instance the newcomer involves the entire management in learning and practicing new forms of behavior that seek to tap and release the creative resources of many people. Again, as in the previous phase, the method for obtaining solutions is based on a *shared* power concept. Here the emphasis is placed on the use of collaboration and participation in developing group solutions to the problems identified in Phase III.

The potency of this model for obtaining both quality decisions and high commitment to action has been demonstrated repeatedly in research. In three successful changes, the model was introduced as a part of the Phase III diagnosis sessions, with the newcomer either presenting it through informal comments or subtly conveying it through guiding actions as the attention of the group turned to the search for a solution. In two other studies, formal training programs were used to introduce and to help implement the model. For all successful changes, the outcome is essentially the same—a large number of people collaborate to invent solutions that are of their own making and that have their own endorsement.

It is significant that none of the less successful changes reach this fourth stage. Instead, the seeds of failure, sown in the previous phases, grow into instances of serious resistance to change. As a result, top management in such cases falls back, gives up, or regroups for another effort. Because these studies conclude their reports at this stage, we are not able to determine the final outcome of the less successful change attempts.

V. Experimentation and Search

Each of the successful change studies reports a fifth stage—that of "reality testing" before large-scale changes are introduced. In this phase not only the validity of specific decisions made in Phase IV, but also the underlying model for making these decisions (*shared power*), falls under careful organization scrutiny. Instead of making only big decisions at the top, a number of small decisions are implemented at *all* levels of the organization. Further, these decisions tend to be regarded more as experiments than as final, irreversible decisions. People at all organization levels seem to be searching for supporting evidence in their environment— e.g., dollar savings or higher motivation— before judging the relative merits of their actions. This concern is reflected in the comment of a consultant involved in one successful change:

> As might be expected, there was something less than a smooth, unresisted, uncomplicated transition to a new pattern of leadership and organizational activity. Events as they unfolded presented a mixture of successes and failures, frustrations and satisfactions . . . With considerable apprehension, the supervisors agreed to go along with any feasible solution the employees might propose.

This atmosphere of tentativeness is understandable when we think of a power structure undergoing change. On the one hand, lower-level managers are undoubtedly concerned with whether top management will support their decisions. If lower-level managers make decisions that fail, or are subsequently reversed by top levels, their own future careers may be in jeopardy. Or, on the other hand, if higher-level managers, who are held responsible for the survival of the firm, do not see tangible improvements, they may revert to the status quo or seek other approaches to change.

Thus, with these experimental attempts at change and the accompanying search for signs of payoff, there begins a final stage in which people receive the results and react to them.

VI. Reinforcement and Acceptance

Each of the studies of successful change reports improvements in organization performance. Furthermore, there are relatively clear indications of strong support for change from all organization levels. Obviously, positive results have a strong reinforcing effect—that is, people are rewarded and encouraged to continue and even to expand the changes they are making. We see this expansion effect occurring as more and more problems are identified and a greater number of people participate in the solution of them. Consider this comment by a foreman in one study:

> I've noticed a real difference in the hourly workers. They seem a lot more willing to work, and I can't explain just why it is, but something has happened all right. I suppose it's being treated better. My boss treats me better because he gets treated better. People above me listen to me and I hope, at least, that I listen to my people below me.

The most significant effect of this phase is probably a greater and more permanent acceptance at all levels of the underlying methods used to bring about the change. In each of the successful changes, the use of *shared* power is more of an institutionalized and continuing practice than just a "one-shot" method used to introduce change. With such a reorientation in the decision-making practices of the power structure, it hardly appears likely that these organizations will "slip back" to their previous behavior.

LOOKING AHEAD

What is needed in future changes in organization is less intuition and more consideration of the evidence that is now emerging from studies in this area. While it would be unwise to take too literally each of the major patterns identified in this article (future research will undoubtedly dispel, modify, or elaborate on them), their overall import suggests that it is time to put to bed some of the common myths about organization change.

As I see it, there are four positive actions called for.

I. *We must revise our egocentric notions that organization change is heavily dependent on a master blueprint designed and executed in one fell swoop by an omniscient consultant or top manager.*

The patterns identified here clearly indicate that change is the outgrowth of several actions, some planned and some unplanned, each related to the other and occurring over time. The successful changes begin with pressure, which is unplanned from the organization's point of view. Then the more planned stages come into focus as top management initiates a series of events designed to involve lower-level people in the problem-solving process. But, even here, there are usually unplanned events as subordinates begin to "talk back" and raise issues that top management probably does not anticipate. Moreover, there are the concluding stages of experiencing success, partly affected by conscious design but just as often due to forces outside the control of the planners.

II. *We too often assume that organization change is for "those people downstairs," who are somehow perceived as less intelligent and less productive that "those upstairs."*

Contrary to this assumption, the success patterns point to the importance of top management seeing itself as part of the organization's problems and becoming actively involved in finding solutions to them. Without the involvement and commitment of top management, it is doubtful that lower levels can see the need for change or, if they do, be willing to take the risks that such change entails.

III. *We need to reduce our fond attachment for both unilateral and delegated approaches to change.*

The *unilateral* approach, although tempting because its procedures are readily accessible to top management, generally serves only to perpetuate the myths and disadvantages of omniscience and downward thinking. On the other hand, the *delegated* approach, while appealing because of its "democratic" connotations, may remove the power structure from direct involvement in a process that calls for its strong guidance and active support.

The findings discussed in this article highlight the use of the more difficult, but perhaps more fruitful, *shared* power approach. As top managers join in to open up their power structures and their organizations to an exchange of influence between upper and lower levels, they may be unleashing new surges of energy and creativity not previously imagined.

IV. *There is a need for managers, consultants, skeptics, and researchers to become less parochial in their viewpoints.*

For too long, each of us has acted as if cross-fertilization is unproductive. Much more constructive dialogue and joint effort are needed if we are to understand better and act wisely in terms of the complexities and stakes inherent in the difficult problems of introducing organization change.

■ Moral Mazes: Bureaucracy and Managerial Work

ROBERT JACKALL

Corporate leaders often tell their charges that hard work will lead to success. Indeed, this theory of reward being commensurate with effort has been an enduring belief in our society, one central to our self-image as a people where the "main chance" is available to anyone of ability who has the gumption and the persistence to seize it. Hard work, it is also frequently asserted, builds character. This notion carries less conviction because businessmen, and our society as a whole, have little patience with those who make a habit of finishing out of the money. In the end, it is success that matters, that legitimates striving, and that makes work worthwhile.

What if, however, men and women in the big corporation no longer see success as necessarily connected to hard work? What becomes of the social morality of the corporation—I mean the everyday rules in use that people play by—when there is thought to be no "objective" standard of excellence to explain how and why winners are separated from also-rans, how and why some people succeed and others fail?

This is the puzzle that confronted me while doing a great many extensive interviews with managers and executives in several large corporations, particularly in a large chemical company and a large textile firm. I went into these corporations to study how bureaucracy—the prevailing organizational form of our society and economy—shapes moral consciousness. I came to see that managers' rules for success are at the heart of what may be called the bureaucratic ethic.

This article suggests no changes and offers no programs for reform. It is, rather, simply an interpretive sociological analysis of the moral dimensions of managers' work. Some readers may find the essay sharp-edged, others familiar. For both groups, it is important to note at the outset that my materials are managers' own descriptions of their experiences. In listening to managers, I have had the decided advantages of being unencumbered with business responsibilities and also of being free from the taken-for-granted views and vocabularies of the business world. As it happens, my own research in a variety of other settings suggests that managers' experiences are by no means unique; indeed they have a deep resonance with those of other occupational groups.

WHAT HAPPENED TO THE PROTESTANT ETHIC?

To grasp managers' experiences and the more general implications they contain, one must see them against the background of the great historical transformations, both social and cultural, that produced managers as an occupational group. Since the concern here is with the moral significance of work in business, it is important to begin with an understanding of the original Protestant Ethic, the world view of the rising bourgeois class that spearheaded the emergence of capitalism.

The Protestant Ethic was a set of beliefs that counseled "secular asceticism"—the methodical, rational subjection of human impulse and desire to God's will through "restless, continuous, systematic work in a worldly calling." This ethic of ceaseless work and ceaseless renunciation of the fruits of one's toil provided both the economic and the moral foundations for modern capitalism.

On one hand, secular asceticism was a ready-made prescription for building economic capital; on the other, it became for the upward-moving bourgeois class—self-made industrialists, farmers, and enterprising artisans—the ideology that justified their attention to this world, their accumulation of wealth, and indeed the social inequities that inevitably followed such accumulation. This bourgeois ethic, with its imperatives for self-reliance, hard work, frugality, and rational planning, and its clear definition of success and failure, came to dominate a whole historical epoch in the West.

But the ethic came under assault from two directions. First, the very accumulation of wealth that the old Protestant Ethic made possible gradually stripped away the religious basis of the ethic, especially among the rising middle class that benefited from it. There were, of course, periodic reassertions of the religious context of the ethic, as in the case of John D. Rockefeller and his turn toward Baptism. But on the whole, by the late 1800s the religious roots of the ethic survived principally among independent farmers and proprietors of small businesses in rural areas and towns across America.

In the mainstream of an emerging urban America, the ethic had become secularized into the "work ethic," "rugged individualism," and especially the "success ethic." By the beginning of this century, among most of the economically successful, frugality had become an aberration, conspicuous consumption the norm. And with the shaping of the mass consumer society later in this century, the sanctification of consumption became widespread, indeed crucial to the maintenance of the economic order.

Affluence and the emergence of the consumer society were responsible, however, for the demise of only aspects of the old ethic—namely, the imperatives for saving and investment. The core of the ethic, even in its later, secularized form—self-reliance, unremitting devotion to work, and a morality that postulated just rewards for work well done—was undermined by the complete transformation of the organizational form of work itself. The hallmarks of the emerging modern production and distribution systems were administrative hierarchies, standardized work procedures, regularized timetables, uniform policies, and centralized control—in a word, the bureaucratization of the economy.

This bureaucratization was heralded at first by a very small class of salaried managers, who were later joined by legions of clerks and still later by technicians and professionals of every stripe. In this century, the process spilled over from the private to the public sector and government bureaucracies came to rival those of industry. This great transformation produced the decline of the old middle class of entrepreneurs, free professionals, independent farmers, and small independent businessmen—the traditional carriers of the old Protestant Ethic—and the ascendance of a new middle class of salaried employees whose chief common characteristic was and is their dependence on the big organization.

Any understanding of what happened to the original Protestant Ethic and to the old morality and social character it embodied—and therefore any understanding of the moral significance of work today—is inextricably tied to an analysis of bureaucracy. More specifically, it is, in my view, tied to an analysis of the work and occupational cultures of managerial groups within bureaucracies. Managers are the quintessential bureaucratic work group; they not only fashion bureaucratic rules, but they are also bound by them. Typically, they are not just *in* the organization; they are *of* the organization. As such, managers represent the prototype of the white-collar salaried employee. By analyzing the kind of ethic bureaucracy produces in managers, one can begin to understand how bureaucracy shapes morality in our society as a whole.

PYRAMIDAL POLITICS

American businesses typically both centralize and decentralize authority. Power is concentrated at the top in the person of the chief executive officer and is simultaneously decentralized; that is, responsibility for deci-

sions and profits is pushed as far down the organizational line as possible. For example, the chemical company that I studied—and its structure is typical of other organizations I examined—is one of several operating companies of a large and growing conglomerate. Like the other operating companies, the chemical concern has its own president, executive vice presidents, vice presidents, other executive officers, business area managers, entire staff divisions, and operating plants. Each company is, in effect, a self-sufficient organization, though they are all coordinated by the corporation, and each president reports directly to the corporate CEO.

Now, the key interlocking mechanism of this structure is its reporting system. Each manager gathers up the profit targets or other objectives of his or her subordinates, and with these formulates his or her commitments to his or her boss; this boss takes these commitments, and those of his or her other subordinates, and in turn makes a commitment to *his* or *her* boss. At the top of the line, the president of each company makes a commitment to the CEO of the corporation, based on the stated objectives given by the vice presidents. There is always pressure from the top to set higher goals.

This management-by-objectives system, as it is usually called, creates a chain of commitments from the CEO down to the lowliest product manager. In practice, it also shapes a patrimonial authority arrangement which is crucial to defining both the immediate experiences and the long-run career chances of individual managers. In this world, a subordinate owes fealty principally to an immediate boss. A subordinate must not overcommit this boss, but rather must keep the boss from making mistakes, particularly public ones; the subordinate must not circumvent the boss. On a social level, even though an easy, breezy informality is the prevalent style of American business, the subordinate must extend to the boss a certain ritual deference: for instance, he or she must follow the boss's lead in conversation, must not speak out of turn at meetings, and must laugh at the boss's jokes while not making jokes of his or her own.

In short, the subordinate must not exhibit any behavior which symbolizes parity. In return, he or she can hope to be elevated when and if the boss is elevated, although other important criteria also intervene here. The subordinate can also expect protection for mistakes made up to a point. However, that point is never exactly defined and always depends on the complicated politics of each situation.

Who gets credit?

It is characteristic of this authority system that details are pushed down and credit is pushed up. Superiors do not like to give detailed instructions to subordinates. The official reason for this is to maximize subordinates' autonomy; the underlying reason seems to be to get rid of tedious details and to protect the privilege of authority to declare that a mistake has been made.

It is not at all uncommon for very bald and extremely general edicts to emerge from on high. For example, "Sell the plant in St. Louis. Let me know when you've struck a deal." This pushing down of details has important consequences:

1. Because they are unfamiliar with entangling details, corporate higher echelons tend to expect highly successful results without complications. This is central to top executives' well-known aversion to bad news and to the resulting tendency to "kill the messenger" who bears that news.

2. The pushing down of detail creates great pressure on middle managers not only to transmit good news but to protect their corporations, their bosses, and themselves in the process. They become the "point men" of a given strategy and the potential "fall guys" when things go wrong.

Credit flows up in this structure and usually is appropriated by the highest ranking officer involved in a decision. This person re-

distributes credit as he or she chooses, bound essentially by a sensitivity to public perceptions of fairness. At the middle level, credit for a particular success is always a type of refracted social honor; one cannot claim credit even if it is earned. Credit has to be given, and acceptance of the gift implicitly involves a reaffirmation and strengthening of fealty. A superior may share some credit with subordinates in order to deepen fealty relationships and induce greater future efforts on his or her behalf. Of course, a different system is involved in the allocation of blame, a point I shall discuss later.

Fealty to the "King"

Because of the interlocking character of the commitment system, a CEO carries enormous influence in the corporation. If, for a moment, one thinks of the presidents of individual operating companies as barons, then the CEO of the parent company is the king. His word is law; even the CEO's wishes and whims are taken as commands by close subordinates on the corporate staff, who zealously turn them into policies and directives.

A typical example occurred in the textile company last year when the CEO, new at the time, expressed mild concern about the rising operating costs of the company's fleet of rented cars. The following day, a stringent system for monitoring mileage replaced the previous casual practice.

Great efforts are made to please the CEO. For example, when the CEO of the large conglomerate that includes the chemical company visits a plant, the most important order of business for local management is a fresh paint job, even when, as in several cases last year, the cost of paint alone exceeds $100,000. I am told that similar anecdotes from other organizations have been in circulation since 1910; this suggests a certain historical continuity of behavior toward top bosses.

The second order of business for the plant management is to produce a complete book describing the plant and its operations, replete with photographs and illustrations, for presentation to the CEO; such a book costs about $10,000 for the single copy. By any standards of budgetary stringency, such expenditures are irrational. But by the social standards of the corporation, they make perfect sense. It is far more important to please the king today than to worry about the future economic state of one's fief, since if one does not please the king, there may not be a fief to worry about or indeed any vassals to do the worrying.

By the same token, all of this leads to an intense interest in everything the CEO does and says. In both the chemical and the textile companies, the most common topic of conversation among managers up and down the line is speculation about their respective CEOs' plans, intentions, strategies, actions, styles, and public images.

Such speculation is more than idle gossip. Because the CEO stands at the apex of the corporation's bureaucratic and patrimonial structures and locks the intricate system of commitments between bosses and subordinates into place, it is the CEO who ultimately decides whether those commitments have been satisfactorily met. Moreover, the CEO and trusted associates determine the fate of whole business areas of a corporation.

Shake-ups and Contingency

One must appreciate the simultaneously monocratic and patrimonial character of business bureaucracies in order to grasp what we might call their contingency. One has only to read the *Wall Street Journal* or the *New York Times* to realize that, despite their carefully constructed "eternal" public image, corporations are quite unstable organizations. Mergers, buy-outs, divestitures, and especially "organizational restructuring" are commonplace aspects of business life. I shall discuss only organizational shake-ups here.

Usually, shake-ups occur because of the appointment of a new CEO and/or division

president, or because of some failure that is adjudged to demand retribution; sometimes these occurrences work together. The first action of most new CEOs is some form of organizational change. On the one hand, this prevents the inheritance of blame for past mistakes; on the other, it projects an image of bareknuckled aggressiveness much appreciated on Wall Street. Perhaps most important, a shake-up rearranges the fealty structure of the corporation, placing in power those barons whose style and public image mesh closely with that of the new CEO.

A shake-up has reverberations throughout an organization. Shortly after the new CEO of the conglomerate was named, he reorganized the whole business and selected new presidents to head each of the five newly formed companies of the corporation. He mandated that the presidents carry out a thorough reorganization of their separate companies complete with extensive "census reduction"—that is, firing as many people as possible.

The new president of the chemical company, one of these five, had risen from a small but important specialty chemicals division in the former company. Upon promotion to president, he reached back into his former division, indeed back to his own past work in a particular product line, and systematically elevated many of his former colleagues, friends, and allies. Powerful managers in other divisions, particularly in a rival process chemicals division, were: (1) forced to take big demotions in the new power structure; (2) put on "special assignment"—the corporate euphemism for Siberia (the saying is: "No one ever comes back from special assignment"); (3) fired; or (4) given "early retirement," a graceful way of doing the same thing.

Up and down the chemical company, former associates of the president now hold virtually every important position. Managers in the company view all of this as an inevitable fact of life. In their view, the whole reorganization could easily have gone in a completely different direction had another CEO been named or had the one selected picked a different president for the chemical company, or had the president come from a different work group in the old organization. Similarly, there is the abiding feeling that another significant change in top management could trigger yet another sweeping reorganization.

Fealty is the mortar of the corporate hierarchy, but the removal of one well-placed stone loosens the mortar throughout the pyramid and can cause things to fall apart. And no one is ever quite sure, until after the fact, just how the pyramid will be put back together.

SUCCESS AND FAILURE

It is within this complicated and ambiguous authority structure, always subject to upheaval, that success and failure are meted out to those in the middle and upper middle managerial ranks. Managers rarely spoke to me of objective criteria for achieving success because once certain crucial points in one's career are passed, success and failure seem to have little to do with one's accomplishments. Rather, success is socially defined and distributed. Corporations do demand, of course, a basic competence and sometimes specified training and experience; hiring patterns usually ensure these. A weeding-out process takes place, however, among the lower ranks of managers during the first several years of their experience. By the time a manager reaches a certain numbered grade in the ordered hierarchy—in the chemical company this is Grade 13 out of 25, defining the top $8\frac{1}{2}$ percent of management in the company—managerial competence as such is taken for granted and assumed not to differ greatly from one manager to the next. The focus then switches to social factors, which are determined by authority and political alignments—the fealty structure—and by the ethos and style of the corporation.

Moving to the Top

In the chemical and textile companies as well as the other concerns I studied, five criteria seem to control a person's ability to rise in middle and upper middle management. In the following paragraphs they are discussed in ascending order.

Appearance and dress. This criterion is so familiar that I shall mention it only briefly. Managers have to look the part, and it is sufficient to say that corporations are filled with attractive, well-groomed, and conventionally well-dressed men and women.

Self-control. Managers stress the need to exercise iron self-control and to have the ability to mask all emotion and intention behind bland, smiling, and agreeable public faces. They believe it is a fatal weakness to lose control of oneself, in any way, in a public forum. Similarly, to betray valuable secret knowledge (for instance, a confidential reorganization plan) or intentions through some relaxation of self-control—for example, an indiscreet comment or a lack of adroitness in turning aside a query—can not only jeopardize a manager's immediate position but can undermine others' trust in him or her.

Perception as a team player. While being a team player has many meanings, one of the most important is to appear to be interchangeable with other managers near one's level. Corporations discourage narrow specialization more strongly as one goes higher. They also discourage the expression of moral or political qualms. One might object, for example, to working with chemicals used in nuclear power, and most corporations today would honor that objection. The public statement of such objections, however, would end any realistic aspirations for higher posts because one's usefulness to the organization depends on versatility. As one manager in the chemical company commented: "Well, we'd go along with his request but we'd always wonder about the guy. And in the back of our minds, we'd be thinking that he'll soon object to working in the soda ash division because he doesn't like glass."

Another important meaning of team play is putting in long hours at the office. This requires a certain amount of sheer physical energy, even though a great deal of this time is spent not in actual work but in social rituals—like reading and discussing newspaper articles, taking coffee breaks, or having informal conversations. These rituals, readily observable in every corporation that I studied, forge the social bonds that make real managerial work—that is, group work of various sorts—possible. One must participate in the rituals to be considered effective in the work.

Style. Managers emphasize the importance of "being fast on your feet"; always being well organized; giving slick presentations complete with color slides; giving the appearance of knowledge even in its absence; and possessing a subtle, almost indefinable sophistication, marked especially by an urbane, witty, graceful, engaging, and friendly demeanor.

I want to pause for a moment to note that some observers have interpreted such conformity, team playing, affability, and urbanity as evidence of the decline of the individualism of the old Protestant Ethic. To the extent that commentators take the public images that managers project at face value, I think they miss the main point. Managers up and down the corporate ladder adopt the public faces that they wear quite consciously; they are, in fact, the masks behind which the real struggles and moral issues of the corporation can be found.

Karl Mannheim's conception of self-rationalization or self-streamlining is useful in understanding what is one of the central social psychological processes of organizational life. In a world where appearances—in the broadest sense—mean everything, the wise and ambitious person learns to cultivate assiduously the proper, prescribed modes of appearing. He dispassionately takes stock of himself, treating himself as an object. He analyzes his strengths and weaknesses, and

decides what he needs to change in order to survive and flourish in his organization. And then he systematically undertakes a program to reconstruct his image. Self-rationalization curiously parallels the methodical subjection of self to God's will that the old Protestant Ethic counseled; the difference, of course, is that one acquires not moral virtues but a masterful ability to manipulate personae.

Patron power. To advance, a manager must have a patron, also called a mentor, a sponsor, a rabbi, or a godfather. Without a powerful patron in the higher echelons of management, one's prospects are poor in most corporations. The patron might be the manager's immediate boss or someone several levels higher in the chain of command. In either case the manager is still bound by the immediate, formal authority and fealty patterns of the position; the new—although more ambiguous—fealty relationships with the patron are added.

A patron provides his or her "client" with opportunities to get visibility, to showcase his or her abilities, to make connections with those of high status. A patron cues his or her client to crucial political developments in the corporation, helps arrange lateral moves if the client's upward progress is thwarted by a particular job or a particular boss, applauds his or her presentations or suggestions at meetings, and promotes the client during an organizational shake-up. One must, of course, be lucky in one's patron. If the patron gets caught in a political crossfire, the arrows are likely to find the clients as well.

Social Definitions of Performance

Surely, one might argue, there must be more to success in the corporation than style, personality, team play, chameleonic adaptability, and fortunate connections. What about the bottom line—profits, performance?

Unquestionably, "hitting your numbers"—that is, meeting the profit commitments already discussed—is important, but only within the social context I have described. There are several rules here. First, no one in a line position—that is, with responsibility for profit and loss—who regularly "misses his numbers" will survive, let alone rise. Second, a person who always hits his numbers but who lacks some or all of the required social skills will not rise. Third, a person who sometimes misses his numbers but who has all the desirable social traits will rise.

Performance is thus always subject to a myriad of interpretations. Profits matter, but it is much more important in the long run to be perceived as "promotable" by belonging to central political networks. Patrons protect those already selected as rising stars from the negative judgments of others; and only the foolhardy point out even egregious errors of those in power or those destined for it.

Failure is also socially defined. The most damaging failure is, as one middle manager in the chemical company puts it, "when your boss or someone who has the power to determine your fate says: 'You failed.'" Such a godlike pronouncement means, of course, out-and-out personal ruin; one must, at any cost, arrange matters to prevent such an occurrence.

As it happens, things rarely come to such a dramatic point even in the midst of an organizational crisis. The same judgment may be made but it is usually called "nonpromotability." The difference is that those who are publicly labeled as failures normally have no choice but to leave the organization; those adjudged nonpromotable can remain, provided they are willing to accept being shelved or, more colorfully, "mushroomed"—that is, kept in a dark place, fed manure, and left to do nothing but grow fat. Usually, seniors do not tell juniors they are nonpromotable (though the verdict may be common knowledge among senior peer groups). Rather, subordinates are expected to get the message after they have been repeatedly overlooked for pro-

motions. In fact, middle managers interpret staying in the same job for more than two or three years as evidence of a negative judgment. This leads to a mobility panic at the middle levels which, in turn, has crucial consequences for pinpointing responsibility in the organization.

Capriciousness of Success

Finally, managers think that there is a tremendous amount of plain luck involved in advancement. It is striking how often managers who pride themselves on being hard-headed rationalists explain their own career patterns and those of others in terms of luck. Various uncertainties shape this perception. One is the sense of organizational contingency. One change at the top can create profound upheaval throughout the entire corporate structure, producing startling reversals of fortune, good or bad, depending on one's connections. Another is the uncertainty of the markets that often makes managerial planning simply elaborate guesswork, causing real economic outcome to depend on factors totally beyond organizational and personal control.

It is interesting to note in this context that a line manager's credibility suffers just as much from missing his numbers on the up side (that is, achieving profits higher than predicted) as from missing them on the down side. Both outcomes undercut the ideology of managerial planning and control, perhaps the only bulwark managers have against market irrationality.

Even managers in staff positions, often quite removed from the market, face uncertainty. Occupational safety specialists, for instance, know that the bad publicity from one serious accident in the workplace can jeopardize years of work and scores of safety awards. As one high-ranking executive in the chemical company says, "In the corporate world, 1,000 'Attaboys!' are wiped away by one 'Oh, shit!'"

Because of such uncertainties, managers in all the companies I studied speak continually of the great importance of being in the right place at the right time and of the catastrophe of being in the wrong place at the wrong time. My interview materials are filled with stories of people who were transferred immediately before a big shake-up and, as a result, found themselves riding the crest of a wave to power; of people in a promising business area who were terminated because top mangement suddenly decided that the area no longer fit the corporate image desired; of others caught in an unpredictable and fatal political battle among their patrons; of a product manager whose plant accidentally produced an odd color batch of chemicals, who sold them as a premium version of the old product, and who is now thought to be a marketing genius.

The point is that managers have a sharply defined sense of the *capriciousness* of organizational life. Luck seems to be as good an explanation as any of why, after a certain point, some people succeed and others fail. The upshot is that many managers decide that they can do little to influence external events in their favor. One can, however, shamelessly streamline oneself, learn to wear all the right masks, and get to know all the right people. And then sit tight and wait for things to happen.

"GUT DECISIONS"

Authority and advancement patterns come together in the decision-making process. The core of the managerial mystique is decision-making prowess, and the real test of such prowess is what managers call "gut decisions," that is, important decisions involving big money, public exposure, or significant effects on the organization. At all but the highest levels of the chemical and textile companies, the rules for making gut decisions are, in the words of one upper middle manager: "(1) Avoid making any decisions if at all possible; and (2) if a decision has to be made, involve as many peo-ple as you can so that, if things go south, you're able to point in as many directions as possible."

Consider the case of a large coking plant of the chemical company. Coke making requires a gigantic battery to cook the coke slowly and evenly for long periods; the battery is the most important piece of capital equipment in a coking plant. In 1975, the plant's battery showed signs of weakening and certain managers at corporate headquarters had to decide whether to invest $6 million to restore the battery to top form. Clearly, because of the amount of money involved, this was a gut decision.

No decision was made. The CEO had sent the word out to defer all unnecessary capital expenditures to give the corporation cash reserves for other investments. So the managers allocated small amounts of money to patch the battery up until 1979, when it collapsed entirely. This brought the company into a breach of contract with a steel producer and into violation of various Environmental Protection Agency pollution regulations. The total bill, including lawsuits and now federally mandated repairs to the battery, exceeded $100 million. I have heard figures as high as $150 million, but because of "creative accounting," no one is sure of the exact amount.

This simple but very typical example gets to the heart of how decision making is intertwined with a company's authority structure and advancement patterns. As the chemical company managers see it, the decisions facing them in 1975 and 1979 were crucially different. Had they acted decisively in 1975—in hindsight, the only rational course—they would have salvaged the battery and saved their corporation millions of dollars in the long run.

In the short run, however, since even seemingly rational decisions are subject to widely varying interpretations, particularly decisions which run counter to a CEO's stated objectives, they would have been taking a serious risk in restoring the battery. What is more, their political networks might have unraveled, leaving them vulnerable to attack. They chose short-term safety over long-term gain because they felt they were judged, both by higher authority and by their peers, on their short-term performances. Managers feel that if they do not survive the short run, the long run hardly matters. Even correct decisions can shorten promising careers.

By contrast, in 1979 the decision was simple and posed little risk. The corporation had to meet its legal obligations; also it had to either repair the battery the way the EPA demanded or shut down the plant and lose several hundred million dollars. Since there were no real choices, everyone could agree on a course of action because everyone could appeal to inevitability. Diffusion of responsibility, in this case by procrastinating until total crisis, is intrinsic to organizational life because the real issue in most gut decisions is: Who is going to get blamed if things go wrong?

"Blame Time"

There is no more feared hour in the corporate world than "blame time." Blame is quite different from responsibility. There is a cartoon of Richard Nixon declaring: "I accept all of the responsibility, but none of the blame." To blame someone is to injure him verbally in public; in large organizations, where one's image is crucial, this poses the most serious sort of threat. For managers, blame—like failure—has nothing to do with the merits of a case; it is a matter of social definition. As a general rule, it is those who are or who become politically vulnerable or expendable who get "set up" and become blamable. The most feared situation of all is to end up inadvertently in the wrong place at the wrong time and get blamed.

Yet this is exactly what often happens in a structure that systematically diffuses responsibility. It is because managers fear blame time that they diffuse responsibility; however, such diffusion inevitably means that someone, somewhere is going to become a scapegoat when things go wrong. Big corporations encourage this process by their complete lack of any tracking system. Whoever is currently in charge of an area is responsible—that is, potentially blamable—for whatever goes wrong in the area, even if he has inherited others' mistakes. An example from the chemical company illustrates this process.

When the CEO of the large conglomerate took office, he wanted to rid his capital accounts of all serious financial drags. The corporation had been operating a storage depot for natural gas which it bought, stored, and then resold. Some years before the energy crisis, the company had entered into a long-term contract to supply gas to a buyer—call him Jones. At the time, this was a sound deal because it provided a steady market for a stably priced commodity.

When gas prices soared, the corporation was still bound to deliver gas to Jones at 20¢ per unit instead of the going market price of $2. The CEO ordered one of his subordinates to get rid of this albatross as expeditiously as possible. This was done by selling the operation to another party—call him Brown—with the agreement that Brown would continue to meet the contractual obligations to Jones. In return for Brown's assumption of these costly contracts, the corporation agreed to buy gas from Brown at grossly inflated prices to meet some of its own energy needs.

In effect, the CEO transferred the drag on his capital accounts to the company's operating expenses. This enabled him to project an aggressive, asset-reducing image to Wall Street. Several levels down the ladder, however, a new vice president for a particular business found himself saddled with exorbitant operating costs when, during a reorganization, those plants purchasing gas from Brown at inflated prices came under his purview. The high costs helped to undercut the vice president's division earnings and thus to erode his position in the hierarchy. The origin of the situation did not matter. All that counted was that the vice president's division was steadily losing big money. In the end, he resigned to "pursue new opportunities."

One might ask why top management does not institute codes or systems for tracking responsibility. This example provides the clue. An explicit system of accountability for subordinates would probably have to apply to top executives as well and would restrict their freedom. Bureaucracy expands the freedom of those on top by giving them the power to restrict the freedom of those beneath.

On the Fast Track

Managers see what happened to the vice president as completely capricious, but completely understandable. They take for granted the absence of any tracking of responsibility. If anything, they blame the vice president for not recognizing soon enough the dangers of the situation into which he was being drawn and for not preparing a defense—even perhaps finding a substitute scapegoat. At the same time, they realize that this sort of thing could easily happen to them. They see few defenses against being caught in the wrong place at the wrong time except constant wariness, the diffusion of responsibility, and perhaps being shrewd enough to declare the ineptitude of one's predecessor on first taking a job.

What about avoiding the consequences of their own errors? Here they enjoy more control. They can "outrun" their mistakes so that when blame time arrives, the burden will fall on someone else. The ideal situation, of course, is to be in a position to fire one's successors for one's own previous mistakes.

Some managers, in fact, argue that outrunning mistakes is the real key to managerial success. One way to do this is by manipulating the numbers. Both the chemical and the textile companies place a great premium on a division's or a subsidiary's return on assets. A good way for business managers to increase their ROA is to reduce their assets while maintaining sales. Usually they will do everything they can to hold down expenditures in order to decrease the asset base, particularly at the end of the fiscal year. The most common way of doing this is by deferring capital expenditures, from maintenance to innovative investments, as long as possible. Done for a short time, this is called "starving" a plant; done over a longer period, it is called "milking" a plant.

Some managers become very adept at milking businesses and showing a consistent record of high returns. They move from one job to another in a company, always upward, rarely staying more than two years in any post. They may leave behind them deteriorating plants and unsafe working conditions, but they know that if they move quickly enough, the blame will fall on others. In this sense, bureaucracies may be thought of as vast systems of organized irresponsibility.

FLEXIBILITY AND DEXTERITY WITH SYMBOLS

The intense competition among managers takes place not only behind the agreeable public faces I have described but within an extraordinarily indirect and ambiguous linguistic framework. Except at blame time, managers do not publicly criticize or disagree with one another or with company policy. The sanction against such criticism or disagreement is so strong that it constitutes, in managers' view, a suppression of professional debate. The sanction seems to be rooted principally in their acute sense of organizational contingency; the person one criticizes or argues with today could be one's boss tomorrow.

This leads to the use of an elaborate linguistic code marked by emotional neutrality, especially in group settings. The code communicates the meaning one might wish to convey to other managers, but since it is devoid of any significant emotional sentiment, it can be reinterpreted should social relationships or attitudes change. Here, for example, are some typical phrases describing performance appraisals followed by their probable intended meanings:

Stock Phrase	Probable Intended Meaning
Exceptionally well qualified	Has committed no major blunders to date
Tactful in dealing with superiors	Knows when to keep his or her mouth shut
Quick thinking	Offers plausible excuses for errors
Meticulous attention to detail	A nitpicker
Slightly below average	Stupid
Unusually loyal	Wanted by no one else

For the most part, such neutered language is not used with the intent to deceive; rather, its purpose is to communicate certain meanings within specific contexts with the implicit understanding that, should the context change, a new, more appropriate meaning can be attached to the language already used. In effect, the corporation is a setting where people are not held to their word because it is generally understood that their word is always provisional.

The higher one goes in the corporate world, the more this seems to be the case; in fact, advancement beyond the upper middle level depends greatly on one's ability to manipulate a variety of symbols without becoming tied to or identified with any of them. For example, an amazing variety of organizational improvement programs marks practically every corporation. I am referring here to the myriad ideas generated by corporate staff, business consultants, academics, and a host of others to improve corporate structure; sharpen decision making; raise morale; create a more humanistic workplace; adopt Theory X, Theory Y, or, more recently, Theory Z of management; and so on. These programs become important when they are pushed from the top.

The watchword in the large conglomerate at the moment is productivity and, since this is a pet project of the CEO himself, it is said that no one goes into his presence without wearing a blue *Productivity!* button and talking about "quality circles" and "feedback sessions." The president of another company pushes a series of managerial seminars that endlessly repeats the basic functions of management: (1) planning, (2) organizing, (3) motivating, and (4) controlling. Aspiring young managers attend these sessions and with a seemingly dutiful eagerness learn to repeat the formulas under the watchful eyes of senior officials.

Privately, managers characterize such programs as the "CEO's incantations over the assembled multitude," as "elaborate rituals with no practical effect," or as "waving a magic wand to make things wonderful again." Publicly, of course, managers on the way up adopt the programs with great enthusiasm, participate in or run them very effectively, and then quietly drop them when the time is right.

Playing the Game

Such flexibility, as it is called, can be confusing even to those in the inner circles. I was told the following by a highly placed staff member whose work requires him to interact daily with the top figures of his company:

> I get faked out all the time and I'm part of the system. I come from a very different culture. Where I come from, if you give someone your *word*, no one ever questions it. It's the old hard-work-will-lead-to-success ideology. Small community, Protestant agrarian, small business, merchant-type values. I'm disadvantaged in a system like this.

He goes on to characterize the system more fully and what it takes to succeed within it:

> It's the ability to play this system that determines whether you will rise. . . . And part of the adeptness [required] is determined by how much it bothers people. One thing you have to be able to do is to play the game, but you can't be disturbed by the game. What's

the game? It's bringing troops home from Vietnam and declaring peace with honor. It's saying one thing and meaning another.

It's characterizing the reality of a situation with *any* description that is necessary to make that situation more palatable to some group that matters. It means that you have to come up with a culturally accepted verbalization to explain why you are *not* doing what you are doing. . . . [Or] you say that we had to do what we did because it was inevitable; or because the guys at the [regulatory] agencies were dumb; [you] say we won when we really lost; [you] say we saved money when we squandered it; [you] say something's safe when it's potentially or actually dangerous. . . . Everyone knows that it's bullshit, but it's *accepted*. This is the game.

In addition, then, to the other characteristics that I have described, it seems that a prerequisite for big success in the corporation is a certain adeptness at inconsistency. This premium on inconsistency is particularly evident in the many areas of public controversy that face top-ranking managers. Two things come together to produce this situation. The first is managers' sense of beleaguerment from a wide array of adversaries who, it is thought, want to disrupt or impede management's attempts to further the economic interests of their companies. In every company that I studied, managers see themselves and their traditional prerogatives as being under siege, and they respond with a set of caricatures of their perceived principal adversaries.

For example, government regulators are brash, young, unkempt hippies in blue jeans who know nothing about the businesses for which they make rules; environmental activists—the bird and bunny people—are softheaded idealists who want everybody to live in tents, burn candles, ride horses, and eat berries; workers' compensation lawyers are out-and-out crooks who prey on corporations to appropriate exorbitant fees from unwary clients; labor activists are radical troublemakers who want to disrupt harmonious industrial communities; and the news media consist of rabble-rousers who propagate sensational antibusiness stories to sell papers or advertising time on shows like "60 Minutes."

Second, within this context of perceived harassment, managers must address a multiplicity of audiences, some of whom are considered adversaries. These audiences are the internal corporate hierarchy with its intricate and shifting power and status cliques, key regulators, key local and federal legislators, special publics that vary according to the issues, and the public at large, whose goodwill and favorable opinion are considered essential for a company's free operation.

Managerial adeptness at inconsistency becomes evident in the widely discrepant perspectives, reasons for action and presentations of fact that explain, excuse, or justify corporate behavior to these diverse audiences.

Adeptness at Inconsistency

The cotton dust issue in the textile industry provides a fine illustration of what I mean. Prolonged exposure to cotton dust produces in many textile workers a chronic and eventually disabling pulmonary disease called byssinosis or, colloquially, brown lung. In the early 1970s, the Occupational Safety and Health Administration proposed a ruling to cut workers' exposure to cotton dust sharply by requiring textile companies to invest large amounts of money in cleaning up their plants. The industry fought the regulation fiercely but a final OSHA ruling was made in 1978 requiring full compliance by 1984.

The industry took the case to court. Despite an attempt by Reagan appointees in OSHA to have the case removed from judicial consideration and remanded to the agency they controlled for further cost/benefit analysis, the Supreme Court ruled in 1981 that the 1978 OSHA ruling was fully within the agency's mandate, namely, to protect workers' health and safety as the primary benefit exceeding all cost considerations.

During these proceedings, the textile company was engaged on a variety of fronts and was pursuing a number of actions. For instance, it intensively lobbied regulators and legislators and it prepared court materials for the industry's defense, arguing that the proposed standard would crush the industry and that the problem, if it existed, should be met by increasing workers' use of respirators.

The company also aimed a public relations barrage at special-interest groups as well as at the general public. It argued that there is probably no such thing as byssinosis; workers suffering from pulmonary problems are all heavy smokers and the real culprit is the government-subsidized tobacco industry. How can cotton cause brown lung when cotton is white? Further, if there is a problem, only some workers are afflicted, and therefore the solution is more careful screening of the work force to detect susceptible people and prevent them from ever reaching the workplace. Finally, the company claimed that if the regulation were imposed, most of the textile industry would move overseas where regulations are less harsh.

In the meantime, the company was actually addressing the problem but in a characteristically indirect way. It invested $20 million in a few plants where it knew such an investment would make money; this investment automated the early stages of handling cotton, traditionally a very slow procedure, and greatly increased productivity. The investment had the side benefit of reducing cotton dust levels to the new standard in precisely those areas of the work process where the dust problem is greatest. Publicly, of course, the company claims that the money was spent entirely to eliminate dust, evidence of its corporate good citizenship. (Privately, executives admit that, without the productive return, they would not have spent the money and they have not done so in several other plants.)

Indeed, the productive return is the only rationale that carries weight within the corporate hierarchy. Executives also admit, somewhat ruefully and only when their office doors are closed, that OSHA's regulation on cotton dust has been the main factor in forcing technological innovation in a centuries-old and somewhat stagnant industry.

Such adeptness at inconsistency, without moral uneasiness, is essential for executive success. It means being able to say, as a very high-ranking official of the textile company said to me without batting an eye, that the industry has never caused the slightest problem in any worker's breathing capacity. It means, in the chemical company, propagating an elaborate hazard/benefit calculus for appraisal of dangerous chemicals while internally conceptualizing "hazards" as business risks. It means publicly extolling the carefulness of testing procedures on toxic chemicals while privately ridiculing animal tests as inapplicable to humans.

It means lobbying intensively in the present to shape government regulations to one's immediate advantage and, ten years later, in the event of a catastrophe, arguing that the company acted strictly in accordance with the standards of the time. It means claiming that the real problem of our society is its unwillingness to take risks, while in the thickets of one's bureaucracy avoiding risks at every turn; it means as well making every effort to socialize the risks of industrial activity while privatizing the benefits.

THE BUREAUCRATIC ETHIC

The bureaucratic ethic contrasts sharply with the original Protestant Ethic. The Protestant Ethic was the ideology of a self-confident and independent propertied social class. It was an ideology that extolled the virtues of accumulating wealth in a society organized around property and that accepted the stewardship responsibilities entailed by property. It was an ideology where a person's word was his or her bond and where the integrity of the handshake was seen as crucial to the maintenance of good business relationships. Perhaps most important, it was connected to a predictable economy of salvation—that is, hard work will lead to success, which is a sign of one's election by God—a notion also containing its own theodicy to explain the misery of those who do not make it in this world.

Bureaucracy, however, breaks apart substance from appearances, action from responsibility, and language from meaning. Most important, it breaks apart the older connection between the meaning of work and salvation. In the bureaucratic world, one's success, one's sign of election, no longer depends on one's own efforts and on an inscrutable God but on the capriciousness of one's superiors and the market; and one achieves economic salvation to the extent that one pleases and submits to one's employer and meets the exigencies of an impersonal market.

In this way, because moral choices are inextricably tied to personal fates, bureaucracy erodes internal and even external standards of morality, not only in matters of individual success and failure but also in all the issues that managers face in their daily work. Bureaucracy makes its own internal rules and social context the principal moral gauges for action. Men and women in bureaucracies turn to each other for moral cues for behavior and come to fashion specific situational moralities for specific significant people in their worlds.

As it happens, the guidance they receive from each other is profoundly ambiguous because what matters in the bureaucratic world is not what a person is but how closely his many personae mesh with the organizational ideal; not his willingness to stand by his actions but his agility in avoiding blame; not what he believes or says but how well he has mastered the ideologies that serve his corporation; not what he stands for but whom he stands with in the labyrinths of his organization.

In short, bureaucracy structures for managers an intricate series of moral mazes. Even the inviting paths out of the puzzle often turn out to be invitations to jeopardy.

■ Can Organization Development Be Fine-Tuned to Bureaucracies?

VIRGINIA E. SCHEIN and LARRY E. GREINER

Firmly embedded in most of the organization development (OD) literature—and its professional culture—is the basic ideology

Reprinted, by permission of publisher, from *Organizational Dynamics*, Winter 1977, Copyright © 1977, AMACOM, a division of American Management Associations, New York. All rights reserved.

that organizations need to become more organic systems capable of responding to a rapidly changing environment. Fueling this belief have been the futurists, such as Alvin Toffler in his *Future Shock*, projecting an increase in environmental turbulence and calling for organizations to abandon rigid bureaucratic structures in favor of ad hoc arrangements to cope more effectively with changing events.

OD's action-emphasis similarly holds that bureaucratic organizations need to be "unfrozen" and moved toward an organic state characterized by a matrix structure (or at least by project teams) and by open communications, interdependence among groups, and expanded levels of trust, participation, joint problem-solving, risk-taking, and innovation within groups. Accordingly, the OD change agent employs a variety of organic-oriented techniques centered around team building, encounter sessions, survey feedback, third-party consultation, interface labs, and confrontation meetings.

Despite OD's preoccupation with organic practices, we contend in this article that the millennium of organic organizations is not on the horizon, which in turn causes us to question the relevance of the present OD movement for the great bulk of business and public organizations. The preponderance of evidence, by contrast, shows that bureaucratic structures are still the dominant organizational form, either for an entire firm or for product groups. Such organizations are characterized by pyramidal authority, downward communications, a workforce largely employed on "rational" functions, and the omnipresence of the specialization of labor. Recent surveys of OD activities in these organizations indicate that the new ideology has made few inroads, except in limited settings such as R & D units, experimental plants, occasional training courses, or special task groups.

Why haven't organic structures been more widely adopted? One explanation is that unenlightened managers and conservative business mentalities are simply resistant and slow to change because of past conditioning. Another explanation is that basic human nature is the villain. Warren Bennis offers support for this explanation with the observations that people tend to place self-interest above public interest, cannot tolerate ambiguity and frustration, and are more concerned with power and profit than with human warmth and love. His view as to the unworkability of truth and love runs counter to his earlier writing that bureaucratic structures should be replaced by organic ones built on a foundation of openness and trust. Of special note is that Bennis revised his view after experiencing the realities and frustrations of being an administrator in two academic institutions.

The optimistic OD change agent, however, might still argue that these self-oriented attitudes and values will, if enough effort is applied, change eventually. The pessimist, though, might counter that human beings will always be self-serving, so OD will never be a major force.

An entirely different explanation, providing a way out of philosophical arguments about the nature of human beings, comes from the weight of emerging research by the structural-contingency theorists, most important of whom are Tom Burns, G. Stalker, Joan Woodward, Paul Lawrence, Jay Lorsch, and John Morse. Their trail of evidence leads to the general conclusion that a prime determinant of organizational effectiveness is an organization's fit between its structure and the demands of its environment and technology. Most significant here is the finding that mechanistic, bureaucratic structures are not only appropriate for relatively stable environments and routine technologies but that such structures are more conducive to high performance than organic-adaptive structures in similar environments.

Unknown is just how broad is the scope of stable environments and programmable technologies that are conducive to bureaucratic structures, but Charles Perrow concludes that "moderate routineness continues to characterize almost all large organizations . . . and most of the small ones, [hence] bureaucracy . . . will remain the dominant mode of organization." James Thompson takes another point of view, suggesting that, even with turbulent environments, organizations need to buffer themselves with formal structures and procedures in order to avoid the chaos of succumbing to rapidly changing events.

The consensus among those who have addressed themselves to the issue seems to be that bureaucracies are the predominant form of structure, now and for the foreseeable future—in short, they are here to stay. Managers in these organizations may intuitively recognize the inappropriateness of the organic-adaptive structure to the demands of their routine technology. Hence managerial resistance to organic approaches in bureaucracies may not necessarily be based on their clinging to old values or needs for personal power but rather on their soundly based concern for organizational effectiveness.

THE CHALLENGE TO OD

If we assume that bureaucratic structures will continue to be the dominant organizational form, what are some possible courses of action for organization development? First, it can continue to prescribe universalistic organic change approaches for all organizations. Advocating structural change, however, without considering the technological and environmental demands of the particular organization may only increase resistance to organization development within bureaucracies. More important, the use of current OD techniques in inappropriate situations can easily damage the credibility of OD as a whole.

A second route for organization development is to limit its change techniques to organizations whose complex technical and environmental demands are more congruent with organic structures. But given the high ratio of routine work to complex jobs, and the apparent continuation of such an imbalance, the growth and impact of OD would be severely restricted by this approach.

If organization development is to continue as a vital force for organizational improvement, it seems imperative that a third route be considered—that of expanding and differentiating applied OD to deal with the behavioral problems of *both* bureaucratic and organic structures. Without such an expanded focus, the field runs a serious risk of becoming a narrow and limited force for change and of being applied within a relatively few organizations.

This challenge to organization development to expand its focus and repertoire of approaches comes out of our belief that by returning to an original cornerstone of the OD movement—its focus on dealing with emergent behavioral problems in organizations—it can make a significant contribution to the functioning of traditional organizations. That the need for this expertise exists within bureaucracies is evidenced by examining the work of other behavioral science groups currently operating in bureaucratic settings.

CONTINGENCY THEORY FOR OD

For OD to enhance its effectiveness within bureaucratic structures, what is needed is a conceptual point of view. The absence of conceptual thinking has long plagued OD. Robert Kahn, after reviewing many definitions of the field, concludes that "organizational development is not a concept, but a convenient term for a variety of activities." Without a conceptual framework to direct the application of these activities, methodological and universalistic solutions have tended to predominate.

Our starting point for the development of a framework grows out of the work of the structural-contingency theorists. Just as the choice of a mechanistic versus organic organizational design is contingent upon environment and technology, so too is the appropriateness of an OD change strategy dependent on the uniqueness of each organizational context. Our proposed contingency theory for OD begins with the basic assumption that different structures develop inherent behavioral problems due to the ways in which their particular configuration conditions the behavior of people within them. The dysfunctional behavioral aspects of classical structures have long been noted by sociologists.

Our contingency approach to OD further contends that behavioral diseases emanating from bureaucratic structures are uniquely different from those of organic structures; hence the treatments must be tailored to fit the disease. This contingency view explains why current OD practices both seem to be and are in fact more effective in organic situations. Inherent behavioral problems of matrix structures are typically those of interpersonal conflict, team formation, living with uncertainty, and coping with ambiguous authority relationships. OD techniques focusing on topics like team building, trust, interpersonal communication, assertiveness, innovation, and confrontation are highly relevant in a flowing matrix of enhancing intragroup and intergroup effectiveness.

On the other hand, bureaucratic organizations, with a hierarchical structure and a functionally based design, breed problems of a different kind and, therefore, require solution-oriented approaches of a quite different nature. Problems such as frustration due to limited promotional opportunities and vertically oriented career routes, alienation and boredom of lower-level employees, and inability to develop general managers are major issues that emanate directly from the nature of the structure. Attention to these emergent problems *within* the confines of the bureaucratic structure requires approaches quite different from those appropriate to organic structural problems.

The challenge to OD, in other words, is to develop new approaches designed to treat the diseases endemic to mechanistic structures. As a first step we propose a "fine-tuning" approach as an effective means for OD to impact bureaucratic structures.

FINE-TUNING BUREAUCRATIC STRUCTURES

Fine-tuning refers to a variety of OD interventions designed to sharpen the operations of an organization and free the system of dysfunctional behaviors. It draws on the best of OD—its strong humanistic concern and its knowledge of process—and applies these skills within the constraints of a bureaucratic structure. Two criteria are used simultaneously in the selection of an OD solution strategy: (1) what actions will enhance the quality of working life of the employees and, (2) what approach will not conflict with any existing structural requirements? It seeks to maximize people-oriented changes within the situations bounded by the environmental and technological realities of the organizations. By way of illustration, what follows is a discussion of four critical behavioral diseases we have observed as inherent to bureaucracies and some fine-tuning OD techniques for maximizing the utilization of human resources within these same bureaucratic structures.

1. Functional Myopia and Suboptimization

Functional managers and technicians tend to develop an allegiance to their particular function. Typically they have been "raised" over many years within that function and have acclimated themselves to its norms, sanctions, and language system. This approach is quite effective in developing and concentrating technical expertise on specific and relatively fixed tasks.

A dysfunctional consequence of this specialization, however, can be a myopic point of view toward the entire organization. Each function looks out for itself without appreciating or understanding the value of other functional entities. Behavioral problems such as inter-departmental conflict, lack of planning coordination, and inability to communicate due to knowledge gaps and different vocabularies are typical outcomes of functional myopia.

A variety of standard OD approaches can be used to reduce the negative impact of this form of suboptimizing behavior. Team building is especially relevant for the top-management group, which serves as a behavioral model for the rest of the organization. Only at this level do the functions, of necessity, come together; unnecessary conflict here will diffuse to lower levels, often with heightened intensity.

The chief executive of one large U.S. manufacturing firm recognized that conflict within his top group was creating divisiveness between functions; moreover, even his own behavior was contributing to it by his dealing constantly on a one-to-one basis with each functional head. As a result, he announced a new and simple policy of requiring the top group to meet twice weekly, to focus on operating problems on Thursday morning and on personnel decisions on Friday morning. His principal ground rule for the meetings was that the group should try to reach a consensus on most issues under discussion. One year later, consultant interviews with the CEO indicated that more "company-oriented" decisions were being made; this impression was confirmed in interviews with various functional managers.

Another approach is to assist the top two or three layers of management from all functions to meet off-site for an annual participative planning and budgeting session. For example, TRW, Inc. takes its top corporate executives off-site at least once a year to debate and revise corporate plans in an atmosphere where open criticism is welcome. Consensus and commitment from these senior managers to overall plans and cost controls can minimize functional conflicts later on.

Alternatively, limited structural interventions designed to facilitate goal integration can also be helpful. For instance, a senior coordination group reporting to top management, full-time liaison roles assigned within each function, task forces to create

action programs cutting across the organization, and a corporate profit-sharing scheme for executives can do much to turn political infighting into cooperative problem-solving.

Last, job rotation of high-potential managers can stimulate transfer of perspective and insights from one functional segment to another. For example, in one petrochemical company, the senior management rotates high-potential executives constantly through its major corporate staff groups. The organization planning group, for example, is made up primarily of line managers rotated from various functions, who spend one year in the group before moving on to other functions. The director of this group contends that the managers rotated not only contribute more realistic solutions than professional experts in planning, but also that they develop new perspectives to apply in their next assignments—including becoming more receptive clients for the organization planning group.

2. Vertical Lock-in and Incompetency

Promotion patterns in bureaucracies tend to reveal a close correlation between rank and seniority, with promotion ladders typically restricted to vertical movement within a single function. These practices lend certainty to career paths, promote loyalty, and facilitate the acquisition of tradition and specialized knowledge. Functional organizations would be chaotic and inefficient without these established career practices.

Nonetheless, such vertical "lock-in" has negative consequences for individual growth and organization decision-making. Limited promotional opportunities within functions can cause managerial frustration and boredom. Promotional decisions, when they occur, tend to be based more on tenure and being next in line, rather than on individual competence. Finally, technical knowledge can easily become more valued than managerial ability, causing a shortage of talented general managers who are sensitive to both people and broader company problems.

Numerous change approaches are available to OD practitioners that help in opening up career opportunities and making competency-based personnel decisions within bureaucracies. Assessment centers have proved effective in organizations such as AT & T and IBM in identifying managerial talent and providing more job-related information for promotional decisions. Job posting, as used at Polaroid, can publicize new openings to numerous employees who may wish to apply. Properly designed employee information systems may assist in quickly revealing a range of candidates whose skills fit certain job requirements. Career counseling provides an outlet for managerial frustration, as well as making known aspirations ignored by insensitive superiors. Training programs designed in-house can impart general management skills and stimulate interpersonal sharing of cross-functional knowledge. These and similar programmatic change strategies are all possible within a bureaucracy without altering its basic functional makeup.

Many of these techniques have been brought together in a fascinating career program developed by a major U.S. corporation concerned with its lack of top-management talent. Senior management first developed a list of skills required to be an effective top manager in their company, surprising themselves in the process by producing such a long list. Then they analyzed the array of managerial jobs in the company to determine which jobs tended to develop which skills. Next, they assigned color-coded "job tickets" to jobs with similar skills, such as red tickets for all jobs that emphasized "basic accounting" skills, and blue tickets for all jobs that stressed "staff consulting" skills, and so on through eight colors with different job-skill combinations. Last, a career program in which all managers aspiring to senior levels were expected to pick up the full range of tickets during their early career years was announced and ex-

plained. Each manager, however, was left relatively free to decide in consultation with his or her superiors, on the sequence in which he or she would acquire various job tickets. An employee information system was also developed for top management to identify individual progress in acquiring job tickets, and special training programs were designed to provide "substitute" job tickets.

3. Top-down Information Flow and Problem Insensitivity

The hierarchical and mechanistic nature of bureaucracies lends itself to top-down authority structures and routinization of task efforts. Plans and objectives are typically defined at the top, subdivided by function, and directed downward. Moreover, routine technologies can be programmed in advance by specialists and results predicted based on historical performance. This clearly defined and stable structure serves to effectively allocate work, control costs, specify responsibilities, and convey acquired skills to lower-level employees. Too much autonomy or creativity in a bureaucracy would obviously interfere with the smooth functioning of the system.

However, an almost inevitable cost of this directive and deductive mode of operating is a lack of innovation and sensitivity to emergent problems and to suggestions from below. Top-management decision-making based on past experience, while also being insulated from lower levels, can paralyze or blind management from dealing effectively with nonroutine issues. Minor problems can grow into major crises before coming to top management's attention.

Organization development approaches need to provide new avenues for upward feedback of information and creative thought without significantly altering the everyday downward flow of operating decisions. A "shadow" structure can be introduced in which cross-functional teams meet periodically to assess organization practices and to recommend modifications directly to top management. Varying names have been given to this structural innovation: "reflective" by Larry Greiner, "collateral" by Dale Zand, and "parallel" by Howard Carlson at General Motors. Such a structure enhances the flexibility and problem-solving ability of the organization while maintaining and complementing the hierarchical organization.

The shadow-structure approach is being followed in a Swedish government agency that came under public attack for its ponderous bureaucracy. Six permanent teams that report directly to the director of the agency have been set up. Each group is assigned a critical agency activity to investigate and come up with recommendations in a written report. One group, for example, is examining the computer operations of the agency, while another is analyzing the agency's relationships with other government bureaus. Membership in each group represents a diagonal slice of the organization, ranging from clerical workers to senior managers. They are freed from their regular jobs for at least two days per month; membership is rotated every six months. Numerous changes have already been introduced as a direct result of the groups' reports, such as one in which the information system was revised to include fewer key indices as well as a qualitative report from each supervisor on performance progress in his or her unit.

Another similar technique is the junior board composed of middle managers who meet every few months with senior executives. Off-site conferences, where rank is temporarily set aside, can also be held to identify major problems and discuss impending changes. Elements of both techniques have been combined in one intriguing exercise that a major plant of an aluminum company goes through once a year. First, the top-management group of eight meets for three days to lay out its key goals for the year and to develop a priority list of the major plant problems that need to be solved. Second, the key middle-management group is asked to perform the

same exercise. At the end, the two groups meet for a week to hear their joint conclusions and to work out a common agenda based on small-group meetings that intermingle senior with middle-level managers.

A corporate ombudsman can be established to hear employees' complaints and offer suggestions around blocked channels. Periodic personnel surveys can monitor trends and detect hidden problems. Based on employee attitude survey data indicating dissatisfaction with upward communication, one Canadian financial institution established a corporate ombudsman, who reports directly to the president. Among other activities, this person attempts to resolve employee difficulties by negotiating with their supervisors and managers and has the authority to take any unresolved issues directly to the president. A two-year follow-up of employee attitudes reported a marked increase in satisfaction with upward communication.

Management by objectives (MBO) can be introduced to provide subordinates with a structured opportunity for melding their ideas with overall production goals. The same Canadian financial institution also successfully introduced MBO as far down as the junior-clerical level. Finally, younger high-potential managers can be assigned as temporary assistants to older top managers as a means, not only to enhance career development, but also to make middle-management views available to senior-management deliberations.

4. Routine Jobs and Dissatisfaction

Bureaucracies are born out of the need for economies of scale in production and distribution. There is a large fixed investment in plant and technology. Division of labor becomes the basic rationale for organization structure; efficiency is derived from labor specialization assigned to relatively finite and predetermined tasks sequenced along a production flow. Large numbers of unskilled and inexpensive workers are hired to perform simple and repetitive jobs, and labor is treated as a variable cost. When business turns sour, employees can be laid off; in prosperous times, new workers can be easily hired and trained. First-line supervision—assigning work, monitoring output, and insuring discipline—becomes a critical management post.

Serious behavioral costs are paid for these necessary, but impersonal, economic and organizational logics. Boredom, absenteeism, and even physical deterioration are possible negative impacts of routine jobs. Supervisors feel caught in the middle between production pressures from above and resistance from workers below, and their response is often to overcontrol through tight rules and punishment-centered behavior. Workers thereupon respond with output restriction, grievances, and even sabotage.

A key role for organization development lies in relieving the negative impact of routine jobs. One well-known technique is job enrichment, in which work is redesigned to provide more complexity and autonomy without endangering efficiency. In fact, efficiency may be increased. The Volvo experiment in its Kalmar plant is a notable case in point. Through a complete redesign of the traditional assembly plant, jobs have been arranged so that they are to be performed by relatively autonomous working groups. Considerable freedom exists within groups to schedule production and assign jobs. While production levels have not increased significantly, the high absenteeism and turnover have been lowered dramatically in a plant whose initial costs were only 10 percent higher than in a plant designed along traditional lines. Less often acknowledged is the fact that there are many more jobs in bureaucracies where enrichment cannot occur due to fixed capital investment, the prescribed nature of technology, or limits in worker ability. What can be done under these restrictions? Variety can still be added through job rotation, where workers learn two or three jobs and alternate between them. Or job interest

can be heightened by increasing the visibility of output, as one paper manufacturer found when it simply posted the output of work teams on comparable jobs across shifts, thereby increasing the competitive spirit. Another solution is to revise hiring practices to accommodate more people, such as part-time employees, who do not necessarily expect much from their work beyond a paycheck. Reduced boredom can also be achieved through increasing the employee's opportunity for personal growth off the job, made possible by work-schedule variations—flexible working hours, four-day workweeks, flexible lunch periods, expanded vacation periods, and leaves of absence. All these afford an employee some degree of freedom and opportunity for self-expression not achievable within the job itself.

OD can also be helpful in addressing the problem of alienation between supervisors and workers by considering alternative approaches to supervisory training. In one large insurance company, for example, a flexible-hours program became a vehicle that forced supervisors to place greater trust in employees. Varying work hours made it impossible for supervisors to monitor the work of all employees at all times, thereby causing supervisors to relax their vigilance and eventually recognize that most employees still performed effectively in their absence.

Extrinsic rewards have also gained increased attention in stimulating employee-company goal congruence, such as team bonus schemes, the Scanlon Plan, salary in place of hourly wages, and employee stock ownership plans. OD skills will also be valuable in experiments to include union representatives in management decision-making, either through worker councils or board membership.

The fate of OD? Fine-tuning approaches to organization development are neither glamorous, sexy, nor revolutionary. However, if bureaucracies, by reason of economics, technology, and even human behavior, continue to be the dominant organizational structure, serious attention should be given to making OD more relevant to these organizations. The future growth and impact of OD may hinge on the acceptance or rejection of this challenge.

■ Organizational Diagnosis: Six Places to Look for Trouble with or without a Theory

MARVIN R. WEISBORD

For several years I have been experimenting with "cognitive maps" of organizations. These are labels that would help me better describe what I saw and heard, and understand the relationships among various bits of data. I started this endeavor when I realized that though I knew many organization theories, most were either (1) too narrow to include everything I wished to understand or (2) too broadly abstract to give much guidance about what to do.

This article represents a progress report on my efforts to combine bits of data, theories, research, and hunches into a working tool that anyone can use. It is one example of a process I believe goes on among practitioners that is neither well documented nor well understood. The process does not take place in a mode consistent with the protocols of social science research. It is not tied to any particular theory, nor is it subject to easy translation into research instruments. It is not intended to prove or disprove hypotheses. Rather, it represents what Vaill calls a "practice theory"—a synthesis of knowledge and experience into a concept that bears "some relation to public objective theories about organizational situations, but in no sense [is] identical to them."

I think this accurately describes what I have been calling, for want of a more elegant name, the "Six-Box Model." This model (exhibit 5.7) has helped me rapidly expand my diagnostic framework from interpersonal and group issues to the more complicated contexts in which organizations are managed. It provides six labels, under which can be sorted much of the activity, formal and informal, that takes place in organizations. The labels allow consultants to apply whatever theories they know when doing a diagnosis and to discover new connections between apparently unrelated events.

We can visualize exhibit 5.7 as a radar screen. Just as air controllers use radar to chart the course of aircraft—height, speed, distance apart, and weather—those seeking to improve an organization must observe relationships among the boxes and not focus on any particular blip.

Organizational "process" issues, for example, will show up as blips in one or more

Reprinted from Marvin R. Weisbord, "Organizational Diagnosis: Six Places to Look for Trouble with or without a Theory," *Group & Organization Studies,* vol. 1, no. 4 (December 1976), 430–447. Copyright © 1976 by University Associates, Inc., with permission of Sage Publications, Inc. References deleted. See original work.

EXHIBIT 5.7   The Six-Box Organizational Model

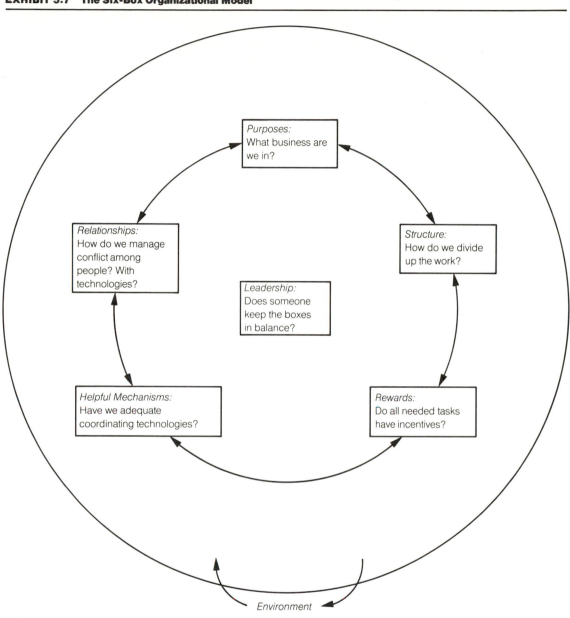

boxes, signaling the blockage of work on important organizational tasks. (Process issues relate to *how* and *whether* work gets done, rather than *what* is to be done.)

Unfortunately, such issues too often are seen as the result of someone's personality. For example, the failure of a group to confront its differences may be diagnosed as the inability of one or two people to assert themselves. Yet, if the consultant were to look closely, he might find that no one in the organization confronts, independent of the assertion skills they may have. Those who do confront may be considered deviant and may be tolerated only to the extent that they have power.

From a management standpoint, it is probably more useful to think of process issues as systemic, that is, as part of the organization's management culture. This culture can be described as:

1. "Fit" between *organization* and *environment*—the extent to which purposes and structure support high performance and ability to change with conditions; and/or

2. "Fit" between *individual* and *organization*—the extent to which people support or subvert formal mechanisms intended to carry out an organization's purposes.

The relationship between individual and organization is the basis for many important books in the organizational literature. McGregor argued that a better fit might be attained under Theory Y assumptions (people like to work, achieve, and be responsible) than Theory X assumptions (people are passive, dependent, and need to be controlled). Blake and Mouton devised elaborate change strategies (variations of "Grid" theory) based on the notion that productivity and human satisfaction need not be mutually exclusive.

Maslow struggled in his last years to reconcile employee self-actualization—personal growth and creativity—with an organization's needs for structure, order, and predictability. Argyris has written extensively on the potential incompatibilities of individuals and organizations and the threat that bureaucratic structures pose to self-esteem.

In the last ten years, both managers and consultants have become much more conscious of organizations as open systems in which structure and behavior are heavily influenced by environment. Lawrence and Lorsch compared high- and low-performance businesses in terms of structural requirements—based largely on rate of change in business technology and environment—and came up with a contingency theory: the way subunits of an organization are structured depends not only on their functions but on environmental factors, which results in different policies and procedures for different organizations.

Sociotechnical theorists such as Trist have tried to reconcile structured technologies and work systems with people's individual and social needs, theorizing that high performance equals an optimum balance between technology ("task") and people ("process").

Each of the possible frameworks highlights important organizational issues; each has been the basis for useful interventions in the organization development repertoire. Yet, none is an adequate tool for the management of an entire organization without an expansion of concepts.

Management needs a view simple enough, and complete enough, to improve the quality of its decisions. What follows is a description of how the Six-Box Organizational Model can be used to put into perspective *whatever* theories and concepts a consultant already knows along with *whatever* problems present themselves in diagnosing an organization's problems.

The circle in exhibit 5.7 describes the boundaries of an organization to be diagnosed. *Environment* means forces difficult to control from inside that demand a response—customers, government, unions, students, families, friends, etc. It is not always clear where the boundaries are or should be. Although such a system can be characterized accurately as "open," its rationality depends on partially closing off infinite choices. Deciding where the boundary lies is an act of reason wed to values, for there are no absolutes.

The consultant may find it necessary to set boundaries arbitrarily so that a diagnosis can proceed. I do this by picking a unit name (i.e., XYZ Company, ABC Department, QUR Team) and listing groups or individuals inside the boundary by virtue of dollar commitments, contract, or formal membership. Within the boundaries, the boxes interact to create what is sometimes called an input-output system, whose function is to transform resources into goods or services. Exhibit 5.8 illustrates the Six-Box organization/environment using input-output terms. Given that organizations func-

EXHIBIT 5.8   The Six-Box Organizational Model Using Input-Output Terms

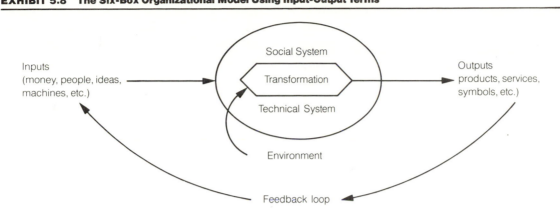

tion or do not function depending on what is going on in and between each of the six boxes, a consultant has a basis for doing an organizational diagnosis.

FORMAL AND INFORMAL SYSTEMS

Within each box are two potential trouble sources—the formal system that exists on paper and the informal system—or what people actually do. Neither system is necessarily better, but both exist. In doing a diagnosis, it helps to identify blips in each system and to attempt to define the relationships among them.

Diagnosing the formal system requires some informed guessing, based on knowledge of what the organization *says*—in its statements, reports, charts, and speeches—about how it is organized. The guessing comes after comparing its rhetoric with its environment and making a judgment about whether everything fits—whether society will value and underwrite an organization with such a purpose and such a means of organizing itself. Much expert consultation is aimed at bringing organizational rhetoric into better harmony with the outside world.

However, in every organization there is another level of behavior—what people actually do. Diagnosing these informal systems is sometimes called "normative" diagnosis. It focuses on the frequency with which people take certain actions in relation to how important these actions are for organizational performance. Normative behavior usually determines whether otherwise technically excellent systems succeed or fail, because normative behavior indicates the degree to which the system as designed meets the needs of the people who have to operate it. Sometimes norms cannot be changed informally, so there is a need to study relationships *between* the two levels of analysis. By persisting in such an inquiry, a consultant discovers some of the reasons why the input-transformation-output stream is not flowing as smoothly as it could.

HOW TO COLLECT DATA

Collecting data on which to base a diagnosis can be as simple as brainstorming or as complex as a "grand design" research methodology involving hypotheses, instruments, and computer analysis. Complexity aside, there are four ways to collect data:

1. *Observation.* Watch what people do in meetings, on the job, on the phone, etc.

2. *Reading.* Follow the written record—speeches, reports, charts, graphs, etc.

3. *Interviews.* Question everyone involved with a particular project.

4. *Survey.* Use standard questionnaires or design your own. Surveys are most useful when they ask for information not readily obtainable in any other way, such as attitudes, perceptions, opinions, preferences, beliefs, etc.

All four methods of data collection can be used to isolate the two major kinds of discrepancy—between what people say (formal) and what they do (informal) and between what is (organization as it exists) and what ought to be (appropriate environmental fit). The trick is not to use any particular methods, but to sort the evidence of one's senses into some categories that encourage sensible decisions.

WHERE TO START

There are two main reasons why one might want to diagnose an organization: to find out systematically what its strengths and weaknesses are or to uncover reasons why either the producers or consumers of a particular output are dissatisfied. Because the latter reason is most often the trigger for corrective actions, I suggest starting a diagnosis by considering one major output. Tracing its relationship to the whole system will result in an understanding of the gaps in the organization between "what is" and "what ought to be."

Let us look at one output—say a single product or service—and determine how satisfied the *consumers* are and how satisfied the *producers* are. The central assumption behind this activity is that consumer acceptance, more than any other factor, determines whether an organization prospers or fades. Satisfied consumers generally indicate a good fit with the environment at one major contact point. Without satisfied consumers, producer satisfaction is likely to be unstable.

A consultant must watch for two situations in particular when diagnosing helpful mechanisms. One is the lack of any rational planning, budgeting, control, or measurement systems. In this case, no amount of interpersonal or group process work will "im-

prove" an organization. Second, and worse, is the organization that has budgeting and controls, but no goals that the people doing the work agree are *organizationally* relevant (for them). The latter describes some universities and medical centers, for example, in which financial control systems provide an illusion of rationality that, like beauty, is only skin deep.

OD in such situations is not an *organization* development process at all. The best that a consultant can do is help members make more rational decisions about their own careers, thereby contributing to their personal growth. Certainly there is no interdependency to be negotiated in the absence of agreement about the ends toward which the organization is being managed.

The Six-Box Organization Model is a useful "early-warning system" for a consultant who is trying to decide where and whether to take corrective action. There are three levels of diagnosis that provide clues to appropriate interventions:

1. Does the organization fit its environment? If not, it cannot be developed until the fit can be rationalized and supported.

2. Is the organization structured to carry out its purposes? If not, work on structure is required before an examination of interpersonal and group processes can take on meaning other than personal growth.

3. Are the organization's norms out of phase with its intent? How much discrepancy exists between formal and informal systems? If this is the main problem (as it often is in otherwise successful businesses) most of the management and organization development interventions will apply.

Any diagnostic questions a consultant asks about any of the boxes will yield useful data. Exhibit 5.9 summarizes the important questions about both formal and informal systems. There are as many ways to use these ideas as there are managers. I have offered this practice theory as the basis for starting new teams, task forces, and commit-

Exhibit 5.9 Matrix for Survey Design or Data Analysis

	Formal System (work to be done)	*Informal System* (process working)
1. Purposes	Goal clarity	Goal agreement
2. Structure	Functional, program, or matrix?	How work is actually done or not done
3. Relationships	Who should deal with whom on what? Which technologies should be used?	How well do they do it? Quality of relations? Modes of conflict management?
4. Rewards (incentives)	Explicit System What is it?	Implicit, psychic rewards. What do people *feel* about payoffs?
5. Leadership	What do top people manage? What systems in use?	How? Normative "style" of administration?
6. Helpful Mechanisms	Budget system Management information (measures?) Planning Control	What are they actually used for? How do they function in practice? How are systems subverted?

Note: Diagnostic questions may be asked on two levels:
1. How big a gap is there between formal and informal systems? (This speaks to the fit between individual and organization.)
2. How much discrepancy is there between "what is" and "what ought to be"? (This highlights the fit between organization and environment.)

tees or for helping existing teams decide what they need to do next. Others have adapted the Six-Box Model to screen prospective employers, evaluate the management literature in terms of which issues it illuminates, write job descriptions, and organize research findings. It is also a useful teaching tool in comparing various types of organizations.

Finally, the Six-Box Organization Model provides an easy way of testing the extent to which an intervention seems right. I have used it both to explain and to anticipate my failures and have found that more anticipating means less explaining. In my experience, all interventions that "fail" eventually do so for one of three reasons:

1. The intervention is inappropriate to the problem or organization. (A T-group may improve relationships without surfacing serious deficiencies of purpose, structure, or technology.)

2. The intervention deals with the wrong (less salient) blip on the radar screen. (When the pressing problem is ineffective leadership, a new reward system, no matter how desirable, may not make a difference.)

3. The intervention solves the identified problem, thus heightening issues in other boxes it was *not* designed to solve. An organization can be restructured to better fit its environment without changing norms and relationships that require other interventions.

Management Practice

■ Schlumberchild

An ideal marriage was expected when Schlumberger Ltd., a cash-rich goliath in the oil industry, acquired Fairchild Camera & Instrument Corp., a world leader in a soaring market. Schlumberger needed a way to tap into the fast growth semiconductor field and, with all its cash, Schlumberger had the punch to do it right. Yet the miracle was slow to happen. The question still being raised is: Can a large cash-rich corporation with many levels of authority and bureaucracy adopt to the semiconductor industry, which requires fast decision-making on new products and markets, as well as fast changes in manufacturing process? *Business Week* reported that with about $2.1 billion in undistributed profits in its coffers, Schlumberger expected to arrest the decline of Fairchild, which "dropped from number two to number six in the world rankings of producers of integrated circuits (IC) after having been the industry pioneer and market leader"[1] in the IC field.

Business Week speculated that perhaps Fairchild, under the leadership of former chairman and CEO, Wilfred J. Corrigan, had diversified too much into the consumer products field. Aside from a $70-million loss caused by the ill-fated computer development, Fairchild diverted too much attention away from its more profitable line—metal oxide semiconductor circuits (MOS).

To turn Fairchild around, Thomas C. Roberts, a proponent of the "textbook approach to organization," was named to replace Corrigan. Roberts's analysis of the situation led him to implement his conclusions to decentralize management, redistribute profit-loss responsibilities and reorganize the firm along product and marketing lines.

One year after the acquisition, problems still abound at Fairchild. While the reorganization proposed by Roberts sounds textbook correct, it may have taken too long to implement. And in the semiconductor field where products become obsolete in three years, Fairchild could not afford to take two years to build a good organization. Others in the semiconductor field claim that Fairchild had lost too many good executives; some twenty left in the first year after the takeover. An insider argues that it is the difference in management style between Corrigan and Roberts: "Corrigan placed managers in the position of agreeing with him or leaving, while Roberts has a firm line-of-command approach which minimizes personalities."[2] Others point to a brain drain occurring at Fairchild primarily because the "key employee" bonus program was abolished, an anathema to retaining good people in Silicon Valley, where job-hopping is a widely practiced norm. Industry watchers agree that Fairchild needs to maintain some continuity in operations personnel.

Industry analysts point out that Fairchild is in a heap of trouble. It has been losing industry technological positions for ten years in the semiconductor field; personnel, both management and technical, have been deserting, diversification has been stopped

Based on a report of the merger between Schlumberger, Ltd. and Fairchild Camera & Instrument Corp. reported in *Business Week*, August 11, 1980.

[1] *Business Week*, August 11, 1980.

[2] *Ibid.*

even in cases where mergers with European and Asian firms looked promising, and since the merger the oncoming reorganization has produced instability. According to industry analyst Benjamin M. Rosen, the critical failure at Fairchild is its inadequate MOS capability. Rosen claims, "Fairchild does produce its version of other company's MOS circuits, but it has difficulty designing and manufacturing its own proprietary products." [3] In an industry where MOS have grown from 6 percent to 33 percent of sales, this inability could be very critical.

If failure in the semiconductor field is not damaging enough, Fairchild has been floundering also in the new automatic test systems field. The Automatic Test Systems Group (ATSG), which generates two thirds of Fairchild's operating income, has been plagued by a series of executive defections to competitors. An executive-recruiting firm concludes that Fairchild has been "handing over executives to competitors on a golden platter." [4]

A combination of things—merger, new CEO, reorganization, change in incentive system—may be too much to straighten out in an industry as dynamic as the semiconductor field. Even with large cash infusions from Schlumberger, it will take a herculean effort to make a comeback before time runs out. Analyst Sal F. Accardo from Shearson Loeb Rhoads says, "Fairchild's biggest problem has been an inability to treat people well, and it may take years to turn it around." [5]

---

[3] *Ibid.*

[4] *Ibid.*

[5] *Ibid.*

■ Can John Young Redesign Hewlett-Packard?

A fast-growing high-technology company can easily fall victim to its own success. Explosive expansion can lead to corporate bureaucracy, and sheer overweight can kill the informality and entrepreneurial drive that brought it success in the first place. Hewlett-Packard Co., the giant California producer of electronic instruments and computers, has long stood out as a model for surging companies seeking to avoid such bloat. HP has been able to preserve its ability to innovate by continuing to nurture small entrepreneurial units in the face of extraordinary growth. Sales have climbed at a compounded annual rate of 24.3 percent over the past ten years, as earnings increased tenfold.

The company that started in 1939 when David Packard and William R. Hewlett began making instruments in a Palo Alto (California) garage has grown into the world's largest manufacturer of test and measurement instruments. And in the past decade, HP has gone on to score a second spectacular success in the booming world market for small computers, where it now ranks No. 3 after International Business Machines Corp. and Digital Equipment Corp. (DEC). In fact, in the year ended Oct. 31, HP computer sales for the first time outstripped those of instruments. Total sales hit $4.25 billion, and net income rose to $383 million.

But there are signs that HP's dramatic growth in computers is colliding with its unique entrepreneurial culture, and that the clash is threatening both. The decentralized management style that HP has forged over the years—one that assigns the design and manufacturing of products to the individual divisions and gives the sales responsibility to separate marketing groups—has resulted in overlapping products, lagging development of new technology, and a piecemeal approach to key markets. Indeed, HP often comes across to users as "three or four companies that don't seem to talk to each other," says William M. Crow, manager of a worldwide association of HP computer users that is based in Los Altos, California.

Examples of this corporate confusion are growing. Crow points to HP's Computer Peripheral Group in Boise, Idaho, which pushed a new printer as having extensive graphics capabilities. "A lot of users of HP–3000 computers rushed out to buy the printer, only to find that the operating software [for their computers, which were made by another HP division] wouldn't allow them to use it for graphics—and won't to this day," he says. "If anything is frustrating for the [computer] user, it's that divisional structure."

Such problems are swallowing up more and more of the time of John A. Young, president and chief executive officer, who five years ago was given the tough job of taking over the management of HP from its founding fathers and keeping the company on its growth track. "Becoming a computer company has had a dramatic effect on our company," Young says. His biggest challenge, he adds, "is to orchestrate the divisions and provide a strategic glue and direction for the computer effort, while keeping the work units small."

To resolve the conflict between these aims, the HP CEO has launched several programs to improve planning, coordinate marketing, and strengthen HP's computer-related research and development efforts. But so far he has been unwilling to make the sweeping changes that might erode the value that HP derives from what it calls the "HP way" of running the company. "Having small divisions is not the only way to organize a company, but having organizations that people can run like a small business is highly motivational, especially for professionals," he says. "Keeping that spirit of entrepreneurship alive is very important to us."

Some industry experts believe Young will have to make far more changes in HP's corporate structure than he has to date. While they agree that professional motivation is essential, many of them wonder whether Young has done enough, or moved fast enough, to keep HP on the leading edge of the computer industry. First and foremost, experts say, HP must recognize that a coordinated marketing program is rapidly becoming more important for success than sheer engineering prowess.

"There was a lot of product overlap at IBM, too, until its recent reorganization," says Grant S. Bushee, who follows small computers for InfoCorp, a Cupertino (California) market research company. "HP has the same problems, but it just hasn't dealt with them yet."

The moment of truth is likely to come for HP in computers next year, when—or if—the nation's economy recovers. HP has come through the current recession with strong profits, unlike archrival Digital Equipment, which recently reported its first decline in quarterly earnings in seven years. At the same time, HP has piled up cash reserves of $400 million with virtually no debt, thanks to Young's sophisticated use of financial controls that, for example, let HP chop both accounts receivable and inventories from about 28 percent of sales in the early 1970s to well under 20 percent today.

But looking only at the balance sheet could be deceiving. The company is still riding on the momentum of older products introduced several years ago and markets rapidly nearing saturation. While HP remains the second-largest maker of general-purpose minicomputers, it has not kept up in such important, faster-growing areas as business systems or personal computers. HP's market share has slipped in these products in the past two years.

And when the economy recovers, notes E. David Crockett, a former HP manager who is now a market researcher at Dataquest Inc., "the upturn is likely to be strongest in areas such as personal computers and office automation, where HP's strength is unproven."

What is more, the transition of power from Messrs. Hewlett and Packard to Young was relatively slow, allowing the buildup of some serious problems that are only now starting to be tackled:

■ In research, HP's famed central laboratories had until recently failed to make a mark in computer science. As recently as two years ago, HP Labs had only 50 of its 200 professionals working in the computer field. Reflecting the personal interest of longtime R & D head Bernard M. Oliver, the labs focused on physical-science problems instead of the software and design issues crucial to developing new computers. Even in some hardware projects, says David Lam, a former HP researcher, "objectives often weren't well defined, and there would be tremendous delays."

■ In personal computers, HP entered the field late and still holds only a 4 percent unit share of the world market, according to Dataquest. "In terms of price and performance, HP is certainly competitive," says one personal computer analyst. "But they don't have a good understanding of how this market works." As a result, HP has had trouble lining up good dealers and outside software

companies to write programs for its computers.

■ In minicomputers, HP has been unable to develop a follow-on product to its enormously successful HP–3000 computer. Even though the power of the 3000 has been continually increased since it was introduced in 1972, some observers feel it has been outdated by machines from DEC, Prime Computer Inc., and others. "Technically, it's obsolete," says William E. Foster, president of Stratus Computer Inc., of Natick, Mass., and a former HP engineering manager. "It's 1968 architecture, and this is 1982."

Even so, it is highly unlikely that there will be any major tampering with HP's structure as long as the two founders remain on the scene. Both Packard, 70, and Hewlett, 69, are now semiretired. But as board chairman and chairman of the executive committee, respectively, they continue to wield enormous influence.

Packard, who does not plan to retire fully, believes that the company's current divisional structure makes most sense in the $2 billion instrument side of the business. In that area, HP's sixteen instrument divisions face small competitors, and the market segments are sharply defined. But Packard insists that the divisional structure can also work in the computer field. "It's better to stay with something that you know how to manage," he declares, "than try to do something new."

Rebuilding the Folklore

Young's efforts to revamp HP have been hindered not only by the conservatism of Packard, Hewlett, and the HP board, critics suggest, but also by the background of much of the company's top management. They point out that most of the company's senior executives—even those running computer operations—got their start on the instruments side, although data products now account for more than half of HP's sales.

"The remaking of HP won't be complete until the bulk of senior management jobs are filled with people who got their hands dirty in the computer business," says one former manager.

Young, an athletic-looking 50-year-old who capped his engineering degree with an MBA from Stanford University, denies that he has been restrained by the founders' continued presence. Still, outsiders point out that Young's first priority was to transfer the mantle of authority from the company's almost legendary founders. "The biggest challenge he faced was to rebuild the folklore and move it to the new team," says L. William Krause, a former HP division manager who left in 1980 to head 3Com Corp. One reason Young succeeded in this, Krause adds, was that "he didn't come in as a cold-hearted gunslinger and start firing people."

For example, in the R & D area, Young waited until Oliver retired as R & D chief last year before making a clean break with the past. To head HP Labs, Young appointed John L. Doyle, the company's former personnel director, who was known for his ability to articulate HP's entrepreneurial culture. "It was not science but management we needed to emphasize in getting HP Labs reorganized," Young explains. Then, to generate the new products needed to carry the company to greater heights when business picks up, Young followed HP's classic prescription for success in high technology by raising R & D spending to more than 10 percent of sales from 8.8 percent two years ago.

Doyle has already recruited a team of 220 computer-oriented professionals, including several key researers from IBM, Burroughs, SRI International, and other leading computer organizations. And he has started forming research partnerships with universities for the first time. He is also working to couple HP Labs more closely to the strategy-setting committees of the company's operating groups. Declares Doyle, "We want to be sure that HP Labs is as pre-

eminent in computers as it is in instruments."

A bigger challenge for Young may be to negotiate the transition from general-purpose business computers to data-processing systems for specific applications. HP has traditionally concentrated on marketing technically sophisticated products and leaving the applications details to its customers—either end users or software companies that tailored a computer for specialized needs and resold it.

But the spread of computing out of traditional corporate data processing departments and the skyrocketing cost of programming are forcing a change to vertical marketing directly to specific industries. "HP is a classic case of the engineering-driven company confronting a marketing-driven world—they should restructure to acknowledge that," says one computer industry expert.

If the company is to carry off this assignment, however, it will have to do a better job of coordinating the activities of its twenty-two information processing divisions. "HP is not organized very well to do vertical marketing," says InfoCorp's Bushee. "The best thing they can do is team up with [applications] software specialists." Besides doing that, HP is also starting to acquire small companies to get the necessary applications skills. In addition, it has set up its first applications marketing division and is staffing it with specialists from other industries.

A computer strategy council, set up by Young to improve the coordination of the company's computer divisions, is redefining HP's role in the market. Under the leadership of Executive Vice-President Paul C. Ely, Jr.—a 50-year-old engineer who earned his spurs in HP's microwave instruments operation—the council addresses strategic issues ranging from product introductions to data communications standards.

As a result of that effort, HP last year bet on an applications-oriented marketing strategy called Manufacturers' Productivity Network (MPN) to serve as a blueprint for its product development work in the 1980s.

Four Crucial Areas

Choosing manufacturers as a marketing target was logical, Ely explains, since HP has concentrated on selling to manufacturing companies for nearly ten years. That market now generates more than 40 percent of the company's business-computer sales. "If we tried to solve the problems of small business, retailers, and banks, we couldn't do it," Ely says.

As part of that new strategy, HP will zero in on four applications areas that it considers crucial to manufacturing companies: planning and control, factory automation, office systems, and engineering. Because the success of this marketing concept will depend heavily on HP's ability to tie together equipment in each of the four applications areas, the company, more than ever before, is emphasizing customer software and communications network products to link its computers together.

Already, the MPN formula has revealed some holes in HP's product line that the company is racing to fill. In office systems, for example, HP launched a development effort that led to a massive rollout of twenty-seven new products last year.

Surprisingly, the new strategy also pointed up serious gaps in HP's scientific and engineering product lines. Despite its strength in the minicomputer market, HP has never dislodged DEC from its leadership position in that segment. DEC added to its lead in this field in 1978 by bringing out the VAX superminicomputer, which processes thirty-two bits of information at a time, like the more expensive mainframe computers.

HP seemed unable to decide how to respond to the VAX challenge. Under its highly decentralized system, several 32-bit computer development programs were started and then squelched as division managers battled for top-management approval.

"There was endless bickering over what to do," recalls John V. Sell, a former HP engineer who left to help found Ridge Computers Inc., a maker of the 32-bit minis.

The issue was settled at least in part by the dramatic success of the Desktop Computer Div. in Fort Collins, Colorado, in developing a 32-bit microprocessor, the key to a superminicomputer. Once this complex chip was developed, Young and Ely created a special project—code-named Dawn—to pull together the resources of many HP divisions to develop the computer.

So important was this project that Young took the unprecedented step of naming Fred W. Wenninger as "program manager" with broad powers to tap many HP divisions for necessary components or software. In the past, new products have always come from individual divisions or from small teams in the central HP Labs. This time, says Douglas C. Chance, general manager of HP's Technical Computer Group, "we did just the opposite of taking a small group of engineers and sticking them in the basement."

Wenninger, an easygoing Fort Collins engineer who farms 7,000 acres of wheat in his spare time, quickly put a half-dozen of the widely scattered HP divisions into lock-step on the $100 million Dawn project. And on Nov. 16, less than two years after the integrated-circuit technology that made Dawn possible was announced, HP introduced the HP–9000. Considered by some the ultimate personal computer, the HP–9000 packs the power of a 32-bit mainframe into a unit small enough to sit on a desk.

HP's many divisions have not seen the last of the program management concept. The company is now trying a modified version in a bid to bring order to its chaotic position in personal computers. Three HP groups sell them: the Corvallis (Oregon) Personal Computer Group turns out a handheld computer along with HP's Series 80 personal computer line; the Computer Terminals Group makes personal office computers; and the Technical Computer Group makes a line of desktops for engineers, now headed by the 9000. These three units have not worked with one another, and their pricing and marketing strategies have been off target. "These markets have grown and overlapped," says InfoCorp's Bushee. "But HP's organization hasn't changed to accommodate that."

In the past, HP has stressed good profitabilty over large market share. But obtaining a large share in the personal computer market may be the key to long-term profitability. The reason: In today's applications-driven market, consumers want machines that run the most software, and entrepreneurial programmers are writing software for the best-selling machines to boost their own sales. In such a market, low market penetration could be fatal.

As a first step toward better coordination of personal computer efforts, Young last summer appointed Cyril Yansouni, 40, general manager of the Computer Terminals Group, as program manager for personal computers. Yansouni, an Egyptian-born, Belgian-trained engineer who had previously headed HP's Grenoble (France) Division will be more of a strategic coordinator than a project leader. He is already working with the three divisions to align product design and software strategies.

The first fruits of this cooperation appeared in early November, when HP announced two new personal computers—the HP–120 from the California-based Computer Terminals Group and the Model 16 from the Technical Computer Group—that look alike and use the same peripheral products.

Placating the Dealers

Personal computer marketing is also being coordinated for the first time under Yansouni. This effort, HP hopes, will end the problems that it encountered with its full-service dealers. Many of those dealers had started refusing to handle the HP products because they were getting no better dis-

counts than the discounters and mail-order houses they were competing against—even though they had to provide service. To cut manufacturing costs so that HP can be competitive with the highly efficient Japanese producers barreling into the market, Yansouni is looking for ways to automate production and to force the divisions to share components to a greater degree than they are accustomed to.

Young's efforts to improve coordination clearly seem to be having some success. "Now we see a lot of products coming out of cross-divisional development projects," says Crow, the HP Computer Users Group manager. He adds, "There is clearly a marketing and development effort to pull things together."

But all this planning and coordination are apparently threatening the entrepreneurial spirit of HP's divisions. Even though Young has stopped far short of a complete overhaul at HP, the changes he has made so far have been wrenching enough at the division level to help trigger a wave of defections that is deeply troubling for a company that has never had turnover problems.

Former employees speak glowingly of HP's ability to recruit the best talent from the best engineering schools and to move young engineers quickly into significant jobs in an informal environment. But the drift toward centralized planning does not sit well with people trained to be entrepreneurial, notes Fred M. Gibbons, a former HP manager and now president of Software Publishing Corp. in Mountain View, California. "They don't want to get involved in organizational problems," he says. "They want to get out and 'take the hill.'"

Young was concerned enough recently about the health of HP's entrepreneurial spirit to commission a survey of 12,000 employees, which he says demonstrated that "all the traditional things are still working." Nevertheless, HP has tuned up an already liberal benefits program and launched new efforts to improve communication with employees, especially when divisions are split up or moved.

HP is probably powerless to stop the loss of upwardly mobile managers to the proliferating new companies in the San Francisco Bay area. Nor can it fully reconcile the bureaucratic demands of the computer business with its entrepreneurial traditions. "We're constantly dealing with the trade-offs" between those requirements, Young says. "We work hard at creating an exciting environment, but in the computer area interdependence is also very important."

If HP can solve this conflict, it will have written another chapter for the management textbooks. And outsiders are eagerly watching to learn how HP achieves this balance because its organization and style have served as models at other high-tech companies. "That management style is important to stimulate creativity," says an executive at Rolm Corp., a California maker of telecommunications equipment that has borrowed HP concepts. "It would certainly be nice if it can be made to work."

■ Plant Democracy at National Foods

PART I

The opening of a new pet food processing plant at Omaha, Nebraska, gave the National Food Company (NF) an opportunity to design its organization structure in a manner that incorporates modern design principles. Utilizing the design principles of (1) *participation*, an attempt to distribute power throughout the organization and (2) *autonomy*, creation of independent work teams, NF designed a new factory system aimed at overcoming problems that beset other food processing plants. The specific goals of the new factory system, according to T.K. Nunley, manager of organizational development at NF, included maximum machine utilization, minimum waste, low distribution costs, low productivity costs, and low absenteeism and turnover. Many of the functions traditionally the prerogatives of management were designed to be perfomed by the workers. The aim of the new system was to have workers make job assignments, interview prospective employees, schedule coffee breaks, and decide on pay raises. Having workers perform these duties was NF's way of attempting "to balance the needs of the people with the needs of the business," according to Nunley.

This case is based largely on an experience of General Foods Corporation as reported in "Stone-

walling Plant Democracy," *Business Week*, March 28, 1977, pp. 78–82.

■ ANALYSIS QUESTIONS

1. If you were asked by Nunley to react to his design ideas and goals, what would you tell him? Why?

2. Do you think a new structure alone will create the behaviors and outcomes that Nunley expects? Discuss.

3. As an organizational development attempt, is the structural design enough, or is more needed to produce the results desired?

■ DO NOT READ UNTIL TOLD TO DO SO BY YOUR INSTRUCTOR.

PART II

The factory system designed by a NF task force working with a professor from Harvard Business School eliminated some layers of management and supervisory personnel and assigned three areas of responsibility to self-managing work teams—processing, packaging, and shipping. Each of the shift teams has seven to fourteen members who decide how to share authority and responsibility for a variety of tasks. For example, a processing team not only handles the actual pet food manufacturing, but also is responsible for unloading raw materials, maintaining equipment, inspecting for quality control, engineering how the work should be performed, and deciding on the size of pay raises for team members.

Work is directed by a team leader described as a "coach," rather than a supervisor or foreman. Work is made less boring by allowing team members to rotate between monotonous and interesting jobs. Pay is determined by the number of tasks each member masters and performs. The teams make necessary management decisions. To reduce perceived heirarchical status differences, NF removed some of the traditional management symbols. For example, there is now a common entrance for employees and management, and reserved parking spaces for management have been eliminated.

■ ANALYSIS QUESTIONS

1. Estimate the efficiency of the factory system designed by the NF task force with respect to:

   a. Production costs per unit: _____ Higher _____ Unchanged _____ Lower

   b. Employee turnover: _____ Higher _____ Unchanged _____ Lower

   c. Absenteeism due to lost time because of accidents: _____ Higher _____ Unchanged _____ Lower

2. Will the above design produce short-term changes, long-term changes, or no change at this plant? Why? What will it take to make it a long-term change?

▪ DO NOT READ UNTIL TOLD TO DO SO BY YOUR INSTRUCTOR.

PART III

The new factory system installed at the Omaha plant of NF was heralded as a model for the future and Nunley, who proclaims it as being "very successful," indicated that NF is applying a similar system at another dog food plant in St. Louis and at a coffee plant in Maryland. Reports indicate that NF may eventually install a similar system at two plants in Mexico and among white-collar workers at the headquarters organization in Stamford, Connecticut. Even the former manager of NF's Omaha and Milwaukee plants, James T. Lyman, who was a critic of the new system, admits, "Based on both the economic results and the quality of working life, it can be considered a success."

There remains little doubt that NF has met many of its goals. Unit costs are 6 percent less than in other plants using a traditional factory system. This, says Nunley, should amount to a savings of over $1.2 million in one year. Employee turnover is only 7 percent and the plant has not experienced a lost time accident in three and one-half years.

▪ ANALYSIS QUESTIONS

1. How close were your estimates of production costs, turnover, and absenteeism due to lost time for accidents? How can you explain the differences?

2. Is this outcome what you expected? Why, or why not?

▪ DO NOT READ UNTIL TOLD TO DO SO BY YOUR INSTRUCTOR.

PART IV

Management analysts and former employees of the Omaha plant reveal a story that is somewhat different from the one released by National Foods. Critics say that after the initial euphoria, the new factory system, confronted by indifference and open hostility from some of the NF managers and staff specialists, has been modified several times.

"The system fell apart. It didn't work in practice," says one former manager. Another ex-employee adds, "It was both successful and unsuccessful. From an economic point of view, it was an absolute success, but from a human and organizational standpoint, it created a power struggle. It was much too threatening to both managers and staff specialists." He predicts that the plant will eventually be switched to a more traditional factory system.

The major problem was not that workers cannot manage their own work, as much as that some management and staff personnel felt their own positions were threatened by the workers' good performance. A management analyst suggested that the system, built around the team concept, was not compatible with NF's bureaucracy. NF's attorneys, fearing reaction from the National Labor Relations Board, opposed the concept of allowing team members to make pay raise decisions. Staff specialists feared the loss of prestige and even their positions, because the teams were doing some of their work. Personnel managers objected because the team members made hiring decisions and performed some of the other personnel functions like screening, training, and so on. Engineers resented engineering work being done by the team members. Quality control personnel saw an erosion of their functions since team members were responsible for some quality control work.

Another ex-employee, who was enthusiastic about the new system when it was first installed, saw it deteriorate. "Creating a new system is one thing, maintaining it is different," she claims. "There were pressures almost from the beginning, and not because of failures. The basic reason was power. The new arrangement contradicted corporate policy. People like stable states. This system has to be changing otherwise it will die. Why allow worker discretion to make changes and then turn around and freeze the system?"

The ex-plant manager felt that any time a structural change is made, one should not be surprised by unanticipated consequences.

If you have industrial engineers who have been designing work based on traditional

principles for many years, they get anxious and threatened when they are thrown into a plant where the workers are doing job design. The personnel people are also threatened by the loss of functions they have performed in the past, and on top of that the personnel people must deal with a whole new set of problems such as the power struggle, peer complaints about pay raise decisions, etc. Controllers want someone from their own fraternity in the system, and so on. Plant democracy does not eliminate problems, all it does is create a new set of problems. As a result, pressures build up, the system starts to fragment, and when you fragment it, you also degrade it.

Consequently critics point out, there has been a slow "stiffening and tightening" in the Omaha system, such as more job classifications, more supervision, less participation, and so on. NF has added seven managment positions to the plant including a plant industrial engineer, a controller and a manufacturing service manager. NF claims that the additions were due to plant expansion, but critics believe that it was more due to the "tightening up" of the system. A management analyst suggests that the modifications have caused a slight decrease in quality, a buildup of minor problems because of fewer team meetings, and increased competition between shifts.

Another problem area is pay. As the new system was implemented, team members who were voting on pay raise decisions began to feel peer pressure and stress. "You work with one person for several years and you get to be pretty good friends. Then it is difficult to be objective in deciding on pay raises," says one worker. "Moreover, the equal-pay-for-equal-work principle begins to break down."

Managers at the Omaha plant feel that their careers at NF have been jeopardized by getting involved in the new system. Along with the ex-plant manager, another manager who has since departed, says, "They felt we had created something that the corporate management couldn't handle, so their guys were sent in and we were forced out. By being involved in the new system at Omaha, I ruined my career at National Foods." Such skepticism exists even with some of the managers who have remained at the Omaha plant, and it affects all the work teams. One team member said,

"Every time we make a mistake, I wonder if Stamford thinks that maybe it could have been avoided if the plant were operated by a traditional system." But even so, he adds, "This is the best place I've ever worked."

■ ANALYSIS QUESTIONS

1. The big question is whether or not the Omaha system will continue to erode or renew itself. As a consultant to National Foods headquarters, what would you recommend? As a consultant for the Omaha plant, what would you recommend?

2. What are the forces now in the Omaha system that may affect the implementation of future change?

3. How do you think Greiner and Schein would react to these developments, i.e., did an organic-based O.D. effort fail (Schein and Greiner reading)?

■ The White Knights Are Coming!

On February 19, 1982, D–Day for the merger of Wareham Corporation and Piedmont, Inc., many employees at Wareham—from clerk to executive—received a familiar message: "Your services are no longer needed by the company." The anticipation in industry circles was that the acquired firm—Wareham—would prosper under Piedmont; the "white knight" turned out to be somewhat black for the disappointed employees. Such disappointments should

be expected for, according to merger experts, "There is no such thing as white knights, at best there are only gray knights." Takeovers usually occur because one or both partners face critical problems that they cannot solve easily alone. To expect "rosy" solutions is unrealistic. Many surprises occur as a result of a takeover.

Acquired companies invariably lose some of their independence. If top managers are not canned as they were at Wareham, they find themselves reporting to a new level of management above them. The parent company usually inserts its own managers to make the important decisions until it can fig-

Inspired by a report on the merger between the Sunbeam Corp. and Allegheny International Inc. by Lawrence Ingrassia, *Wall Street Journal,* July 7, 1982.

ure out what to do with the extra layer of acquired managers. In the meantime, the white knight discovers the shortcomings and weaknesses of the acquired managers and employees leading to the second surprise. Invariably the acquired company is short on technological capacity, experiencing a diminishing market share, harboring an aging management, coddling spoiled employees, stagnating in the R&D area, patching up obsolete equipment, etc.

The second surprise is exacerbated in cases in which the parent company pays more per share for the acquired company's stock than it is worth. This happens especially in situations in which the parent company engages in a bidding war with others interested in the takeover.

The parent company often turns out to be a white knight for the shareholders of the acquired company. For example, according to the *Wall Street Journal*, Wheelabrator-Frye, Inc., late in 1980, paid close to 100 percent over the market price to buy McDermott Inc. because there were several firms bidding to acquire it. The lay-offs initiated by Wheelabrator the day after the acquisition ended up furloughing more than 1,500 Pullman employees of McDermott Inc. Similar dismissals have occurred over and over in other mergers.

The shareholders of Wareham profited from the merger bidding that occurred prior to the takeover by Piedmont. Wareham stock had been priced in the low 30s prior to the takeover, yet Piedmont acquired Wareham for $41 per share in cash and preferred stock. Wareham's management did well for its shareholders but not for its employees. The surprises started immedi-

ately when Piedmont chairman criticized the past performance of Wareham, followed by dismissal of about 160 members of Wareham's corporate staff. The lucky ones, twenty-one of them, received "golden parachute" dismissals that is, executive termination contracts paying one to two years of salary. Other not-so-lucky managers received twelve weeks of severance pay, professionals got eight weeks, and clerical employees received four weeks severance pay alone with one week's pay for each year of service.

The axing was hard to accept since many employees had been optimistic about the takeover. One executive stated "I had nothing but positive thoughts. I thought this would be a good opportunity for our company to grow. Rumors had it that Piedmont would inject much needed capital for modernization and growth."

Another manager, who was more realistic, indicated that he too would do the same thing, "Piedmont paid $41 per share and Wareham is not worth it. They didn't anticipate the low-profit performance they got in the deal."

Mergers sometimes work out better for both parties, especially when each needs the other. The recent takeover of Marathon by U.S. Steel resulted in some preferential treatment for the acquired managers of Marathon. U.S. Steel needs the oil expertise of the Marathon executives. Consequently, U.S. Steel's 5 percent cutback in executives and the suspension of the executive-incentive compensation plan was not applied to Marathon. There are some white knights still but many of them turn out to be gray or black.

■ Playing the Game in 1492

AL CHARMATZ

Your Excellency:

Please convey word of this victory to our most illustrious King and Queen. Glorious news! The Expedition to the Indies has returned safely, having discovered and claimed new lands!

After sailing for seventy days, at 2 A.M. on October 12, 1492, we first sighted land. We sailed for a further three months, exploring, charting, sighting, and landing on many islands, meeting natives, and trading for objects of gold.

In December we lost the Santa Maria on a reef. On March 4th the Nina anchored at Lisbon for refit and returned to our home port with the Pinta on March 15.

We will make celebrations and give solemn thanks for the great exaltation which this victory will have.

> Christopher Columbus
> Admiral of the Ocean Sea

To: C. Columbus, Admiral of the Ocean Sea (AOS)
From: Program Manager/Dept. of Discoveries
Leon and Castile National Sea Laboratory
Symbol: PM/DOD (LACNSL)
Subject: Operational Procedures

1. Because our reorganization occurred while you were away on official travel

your lapse from proper procedures will be overlooked this time. However, in the future you will refrain from communicating with the Sovereigns.

2. You will submit your program plan for a proposed second voyage across the Western Ocean directly to this office.

To: C. Columbus, AOS
Fm: Chief, Administration
Subj: Matrix Management System

1. Because LACNSL has expanded and accepted increased responsibilities, we have instituted new regulations and reorganized our management structure, applying the management procedures that have proven so effective in the Department of Exploration (DOE).

2. In this matrix management system each employee knows exactly who his supervisors are. In its ultimate form he is placed within a line or functional organization: pilot-navigators in the Navigation Division, seamen in the Labor Division, cabin boys in the Supernumerary Division, soldiers in the Protective Force Division, clerks and pursers in the Personnel Administrative Division, etc. Individuals are then selected and assigned to specific programs. Their work is directed by the line managers with coordination by the program managers. They report in both directions (vertically, within the line organization, and horizontally, to the program manag-

First printed in *Analog Science Fiction/Science Fact,* January 5, 1981, pp. 73–79, under the title "Sailing Through Program Management." Reprinted by permission of the author and publisher.

er) as circumstances require. Certain individuals may work on several programs simultaneously and thus report to a number of program managers. Rumors of simultaneous assignments to different fleets are false.

3. In your specific situation, voyages of discovery are handled by Program Managers in the Department of Discoveries (PM/DOD). Specialists in details of the areas to be searched are placed in the appropriate Explorations functional organization; you are in Western Explorations (WX) Division.

To: PM/DOD
Fm: C. Columbus, Admiral of the Ocean Sea
Subject: Personnel Reassignment

Assigning people to Divisions by discipline means you are breaking up good, established teams. Our crews and officers have built up special expertise and have high morale, which we will need for our Second Voyage.

Furthermore, you cannot pirate our people to staff your expanding program offices if you expect us to do well in the future.

To: C. Columbus, AOS
Fm: PM/DOD
Subj: Personnel Complaints

1. Piracy is a hanging offense and you will not use that word.
2. We decided it is most efficient to assign people to Divisions by discipline (Navigation, Labor, etc.) even if it did mean breaking up established teams. For too long, special tasks and programs have been assigned to small teams. The crews of your three previous vessels are prime examples of this elitism. We have decided the overall organization will benefit if we rotate personnel to

new assignments as the tasks open up, thus ensuring a more universal distribution of skills. That explains why we have reassigned your pilot-navigator to the Northern Fleet, searching for the Isles of the Blessed. Your new pilot-navigator is a recent graduate of the Famous Navigators School and we are sure he will do an excellent job. As a new graduate his salary is lower, which will help your budget.

3. You seem to be unable to understand the rationale behind reassigning personnel, with your whining about "morale" and "breaking up good teams." From the viewpoint of management, "everyone in his box and a box for everyone" simplifies our task immensely. If individuals are assigned to functional organizations that they believe they do not belong in, it is their own fault; they should have planned ahead when they began their apprenticeship. Morale problems, if they really exist, are your concern and not that of the management. You, not we, have the responsibility of getting the assigned task done. The best organizational experts and consultants have told us we are correct, and we see no need for another Employee Attitude Survey. You sailors are all complainers, anyway.

To: C. Columbus, AOS
Fm: PM/DOD
Subj: Written Reports

1. Because some interest in your first voyage has been expressed by the funding agency, our office has decided to publish formal reports.
2. You will furnish us with two reports, an unclassified one written in the style of "Scientific Spaniard" and a classified document. The second report will be classified S–NSI (Secret-National Sea Information) and must be classified by paragraph.

To: C. Columbus, AOS
Fm: Parking Compliance Office
Subj: Parking Violation

1. Parking regulations have been established and will be found in the Supervisors' Manual. You are in violation in the following respect: Ocean-going vessels are divided into two categories, compact and full-size. Vessels with cargo capacity of fifty tonnes burthen or greater are defined as full-size.

2. On 14 March 1493, you dropped anchor on the Nina and the Pinta in the compact vessel portion of the roadstead.

3. A citation has been issued and you are fined, which fine shall be deducted from your wages.

4. If you wish, you can file a written complaint to the Parking Hearing Officer, who will render a decision which will be final and binding on all parties.

To: Parking Hearing Officer
Fm: C. Columbus, Admiral of the Ocean Sea
Subj: Parking Violations—Nina and Pinta

On March 14, 1493, our ships returned from a seven-month voyage. Upon arrival in the roadstead we found mooring buoys labeled ''C,'' which we believed meant ''Caravel,'' not ''Compact.'' I appeal the fine on the basis of not having been notified of these procedures.

By the way, I cannot find anything on this subject in the Supervisors' Manual. The manual is so overcrowded now that I cannot fit new bulletins into it as they are issued. Surely, the sign of a decadent organization must be an overweight manual of procedures. We have rules and regulations for everything, with procedure more important than substance.

To: C. Columbus, AOS
Fm: Parking Hearing Officer
Subj: Parking Violations

1. Rejected, Ignorance is no excuse.

To: C. Columbus, AOS
Fm: Fiscal Management Office
Subj: Call for OPLANs

1. You will prepare an Operating Plan for Fiscal Years 1493 and 1494, which shall include a month-by-month projection of costs, expressed in terms of both manpower and money. You are to count on-board support people (cabin boys, clerks) as 0.5 Full Time Equivalents; everyone else is one FTE each. You should indicate an expected attrition caused by scurvy, fights, storms, hostile natives, sea serpents, etc., and you should account for this diminution of staff. You are, of course, authorized to recruit help from the natives; carry them as non-salaried crew members.

2. You have not yet submitted your formal work statement (Revisable Program Description) to us and to PM/DOD for FY 1493–1498. You claim that you will search, search, and search again until you find the direct route to the Indies. We require that you submit your plan for search and research, with milestones, expected discoveries, and the benefits therefrom.

To: Fiscal Management Office
Fm: C. Columbus, Admiral of the Ocean Sea
Subj: Planning Documents

I cannot go into detail you require regarding a five-year search plan or work statement. If I knew what I would be doing in five years I would be doing it now.

In costing-out the annual OPLANs I find the indirect costs (overhead) are rising excessively. Currently at 60 percent of direct (salary, etc.) costs, they seem to be increasing by ten points per year. If this continues, in FY 1498 they will equal 110 percent of direct costs. Can you find a way to control them?

Also, the 5 percent surcharge imposed by the Program Managers Office is excessive. I resent having to subsidize those who are harassing me. Do you realize that we have to teach the managers what we do, so they can then supervise us?

To: C. Columbus, AOS
Fm: Fiscal Management Office
Subj: Financial Policies

1. It is true that indirect costs are increasing. However, they are calculated as a fraction of your direct costs. If you do not gain control of your direct costs and operating and maintenance costs, you will be forced to reduce the wages of your crews or sail with fewer personnel or ships. We intend to cut the fat from your budget.

2. You should be pleased to learn that we have decided to maintain the ratio of in-house managers to staff at the current level. We realize that the managerial staff cannot continue to expand, so we have recently sent a Request for Quotations to outside agencies, seeking management, administrative, and technical skills. These organizations will assist us in coordination and management. The cost will come out of overhead.

To: C. Columbus, Admiral of the Ocean Sea
Fm: WX-Division Leader
Subj: Harassment

You are fortunate that the managers ask you to teach them before they begin supervision. Other fleet commanders have not been so lucky. Hang in there.

To: C. Columbus, AOS
Fm: PM/DOD
Subj: Planning

1. Your long-range plans have been reviewed by the SMG (Senior Management Group) and our consultants, the DODDERERs (Deputy Over-Directors Doing Early Retirement and Extended

Research). They find your plans elusive and insubstantial. More detail is required.

To: PM/DOD
Fm: C. Columbus, Admiral of the Ocean Sea
Subj: Paperwork

Is it true that paper is now our most important product?

To: C. Columbus, AOS
Fm: Equal Employment/Affirmative Action
Subj: Employment Conditions

1. During your recent voyage you claimed new territories for the Crown.

2. In your OPLAN you describe the natives you recruited as "unpaid crewmen." Although these crewpersons are not full citizens they live in Crown territory and must be accorded the rights of citizens. They must receive the minimum wage. Furthermore, you will prepare a training plan to upgrade their qualifications so they will become eligible for more responsible positions.

To: C. Columbus, AOS
Fm: Associate Director for Exploratory Sciences
Subj: Performance Appraisals

1. Please prepare evaluations of your senior staff, describing their assignments and performance during the recent voyage. In turn, they will prepare evaluations of their subordinates.

2. This year, we will include a summary word describing each employee's overall performance: outstanding, very good, satisfactory, marginal, or unsatisfactory. Note that, by definition, "outstanding" requires consistently exceptional performance. "Satisfactory" means that the job requirements are being met.

3. You should have very few outstanding people, probably no unsatisfactory per-

formers, and very few marginal ones. Effectively, you will be categorizing your personnel as satisfactory or very good. Please try your best, especially in selection of the one-word summary. Remember a key part of the Hippocratic Oath: "First, do no harm."

To: PM/DOD
Fm: C. Columbus, Admiral of the Ocean Sea
Subj: Publications

Our article appeared in *Scientific Spaniard* under your name, not mine, and the acknowledgements were omitted! Explain this theft!

Our classified article appeared verbatim in *Nautical Week and Sea Technology*, including the figures, charts, graphs, and tables. Only the classification labels were removed. This is an obvious violation of security regulations. Also, the only name mentioned is yours!

To: C. Columbus, AOS
Fm: PM/DOD
Subj: Publications

1. Obviously only the names of Program Management personnel should appear on external publications. It is our function to interface with outside agencies. Our sponsors, the funding agencies, deal with us routinely and would only be confused if we brought in the names of people they have not met.
2. Classification is what we say it is. *Nautical Week* would not even look at our reports, let alone publish them, if they were not classified.

To: C. Columbus, AOS
Fm: Parking Compliance Officer
Subj: Parking Violation

1. Our records show this is your second violation.

2. Yesterday a small, oar-propelled craft, safety-rated for six persons, was tied up along the Full-Size Vessel section of the pier.
3. As commanding officer you are responsible. You are hereby issued a citation and informed that a fine has been imposed, which will be deducted from your wages.
4. Future violations will be met with administrative measures, commencing with a suspension from duties without pay.
5. You may pursue the established grievance or administrative review procedure (see the Supervisors' Manual on Corrective Actions and Administrative Review).

To: C. Columbus, Admiral of the Ocean Sea
Fm: WX-Division Office
Subj: Appraisal of Your Performance

We really wish we could have rated your performance during the current review period as "outstanding." However, the definition requires consistently exceptional performance and we find from the log books that several periods of time elapsed during which you did not discover new lands. Furthermore, you did lose the Santa Maria. We would have rated your performance only as "very good" for those reasons.

However, the program manager who has cognizance over your activities has direct input into your performance appraisal. He stated his displeasure at your failure to provide the necessary documentation and other paperwork he asked for. He could not rate you as "unsatisfactory" because of your positive accomplishments, but wished to rate your performance as only "marginal." We compromised and your performance rating is "satisfactory."

For "Development Plans" the program office expects you to devote more attention to following procedures established by the organization.

To: WX-Division Office
Fm: C. Columbus, Admiral of the Ocean Sea
Subj: My Performance Appraisal

So you call me a C student!

To: PM/DOD
Fm: C. Columbus, Admiral of the Ocean Sea
Subj: Scurvy

On long voyages crewmen are coming down with scurvy. Can you work on finding a cure?

To: C. Columbus, AOS
Fm: PM/DOD
Subj: Advanced Development Program

1. You asked that a cure be found for scurvy.
2. You were able to return from your voyage with most of the crew alive, so this appears to be a needless expenditure; we must watch our budget.
3. Solution to the problem of scurvy is of long-term interest and we encourage your work in this field. We suggest you prepare a program plan and submit it to the Office of Advanced (Nonprogrammatic) Research and Development. We have no funds that we can dedicate to this task. Perhaps you can obtain funding from them.

To: C. Columbus, AOS
Fm: Training Office
Subj: Upgrading of Native Crewpersons

1. We understand you are having problems qualifying for higher ratings the crewpersons you acquired on your Western voyage. We would like to help.
2. We have reorganized the Training Office with enlarged staffing, so now we can take on training of non-citizens. We also have instituted a bilingual education program.
3. Unfortunately, we cannot send the crewpersons to our special school because the "travel-for-training" budget has been cut.
4. However, be assured that we have every confidence in our capability to help your people. We have correlated our Figures-of-Merit (number of training office personnel per student, and cost of training per student) and find them both in phase and increasing, so we know we are doing well. We are doing very well indeed.

To: All Employees
Fm: Director
Subj: Family Days

1. On the second weekend in June all facilities and vessels will be open to the public.
2. You will arrange displays, tours, and demonstrations. They must not interfere with the orderly pursuit of work. All areas will be clean and safety hazards eliminated. Money will be taken from the Recreation Fund and used to pay for minstrels to entertain the visitors.

To: Master Supervisors List
Fm: Administration
Subj: Professional Titles

1. The Senior Management Group (SMG) has decided that all employees should be numerically graded. We will start with the seamen (SMs), giving them a rating level of SM–1 up through SM–9.
2. You will assign a rating number to each SM, based on your evaluation of qualifications and performance, considering training, education, experience, seniority, and general worth to the organization. Guidelines will follow.
3. It is imperative that all SMs agree that the rating level assigned them is fair. Remember, they will compare their ratings against those of their colleagues pulling on the same capstan bar or setting the same sails, and they know their own worth at least as well as you.

4. We are certain that once we have a box for everyone and everyone in his box the organization will run more smoothly.

To: C. Columbus, AOS
Fm: Equal Employment/Affirmative Action
Subj: Underutilization of Minorities

1. After SMs were given numerical ratings we determined that there is an underutilization of minorities (from the new Western islands) in upper levels.
2. It is our policy that certain goals be met, for which purpose this department will work closely with you.

To: C. Columbus, AOS
Fm: PM/DOD
Subj: PM Representation

1. Should your second voyage be approved, representatives of the Program Manager will accompany you for the purpose of negotiating with the Great Khan. Our office will contract for the exchange of goods and services and will arrange delivery schedules. You will not conduct any negotiations by yourself. Any meetings must be attended by our official representatives. Those individuals will have the final say, and will inform you of your responsibilities in meeting the cargo delivery schedule, etc. Failure to comply with the schedules will reflect adversely upon your next performance appraisal.
2. We are certain we will have your cooperation, especially if you wish to have your theories vindicated. Remember, we have many junior Program Managers who have not yet been to sea and who are eager to go. Several will be aboard as observers, critiquing your decisions and debriefing you at the end of each watch. They will send periodic letter reports by carrier pigeon. We will judge the success of your next voyage by the regularity of those reports and their description of how well you

function as a member of the LACNSL team.

To: WX-Division Leader
Fm: C. Columbus, Admiral of the Ocean Sea
Subj: Options

I believe I have only two choices left: follow these fantastic procedures or take early retirement. Have you any advice?

To: C. Columbus, AOS
Fm: WX-Division Leader
Subj: Options

Hang in there; sanity must return.

By the way, I am approaching the mandatory retirement age myself and will be leaving soon. Have you considered applying for my job? It involves desk work instead of field work and a different degree of harassment, of course.

To: Director
Fm: C. Columbus, Admiral of the Ocean Sea
Subj: Is Paper Really Our Most Important Product?

The enclosed files (three mule-loads' worth) will show you the difficulty I have had in getting my job done. Can you help?

To: PM/DOD and WX-Division
Fm: Director
Subj: Columbus

1. Who is this C. Columbus person? My office has never heard of him.

To: WX-Division Leader
Fm: C. Columbus, Admiral of the Ocean Sea
Subj: Options

No thanks; I wouldn't want your job. At least I can go to sea now and then.

I had considered moving West to the Leeward Lisbon Laboratory (LLL) but they discovered hybrid matrix management before we did, so they must be in even worse condition. I cannot set up my own company of merchant adventurers and explorers because of the government monopoly, so I will indeed just "hang in there." I will be going to sea soon; I may even decide to come back.

To: C. Columbus, AOS
Fm: WX-Division Leader
Subj: Second Voyage

Afraid it's too late. This morning, without notifying us, the PM/DOD sent the fleet to sea. They encountered a severe storm and went down with all hands. It will be interesting to see how they get out of this one.

To: Director
Fm: PM/DOD
Subj: Investigation into the Loss of C. Columbus' Fleet

1. A court of Inquiry, consisting of members of PM/DOD and the DODDERERs, has investigated the loss of the C. Columbus fleet.

2. We concluded that loss of the fleet was caused by the failure of C. Columbus (formerly AOS) to make adequate preparations and to follow the prescribed procedures.

3. We recommend that C. Columbus be tried and executed.

4. Furthermore, it is apparent that this failure to adequately prepare for sea was due in part to our inability to exercise sufficient and close supervision over day-to-day details. Thus we further recommend that the Project Manager's staff be enlarged, including supplementary in-house personnel, resident consultants, and outside contractors.

To: PM/DOD
Fm: Director
Subj: Court of Inquiry Findings and Recommendations

1. Accepted.

Exercises

■ Remloph Manufacturing Company

Organizations are constantly under pressure to change and to maintain the status quo simultaneously. These forces for change and stability may originate internally or from external sources including, for example, technology, social custom, government regulation, and competition. A manager's perception of the organization's needs is influenced by his or her position in the organization. Gaining an overall awareness of the problems, distinguishing them from their symptoms, and synthesizing the information into a plan of action is difficult for managers who may be either overinvolved in a problem or insulated from it.

The exercise provides the opportunity for groups of participants to develop an appropriate strategy for gathering information about an organization's needs, implementing their strategy for developing an initial diagnosis, and receiving feedback on their approach, diagnosis, and implementation.

Directions—Role Players

1. Your instructor will select role players and assign each one to a particular role.
2. Each role player should carefully review the letter and organization chart received from Remloph, Exhibit 5.10, and role-playing instructions of the role assigned by the instructor.
3. Each role player should be prepared to be interviewed by each consulting team.
4. Role players will be required to provide feedback to the consulting teams on their intervention approaches and presentations.

Directions—Consulting Teams

1. Your instructor will set up consulting teams.
2. Each team should carefully review the letter and organization chart received from Remloph, Exhibit 5.10, and develop a strategy for gathering information.
3. Each team will have appointments with the role players it wishes to interview.
4. Each team will then implement its intervention approach.
5. Each team will prepare and present its initial findings and recommendations for the future.
6. The presentations will be discussed and evaluated.

Developed by David D. Palmer, University of Connecticut, and W. Alan Randolph, University of South Carolina.

Remloph Manufacturing Company

Dear Consultants:

As I mentioned during our recent phone conversation, my company has been experiencing some difficulties of late--sales and profits have declined over the past several years. While the increased number and strength of our competitors may account for part of our problem, I suspect that some internal problems exist and that they have contributed to our difficulties. Your consulting firm comes highly recommended as one that may be able to provide the help necessary to resolve these problems.

We are a medium-sized manufacturer of materials handling and storing equipment, including conveyors, hoists, casters, shelving, parts bins, and related equipment. The firm, founded fifteen years ago, currently employs about 2,000 people. Except during the first two years and the last three years, Remloph experienced rapid growth in sales and profits. Profits have declined 15 percent in the last three years. Two new local competitors began operations within the past three years and have gained a sizable share of the market. Several middle managers who left Remloph during the last few years have joined these new companies.

I would like you to meet with several key people. After your meetings with them, you should present your initial findings and suggestions about how to proceed in collecting additional information and in defining and implementing solutions. If your suggestions are accepted, we can then work out the details of our consulting arrangement.

I think you should talk to the following people: myself, Vice-President of Personnel, Vice-President of Manufacturing, and the Production Manager. Accordingly, at a recent meeting I have announced my decision to have you come in and have advised them that you will set up the necessary appointments. Some background on these personnel may be valuable to you.

I started the company when I was thirty years old,
and for many years was involved in all major decisions. In addition, during the earlier years I contributed some ideas that led to the development of
several new products and major product changes. Over
the last few years I have begun to delegate more authority.

The Vice-President of Personnel, 35 years old, was
hired into that position four years ago, has an MBA
and several years of personnel experience. The VP of
personnel is very innovative and has introduced several training programs for us during the past several
years.

The Vice-President of Manufacturing, 56 years old, is
a loyal and dependable member of the management team
who has been with the firm since its inception and
has been Vice-President for the last five years. The
Vice-President started as a production employee and
moved up through the management ranks while going to
night school to earn an engineering degree.

The Manager of Production, 40 years old, came to our
firm ten years ago with a BS in engineering and began
as the assistant Manager of Production. The promotion to Manager of Production occurred when the previous manager was promoted to VP of Manufacturing. I
have attached an organization chart that I drew up
several years ago so that you can see how we operate.

I look forward to hearing from you.

Sincerely,

A Remloph

President
Remloph Manufacturing
Company

EXHIBIT 5.10   Remloph Manufacturing Company Organization Chart

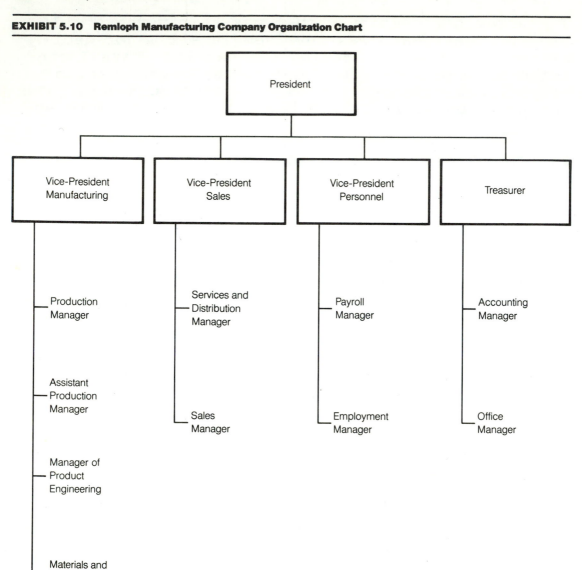

■ Video-Tronics Division

To the casual observer, an organization appears rather complex, often betraying the machine-like qualities assumed in the organizational chart. Given a specific organizational structure, it is possible to generate a variety of potential pathological outcomes that may or may not emerge during the life of the organization. The view that is being posited here is that while an organization's structure can and does have impact on emergent behavior, the dysfunctional properties of that behavior may include a wide continuum of responses. Nevertheless, the serious student of organization would be remiss not to trace such outcomes back to the structural roots. Often the search for structural issues is hampered by behavioral disguises, which are more of a symptom than a cause.

In this exercise, you will be confronted by symptoms of organizational problems. Much like a pathologist, you will have to examine the anatomic deviations from the norm and attempt to diagnose the organizational disease. As an investigator, you will want to examine the basic anatomy (Exhibit 5.11) and begin to gather pieces of information from organizational members to aid you in your analysis. Unlike the pathologist and much like the surgeon, you will have to go beyond diagnosis and develop a strategy for action.

Video-Tronics Division Background

The Video-Tronics Division, a designer and manufacturer of video games for home and commercial use, is part of a multinational conglomerate. The Division was formed three years ago to better utilize surplus engineering talent from the parent company. As an experiment, the entire division management was recruited from young corporate talent. As a result, the average manager is thirty years of age and has a MBA. To the delight of the parent organization, the new division was producing a profit by its second year of operation. The experiment was deemed a complete success until about six months ago when the Division Manager reported having increasing difficulty in dealing with all the "young tigers" who manage the division. There seems to be a lot of unrest and discontent among managers at Video-Tronics and three managers have privately requested transfers to other divisions. While sales were increasing, the profit margin showed a decline in the first two quarters of this year. Annual sales last year were $248 million with a profit margin before taxes of 15 percent. This year sales should exceed $275 million but the profit margin has slipped to 7 percent. The Division Manager has asked some consultants to take a look at the current situation. The following descriptions briefly define the tasks of each department.

Sales Department	Responsible for all selling, marketing research, and advertising activities
Manufacturing Department	Responsible for the production, inspection, and shipping of all products
Engineering Department	Responsible for all engineering functions. Each engineering group has its own head with the following responsibilities:

Mechanical Designs the game's chassis and mechanical components (levers, plastic handguns, steering wheels that attach to chassis)

Electrical Designs the theoretical systems and game program's circuitry; creates new game ideas

Manufacturing Designs equipment to effectively produce plastic chassis and parts, as well as equipment to produce internal electrical components such as printed circuit boards

Industrial Work and job design to produce products as efficiently as possible, including plant layout, time and motion study, cost effectiveness studies; responsible for cost estimating and packaging designs

Purchasing Department Responsible for the procurement of all raw materials and inventory control on finished goods and raw materials

Exhibit 5.11 indicates how Video-Tronics was organized.

EXHIBIT 5.11 Organizational Chart Highlighting Video-Tronics Division

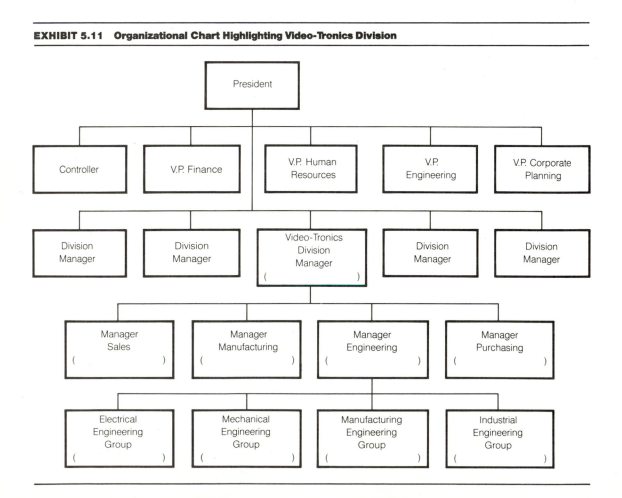

Directions—Video-Tronics Role Players

1. As part of the role-playing group, your task will be to determine an organizational issue that your group will have to role play as members of the Video-Tronics Division. Your instructor has a list of suggested issues for your group to consider; however, your group is encouraged to develop its own problematic issues that it would like to act out. Your group should determine who will play which role and how each role should be presented. Special effort should be made not to give away the underlying issues you are attempting to portray, but rather to indicate only the symptoms of the problem. Each consulting group may ask different questions during the interview that you should try to answer. You are free to make up answers that are consistent with your role in Video-Tronics. However, this is *not* a soap opera—there is no need to create roles that are personally entwined or out of the ordinary.

2. Your instructor will present an interview schedule, which the consulting teams will follow, and designate each role player's office space. When instructed, you should go to your specific office space and prepare to receive various consulting teams. You should terminate each designated interview session *promptly*. Interviews will last twenty minutes.

3. You should be prepared to articulate *internal* as well as *external* forces influencing Video-Tronics. In addition, have some ideas about why the profit margin is slipping drastically.

Directions—Video-Tronics Consultants

1. Your task as a consulting team will be to conduct a series of sensing interviews with key Video-Tronics Division personnel in order to obtain data to diagnose organizational problems. Your instructor will provide an interview schedule that must be followed closely. You will have to prepare your interview questions. An interview schedule and notes form is provided for your use. Also, you should review the *Sensing Interview Suggestions* to prepare for your first interview. Interviews will last twenty minutes.

2. After the interviews your team should pool its knowledge and develop a diagnosis of the Video-Tronics Division. In addition, your team should formulate a plan of action to deal with the problems and issues identified. Below are some guidelines for diagnosis and action planning. Your team will be expected to present its diagnosis and action plan.

3. The management team will evaluate your overall performance as a consulting team using the *Video-Tronics Presentation Evaluation* form provided.

Diagnosis and Action Plan Guidelines

Diagnosis

1. Present the specific organizational problems you have identified (your summary statements based on common themes from the interviews). Note: Demonstrate the validity of each problem statement using as evidence citations of specific examples of actual comments gathered. (Harvey and Albertson reading)

2. Carefully assess the degree to which Video-Tronics is receptive to and ready for change:
   a. What pressures exist? Internal as well as external. (Greiner reading)

b. What major driving and restraining forces are operating with respect to Video-Tronics present state of equilibrium, i.e., its present profit margin?

Action plan

In this section we are looking for you to make recommendations on how to solve the problems you have identified in your diagnosis. While our readings suggest that consultants/change agents should avoid making recommendations without some shared approach to defining the problem and alternatives, a consultant/change agent must be prepared to provide some theoretical and practical guidance on possible solutions. Few consultants/change agents enter a management diagnosis session without some clear ideas about plausible solutions that the client may be helped to "see." Therefore, you are asked to present your *macro solutions* for Video-Tronics.

1. What specific changes in Video-Tronics would you recommend? Note: Be sure solutions address the problems you identified in your diagnosis.

2. Explain specifically how you see your changes resulting in more effective performance at Video-Tronics, i.e., how do you see your solutions working out in practice in the future. Lay out a scenario.

3. In light of your solutions and knowledge of the change forces present at Video-Tronics, how would you recommend your solutions be implemented? Provide some detail on how you would go about initiating an organizational development effort. (Use readings in Part 5 as a basis for your recommendations.)

Note: Your instructor will indicate the length and format of your presentations.

VIDEO–TRONICS INTERVIEW SCHEDULES

TEAM A

	Title	Name	Location	Interviewer
Session 1 (From/To) ___/___	Optional *			
	Optional *			
	Optional *			
Session 2 (From/To) ___/___	Div. Mgr.			
	Mgr. Sales			
	Mgr. Eng.			
Session 3 (From/To) ___/___	Mgr. Mfg.			
	Mgr. Purch.			
	Head Elec. Eng.			
Session 4 (From/To) ___/___	Head Mech. Eng.			
	Head Mfg. Eng.			
	Head Ind. Eng.			

* You may use this time to *observe* any interview but not participate. (*Only one member per team may go as an observer to each interview.*)

TEAM B

	Title	Name	Location	Interviewer
Session 1 *(From/To)* ____/____	Div. Mgr.			
	Mgr. Sales			
	Mgr. Eng.			
Session 2 *(From/To)* ____/____	Optional *			
	Optional *			
	Optional *			
Session 3 *(From/To)* ____/____	Head Mech. Eng.			
	Head Mfg. Eng.			
	Head Ind. Eng.			
Session 4 *(From/To)* ____/____	Mgr. Mfg.			
	Mgr. Purch.			
	Head Elec. Eng.			

 * You may use this time to *observe* any interview but not participate. (*Only one member per team may go as an observer to each interview.*)

TEAM C

	Title	Name	Location	Interviewer
Session 1 *(From/To)* ____/____	Mgr. Mfg.			
	Mgr. Purch.			
	Head Elec. Eng.			
Session 2 *(From/To)* ____/____	Head Mech. Eng.			
	Head Mfg. Eng.			
	Head Ind. Eng.			
Session 3 *(From/To)* ____/____	Optional *			
	Optional *			
	Optional *			
Session 4 *(From/To)* ____/____	Div. Mgr.			
	Mgr. Sales			
	Mgr. Eng.			

 * You may use this time to *observe* any interview but not participate. (*Only one member per team may go as an observer to each interview.*)

TEAM D

	Title	Name	Location	Interviewer
Session 1 (From/To) ____/____	Head Mech. Eng.	_____	_____	_____
	Head Mfg. Eng.	_____	_____	_____
	Head Ind. Eng.	_____	_____	_____
Session 2 (From/To) ____/____	Mgr. Mfg.	_____	_____	_____
	Mgr. Purch.	_____	_____	_____
	Head Elec. Eng.	_____	_____	_____
Session 3 (From/To) ____/____	Div. Mgr.	_____	_____	_____
	Mgr. Sales	_____	_____	_____
	Mgr. Eng.	_____	_____	_____
Session 4 (From/To) ____/____	Optional *	_____	_____	_____
	Optional *	_____	_____	_____
	Optional *	_____	_____	_____

* You may use this time to *observe* any interview but not participate. (*Only one member per team may go as an observer to each interview.*)

Sensing Interview Suggestions

The aim of a sensing interview is to observe and gather data to be used later in diagnosing the organization. The following suggestions may be useful in achieving these aims.

A. Data gathering

1. Set up the interview by having your key questions in front of you within easy visual distance.
2. Start the interview with easy-to-answer, low-threat questions, then advance to more difficult ones.
3. Consider asking four types of questions
   a. *general lead questions* designed to explore and probe as well as give you a general sense of the organization, e.g., "In your opinion what problems does the organization face at the present time?"
   b. *educated guess questions* designed to give you more information about particular problems that you suspect may exist based on your initial impression of the organization (its structure, environment, products, past problems, etc.), for example, in a matrix organization one may want to ask about dual authority relationships
   c. *continuation/elaboration lead questions* designed to allow the interviewee to continue talking or to elaborate on the issue at hand
   d. *testing questions* designed to test the accuracy of the assumptions that you are making; this is a way of testing your hunches as you experience initial contact with the organization

4. Use exploratory, open-ended questions rather than questions that yield a yes or no response.

5. Listen actively for both verbal and nonverbal responses made by the interviewee. Avoid hearing only what you want to hear or came prepared to hear. When you start clarifying the interviewee's statements for him or her instead of asking for clarification, you have gone too far.

B. Development of climate

Conveying to the interviewee your desire to understand the organization is a crucial step in developing an effective relationship. The following styles foster an understanding climate within the interview setting.

1. *Restating* repeating a statement made by the interviewee aimed at making certain that you heard exactly what the interviewee said. It should be a word-for-word replay.

2. *Paraphrasing* a demonstration using your own words to show that you understood what the interviewee said.

3. *Mirroring* a technique by which you play back the interviewee's feeling experienced during the interview.

4. *Summarizing* a way of integrating the different data being conveyed by the interviewee. This fosters a climate of understanding.

Diagnosis

The diagnosis relies largely on the quality of the raw data and observations gathered during the sensing interview and the way the data is organized for the analysis.

A. Quality of data

1. With the approval of the interviewee, take notes on the comments expressed during the interview and record especially feelings-oriented and evaluative responses.

2. Accuracy is very important. Try to record as accurately as possible statements made by the interviewee and observations you gathered during the initial contact with the organization. Remember this is your raw material for the diagnosis.

B. Organization of data

1. Sort the data gathered in all the interviews into common themes using nonevaluative labels, e.g., if several comments have been gathered concerning organizational structure, then list under this label all the relevant comments such as:

   Organizational Structure
   a. "This Division is poorly organized."
   b. "Research does not belong in this Division."
   c. "The Division structure makes no sense."

   Other common themes might include: strategy, company policy, interunit behavior, top leadership, decision-making, power/trust, communications, organizational climate.

2. Make a summary statement for each theme. Since the summary statement is a summary of the subjective comments made by the interviewees, it should be evaluative in nature. A summary statement that can be drawn from the comments made above under the or-

ganizational structure theme is, "People feel the division is poorly organized, which reduces organizational clarity and results in confusion."

Summary statements provide the basis for developing action plans.

VIDEO-TRONICS PRESENTATION EVALUATION

Rate each consulting team on the following five-point scale on each of the dimensions noted below.

	Poor 1	Fair 2	Average 3	Good 4	Excellent 5

Dimensions Rated	Team A	Team B	Team C	Team D
Sensing Interview:				
1. Building rapport				
2. Quality of questions				
3. Skill in asking questions				
Subtotal				
Diagnosis:				
1. Identification of organizational problems (How many problems did they identify accurately?)				
2. Support of problem statements with evidence from interviews				
3. Evaluation of Video-Tronics' receptivity and readiness to change (Identification of major forces, internal and external)				
Subtotal				
Action Plan:				
1. Identifying solutions that fit problems identified in diagnosis (Are they *macro* solutions?)				
2. Strength of explanation as to how solutions will solve Video-Tronics' problems in the future				
3. Usefulness of solutions (Given your knowledge of the problems that exist, are their proposals practical or workable?)				
4. How workable is their proposed approach to *implementation* in light of readings and your knowledge of Video-Tronics?				
Subtotal				
Total Evaluation (Points)				

Maximum Points 50, Minimum 10

■ Organizational Dry Rot Index: A Project

Like a burlap bag that has aged, an organization may not give an outward appearance of "dry rot" until some pressure is applied. Then the fabric begins to fall apart. John Gardner has outlined nine requirements that prevent dry rot by allowing organizational renewal. These requirements exist in varying degrees by organizations. The Organizational Dry Rot Index includes the nine requirements Gardner believes reflect the potential an organization has for renewal.

Select an organization to examine for the purpose of evaluating its potential for renewal. Interview managers at several levels and some nonmanagers to collect data using the Organizational Dry Rot Index. To rate an organization, circle the best description under each requirement statement. In addition to rating each requirement, space is provided for you to record any supporting observations you have about the organization.

Your instructor will provide further information on how your project results should be prepared.

Requirement 1: The organization must have an effective program for the recruitment and development of talent.

A shortage of talent and/or developmental programs exists		Some talent exists but much is being wasted		A steady supply of highly trained and motivated personnel exists
1	2	3	4	5

Supporting observations: _____

_____

_____

_____

Requirement 2: The organization must be a hospitable environment for the individual.

No "sparks" of individuality are present		Some idea people are present but too often smothered		Individuality is encouraged and supported
1	2	3	4	5

Supporting observations: _____

_____

_____

_____

Based on John W. Gardner, "How to Prevent Organizational Dry Rot," *Harper's Magazine*, October 1965, pp. 20–26.

Requirement 3: The organization must have built-in provisions for self-criticism.

Those in power are often self-deceived and fail to see what is really going on		Certain organizational members are allowed to criticize the organization but many more are not afforded the luxury		An atmosphere exists in which uncomfortable questions can be asked of those in power
1	2	3	4	5

Supporting observations: _____

_____

_____

_____

Requirement 4: The organization must have a fluidity of internal structure.

Jurisdictional boundaries are set in concrete		Some room for flexibility exists but boundaries tend to be relied upon		Jurisdictional lines are not sacred
1	2	3	4	5

Supporting observations: _____

_____

_____

_____

Requirement 5: The organization must have an adequate system of internal communication.

A guarded, often unspoken, formal system prevails		Some obstacles present		An open, sharing, and spontaneous system prevails
1	2	3	4	5

Supporting observations: _____

_____

_____

_____

Requirement 6: The organization must have some means of combating the process by which members become prisoners of their procedures.

Total reliance on and subservience to procedures		Procedures are invoked mostly in cases of dispute		Procedures are perceived as means to ends and not ends in themselves
1	2	3	4	5

Supporting observations: _____

_____

_____

_____

Requirement 7: The organization must have some means of combating the vested interests that grow up in every organization.

Members and their subunits hold on ferociously to their turf

Changes encounter moderate resistance but the organization's interests prevail

Members accept the notion that in the long run everyone's overriding vested interest is the continuing vitality of the organization

1   2   3   4   5

Supporting observations: _____

_____

_____

_____

Requirement 8: The organization is interested in what it is going to become and not in what it has been.

Members rest on their laurels and pay homage to the organization's historical roots

Members look forward to the future but are constrained by the organization's past

Members habitually look ahead and develop contingencies to cope with the future

1   2   3   4   5

Supporting observations: _____

_____

_____

_____

Requirement 9: The organization must have members who have strong convictions developed in an atmosphere that strives toward continual improvement.

Most members are apathetic and lack commitment to the organization's development

Members tend to get worn down by their continued efforts to change the organization

Members have a strong belief in the notion that it really makes a difference whether they do well or poorly

1   2   3   4   5

Supporting observations: _____

_____

_____

_____

■ The H.E./L&P Merger

Any time one organization takes over another there are bound to be some differences of opinion about what changes are necessary as the transition occurs. In this exercise you have an opportunity to play a part in how the initial stages of such a transition come about.

Directions

1. In preparation for this exercise everyone should read "A Brief Note on Force-Field Analysis" provided at the end of the exercise.
2. Your instructor will assign you to one of two teams—the Hayes management team or the Lorrilard transition team.
3. When instructed, you should read *only* the background provided for your team and begin working on the tasks outlined. Your instructor will indicate how much time is available for each phase of the exercise.

■ DO NOT READ UNLESS INSTRUCTED TO DO SO

Background for the Hayes Electric Management Team

You are part of the management team at the Hayes Electric Company (H.E.). Recently a major conglomerate, Lorrilard & Pullman (L&P), acquired your company for $250 million. For the most part you are quite excited about this merger because Lorrilard can infuse the needed capital to put Hayes into the big time. Your team has been asked, in the week before new management takes over, for its input on changes necessary. Lorrilard has assured you that the present management team will remain intact provided you are willing to help facilitate any needed changes.

Hayes has been a family owned and operated business for fifty years. Mr. Hayes, the president, and only grandchild of "Pop Hayes" the founder, has been offered a position as special consultant. A general manager has yet to be named to take the helm of Hayes, but Lorrilard top management has indicated a willingness to consider promoting one of the present Hayes's managers.

Your team has selected the vice-president of manufacturing _____ [Fill in one team member's name here.] to serve as the chairperson of your team. You have selected this person because of his/her expertise in manufacturing and electronics and because the team agrees that Hayes could benefit if he/she were named general manager. In addition, you feel the strength of your management team lies in the production/engineering areas.

Hayes produces a variety of small household appliances—hair dryers, mixers, blenders, etc. While Mr. Hayes, your president, was an idea man, he was incompetent as a financial manager and consequently was unable to obtain the funding for new equipment badly needed to remain competitive. At a *minimum,* Hayes will require an *immediate* $25 million in capital investment to make a solid turnaround. At the time of merger negotiations, this fact was somewhat played down. In fact, figures in the $5–7 million range were frequently cited, coupled with a caveat that this would not be enough in the long run. Your team did not want to scare off potential buyers, especially Lorrilard, which, as a multi-billion dollar conglomerate, should find your capital improvement needs a drop in the bucket.

Hayes has been experiencing a steady decline in profits for the last five years, and in the last two years incurred losses of $5 million and $6 million respectively on sales revenues of $150 million each year. As a management team, you attribute most of these losses to three factors: (1) poor financial management by Mr. Hayes, who also served as treasurer; (2) a steady decline in the quality of your products because of old and poorly maintained equipment; and (3) some long-term customer reluctance to stock your products, given premium prices, because quality has been declining.

The entire management team is committed to Pop Hayes's motto: "Quality always sells." The company was founded on this notion and consequently emphasized quality over price, and durability over style. Your products have always enjoyed the reputation of being the Cadillac of the small-appliance industry. Unlike some of your competitors, your workers are all skilled craftsmen—making your product more labor intensive *but* of much higher quality. Your workers are also loyal Hayesites. Given that Hayes is the major employer in your small town and given Pop Hayes's philosophy to pay his people quite well, you have never been unionized—in fact, you are almost like one very large family. The recent agreement by the Hayes family to sell has strained this family feeling; however, your management team was able to dampen some employee attempts to unionize "before it's too late."

Your team feels strongly that the Hayes tradition can be profitable again and you feel the vice-president of manufacturing is just the person to lead you into a new era of "quality always sells."

Your task

You have been asked by the top management of Lorrilard to submit a written proposal on the changes you recommend as the takeover is completed. Your proposal is to be sent to the head of Lorrilard's transition team, which has agreed to send you a copy of the transition team's proposals as well.

1. Your team should first prepare a force-field analysis to diagnose the present level of profitability at Hayes and to determine what driving and restraining forces need to be altered to improve profitability.

2. Once the force-field analysis is complete, your team should prepare a memo outlining your proposals. Be sure to include your recommendations on the general manager position, the necessary capital investment outlays, and any supporting information.

3. The instructor will tell you when your memo is to be delivered and will also obtain a copy of the Lorrilard team's proposal as agreed. Once your team has reviewed their proposal, you are asked to respond to it in a second memo written to the Lorrilard transition team.

4. After exchanging and reviewing the second set of memos, a pre-takeover meeting will be called at Lorrilard headquarters (front of room) between the two teams. Two members of your team will be asked to attend; the other members may act only as observers. At this meeting all necessary changes must be finalized.

■ DO NOT READ UNLESS INSTRUCTED TO DO SO

Background for the Lorrilard Transition Team

You are part of a transition team organized by your company, Lorrilard & Pullman (L&P), to facilitate takeover of a recent acquisition—the Hayes Electric Company (H.E.). Your company acquired Hayes for $250 million. Your top management has asked Hayes, in the week before takeover begins, to submit any change proposals it feels are necessary. Your team is also to prepare its own change proposal. While your team has been given the final authority to make changes, you are willing to consider the Hayes management's proposals. Lorrilard has assured Hayes's present management team that it will remain intact provided it is willing to help facilitate needed changes; the Hayes people have responded enthusiastically.

Hayes has been a family owned and operated business for fifty years. Mr. Hayes, the president and only grandchild of "Pop Hayes" the founder, has been offered a position as special consultant. A general manager has yet to be named to take the helm of Hayes although the vice-president of manufacturing has been selected by the Hayes management team to chair their merger team. While Lorrilard is generally willing to consider promoting a manager from within an acquired company, the candidate must be acceptable and compatible with Lorrilard's views.

Hayes produces a variety of small household appliances—hair dryers, mixers, blenders, etc. The president, Mr. Hayes, was an idea man but totally incompetent as a financial manager. Hayes' managers have indicated in earlier meetings an investment of $5–7 million dollars would be sufficient to provide the necessary new equipment needed to turn Hayes around. While they are probably being overly optimistic about the impact of such a small investment, you have been told by your top management that you cannot invest one cent in Hayes for at least one to two years. At the time of the merger negotiations, your top management ignored your team's advice that Hayes was not worth more than $200 million, given the equipment it needs, and got into a bidding war that pushed the offer $50 million too high.

Hayes has been experiencing a steady decline in profits for the last five years, and in the last two years incurred losses of $5 million and $6 million respectively on sales revenues of about $150 million each year. Your own analysis of these losses uncovered several factors. First, there is Mr.Hayes's poor financial management—he served as treasurer, but didn't even know the fundamentals of basic cash-flow management. Second, there is an overpaid and under-utilized workforce—Hayes is located in a small town and is its major employer with a non-union shop in which all workers are treated and paid as craftsmen. Employees are exceptionally loyal to the company and management is very loyal to its "family" of workers. Clearly an incentive system would separate the "wheat from the chaff" at Hayes. Third, management hangs onto an outmoded strategy, which was started by "Pop" Hayes, that "Quality always sells." This strategy has led the company to emphasize quality over price, and durability over style. Yes, they do produce the Cadillac of small appliances but the market share has been going to the cost-effective, less durable producers who have a flair for style, price, and what sells. Fourth, quality has been slipping because of old and poorly maintained equipment. Given Hayes's emphasis on "handmade" or labor-intensive quality being built in, craftsmen are still using methods of manufacturing on a number of smaller parts that could and should be made on modern, fully automated equipment.

The initial impetus for buying Hayes was your marketing research projections that said a number of new households will be started in the next ten years as the baby-boom generation sets up house. You saw an opportunity to acquire a company with a highly reputable name brand in need of a major overhaul. Clearly, a strong market-oriented general manager is needed—making it unlikely to promote someone from Hayes's existing production/engineering-oriented management team. However, the overzealous bidding war for Hayes has created a bit of a dilemma: your plans to invest $50 million in new automated equipment have to be shelved for at least one or two years. However, some short-term options are possible, including emphasis on worker productivity, layoffs of some of the "craftsmen" and subcontracting their work to more automated manufacturers, redesign of present products to incorporate less expensive electronic components, and the establishment of a strong marketing orientation in management to increase sales by pricing more competitively to keep Hayes afloat until money is available to automate fully.

Your task

You have been given the responsibility to prepare the final transition plan for Hayes. This plan should include all the changes you feel are necessary. Your proposal will be sent to the Hayes management team for review and reaction. In addition, the Hayes team has been told to send you a copy of its proposal for reaction as well.

1. Your team should first prepare a force-field analysis to diagnose the present level of profitability at Hayes and to determine what driving and restraining forces need to be altered to improve profitability.

2. Once the force-field analysis is complete, your team should prepare a memo outlining your proposals. Be sure to include your recommendations on the general manager's position, plus any other changes you feel need to be initiated.

3. The instructor will tell you when your memo is to be delivered and will also obtain a copy of the Hayes management team's proposal as agreed. Once your team has reviewed this proposal, you are asked to respond to it in a second memo written directly to the Hayes management team.

4. After exchanging and reviewing the second set of memos, a pre-takeover meeting will be called at Lorrilard headquarters (front of room) between the two teams. The Hayes team has been told to send two of its managers, you will be allowed to send up to four members of your team; the other members may act as observers. At this meeting all necessary changes must be finalized by your team. Your team should decide the format of the meeting and have someone chair it. Remember, final changes must be announced by a spokesperson for your team at the end of this meeting.

■ A Brief Note on Force-Field Analysis

No institution or organization is exempt from change. Today the student who returns to his alma mater ten years after graduation can expect to find changes not only in personnel but also in personnel policies and teaching practices. The executive returning to the firm where

Adapted from "Change Does Not Have to Be Haphazard," Kenneth D. Benne and Max Birnbaum, *The School Review*, Volume LXVIII, Number 3 (Autumn, 1960), pp. 283–297. Copyright © The University of Chicago Press.

she once worked, the nurse going back to her old hospital, the social worker visiting his agency—all can expect to find sweeping changes.

It is fairly easy to identify changes in institutional patterns after they have occurred. It is more difficult to analyze changes while they are going on and still more difficult to predict changes or to influence significantly the direction and the tempo of changes already underway. Yet, more and more, those who have managerial functions in organizations must analyze and predict impending changes and take deliberate action to shape change according to some criteria of progress. The planning of change has become part of the responsibility of management in all contemporary institutions, whether the task of the institution is defined in terms of health, education, social welfare, industrial production, or religious indoctrination.

Whatever other equipment managers require in analyzing potentialities for change and in planning and directing change in institutional settings, they need some conceptual schema for thinking about change. This need stems from the profusion and variety of behaviors that accompany any process of change.

One useful model for thinking about change has been proposed by Kurt Lewin, who saw behavior in an institutional setting not as a static habit or pattern but as a dynamic balance of forces working in opposite directions within the social-psychological space of the institution.

Driving Forces and Restraining Forces

Take, for example, the production level of a work team in a factory. This level fluctuates within narrow limits above and below a certain number of units of production per day. Why does this pattern persist? Because, Lewin says, the forces that tend to raise the level of production are equal to the forces that tend to depress it. Among the forces tending to raise the level of production might be: (a) the pressures of supervisors on the work team to produce more; (b) the desire of at least some team members to attract favorable attention from supervisors in order to get ahead individually; (c) the desire of team members to earn more under the incentive plan of the plant. Such forces Lewin called "driving forces." Among the forces tending to lower the level of production might be: (a') a group standard in the production team against "rate busting" or "eager beavering" by individual workers; (b') resistance of team members to accepting training and supervision from management; (c') feelings by workers that the product they are producing is not important. Granted the goal of increased productivity, these forces are "restraining forces." The balance between the two sets of forces, which defines the established level of production, Lewin called a "quasi-stationary equilibrium." We may diagram this equilibrium as follows:

According to Lewin, this type of thinking about patterns of institutionalized behavior applies not only to levels of production in industry but also to such patterns as levels of discrimination in communities; atmosphere of democracy or autocracy in social agencies; supervisor-teacher-pupil relationships in school systems; and formal or informal working relationships among levels of a hospital organization.

According to this way of looking at patterned behavior, change takes place when an imbalance occurs between the sum of the restraining forces and the sum of the driving forces. Such imbalance unfreezes the pattern; the level then changes until the opposing forces are again brought into equilibrium. An imbalance may occur through a change in the magnitude of any one force, through a change in the direction of a force, or through the addition of a new force.

For examples of each of these ways of unfreezing a situation, let us look again at our original illustration. Suppose that the members of the work team join a new union that sets out to get pay raises. In pressing for shifts in overall wage policy, the union increases the suspicion of workers toward the motives of all management, including supervisors. This change tends to increase the restraining force—let's say restraining force b'. As a result, the level of production goes down. As the level of production falls, supervisors increase their pressure toward greater production, and driving force a increases. This release of increased counterforce tends to bring the system into balance again at a level somewhere near the previous level. But the increase in magnitude of these opposed forces may also increase the tension under which people work. Under such conditions, even though the level of production does not go down very much, the situation becomes more psychologically explosive, less stable, and less predictable. Hence, while the place to begin change is at those points where some stress and strain exist, one should ordinarily avoid initiating change at the point of greatest stress.

A war that demands more and more of the product that the work team is producing may convert the workers' feeling that they are not producing anything important (restraining force c') to a feeling that their work is important and that they are not working hard enough. This response will occur provided, of course, that the workers are committed to the war effort. As the direction of force c' is reversed, the level of production will almost certainly rise to bring the behavior pattern into a state of equilibrium at a higher level of productivity.

Suppose a new driving force is added in the shape of a supervisor who wins the trust and the respect of the work team. The new force results in a desire on the part of the work team to make the well-liked supervisor look good—or at least to keep him/her from looking bad—in relation to colleagues and superiors. This force may operate to offset a generally unfavorable attitude toward management.

These examples suggest that in change there is an unfreezing of an existing equilibrium, a movement toward a new equilibrium, and the refreezing of the new equilibrium. Planned change must use situational forces to accomplish unfreezing, to influence the movement in generally desirable directions, and to rearrange the situation, not only to avoid return to the old level but to stabilize the change or improvement.

This discussion suggests three major strategies for achieving change in any given pattern of behavior: the driving forces may be increased; the restraining forces may be decreased; or these two strategies may be combined. In general, if the first strategy only is adopted, the tension in the system is likely to increase. More tension means more instability and more unpredictability and the likelihood of irrational rather than rational responses to attempts to induce change.

It is a well-known fact that change in an organization is often followed by a reaction toward the old pattern, a reaction that sets in when pressure for change is relaxed. This raises the problem of how to maintain a desirable change. Backsliding takes place for various reasons. However, quite often those affected by the changes may not have participated in the planning enough to internalize the changes that those in authority are seeking to induce; when the pressure of authority is relaxed, there is no pressure from those affected to maintain the change.

†